S0-ATL-824

RADIO AND TELEVISION ACTING

Criticism, Theory, and Practice

RINEHART RADIO SERIES

Erik Barnouw	RADIO DRAMA IN ACTION
Rome Cowgill	WRITING FOR RADIO
Edwin Duerr	RADIO AND TELEVISION ACTING
H. William Fitelson	THEATRE GUILD ON THE AIR
Ben G. Henneke	THE RADIO ANNOUNCER'S HANDBOOK
Walter and Rome Krulevitch	RADIO DRAMA PRODUCTION A Handbook
Ernest LaPrade	BROADCASTING MUSIC
William B. Levenson	TEACHING THROUGH RADIO
Max Wylie	RADIO AND TELEVISION WRITING (A Revision)

RADIO AND TELEVISION ACTING

Criticism, Theory, and Practice

by EDWIN DUERR

Radio and Television Supervisor, Young & Rubicam, Inc.
Formerly Director, The University of California Little Theatre

RINEHART & COMPANY · INC · *Publishers* · *New York*

Printed in the United States of America

To F.H.D. and C.A.D.,
who always believe that radio and television acting
could be better than it is

Preface

Surprisingly little has been written about professional radio acting, perhaps because we who are occupied with the day-to-day chores of commercial radio are usually too busy to do much thinking or writing about it; and almost nothing has been written about television acting, perhaps because we are all so new in the medium. Yet a number of us have longed to see their theory and practice organized and evaluated.

With ulterior motives, then—after fifteen years spent in teaching and directing actors in the legitimate theatre, both professional and nonprofessional, and after six additional years in New York City working with actors in all manner of top-flight radio and television shows—I have somehow managed to squeeze out enough time to examine a vast amount of radio and television acting, and to read and think and argue about it. The result is this book for actors and directors.

Largely it is a work of compilation, but three not-so-vague convictions of my own hold it together and shape it. The first is that a student handbook can be justly criticized for placing too much attention on the mechanics and not enough on the more basic problems of creativeness. I have therefore tried to avoid that departmentalized error. My basic topic throughout is *acting,* not merely studio mechanics. Only after a student has learned to act should he specialize in the few peculiarities of reading before a microphone or of performing before the cameras. Mere effectiveness in the radio and TV studio will never automatically make him a first-rate actor.

The second conviction is that most students not only want to learn the practical business of how to act for radio and television—"You can teach us these procedures soon enough"—but hope to discover how they can bring a better kind of acting to the air waves. I have therefore given more space to what radio and video acting can ideally be than to what they actually are in current practice.

The third conviction is that radio and television acting are far from being something new under the sun. I have therefore purposely tried by means of frequent quotations from hither and yon to call attention to the heritage and tradition of the old, old art of acting.

My stanch loyalty to the aesthetic of Stark Young is everywhere in evidence; and I have gratefully pilfered treasure from Bernard Shaw, Wayland Maxfield Parrish, and others, as well as from my colleagues at the University of California, Cornell and Western Reserve Universities, Carnegie Institute of Technology, and the Young & Rubicam advertising agency.

Grateful acknowledgment is made to authors, publishers, and other holders of copyright for permission to quote from published and unpublished plays and scripts. Special notice should be taken that these permissions are restricted to this one use in *Radio and Television Acting.* Other persons desiring to use these scripts and plays in any way whatsoever must obtain permission from the copyright owners.

I am also indebted to Janet Cohn, who started me in radio, and to House Jameson, who started me on this book.

E.D.

New York,
January, 1950

Contents

	Preface	vii
I	THE NATURE OF ACTING	1
II	VOICE AND SPEECH	31
III	MICROPHONE TECHNIQUES AND PROCEDURES	59
IV	MICROPHONE READING: MEANING	97
V	MICROPHONE READING: MEANING (Continued)	121
VI	CHARACTERIZATION: ACTION	155
VII	MICROPHONE READING: ILLUSION OF THE FIRST TIME	183
VIII	MICROPHONE READING: CONTACT	221
IX	CHARACTERIZATION: MOTIVATION	259
X	MICROPHONE READING: CIRCUMSTANCES	289
XI	EMOTIONAL AND COMEDY ACTING	321
XII	MOTION	351
XIII	MICROPHONE READING: STRUCTURE (DIRECTING)	371
	Play Lists and Recordings	407
	Index to Exercises	411
	Index to Selections and Authors	411
	Index to Subjects	414

RADIO AND TELEVISION ACTING

Criticism, Theory, and Practice

I plead then that acting is potentially an artistic profession, and that by training and practice a person can qualify himself or herself to come to a manager or author and say, ". . . I know my vowels and consonants as a phonetic expert, and can speak so as to arrest the attention of the audience whenever I open my mouth, forcibly, delicately, roughly, smoothly, prettily, harshly, authoritatively, submissively, but always artistically just as you want it. I can sit, stand, fall, get up, walk, dance, and otherwise use my body with the complete command of it that marks the physical artist." An actor might know all this, and yet, for want of the power to interpret an author's text . . . never, without coaching, get beyond Rosencrantz or Seyton. It is, therefore, only the minimum qualification of a skilled stagehand; and if an actor is not that, then he is merely a stage-struck unskilled laborer or handyman, and his "conceptions" of Ibsen or Shakespeare are mere impertinences.

BERNARD SHAW
Dramatic Opinions and Essays

To create in this medium of himself the actor needs technique. Acting is a language in the theatre which must be learned. Without technique the actor cannot know the resources of rhythm, what tempo is, what the voice means to such ends as his, or how to recognize effects when he does get them, to retain from these what is most expressive and to repeat it when he wills. Through the avenue of technique the actor approaches all wit, elevation, variety and depth of style. Through his technique he establishes that firm outline that divides his creation from reality and heightens it into art. Without technique, however wonderful his own quality may be, he has no language to speak. Through technique he learns the use of his medium. Through technical labor he gets an intellectual discipline that helps to clarify his ideas; which in their turn are developed by this search for their right technical form.

STARK YOUNG
The Theatre

The broadcasters are only interested in selling time. The advertisers are only interested in selling their products. No one is interested in the show or the actor.

FRED ALLEN

Chapter I . . THE NATURE OF ACTING

1

Radio and television acting, though new to the theatre, are not so unique that they can be separated from the general field of acting. Yet in their bustling toward so-called success many would-be radio and video performers overlook this obvious truth. They forget that radio, television, film, and theatre acting are almost identical activities. They seem to conclude, with a curious and fatal lapse of logic, that they can forego any familiarity with acting's age-old fundamentals. The result of this error is continuously apparent in the major New York and Hollywood broadcasting studios where too many young actors are attempting to become experts by accident—are trying, by what methods they know not, to achieve what they know not. They are, strangely enough, actors who do not know what acting is.

Perhaps it would be kinder to say that most young actors take for granted that they know what acting is. Everyone knows what acting is! Some two hundred years ago Mr. Partridge in *Tom Jones* knew what acting was. When he saw David Garrick as Hamlet, he boasted,

> ". . . why, I could act as well as he myself. I am sure, if I had seen a ghost, I should have looked in the very same manner, and done just as he did. And then, to be sure, in that scene . . . between him and his mother where you tell me he acted so fine, why, Lord help me, any man, that is, any good man, that had such a mother, would have done exactly the same."[1]

Today one of Arthur Kober's characters in a *New Yorker* sketch also knows what acting is when he says, "I figger things like this here. I figger when I get a script, how would the people in the script act suppose they were in real life. Get me?"[2] Even that revered teacher of acting, Constantin Stanislavski, advises his students to enact a fiction truthfully by merely asking themselves, "What should I do if this really happened?"[3]

Yes, everyone is sure he recognizes good acting when he sees it, is certain that he could easily become an actor provided he wanted to become one. Acting is simple: acting is just getting up on the stage, or in front of the camera or the microphone, and imitating other people.

Yet if imitation is all there is to acting, by quick majority vote, why did the great French actor Talma maintain that it would require a period of at least twenty years before a student could "present to the public a series of characters acted almost to perfection"?[4] He did not prescribe twenty years for mastering only impersonation. Long ago he ventured to suggest that there is more, much more, to acting than merely behaving like other people, easy as that is for some actor candidates and difficult as it is for others. Today the experts tend to believe with him that a mimetic talent is helpful but that the ability to imitate others is not enough in itself to make an accomplished actor. If likeness is all, people like Johnny Bear, in the Steinbeck-Ricketts *Sea of Cortez,* who can reproduce any conversation he hears with phonographic accuracy, in the exact words and voice of the speaker, would be actors. The dull thud of truth, however, is that they rarely are.

So, like everyone else, young actors are wrong in believing that acting is only "imitating other people." They are no more perceptive in their judgment than the average man. According to Stark Young, the most astute of American theatre critics,

> Without practice or familiarity or study the average man knows no more about acting than he does about architec-

[1] Henry Fielding, *The History of Tom Jones,* Book XVI, Chap. 5.
[2] Arthur Kober, *The New Yorker,* March 11, 1933, p. 55.
[3] Stanislavski, *An Actor Prepares,* p. 137.
[4] Talma, *Reflections on the Actor's Art,* p. 23.

ture or music . . . . One must have seen it often and intelligently, have endured boredom and ecstasy, have made comparisons through experience and repetition, have formed in one's mind ideas and models of what one thinks admirable. In spite of the seeming nearness and reality of acting to the average man, there is no reason to believe that he is any more a judge of it than he is of any other art.[5]

That is the important and yet swoonless word—art. The one basic point that most young actors might well learn is that acting is, or can be, an art. Of course they frequently call themselves artists, but rarely do they understand what an art is and therefore what acting as an art must be. If they did, they might better perceive what they are aiming to accomplish, and why; they might discover methods and procedures that would be somewhat more rewarding than a mere reliance on instinct and luck, on personality and mimicry and whatnot. They need, for the moment, to forget their "mikes" and cameras and to examine the general field of acting, or acting considered as an art, since, as André Gide says, "The great mistake of actors is to make naturalness triumph where art should."[6]

2

Art, however, is a slippery term; it eludes final definition. Consequently there are as many definitions going the rounds as there are cures for colds, and one will work for one person and another for another. Art is especially difficult to define for an actor, since analysis is often an enemy to his gift of sensibility. Yet, despite the declaration of George Jean Nathan that if he were ever Secretary of Culture he would burn all the books that define art, the term must be serviceably defined. No one learns much when an actor says, in the manner of St. Augustine, that he knows what an art is provided you don't ask him.

First, then, in order to banish too much cathedral hush in his hunt for the meaning of art, the actor (stage, screen, or radio) might keep in mind critic Harry Levin's statement that "all art is a game, the object of which is to make the problems of life and death—with as much insight, skill, and originality as possible—a source of enjoyment."[7] Only after you have been more or less relaxed by that refreshing observance should you go on to find that among those who have had the time and skill to search out such things it is rather generally agreed that art is not life, is not a carbon copy of something in reality, is not the mere duplication of an actual event or experience, is not limited to a mere recording or reproduction of the objective world. Art is infinitely more than that; it is the revelation of *a state of mind and spirit* resulting from experiences in the world. No genuine artist is content with copying an object or an event down to the smallest detail merely to enable others to recognize it. The artist does, is driven to do, something else. He puts *himself* into what he creates. He does whatever is necessary and whatever he can to the object or the event he has experienced—eliminating this part or that, adding this or that, heightening here and there, rearranging the sequence, and so forth—all for the purpose of communicating to others, in the way or medium he has chosen, the quality of his own peculiar experience. Positive that in life no two people ever react identically to the same object or event, the artist wants others to respond to *his own individual experiencing* of an object or an event. He therefore designs, or organizes, his perceptions so that something new, his unique attitude or idea, comes into existence.

To put all this another way, in nature, in life around us, a wave is a wave, a tree is a tree, a miser is a miser, a mother's grief over her dead son is a mother's grief over her dead son. In art, however, this wave, this tree, this miser, this grief is something else, is something additional. In art the wave, for instance, has in it Winslow Homer's attitude toward it. In art the tree is Corot's tree or Rousseau's, not God's. In art the miser is not merely the duplication of any old miser; he is Silas Marner or Scrooge or Harpagon, each seen through the distinctive temperament of a George Eliot or a Dickens or a Molière. In art the mother's grief over her dead son is, for example, what Synge found in such grief and how he used what he found as a functional part of *Riders to the Sea* to express his individual idea. In art, according to Zola, nature is seen through a temperament.

All the foregoing is somewhat adequately summed

[5] Young, *Theatre Practice*, p. 5.

[6] André Gide; quoted by Jean-Louis Barrault, in an interview by Luce and Arthur Klein, *Theatre Arts Monthly*, XXXI (October, 1947), p. 26.

[7] Harry Levin, *James Joyce* (Norfolk, Conn.; New Directions, 1941), p. 177.

up in Tolstoy's well-known contention that art is "an activity by means of which one man, having experienced a feeling, intentionally transmits it to others."[8] That is to say that in art a unique experience is somehow so intensified and clarified that one man's emotion (since an emotion always attaches itself to events and objects) is transmitted to an audience. In art an attitude toward life comes into being designed for distribution. And the emotional quality of that experience, or attitude, or idea, can be appreciated in and for itself or can be evaluated for its effect on actual living.

J. W. N. Sullivan, writing about the spiritual development of Beethoven, is sure that

> we cannot say that art communicates knowledge, as science does . . . . But what art does is communicate to us an attitude, an attitude taken up by the artist consequent upon his perceptions . . . . It is characteristic of the greater art that the attitude it communicates is felt by us to be valid, to be the reaction to a more subtle and comprehensive contact with reality than we can normally make . . . . The colossal and mastered experience which seems to be reflected in the Heilgesang of the A minor quartet, for instance, is, we may be confident, indicative of more than the peculiarities of Beethoven's neural organization. The perceptions which made that experience possible were in no sense illusory; they were perceptions of the nature of reality, even though they have no place in the scientific scheme. Beethoven does not communicate to us his perceptions or his experience. He communicates to us the attitude based upon them.[9]

If, then, in your search for the essence of an art, you want a brief working definition, you might well cling to Theodore Meyer Greene's finding that "in a work of art (a) reality is (b) interpreted, and (c) expressed in a distinctive way."[10] You should, however, be positive that you understand thoroughly the meaning of that "a," "b," and "c."

a) Any stage, screen, or radio actor can readily understand the importance of the first term, "reality." The only danger is that he may be overenchanted with it and with the truth that art stems from life and cannot for long be cut off from life. Cherishing actuality in all the richness of its objects and events, he will often aim only for verisimilitude in his creations, will tend to become pleased with his ability merely to copy life. In so doing he can be rightly proud of his skill at authentic reproduction, but he can be an artist only in so far as he is aware of, and adds, an attitude or a personal interpretation to the character he acts.

b) Greene's second term, "interpreted," thereby at once ascends to its position of paramount importance in art. Yet for an actor this importance of interpretation is likely to seem much too intricate, a labyrinth of wheels-within-wheels. He will promptly raise his hands and eyebrows in horror when told that always in acting as an art he must first take cognizance of the playwright's interpretation of reality, and then, secondly and inescapably, add his own interpretation. He should realize, however, that this matter of interpretation is not nearly so complex as it sounds. All it means is that the actor, when creating a role, must go for his material not only to nature but to the playwright and to himself.

From the playwright—from the script by an O'Neill, a Corwin, or a Nunnally Johnson—the actor must discover what the temperament of the playwright is and *what he has done to actuality* in order to communicate his unique perception to an audience. The actor as artist must be true to nature *as experienced by the playwright.* He must, in a sense, verify it—or at least comment on it. He should neither distort nor ignore it.

The actor needs to remember that Iago and Mrs. Alving, for example, do not exist in nature. They are imagined characters. Actually there are no such people in reality or in memory whom the actor or actress can use as full-fledged models. The choice from reality has already been made by the playwright, and interpreted by him, and utilized by him in a design. Iago and Mrs. Alving already have in their lifelike make-ups the attitudes of their respective playwrights toward them. Iago is a man seen through the temperament of Shakespeare; Mrs. Alving is a woman seen through the temperament of Ibsen. Thus, since the essential truth about these characters is that they are *not* actual, the actor cannot correctly rely only on the objective world for the total substance and form of his characterization. He must, of course, always turn to nature in preparing his roles, since the artist creates "from discoveries and experiences in the lives of his people, not from the lucubra-

[8] Leo Tolstoy, *What Is Art and Essays on Art* (1898), translated by Aylmer Maude (London: Oxford University Press, 1930), see pp. vi and 121 ff.

[9] Sullivan, *Beethoven,* pp. 23–24. Reprinted with the permission of the publisher, Alfred A. Knopf, Inc.

[10] Theodore M. Greene, *The Arts and the Arts of Criticism* (Princeton: Princeton University Press, 1940), p. 230.

tions of sciolists and eremites."[11] Yet he must *also* try, in so far as he is an artist, to assist the playwright in communicating his perceptions, his qualities. He must strive to create his character as a functional part in the theatrical expression of an idea.

An elementary indication of what is meant by enacting the playwright's attitude or idea will be found in entertainments such as those in which three brief skits about the same domestic triangle are acted, let us say, as written (1) by Eugene O'Neill, (2) by Somerset Maugham, and (3) by Noel Coward. The actors playing the parts will demonstrate in their three distinctly different delineations, even if only in burlesque fun and in broad terms, the truth that actors can play from the point of view of the playwright. (If Noel Coward has written all three of the sketches, the actors will play from Mr. Coward's idea of O'Neill, of Maugham, and of himself.)

Aeschylus, Sophocles, Euripides, von Hofmannsthal, Robert Turney, Robinson Jeffers, and Eugene O'Neill have created seven widely different characters for Electra, all from the identical source, for seven different responses to her story. St. John Ervine's Shylock in *The Lady of Belmont* and Ari Ibn-Zahav's in *Shylock and His Daughter* are not Shakespeare's Shylock—and his was changed considerably from the source. The *Amphitryon*'s of Plautus, Molière, and Behrman are each the expression of a different personality. Similarly, Abraham Lincoln is not the same person to John Drinkwater that he is to Robert E. Sherwood. In short, and to repeat, in every play reality has already been interpreted; therefore the actor must go to the playwright for an idea, must act that idea, and must communicate it to others.

If the actor asks why he should go to himself as well as to nature and to the playwright for the material of his characterization, the answer is that the actor is always himself in the theatre. He never actually *is* the character he plays. Only as himself can he perform the artist's job of expressing an attitude toward reality. His intelligence, sensibility, voice and body—all the things he is—are, in acting, the medium by which he communicates to others his conception of a playwright's idea via a character. If he aims only to *be* a person other than himself, if he aims to *be* Electra or Shylock, then he evades his artistic responsibility of playing from an idea, because no real person in actual life is ever consciously and intentionally making another's comment on himself or giving another's preconceived notion of himself to an audience. No real person in actual life (for instance, no Tom Higgins in Newton, Kansas) is a functional part of a playwright-made design that expresses an idea. No real person in actual life has matter that he must get over the footlights or a microphone to an audience. Therefore the actor as artist cannot try to *be* the character; he must *act* the character in terms of himself. He must "keep the minutes of his own meeting" with the playwright.

c) Greene's third term, "expressed in a distinctive way," refers to the medium in which the artist has chosen to express the quality of his experience, or his attitude or idea. Eric Newton, a critic of sculpture and painting, helps clear up this point about the medium, or the expression of an interpretation of reality in a distinctive way, when he finds that to say, "'That picture of the Madonna is beautiful' is merely an extremely compressed way of saying, 'In that picture the artist has succeeded in communicating to me certain of his own personal excitements about Madonnahood *and about line and colour.*' In looking at it I begin to share those excitements. Having looked at it I shall never feel quite the same again about Madonnas *or about the interplay between dark blue and gold.*"[12] The references to "line and color" and to "dark blue and gold" are references to the medium used, the distinctive method of expression. In the same way, having witnessed a performance of *Othello,* an audience should perhaps say, "I shall never feel quite the same again about Othellos (or about jealousy) or—and this is the important point concerning the medium—about the interplay between the vocal and the visual, about color, about men and women in movement, about the glories and the infinite varieties of human speech."

In short, the actor as artist ought constantly to be aware of the distinctive *way* in which he is creating; he should always remember he is in and of the theatre; he must master, not ignore, the conventions of his medium.

[11] Thomas Craven, in a review of Cassou's *Picasso* and Mackenzie's *Understanding Picasso,* New York *Herald Tribune,* January 5, 1941, Books Section, p. 4.

[12] Eric Newton, *European Painting and Sculpture* (Harmondsworth, Middlesex, England; Penguin Books, 1941), p. 29.

3

Following this perhaps all too sudden knowledge of what an art is, you as the actor may at first be as perplexed as the poor hundred-legged centipede who became so involved in the theories of how to be a pedestrian that, after walking easily for months, it could no longer decide which foot to put forward first, and so stood still and confusedly starved to death. Finally, though, once you have done even a little concentrated thinking about art, you should be better prepared to understand the potentialities of acting. You may be ready to define, if only for yourself, the activity in which you are engaged.

Definitions of acting as an art are not many; even the theatre theologians more often than not by-pass defining exactly what they are talking about; they are satisfied with drowsy generalities. Yet Stark Young has composed a well-nigh infallible definition, as follows:

> Acting is an art in which the artist uses himself, his body and voice, as a medium. The actor takes from a drama a person and the dramatist's comment on the person; he brings his inspiration and technique to the dramatist's imagination. This creation of the dramatist's he restates in terms of acting, bringing into existence a new creation that was not there before. This creation has then to be restated in relation to the whole play . . . and by this it becomes a part of another body, of the whole theatre work that is to be created.[13]

Someone else has said that acting is life "reorganized and designed by an artist, whose purpose it fulfills."

The actor, however, usually wants a less esoteric definition, one that is aesthetically sound but practical. He seeks to learn by virtue of what principles, rules, and practices-to-be-discovered or already known the actor as artist works. He hopes to understand how an actor forms more or less an artistic habit of creating for the theatre in conscious accordance with correct method.

Such a definition can be attempted as follows: Acting —which is always action—demands a concentration of the intelligence and sensibility on seven elements, or regulators, which, when totaled, *differentiate it from action in life.* The actor must concentrate on

1) all the necessary imagined circumstances,

2) around an imagined character,

3) with a completely imagined objective—

4) all based upon a sense of truth;

5) and all functional to the expression of the playwright's attitude or idea as embodied in the script, and

6) the actor's own comment on that idea—

7) and all given an appropriate theatrical form for the purpose of artistic communication with an audience.

From some such definition of the art of acting—when it is reread and reread, and examined for all its implications, and then carefully assimilated—the actor (stage, screen, or radio) can in some measure determine what he is doing and why. From such a definition he can discover wherein most of the teachers and critics of acting today are only the one-eyed leading the blind, since, in their conceptions of acting, they usually include no more than the first four elements.

Moreover, if it is true that in the United States acting is the only profession in which the student is normally expected to be his own teacher, perhaps in something like the aforementioned definition both the actor candidate and the professional actor, averse as they usually are to theories, can find a method that can be followed and a technique that can be practiced to perfect whatever talents they possess. "What the theatre needs," Sir Cedric Hardwicke stated in an interview, "is more actors who are hard-working technicians and not many who act 'intuitively' the way some piano players play 'by ear.'" When Fanny Kemble wrote in 1863 that the art of acting has "neither fixed rules, specific principles, indispensable rudiments nor fundamental laws,"[14] the dear lady was talking fantasy through her old-fashioned hat.

4

Once the art of acting has been somewhat serviceably defined, the radio actor, in order better to know his more specific business, need only discover wherein radio acting differs—not in fundamentals, but differs nonetheless—from acting in general. Those differences, perhaps disputable, are several:

1) Radio acting is directed only toward the ear of the listener. A radio production is a combination restricted to sound effects, music, and the words of the playwright as voiced by the actors.

[13] Young, *The Theatre,* p. 105.

[14] Fanny Kemble; quoted by Montrose J. Moses, "Royal Roads to Acting," *Theatre Arts Monthly,* X, 12 (December, 1926), 832.

2) Radio acting is read from a script; it makes no demands whatsoever on memorization.

3) Radio acting, because of its mechanical setup, eliminates most of the customary possibilities for fruitful contact of one actor with another.

4) Radio acting, in bondage to a clock, is usually limited to brief rehearsals and to a single performance that is sustained only for a short period—an hour, a half-hour, fifteen minutes.

5) Radio acting calls for many quick and arbitrary transitions from one mood or set of circumstances or time sequence to another.

6) Radio acting is aimed at an audience of millions of people whose presence is not felt and who are not assembled in a theatre.

7) Radio acting, like film acting, often foregoes traditional theatrical projection "to the last row in the gallery."

The basic differentiation between radio acting and all other kinds of acting is, of course, that it is only auditory, that it forfeits all visual appeals for an audience. As a consequence there are those who say that artistic communication is thereby crippled; there are those who maintain that the theatre is primarily a place for seeing, and that to limit acting to the voice is to eliminate the essential. All such enemies of only the oral should weigh Lane Cooper's assertion that ". . . . every bit of literature properly so-called that history has to show is intended, not for the eye primarily, but for the ear. Every line of Shakespeare, every line of Milton, is meant to be pronounced, cannot be duly appreciated until it is pronounced."[15] In addition, they should return to Aristotle's point that in Tragedy, for instance, "the Plot should be so constructed that, even without help from the eye, one who simply hears the play recited, must feel the chill of fear, and be stirred with pity, at what occurs."[16]

Yes, all the values of a radio actor's work reside in reading. Yet to that reading the test of acting as an art can be applied.

The television actor, in order to know his specific business, needs to discover wherein video acting differs, although not in essentials, both from acting in general and from acting in radio. The differences, again perhaps somewhat arbitrary, are several, and important. Unlike radio acting:

1) Television acting depends on memorization of the words of the script.

2) Television acting is directed simultaneously at both the ear and the eye of the audience, is seen as well as heard. Like radio acting, it differs from acting in general in the last four of the previously listed seven items: bondage to a clock, quick and arbitrary transitions, huge audiences not assembled in a theatre, and a lack of traditional theatre projection.

5

And now let us drop from the clouds of theory back to earth.

In the official files of the American Federation of Radio Actors in New York City alone there are approximately 3,000 paid-up members. This total may be taken as a rough census of accepted and accredited professionals. The sobering fact, however, is that more than 50 per cent of the radio acting in New York City is done by 20 per cent of the members of AFRA. "They are the dependable troupers," as Robert J. Landry points out. "Studio-wise, quick to grasp direction, agile and adept, they are preferred-list choices for any program producer."[17] Marjorie Morrow, CBS casting director, states that of the radio actors in New York City "eighty per cent (which means 2,400 actors and actresses) are earning less than $20 a week."[18] The average salary for actors giving their full time to radio in 1947, according to a study conducted by the United States Department of Labor, was only $3,100. The figures for television actors are, and will continue to be, just as frightening. Because of the high production costs involved, television employment and salaries are not likely to equal for some time to come the average figures for radio. The conclusion to be drawn from this state of affairs is that the young actor who courts art or success, or even employment, must be competently trained.

Technical training and skill can be acquired by practice, but the results cannot always be sterling unless the actor candidate possesses a special sort of talent

[15] Lane Cooper, *Two Views of Education* (New Haven: Yale University Press, 1922), p. 115.

[16] Lane Cooper, *Aristotle on the Art of Poetry; An Amplified Version. . . .* (New York: Harcourt, Brace and Company, 1913), see pp. 27–28, 44.

[17] Landry, *This Fascinating Radio Business,* p. 269.

[18] Marjorie Morrow, "Precarious Pursuit," New York *Times,* December 28, 1947, p. X–11.

for acting. Talent can be cultivated, but it is largely inborn. Talent "is something one has or has not. You can develop it by hard work, but to create it is impossible."

A radio actor, before he proceeds to study and to practice his art, ought to know at least five of the attributes of talent that he must possess:

1) A voice that goes out magnetically and individually over the air lanes, "a voice that may express to its hearers a sense of things that the speaker neither intends nor could understand," "a voice whose life is at once contagious for the hearer," a voice that should have in it a quality somehow theatrical, that should in some baffling way immediately click.

2) A time sense, an instinct for pause and cues and beat, an awareness of retardation and acceleration, a feeling for rhythm, which Richard Boleslavsky has attempted to define as being "the orderly, measurable changes of all the different elements in a work of art . . . ."[19]

3) A gift of mimicry, an ear for all the oral manifestations, both eccentric and general, of different personalities, an ability to capture the *essence* of speech as heard in life—to which must be added the related awareness of tone.

4) Sensibility, the development of the five senses to so acute a degree that the nature of true contacts with the world can be recalled at will; sensibility that is, according to Henry James, "a kind of huge spider-web of the finest silken threads suspended in the chamber of consciousness, and catching every air-borne particle in its tissue . . . it takes to itself the faintest hints of life, it converts the very pulses of the air into revelations."[20]

5) Imagination, the ability to invent, to make new combinations from knowledge and past experience, and to enter inside both a character and a happening with full emotional understanding; imagination that is, like perception and memory, a mode of apprehension. Every word the actor speaks should be "the result of the right life of the imagination."

A television actor ought to know the three *additional* attributes of talent that he must possess:

1) A photogenic face—features that are not necessarily beautiful but so planed and proportioned and sharply defined that they film effectively.

2) A projective personality, a quality that can hold the viewers, that "will flow out from the screen and envelop the audience without seeming to work at it."

3) Pantomimic skill—complete command of bodily movement, gesture, and facial expression.

With some such prerequisites in talent the actor is ready to prepare himself for working, perhaps creating, in radio and in television.

[19] Boleslavsky, *Acting*, p. 112.

[20] "The Art of Fiction" (1884), in *Partial Portraits* (1888), quoted in F. O. Matthiessen, *The James Family* (New York: Alfred A. Knopf, Inc., 1947), p. 359.

DISCUSSION

Examine very carefully and discuss in class the following statements:

1. Through art we express our conception of what nature is not. (Picasso)

2. Art does not consist in repeating conscientiously everything we see and hear. Art consists in conjuring up, with the help of familiar symbols, the things that are not ordinarily perceptible to human eyes and ears. (C. A. LeJuene)

3. Art is not Magic, *i.e.*, a means by which the artist communicates or arouses his feelings in others, but a mirror in which they may become conscious of what their own feelings really are: its proper effect, in fact, is disenchanting. (R. G. Collingwood)

4. Art is man added to nature. (Bacon)

5. To effect . . . an intensification and clarification of experience is the province of art. (Irwin Edman)

6. Art is the communication of a conception in terms of a medium. (Eric Newton)

7. Art is . . . a representation of life and the emotions of life, but cut loose from immediate action. Action may be and often is represented, but it is not that it may lead on to a practical further end. The end of art is in itself. (Jane Harrison)

8. Art is the creation of meaningful patterns of experience, or the manipulation of human experience into meaningful patterns. (Stanley Edgar Hyman)

9. A memoir is history; it is based on evidence. A novel is based on evidence plus or minus X, the unknown quantity being the temperament of the novelist, and the unknown quantity always modifies the effect of the evidence, and sometimes transforms it entirely. (E. M. Forster)

10. . . . my own definition of art—the shortest with which I am familiar: articulate vision. (Edward Alden Jewell)

11. Art keeps alive the power to experience the common world in its fullness. It does so by reducing the raw materials of that experience to matter ordered through form. (John Dewey)

12. The aim of art is to represent not the outward appearance of things, but their inward significance; for this, and not the external mannerism and detail, is true reality. (Aristotle)

13. Art, if it is to survive and to function as a civilizing instrument, must administer to the cause of humanity; it must share and intensify the convictions of those who still have faith in the ultimate triumph of the human spirit. It cannot be separated from the people. (Thomas Craven)

14. . . . in objects created to arouse the aesthetic feeling we have an added consciousness of purpose on the part of the creator, that he made it on purpose not to be used but to be regarded and enjoyed . . . . And when we come to the higher works of art . . . . We feel that he has expressed something which was latent in us all the time, but which we never realized, that he has revealed us to ourselves in revealing himself. (Roger Fry)

15. Art is the desire of a man to express himself, to record the reactions of his personality to the world he lives in. (Amy Lowell)

16. Art is a weapon in the class struggle. (John Reed Club)

17. Art was originally concerned with the effort to assert the reality of things not present in the world of nature at all, with the effort to render concrete by pictorial representation that which is thought and spiritually real. (Otto Rank)

18. But a vital art work comes always from a cross between art and life: art being of one sex only, and quite sterile by itself. Such a cross is always possible: for though the artist may not have the capacity to bring his art into contact with the higher life of his time, fermenting in its religion, its philosophy, its science, and its statesmanship . . . he can at least bring it into contact with the obvious common passions of the streets. (Bernard Shaw)

19. I have no right to consider anything a work of art to which I cannot react emotionally. (Clive Bell)

20. To see anything as art means that you do not see it as a duplicate of something in life . . . . You judge its truth by its intentions, its essential idea. The history of any art is a history of man's states of mind and spirit, not of the objective world around him. (Stark Young)

21. Art is the intense expression of inner feeling through plastic means alone. (Gustave Moreau)

22. Art . . . is the mediatress between, the reconciler of nature and man. (Coleridge)

23. A musical composition is a musical phenomenon that emanates from the whole man, equipped with all his sensory resources and armed with his intellect, a form of speculation of which the elements are sound and time. (Stravinsky)

24. You see, what you don't understand is that acting isn't nature; it's art, and art is something you create. Real grief is ugly; the business of the actor is to represent it not only with truth but with beauty. (Somerset Maugham)

25. The artist says, "I will make that event happen again, altering its shape, which was disfigured by its contact with other events, so that its true significance is revealed"; and his audience says, "We will let that event happen again by looking at this man's picture or house, listening to his music or reading his book." It must not be copied, it must be remembered, it must be lived again, passed through those parts of the mind which are actively engaged in life . . . while at the same time it is being examined by those parts of the mind which stand apart from life. At the end of this process the roots of experience are traced; the alchemy by which they make a flower of joy or pain is, so far as is possible to our brutishness, detected. What is understood is mastered. (From *Black Lamb and Grey Falcon,* by Rebecca West. Permission to use this selection has been given by Rebecca West and The Viking Press, Inc. NOTE: This excerpt may be used only in the classroom and in no case on the radio or the stage, professionally or in any other way.)

SELECTED READINGS

General:

Irwin Edman's *Arts and the Man; A Short Introduction to Esthetics* (New York: W. W. Norton & Company, Inc., 1939) is both popular and thought-provoking. Read Chap. I, "Art and Experience," pp. 11–35; and Chap. II, "Art and Civilization," pp. 36–58.

Roger Fry has much that can be profitably read in his *Vision and Design,* first published in 1920 (Harmondsworth, Middlesex, England: Penguin Books, 1937). See especially the chapters, "Art and Life," pp. 11–21; "An Essay in Aesthetics," pp. 22–39; "Art and Science," pp. 71–75; "Giotto," pp. 112–148; "The Art of Florence," pp. 149–154; "Three Pictures in Tempera by William Blake," pp. 176–180; and "Retrospect," pp. 229–244.

J. W. N. Sullivan is illuminating in *Beethoven; His Spiritual Development* (New York: Alfred A. Knopf, Inc., 1944). Read Book One, "The Nature of Music," Chap. 1, "Art and Reality," pp. 3–24; Chap. 2, "Music as Isolated," pp. 25–37; and Chap. 3, "Music as Expression," pp. 38–58.

F. O. Matthiessen perceptively examines the nature of literature in *American Renaissance; Art and Expression in the Age of Emerson and Whitman* (New York: Oxford University Press, 1941), 678 pp.

Lascelles Abercrombie is worth reading in "Communication versus Expression in Art," *The British Journal of Psychology,* XIV (July, 1923), 68–77.

Percy Fitzgerald writes pointedly in *The Art of the Stage, as Set Out in Lamb's Dramatic Essays, with a Commentary* (London: Remington & Co., 1885). See especially in the "Commentary" the section, "Stage Illusion," pp. 225–255.

Alexander Bakshy is difficult but seminal in his chapter, "The Aesthetic of the Theatre," in his *The Theatre Unbound* (London: Cecil Palmer, 1923), pp. 65–107.

Stark Young is the most astute of all the critics of acting. Highly recommended is "Acting," in his *Theatre Practice* (New York: Charles Scribner's Sons, 1926), pp. 1–37. See the same article in his *The Flower in Drama* (New York: Charles Scribner's Sons, 1923), pp. 1–39. Also there is the excellent chapter, "The Actor," in his *The Theatre* (New York: Doubleday & Company, Inc., 1927), pp. 98–120. Both articles are indispensable to the actor who wishes to understand acting as an art.

Constantin Stanislavski's chapter, "When Acting Is an Art," in his *An Actor Prepares,* translated by Elizabeth Reynolds Hapgood (New York: Theatre Arts, Inc., 1936), pp. 12–30, gives an opposing point of view.

Special Topics:

Sensibility:

See Chap. II, "Sensibility," pp. 5–16; and Chap. III, "Observation," pp. 17–25, for many valuable exercises in *Modern Acting; A Manual,* by Sophie Rosenstein, Larrae A. Haydon, and Wilbur Sparrow (New York: Samuel French, Inc., 1936).

Read the delightful "The Fifth Lesson: Observation," in Richard Boleslavsky's *Acting; The First Six Lessons* (New York: Theatre Arts, Inc., 1933), pp. 89–102.

Imagination:

See Chap. IV, "Imagination," in Stanislavski's *An Actor Prepares,* pp. 51–67.

Read sometime *The Road to Xanadu; A Study in the Ways of the Imagination,* by John Livingstone Lowes (Boston: Houghton Mifflin Company, 1927), 639 pp.

For an advanced examination of the topic, see *Coleridge on Imagination,* by I. A. Richards (New York: Harcourt, Brace & Company, Inc., 1935). Read especially Chap. III, "The Coalescence of Subject and Object," pp. 44–71; and Chap. IV, "Imagination and Fancy," pp. 72–99.

Study Edward A. Armstrong's *Shakespeare's Imagination; A Study of the Psychology of Association and Inspiration* (London: Transatlantic Arts, Ltd., 1946), 191 pp.

Some Standard Books on Acting:

[Hill, John] *The Actor; or, A Treatise on the Art of Playing. . . .* London: R. Griffiths, 1755, 284 pp. A sequel to a book of the same title, and by the same author, published in 1750; both books are largely translated from Rémond de Sainte-Albine's *Le Comédien* (Paris, 1747).

Diderot, Denis, *The Paradox of Acting* (1770–1778; 1830), translated by Walter Herries Pollock. London: Chatto & Windus, 1883, 108 pp.

Talma, Francois J., *Reflexions on the Actor's Art* (1825), translator unknown, *Papers on Acting IV.* New York: Dramatic Museum of Columbia University, 1915, pp. 5–41.

Lewes, George Henry, *On Actors and the Art of Acting.* London: Smith-Elder & Company, 1875, 278 pp.

Coquelin, Constant, *Art and the Actor* (1880), translated by Abby Langdon Alger, *Papers on Acting II.* New York: Dramatic Museum of Columbia University, 1915, pp. 39–88.

The Art of the Actor (1886), translated by Elsie Fogerty. London: George Allen & Unwin, Ltd., 1932, 106 pp.

The Art of Acting; A Discussion by Constant Coquelin, Henry Irving, and Dion Boucicault, Papers on Acting II. New York: Dramatic Museum of Columbia University, 1916, "Actors and Acting (1887), pp. 5–42; "A Reply to Mr. Henry Irving," pp. 63–82; and "A Reply to Mr. Dion Boucicault," pp. 83–93.

Rapoport, I., "The Work of the Actor," translated by Ben Blake and Lyuba Vendrovskaya. *Theatre Workshop,* I, No. 1 (October-December, 1936), 5–40. The same article appears in *Acting; A Handbook of the Stanislavski Method,* edited by Toby Cole (New York: Lear Publishers, Inc., 1947), pp. 36–68.

Pudovkin, V. I., *Film Acting . . .*, translated by Ivor Montagu. London: George Newnes, Ltd., 1935, 153 pp.

Radio:

Anderson, John, "Notes on Radio," *Theatre Arts Monthly,* XXVIII, No. 6 (June, 1943), 341–346.

Arnheim, Rudolf, *Radio,* translated by Margaret Ludwig and Herbert Read. London: Faber & Faber, Ltd., 1936, 296 pp. See especially Chap. 7, "In Praise of Blindness; Emancipation from the Body," pp. 163–204. Consult also Chap. 1, "The Imagery of the Ear," pp. 21–26; Chap. 2, "The World of Sound," pp. 27–51; Chap. 3, "Direction and Distance," pp. 52–94; and Chap. 5, "Sequence and Distance," pp. 105–125.

Chase, Francis, Jr., *Sound and Fury; An Informal History of Broadcasting.* New York: Harper & Brothers, 1942, 303 pp.

Cott, Ted, *How to Audition for Radio. . . .* New York: Greenberg, Publisher, 1946, 142 pp.

Denison, Merrill, "The Actor and Radio," *Theatre Arts Monthly,* XVII, No. 11 (November, 1933), 849–855.

"The Broadcast Play," *Theatre Arts Monthly,* XV, No. 12 (December, 1931), 108–111.

Gielgud, Val, "The Actor and the Broadcast Play," *Theatre Arts Monthly,* XV, No. 2 (February, 1931), 119–122.

"The Broadcast Play," *Theatre Arts Monthly,* XIV, No. 11 (November, 1930), 956–962.

"Side Lights on the Broadcast Play," *Theatre Arts Monthly,* XV, No. 6 (June, 1931), 479–484.

"What Hope Radio Drama?" *Theatre Arts Monthly,* XVIII, No. 4 (April, 1934), 307–309.

Herzog, Herta, "On Borrowed Experience; An Analysis of Listening to Daytime Sketches," *Studies in Philosophy and Social Science,* IX, No. 1 (1941), 65–95.

Hughes, Richard, "The Second Revolution: Literature and Radio," *Virginia Quarterly Review,* XXIII (Winter, 1947), 34–43.

Julian, Joseph, "An Actor Analyzes Radio Acting," *Variety,* January 15, 1941, p. 30. (See also comments on the article in the issue of January 22, 1941, p. 34.)

Landry, Robert J., *This Fascinating Radio Business.* Indianapolis: Bobbs-Merrill Company, 1946, 343 pp. A general discussion.

Reis, Irving, "Techniques in Radio Drama," *Education on the Air; Eighth Yearbook of the Institute of Education by Radio,* edited by Josephine H. MacLatchy. Columbus: Ohio State University Press, 1937, pp. 211–217.

Robson, William N., "Dramatic Programs," *Education on the Air; Ninth Yearbook of the Institute for Education by Radio,* edited by Josephine H. MacLatchy. Columbus: Ohio State University, University Press, 1938, pp. 179–187.

Rose, Oscar, *Radio Broadcasting and Television; An Annotated Bibliography.* New York: H. W. Wilson Company, 1947, 120 pp. Imperfect, but helpful.

Tyler, Kingdom S., *Modern Radio.* New York: Harcourt, Brace & Company, Inc., 1944, 238 pp. A nontechnical explanation of technological matters, such as the control room, radio tubes, the transmitter, antennas, receivers, and the like.

Tyson, Raymond, "Acting for Radio," *Quarterly Journal of Speech,* XXV, 4 (December, 1939), 634–640.

Waller, Judith C., *Radio—The Fifth Estate.* Boston: Houghton Mifflin Company, 1946, 483 pp. An excellent survey.

EXERCISES

A note needs to be written about these exercises. Nobody will want to perform them; everyone will want to skip them and get on to the actual performance of radio plays. That attitude is fatal. No student should be exposed to actual radio scripts—or, no script should be exposed to the student—until he has had long practice in plain reading before the microphone.

Each of the following "curious" selections, differing widely in style, content, and objective, is the sort of material all radio actors are often called on to deliver in front of a microphone. Mostly they are examples of what acting is *not*. Therefore the question to be asked after a student reading of each of the selections is: "*Why* was that reading *not* acting as defined in the chapter just studied?" The reading of each of the selections should be examined and discussed from this point of view. In no better way can the student begin to learn—first, by definition, and finally in his very blood and bones—what acting is and what it is not. In no better way can he learn that not all microphone reading is acting.

Perhaps each selection that on being read turns out to be nonacting can be read again with a change of attitude and concept and thus translated into an example of acting. Can this be done? And if so, how? If not, why not?

Perhaps another question can be discussed: "Is there any great difference between material written for the eye and material written for the ear?"

The instructor ought to arrange the assignments so that each student is given no more than five or ten minutes for preparing the selection to be read at the microphone. Radio performers do not have all day to prepare.

The exercises should be supplemented, of course, by additional selections that the students and the instructor bring to class—especially selections from plays as examples of what acting truly is.

1. INTERNATIONAL SILVER*

MOTHER: Nancy, honey, there'll be five candles on your next birthday cake.

What a big girl you're getting to be! Big enough to tie your own shoes . . . and to make comic experiments with my lipstick. Big enough to help me set the table . . . and to notice the fresh flowers, the shiny forks and spoons.

Maybe you didn't choose the richest parents in the world, Nancy. But you're going to have the nicest life we can give you. A house doesn't need to be big and fancy for things to be done right in it.

I want you to grow up to be — Well, I guess the word is 'gracious.' It's because memories are important that I put on the pretty housecoats that you admire, and use our beautiful International Sterling at every meal.

I always thought that when I had a little girl like you, I'd want her to be used to nice things . . . like real 'family silver' that not

* By Kay Roberts, from *Life* Magazine, November 18, 1946, p. 63. Reprinted with the permission of International Silver Company, Meridian, Conn.

only <u>looks</u> wonderful, but is real and solid all the way through.

You see, darling, our International Sterling is so <u>very</u> good that we can use it always . . . And it won't wear out. It just gets lovelier and lovelier.

We couldn't have anything nicer if we lived in a castle like the ones in your storybooks.

2. EDDIE CANTOR SHOW*

CANTOR: Luba, you look gorgeous! (SIGHS) And that evening gown!

MALINA: Oh, it's more suitable for <u>formal</u> wear. This gown hardly fits around the house.

CANTOR: Say, it hardly fits around you. Now listen, Luba . . .

MALINA: Don't you think that first you should allow me to introduce yourself to me?

CANTOR: Oh, I'm sorry. This is Harry von Zell, and I'm Eddie Cantor.

VON ZELL: Eddie thought you'd recognize him by his pop eyes.

MALINA: From where I'm standing <u>both</u> your eyes are popping!

CANTOR: Oh — eh — We were just admiring your house. It's so lovely. It must have cost you a lot of money.

MALINA: No, I got it very cheap.

CANTOR: Well, I'm glad you moved in. Luba, we're neighbors. I live right next door to your house.

MALINA: That's why I got it so cheap!

VON ZELL: (LOW) Eddie, aren't you going to ask Luba Malina about her station wagon?

CANTOR: (LOW) Not yet, Harry. We'll sneak into it gracefully. (UP) Say, Luba, what do you think of American men?

MALINA: Oh, American men are so different from the Russians. You see, in Russia when a man is in love with a girl he gives her wonderful gifts . . . like chickens and turkeys and pigs and geeses. But what does a man give you here? (BELITTLING) Minks and sable and silver foxes and diamonds and annuities.

* By Joe Quillan, Johnny Rapp, Izzy Elinson, and Johnny Quillan. Reprinted through the courtesy of Eddie Cantor.

CANTOR: Luba, what's wrong with minks and sables and silver foxes and diamonds?

MALINA: Nothing. I love them.

CANTOR: You wear them?

MALINA: No, I sell them and buy chickens and turkeys and pigs and geeses.

CANTOR: Luba, I can see why men shower you with gifts. You're so lovely. You have such gorgeous black hair, such flashing dark eyes . . .

VON ZELL: Yeah, and such a beautiful station wagon!

CANTOR: Harry!

MALINA: Oh, you like my station wagon?

VON ZELL: Luba, would you mind if we borrowed it?

MALINA: Why, not at all . . . But I do think you should leave something with me as a deposit.

CANTOR: She's right, Harry.

VON ZELL: But what can we leave with her?

CANTOR: Me.

VON ZELL: You? (LAUGHS)

MALINA: Boys, I will lend you my station wagon on one condition. You must have it back here by six o'clock.

CANTOR: Six o'clock. And we can have the car now?

MALINA: Yes. The bumpers is loose, the fenders is loose, but still I will lend it to you.

VON ZELL: Oh, a lend-loose.

CANTOR: Stop that, Harry! And don't worry, Luba. We'll have your station wagon back on time.

MALINA: Eddie, my little boiled potato, before you go let me give you a kiss.

CANTOR: A kiss, Luba?

MALINA: Yes. One kiss from me and I know you come back.

CANTOR: One kiss from you and I no go away.

3. JOE COOK'S BASEBALL YARN*

JOE COOK: The score was tied — five to three — in favor of us. We needed six runs to win. Babe Ruth's grandfather was pitching. I was playing

* From *American Vaudeville*, by Douglas Gilbert (New York: Whittlesey House, 1940), pp. 257–258. Reprinted with permission.

second base and right field, as I was too good for one position. We have four men on base — two men on second, one a little short guy the umpire couldn't see.

My manager says to me — "Mr. Spalding" (I went under the name of Spalding in those days; saved me autographing baseballs), he says, "You're next at bat." So I turned to our bat boy, little Gerry Nugent, and says, "Gerry . . ." He says, "What is it, Mr. Delehanty?" (I went under the name of Delehanty for some time.) I says, "Bring me my bat." So Gerry and three other fellows carried my bat over for me. I used a telegraph pole for my bat in those days. I was very tall at one time but I have been out in the rain.

Well, sir, I crouched down in that well-known pose of mine; the ball comes sailing over the pan. I land into the old apple and she goes sailing right over center field fence, and at that I topped the ball. I started for first base. The crowds were hollering: "Hurrah for Weber" (they knew me under the name of Weber). The fans were cheering, bands playing, the King and Queen throwing kisses to me. The railroads started running excursions into the park. The crowd started to throw money at me. I picked up over $9,000 on my way to first base alone and put it in an old steamer trunk I always carried on my back when I ran bases. I light out for second base — third, fourth, fifth, sixth — this was a double header we were playing — and just as I am sliding home the umpire, Daniel Boone — Daniel Boone was umpiring — yells out — "Foul Ball!"

4. REBECCA*

MRS. DE WINTER: Last night I dreamt I went to Manderley again. It seemed to me I stood by the iron gate leading to the drive and for a while I could not enter, for the way was barred to me . . . Then, like all dreamers, I was possessed of a sudden with supernatural powers and passed like a spirit through the barrier before me . . .

The drive wound away in front of me, twisting and turning as it

* From the screen play by Robert E. Sherwood and Joan Harrison, based on the novel by Daphne du Maurier. Reproduced through the courtesy of Vanguard Films.

had always done, but as I advanced I was aware that a change had come upon it. Nature had come into her own again, and, little by little, had encroached upon the drive with long, tenacious fingers.

On and on wound the poor thread that had once been our drive, and finally there was Manderley — Manderley, secretive and silent. Time could not mar the perfect symmetry of those walls . . .

Moonlight can play odd tricks upon the fancy — and suddenly it seemed to me that light came from the windows . . .

And then a cloud came upon the moon and hovered an instant like a dark hand before the face. The illusion went with it and the lights in windows were extinguished.

I looked upon a desolate shell — with no whisper of the past about its staring walls . . . We can never go back to Manderley again. That much is certain. But sometimes in my dreams I do go back — to the strange days of my life —

5. WE THE PEOPLE: *DEAF CONGREGATION'S MINISTER**

POSSEHL: Two men were holding him and he was still struggling to get to the window. I made signs with my hands and told him to sit down. I asked the detective if we could be alone. I talked with him for a half hour, and through him I got my first glimpse of the world I never knew existed — the world of the deaf.

WEIST: It is a strange world, I imagine, Reverend Possehl.

POSSEHL: At times not as strange as it is cruel. That man wanted to commit suicide because he found it impossible to get a job. Well, I got that man a job and I found a career for myself. I studied for the ministry. I wanted to be a minister for the deaf.

MARGARET: Mr. Weist, it was certainly a fortunate day for the deaf when Reverend Possehl went to that hotel in St. Louis. My mother is deaf. And like so many totally deaf people, she finds it difficult to speak clearly. So without St. Matthew's she would have led a much lonelier life. You see, a deaf person gets very little spiritual satisfaction in the

* By James O'Neill. Reproduced through the courtesy of the author.

regular church ceremony. There's a barrier between him and the rest of the congregation. But not at St. Matthew's.

WEIST: Miss Borgstrand, just what is the difference in the service at St. Matthew's?

BORGSTRAND: Reverend Possehl conducts the service both in sign language and orally. The congregation responds to his prayers with signs. The choir sings their hymns with their fingers, getting the rhythm of the song from the vibrations of the organ. There's real beauty in their service. The church services are just one aspect of what Reverend Possehl does for his 250 members. Since the deaf are cut off from all sorts of amusement, Reverend Possehl shows them silent movies at the church. He arranges roller-skating parties, and helps them get jobs also. He even marries them. There is little he doesn't do for them.

POSSEHL: Thanks for the nice things you have just said, Margaret, but I'm afraid you're praising me for things my congregation did — not I. I am grateful to them for the chances to participate in their world. It is a full and satisfying life.

6. GORDON MACRAE SHOW: *THE MOUSE THAT PLAYED THE MINUET**

MACRAE: This was not an ordinary little mouse. No, sir. This mouse lived in a rich lady's home, and every afternoon he would run from the pantry to the music room. In the corner of the music room stood a beautiful golden harp. The mouse would run up and down the strings of the harp making a sound like this . . .

(MUSIC: HARP ARPEGGIO)

MACRAE: A big bulldog lived in the house too. He enjoyed music and he liked to hear the mouse play the minuet. But he was just like some people you and I know. The very minute the concert would start, his eyelids would get heavy and he would yawn . . .

(SOUND: YAWN)

MACRAE: Soon he would be fast asleep, dreaming of eating pork chops and chasing fat, gray alley cats. He would snore too . . .

(MUSIC: BASS CLARINET)

* By Paul Peterson, from the GORDON MACRAE SHOW, August 29, 1947. Reprinted through the courtesy of the author.

MACRAE: Now . . . out in the backyard was a high board fence. And one day a fat gray cat came down the alley dragging an old guitar. He climbed on the fence, swung over the gate, and began to rock back and forth like this . . .

(MUSIC: GUITAR THEME)

MACRAE: Then suddenly he heard the mouse playing the harp, and he stopped to listen . . .

(MUSIC: HARP MINUET FAINTLY . . . SUSTAIN UNDER)

MACRAE: There was something about that music that made his mouth water. So he jumped off the gate, crossed the backyard, and peeked through the window. And no wonder his mouth watered, for there was the roundest, fattest little mouse he had ever seen. Oh, my, how he wanted to catch that mouse! So he sat down and waited for the mouse to finish his song.

7. INTERVIEW IN PM*

YOUNG ACTRESS: I spent all my time in Hollywood being photographed. All they wanted to do was stick me on a white horse with pink plumes and feathers and everything. They made me a blonde and spent all their time glamorizing me. I didn't care if I had dirt on my face or how I was dressed — I just wanted to act. Finally I decided to do a Pygmalion in reverse. I dyed my hair back to its original color — brown — and wore very simple clothes. When Anita Loos and Josh Logan auditioned me for the role in Happy Birthday, they told me I wasn't sufficiently glamorous. I had to dye my hair a flaming red and wear it in an upsweep before I could get the part . . . I love to cook. I'm an excellent cook. I'd much rather entertain and play hostess than go out to a night club. And actually it's far less expensive. I think that people who are always going to night clubs are seeking something. The people in night clubs never look happy to me . . . I don't like pretty men. I'm partial to writers — good writers. Generally, you find the men in that category — they're not good-looking or hand-

* By Ira Peck, from *PM* (New York *Star*), December 29, 1946, p. M18. Reprinted with the permission of the *Star*.

some men — know more about people — they understand the little things, and they know how to handle women better. You know the song that Sinatra sings — "Try a Little Tenderness"? Well, believe me, that goes a long way with women. If I make a date with a man, that means I'm giving him my time and attention for an evening, and I expect he'll do the same. I'd be untrue to myself if I spent a lot of time with someone I didn't like.

8. INNER SANCTUM MYSTERY RADIO SHOW: *BURY ME NOT**

HOST: Good evening, friends of the Inner Sanctum. This is your host — inviting you in through the squeaking Door. Come in, won't you? And have yourselves a grisly time. Tonight is bingo night, and we're giving away a free set of coffins. Of course, the winner will have to be a corpse. But who knows? You may be the lucky stiff . . . (CHUCKLES) Come on — take a chance. That old casket of yours never did look good on you. In fact, I wouldn't be seen dead in it . . . (CHUCKLES)

***

Tonight's Inner Sanctum story is all about a woman who died twice — but was only buried once. The story begins with a storm — (THUNDER AND RAIN UNDER) — a storm that hung like an ominous shadow over the valley in which it was trapped. For three days and nights it poured . . . unmercifully . . . until every stream for miles around was swollen with its rage. And in every house along the river bank troubled faces stared into the night . . .

9. ARROW SHIRTS†

BILL: Saay, what's this I hear about you and that actor?

JEAN: Why — uh — you mean my old friend Cyril?

BILL: That's right — the heart-throb boy. I heard he took you to lunch today.

* By Robert Sloane. A radio presentation, not an adaptation of an Inner Sanctum Mystery novel. Reproduced through the courtesy of the author and Simon & Schuster, Inc., Publishers.

† By Sam Walker, from *The New Yorker,* December 7, 1946, p. 117. Reprinted through the courtesy of Cluett, Peabody & Company, Inc.

JEAN: Why, yes, darling. He wanted me to do him a favor.

BILL: Oh, he did, did he? I'll damage that profile of his beyond repair. I'll —

JEAN: Now take it easy. He has a problem.

BILL: I'll give him a problem, all right. I'll —

JEAN: You see, he admires your Arrow shirts so much. He was telling me how no other shirt was as flattering to a man's looks. Something about trim collars and a Mitoga figure-fit —

BILL: Just what is this leading up to?

JEAN: Well, he said that since he hasn't been able to get Arrow shirts his fan mail has fallen off —

BILL: So —

JEAN: He's in a new show — opens tomorrow night. And he said he'd get us two tickets, first row center, if —

BILL: Uh-oh. Now I catch on —

JEAN: — if I could possibly persuade you to let him have one of your new Arrow white shirts. Will do?

BILL: O.K. — but opening night only. Then I want my Arrow shirt back!

10. THE MARCH OF TIME*

VANVOORHIES: . . . and in Washington, at the United States State Department, newshawks have been waiting since morning for an interview with Cordell Hull, are ushered into the presence of a grave and deadly serious Secretary of State.

HULL: I'm sorry to have kept you waiting, gentlemen.

REPORTERS: MURMURS AND AD LIBS.

ONE: Mr. Secretary, the situation in Europe is so acute, we feel it is proper to ask that you explain the attitude of the government . . . give the public your appraisal of the crisis.

HULL: One person can appraise the situation as well as another, gentlemen.

THREE: Is it true that you have discussed the situation with President Roosevelt?

HULL: Whenever developments require it. I talk with the President every day.

ONE: Mr. Secretary, will you tell us how many American nationals are in the danger zone?

HULL: Yes, I can tell you that. There are 12,000 in France, almost 6,000 in Germany, and more than 5,000 in Czechoslovakia. Altogether about 23,000.

TWO: Are any arrangements being made to care for them in case of war?

HULL: Our envoys already have their instructions. They have full discretion to deal with any emergency which would require evacuation of American nationals. In Prague and other posts there are bombproof shelters, and American consular authorities have arranged facilities for our citizens.

(DOOR OPENS OFF)

AIDE: (COMING ON) Excuse me, Mr. Secretary. The President is calling from Rochester.

HULL: You must excuse me, please, gentlemen.

(SOUND OF NEWSHAWKS EXITING)

Good morning. Goodbye.

(RECEIVER OFF HOOK)

Hello . . . Hello, Mr. President.

11. THE LIFE OF SAMUEL JOHNSON*

E: From the experience which I have had, — and I have had a great deal, — I have learnt to think better of mankind.

JOHNSON: From my experience I have found them worse in commercial dealings, more disposed to cheat, than I had any notion of; but more disposed to do one another good than I had conceived.

J: Less just and more beneficent.

JOHNSON: And really it is wonderful, considering how much attention is necessary for men to take care of themselves, and ward off immediate evils which press upon them, it is wonderful how much they do for others. As it is said of the greatest liar, that he tells more truth than falsehood; so it may be said of the worst man, that he does more good than evil.

* By James Boswell (1791). AETAT. 69, Friday, April 3, 1778.

BOSWELL: Perhaps from experience men may be found happier than we suppose.

JOHNSON: No, Sir; the more we enquire we shall find men the less happy.

P: As to thinking better or worse of mankind from experience, some cunning people will not be satisfied unless they have put men to the test, as they think. There is a very good story told of Sir Godfrey Kneller, in his character of a justice of the peace. A gentleman brought his servant before him, upon an accusation of having stolen some money from him; but it having come out that he had laid it purposely in the servant's way, in order to try his honesty, Sir Godfrey sent the master to prison.

JOHNSON: To resist temptation once, is not a sufficient proof of honesty. If a servant, indeed, were to resist the continued temptation of silver lying in a window, as some people let it lie, when he is sure his master does not know how much there is of it, he would give a strong proof of his honesty. But this is a proof to which you have no right to put a man. You know, humanly speaking, there is a certain amount of temptation, which will overcome any virtue. Now, in so far as you approach temptation to a man, you do him an injury; and, if he is overcome, you share his guilt.

P: And, when once overcome, it is easier for him to be got the better of again.

BOSWELL: Yes, you are his seducer; you have debauched him. I have known a man resolve to put friendship to the test, by asking a man to lend him money, merely with that view, when he did not want it.

JOHNSON: That is very wrong, Sir. Your friend may be a narrow man, and yet have many good qualities: narrowness may be his only fault. Now you are trying his general character as a friend, by one particular singly, in which he happens to be defective, when, in truth, his character is composed of many particulars.

12. THE FALL OF THE CITY*

ANNOUNCER: There's the shout now: he's done:
He's climbing down: a great speech:

* From *The Fall of the City: A Verse Play for Radio.* Copyright, 1937, by Archibald MacLeish. Reprinted with the permission of the author.

They're all smiling and pressing around him:
The women are squatting in full sunlight;
They're opening packages: bread we'd say by the look —
Yes: bread: bread wrapped between corn leaves:
They're squatting to eat: they're quite contented and happy:
Women are calling their men from the sunny stones:
There are flutes sounding away off:
We can't see for the shifting and moving —
Yes: there are flutes in the cool shadow:
Children are dancing in intricate figures:
Even a few old men are dancing. . . .
That's odd! The music has stopped. There's something —
It's a man there on the far side: he's pointing:
He seems to be pointing back through the farthest street:
The people are twisting and rising: bread in their fists. . . .
We can't see what it is. . . . Wait! . . . It's a messenger.
It must be a messenger. Yes. It's a message — another.
Here he is at the turn of the street trotting:
His neck's back at the nape: he looks tired . . .

13. ANATOMY OF SOUND*

WOMAN: How would you like to get up before an audience of five million people and introduce yourself? Would you rap on the edge of a glass with a spoon to get attention, like this? (RAPPING ON GLASS) Do you think that would quiet such an audience? Would you clear your throat like this? (CLEARS THROAT) Or would you try to ride over their noise by shouting through a public address system the traditional salutation? (OVER A PUBLIC ADDRESS AMPLIFIER, AS THOUGH TRYING TO STOP A HUBBUB) Ladies and gentlemen! (NORMAL MIKE) And assuming you got the five million to quiet down, how would you then proceed to introduce yourself? You, standing alone on a stage with a battery of lights trained on you as though you were a night baseball game, only bigger.

* From *More by Corwin,* by Norman Corwin. Reprinted with the permission of Henry Holt and Company, Inc. Copyright, 1944, by Norman Corwin.

Suppose some of your audience were playing bridge and others arguing and still others reading newspapers? Would that terrify you? It would me, I know — except that at this moment when I am addressing five million people and thousands of them are playing bridge and talking across my voice and riding in automobiles and reading things, I'm not at all terrified. That's because there are four walls of a radio studio around me, and I cannot see your faces. I cannot see 246,197 cigarettes light up in the dark across eight million square miles of continent. And so it becomes relatively easy to get on with perfect strangers. Seclusion has an etiquette of its own. I will introduce myself to these strangers after a token sound to separate an informal prologue from a formal introduction.

14. THE ART OF MURDER*

Q. Now, suppose you had to deal with a sleeping man, and it was your object to get down his throat without his knowing it a liquid, the administration of which to the lips or throat would cause great pain — do you agree it would be a very difficult or delicate operation?

A. I think it would be an operation which would often fail, and might often succeed.

Q. Would not you look on it as a delicate operation?

A. I should look on it as a delicate operation, because I should be afraid of pouring it down the windpipe.

Q. That is one of the dangers you contemplate?

A. Yes.

Q. If it got into the windpipe, there would be spasmodic action of the muscles, would there not?

A. At the stage when you had come to the conclusion that you could do it, there is insensibility or partial insensibility, the rejection of the liquid by the windpipe would be probably less active than when the patient was awake.

* From "The Luck of Adelaide Bartlett," in *The Art of Murder,* by William Roughhead (New York: Sheridan House, Inc., 1943), p. 152 (from evidence of Dr. Thomas Stevenson, Trial, pp. 220–221). Reprinted with the permission of the publishers.

Q. If the patient got into such a state of insensibility as not to reject it, it would go down his windpipe and burn that?

A. Probably some of it might go down his windpipe.

Q. If it did so, it would leave its traces?

A. I should expect to find traces after death, unless the patient lives for some hours.

Q. Of course a great many post-mortem appearances are changed if the patient lives for some hours?

A. Yes.

Q. Not only by the chloroform disappearing, so to speak, but also other changes incidental to a post-mortem condition?

A. Yes.

Q. And if the post-mortem examination had been performed, as Mrs. Bartlett wished it to be, on the very day on which death took place, there would have been still better opportunity of determining the cause of death?

A. Yes.

15. THE ALDRICH FAMILY, #432*

ANNOUNCER: You know — people in Centerville are always so friendly! . . . smart, too! Like yesterday when I bumped into Agnes Lawson's mother coming out of the grocery shop . . .

MRS. LAWSON: (COMING ON) Oh, hello, Mr. Weist! So glad to see you! Only now I have to rush!

ANNOUNCER: What's your hurry, Mrs. Lawson?

MRS. LAWSON: Well, I've got to get supper under way! And you know how my husband is about his desserts! Well, maybe you don't, but anyway he is!

ANNOUNCER: Desserts? . . . my favorite subject! What's yours for tonight?

MRS. LAWSON: Oh, Frank's favorite. And it doesn't take long to cook . . . only about five minutes! Then I'll let it cool, and maybe serve it with sliced bananas and —

ANNOUNCER: I'm fascinated, Mrs. Lawson! What is this dessert?

MRS. LAWSON: Mr. Weist, I told you! Frank's favorite! . . . JELL-O Butterscotch Pudding!

* A commercial by Florence Clisbee. Reproduced through the courtesy of the author and General Foods Corporation.

ANNOUNCER: Ah, JELL-O Butterscotch Pudding! . . . with that old-time buttery brown-sugar goodness, mellow and smooth as cream! But how about JELL-O Chocolate Pudding . . . with that rich, true chocolaty flavor!

MRS. LAWSON: Why, that's Frank's second favorite dessert!

ANNOUNCER: And, of course, JELL-O Vanilla Pudding . . . with that wonderful vanilla delicacy!

MRS. LAWSON: How odd you should mention it! That's Frank's third favorite dessert!

ANNOUNCER: Right! All three JELL-O Puddings — Vanilla, Chocolate, and Butterscotch — are rich and distinctive . . . with that old-fashioned HOMEMADE goodness! A trio of treats!

MRS. LAWSON: What I like is they're nourishing too . . . made with milk.

ANNOUNCER: You bet! So try one, try all, friends! JELL-O Vanilla . . . Chocolate, and Butterscotch Puddings! You never tasted anything better!

16. MY LAST DUCHESS*

FERRARA: Sir, 'twas not

Her husband's presence only called that spot
Of joy into the Duchess' cheek: perhaps
Fra Pandolf chanced to say, "Her mantle laps
Over my lady's wrist too much," or "Paint
Must never hope to reproduce the faint
Half-flush that dies along her throat": such stuff
Was courtesy, she thought, and cause enough
For calling up that spot of joy. She had
A heart — how shall I say? — too soon made glad,
Too easily impressed: she liked whate'er
She looked on, and her looks went everywhere.
Sir, 'twas all one: My favour at her breast,
The dropping of the daylight in the West,
The bough of cherries some officious fool
Broke in the orchard for her, the white mule
She rode with round the terrace — all and each

* From the poem by Robert Browning.

Would draw from her alike the approving speech,
Or blush, at least. She thanked men, — good!
but thanked
Somehow — I know not how — as if she ranked
My gift of a nine-hundred-years-old name
With anybody's gift.

17. THE CANDID MICROPHONE, #18: *THE LOST SHOE**

Now listen to what happened when the man with the hidden microphone stepped into a shoe salesman's shoes.

A: I've showed you about twenty-two shoes and I don't think I can find anything you like.

W: Well, I'm sorry then.

A: You . . .

W: There's nothing you can do for me then.

A: No. Did you happen to see your other shoe?

W: No, you took it off.

A: Ah . . .

W: It must be around here.

A: I don't know where the other one is.

W: You took it off and you put it down . . .

A: It isn't any place around here. And ah . . . I don't . . .

W: Maybe someone kicked it under another chair.

A: No . . . Maybe . . . but I'm looking. I don't see a thing of it.

W: Well, I'm sure no one walked out with it.

A: No, I don't think so. Eight-double-A. I . . . I'll go back and look for it. I might of put it back there.

(MUSIC: SEVEN SECOND SNEAK BRIDGE)

A: It just can't be found right now. I —

W: Well, standing here and talking to me is not finding my —

A: No, madam. I went back there. I just went back there. I —

W: And what did you do? You just went back there and came right back.

A: (UNDER) I don't see anything there but boxes of shoes.

* Reproduced through the courtesy of Allen A. Funt Productions.

W: You find my shoe.

A: Are you sure you came in with two shoes?

W: Yes, I am. And —

A: Nobody's going to take one shoe.

W: No, I don't think they would.

A: I don't want to waste any more of your time.

W: I want to see the manager.

A: I'm the manager.

W: You're the manager!

A: I'm the manager, yes. I wait on customers sometimes, but I'm the manager.

W: Is there another manager in the store?

A: What do you mean — another manager? How many managers do you think we have around here? There's only one manager.

W: Well, there should be more than one with you around.

A: Well, I'm trying to help you.

W: You're not helping me by sitting there and talking to me.

A: I want you to go out and come back and we'll find your shoe.

W: You find my shoe while I'm sitting here!

18. INTERMISSION TALK: *PHILHARMONIC SYMPHONY SOCIETY OF NEW YORK**

DEEMS TAYLOR: Do you know, I'm afraid I think it's a good thing that we do hear so much cheap humor and bad sentiment and bad music on the radio. Mind you, I think it would be an even better thing if we heard nothing but good stuff on the radio — if everybody wanted to hear it. But as long as there are people who want to hear bad stuff, they should be allowed to listen to it if it isn't obscene or criminal. Because if they're not allowed, they won't listen to anything else. Now I know that in some countries broadcasting is in the hands of certain persons who are so confident of the infallibility of their own taste that they undertake to decide what is or is not good for the public to hear on the radio. They allow the public to hear only such music as is, in their opinion, "good" music. It's my guess that large portions of the population simply turn their radios off when some of that "good" music

* By Deems Taylor, broadcast December 11, 1938. Reprinted through the courtesy of the author.

is being played. It's one thing to offer a listener something, and it's another thing to get him to listen. So long as his receiving set is working, no matter how low his tastes are, you always have the chance of luring him into hearing and learning to like something better than what he thought he liked; in other words, of elevating his taste. But you can't elevate a man's taste through a dead radio.

19. ARTHUR GODFREY'S TALENT SCOUTS*

GODFREY: Hello. This is Godfrey . . . the sweeter Peter Lorre. Well, I just got back from my first vacation from radio in ten years. I didn't really need it. MY LISTENERS did! It was nice going to my farm in Virginia. I'd been away so long my youngster didn't recognize me. When he saw me coming along the road he started to scream — A watchdog, in diapers.

Well, this is the Talent Scout show, and once more five talented acts found by you, the public, will be presented to the rest of the country with this question mark: Are they as good as the people who found them think they are? And if they are, what are we going to do about it? Well, we'll do plenty, believe me.

Right now let me tell you that if you haven't as yet received an answer to the letters you wrote us, please be patient. We have a large staff working on nothing else but answering our correspondence, and right now she's a very tired girl. Seriously, we have eight girls at work all day and every day, and we'll catch up to your letter soon.

But after all, that's "soon," but this is right now. So after I tell you all the talent gets $100 and the talent scout $25, let's meet our first talent scout, Mr. Kale Mody.

GODFREY: That's a very unusual name, sir. May I ask where you are from?

MODY: I come from Bombay, India.

GODFREY: You sure travelled an awfully long distance just to make yourself twenty-five bucks. Why ARE you here, Mr. Mody?

MODY: I came to America twenty months ago to study at New York University.

* By Kenny Lyons. Reproduced through the courtesy of Kenny Lyons, Arthur Godfrey, and the Columbia Broadcasting System.

GODFREY: A college education is a wonderful thing. It's too bad so few college graduates get one. What are you majoring in?

MODY: Business Administration. I just finished my courses in the fall of this year, and next I go to Harvard.

GODFREY: You have the right accent for it, I'll tell you that. Whom are you scouting for tonight, Mr. Mody?

MODY: A young lady named Chris Adams. A very attractive young lady.

GODFREY: He's here twenty months and he's found something most guys never find in twenty years. How did you meet her?

MODY: Her father and mine are business associates. My father wrote her father I was coming over here, and an appointment was arranged between Chris and me. After we met I heard her sing, and I thought she was entitled to the chance you offer on this program.

GODFREY: Where had she sung before, sir?

MODY: Her first job was with Richard Himber's orchestra when she was sixteen. After that she went with Dean Hudson's band, and up until a month ago she was singing with Ray McKinley. This is her first try on her own.

GODFREY: Well, let's let her (BRITISH) have a go at it, shall we, old man?

MODY: Righto.

GODFREY: Cheerio, pip pip, and thank you, old fellow. Ladies and gentlemen, the singing cutie of the boy from Bombay . . . Chris Adams.

20. DESCENT OF THE GODS*

ANNOUNCER: We interrupt the program of the Four Horsemen to bring you the following bulletin:

NEWSCASTER: Boston, Massachusetts. Police and civic authorities are puzzled over the appearance early tonight of a beautiful woman claiming to be the goddess Venus. Astonished spectators reported that she descended on a brilliant shaft of light on Boylston Street, in the heart of the city, shortly after eight. At first she was mistaken for movie exploitation in connection with the opening of a new picture at Keith's.

* From *More by Corwin,* by Norman Corwin. Reproduced by permission of Henry Holt and Company, Inc. Copyright, 1944, by Norman Corwin.

Asked what she was doing in Boston, she said she had read a reference to that city as the Hub of the Universe and wanted to see what a hub of the universe looked like. The case has been referred to the immigration authorities. A public hearing will be held tomorrow. For further details read your newspaper.

ANNOUNCER: We now return you to the program of the Four Horsemen.

Chapter II . . VOICE AND SPEECH

1

When Salvini declared that three things are necessary in order to act: "first—voice, second—voice, and third—voice,"[1] he undoubtedly made some gorgeous sounds, if not complete sense, while resonantly overemphasizing his point. The truth of the matter is that the voice is not, as some would have it, "the ultimate mark of the good or bad actor" nor, more eloquently, "the justification of the theatre." Actually, it is no more than "the actor's most potent instrument of expression." That is importance enough to claim for the voice in acting; it is considerable.

Because an actor's voice is his most prominent and influential medium, you can say of it, whether on stage or on the screen or at the microphone, that it must somehow be more expressive than an everyday, bread-and-butter voice. You can say, as Stark Young does, that

> . . . the tone an actor uses can move us more than any other thing about him. The word he speaks gives the concept . . . but the voice may be anger itself or longing, and may go straight, as music does, to the same emotion in us . . . . The voice in our theatre is used almost entirely as an articulate medium. But a part of every truth is its inarticulateness: all the half-conscious elements, delicate implications, the radiant and shadowy emanations that make up every human truth, and that words can never express. And sound itself has significance. The articulate meaning of the word *pain* is a symbolistic accident; the sound of it goes vaguely but farther in . . . .
>
> Things for which there are no words, which rule us without sharing their counsels with us, which have no outlines or patterns in our thinking but which move in us like the wind through the world, which are ourselves indeed and carry us beyond ourselves, all these can sound express or arouse.[2]

[1] Salvini; quoted in "The Actor's Creative Work," by I. Sudakov, *Theatre Workshop,* I (January–March, 1937), p. 39.

[2] Young, *Theatre Practice,* pp. 160–161, 157; cf. *The Theatre,* p. 34.

You must say more than that, though, about the radio actor's voice. It ought to be even more expressive than the stage or screen actor's voice, because it is the only bridge between the playwright's text and the audience. It should do more than other voices do. It must indicate many things that cannot be seen: it must to some considerable extent include in itself the make-up and costume, all movements and gestures and business, and the various scenes of the action. In short, you are compelled to conclude that the talents of a radio actor count only in so far as they are evidenced in his voice.

Since the voice, then, is the radio actor's only instrument of expression, it is too important ever to be merely taken for granted. Yet something there is in too many radio performers that illogically minimizes vocal training, that lazily accepts inadequate voices and deplores as incidental or wasteful any time spent on voice improvement. Perhaps the cause of this general antipathy to training the voice is a mistaken notion, such as the following: "Stanley in Tennessee Williams' *A Streetcar Named Desire* never took any voice lessons; so why should I have to practice vocal exercises in order to act the role?" (Where and when will such specious arguments ever end?) Whatever the cause, so long as radio voices are untrained, their characteristics are likely to be "apart from bad enunciation, a tone driven through the nose, an inflexible upper lip, a very insecure placement in the throat." Just so long will anyone who auditions novice radio performers be continually astounded at the poor quality of the voices heard—voices that are thin, harsh, bleak, monotonous, and completely lacking in individual color or warmth. Just so long will the radio actors themselves be frequently baffled and balked because their voices cannot do what is demanded of them.

The voice of the radio actor needs to be trained, and can be trained. A pleasing and expressive voice "is no more a 'gift of God' than is the tone from any other musical instrument, like a piano or violin."[3] It does not just happen eventually—like a paunch. The ingredients of a first-rate voice—good tone, flexibility, and proper articulation—are not contagious; no one ever "catches" them. Nor do these vocal virtues ever come to anyone as surprise legacies one day from out of the blue. Radio actors have to try for them.

2

In trying for good tone the radio actor needs to develop, according to Wayland Parrish, (1) a firm support that comes from diaphragmatic-abdominal breathing, (2) a freedom from strain and tension that comes from a so-called relaxed throat, and (3) a pleasing color or quality that comes from well-balanced resonance.[4]

1) Cultivation of good tone demands, first of all, correct and efficient breathing. The well-known voice teacher, Frances Robinson-Duff, insists, "I couldn't possibly teach anyone to speak well without teaching him first of all . . . how to breathe properly." The fault with many voices is a lack of breath, or badly managed breath, during utterance. Therefore the skills to be developed in breathing, as listed by Grant Fairbanks, are three: (a) expansion and contraction in the proper regions of the torso, (b) controlled expiration during speech, and (c) inspiration during the natural pauses.[5]

a) The wrong method of breathing is high-chest breathing, or the chest-expansion kind practiced in every gymnasium. This is inefficient for microphone speech because it is fatiguing, because it increases tensions in the throat area, and because it offers no firm control over expiration. The right method of breathing is diaphragmatic, or natural, breathing—an expansion and contraction of the body just above the belt line—the breathing, for instance, of the basketball player as he lies stretched out on the floor during a time-out period.

In inhalation, the diaphragm contracts and takes a lower position across the body. In doing so it gives the lungs more room above and displaces the visceral organs below, causing them to bulge outward at the waistline. In exhalation, the abdominal muscles crowd the viscera inward, causing them to bulge upward against the diaphragm, forcing it back to its high arched position, and so expelling the air from the lungs.[6]

b) During vocalization the problem is to control carefully the exhalation of breath, the gradually relaxing diaphragm. Many radio actors habitually and wrongly allow more breath to escape at the beginning of a phrase than toward the end, while others habitually expire a large fraction of their breath immediately after inspiration, *before* beginning a new phrase, or on the first word. The actor must practice to perfect a *steady* exhalation by hardening the abdomen, since evidence shows that contraction is steady in good voice usage, jerky in poor.

c) As for inspiration during utterance, the radio actor can avoid "running out of breath" or requiring special stopping places for the sole purpose of replenishing his breath supply, if he will pause as often as he should and learn to use the pauses to ventilate his lungs. The remedy is as simple as that. Moreover, since "it is easier to take a shallow breath than a deep one" and "since inspirations may be frequent in average speech, they may also be shallow."[7] Frequent shallow breathing is required in front of radio's extremely sensitive microphones—unless the sound of the actor's breathing is desired as an essential part of the dramatic effect.

2) Cultivation of tone demands, second, a so-called relaxed throat, since "a good voice is one that seems to flow through the throat as if there were nothing there to interrupt it." Usually when the radio actor is ill-prepared, rushed, nervous, uncertain, self-conscious, or trying too hard, he tightens his jaw, neck, or shoulders; and always as a result his vocal quality is sure to be impaired. In all such instances he must learn to do just the opposite: he must relax the interfering muscles. He must learn how to speak without strain and wrong and unnatural tensions.

3) Finally, cultivation of good tone demands a clear, pleasing resonance or "voice placement." The encouraging truth here is that *any weak voice can be substantially improved*—within limits. Always "a better habit of resonance may be developed by improving the habits

[3] Floyd S. Muckey, *The Natural Method of Voice Production* (New York: Charles Scribner's Sons, 1915), p. 112.

[4] Wayland Parrish, *Reading Aloud; A Technique of the Interpretation of Literature,* 2nd ed., rev. (New York: The Ronald Press Company, 1941), p. 196.

[5] Fairbanks, *Voice and Articulation Drillbook,* pp. 134–135.

[6] Parrish, *op. cit.,* p. 185.

[7] Fairbanks, *op. cit.,* p. 133.

of the tongue, palate, and lips, but the material substance of the human resonators cannot be changed. A voice is what it is, and is distinguishable from other voices, partly because of such individual factors as hardness of gums, shape of the mouth-arch, thickness of cheeks, etc."[8] All the radio actor need aim for, in the opinion of Parrish, is a voice "which carries to the vowels the same balance of resonance as is found in the hummed *m*. This . . . probably brings us as near as we can come to a satisfactory solution of the problem of tone placement."[9]

3

In trying for greater vocal flexibility the radio actor should utilize the flexibility he already has, in most instances, if he but knew it. According to Henrietta Prentiss,

> . . . each of us has many qualities of voice, one of which we habitually over-use. The shrill yip yapping of the flapper, the growl of the paterfamilias, the dry incisiveness of the mathematician, each of these is not the one and only voice of its possessor. If the girl fall in love the whole timbre and range of her voice are transformed. If the father hold his infant in his arms there is an unaccustomed clearness and sweetness in his voice. If the scientist celebrate a victory there is a ring and sparkle in his words rarely heard in the classroom. Even a pessimistic college or dramatic school student in a required course in voice training can be happily moved from her conviction that "her voice," poor thing though it may be, is irrevocably and unchangeably hers, if you remind her that her family can always detect the "man at the other end of the line" by the change in the quality of her voice, however guarded her remarks.[10]

Instead of limiting himself to an habitual three or four notes in his voice—"a hopelessly inadequate range for even the most bovine existence"—instead of using less vocal range at the microphone than he uses in normal, everyday conversation, the radio actor should try to make his *natural* pitch level his *habitual* pitch level. They are not always identical. Everyone has a certain natural pitch level, determined by the characteristics of his mechanism, at which his voice is most efficient for speech. Yet most persons, especially before a microphone, tend to limit this natural level to a narrower habitual level. There are tests by which the actor can determine his habitual and natural pitch levels (see Fairbanks, pages 166–171) and thereby discover whether he is using his voice most efficiently for the greatest flexibility.

(Research has shown, according to Fairbanks, that the pitch levels of superior adult male speakers are located very close to C_3, one octave below middle C on the musical scale, while those of superior adult female speakers approximate $G\sharp_3$, two tones below middle C. "Although these values may be recommended as the *optimum* or *best* pitch levels for the two sexes, they cannot be enforced rigidly with all speakers because of the individual structural differences.")[11]

In checking his vocal flexibility still further the radio actor should know that "superior speakers have average total singing ranges including falsetto of approximately 22 to 24 notes, or 18 to 20 musical tones."[12] Therefore any radio actor with a range less than 15 tones should make a systematic attempt to increase it by daily drill.

All in all, as Henrietta Prentiss observes,

> The actor of fine technique has a hundred natural voices, each one adding its expression and emphasis and character revelation quite simply and fluently to any part he creates. A fine actor does not affect one voice or speech for a king and another for a pauper; he has those voices and a whole range between, and they are set free as he develops his characterization. New experiences do not foist new voices upon us. They reveal the many facets of our voices. In the same way, voice training and exercises in interpretation bring out our varied vocal qualities and make us unwilling to express ourselves habitually in our most commonplace.[13]

4

In trying for correct articulation the radio actor ought to learn, as Shaw said in all solemnity, "how to pronounce the English alphabet clearly and beautifully from some person who is at once an artist and a phonetic expert."[14] While it is not the actors' duty to set the speech standards of a country, it is their shame to enunciate badly—to substitute sloppily one vowel for

[8] Parrish, *op. cit.*, p. 195.

[9] *Ibid.*, p. 196.

[10] Prentiss, "The Master Key to Understanding," p. 588.

[11] Fairbanks, *op. cit.*, pp. 168–169.

[12] *Ibid.*, p. 169.

[13] Prentiss, *op. cit.*, p. 599.

[14] George Bernard Shaw, *Dramatic Opinions and Essays,* edited by James Huneker (New York: Brentano's, 1906) I, p. 27.

another, "sod" for "sawed," "putt" for "put," or "min" for "men"; to substitute the voiced consonant for its voiceless correlative, "medal" for "metal," or "wading" for "waiting"; to slight, to distort, or to omit the proper sounds.

The radio actor, furthermore, has to watch his hisses. Microphones do rude, steamlike things to *s, ch,* and to several somewhat similar sibilant sounds. He must by practice learn to "swallow," to minimize, them.

As Shaw wrote to Ellen Terry,

When people intend to play the piano in public they play scales for several hours a day for years. A pupil of Leschititsky (Paderewski's master) comes before the public with steel fingers, which gives a peculiar quality and penetration even to pianissimo notes. *An actress should practice her alphabet in just the same way, and come before the public able to drive a nail up to the head with one touch of a consonant. For want of this athleticism, people get driven to slow intonings, and woolly execution.*[15]

5

The full subject of voice training is a large and highly technical one, and is therefore better left to specialists. A complete discussion of voice and speech, with exercises, would require another book, a book within this one. What can be said here, however, and said emphatically, is that *some intensive work in voice training ought to be a prerequisite for any study of radio acting.* Yet expert voice and speech teachers are rare; Tom-Dick-and-Harry poseurs are everywhere and can do much harm. As a result, the ambitious radio actor is often forced to become his own teacher by turning to some of the better books on the subject.

Three such books can be highly recommended. The first is *The Voice; How to Use It, with Exercises for Tone and Articulation,* by Sarah T. Barrows and Anne E. Pierce (Magnolia, Mass.: The Expression Co., 1933), 172 pages. Part I includes exercises for relaxation, breathing, voiced and voiceless sounds, and the articulators; Part III includes exercises for vowel tones, voice quality, and resonance. The second is *Voice and Articulation Drillbook,* by Grant Fairbanks (New York: Harper and Brothers, 1940), 234 pages, which is at its best in Chapters II, III, and IV on vowel articulation, diphthong articulation, and consonant articulation, and includes extensive exercise material. The chapters on breathing and on voice quality also furnish profitable reading and exercises. The third is *An Introduction to the Phonetics of American English,* by Charles K. Thomas (New York: The Ronald Press Company, 1947), 181 pages. One chapter, "The Mechanism of Speech," is a clear summary of the subject, and the rest of the book is authoritative in its examination of the sounds in English.

With the help of these three books any radio actor can refute Shaw's observation that "actors and actresses never dream nowadays of learning to speak."[16]

6

For the correct pronunciation of commonplace words every radio actor should own *A Pronouncing Dictionary of American English,* by John Samuel Kenyon and Thomas Albert Knott (Springfield, Mass.: G. & C. Merriam Co., 1944), 484 pages. This "dictionary of colloquial English, of the everyday unconscious speech of cultivated people—of those in every community who carry on the affairs and set the social and educational standards of those communities," uses the symbols of the International Phonetic Alphabet. It is indispensable.

7

Closely related to proper breathing and correct articulation is the radio actor's rate of speaking. How quickly or how slowly should he read his lines? The immediate and correct answer is that generally he ought to speak more quickly than his colleagues on stage and on the screen. Since he is denied the support and filling-in of movements, gestures, stage business, and facial expressions, he must be trained in speed of enunciation and delivery of lines. Only in the daytime serials can the actor take his naturalistic time. Here, because housewives going about their daily tasks give only intermittent attention to the radio plays they are tuned to, the actor can perhaps use pauses wide enough to drive Stanislavski through in a Chevrolet coupé. Elsewhere on the air lanes, however, the actor has to keep things moving along.

[15] George Bernard Shaw and Ellen Terry, *Ellen Terry and Bernard Shaw; A Correspondence,* edited by Christopher St. John (New York: G. P. Putnam's Sons, 1931), p. 171.

[16] Shaw, *op. cit.,* I, 243.

Research has discovered that the rate for radio speakers—though not necessarily for actors—is likely to be too rapid if it exceeds 185 words a minute or too slow if it is less than 140 words a minute. (You can quickly measure your reading rate by the test included in Fairbanks, page 144.) To furnish you with a base for measurement, Franklin Delano Roosevelt spoke between 110 and 135 words a minute, and certain news commentators have gone as high as 225 words a minute. Radio actors sometimes speak as slowly as Franklin Roosevelt, but more often they speak almost as rapidly as the news commentators.

Yet, as Stark Young warns,

> For this speed, of course, there would have to be concentration on the precise accent of word and on the sense accent; and there would have to be trained lips, tongue, and breathing. There would have to be vivacity of tone, concentration on the values of emphasis and idea, and smart accuracy of phrase. But what else is an artist . . . for? [17]

The secrets of brisk utterance at the microphone are two: smart picking up of your cues and an avoidance of taking the tempo of your speech from the speech that has just been spoken. As Young concludes,

> A study of tempo by our actors would help mend two of the worst faults . . . monotony and lack of speed. And the achievement of more variety and speed would help to clear away the idly imitative, the realistic clutter now so much in the way of the art of the theatre. And finally a study of tempo leads to better diction, to more flexible characterization, and to a sharper impress of the dramatic pattern involved.[18]

8

In summary, then, the radio actor's voice should ideally give an audience beauty of tone, wide flexibility, correct articulation, and (especially for verse) a grace of measure, together with evidence of rich feeling and fine intelligence "without which those technical qualities would soon become monotonous." These virtues are the product of correct vocal training.

Ideally there is something else a radio actor's voice ought to do, an additional something that is usually neglected in training. The best actor's voice should have in it and give to an audience a sense of style. This means a constant variation in the quality of the voice to suit the kind of play it carries. It means, as Young elaborates the point, that

> in a comedy of manners like the *School for Scandal* the voice should be clear, finished, the lips expert, the tongue striking well on the teeth; the tone would go up and down but always be sure of its place in the throat, be crisp, shining, in hand, like the satin and gold of the furniture and costumes, the rapier at the wrist, the lace over it, the wordliness and the wit. In Chekov it would have the last naturalness, every closeness to feeling and impulse that the moment reveals. In Shakespeare a range of elaborate music, suited to the style, clearness, with warmth of poetic emotion. In D'Annunzio's drama the voice would have to be rich and sensuous, metallic, shading infinitely, the voice of a degenerate god. And so on through the styles and moods of all drama.[19]

And so on through the different styles of radio playwrights such as Corwin, Oboler, Goldsmith, Carrington, Quinn, Perl, and Alexander.

SELECTED READINGS

General:

Aikin, William A., *The Voice; An Introduction to Practical Phonology* (2nd ed.). New York: Longmans, Green & Company, Inc., 1910, 159 pp.

Anderson, Virgil A., *Training the Speaking Voice.* New York: Oxford University Press, 1942, 387 pp.

Barrows, Sarah T., and Anne E. Pierce, *The Voice: How to Use It, with Exercises for Tone and Articulation.* Magnolia, Mass.: The Expression Co., 1933, 172 pp.

Beiswanger, George, "The Power behind the Tone," *Theatre Arts Monthly,* XXIV, No. 10 (October, 1940), 735–744.

Cantril, Hadley, and Gordon W. Allport, "Voice and Personality," in their *The Psychology of Radio.* New York: Harper & Brothers, 1935, pp. 109–126.

Corson, Hiram, *The Voice and Spiritual Education.* New York: The Macmillan Company, 1923, 198 pp.

Curry, Robert, *The Mechanics of the Human Voice.* New York: Longmans, Green & Company, Inc., 1940, 205 pp.

Curry, Samuel S., *Mind and Voice; Principles and Methods in Vocal Training.* Magnolia, Mass.: The Expression Co., 1910, 456 pp.

Daggett, Windsor P., "The Delivery of Words," *Theatre Arts Monthly,* XIV, No. 7 (July, 1930), 614–618.

[17] Young, *Theatre Practice,* p. 44.
[18] *Ibid.,* p. 45.
[19] *Ibid.,* pp. 159–160.

"Hans across the Sea," *Theatre Arts Monthly,* IX, No. 10 (October, 1925), 655–660.
"The Lineage of Speech," *Theatre Arts Monthly,* IX, No. 9 (September, 1925), 597–604. Also in *Theatre,* edited by Edith J. R. Isaacs (Boston: Little, Brown & Company, 1927), pp. 35–36.
"The Sound of English," *Theatre Arts Monthly,* X, No. 1 (January, 1926), 25–31.
"The Voice and the Magic Word," *Theatre Arts Monthly,* IX, No. 6 (June, 1925), 366–373.
"Ugly Words," *Quarterly Journal of Speech,* VIII, No. 3 (June, 1922), 266–270.

Dodds, George R., and James D. Lickley, *The Control of the Breath.* London: Oxford University Press, 1925, 65 pp.

Fairbanks, Grant, *Voice and Articulation Drillbook.* New York: Harper & Brothers, 1940, 234 pp.

Holmes, F. Lincoln D., "Resonance," *Quarterly Journal of Speech,* XXI, No. 2 (April, 1935), 216–224.

Huyck, E. M., and K. D. A. Allen, "Diaphragmatic Action of Good and Poor Speaking Voices," *Speech Monographs* 4 (1937), 101–109.

Kenyon, Elmer, "Speech Standards in the Theatre," *Quarterly Journal of Speech,* XII, No. 3 (June, 1926), 196–199.

Lumley, F. H., "Rates of Speech in Radio Speaking," *Quarterly Journal of Speech,* XIX, No. 3 (June, 1933), 393–403.

Pear, Tom H., *Voice and Personality as Applied to Radio Broadcasting.* New York: John Wiley & Sons, Inc., 1932, 247 pp.

Prentiss, Henrietta, "The Master Key to Understanding," *Theatre Arts Monthly,* X, No. 9 (September, 1926), 587–592.
"Our Speech Standards," *Quarterly Journal of Speech,* XIV, No. 2 (April, 1928), 189–195.
"The Training of the Voice," *Studies in Speech Training and Public Speaking for Secondary Schools,* edited by A. M. Drummond. New York: Appleton-Century-Crofts, Inc., 1925, pp. 63–75.

Stanley, Douglas, *Your Voice, Applied Science of Vocal Art—Singing and Speaking.* New York: Pitman Pub. Corp., 1945, 306 pp.

Thomas, Charles K., *An Introduction to the Phonetics of American English.* New York: The Ronald Press Company, 1947, 181 pp.
"Voice and Speech," in James A. Winans, *Speech Making.* New York: Appleton-Century-Crofts, Inc., 1938, pp. 452–478.

Young, Stark, "The Voice in the Theatre," in his *The Flower in the Drama.* New York: Charles Scribner's Sons, 1923, pp. 85–92. The same essay appears in his *Theatre Practice* (New York: Charles Scribner's Sons, 1926), pp. 156–163.

Pronunciation:

Dolman, John, Jr., "Notes on Pronunciation," in his *The Art of Play Production* (rev. ed.). New York: Harper & Brothers, 1946, pp. 245–249.

Gray, Giles W., "Sidelights on the Pronunciation of English," *Quarterly Journal of Speech,* XVIII, No. 4 (November, 1932), 546–560.

Greet, W. Cabell, *World Words; A Guide to Pronunciation of Names and Places in the News* (rev. ed.). New York: Columbia Univ. Press, 1948, 528 pp.

Kenyon, John Samuel, and Thomas Albert Knott, *A Pronouncing Dictionary of American English.* Springfield, Mass.: G. & C. Merriam Co., 1944, 484 pp.

Mencken, H. L., *The American Language; An Inquiry into the Development of English in the United States* (4th ed.). New York: Alfred A. Knopf, Inc., 1936. Read Chap. VII, "The Pronunciation of American," pp. 319–378. Also read the extended enlargement of the same topic in *Supplement Two* (New York: Alfred A. Knopf, Inc., 1948), pp. 3–270.

Dialects:

Herman, Lewis Helmar, and Marguerite Shalett Herman, *Manual of American Dialects for Radio, Stage, and Screen.* New York: The Ziff-Davis Publishing Company, 1947, 326 pp.
Manual of Foreign Dialects for Radio, Stage and Screen. New York: The Ziff-Davis Publishing Company, 1943, 416 pp.

Dialecton—European (Phonograph Records). Four 10-inch records, eight sides—French, German, Spanish, Italian, Swedish, Greek, Russian, and Yiddish—plus instruction book. Dialecton, Inc.: 250 West 49th Street, New York City 19.

DRILLS

The following common classroom drills have been found to be most helpful in correcting basic faults.

A. *Breathing:*

1. Stand erect, hands on your hips, and then suddenly draw in your breath through your mouth as if you were greatly frightened. Locate and note the action of the breathing muscles. Repeat the exercise several times.
2. Stand erect, place your hands so that your thumbs touch your lower ribs at the sides and your fingers

extend over your abdomen; then alternately inhale and exhale as in panting. Do this slowly at first, then quickly. Once again notice the action of the breathing muscles.

Next, inhale as much as possible, letting your ribs and abdomen push out against your hands. Making the inspiration as long as the expiration, repeat ten times.

Next, repeat the same exercise, but gradually increase the speed of the inhalation and slow down the exhalation until the former is very rapid and the latter very slow. Repeat ten times.

3. Take a complete but easy breath through your nose. Hold your breath for two counts; then exhale a small amount through slightly opened lips to two counts; then hold again for two counts; then exhale again; and so on until your breath is exhausted. Repeat ten times.
4. Take a complete and easy breath to a count of three or four, and then exhale steadily to the same count, keeping the flow of your breath even. Repeat ten times.

   Expend the breath while whispering "ah." Whisper as long as possible, using a slow and steady expiration. Repeat five times.
5. Take a complete and easy breath, and then gradually expend it with a sustained hum. Repeat five times.
6. Count aloud as far as possible on one breath.
7. Articulate "b" as many times as possible on one breath.
8. Sustain "ah" comfortably, starting the tone softly and then gradually increasing the volume until the tone becomes very loud. The quality of the tone should not alter with the change of volume.
9. Laugh as long as possible on one breath, using the sound "ha," and contracting after each "ha."
10. Shout a single word like "No!" "Don't!" "Help!" three times on one expiration, contracting for each shout.

B. *Tone:*

1. Sustain a normal "ah" as long as possible. As you make the sound, alternately pinch and release your nostrils with your finger and thumb. If the sound of the "ah" is properly nonnasal, there will be no perceptible change in vocal quality.
2. Close your teeth and say "ah" loudly; then, without interrupting the sound, open your mouth wide enough to place two fingers, one above the other, between your teeth. Note how the volume of the tone is increased. Form the habit of opening your mouth well when speaking.
3. Hum the consonant "m." Then open your mouth slowly, avoiding any change of the "feel" of the tone, and change from "m" to "ah." Then gradually close your mouth again without stopping the tone or changing the placement. Repeat this slow alteration of "m's" and "ah's" until your breath is exhausted.

   Beginning with the hummed "m," change to "ah" and hold it as long as your breath lasts, keeping the tone full and steady. Make the tone round and full, and try to "feel" its reverberations.

   Repeat by replacing "ah" with each of the vowel sounds.
4. Intone the sound "ing," keeping the tone rich and full. Note again the "feel" of the vibrations.

   Now alternate between the sounds "ing" and "ah," but avoid any change in the fullness of the resonance. (But note that the "ing" sound will be properly nasal and that "ah" will not.)
5. Repeat such words as "rhythm," "moan," "thumb," "boom," "scene," "palm," emphasizing and projecting the final consonant sound.

C. *Relaxed Throat:*

1. Simulate a yawn, and then note—and try to retain—the throat relaxation that follows.

   Simulate raising a glass of water to your lips, open them to drink, and then note—and "feel"—the throat relaxation.
2. Open your mouth as you would for saying "ha," take an easy breath through your mouth, and then—without tensing or moving your throat or tongue—exhale through your mouth slowly. Repeat several times.

   Next, take your breath as before, start exhaling as before, but after your breath is well started, merge it into the easiest possible tone, using "ha." Make this tone easily, leaving all your muscles completely relaxed. Repeat ten times.

   Repeat the same exercise, but this time start the tone as you start to exhale, keeping the same open, soft quality. Repeat several times. Try the same exercise on different pitches.
3. Relaxing your muscles completely, let your jaw drop; then let your head fall forward after it. Then, with your neck and jaw completely relaxed, shake your head quickly from side to side until you can feel your jaw flap back and forth.

   Next, with your jaw relaxed, lazily say "hoh," "hai," "hoh," "hum" several times in succession.

4. Let your jaw drop and your head fall forward after it. Then say lazily and slowly "lah," "lah," "lah"; "mah," "mah," "mah." Repeat five times.
5. Say "yah," "yah," "yah," letting your jaw drop lazily and loosely for each syllable, your tongue going with your jaw. Repeat five times.

D. *Pitch Changes:*

1. Make up ten two-word sentences. Then read each sentence aloud, with the slightest of pauses between them, and with a definite upward shift of pitch for the second word. Repeat these two-word sentences with a downward pitch to the second word. Notice what change of pitch can do for meaning.
2. Notice your shift upward or downward in the following sentences in accordance with the meaning intended:
   a. If you don't go, I'll scream.
   b. She won't answer; let's go.
   c. I repeat—I didn't do it.
   d. Now that I remember, I did meet her.
   e. The sign said, "Norwalk 5 miles."
   f. Give them one more minute, then break down the door.
   g. He'll come if we invite him.
   h. Did you do it, or didn't you?
   i. If you don't write, I will.
   j. He came in the room and just looked at us.
3. Take a simple sentence like, "Will you type the envelope for me?" noticing carefully on which word the emphasis is placed and where the voice rises and falls for different meanings.
   Repeat the sentence several times, each time emphasizing a different word. Again notice the rise and fall of the voice.
   Always concentrate on meaning, not on vocal decoration.
4. Read the following, and similar, questions first with a downward intonation—or general pitch movement; then read them with an upward intonation:
   a. Where are you going?
   b. Why can't I go?
   c. Is she in danger?
   d. Why do you agree with him?
   e. Who turned out the light?
   f. Do you want to bet?
   g. Why did he say that?
   h. Who invited her?
   i. What did I tell you?
   j. How many miles did you say?
5. Read the following, and similar, sentences with a downward inflection. Then read each of them with an upward inflection.
   a. Don't forget to write.
   b. Let's have lunch tomorrow.
   c. You carry the large package.
   d. That isn't what I said at all.
   e. Now I'm ready.
   f. This is too much.
   g. It isn't for me to say.
   h. Don't worry—he'll get along.
   i. What do you mean by saying a thing like that?
   j. I saw her downtown just yesterday.

EXERCISES

A. BREATHING WHILE READING

Find the typical breathing pauses in the following selections, noting that they will all agree with interphrasal pauses. Do the same for the selections at the end of Chapter I.

1. THE PEOPLE WITH LIGHT COMING OUT OF THEM*

YOUNG MAN: All the people in this block are like that. Like Bailey and Pete, and his boy Dominick, and Mike Okagawa, and the old man, and his granddaughter. But this block's no different from any other block in any other town in America. People are like that all over the place, and when you've got people with light coming out of them, like it comes out of these people, then you've got light coming out of their houses and the streets they live on, and the towns where these streets are, and the whole land where these towns are. You hear 'em coming to life in the morning, the alarm clocks ringing, the faucets running, and everybody getting up to start another day. You know they're happy people because they belong to a happy nation. They're free people and they're glad to be alive. I've done a lot of looking around all over this country, because that's my work, and everywhere I've gone — from the biggest city to the smallest town — I've seen people with light in 'em. Human people. People who are young and friendly and kind — Oh, I know. I've seen bad people, too — all kinds of 'em — but I looked a long time, and it's gotten so that I can see right through people who look as if they're bad. But they're not bad — they're having trouble — they're up against something — things have gone wrong — they've lost faith — they need more things than they've got — they're out fighting because they don't know what else to do about the trouble — but even these people are good people. Something's pressing against their spirits, hurting 'em. Everything isn't perfect in any block of any town or city in this country, but in this country it's always trying to improve — it's always working at the job, the same as a painter's got to work at a picture he's painting.

* By William Saroyan. Reprinted with the permission of the author.

2. DESCENT OF THE GODS*

VENUS: Here in the New World as in the Old, you mortals love beauty and you love love. The millions of you want to look beautiful and well to others and yourself: the girl at the machine, the elevator boy, the typist and the shipping clerk; the busy housewife, straightening the house before she goes to town to meet her husband; the school-girl, primping in the corridor; the plowman on the prairie, bronzed by summer, waiting to see Mary on Sunday morning — they all want good looks: each last one likes the smell of new, clean things to wear and pretty baubles for his best girl or her best fellow. Some cannot afford to buy a hair-do or to straighten out their teeth; others wear their good clothes only once a week; some never, having none to wear; but always they are hoping things will be better; always they would like to earn a little more, to stay ahead, to put a little by. And as for love, who would not be a part of that? How low must one be before he cannot dream of loving and being loved? No, my domain will never shrink, Old World or New, or never still . . .

3. THE ADVENTURES OF OZZIE AND HARRIET†

ANNOUNCER: (EXCITED) How do you do, ladies and gentlemen. This is Verne Smith speaking to you from the vacant lot at the corner of Rogers Road and Elm Street and bringing you a play-by-play description of the great annual football classic between the Rogers Road Pelicans and the Gardner Street Tigers. There's an enthusiastic crowd here this afternoon — must be twenty-five people. It's the second quarter of the game, and the Rogers Road Pelicans are leading by a scant six points. Score: Gardner Street Tigers 66 — Rogers Road Pelicans 72.

There's a slight delay out there on the field at the moment, but fortunately the situation is in the capable hands of that well-known football expert — that master of gridiron strategy — Ozzie Nelson. At the start of the game Ozzie was merely a spectator . . . but not for

* From *More by Corwin*. Reproduced by permission of Henry Holt and Company, Inc. Copyright, 1944, by Norman Corwin.

† By Ozzie Nelson and staff. Reproduced through the courtesy of Ozzie Nelson.

long. Knowing of his inexhaustible fund of football know-how and cunning, the kids have asked him to help out. Yes, folks, Ozzie is going to referee! (WHISTLE) There's time in . . . The Tigers are into the huddle . . . up to the line . . . it's a three man line, eight quarterbacks in the backfield. Rickey Nelson getting ready to center the ball. He's doing a great job out there — playing center for both sides. The ball is snapped . . . It's going to be a pass . . . No, he's going to run with it . . . He changed his mind . . . He changed it again . . . He's going to throw it . . . It's a long high spiral . . . There goes Ozzie . . . He's got his eye on the ball. Look out, Ozzie! Ouch! (HE GROANS) Right in the eye! He got his eye a little too close. There's going to be a penalty. He's calling the ball back. Oh-oh, the Tiger rooting section doesn't like it. Fifteen yards for unnecessary roughness, Ozzie says. There's an argument out there. Oh-oh! He's reversed his decision. The play was good. The Tigers get a twenty yard gain. Oh-oh! The Pelican's rooting section doesn't like that. Another argument out there . . . Ozzie's right in the middle of it. Wait a minute . . . there's another decision. Ozzie says take the play over. Oh-oh! The crowd doesn't like that either. They're still arguing out there. And here's another substitution . . . Ozzie Nelson is coming out of the game!

4. MICHAELA*

MICHAELA: Of course, since we're looking for causes . . . it's possible my hatred of my step-father has something to do with it. My own father died when I was a year old, and I never really knew any father except Willard Lanier. He was big, with thick, big hands. And he had a way of looking at me as though he'd just thought of something diabolically funny to do to me and was just waiting when I wasn't looking. He had a bad temper, and he hit my mother lots of times. I hated him! I hated to be in the same room with him. I felt dirty if I was breathing the same air. I used to hold my breath when he came near me. He only hit me once . . . I was out with some boy. We went to a dance and I came

* By Robert Presnell, Jr. Reproduced through the courtesy of the author.

home. I was fifteen . . . close to sixteen. And we got home at one-thirty and the boy kissed me good night, and Willard Lanier saw us. He hit me with the back of his hand . . . but he hit the boy with his fist and hurt him. And, of course, I never saw him again. Soon after that I ran away. I wrote a note to Mother and tried to explain . . . and said not to worry . . . I worked as a waitress for a while . . . then in a department store . . . and then as a receptionist. It was easy to get jobs . . . if there was a man doing the hiring. They always went out of their way to make my jobs better, but I didn't have anything to do with them, and eventually I got fired. I'd like to be a shop girl, or an office girl . . . or maybe even a school teacher. But I haven't got a chance because I'm beautiful.

5. COLUMBIA WORKSHOP: *NINE PRISONERS**

WADE: My name is James Wade. I was the youngest in Corporal Foster's squad when we went to the ravine, but I was the oldest man in the world coming back. My father was a clergyman, and I was going to be a clergyman, just like him. But I knew I could never preach to men of justice, love, and mercy. Those things had vanished from the earth . . . they were no more . . . if, indeed, they ever existed as more than words. Perhaps it would not have shook my faith so if Captain Matlock hadn't lined us up, next day, and marched us all to chapel. I could never trust men again. I've been back to that ravine, once, since that day. The pits and scars have all gone from the land. Abandoned trenches and shell-holes are now a solid mass of gently sloping vines that ripple all day in the wind. You can tell the places where the men died. The grass is more green. Poppies grow more red, and the cornflowers more blue. Perhaps that's because the soil is fertilized by the blood and bodies of those who fell. More likely it's because God is so sickened with the things men do to each other that he covers the places where they have

* From *Nine Prisoners,* dramatic version copyright, 1939, by Brian Byrne; original story, *Nine Prisoners,* by William March, copyright, 1931, by *The Forum Magazine.* In *Columbia Workshop Plays,* edited by William Coulter; copyright, 1939, by Columbia Broadcasting System, Inc.

NOTE: Permission to quote must be obtained in writing from Columbia Broadcasting System, Inc., and from Harold Ober.

been as quickly and as completely as possible. They say that war makes beasts of men, but I say beasts of men make war.

6. THE EMPTY NOOSE*

WOMAN: Our prayers had been answered. Their soldiers were coming, but their guns had been aimed beyond our town, and our buildings were still standing. We were in the woods, watching close by, when they came, fast in their tanks and trucks, and they were speeding ahead, most of them. Maybe . . . maybe . . . We looked at each other with hope. The last group stopped suddenly in the square. And in an hour there was not a home or a shop, not even a barn that was not burned to the ground. And then they came for us, beating in the woods, like for animals, rounding up our people one by one, dragging them to vans, loading them in, driving them away. They did not find me. Later I saw the flames die down, I alone, and there was no town, and there never will be. About the people, my family and my neighbors, I never will know. Ashes, everything ashes . . . everybody . . .

B. HISSES AND MISSES

Practice minimizing the hisses in the following contrived sentences.

1. Sam is saying something nice which we shouldn't miss.
2. It certainly sounded as if my niece's voice came from inside the house.
3. Are you so sure you'll miss us if we dress like this?
4. Our horse Susy once kept up a steady pace for six miles.
5. Your sister asked you to please pass the sauce dishes.
6. His plays always manage to succeed because of their surprises.
7. My second cousin sent us some daisies and some roses.
8. This moss-green sofa is the softest to touch in the store.

* This script was written by Arnold Perl and broadcast over the Columbia Broadcasting System on October 16, 1946. Copyright, 1946, by Columbia Broadcasting System, Inc.

9. This is the seasonal sale of small-size dresses for young misses.
10. Nowadays she always washes her dishes in machines.
11. As soon as he finishes we'll give him a swift push over the edge.
12. The small shop I discovered sold brushes, watches, and silk shawls for cash.
13. In a flash the six of them rushed down to the seashore.
14. She always washes her radishes first and serves them fresh.
15. At the close of his speech each of us is to march into the church kitchen for some lunch.
16. There was a sizable commotion in the bushes — then a sudden hush.
17. Yes, I'll sell you some fresh fish if that's what your father wishes.
18. Camouflage uses visual illusion.
19. A soda always fizzes better than it tastes.
20. Her sweet face flushed as she insisted her prestige had been damaged.
21. No spinster will risk making such simple decisions.
22. The blaze, fanned by breezes, burned the houses and garages to ashes.
23. There are risks we assume while watching wasps.
24. A small sphinx was placed on the edge of each of the desks.
25. The avaricious man grasps, seizes, and takes surprising chances.

C. VOICE QUALITIES

In the following selections the actor has to change his voice quality—has to find one of his other voices. Additional examples should be brought to class. Examples of "voice doubles" are purposely *not* included here since they come more properly under the heading of characterization.

1. THE SECOND MRS. BURTON, #443*

TERRY: (SOTTO: HERSELF) The whole trouble is — I either work too fast, or I just plain haven't enough to do.

(MUSIC: STING)

TERRY: (HER UNSYMPATHETIC CONSCIENCE: SOTTO) Oh, no. Your trouble is — you have enough to do, but you don't do it, Terry. You start things you never finish. What happened to those great plans of yours to go on with your designing? You made a start —

(MUSIC: STING)

TERRY: (HERSELF) But Ted Miller discouraged me. He said that designing clothes didn't mean anything. He said I should — paint, not just design.

(MUSIC: STING)

TERRY: (CONSCIENCE) What if he did? Is his word law? Is his judgment infallible? Do you have to believe everything he says?

(MUSIC: STING)

TERRY: (SELF, SLOWLY) No . . .

(MUSIC: STING)

TERRY: (CONSCIENCE) Then why do you? That's only an excuse, Terry. It isn't a sensible reason. You know perfectly well what Ted Miller wants you to do. That doesn't mean it's the right thing for you. Who's running your life anyway?

(MUSIC: STING)

TERRY: (HERSELF) I am. (HALF SMILE) But Ted would like to.

(MUSIC: STING)

TERRY: (CONSCIENCE) The question is — do you intend to let him?

(MUSIC: STING)

TERRY: (HERSELF) NO! Why should I?

(MUSIC: STING)

TERRY: (CONSCIENCE) Why, indeed? Don't ask me. He's already interfered more than I would have let him. Oh, I'm not saying he means to do you harm. But I am saying that if you don't watch out, you may do yourself some serious harm. (POINTEDLY) And Stan.

(MUSIC: STING)

* By Martha Alexander. Reproduced through the courtesy of the author.

TERRY: (HERSELF) Stan? Oh, no! I'd never do Stan any harm. I'd do anything to save him from harm!

(MUSIC: STING)

TERRY: (CONSCIENCE) Do you think listening to Ted Miller does Stan any good?

(MUSIC: STING)

TERRY: (HERSELF) Why, I don't think it does him any harm. Ted's just a boy. I don't take anything he says seriously. Why — compared with Stan, he's — he's nothing to me. Nothing. No more important than a little drop of water.

(MUSIC: STING)

TERRY: (CONSCIENCE) But a man named Plutarch once discovered that water, continually dropping, would wear the hardest rock hollow. Do you think you're wiser than Plutarch?

2. INNER SANCTUM MYSTERY RADIO SHOW: *THE HORLA**

MARTIN: So . . . you came back again.

HORLA: (THE SAME ACTOR'S VOICE . . . CHANGED IN QUALITY) Again . . .

MARTIN: I never heard your voice before while I was awake.

HORLA: Awake . . .

MARTIN: Who are you?

HORLA: You . . .

MARTIN: Tell me your name. (PAUSE) What is your name?

HORLA: (PAUSE) Horla.

MARTIN: Horla?

HORLA: Horla.

MARTIN: Then you do understand when I speak to you?

HORLA: Yes.

MARTIN: Why have you not spoken to me before?

HORLA: I did not choose to.

MARTIN: What do you want with me?

HORLA: I thought . . . you knew.

* By Milton Lewis. A radio presentation, not an adaptation of an Inner Sanctum mystery novel. Reproduced through the courtesy of the author and Simon & Schuster, Inc., Publishers.

MARTIN: No. I imagined all sorts of things, but I never knew. What do you want with me?

HORLA: If I tell, you will resist. And it will only be worse if you resist.

MARTIN: What do you mean?

HORLA: Don't be a fool. Don't you understand yet?

MARTIN: No.

HORLA: I will tell you this. To resist me is impossible. I will come to you when you sleep, when you are helpless. After each visit you will be more and more under my power, until finally you will become my complete slave, to do with as I will.

3. THE SECOND MRS. BURTON, #392*

TED: (SLIGHTLY OFF, SLIGHTLY FEY. NOTE: CHOOSE YOUR OWN PIXIE VOICE — THE ONLY REQUIREMENT IS THAT IT SHOULDN'T BE IMMEDIATELY RECOGNIZED AS TED'S) Terry. Ter-ry!

TERRY: (AUTOMATICALLY) Yes? (BEAT) Who called me? (ADDRESSING HIM) Brad?

TED: (STILL FEY) Brad is two blocks away — playing baseball in a vacant lot. He just struck out. He's — blushing.

TERRY: Who is that? Where's that voice coming from? (ADDRESSING HIM) Stan?

TED: (STILL FEY) Mr. Burton's tending to business as usual. He just told a woman who asked for a "large" girdle that she should have "colossal." No sale.

TERRY: (SPOTTING HIM) Well, when — Oh, Ted! Ted Miller, come down from there!

TED: (NATURAL VOICE, GRINNING) Hello.

TERRY: What on earth are you doing up in that tree? Playing "bird"?

TED: (CLIMBING DOWN) Waiting for you.

TERRY: Did you expect me to come on the wing?

TED: (COMING ON) I was afraid you wouldn't come out at all if you saw me sitting out here.

TERRY: Why? You don't scare me.

TED: I wish I did.

* By Martha Alexander. Reproduced through the courtesy of the author.

4. IVORY TOWER*

ELSA: (SPEAKING IN A HALL) Children! Children, listen to me!

(MURMUR OF CROWD)

ELSA: Lies! All I taught you were lies! Lies! Lies! There is no glory in war! War is gas tearing at your lungs and screaming bullets in your eyes! Children, listen! There is no God but the true God, and all men have his blood in them; so they are all your brothers! This man sitting here is a man like all men, and he will die, but this truth will live — liberty is the greatest right of man, and nations are great only when each man is free to reach for the greatness within himself! Children, this is the truth. Children! The truth!

(MUSIC: STREAM OF CONSCIOUSNESS BEHIND)

ELSA: (SPEAKING THOUGHTS IN HER MIND — WITH A DEFINITE VOCAL CHANGE) And so I said it . . . there in the great hall . . . and they heard, and their fathers, and their mothers . . . And the little man sitting there heard . . . When I had finished . . . silence . . . I turned — my eyes were so filled with tears for the days I had lost being afraid that I — I could hardly see as I walked out into the street — the long road to this, my garden . . . So I wait . . . for them. Yes, they will come for me . . . I could run . . . but no, I will wait . . . If I run, the children will doubt . . . If I stay, they will remember . . .

5. COLUMBIA WORKSHOP: *DANIEL WEBSTER AND THE SEA SERPENT*†

CHEERFUL VOICE: There ain't nobody kin fish like Daniel Webster. I'll wager my best cockerel he brings back a cod twice as big as anyone else hooks . . . an' that goes fur haddock, too.

STRONG VOICE: Ain't no use bettin' on a sure thing, Zeb. Daniel can't be beat at fishin', nor anything else.

AWED VOICE: I heard tell that when he goes trout fishin' down to his farm at Marshfield, the trout leaps right outta the water into his pockets.

* By Arch Oboler. Reprinted with the permission of the author.

† From *Daniel Webster and the Sea Serpent,* dramatic version copyright, 1939, by Sheldon Stark; original story, *Daniel Webster and the Sea Serpent,* by Stephen Vincent Benét, copyright, 1937, by Stephen Vincent Benét. In *Columbia Workshop Plays,* edited by William Coulter; copyright, 1939, by Columbia Broadcasting System, Inc.

NOTE: Permission to use must be obtained from Columbia Broadcasting System, Inc.

CHEERFUL VOICE: Sure. They know it ain't no use fightin' agin' Daniel!

GLOOMY VOICE: He hadn't oughta be wastin' his time fishin'. He oughta be down to Washington right now, takin' care of that treaty with the British.

(GENERAL LAUGHTER)

CHEERFUL VOICE: Trouble with you, Jonas, you allus look at the dark side o' things.

GLOOMY VOICE: (STUBBORN) He oughta be down to Washington. That Lord Ashburton the British sent over ain't no easy man to get the best of.

STRONG VOICE: We whipped 'em in the Revolution an' in 1812. An' if it comes to fightin', we kin whip 'em again!

GLOOMY VOICE: That won't stop them British from boardin' an' searchin' our ships. They do it all the time.

CHEERFUL VOICE: Say, Daniel will take care of that, don't doubt it, Jonas. He'll let his voice out on that Lord Ashburton, an' when he's through, Lord Ashburton'll just say: "Well, Mr. Secretary of State, I guess you're right. Us British won't board an' search your ships at sea no more."

STRONG VOICE: By the Thirteen Originals, that's true. Ain't Daniel Webster the defender of the Constitution? He'll get a rock-bottomed, copper-riveted treaty outta those blue-blooded Britons.

AWED VOICE: They say when Daniel Webster speaks the thunder rolls an' the birds stop chirpin'.

GLOOMY VOICE: He oughta be down to Washington 'stead of out fishin'.

CHEERFUL VOICE: Good day fur it. Calm as a mill pond, with a haze lyin' close. The cod oughta be runnin' thick. There's nobody kin beat Daniel when it comes to fishin' — or anything else. He'll be our next President, sure.

GLOOMY VOICE: He oughta be down to Washington, catchin' that treaty, 'stead of catchin' cod.

D. PRONUNCIATION

In one month's intermittent listening to the radio the following list of 400 commonplace words were at one or more times mispronounced. Check the Kenyon-Knott *Pronouncing Dictionary* for preferred pronunciations.

abdomen
absent (v)
absorb
accompanist
accurate
acquaintance
actually
acumen
address (n)
admirable
adolescence
adult
advance
advantage
adventurer
advertisement
again
aghast
alien
alimentary
allegiance
allude
American
annual
anti-
anybody
anyway
applicable
appreciate
apprehend
apprentice
arctic
ascetic
assess
associate (n, adj)
athletic
attitude
augment
autopsy
aviation

baccalaureate
bachelor
bacillus
bade
balsam
banal
bandage
bandit
baptize
batik
because
beloved
beneficiary
bestial
beverage
bird
bisect (v)
blouse
boisterous
bona fide
brand-new
broad-minded
brooch
burglar

cabbage
cacao
calculate
camera
camouflage
candidate
capsule
carousel
catholic
cavalry
censorship
celluloid
century
chastise
chemise
chivalric
circumstance
civilization
clandestine
clientele
clothes
codicil
collateral
comfortable
company
compliment
comptroller
conflict (v)
consul
contemporary
coroner
counselor
counteract
coupon
courtier
cuckoo
culinary

dais
data
debacle
decadence
deciduous
décor
decorative
defects
deliberative
demonstrable
denture
derisive
desperado
despicable
destitute
detail (n)
deteriorate
devil
dewy
diamond
diaper
dictionary
difference
difficult
direction
disobey
dissolute
distinguished
divan
docile
dramatis personae
duel
duke
duplex
duplicate
durable
duress
duty

ebullience
economical
education
either
elaborate (adj)
elementary
elephant
elevated
elucidate
emperor
employees
en route
ensemble
entertain
enumerate
equator
era
err
execution
experiment
exquisite
extant
extol
extraordinary

family
fast
feature
federal
ferment
fertile
fiancé
figure
finance (v)
foliage
forehead
formidable
frailty
frantic
frigid

gallery
gangrene
gasoline
general
genuine
ghastly
girl
going
gossamer
gourd
government
granite
gratitude
grease (v)
grocery
guillotine

habit
harass
hautboy
height
herculean
hereditary
heroically
history
homage
horrible
horror
hosiery
hospitable
hover
hysteria

identify
illicit
illustrate
impious
importune
impoverish
incongruous
incubate
individual
indubitable
ineffectual
inquiry
inseparable
institution
insufferable
insulate
intellectual

interest (v)
interesting
introduce
invalid
irrefutable
itinerary

jewel

ketchup
khaki
kindergarten

laboratory
lambaste
lamentable
largess
lathe
length
lettuce
lever
liberal
licorice
liege
literary
loss
lurid

macabre
malice
malleable
manual
manufacture
market
marquee
matinee
measurable
medieval
memorable
men
menial
merciful
mien
milk
miscellany
miserable
mongrel
moustache
multiply

multitude
mundane
murderer
mystery

naked
natural
negligee
neither
new
nonsense
noncombatant
notice
numeral

occult
off
office
omen
on
onus
opera
opportune
ordinary
ornery

palace
particularly
partner
pendulum
percolate
perfume
pianist
pilgrim
pitiful
placate
pleasurable
poem
political
popular
practical
premature
preposterous
privilege
prosecute
punctual
pursue

quart
quandary
quantity

rancid
rapid
rationing
readily
really
realty
recess (n)
reconnoiter
recuperate
reference
reproduce
research
resin
reservoir
revocable
rind
rinse
robust
romance (n)
route

sacrifice
salary
sandwich
satiety
secretive
separate (adj)
service
several
shone
silence
simultaneous
slavery
slippery
solace
solicit
soot
sophomore
sordid
sovereign
species
spiritual
status quo
stomach
strata
striped (adj)
stupid
substitute
suburb
suffrage

summit
surmise (n)

tacit
tantalize
temperament
temperate
tennis

theory
tomato
transact
tube
tumult
tune

unaccompanied
unsavory

valid
valuable
variegated
various
vegetable
via
violent
virtual
visualize

vouchsafe

walrus
was
wash
water
wept
wrestle

E. CHARACTERISTIC PRONUNCIATION

Consult in Constance Smedley's *Greenleaf Theatre Elements II. Speech* (London: Duckworth, n.d.) the exercises for characteristic pronunciation for roles in Goldsmith's *She Stoops to Conquer,* pages 20–25.

F. RATE OF SPEECH

Compare your own rate of speaking with the actual broadcast timings for the following selections. But *don't* use them as a mechanical regulator.

1. THE SECOND MRS. BURTON, #435*

STANLEY: No, I don't think it will harm her. It'll do Marion good to take care of Bill. If she does it.

TERRY: (SLIGHT PAUSE) Stan — do you think Marion really loves Bill?

STANLEY: (SLIGHT PAUSE) Do you think Marion's capable of really loving anyone, Terry?

TERRY: She loved you (15 SEC) for several years.

STANLEY: No, she didn't, honey. She loved a mental picture of herself playing the role of "my wife." That's all. And when the picture began to bore her, I began to bore her. She'll take good care of Bill, if the role of "martyred (30 SEC) wife" appeals to her. But if any other mental picture appeals to her more, she won't. At least, that's my guess.

TERRY: What if he should die, Stan?

STANLEY: (SLIGHT PAUSE) Well — I imagine Marion would be the most attractive widow Dickston ever saw (45 SEC) — for a while. Then I imagine she'd remarry and start all her troubles all over again.

TERRY: (SLIGHT PAUSE) Do you feel sorry for Marion?

* By Martha Alexander. Reproduced through the courtesy of the author.

STANLEY: For Marion? Not very. I'm sorry about Bill.

TERRY: I feel sorry for Marion. (60 SEC)

2. Another scene—exactly one minute actual playing time—from the same script

MARION: No . . . I don't suppose we're utterly impossible, Bill. But we're difficult. We're not an easy pair to — mesh.

BILL: (REPEATING) Mesh. Yeah — that's what we need. (15 SEC) We've got to learn to align ourselves to each other — like gear-teeth, huh?

MARION: First of all we have to get you well.

BILL: We can do it. We can, can't we, Marion?

MARION: I — Yes, I think so, Bill. But not tonight. (30 SEC) You must get to sleep. And I must get to the drugstore.

BILL: (SIMPLY) I love you, Marion. It may seem like a funny kind of love to you sometimes. But it's all I've got. I've never (45 SEC) given it to anybody else.

MARION: I know, dear. (DUTIFULLY) I love you, too.

BILL: "I love you, too." Okay. I'll go to sleep — saying that over and over to myself. (60 SEC)

3. MYSTERY THEATRE: *NEMESIS**

DAVE: Now look, Phyllis – I didn't want to kill him. I just wanted to give you a divorce so we could get married. I'd give my right arm to bring him back to life.

PHYLLIS: If we only could . . .

DAVE: But we can't. So what are we going to do? Let our lives go to the devil, or make the best of it? (15 SEC) (PAUSE) I love you, honey.

PHYLLIS: I love you, Dave. (PAUSE) I'll be all right.

DAVE: That's better. Now . . . the coroner's inquest is tomorrow afternoon. You'll have to testify.

PHYLLIS: I know. (30 SEC) (PAUSE) He was jealous. He was afraid of losing his job . . .

DAVE: That's it. Go on.

* By Paul Monash. Reproduced through the courtesy of the author.

PHYLLIS: He threatened to kill himself before, but I never took him seriously . . .

DAVE: And then tonight . . .

PHYLLIS: . . . he was brooding — (45 SEC) wanted to be alone. I was in the bedroom when I heard a shot. I went in, found him, called the police. That's all.

DAVE: Good. (60 SEC).

4. Another scene—exactly one minute actual playing time—from the same script

PHYLLIS: (COMING ON) Well, what did he say? What did he tell you?

DAVE: What did he tell me? What's the difference — the guy's nuts. (5 SEC)

PHYLLIS: But what did he say?

DAVE: He gave me a lot of stuff about counter-electricity . . . ("What's that?") It doesn't matter. The thing is — he keeps insisting that he killed Jack.

PHYLLIS: But how — how could he say that?

DAVE: Now look — just keep your voice down, huh? ("Yes, yes.") Okay. He's a nut. (20 SEC) Fine. But he knows how we killed Jack. He says he shot him with his own gun — pressed it against him and shot him.

PHYLLIS: But then — (SHE STOPS)

DAVE: You've got a bright idea?

PHYLLIS: Why don't we just let him go on saying it? (35 SEC)

DAVE: Because he'll break down after a while and admit the truth — admit he was miles from Waverly Place last night. But in the meantime the cops will be investigating his angles — I know how they work — and maybe they'll stumble on the fact that I did it.

PHYLLIS: What can we do? (50 SEC)

DAVE: You can sit tight — you'd better sit tight — while I do the only thing left to do . . . find out where that nut Graham was last night and fix him with an alibi. (60 SEC)

5. PORTIA FACES LIFE, #1819*

WALTER: I'd rather see the reporters at the studio than have the house swarming with them. Then, too, I promised Leslie Palmer she could have that rewrite on one of the scenes of "Challenge" by this evening.

DAISY: It seems a shame you should have to be workin' today of all days.

WALTER: (CHUCKLING) Somebody's got to keep the lady on my left (15 SEC) in mink coats. I'll be home early — so you won't mind, will you, sweet?

(A PAUSE WHILE PORTIA NODDING SLEEPILY DOESN'T HEAR)

DICKIE: You know what, Walter? Mom's gone to sleep. Hey, Mom!

PORTIA: (STARTLED) What! What are (30 SEC) you talking about? I'm wide awake, Dickie.

WALTER: Look at me. (HE CHUCKLES) You're about as wide awake as an owl at high noon. The bed's the place for you, and that's where you're going.

PORTIA: No . . . no, (45 SEC) it's just that I feel so relaxed and contented.

WALTER: You'll feel even more so in bed.

PORTIA: But really, Walter, I don't want —

WALTER: (INTERRUPTING) We're going to get something settled right here and now, Mrs. Manning. I'm the boss in this house. (60 SEC)

6. Another scene—one minute actual playing time—from the same script

WALTER: Don't grin at me. I really mean it.

PORTIA: You say the nicest things, darling.

WALTER: Now — enough of this monkey business. You're going to sleep — remember?

PORTIA: Yes, boss.

WALTER: (CHUCKLING) I should bounce you into that bed good and hard for being such a sassy little devil, but you're so darned nice to hold (15 SEC) I don't want to let go of you.

PORTIA: You're going to get very tired if you don't. I'm a big girl, you know.

WALTER: Sometimes you are. Sometimes you're a very wise, wonderful woman . . . and then again you're just a baby . . . a cute baby who gets kissed (30 SEC) when she ought to get spanked. And the next time she gets uppity with me I'm going to turn her over my knee and paddle her till she hums.

* By Mona Kent. Reproduced through the courtesy of the author and General Foods Corporation.

PORTIA: Walter, darling, there's a law against beating your wife.

WALTER: Not when my wife needs it — and she does . . . sometimes. (45 SEC)

PORTIA: If you ever do it I'll scream.

WALTER: And I'll put my hand over your mouth and keep right on until I've finished the job.

PORTIA: I'll bite your thumb.

WALTER: I wouldn't put it past you. And I'd probably get a bad case of hydrophobia from it.

PORTIA: Then we'd have to shoot you. (60 SEC)

7. THE ALDRICH FAMILY, #418*

(DOOR BANGS ON)

MRS. ALDRICH: (OFF) Sam, is that you?

MR. ALDRICH: (CALLING) Where are you?

MRS. ALDRICH: (COMING ON) My goodness, what are you doing home in the middle of the morning?

MR. ALDRICH: Alice, we're rich!

MRS. ALDRICH: What?

MR. ALDRICH: Mr. Kelly was just in my office, and he said to drop the suit against the Enterprising Enterprises outfit —

MRS. ALDRICH: But, dear, why —

MR. ALDRICH: Because they want to buy the Circus! And I'm going to handle the whole deal.

MRS. ALDRICH: Sam, you aren't making sense.

MR. ALDRICH: Look, Alice — Mr. Kelly got a phone call last night from the President (15 SEC) of Enterprising Enterprises, and the fellow started talking about buying the Circus.

MRS. ALDRICH: Sam, please sit down. You're all flushed.

MR. ALDRICH: But as soon as Kelly mentioned prices something happened to their connection, and he hasn't been able to locate them.

MRS. ALDRICH: Is that all you have to do? Locate them?

MR. ALDRICH: Yes, Alice. The Circus hasn't been doing too well lately, and if

* By Patricia Joudry and Del Dinsdale, based on characters originated by Clifford Goldsmith. Reproduced through the courtesy of the authors and Clifford Goldsmith.

that firm is willing to go anywhere near (30 SEC) half a million, we're going to snap them up.

MRS. ALDRICH: Half a million? Is that dollars, dear?

MR. ALDRICH: Yes! And I'm to get a ten percent commission! Alice, ten percent of half a million dollars!

MRS. ALDRICH: That's fifty thousand! Sam, let's both sit down. (45 SEC)

8. Another scene—exactly one minute actual playing time—from the same script

HENRY: Look, why don't we earn our own money?

HOMER: How?

HENRY: Work.

HOMER: Work?

HENRY: Sure.

HOMER: What's the matter with you, Henry?

HENRY: Why not? We could carry water for the elephants.

HOMER: Have you any idea how much water an elephant's trunk holds?

HENRY: It wouldn't do any harm to ask, would it?

HOMER: Ask an elephant? (15 SEC)

HENRY: No, Homer, the Circus Manager! Come on — he's got an office down at the Fair Grounds.

HOMER: (FADING SLIGHTLY) But, Henry, the Circus doesn't get in till tomorrow.

HENRY: (FADING) I know, but this man is down there selling tickets and putting up signs.

(DOOR OPENS OFF)

MRS. ALDRICH: (COMING ON) Henry.

HOMER: (OFF) Listen, let's not be hasty about this.

(DOOR CLOSES OFF)

MRS. ALDRICH: (ON) Henry, come back! (30 SEC) I have something for you!

MR. ALDRICH: (ON) What's that?

MRS. ALDRICH: Oh, dear!

MR. ALDRICH: Is that money you have in your hand?

MRS. ALDRICH: Sam, the Circus only comes to town once a year.

MR. ALDRICH: Now, dear, I know you can't help being a mother . . .

MRS. ALDRICH: What?

MR. ALDRICH: But do you intend letting Henry go through life leaning on you like a crutch (45 SEC)?

MRS. ALDRICH: Sam, what do you mean by calling me a thing like that?

MR. ALDRICH: I didn't call you anything! I just want you to let Henry earn his own way. He's got a head on his shoulders. Why not let him use it?

MRS. ALDRICH: But, dear, do you think we should make him do a thing like that all of a sudden? (60 SEC)

Chapter III . . MICROPHONE TECHNIQUES AND PROCEDURES

1

Some techniques and procedures are so simple that they require no elaborate explanations. As yet, thank Heaven, no one has written out intricate instructions concerning how to hold a skillet—how to take it down from the hook, at what precise position to place it over the gas burner, how to grease it, or how to manipulate it variously for the frying of either bacon or eggs. Such instructions in the obvious are needless. Intricate and esoteric instructions in microphone techniques and procedures are just as needless. As Arch Oboler points out,

> No matter what the phony "Get-on-the-radio-in-ten-easy-lessons" schools tell you, it's all quite simple. When you speak loudly, you step away from the microphone. When you speak softly, you come in closer. When you are supposed to be leaving a scene, you speak as you walk away from the microphone. If the fade is to be abrupt, you turn your head away as you speak and as you walk, or else you walk sideways away from the microphone instead of backward, since most microphones cut off sharply when one moves from them on a parallel line to the face of the microphone.
>
> Of course, there are other simple little microphone tricks which one learns through experience, such as coming to within eight or ten inches of the microphone and speaking very softly when one wishes to indicate an extremely intimate tone, or turning one's head away from the microphone when the action calls for a sudden extremely loud tone—but the basics are simply a matter of working about two feet away from the microphone and speaking directly into it in ordinary scenes, and turning one's head or taking a long step backward when there is to be a great deal of voice used.[1]

Anyone can learn most of the essentials of microphone behavior by watching carefully several broadcasts of plays. The simplicities about microphones, about speaking in front of them, about marking scripts, and about rehearsal procedures can therefore be quickly listed.

2

Principally because the microphone's two dead sides offer the opportunity of creating subtler shadings of sound perspective (the illusion of depth or third dimension), but also because it can accommodate a large number of actors, the type most widely used today for the broadcasting of plays is the bidirectional-velocity or ribbon microphone. As described by Earle McGill, it "is bi-directional in response, allowing equal pickup from front and back. Sound waves *from either direction* along an axis perpendicular to the plane of the ribbon have the maximum effect . . . ; sound waves approaching the microphone from a direction in the same plane as the ribbon have no effect on it."[2]

The radio actor must know how to speak on this microphone from at least five basic positions: (1) on mike, (2) off mike, (3) coming on, or fading in, (4) fading, and (5) behind a door or similar obstruction.

Fundamental to all these positions, however, is the fact that radio is a thing of intimacy. "In other words, where the very mechanics of the theatre make it necessary to project one's voice sufficiently to be heard in the last row, in the medium of radio every listener is standing right before the actor and there must be an under-emphasis in both the coloring and the projection of the speech. There, in a vitamined, fortified-chocolate capsule," according to Oboler, "is the basic prerogative of acting for the radio medium: the continued recognition of the fact that one is performing in an intimate medium to an audience of one whose loud-speaker is as close to you as you are to the microphone."[3]

[1] Arch Oboler, "Notes on Acting and Production," *This Freedom* (New York: Random House, Inc. 1942), pp. xvi–xvii.

[2] McGill, *Radio Directing,* cf., pp. 11–12.

The velocity microphone, with its live and dead areas, can be diagramed as follows:

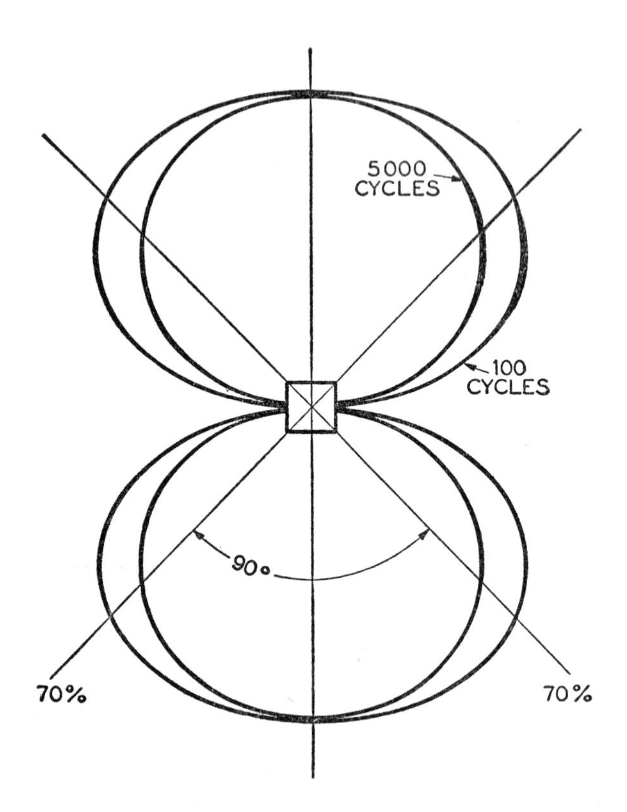

The louder the radio actor speaks "on mike" the more danger there is that his tones will disrupt the transmitting equipment. Whenever the actor blasts or raises his voice too much, the engineer in the glassed-in control room must, for precaution's sake, "sit on the actor's voice" or hold it down within prescribed limits. This holding down cramps the voice, restricts it, makes it sound one-toned and monotonous. The voice therefore forfeits its potentialities for natural variety. In order, then, to retain a full and rich flexibility the radio actor speaks only loud enough to be heard by his associates at the microphone. The problem of theatrical projection does not exist.

Also fundamental to the five basic microphone positions is the fact that "equal distance positions are incompatible with good voice balance." In other words, you as the radio actor do not always stand the same distance from the microphone for any one of the positions; nor do you always stand at the same distance from the microphone as does your partner in the same perspective. Your distance is often governed by the voice qualities of your partners. With one partner your on-mike position may be one distance; with another partner the on-mike position may be slightly different. This variation is caused by the fact that "when two actors share one microphone, the control engineer has but one control factor to accommodate both voices." "Therefore," according to Ted Cott, "if an actor with a voice weaker in tonal quality than yours is playing opposite you, his voice is balanced by giving him a position closer to the microphone."[4]

All in all, the radio actor uses his microphone distances and his voice so that modulating by the engineer will be at a minimum.

1) In general, when speaking on mike the actor stands from one foot to eighteen inches away from it, and talks directly into it without too much rocking back and forth, and uses only enough volume to address a person four feet distant. He carefully maintains this position throughout a scene that has in it no perspective changes. (If the microphone is either too high or too low for his or his partner's shared comfort, he simply lowers or raises it—even in the middle of an actual broadcast—since this can be done quickly and quietly with practice.)

Sometimes, however, depending on such variable factors as the acoustics of the studio, the kind of microphone used, the balance with other actors, or the kind of play being broadcast, the actor can stand as far as three feet away from the microphone or move in to within three inches of it for the on-mike position. In the very intimate scenes from THE SECOND MRS. BURTON or PORTIA FACES LIFE, for instance, the actors usually stand a little closer to the microphone than they do for the less intimate scenes in MYSTERY THEATRE. In a bright comedy like THE ALDRICH FAMILY, on the other hand, the actors habitually stand a bit more than a foot away from the microphone and speak up more loudly.

For an emergency cough or sneeze or clearing of the throat the actor moves to the dead side of the microphone and simultaneously turns away from it.

Often an actor has to move from an on-mike position at one microphone to an on-mike position at another microphone. Since many directors, especially when large casts are called for, use two cast microphones set

[3] Oboler, *op. cit.*, pp. xiv–xv.

[4] Ted Cott, *How to Audition for Radio* (New York: Greenberg, Publisher, 1946), p. 9.

up from ten to twenty feet distant from each other, it is often desirable for the actor who finishes a scene with one partner at microphone A to cross to microphone B for a long scene with another partner. The actor making the cross simply does so while his new partner is reading a speech long enough to cover the cross.

2) In the off-mike position the actor generally stands about eight feet away from the microphone either in the dead or in the live area, depending on whether an effect of more or less distance is wanted. Here, from Fletcher Markle's *Sometime Every Summertime,** is a typical off-mike effect:

* Copyright, 1945, by Fletcher Markle. Included in *Radio's Best Plays,* published by Greenberg Publisher, 1947.

MCFEDRIES: Beginning the next morning, after a long night sitting out on the porch getting to know each other, we talked back and forth as if we were all living in the same cottage, ignoring the 100 yards that separated us.

FRAN: (FAR OFF, AT THE NEXT COTTAGE, SHOUTING) Charlie! You going down to the beach?

MCFEDRIES: It's Fran.

HAYES: (ON, SHOUTING BACK) I'm ready whenever you are. Now?

FRAN: About two minutes.

HAYES: Right.

HELEN: (OFF, SAME PERSPECTIVE AS FRAN) You going down, Mac?

MCFEDRIES: (ON, SHOUTING BACK) Sure, Helen.

HAYES: Better get into your trunks.

MCFEDRIES: (ON, SHOUTING) I'll be just a shake getting changed. We'll pick you up.

HELEN: (OFF) Okay.

3) In coming on, or fading in, the actor usually makes his entrance about eight feet away from the microphone in the live area and moves steadily toward it while speaking, or he can make his entrance much closer to the microphone if he starts in the dead area and curves around to an "on" position. Here is an "ad lib" coming on from Arch Oboler's *Special to Hollywood:**

* Reprinted with the permission of the author.

BOB: (FAR OFF) Pilot, what's happened?

SAM: (FAR OFF) I don't know. I don't!

BOB: What is it? What's happened? (THEY CONTINUE TO AD LIB FAR BACK DISCUSSING ENGINE FAILURE)

LONA: What is this? Mark, what did he chase off for? We are landing, aren't we? Then what's there to get so excited about?

MARK: The — the engine's stopped.

LONA: Will you stop saying that? So what!!

MARK: W-we're not due in for an hour yet!

LONA: Something's wrong! (FADING) Pilot, what's the matter? Pilot!

MARK: (THROUGH ABOVE FADE) Lona! Lona, wait! Lona!

(FAST FADE-IN OF BOB AND LONA TALKING A MILE A MINUTE TO PILOT. AD LIBS, SUCH AS, "WHAT'S THE BIG IDEA?" — "WHY ARE WE LANDING HERE?" — "WHAT'S THE MATTER WITH THE ENGINE?" — "WHAT KIND OF A PILOT ARE YOU, ANYWAY?" — ETC.)

MARK: (JOINS IN) No, no, let me talk to him! Listen, you — what's the matter? Why don't you answer? I'm paying for this — answer me! What are you up to?

PILOT: Shut up! Shut up, all of you! Shut up, I say!

4) In fading, this method of coming on is simply reversed, as illustrated in the following example from the COLUMBIA WORKSHOP script for *A Trip to Czardis,** adapted by James and Elizabeth Hart from the story by Edwin Granberry:

* From *A Trip to Czardis,* dramatic version copyright, 1939, by James and Elizabeth Hart; original story, *A Trip to Czardis,* by Edwin Granberry, copyright, 1932, by *The Forum Magazine.* In *Columbia Workshop Plays,* edited by William Coulter; copyright, 1939, by Columbia Broadcasting System, Inc.

NOTE: Permission to use must be obtained in writing from Columbia Broadcasting System, Inc.

JIM: I never see sech a place as Czardis. Papa takened me one time he were goin' to market. You were too little then, and he were feared you'd get tuckered. You started up whimperin' jest as we drove off, and papa jumped outen the wagon and run back and told you, "Don't take on, Dan'l. Soon's you get to be six, I'll bring you, too, and we'll have us a right fine time." (FADING) Hit were terrible long ago that papa takened me, but I can see it all plain, just like it was happenin' now . . .

(THE BABBLE OF MANY VOICES AND CRIES OF MARKET VENDORS COME ON . . . AND THEN FADE)

VOICES: 'Taters! Sweet 'taters! Pick 'em up, gents. Pick 'em up! Grapefruit, oranges, and lemons! Grapefruit, oranges, and lemons! Floridy's finest, ladies! Floridy's finest! Fresh, fresh fish! Fresh, fresh fish! Redsnapper! Redsnapper! Right out of the gulf, folks! Right out of the gulf!

5) In giving the effect of speaking from behind a door the actor can either speak from the dead side of the microphone or, holding his script directly in front of his face, read his lines from the live side. Ferenc Molnar's *The Guardsman,** as adapted by Arthur Miller for THEATRE GUILD ON THE AIR, is an excellent through-the-door scene:

* From *The Guardsman,* by Ferenc Molnar, published by the Liveright Publishing Corporation. Translated by Grace I. Colbron and Hans Bartsch; original play copyright, 1924, by Hans Bartsch. All rights reserved therein, particularly all broadcasting and television rights. Radio adaptation by Arthur Miller. Reprinted with the permission of Hans Bartsch, Ferenc Molnar, Arthur Miller, and the Liveright Publishing Corporation.

MARIE: (FADING) I — I'd better do my face. I'll be in my room if anyone wants me.

(DOOR CLOSES OFF)

BERNHARDT: (OFF) Franz! What are you doing here? (COMING ON) What's the matter?

FRANZ: I'm believing that I wasn't with her last night.

BERNHARDT: You weren't with — ? (LAUGHS) Perhaps you weren't! Is there anything you can't believe if it's necessary?

FRANZ: Never mind about that. I've got control of myself now. Where's that valise? Oh, yes.

BERNHARDT: What in the world are you doing?

FRANZ: (QUIETLY) Now comes the moment when her lying is not going to help her any.

BERNHARDT: (QUIETLY) The uniform? Franz, you're not going to . . .

FRANZ: Hold that boot for me.

MARIE: (FROM THE NEXT ROOM) Who came, Franz?

FRANZ: (PROJECTING) Just Bernhardt? (SOTTO VOCE) Quick, where's the beard?

MARIE: Why don't the two of you go to a cafe before we have dinner?

FRANZ: (PROJECTING) Splendid idea! Hurry and dress, dear. You'll come along?

MARIE: No, I'll rest a while.

FRANZ: Not expecting someone, are you? (SOTTO VOCE) Buckle my sword on, Bernhardt.

MARIE: That's a funny question.

FRANZ: Then why should I go out?

MARIE: Do go out — even for half an hour. Can't you understand? After this dreadful scene I'm a wreck. Tell Bernhardt about the fire in Olmutz. The theatre in Olmutz burned down, Bernhardt.

BERNHARDT: You don't say!

FRANZ: Yes, and the firemen ended up two hundred miles away drinking tea in my apartment.

MARIE: Oh, stop it!

BERNHARDT: (SOTTO VOCE) Button the cloak. Your pants will show.

For all these basic microphone positions it is generally a rule in radio that in every scene someone must always be on mike; in other words, the microphone must always be with someone. Rarely are all the voices and sound effects off mike as they are, perhaps unradiolike, in the following excerpt from Arthur Arent's adaptation of George Kelly's *The Show-Off** for THEATRE GUILD ON THE AIR:

* By George Kelly. Copyright, 1924, by George Kelly, published by Little, Brown & Company. Radio adaptation by Arthur Arent, in H. William Fitelson's (ed.), *Theatre Guild on the Air,* published by Rinehart & Company, Inc.

(DOORBELL RINGS)

AMY: See who's at the door, Aubrey. (FADING) I'm going down to the drugstore and telephone the hospital to see how Pop is.

AUBREY: (CALLING) Go ahead, ole girl. I'll take care of whoever it is.

(DOORBELL RINGS AGAIN)

AUBREY: (SINGING AS HE FADES) I'm coming . . . I'm coming.

(RECEDING FOOTSTEPS . . . DOOR OPENS OFF)

GILL: (OFF) Good evening. Is this where Mr. Fisher lives?

AUBREY: (OFF) Yes, this is Mr. Fisher's residence. Won't you step inside?

(FOOTSTEPS COMING ON)

GILL: (COMING ON) I got some things of his here that the boss ast me to leave.

AUBREY: (ON) I'm Mr. Fisher's son-in-law.

In the radio scheme of things the microphone should have remained with Aubrey. He should not have faded as he sang, "I'm coming," his footsteps should have stayed on mike, and the door should have been opened on mike.

A similar scene is correctly microphoned in the Jeffrey Dell, C. S. Forester, and Gerald Holland script for *Payment Deferred** on THEATRE GUILD ON THE AIR:

* By Jeffrey Dell, based on the novel by C. S. Forester. Copyright, 1934, by Samuel French, Ltd. Radio adaptation by Gerald Holland. Used by arrangement with the authors and Samuel French, Ltd. In H. William Fitelson (ed.), *Theatre Guild on the Air,* published by Rinehart & Company, Inc.

(DOORBELL RINGS)

WINNIE: Shall I answer it, Mother?

ANNIE: Yes, dear, see who it is. Now, Will — don't look like that.

(WINNIE'S FOOTSTEPS FADE . . . DOOR OPENS OFF)

JIM: (OFF) Is Mr. Marble at home?

WINNIE: (OFF) Will you come in, please? He's in the living-room.

JIM: (OFF) Oh, thanks, miss.

WILL: (ON, IN A FRIGHTENED WHISPER) That's not Charlie. It's Evans' man. I know it!

ANNIE: (ON) Wait now . . .

WINNIE: (COMING ON) Right in here, sir . . . Father, it's somebody for you.

WILL: (SHAKEN) For me?

JIM: (COMING ON) Oh! Good evening! Sorry if I scared you. You look as if you'd seen a ghost! Mr. Marble, isn't it?

In changing scenes *at the microphone* the mike is passed like a football from one party to another so that someone is always on mike. In the following scene from THE ALDRICH FAMILY, #445,* by Patricia Joudry and Del Dinsdale, the microphone is first with Henry in the living-room; then, as Mr. Aldrich comes on mike, he takes it, so to speak, from Henry and carries it from the living-room into the hall—and a change of scene has been effected:

* Reproduced through the courtesy of the authors and Clifford Goldsmith.

HENRY: Look, would you sort of accidentally drop over to Kathleen's? And without letting her know what you want, sort of find out if she's asked anybody else to the dance, huh?

HOMER: Well, I guess I could try.

(PHONE RINGS OFF)

MR. ALDRICH: (OFF) I'll get it!

HENRY: (CALLING) Is that the phone?

MR. ALDRICH: (COMING ON CALLING) Never mind, Alice! I'll get it.

HENRY: I'll get it, Father. (FAST FADING) Father, wait — I'll get it.

MR. ALDRICH: I'm coming, Alice! Tell Bob to hold on.

HENRY: (OFF) But, Father — ?

MRS. ALDRICH: (COMING ON) Sam, it isn't Bob Anderson. (INTO PHONE) I'm sorry, but you have the wrong number.

(RECEIVER DOWN)

MR. ALDRICH: A wrong number? Alice, are you sure?

MRS. ALDRICH: Really, dear, I wish you'd settle down with a nice book.

All voices other than those emanating from these five basic positions are created by the engineer. By using a filter microphone—where the tone characteristics are changed by mechanically eliminating or augmenting the frequencies—he creates the telephone voice, the ghostly voice, and so forth. By using an echo chamber —a bare room in which a microphone picks up the reverberation of sound and feeds it back to the control board—he creates the resonant effect of voices coming from a vaulted castle, a tunnel, a vast auditorium, and the like.

For example, in the Giant scene of his *The Odyssey of Runyon Jones,* Norman Corwin achieved complete isolation so that Runyon could sound small and the Giant big by placing the boy in a dead booth—a small, four-walled, portable studio-within-a-studio—and by reducing the level of his microphone there. The Giant therefore had the whole studio to himself, and in addition used an echo chamber. In Corwin's *It Seems Radio Is Here to Stay,* Whitman, who is dead, spoke with a far-off, mystical quality on a filter microphone. In the same play the Whisperer, who has to sound as if he were speaking across sidereal distances, whispered over a dynamic or moving-coil microphone—the other main type in common use—which is most frequently either unidirectional or nondirectional.

3

In addition, then, to concentrating on his acting the radio performer must constantly—almost instinctively —watch his distances from the microphone. He also must do three other things in rehearsals and while on the air: he must continually look for the director's signals from the control booth, he must listen and wait for certain sound effects, and he must keep his place in the script.

Directors must throw all cues for starting a new scene immediately following a music bridge, because the actors cannot hear the music as the audience hears it. Also, cues often have to be thrown to the actor following an announcer's lead-ins or interpolated narration, as well as for terminating pauses, and for speaking in the middle of or at the end of certain sound effects. A radio actor therefore has to learn to take his proper position at the microphone, to look toward the director for a starting cue, and then to turn back to his next speech in the script without losing his place or reading the wrong lines.

Between scenes, during the music bridges, the cast usually looks to the director for a speed-up or slow-down signal—although such signals are not as frequent in radio as they once were. Lest actors speed up or slow down too much they should realize that in a twenty-page script an acceleration or retardation of only three seconds a page equals an over-all change of one minute. Most actors, losing their heads at such speed-up or slow-down signals, tend to increase or decrease their rate of speaking too much. In most cases a five-second change a page in the rate of speaking is sufficient—and is relatively simple to accomplish.

Obviously radio actors must listen to the sound man, or wait for a cue from the director; otherwise they may easily make such mistakes as speaking into a telephone before the receiver has been lifted from its hook or coming into a room before the door has been opened. The wiser directors will allow the sound man to make his sound effects from cues in the script, instead of taking them from the control room, and will let the actors listen for their own sound effects.

It is common practice, when a new scene starts after a music bridge and there are two or more actors sharing a microphone, for the actor who is to begin the scene on a cue from the director to take a position at the microphone facing the control room.

An actor usually leaves his seat and comes to the microphone during a music bridge or from five to six speeches before he must take part in the scene; he takes a position established at the rehearsals. From experience at rehearsals he knows when he must move slightly away from the microphone in order to give room for another actor on the same side; he knows also exactly how he must manage to thrust himself forward in a group in order to speak on mike.

At the microphone the radio script is usually held in one hand; the other hand is left free to lift the finished page of script and place it quietly behind the other pages. Finished pages are *not* dropped to the floor.

4

An experienced radio actor will no more think of coming to a rehearsal without at least two soft black lead pencils than he would think of coming without his two eyes. In one sense the rehearsal for a radio play is "a time for marking scripts." A script that has not been marked is a script that has not been rehearsed. A radio actor customarily uses seven different kinds of script markings:

1) At the first reading, as soon as he has unclipped his script into loose pages, he goes through them all, circling his character's name in the margin and drawing a black line across the page at the termination of each of his speeches. The illustration opposite, from *The*

*Great Mellagio,** by Ethel Harris Gregory, broadcast on MYSTERY THEATRE, shows how this is done.

2) Next, the radio actor checks his page numbers. If, for instance, there are two pages numbered "11" he changes the second one to "11A"; if there is no page "11" he renumbers page "12" so that it reads "11–12." If during the rehearsals any pages are cut or added he promptly follows the same procedure so that he will not be confused by the pagination when checking his script just before going to the microphone.

3) Then he marks his script with an advance indication of all the scenes in which he participates. If a scene in which he takes part starts on page 5, and especially if he has the first speech on that page, he usually draws a large black arrow, pointing to the bottom, in the margin of page 4.

4) During the rehearsal, on instructions from the director, the actor marks with the word "CUE" every speech in which he must wait for a cue from the director.

5) During the rehearsal he makes all necessary notations for mood, interpretation, change of pace, motivation, and the like in the margin of the script.

6) During the rehearsal and in the sessions afterward he writes in as legibly as possible, usually printing, all the script changes.

7) He carefully marks all script cuts.

```
NICK:      You gotta divorce him.
AUGUSTA:   You know that's out.  How can I talk to him?
           He's so broody and irritable.
NICK:      Then I'll talk to him.
AUGUSTA:   What's the good?  You know he won't let me go.
           He's been walkin' around in a daze since his
           mother died.  He gets into such black moods...
           I think he's gonna kill himself.
NICK:      That's all you got to say?
AUGUSTA:   What can I say?
NICK:      (COLDLY) Okay.  Then I'm washed up.
AUGUSTA:   (SOBBING) No!  I love you.  You know I love you.
           But I'm trapped.
```

A page of correctly marked radio script will look something like the specimen on page 68, from *Leave It to Ethel*,† by Jerry Rice and Bill Stuart, produced on SILVER THEATRE.

5

The actual rehearsal schedules for three widely differing radio programs will quickly show the actor how little time he has for the preparation of his performance.

Though many daytime serials, the soap operas, rehearse only one hour for each fifteen-minute broadcast, the time used daily by the cast of THE SECOND MRS. BURTON is one hour and a half. Two hours would be

* Reproduced through the courtesy of the author.

† Reproduced through the courtesy of the authors.

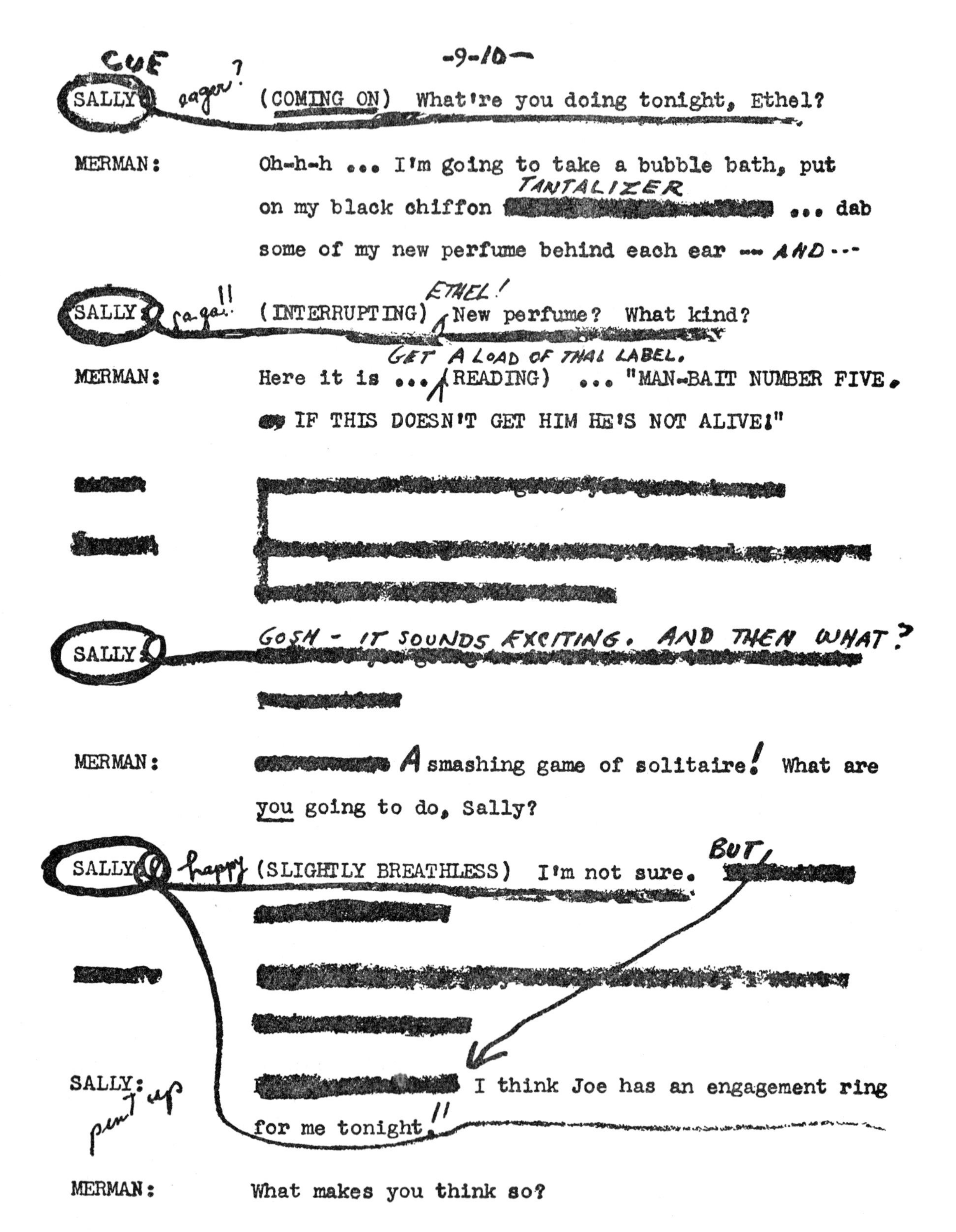
CUE
-9-10-
SALLY: eager? (COMING ON) What're you doing tonight, Ethel?
MERMAN: Oh-h-h ... I'm going to take a bubble bath, put on my black chiffon TANTALIZER ... dab some of my new perfume behind each ear -- AND ---
SALLY: eager!! (INTERRUPTING) ETHEL! New perfume? What kind?
MERMAN: Here it is ... GET A LOAD OF THAT LABEL. (READING) ... "MAN-BAIT NUMBER FIVE. IF THIS DOESN'T GET HIM HE'S NOT ALIVE!"
SALLY: GOSH - IT SOUNDS EXCITING. AND THEN WHAT?
MERMAN: A smashing game of solitaire! What are you going to do, Sally?
SALLY: happy (SLIGHTLY BREATHLESS) I'm not sure. BUT,
SALLY: pent up I think Joe has an engagement ring for me tonight!!
MERMAN: What makes you think so?

nearer the ideal for most of these programs. THE SECOND MRS. BURTON actors begin work at 12:30 each day, and go on the air at 2 o'clock EST. The time is apportioned as follows:

12:30 to 1:00—First reading by the cast around a table; cuts for time, already prepared by the director, given; comments.
1:00 to 1:30—Perhaps two run-throughs of the script—about ten or eleven minutes of playing time excluding the commercials, announcer's lead-ins, and opening and closing signatures—with all sound effects. The comments of the director after the first run-through are incorporated in the second microphone reading. Often, especially when the sound effects are many or complex, there is time for only one microphone reading.
1:30 to 1:45—Complete dress rehearsal with music, announcer, and commercial voices. This rehearsal is accurately timed at each fifteen-second mark.
1:45 to 1:55—Final cuts and comments.
2:00 to 2:15—On the air.

A straight dramatic show like THE MYSTERY THEATRE, with no characterizations set, since there is a complete new story with a new cast each week, rehearses for a total of six hours for each half-hour broadcast. Because of the elaborate sound effects used almost every week, the cast could often profitably use an additional hour or more. The rehearsal time is apportioned as follows:

Nine days before the actual broadcast the cast is given an hour-and-a-half call for purposes of reading script. During the first half hour of this so-called rehearsal the cast listens to the director's analysis of the play and then, sitting around a table, reads it through once. After this, with the host and the announcer, and with filler-in or stock musical bridges, the entire script is put on microphone with sound effects and in its customary format. The program is accurately clocked at each fifteen-second mark.

Since this is primarily a script instead of a production rehearsal, the cast is then dismissed, and a long story conference with the writer follows. Suggestions are given for rewriting the story, when necessary, and for cutting it down to the playing time of an average script, about twenty-one minutes.

On the day of the broadcast the remaining four and one-half hours are apportioned as follows:

11:00 to 11:30—First reading by the cast around a table of the revised and cut script with comments by the director on characterizations, style, mood, pace, and the like.
11:30 to 2:00—A scene-by-scene—not necessarily in correct sequence—microphone rehearsal of the script with full sound effects. Some scenes are run on microphone only once or twice; some scenes are rehearsed many more times.
1:30 to 2:00—Orchestra rehearsal (in another studio).
2:00 to 2:15—Commercials rehearsed.
2:15 to 2:45—Complete dress rehearsal—as if it were an actual air performance—with the script clocked every fifteen seconds.
9:30 to 10:00—Script changes and cuts given to the cast; additional microphone rehearsals of certain scenes.
10:00 to 10:30—On the air.

A comedy show like THE ALDRICH FAMILY, even though two thirds or more of the actors in each week's cast are already definitely set in their characterizations, rehearses eight and one-half hours for each weekly half-hour broadcast.

Eight days before each broadcast a two-hour script rehearsal is held. The procedure here is about the same as that for MYSTERY THEATRE except that there is more time for directorial comments and suggestions to the actors.

On broadcast days the six and one-half hours given over to the production rehearsal are apportioned as follows:

10:00 to 10:30—First reading of the revised script by the cast around a table.
10:30 to 10:45—Cuts and script changes agreed on by the writers and the director.
10:45 to 11:00—Cuts and changes given to the cast.
11:00 to 1:00—A scene-by-scene—not necessarily in correct sequence—microphone rehearsal with all sound effects.
1:00 to 2:00—Lunch.
2:00 to 2:15—Finish any leftover scenes.
2:15 to 2:45—First straight run-through for continuity—with sound, but without the announcer, music, and commercials.
2:45 to 3:05—Director's comments to the cast.
3:05 to 3:30—Orchestra rehearsal.
3:15 to 3:30—Commercials rehearsed.
3:30 to 4:00—Complete dress rehearsal—as if it were an

actual air performance—with the program clocked every fifteen seconds.
6:30 to 7:00—Script changes and cuts given to the cast in the conference room, and each change read across for checking purposes.
7:00 to 7:30 or 8:00—Director's comments to the actors on the playing of the various scenes.
7:00 to 7:30—Orchestra rehearsal in studio.
7:30 to 8:00—Used, when possible, as a relaxation period.
8:00 to 8:30—On the air.
11:30 to 12:30—Repeat performance for the West Coast.

It is important to note that both MYSTERY THEATRE and THE ALDRICH FAMILY are unusual in following the practice of having weekly advance reading of the scripts. Most radio programs are not so farsighted; therefore many script revisions have to be made during the rehearsal period; and all time taken up with script cuts and changes is time taken away from the actors' rehearsal. Too often for either comfort or perfection the actors are penalized by being asked to perform on the air with only one microphone run-through of the script! What is worse—too often many actors feel that if they do more than one microphone run-through they are in danger of going stale!! Whereupon the judicious must wince.

SELECTED READINGS

McGill, Earle, *Radio Directing*. New York: McGraw-Hill Book Company, 1940. Read especially Chap. 7, "Microphone Rehearsal," pp. 115–144; Chap. 8, "The Dress Rehearsal and Air Show," pp. 145–168; and Chap. 11, "Production Script of *Christ of the Andes* (by Bernard C. Schoenfeld) with Analysis," pp. 227–268.

EXERCISES

The following selections in microphone positions should be practiced again and again until the radio actor knows his distances as if by instinct. It would be ideal if each student could have a recording made of his work in these exercises so that he could hear what his voice sounds like in the on, off, coming-on, fading, whisper, and shouting positions.

A. COMINGS ON

1. DAVID HARDING—COUNTER-SPY, #158*

(VERY FAINTLY) (THE MONASTERY BELL TOLLS — RING ABOUT EVERY TWELVE SECONDS THROUGHOUT - VERY, VERY DEEP AND LOW)

ANNOUNCER: Six weeks ago, as the shadows of evening spread over the sagebrush, a young woman — attractive, slight, pale — knelt beside one of the gravestones and prayed . . .

(TOLL OF BELL)

ELRA: (COMING ON) " . . . Las necessidades y enredos de nuestra vida, danos sincero amor de los pobres, mucho confianza en Dios y alto aprecio de la vida eterna, a la cual se ordena toda la vida temporal . . . "

(SHE STOPS — THE BELL TOLLS — SLOWLY SHE WALKS ALONG THE GRAVEL PATH FOR ABOUT SIX SECONDS)

CARLTON: (OFF — VERY, VERY SLIGHT SPANISH ACCENT) You look so lonesome. May I speak to you?

(WALKING STOPS)

CARLTON: (COMING ON) I could not help watching. With the setting of the sun — you silhouetted against that mesquite tree in the distance — it was like an old painting of a monastery garden.

ELRA: (PAUSE) Who are you?

CARLTON: Just a person who is perhaps lonesome — like you.

2. A WOMAN'S LIFE, #2085†

BARBARA: (OFF) Carol? Michael?

CAROL: (PROJECTING) Coming right in, Babs. (LOW) Please, Michael, nothing about what you were just saying to <u>them</u>.

* Excerpt from DAVID HARDING, COUNTER-SPY, written by Phillips H. Lord.

† By Julian Funt. Reproduced through the courtesy of the author.

MICHAEL: (LOW) The marriage?

CAROL: No, the other things.

MICHAEL: Well, of course not.

BARBARA: (COMING HALF ON) Do you hear voices, Tom? Strangely familiar voices?

TOM: (HALF-ON) Vaguely.

CAROL: Hello, Tom. Were you starting to get worried?

TOM: (COMING ON) No. Not really. But —

BARBARA: (COMING ON) They know your name! And they look — Yes, very much like dear old Uncle Michael and Aunt Carol who went out that very door for a short walk one lovely spring night.

3. HELEN KELLER*

MRS. KELLER: What dress do you want to wear? This one — No? (TROUBLED) Look, Helen, look at me . . . Your red one? — No? The blue one with the crinkled violets? . . . Helen! You don't seem to care! . . . Why don't you look at me, dear? . . . Why are you so listless? . . . Oh — (CALLING) Arthur! Arthur!

CAPT. KELLER: (OFF) What is it, Kate?

MRS. KELLER: Please — Arthur. Come up here a minute.

CAPT. KELLER: Sure. What is it? (COMING ON) What's the matter?

MRS. KELLER: I don't know. Arthur, I —

CAPT. KELLER: (INTERRUPTS) How's Helen today? How's my baby?

4. THE STORY OF GUS†

GUS: Anyway, I didn't do nothin' about it, and the kid went to work in the place with us, and the only thing that bothered me was that I wasn't settin' him an example. But there was nothin' I could do, see, because Theresa was too smart for me. Every day she'd corner me and start talkin' . . .

(SOUND OF ENGINES OUT)

THERESA: (FADING IN WITH AD LIBS TO) . . . on your mind. I know just what you're going to tell him, and I wish you wouldn't, Gus.

* By Ethel Deckelman. Reprinted with the permission of the author.

† By Arthur Miller. Reproduced through the courtesy of the author.

GUS: Why, what am I going to tell him?

THERESA: About the ships. About how you sailed all over the world. I never told him you were a sailor, and I don't want him to know.

5. MYSTERY THEATRE: *DOUBLE DISASTER CLAUSE**

BARBARA: The moment Prosper left me I ran downstairs and got out my car and drove back to Hugo's house, driving slowly enough so that Prosper's taxi would get there first. I let myself into the house by the side door . . .

(DOOR OPENS ON)

PROSPER: (OFF) I'm as fully aware of the circumstances as you are, Hugo!

HUGO: Then what the devil's come over you anyhow! Are you out of your mind?

BARBARA: (PAUSE) I heard angry voices coming from the library . . . and I crept closer and stood outside the library door . . . listening!

PROSPER: (COMING ON UNTIL FULL) Hugo, I'm trying to be reasonable and civilized about this. Barbara won't marry either of us probably without the other's consent and blessing. Will you give Barbara up?

HUGO: No, I will be hanged if I will!

PROSPER: You're not in love with her!

HUGO: Not in love with her! You are out of your senses!

B. FADINGS

1. THE MAN BEHIND THE GUN: *THE DEATH OF AUNT AGGIE*†

HARRY: (AWKWARD) Well, be seeing you.

MABEL: Wait, Harry. Would — would you kiss me once for luck?

HARRY: Aw, gee, Mabel — right in front of everybody?

VOICE: (OFF, SWEETLY) Aw, go ahead and kiss her. We ain't looking. (LAUGHTER)

ANOTHER: (OFF) How about me, lady? Won't I do? (MORE LAUGHTER)

HARRY: (ROARING) Pipe down, you lugs! (IN and DOWN) You see how it is, Mabel. They'll kid the pants off me.

MABEL: Okay, Harry. Next time, huh?

HARRY: Yeah, sure, Mabel. Next time. (FADING) Well — be seeing you.

* By Milton Geiger. Reproduced through the courtesy of the author.

† By Ranald MacDougall. Copyright, 1949, by Columbia Broadcasting System, Inc.

VOICE: (OFF — HEAVY DISAPPOINTMENT) Aw, he ain't gonna kiss her!

CHORUS: (OFF — VERY SADLY) Awwwwwww.

HARRY: (SAME PERSPECTIVE) Aloha, Mabel.

CHORUS: Aloha, Mabel.

(THE BOAT STARTS AWAY)

MABEL: (PROJECTING) Aloha, Harry. Good luck. (A PAUSE) Don't forget! Come back! Come back!

HARRY: (FAINTLY) I'll come back. Aloha.

MABEL: (TO HERSELF) Aloha, Aloha, Harry.

2. THE ALDRICH FAMILY, #445*

KATHLEEN: How could Henry do a thing like that to me?

AGNES: My goodness, Kathleen, you tore up his letter — just when it was getting good!

(DOORBELL RINGS)

KATHLEEN: (FADING) I'm going up to my room.

MRS. ANDERSON: (OFF) What's the matter, dear?

KATHLEEN: (OFF) Nothing, Mother.

AGNES: (SHOUTING) Kathleen! Your doorbell's ringing!

MRS. ANDERSON: (COMING ON) Agnes, what's the matter with Kathleen? She just bumped into me with her eyes closed.

AGNES: (FADING) The fact is, Mrs. Anderson, she just had her eyes opened!

(DOORBELL RINGS AGAIN)

MRS. ANDERSON: My goodness!

AGNES: (OFF) Kathleen!

(DOOR OPENS ON)

MR. ALDRICH: Afternoon, Mrs. Anderson.

MRS. ANDERSON: Well, Mr. Aldrich! Won't you come in?

3. THE STATES TALKING†

(THE LAUGHTER SWELLS UP SO THAT THE SPEAKING VOICES ARE SHOUTING ABOVE IT)

* By Patricia Joudry and Del Dinsdale, based on characters originated by Clifford Goldsmith. Reproduced through the courtesy of the authors and Clifford Goldsmith.

† By Archibald MacLeish. Reprinted with the permission of the author.

A VOICE: Stayed home and stuck to their kin says New Mexico.

A VOICE: Stayed home and married their kind says Missouri.

A VOICE: Married their cousins who looked like their mothers says Michigan.

A VOICE: The pure-bred breed! says Texas.

A VOICE: How could they help it? Who would they marry? says Florida. Who could they find?

A VOICE: The girls they left behind us says Missouri.

(THE LAUGHTER, NOW A TREMENDOUS SHOUT, BEGINS TO RECEDE)

A VOICE: That's them! The girls we left behind! They married the girls we left behind says Wisconsin!

A VOICE: So that's it. So that's who! says Connecticut.

A VOICE: So that's all! East of the sea! says Ohio.

A VOICE: So that's all! says Missouri. All for that! All for the pure-bred girls we left behind!

(THE LAUGHTER FADES . . . THE VOICES PAUSE, FADE)

A VOICE: (FADING) Surf on the reefs says Maine. Ice on Penobscot . . .

A VOICE: (FADING) There's talk says Iowa.

(FAR OFF AND FAINTLY THE LAUGHTER RISES AGAIN AND RECEDES)

A VOICE: (FADING) Talk says Illinois.

A VOICE: (FADING) Bells on the Old Orchard . . . bells at Ogunquit.

(PAUSE)

A VOICE: (FADING) Clash of the corn in the wind says Illinois.

4. COLUMBIA WORKSHOP: *MERIDIAN 7-1212**

FAWCETT: May we go right into the office? I'd like to listen for a while.

BRADLEY: Certainly. But we'll have to whisper if you want to talk to me in there. It might be picked up on the mike.

FAWCETT: Of course.

(DOOR OPENS ON)

OPERATOR: (OFF) . . . the signal the time will be eleven forty and one-quarter. (TONE)

BRADLEY: (WHISPERING) Sit down, Mr. Fawcett.

* By Irving Reis.

FAWCETT: Thanks. (PAUSE) Mr. Bradley, is it possible for us to trace a few calls? I'd like to find out just why people use the service. Is it because their watches stop . . . or what?

(OFF) When you hear the signal the time will be eleven forty and one-half. (TONE)

BRADLEY: Unfortunately I can't do anything about that. All the calls come in on the dial system, and you can't trace dials.

(OFF) When you hear the signal the time will be eleven forty and three-quarters. (TONE)

FAWCETT: That's too bad. It would be interesting to know. Could you offer a guess from personal knowledge? We could quote you.

(OFF) When you hear the signal the time will be eleven forty-one. (TONE)

BRADLEY: (STARTING TO FADE) Your guess would be as good as mine. Time plays an important part in the lives of people in a big city. We get several hundred calls an hour. It may be people trying to make a train connection . . . somebody in bed who's too lazy to get up and look . . . (OFF NOW) someone with a watch that stopped.

(OFF, COMING ON) When you hear the signal the time will be eleven forty-one and one-quarter. (TONE)

(ON MIKE NOW) When you hear the signal the time will be eleven forty-one and one-half. (TONE) When you hear the signal the time will be eleven forty-one and three-quarters. (TONE)

FAWCETT: Yeah. Well, I'll write all that down.

5. BEAUTIFUL SILENCE*

RANDY: There's a bomb under this house and they won't believe it. I can hear it, Doctor! They won't leave! They'll be killed! The house is going to

* By M. H. Swanton. Reproduced through the courtesy of the author.

blow up. (FADING SLOWLY) Talk to them. Tell them I'm not crazy! Jeff . . . talk to him. He'll tell you I'm . . . . Talk to him . . .

JEFF: Easy, old boy. Hello, Doctor. No . . . of course not. There's no ticking. It's his imagination . . . . Yes, just like the first time. (FADING) We were sitting here in the living-room when . . . . Yes . . . . (CONTINUED FADING AD LIB)

RANDY: I ran down the side street . . . one block . . . two blocks . . . I was safe now. I was alone in the church. It was all over and done with.

C. OFF MICROPHONE

1. TALES OF WILLIE PIPER*

WILLIE: Look at my pajamas! Grease all over!

MR. WESSEL: Only on the pants. The top's good for another week.

WILLIE: Sure, but if I sent the pants to the laundry one week, and the top the next week, how am I going to get straightened out?

MR. WESSEL: Odd weeks you can wear your undershirt.

WILLIE: Without arms! Gee whiz, winter's coming! And look at my undershirt! How do you think I — (ALARMED) Hey! Where's my undershirt?

MR. WESSEL: I dunno.

WILLIE: Listen, Mr. Wessel, did I hang it on the handlebars last night?

MR. WESSEL: You did?

MRS. GREENE: (OFF, THROUGH DOOR, CALLING) Willie! Willie Piper!

WILLIE: (LOW) Oh, boy! We woke up Mrs. Greene.

MR. WESSEL: (LOW) Make believe we're not up yet.

MRS. GREENE: (OFF) Mr. Wessel! Willie!

WILLIE: (LOW) She knows we're up.

(DOOR OPENS ON)

WILLIE: (CALLING) Yes, Mrs. Greene? Good morning.

MRS. GREENE: (OFF) What happened up there?

WILLIE: Why . . . I just got out of bed, Mrs. Greene — that's all.

MRS. GREENE: Didn't I hear some glass break?

WILLIE: You did? Well . . . Mr. Wessel just got out of bed too. And we're having a little trouble with my pajamas.

* An audition script, by Samuel Taylor. Reproduced through the courtesy of the author.

MRS. GREENE: What are you trying to do — frame them?

WILLIE: What?

MRS. GREENE: Be a little more quiet. People are still trying to sleep down here.

WILLIE: Oh, sure, Mrs. Greene. You haven't got anything to worry about. And, Mrs. Greene, if you should happen to notice an undershirt down in the alley . . . Mrs. Greene? . . . Boy!

2. THE ALDRICH FAMILY, #436*

MR. ALDRICH: Mr. Bradley, I just don't know how to apologize enough.

MR. BRADLEY: Never mind, Mr. Aldrich. I'm glad you made it in time for the Student Court. Shall we go in?

(DOOR OPENS ON)

After you.

MR. ALDRICH: Thank you.

(DOOR CLOSES)

Well, Henry!

HENRY: (OFF) Oh, gee whiz! (COMING ON) Father, I was hoping . . . That is, Mr. Lawson told me you'd left.

MR. ALDRICH: I came back. Are you functioning in the Court today, Henry?

HENRY: Functioning? In a way.

MR. BRADLEY: You're defending someone, Henry?

HENRY: Yes, sir. You might say I am.

MR. ALDRICH: Good, son. I'll see you later.

HENRY: (FADING) Yes, sir. I guess you will.

MR. BRADLEY: A chip off the old block, eh, Mr. Aldrich?

MR. ALDRICH: Yes, indeed!

MR. LAWSON: (COMING ON) Hello, Sam. I see you finally made it all right.

MR. BRADLEY: (PROJECTING) All right, let's begin, your Honor.

STRINGBEAN: (OFF) Now, Mr. Bradley?

MR. BRADLEY: Now.

STRINGBEAN: But we only have one case and — well, couldn't we postpone it a week?

* By Norman Tokar and Ed Jurist, based on characters created by Clifford Goldsmith. Reproduced through the courtesy of the authors and Clifford Goldsmith.

MR. BRADLEY: We could not. Charley, you're the Prosecutor, aren't you?

CHARLEY: (OFF) Yes, sir.

MR. BRADLEY: Well, begin.

CHARLEY: But, Mr. Bradley, when I handed this guy his summons I didn't realize his fath — That is — I don't think he's guilty.

MR. BRADLEY: You don't?

CHARLEY: Not that guilty.

MR. BRADLEY: Suppose we let the Court decide? Proceed.

CHARLEY: Yes, sir. Well, Stringbean . . .

STRINGBEAN: Yes?

CHARLEY: I don't know how to begin.

MR. ALDRICH: (ON, LOW) Mr. Bradley, may I interrupt?

MR. BRADLEY: Certainly, Mr. Aldrich.

MR. ALDRICH: (PROJECTING) Might I suggest that the Prosecutor address the Court as your Honor?

CHARLEY: The Court?

MR. ALDRICH: The Bench.

CHARLEY: What bench?

MR. ALDRICH: Stringbean.

CHARLEY: Oh. Well, the whole thing is, Stringbean, your Honor . . .

MR. ALDRICH: No, no, I'm afraid that isn't quite it, Charley. (LOW) Mr. Bradley, perhaps if I might be allowed to take over . . . ?

MR. BRADLEY: Of course, Mr. Aldrich. (PROJECTING) Step down, Charley.

MR. ALDRICH: Will someone read the charges, please?

STRINGBEAN: (COMING ON) Go ahead, Charley.

CHARLEY: (ON) Well, the charges are . . . Loitering, going to lockers at the wrong time, breaking and entering, bribing an officer, and blocking traffic.

MR. ALDRICH: Well! That sounds pretty serious. Who is it?

CHARLEY: Is that important?

MR. ALDRICH: I would think so. Your Honor, call the defendant to the stand.

STRINGBEAN: Yes, Mr. Aldrich. (PROJECTING) Henry Aldrich, take the stand.

MR. ALDRICH: Who?

MR. BRADLEY: (OFF) What's that?

CHARLEY: I tried to tell you, Mr. Bradley.

MR. ALDRICH: Henry!

HENRY: (COMING ON) Hello, Father.

MR. BRADLEY: (OFF) Mr. Aldrich, perhaps it would be wiser to postpone —

MR. ALDRICH: Not at all, Mr. Bradley. Will the defendant please take the stand?

HENRY: (ON) Yes, Sir.

MR. ALDRICH: Now — guilty or not guilty?

HENRY: Guilty.

3. THE CLINIC*

NURSE: You'll sleep better tonight. It's hard the first night. Dr. Beems will be here in a minute.

LIBBEY: The X-rays done?

NURSE: Oh, sure. You're down for surgery tomorrow, aren't you? Bed high enough?

LIBBEY: Yes.

NURSE: (FADING) He'll be here in a minute.

BED #2: (FAR OFF) See in the paper about all those nickels, Mr. Michaels?

BED #4: (OFF) I didn't see the paper yet.

BED #2: Someone threw a lot of nickels from the Empire State Building. They had a traffic jam a mile long.

BED #4: Nickels?

BED #2: Two women fainted, and some guy had his fingers smashed.

DR. BEEMS: (FAR OFF) Be right there, nurse. (COMING ON) Put on your bathrobe and come with me, Mr. Libbey.

4. THEATRE GUILD ON THE AIR: *ON BORROWED TIME*†

PUD: Gramps, I want to steal an apple, too. Boost me up the tree.

GRAMPS: You don't have to steal. Oh, all right. One — two — up you go!

(HOISTING PUD INTO APPLE TREE . . . LEAFY RUSTLE)

* By Ted Key. Copyright, 1940, National Broadcasting Company, Inc.

† From the play by Paul Osborne, taken from the novel by Lawrence Edward Watkin. Copyrighted, 1937, by Paul Osborne. Radio adaptation by Paul Peters, in H. William Fitelson (ed.), *Theatre Guild on the Air*, published by Rinehart & Company, Inc.

PUD: (OFF) You know, Gramps, I can't get down till you let me.

GRAMPS: Why not?

PUD: Because you wished nobody could come down till you let them. That was your good-deed wish. Then you did another good deed and that makes it stick double.

GRAMPS: (PROJECTING) Did it? Well, now, I'm liable to keep you there all week. Maybe a hundred years. Depends on how I feel. I think I'll stroll down to Milbaur Park and pick up a few fossils for our collection.

PUD: Wait a minute. I'm coming with you.

(RUSTLE OF LEAVES)

(IN ALARM) Gramps, I can't let go!

GRAMPS: (LAUGHING) Course you can't. You're going to hang onto that limb till I release you from my magic spell.

PUD: (FRIGHTENED NOW) Let me down, Gramps. Please! My arm is tired.

GRAMPS: (LAUGHING) Now, now, sonny. You can't go breaking my spell like that.

PUD: (SCREAMING IN TERROR) Gramps, let me go! (HE CRIES) Please, Gramps, please!

5. THE LITTLE ONE*

HELEN: Phil, you make me sick the way you always pick on little things like that and blow them up.

PHIL: Little things!

HELEN: Yes, little things.

PHIL: Little things my foot! I just hate to see him get away with it.

HELEN: Sometimes you make me so mad I could . . .

PHIL: Spit?

HELEN: Worse than that.

NARRATOR: That's the way it usually went. Phil and Helen at each other's throats from the word go. They didn't mean all the things they said . . . but you know how it is. They'd get all heated up and start calling each	PHIL: (OFF) For heaven's sake, Helen, either say something and stick at it or shut up. HELEN: (OFF) If that's the way you feel about it there's no use discussing anything, is there?

* By Al Morgan. Copyright, 1942, by Al Morgan. Reproduced through the courtesy of the author.

other names. I guess there are people like that in all groups. The rest of us would just sit around and watch them go at each other. You know, if this was a movie, they'd wind up in each other's arms. But this isn't a movie, so they just went along like that, fighting each other.

PHIL: (OFF) You're darn right there isn't. Start talking about something and you make it personal right away.

HELEN: You've got so many cock-eyed ideas.

PHIL: Thanks.

HELEN: Shut up and have a drink.

D. THROUGH DOORS

1. MYSTERY THEATRE: *THE CREEPER**

GEORGIA: Yes?

DOORMAN: (OUTSIDE DOOR) This is the doorman, Mrs. Grant.

GEORGIA: Yes?

DOORMAN: The druggist sent over your medicine . . .

GEORGIA: My medicine. Oh, yes, I forgot. In just a minute — No, no! Never mind! Go away!

DOORMAN: But, Mrs. Grant —

GEORGIA: No, no, no! I'm perfectly all right! I don't need it. Go away. Please go away! I don't want to see anyone.

DOORMAN: Very well, Mrs. Grant.

(PAUSE)

GEORGIA: Oh, thank the Lord! Thank the Lord! Any minute now . . . another knock at the door . . . or a ring . . . (SHE GASPS AS)

(DOORBELL RINGS)

GEORGIA: Wh — Who's there?

MRS. STONE: (OUTSIDE DOOR) It's me, dear. Mrs. Stone.

GEORGIA: Oh. What do you want?

MRS. STONE: Why, I've been worried about you. Are you ill?

GEORGIA: No, I'm all right, Mrs. Stone. I'm feeling — fine.

(RATTLING OF DOORKNOB)

MRS. STONE: Open up, dear. Don't you want me to keep you company?

GEORGIA: N-no, thank you. I . . . was just . . .

(MORE RATTLING)

(YELLING) Stop it!

MRS. STONE: Oh, do let me in, silly, and we'll —

GEORGIA: No, no, no! Go away! I'm going to sleep. Go away. You hear me — go away!

2. TALES OF WILLIE PIPER, #5*

GILLESPIE: But you've got plenty to eat, haven't you, Martha? Look at all the fish there!

MARTHA: Yes, why don't we give a fried fish party! Where's Mr. Bissel? He usually drops in around this time. Why isn't he coming for supper?

WILLIE: (NERVOUSLY) Oh, I don't think he'll be around, Martha. He's probably working late at the telegraph office tonight.

(KNOCKING ON KITCHEN DOOR OFF)

MR. BISSEL: (OFF) Hey, Willie! Martha! Are you eating?

WILLIE: Huh? (CALLING) Who's that?

MR. BISSEL: It's Mr. Bissel. Don't let me disturb you if you're eating.

WILLIE: Mr. Bissel!

MARTHA: (GRANDLY) No, come in, Mr. Bissel! You're just in time! Do you like fried fish?

GILLESPIE: Now, Martha, I think it'd be too much for you to have him, too.

WILLIE: (CALLING) Sure, Martha, I'll get rid of him. Hey, Mr. Bissel . . .

MARTHA: (FADING) What difference does it make?

(KITCHEN DOOR OPENS ON)

WILLIE: Mr. Bissel?

MR. BISSEL: Here I am, Willie. Hold the door open. I want to bring my bicycle in the kitchen.

WILLIE: Mr. Bissel, look — Martha's sort of nervous tonight, see, and —

MR. BISSEL: You mean she'd rather not see my bicycle?

WILLIE: She'd rather not see you.

MR. BISSEL: Eh?

* By Samuel Taylor. Reproduced through the courtesy of the author.

WILLIE: I mean for supper. We've got company. But — well, if you want to come over later, we'll save you a piece of apple pie.

MR. BISSEL: That sounds fine, Willie. (FADING) I'll go along down to the Public Library and read a couple of papers and be back in an hour.

WILLIE: (CALLING) Okay, Mr. Bissel. And thanks.

(DOOR CLOSES ON)

(CALLING) Martha, it's okay. He doesn't want to stay for supper.

MARTHA: (COMING ON) Thank you, Willie.

GILLESPIE: (COMING ON) She's all right now, Willie. Look, she's smiling! Nothing to worry about.

3. MYSTERY THEATRE: *NOW YOU SEE HER**

ELAINE: Please . . . don't leave me alone.

DOCTOR: Mr. King, are you leaving?

KING: Well, I —

DOCTOR: Mr. King — !

KING: All right! (PROTEST FROM ELAINE) I'll be right in the next room.

(FOOTSTEPS ON . . . DOOR OPENED ON AND CLOSED) (WE STAY IN KING'S PERSPECTIVE AND HEAR THE DOCTOR AND ELAINE TALKING THROUGH THE DOOR)

DOCTOR: (OVER ELAINE'S SOBBING) Now, Miss Vickers . . . you've been under tension for quite some time. Your nerves have given away . . .

KING: (ON, TO SELF) Eavesdropping is permissible under the circumstances.

DOCTOR: You are beginning to suffer hallucinations about some imaginary sister. These delusions have the appearance of reality to you, but they aren't true. Are they, Miss Vickers? (MUFFLED PLEADING FROM ELAINE) You know they aren't true. This is a trick you are playing on yourself.

KING: (ON, TO SELF) I don't trust that old saw-bones.

DOCTOR: You'll realize it as soon as you've had some rest. (SLIGHT PAUSE) Now . . . just take this capsule.

KING: Capsule!

DOCTOR: (OVER ELAINE'S STRUGGLES) Very well, if you won't take the capsule, I'll have to administer the hypodermic.

(ELAINE SCREAMS)

(DOOR FLUNG OPEN)

* By Paul Monash. Reproduced through the courtesy of the author.

KING: Oh, no, you don't!

(RUNNING FEET ON . . . TINKLE OF GLASS)

DOCTOR: (ON) You fool! You've smashed my hypodermic!

KING: And just in time, too.

DOCTOR: You idiot! I could kill you!

KING: I have no doubt of that. Now get out of here.

DOCTOR: (FADING) Never . . . never in all my life have I seen —

(DOOR OPENED OFF)

(OFF) Such maniacs!

(DOOR SLAMMED)

4. THE ALDRICH FAMILY, #431*

MRS. LAWSON: Have you decided what you're going to do, Mrs. Aldrich?

MRS. ALDRICH: Yes . . . I think I'll phone him!

MR. ALDRICH: What's that?

AGNES: (OFF) Mother!

MR. LAWSON: Lucille, does Agnes have to yell like that?

MRS. LAWSON: (SHOUTING) Agnes, your father says not to yell like that!

AGNES: I'm not yelling, Mother! I'm just saying goodbye.

MRS. LAWSON: (SHOUTING) Well, come on in here and let's see how you look.

AGNES: Mother, I can't possibly! I was due at Kathleen's party half an hour ago.

MRS. ALDRICH: (GETTING UP) Excuse me.

MR. ALDRICH: (FADING) Alice, where are you going?

MRS. ALDRICH: (CALLING) I'd like to see how Agnes looks. I'll be right back.

MR. LAWSON: (OFF) Mr. Aldrich, did your wife bid or didn't she?

MRS. ALDRICH: Oh, Agnes.

AGNES: (COMING ON) Hello, Mrs. Aldrich. Goodbye.

MRS. ALDRICH: Wait, dear. (LOW) Would you consider doing something for me?

AGNES: (LOW) Sure, Mrs. Aldrich. What?

* By Patricia Joudry and Del Dinsdale, based on characters by Clifford Goldsmith. Reproduced through the courtesy of the authors and Clifford Goldsmith.

5. BABY SNOOKS*

DADDY: Hmm. Nobody seems to be here. I wonder where Snooks is? She's not in the closet. She's not in back of the bureau.

SNOOKS: (OFF) She's under the bed!

DADDY: Oh! ha ha ha. I found her. She is under the bed. (EFFORT OF GETTING DOWN) And someone's with her. It looks like a little teddy bear.

SNOOKS: (SLIGHT OFF, MUFFLED) No, it isn't.

DADDY: Then what is it?

SNOOKS: A great big giant, and if you don't go away it'll eat you up!

DADDY: Now you wouldn't let him eat me up, would you, Snooks?

SNOOKS: (CUTELY) Wouldn't I?

DADDY: Well, I'm not afraid of him. Come on out and fight, Giant! (PAUSE) Well, why don't you come out and fight?

SNOOKS: (SMALL VOICE) He went away.

DADDY: That's good. Do you have any idea where Oscar is?

SNOOKS: No.

DADDY: Too bad. Because I have a shiny new coin for him.

SNOOKS: You do?

DADDY: Yes.

SNOOKS: Oh, Daddy!

DADDY: What?

SNOOKS: Here comes Oscar now!

DADDY: Wonderful! Ask Oscar if he wants a great big nickel.

SNOOKS: All right. (WHISPERS — AND THEN) He says he'd rather have a teeny, weeny dime.

E. WHISPERS

1. ADVENTURES OF THE THIN MAN: *THE CASE OF THE CROWDED COFFIN*†

EB: What're we going to do about it?

NICK: I have the cops outside. They've surrounded the building. But I pulled one more trick that may bring results.

NORA: Not a trick on that vampire, Nick?

* By Jesse Oppenheimer and Mac Benoff. Reproduced through the courtesy of the authors.

† By Milton Lewis, based on characters originated by Dashiell Hammett. Reproduced through the courtesy of the authors.

NICK: Yes, Baby. I hinted that I might like to split the take on the buried loot if she'd throw me a patsy to take the rap for the murders. She pretended to know nothing about it, but —

(NOISE OFF)

NORA: (LOW) Nick . . . someone's coming down here!

NICK: (LOW) Yeah. And I don't want them to know we're here. Eb, get into that coffin over there! And pull the lid down!

EB: (FADING) All right.

(COFFIN LID CLOSES OFF)

NICK: (LOW) There's only one other empty one here. Get in, Nora. I'll share it with you.

NORA: That's what I call true devotion . . . sharing the same coffin.

NICK: Keep quiet, and move over.

NORA: (LOW) I can't do either if you don't cooperate. Ow! Don't be a hog!

NICK: Now I'll close the lid . . . except for a crack.

(COFFIN LID CLOSES)

(ON ECHO) There.

(DOOR OPENS AND CLOSES OFF)

NORA: (WHISPERING) Who came in?

NICK: (WHISPERING) The undertaker, Richard Mayo . . . and his wife.

MAYO: (OFF) But, Jane, why'd you have to take me down here now?

JANE: (OFF) Because it's very important, Richard. I want you to sign those papers tonight, dear.

MAYO: I still don't see why it can't wait until tomorrow.

JANE: You're not very well, darling. You may not be able to do it tomorrow.

MAYO: Really, Jane? That doesn't sound so cheerful. Where are they?

JANE: I have them right here.

MAYO: What does it say? I haven't my glasses — can't read a thing.

JANE: It's just a contract, darling. You know I wouldn't ever do anything silly. Sign there.

MAYO: Very well.

JANE: And now, Richard, you'd better take one of these pills.

NICK: (WHISPERING) Okay, Baby. Here's where I get out.

(COFFIN LID OPENS)

(PROJECTING) Mayo! Don't take that pill!

MAYO: Jane! What's a live person doing in one of my coffins?

NORA: (PROJECTING) We were just testing it for size.

MAYO: Why, it's Nick and Nora Charles!

JANE: Yes. And if they had any sense they'd have stayed in that casket . . .

(COFFIN LID OPENS OFF)

EB: (OFF) Don't reach in your pocket, Mrs. Mayo. I have you covered from here!

JANE: Another comedian heard from! Well, you —!

(SHOTS)

EB: (OFF) The next one won't give your hair a wave, Mrs. Mayo. Take her gun, Nory.

NORA: I have it.

JANE: (ON) Well? So what?

NICK: So, dear Jane, this paper you made your husband sign is a complete confession to the murder of Pete the Pigeon and Boscoe Brant. It's also a suicide note.

MAYO: (ON) Suicide? Why, I have no reason to commit suicide.

NICK: But you would have just the same . . . if you had swallowed the pill, Mr. Mayo. Your wife was going to murder you.

2. THE FALL OF THE CITY*

ANNOUNCER: They stand in the slant of the sunlight silent and watching.
The silence after the drums echoes the drum beat.
Now there's a sound. They see him. They must see him!
They're shading their eyes from the sun: there's a rustle of whispering:
We can't see for the glare of it. . . . Yes! . . . Yes! . . .
He's there in the end of the street in the shadow.
We see him!
He looks huge — a head taller than anyone:
Broad as a brass door: a hard hero:
Heavy of heel on the brick: clanking with metal:
The helm closed on his head: the eyeholes hollow.

* From *The Fall of the City; A Verse Play for Radio.* Copyright, 1937, by Archibald MacLeish.

He's coming! . . .

He's clear of the shadow! . . .

The sun takes him.

They cover their faces with fingers. They cower before him.

They fall: they sprawl on the stone. He's alone where he's walking.

He marches with rattle of metal. He tramples his shadow.

He mounts by the pyramid — stamps on the stairway — turns —

His arm rises — his visor is opening . . . .

(THERE IS AN INSTANT'S BREATHLESS SILENCE: THEN THE VOICE OF THE ANNOUNCER LOW — ALMOST A WHISPER)

There's no one! . . .

There's no one at all! . . .

No one! . . .

The helmet is hollow!

The metal is empty! The armor is empty! I tell you

There's no one at all there: there's only the metal:

The barrel of metal: the bundle of armor. It's empty!

The push of a stiff pole at the nipple would topple it.

They don't see! They lie on the pavings. They lie in the

Burnt spears: the ashes of arrows. They lie there . . .

They don't see or they won't see. They are silent . . .

The people invent their oppressors: they wish to believe in them.

They wish to be free of their freedom: released from their liberty —

The long labor of liberty ended!

They lie there!

3. WHEN A GIRL MARRIES, #1609*

Harry and Ann are walking down the long corridor toward Mr. Darrow's office.

(FOOTSTEPS)

ANN: (LOW) Why is his office so far away from his secretary?

HARRY: That's one of his eccentricities.

ANN: But I don't understand?

* By Elaine Carrington. Reproduced through the courtesy of the author.

HARRY: He wants to be off by himself.

ANN: Where he won't be disturbed by man or beast?

HARRY: That's it.

(FOOTSTEPS STOP)

HARRY: (WHISPERING) Sit down here, Ann. I'll go in first.

ANN: (WHISPERING FADING) You'll let me know — ?

HARRY: (PROJECTING) I'll be right out.

(KNOCK ON DOOR)

DARROW: (INSIDE) Come in.

(DOOR OPENS ON)

HARRY: (PROJECTING) How are you, Mr. Darrow?

DARROW: (OFF) Harry! Come in — take a chair.

HARRY: Thank you.

(DOOR CLOSES)

DARROW: (COMING ON) I understand you've been scouting around to find a receptionist for us?

HARRY: Well, it just so happens a very good friend of ours is looking for that kind of job.

F. SHOUTS, SCREAMS, LOUDNESS

1. THE BIG STORY, #40: *MURDER ON SEVENTY-SEVEN**

REDDEN: You loved your wife?

GRAHAM: You've asked me that over and over. The same question . . .

REDDEN: Answer the question.

GRAHAM: Yes, yes, yes!

REDDEN: And there was no other woman?

GRAHAM: No, I told you. No, no!

FRANK: And you positively identify John McCabe as the killer?

GRAHAM: (LOUDLY) How many times are you going to ask me that? Why are you asking me the same questions over and over?

REDDEN: Answer the question, Mr. Graham.

FRANK: Did John McCabe kill your wife?

GRAHAM: (LOUDLY) Yes, yes, yes!

* By Max Ehrlich. Reproduced through the courtesy of the author and the producer of THE BIG STORY.

REDDEN: Now then, Mr. Graham . . .

GRAHAM: (SHRIEKING) Stop it, stop it, stop it!!!

FRANK: Stop what, Mr. Graham?

GRAHAM: That pounding sound. That heartbeat . . .

REDDEN: You can't hear your heart beat on the lie detector, Mr. Graham.

GRAHAM: (YELLING) I tell you I hear it, I hear it! It's driving me out of my mind!

REDDEN: The lie detector makes no sound, Mr. Graham.

GRAHAM: (HYSTERICALLY) I hear it, I tell you! And I can't stand it, I can't stand it! This box . . . it's driving me crazy!! I'm going to smash it to bits!

(A SPLINTERING CRASH)

FRANK: (QUIETLY) Well, Graham?

GRAHAM: (SOBBING) All right, all right. I did it. I killed Ellen. There was another woman . . . a woman in Moline. I never loved Ellen. I had to get rid of her. So I shot her.

2. THE WOMEN STAYED AT HOME*

CELIA: I love you, Carl. I love you, Carl! So I said it. And his arms came close around me . . . and there was no earth or sky or death. (PAUSE) The days after that? Days that stood still in wonder — and then in rush were gone. Warm days — lazy days — wonderful days — days when the sky reached down and lifted us to the clouds, and we — Oh, Carl . . . Carl . . . (PAUSE) And then a new day — a morning — sun awakened me . . . stretched out my hand . . . (OFF, SHARPLY) Carl! No! Carl, where are you? (BUILDING) Carl, where are you? (UP, CRYING OUT) Carl! (DOWN) Gone — gone — I cried . . . Not very long . . . You see, I understood. Always, in our days together, there'd been a cloud, and with each passing day that cloud would have grown larger until there was no warmth of sun for us. The cloud of fear — that someone of the village would see us — see him — and seeing him — end my world for me. And he knew that . . . And so he went away. Where? I don't know. I like to think

* By Arch Oboler. Reprinted with the permission of the author.

he took a boat during the night and sailed out to sea in it back to where he came from . . . Back to <u>his</u> small village by the cliffs . . . I like to think that.

3. MYSTERY THEATRE: *DOUBLE DISASTER CLAUSE**

RAY: Well, yesterday I told you both men were instantly killed. I was wrong. Today's medical investigation proves beyond any shadow of a doubt that Hugo lived a minute or so longer than Prosper.

BARBARA: Poor Hugo!

RAY: It's pretty wonderful of you to think only of his final moments instead of yourself and the $200,000.

BARBARA: (BROUGHT UP SHORT) Why? What do you mean?

RAY: Prosper died first.

BARBARA: (GETTING PANICKY . . . A BIT SHRILL AND EDGY) You <u>said</u> that!

RAY: Therefore his insurance went to his survivor and first beneficiary — Hugo.

BARBARA: But Hugo died a minute later!

RAY: But you weren't mentioned in <u>his</u> policy at all. It all stops with Hugo.

BARBARA: (LOUDLY) Then I don't get the $200,000?

RAY: Under the circumstances, Barbara —

BARBARA: (HIGHER) How much <u>do</u> I get?

RAY: You don't understand, Barbara. You don't get anything.

BARBARA: (ALMOST A HARSH SCREAM: TERRIBLY) What!! (THEN PELL MELL) What do you mean — I don't get anything? What are you trying to pull here?

RAY: Barbara . . .

BARBARA: (LOUDLY) You and your company and your purchased doctors and your slick lawyers — what are you up to?

RAY: Barbara, I told you. According to —

BARBARA: I know you told me, and you lie in your teeth! You lie, do you hear? You're all lying! (HYSTERICAL NOW) They couldn't tell who died first! You said yourself no one could live a second with such injuries!

RAY: I know, but —

* By Milton Geiger. Reproduced through the courtesy of the author.

BARBARA: (SCREAMING) No one got out of that wreck! I watched and no one got out. Do you hear me — no one!!

RAY: (STUNNED) What did you say, Barbara?

BARBARA: Burning gasoline all over, lighting up the rain, lighting up the river like a torch — no one could live!

RAY: Barbara, why didn't you tell me where you were when it happened?

BARBARA: (FURIOUSLY) I'll sue you! I'll sue your dirty company for everything they've got!!

RAY: (TOPPING HER ACCUSINGLY) I asked you a question, Barbara!

BARBARA: (STILL LOUD) After all, $200,000 is big news for any newspaper in . . . in the . . . (STOPS, REALIZING A LITTLE NOW) Wh . . . what?

RAY: You didn't tell me you'd seen the accident. (PAUSE) Accident? I wonder! I'm beginning to wonder!

BARBARA: (SCREAMING) Get out of here! GET OUT OF HERE!

4. MYSTERY THEATRE: *THE COMIC STRIP MURDER**

HANLEY: The most ingenious part of the whole thing was calling me in on the case. If I had believed the story she just got through weaving for me . . . and if she had shot you . . . it would have been a clear-cut case of self-defense . . . with the District Attorney as her star witness! But they always slip up somewhere.

JULIA: (IN A HARD VOICE) What do you mean? How?

HANLEY: You forgot that today was your wedding anniversary.

JULIA: So?

HANLEY: And I was just lucky enough to find that out. Mrs. Stetson, a man who is going to murder his wife doesn't arrange a surprise party for her at midnight! He —

(FEET SCURRY OFF)

(LOUD AND EXCITED) Mrs. Stetson, come back here! Stay away from that parapet!

MARK: (SHOUTING) Julia, don't! Don't climb over! Come back!

JULIA: (OFF) If you don't like it come and get me!

* By Frederic A. Methot. Reproduced through the courtesy of the author.

MARK: Mr. Hanley, stop her! She's trying to walk along the ledge and then escape down the fire-escape!

HANLEY: It's fifty stories down! She's mad! She's —

MARK: (SHOUTING) Julia, look out! Julia, you're going to —

JULIA: (STARTS A SCREAM OF HORROR WHICH FADES AS SHE FALLS)

HANLEY: Good Heavens!

MARK: Julia . . .

G. KISSES

The actor kisses his loved one simply by kissing the back of his own hand in front of the microphone. Practice this "trick" in the following, and similar, excerpts.

1. A WOMAN'S LIFE, #2086*

MADELINE: If you took me in your arms, kissed me, that night . . . Well, it might give you at least part of the answer.

SCOTT: Madeline! My dearest!

(KISS)

SCOTT: I don't think . . . No, I know I've never been more completely happy in my whole life.

2. ADVENTURES OF THE THIN MAN: *THE CASE OF THE BLEEDING LIPSTICK*†

NICK: And putting your arms around me will get you nowhere.

BELINDA: Darling, when that gets me nowhere I'll blow my brains out.

(KISS)

NICK: Belinda!

BELINDA: Change your mind, Nick?

NICK: No.

BELINDA: (KISS) Yes?

NICK: No!

BELINDA: Yes! (KISS)

NICK: Oh, nuts!

BELINDA: Why?

NICK: You got lipstick on my shirt!

* By Julian Funt. Reproduced through the courtesy of the author.

† By Milton Lewis, based on characters originated by Dashiell Hammett. Reproduced through the courtesy of the authors.

3. MY FRIEND IRMA*

RICHARD: It's all set, Jane. And, really, I wish I knew how to thank you.

JANE: Richard, when a girl stands on her tip-toes and puckers . . . it's not setting-up exercises.

RICHARD: Oh.

(KISS)

JANE: That's better. Well, don't work too hard.

* By Cy Howard and Parke Levy. Reproduced through the courtesy of the authors.

Chapter IV. . MICROPHONE READING: MEANING

1

The dialogue of a radio script is not always as thin and casual and uninviting as it appears to be on the mimeographed pages. If the play is well written the speeches are variously functional and carry meanings that can be enforced by their context and by their connection with life. Even in a radio play a sentence can often accomplish what Eric Bentley finds an Ibsenite sentence accomplishes:

> It sheds light on the character speaking, on the character spoken to, on the character spoken about; it furthers the plot; it functions ironically in conveying to the audience a meaning different from that conveyed to the characters (and it is not merely that the characters say things which mean more to the audience than to them, but that they also say things which, as one senses, mean more to the characters than to the audience);[1]

and finally, each "sentence is part of the rhythmic pattern which constitutes the whole act" or the play.

Success in enriching and vitalizing a play's dialogue therefore depends on the actor's knowing the full meaning of what he says. This point must be underlined and reiterated again and again, since the recurring blight to radio is the actor who does not know the precise meaning of what he is reading. Meaning is rarely simple—is usually complex and full of nuances. For this reason perhaps the best director for a radio play is a machine that blares out to the rehearsing actor at the end of every sentence and every speech the single question: "What do you mean?"

The words people say in a play, as in life, are usually only an indication of the full meaning behind them. Words imply more than they state: "Human speech is merely reticence." Consequently in reading from his script the radio actor cannot, as Goethe observed, "make pretensions to the spirit of the thing while the sense and letter of it are not clear to him."[2] The sense conveyed in reading depends on the intention of the actor. If he has no intention, or a fuzzy one, or an incomplete or superficial one, his reading will betray him, since the influence of the mind on the voice is ever present and always evident. It can be heard in all natural and unstudied utterance where every variation of the tone and tempo of the voice means something—is significant. The voice serves the mind—is, as Quintilian said, "The index of the mind."[3]

In everyday conversation these significant variations of the voice are unpremeditated. In reading in front of the microphone, however, they must be somewhat premeditated; and this practice can best be carried out only when the actor fully understands the meaning of his speeches. In an old book on acting there is the quaint notation that while nature

> . . . deny'd to man the fur of the bear, the talons of the eagle, the wings of the kite, and the strength of the horse, she gave him understanding . . . . Here it is that the greatest discernment of the actor is shown, *in understanding the intent of the author.*[4]

2

Artificial, monotonous, mechanical, superficial, and careless or inaccurate reading are the five most common faults that follow from not comprehending fully the sense of what is being said. Although the types to some extent overlap, each can be examined separately.

[1] Eric Bentley, *The Playwright as Thinker* (New York: Harcourt, Brace & Company, Inc., 1946), pp. 124–125.

[2] Johann W. von Goethe, *Wilhelm Meister;* quoted in Bassett, *A Handbook of Oral Reading,* p. 15.

[3] Quintilian, *Institutio Oratoria,* XI, iii, 62.

[4] [John Hill] *The Actor; or, A Treatise on the Art of Playing . . . .* (London: R. Griffiths, 1755), pp. 22 and 14.

1) Artificial radio reading results from giving more attention to the sound of the thing said than to its sense. Perhaps it derives from the belief, a true one, that speech in art ought to be better than speech in life. That theory, though, always tends to overleap itself; it becomes esoteric and ends by making speech precious and pretentious. Reading born of this theory has in it too much of the elocutionary. According to John Masefield,

> You, who have suffered from the elocutionists . . . have seen their pupils in their spotless pinafores on prize-day, repeating and acting "Little drops of water . . . . Little grains of sand." You know their methods. They have made a child in a pinafore on prize-day a thing that strong men fly from screaming.[5]

If reading on the radio is to be elevated above the quality of everyday conversation it ought not, as a consequence, make a subtraction (or distraction) from the sense intended.

In order to avoid artificial reading the radio actor ought to center his prime attention during rehearsal and performance on the *sense* of what he is saying. If perfect speech and voice work are not instinctive by that time, it is too late. On the air the actor cannot be absorbed with the "prunes and prisms" of perfect diction or intent on "listening to his own voice, caressing its tones, lapping up its curves and resonance." The practical rule, as Richard Whately wrote in his *Elements of Rhetoric* (1828, 1846) is

> . . . not only to pay no studied attention to the voice, but studiously to *withdraw* the thoughts from it, and to dwell as intently as possible on the Sense; trusting to nature to suggest spontaneously the proper emphases and tones . . . . A reader is sure to pay *too much* attention to his voice, not only if he pays *any at all,* but if he does not strenuously *labour to withdraw* his attention from it altogether. He who not only understands fully what he is reading, but is earnestly occupying his mind with the matter of it, will be likely to read as if he understood it, and thus make others understand it . . . . But this cannot be the case if he is occupied with the thought of what their opinion will be of his reading, and, how his voice ought to be regulated; —if, in short, he is thinking about himself, and, of course, in the same degree, abstracting his attention from that which ought to occupy it exclusively.[6]

2) Monotonous radio reading results when there is a flatness of tone throughout, or a sameness in the rise and fall of the sentence patterns, a sameness of accents, inflections, pauses, and the like. At its worst, in the absence of any variety whatsoever, it is dead reading. The monotonous actor is uninterested in what he is saying and seems to lack the sensitivity to qualify, dissect, and shade his meanings; he gives no evidence of vitality, an essential ingredient of art, but reads his lines merely because they come next on the page. According to Lee Emerson Bassett.

> If reading is to have the convincing directness and force of living speech, the keen edge of the mind must be applied with vigor to every word, phrase, and sentence when they are spoken. Thoughtful reading is marked by the variety of utterance characteristic of conversation, and variety is the direct result of thinking at the time of speech. The boy who speaks "The curfew tolls the knell of parting day," when his mind is occupied with thoughts of his lunch, or the afternoon ball game, or his own discomfort as he stands before his fellows, is not likely to put life or reality into the line. Speech, to be convincing and genuine, must be the expression of *active* and *present thinking.*[7]

3) Mechanical radio reading usually results whenever the actor reads his lines largely in accordance with some arbitrary system of script marking. Primer style and primer stuff result, in Henry Irving's opinion, the more the actor is intent "upon the words, and the less on the ideas that dictated them."[8] If the radio actor has nothing but words to speak, he has nothing to say. Nevertheless many actors, forgetting all connection between mind and speech, always copiously mark their scripts to indicate changes in rate, in pitch, in emphasis; they denote the pauses (and their length: "count three"), the inflections, the patterns, the tones. Often they go on mike with as many signs to follow as they have words to speak.

To the adoption of such artificial schemes there are three weighty objections, according to Bishop Whately:

[5] John Masefield, *The Living Voice* (New York: The Macmillan Company, 1925), p. 19.

[6] Richard Whately, *Elements of Rhetoric,* 7th ed., rev. (London: B. Fellowes, 1846), see pp. 348–353; quoted in Parrish, *Reading Aloud,* see pp. 33–35.

[7] Bassett, *op. cit.,* p. 21; see Parrish, *op. cit.,* p. 40.

[8] Henry Irving, "The Art of Acting," in *The Drama* (Boston: Joseph Knight, Publisher, 1892), p. 60.

First, such a system must necessarily be imperfect; because though the *emphatic* word in each sentence may easily be pointed out in writing, no variety of marks that could be invented . . . would suffice to indicate the different *tones* in which the different emphatic words should be pronounced; though on this depends frequently the whole force, and even sense of the expression . . . . It would be moreover a task almost equally hopeless to attempt adequately to convey, by any written marks, precise directions as to the *rate* . . . with which each sentence and clause should be delivered.

Secondly, but were it possible to bring to perfection the . . . system of marks . . . . It is surely . . . a circuitous path . . . when the learner is directed, first to consider how each passage ought to be read; . . . then, to observe all the modulations, etc., of voice, which take place in such a delivery; then to note these down, by established marks, in writing; and, lastly, to pronounce according to these marks. This seems like recommending, for the purpose of raising the hand to the mouth, that he should first observe . . . what muscles are contracted,—in what degree,—and in what order; then that he should, in conformity with these notes, contract each muscle in due degree and in proper order; to the end that he may be enabled, after all, to—lift his hand to his mouth . . . .

Lastly, waiving both the above objections, if a person could learn thus to read and speak, as it were, *by note,* with the same fluency and accuracy as are attainable in the case of singing, still the . . . inevitable consequence would be that (the reader) would betray more or less his studied and artificial delivery; and would, in the same degree, manifest an offensive affectation . . . .[9]

Marking a script is not in itself fatal. A radio actor must mark his script. In the generally accepted opinion of Arch Oboler,

The definite indication of an amateur actor, to a director, is to see a script page which, after hours of rehearsal, is as free of notations as a blank check. Every possible marking should be used as a sign-post to a good performance . . . . A good memory is the leaning-post of the stage actor; a good pencil is the bulwark of the radio performer against the uncertainties of inspiration at the time of actual broadcast.[10]

When the actor marks his radio script he must always be on guard against purely mechanical results. When he underlines words for emphasis, uses lines to indicate pauses and breathing places, and employs other scribbled shorthand interpolations to enable him at a glance to anticipate changes of pace and mood, he should never forget Irving's advice that

. . . the thought precedes the word. Of course there are passages in which thought and language are borne along by the streams of emotion and completely intermingled. But more often it will be found that the most natural, and most seemingly accidental, effects are obtained *when the working of the mind is evident* before or as the tongue gives it words.[11]

In brief, when he marks his script the radio actor should attempt to set down, not the exact manner in which the lines are to be read, but the thought or the motivation behind and the various circumstances surrounding them.

4) Superficial radio reading results when the actor remains on top of his text instead of searching out the hidden subtext, when he misses nuances, when he is content with generalities or mere indications instead of digging out the subtle specifics, when he is incapable of discovering the fine gradations of meaning. Superficial reading is obvious or glib reading, or reading minus the validity of the individual actor's personal experience.

Apparently differences in meaning and a fullness of meaning are nowadays not too important. As John Dewey writes, "We are very easily trained to be content with a minimum of meaning, and fail to note how restricted is our perception of the relations which confer significance. We get so thoroughly used to a kind of pseudo-idea, a half-perception, that we are not aware how half-dead our mental action is."[12] To the old critics and actors reading was superficial when it lacked breadth. And breadth, according to Percy Fitzgerald, "arises from the actor being able to *enrich* a simple sentence, or even a word, with its fullest meaning, with all the associations and illustrations of which it is capable."[13] Unfortunately, many a radio actor, like Neville in Virginia Woolf's *The Waves,* is a clinger to the outside of words.

[9] Whately, *op. cit.*

[10] Arch Oboler, "Notes on Acting and Production," *This Freedom* (New York: Random House, Inc., 1942), pp. xv–xvi.

[11] Irving, *op. cit.*, pp. 83–84.

[12] John Dewey, *Democracy and Education* (New York: The Macmillan Company, 1916), p. 168.

[13] Percy Fitzgerald, *The Art of Acting* (New York: The Macmillan Company, 1892), p. 11.

5) Careless or inaccurate radio reading results when the actor gives the wrong meaning to a sentence or speech. The possibilities for doing this are endless. With every sentence he reads, the radio actor has many choices to make: he can read it this way or that way, one way or five other ways. No sentence has ever been written that can be read in only one way. Yet many radio actors are content to read their speeches as they first interpret them; they do not hunt for the meaning the playwright intended. Other actors perhaps can find the author's intent, and can verbalize about it, and yet in their reading cannot communicate it to others. Still others never seem able to appreciate the shade of difference between one reading and another; further, they never see that it matters much anyhow which way the line is read—despite the fact that the playwright may have written it as he did for the expression of a subtle point.

Warnings to the radio actor to be keenly vigilant for clarity in meaning do not, however, imply that he must make the mistake of believing that there is enshrined somewhere a one and only absolute way of reading each line or speech. While there is a precise meaning to be aimed at for each line and speech in its context, the actor is always entitled to his personal leeway in bringing out that meaning. His task is to communicate in his own way and from his own experience the full rather than the partial meaning, and a right rather than the wrong meaning.

3

Correct or meaningful reading depends, therefore, on thinking through, or understanding completely, the words and groups of words set down by the playwright. To say, though, that the radio actor must understand the individual words he reads, that words can be taken too much for granted, is elementary—and perhaps fruitless. Actors do not carry little dictionaries around with them; and the vocabularies of most radio plays do not often baffle a child of fifteen. All that an actor needs to know about words is that they are not transparent and unchangeable. Each, as Justice Holmes remarked, "is the skin of a living thought, and may vary greatly in color and content according to the circumstances and the time in which it is used."[14] The number of different meanings for a word is almost incredible. *The American College Dictionary*, for instance, lists 55 for "point" and 109 for "run." And J. R. Firth, in *Tongues of Men*, devotes an entire chapter to all the meanings in the phrase "say when."

On the other hand, to say that the radio actor must be aware of words in combinations or groups is not so elementary. Grouping is a somewhat intricate matter and demands his constant attention. Moreover, skill in grouping, or phrasing, is much more important to the radio actor than to his colleagues on the stage and screen. Phrasings are his unseen facial expressions.

"In successful speech," Bassett advises, "words are combined in groups according to the ideas and images the speaker wishes to communicate. Without clear thinking there can be no accurate grouping, and without clear grouping there can be no clear expression of thought."[15] Also, without clear grouping by the actor there can be no perfect reception of the thought by an audience. Quintilian's rule to the effect that "the merit of making proper distinctions (groupings) may perhaps be little; but without it all other merit in speaking would be in vain"[16] is capital advice for the radio actor. Only when he sees meaning in its true units of thought can he grasp it. Only when the lines are "opened out" into their component sections or phrases can the actor addressed "get into" the sentences or speeches. Only thus can the audience receive the meanings in the way that all meaning is received—in smaller units that make up and lead to the whole meaning.

Thoughtful speech is not normally expressed by a uniform succession of words; thought proceeds by word groups, is combined into small units, is phrased. These word groups the actor must discover and utilize (a) by joining the words within each group by uninterrupted utterance, (b) by separating the groups from one another by pause and change of pitch, and finally (c) by relating the groups properly with one another.

For an example of "a," uninterrupted flow, in the line:

A girl who's really fond of her mother would never say a thing like that

the sounds are merged into one continuous flow for the first group ending in "mother," and then into another stream of sound for the second group. Speech is not broken up into separate words. ("No amount of study

[14] Oliver Wendell Holmes, quoted in Parrish, *op. cit.*, p. 44.

[15] Bassett, *op. cit.*, p. 30.

[16] Quintilian, *op. cit.*, XI, iii, 35 and 39.

of the sounds only of a sentence will enable us to recognize the individual words of which it consists.")[17]

As an example of "b," the separation of groups, note this final sentence in Morton Wishengrad's *The Last Inca:*

From beyond the grave and the dry and folded years I say to you . . . hold out your hand and a day will come when we shall put in it a flower that will adorn the world.

Something must be done with the group, "and the dry and folded years"; something must happen in the reading after the word "hand"; and the actor must decide whether the meaning demands a pause after "it" or after "flower." Likewise, in Arthur Laurents' line in *The Face:*

He'd like to shut out the world of mirrors and of other people's eyes which might flinch looking at him

the reader must watch his groupings carefully, or he will muddle the meaning.

As an example of "c," group relationships, examine a speech from John Mason Brown and Howard M. Teichmann's *Many a Watchful Night,* wherein all the groups are variously related to one another:

On the way into battle most men wonder if they will be afraid—and are afraid they will be. No man knows how he will behave under fire until he has been under fire. Then he is never quite certain as to what he will do the next time. There is always the humiliating possibility that he won't take it the way he wants to in the presence of his fellows. That is where pride comes in—a bit of ammunition not officially recognized by the Bureau of Ordnance.

Similarly, the proper relationships of the word groups is the basis of a meaningful reading of Shakespeare. Study, for instance, from the opening speech from *Henry IV,* Part I:

No more the thirsty entrance of this soil
Shall daub her lips with her own children's blood;
No more shall trenching war channel her fields,
Nor bruise her flowerets with the armed hoofs
Of hostile paces: those opposed eyes
Which, like the meteors of a troubled heaven,
All of one nature, of one substance bred,
Did lately meet in the intestine shock
And furious close of civil butchery,
Shall now, in mutual well-beseeming ranks,
March all one way, and be no more oppos'd
Against acquaintance, kindred, and allies:
The edge of war, like an ill-sheathed knife,
No more shall cut his master.

In attempting to relate one group of words to other groups a radio actor often "thinks into" the context various transitional words and phrases, such as "on the other hand," "therefore," "then," "but," "that is," "as a result," "in short." He follows Wayland Parrish's advice and makes "a practice of supplying all this connective tissue of discourse whenever it is omitted."

In his search for the proper groupings the radio actor has only his mind, and perhaps his ear, to guide him. Punctuation—contrary to custom—is no sure guide to the discovery of word groups. Often punctuation is a trap. Sometimes a group is marked off by a comma or a period, but most times it is not; and a comma or a period does not always indicate a pause or a new intonation. Punctuation is for the writer, is for the eye; it shows the grammatical structure of a sentence or a speech. Grouping is for the ear and mind of the listener; it is determined, not by grammatical structure, but by the accretion of images or the progression of ideas and their relationships to one another. Thinking alone dictates the groupings, and thinking proceeds unit by unit, with some units being principal and some subordinate, some contrasting, some echoing, some parenthetical, some reinforcing, some adding to, some qualifying, and so on.

People creating their thoughts as they go along, as in most conversations in life, usually make their groupings clear to their listeners. The radio actor, however, who is *not* creating his thought as he goes along, but reading, must consequently center much of his attention on communicating the correct groupings lest his meaning be blurred, or falsified, or destroyed. He must do this even though the groupings are never absolute. There is no one way to phrase words; they vary with the content of what is being said, with the circumstances, and with the hearers. Sometimes the same passage can be delivered as two groups and then again as many more groups.

Careful grouping for clarity is vastly more important to the radio actor than to the stage and screen actor. The latter, being seen, can help mark off his group-

[17] Henry Sweet, *Primer of Phonetics* (Oxford, Clarenden Press, 1877); quoted by Bassett, *op. cit.,* p. 32.

ings by a movement, a turn of the head, or the slightest gesture or facial expression; he can call for assistance on things that are visible. For the marking out of his groupings the radio actor has only his voice. All meaning is there. In order to improve his reading, then, the radio actor should follow Parrish's advice and first give his attention "to the analysis of thought, to the grouping and inter-relations of logical elements, and later to the analysis of the more subtle elements of mood, emotion, and imagination."[18]

[18] Parrish, *op. cit.*, p. 42.

SELECTED READINGS

George Lyman Kittredge and James B. Greenough write informatively in *Words and Their Ways in English Speech* (New York: The Macmillan Company, 1925), 431 pp. Read especially Chap. XVI, "The Conventional Character of Language," pp. 219–233; Chap. XVII, "Generalization and Specialization of Meaning," pp. 234–258; Chap. XVIII, "Special Processes in the Development of Meaning: Radiation," pp. 259–271; Chap. XIX, "Transference of Meaning," pp. 272–283; and Chap. XX, "Degeneration of Meaning," pp. 284–299.

Stuart Chase's *The Tyranny of Words* (New York: Harcourt, Brace & Company, Inc., 1938), 396 pp., is a popular introduction to semantics.

Lee Emerson Bassett's *A Handbook of Oral Reading* (Boston: Houghton Mifflin Company, 1917) is old but still helpful. See Chap. I, "The Relation of Thought and Speech," pp. 15–29, and Chap. II, "Groupings," pp. 30–50. (Both chapters include exercises.)

Wayland Maxfield Parrish has written the best textbook on reading in *Reading Aloud; A Technique in the Interpretation of Literature* (1933), rev. ed. (New York: The Ronald Press Company, 1941). Study Chap. III, "Method in the Study of Reading," pp. 31–42; Chap. IV, "Interpretation of Logical Content," pp. 43–77; Chap. XIV, "Impersonation and the Art of Interpretation," pp. 384–462 (including many exercises); and Appendix I, "Plato's *Ion*," translated by Benjamin Jowett, pp. 476–487.

EXERCISES

A. READING FAULTS

The following selections should be used in class—with no emphasis on characterization or on circumstances—to demonstrate the five common faults in reading. Each student should be assigned to read one of the exercises *faultily* in various ways for the consideration of the rest of the class. The point is to develop in the students a quick ear for bad reading. Finally each student should attempt to read his assigned sentence or speech for the communication of its precise meaning.

Perhaps some of the selections can be memorized and then delivered over the microphone so that a memorization can be contrasted with a radio script reading. What are the virtues, if any, of memorization? What are the dangers involved in reading from a script?

Some of the selections are from radio scripts; some are from theatre plays. Is it possible to detect any differences between them? Are speeches that are effective in the theatre similarly effective over the microphone?

Additional selections should, of course, be brought to class by the students.

1. THE FALL OF THE CITY*

THE GENERAL: You are foolish old men.

You ought to be flogged for your foolishness.
Your grandfathers died to be free
And you — you juggle with freedom!
Do you think you're free by law
Like the falling of apples in autumn?

You thought you were safe in your liberties!
You thought you could always quibble!
You can't! You take my word for it.
Freedom's the rarest bird!
You risk your neck to snare it —
It's gone while your eyeballs stare!

Those who'd lodge with a tyrant
Thinking to feed at his fire
And leave him again when they're fed are
Plain fools or were bred to it —

Brood of the servile races
Born with the hang-dog face . . .

There's nothing in this world worse —
Empty belly or purse or the

* From *The Fall of the City: A Verse Play for Radio.* Copyright, 1937, by Archibald MacLeish.

Pitiful hunger of children —
Than doing the Strong Man's will!

The free will fight for their freedom.
They're free men first. They feed
Meager or fat but as free men.
Everything else comes after —
Food: roof: craft —
Even the sky and the light of it!

2. THE THREE SISTERS*

OLGA: The bands are playing so gayly, so bravely, and one does so want to live! Oh, my God! Time will pass and we shall forever be dead; they will forget our faces, voices, and even how many there were of us. But our sufferings shall turn into joy for those who will live after us; happiness and peace shall reign on earth, and people will remember with a good word and bless those who live now. Oh, dear sisters, our life is not yet at an end. Let us live. The music is so gay, so joyful, and it seems that in a little while we shall know why we are suffering. If only we knew! If only we knew!

3. OCTOBER MORNING†

DAVE: My son comes into the room. He stands there almost shy, saying "good morning" with an uncertain smile. I have been away for a long time and we are strangers. He looks at me. Now I remember my promise. We will take a walk before breakfast. We will talk of many things and become father and son again. I get up and dress in the army shirt, the stained olive drab, the combat boots. I find an old sweater; then I turn to my son and rub my knuckles across his head and we go.

We walk out through the yard slowly, the feel of home returning. I notice the woodpile is almost empty, a grape vine has climbed out of the arbor and up the birch tree, and there are great bunches of Concords,

* From *The Three Sisters*, by Anton Chekhov, translated by Jenny Covan. Copyright, 1922, 1933, by Coward-McCann, Inc., *The Moscow Art Theatre Series of Russian Plays*, Vol. 4.

† By Millard Lampell. Reprinted with the permission of the author.

heavy and ripe. I reach up and get some and give a bunch to Pete, and we get out down the road, eating the smoky-blue grapes, squeezing the skins and letting the soft meat pop into our mouths.

4. THE WALTZ*

Permission to use this selection has been given by Dorothy Parker and The Viking Press, Inc.
NOTE: This excerpt may be used only in the classroom and in no case on the radio or the stage, professionally or in any other way.

GIRL: I don't want to dance with him. I don't want to dance with anybody. And even if I did, it wouldn't be him. I've seen the way he dances; it looks like something you do on Saint Walpurgis Night. Just think, not a quarter of an hour ago, here I was sitting, feeling so sorry for the poor girl he was dancing with. And now I'm going to be the poor girl. Well, well! Isn't it a small world? And a peach of a world, too. A true little corker! Its events are so fascinatingly unpredictable, are not they? Here I was, minding my own business, not doing a stitch of harm to any living soul. And then he comes into my life, all smiles and city manners, to sue me for the favor of one memorable mazurka. I haven't any idea what his name is. Jukes would be my guess from the look in his eyes. How do you do, Mr. Jukes? And how is that dear little brother of yours with the two heads?

5. SILVER THEATRE: *CRYSTAL*†

KENNETH: I . . . really didn't mean to stare at you. Excuse me. It sounds silly, but — well, there was a painting . . . by an eighteenth century Frenchman . . . Greuze . . . called "Age of Innocence." It was a portrait of a very lovely girl . . . with wide, sad eyes. I used to stare at it in a classroom. You . . . look just like her. It's hard now to admit I was in love with a painting, but it's so. When I saw you . . . it surprised me. And I guess I just resumed staring where I left off. Please forgive me.

And since I've begun I may as well finish. In that instant of recognizing you a curious thing happened. I had the sudden impression that

* By Dorothy Parker, in *The Portable Dorothy Parker* (New York: The Viking Press, 1945), p. 77.
† By Robert Presnell, Jr. Reproduced through the courtesy of the author.

all the time that has passed since I was in that classroom was wiped away. I had the feeling I'd been asleep, dreaming . . . that all that's happened in sixteen years hasn't happened at all. I . . . Oh, but you're a stranger really, not a painting. I don't know why I'm trying to explain this . . .

6. SOMETIME EVERY SUMMERTIME*

MARY: Clem was tall. Clem was very tall and thin, and he looked at me in a funny way when we were first introduced. "Hello, Mary," he said — only in a funny way, like he knew me before, or was scared of me or something. It was at a summer camp I went to one year with Helen Rowley and Frannie Howard. We took a cottage at the camp, the three of us, putting all our vacation money together to pay the rent and have enough for food for two weeks, and everything.

It was a lovely cottage overlooking the lovely bay at the camp, and the three boys were in another cottage just back of us. Clem, I mean, and his friends. Clem talked to Helen one night while she was hanging washing, and then one of Clem's friends — I forget his name — came over later and talked to all of us, and asked us to come and be sociable with our neighbors, and we all went. That was when I met Clem, when we all went over to their place, and he spoke to me in that funny way.

7. THE SECOND MRS. BURTON, #452†

BILL: I don't expect anything of you any more, Marion. That's why I thought it might be a good idea to take Liz along on our trip. I got a feeling that — if I got sick — at least there'd be somebody around to give me my digitalis. Not that you're not capable of doing it. You're one of the most capable women I've ever known. That's — what worries me a little. Sometimes it gives me the feeling that — maybe you're too capable of doing — almost anything. The truth is, Marion, that all of a sudden I've gotten fed up. All of a sudden I can see through you like

* Copyright, 1945, by Fletcher Markle. Included in Joseph Liss (ed.), *Radio's Best Plays,* Greenberg, Publisher, 1947.

† By Martha Alexander. Reproduced through the courtesy of the author.

cellophane. And I'll be honest with you, Marion — now that it's come up. I don't want to take you on this trip. I don't want a second honeymoon with you after all. I want to be reasonably sure — as sure as I can be with this bad ticker — that I'll live to enjoy this trip. You get my point, don't you? It's the way you're staring at me right now that's enough to scare the life out of any man.

8. TWO ON A CLUE*

DEBORAH: Oh, now look, Larry, you can't just sit there and absorb heat and brandy all night when there's so much to be done. You don't seem to realize that my cousin Tom knows this girl. And don't give me that old stuff about that not making any difference, and Tom is nuts and all. That won't work tonight. (GETTING ANGRIER) How would you like it if you were an eighteen year old girl all alone in the world and facing a murder charge? Come on now. Get going and do something about it! Supposing Rosemary were that age and in that kind of trouble? (SMILING AS SHE REMEMBERS) That sweet darling. You know what she did just a couple of hours ago? She came up to my room and . . . Oh, you know . . . started looking out the window the way she does when she's about to make a profound observation. And she said, "Mommy, Daddy's pretty much of a skunk, isn't he?" (LAUGHING) Really she did. And she's right, of course. No, seriously, Larry — you've got to do something about that girl. I can remember when I was eighteen. It's a very difficult age. You don't know whether you're a girl or a woman. I wish there were a way to take every lonely little girl in the world into my arms and — Oh, comfort her somehow or other and make her know that some place in the world there are people who do understand . . . and believe. Larry, if you don't take this murder case I'll kick you right in the shins! How do you like that?

* An audition script by Louis Vites. Reproduced through the courtesy of Frank Cooper Associates.

9. MYSTERY THEATRE: *THE HANDS OF MR. OTTERMOLE**

NARRATOR: Yes, Mr. Whybrow, the man who is about to kill you is just coming into the same fish store. But he isn't going to kill you here among the glossy-eyed fish. No, not here. Not now. So don't turn away, Mr. Whybrow. Look at him. That's right. There's nothing so unusual about him, is there? Just another man wanting to buy a fish. You've seen him before many times on your way home from work. You've spoken to him even as you do now.

****

Quiet but friendly sort of a fellow, your murderer, isn't he, Mr. Whybrow? Yes, it's a friendly world. So take your fish and leave the market and go on to your rendezvous with death.

****

You're almost home now, Mr. Whybrow, but don't hurry so. Take a look around you. It's your last look at the world. And if you knew it you'd look at it more closely. The more slowly you walk the longer you'll enjoy the fragrant air of this evening . . . the longer you'll see the dreamy lamplight . . . and the little shops . . . Pause a moment before you cross Royal Lane. Pause among the houses that shelter the useless and the beaten of London's camp-followers. Hear the music of the people in the streets. It's the last time, Mr. Whybrow, the very last time.

10. RIDERS TO THE SEA†

MAURYA: They're all together this time, and the end is come. May the Almighty God have mercy on Bartley's soul, and on Michael's soul, and on the souls of Sheamus and Patch, and Stephen and Shawn; and may He have mercy on my soul, Nora, and on the soul of everyone is left living in the world. Michael has a clean burial in the Far North, by the grace of the Almighty

* From the radio script by L. K. Hoffman, based on *The Hands of Mr. Ottermole,* by Thomas Burke.

† By John M. Synge.

God. Bartley will have a fine coffin out of the white boards, and a deep grave surely. What more can we want than that? No man at all can be living forever, and we must be satisfied.

B. SENTENCES

The student is to read each sentence many times, once for each of five or more different meanings given him by the class. Many additional single sentences should be brought to class and subjected to this same practice. It might be profitable to take sentences from plays heard on the air.

1. I haven't had a visit from you in a long time.
2. If you want more coffee, ask Nora to bring it into your study.
3. Do you believe in a life after death?
4. I'm not afraid of a fight.
5. He said he'd phone me his answer in five minutes.
6. Come on in the living room. Guess who's here.
7. Gee, I'm hungry. Isn't it about time to eat?
8. I shall go back to the little town on the Pacific Coast where I was raised.
9. Aren't you a little old for that sort of thing?
10. She's gone to bed. She hasn't been sleeping so well lately.
11. What have I done?
12. I won't take this kind of treatment from you.
13. Are you the only boarder Mrs. Hallahan has?
14. Would you accept the presidency if it were offered to you?
15. You were no martyr tonight.
16. Some of them became almost legendary characters because of their deeds.
17. You've opened the window and let in a whole flood of sunshine.
18. I never doubted your ability — not even for an instant.
19. Gosh, you must think I have an evil mind.
20. Why didn't you tell me that before?
21. I've been thinking of very little else since last night.
22. She hasn't had a vacation for three or four years.
23. And you think that personalities had nothing to do with our disagreement?
24. I don't think Joe Marvin's being in town had anything to do with it.
25. You must have been very fond of her.

C. GROUPING (single sentences)

The student should read the following sentences with different phrasings and with pauses of different length in a search for the various possible meanings that can be brought out by grouping.

1. Yes, I do believe Joey needs her in a way he never could need you no matter how much he learned to love you.
2. I can look at the facts and add them up and then tell myself the very same things you've been telling me ever since I met you.
3. But it's always the things we don't know or understand that get us into trouble, isn't it?
4. I'm afraid I wasn't very nice to you the other afternoon when you came over to tell me good-by.
5. If I move I'll see that you always get my new address some way, because if you should ever need me for anything I'll be on tap as long as I live.
6. And I wish that any other stockholder in the store had approached me instead of you.
7. In fact, I wouldn't be surprised if this evening turns out to be only the beginning of many such evenings for all three of us.
8. He said he was sure it would rain or snow or something tomorrow night.
9. I don't understand how you could phone me in that offhand manner and tell me that you were at Susan's and were going to stay for dinner — as if it were a perfectly usual thing that hardly concerned me at all.
10. I warn you that if you suddenly turn on me the way Bill did you're likely to find yourself with a fight on your hands.
11. She told me later that of all the men she ever met he was the most brilliant.
12. When shall we three meet again
In thunder, lightning or in rain?
13. The people of our city will stand together in solving this problem as they have in the past time and time again if only they can find a leader.
14. He said that when the proper time came he would tell all of us — even you — the reason he did what he did on that awful day.
15. Your brother who is about to die wanted me to give you this.
16. I remember the moonlight on that country road and the crickets chirping against the silence, and the two of us sitting there a long time, holding hands and dreaming.

17. Go down to the tenement district and look at all those poor families huddled together there like cattle and then ask yourself whether something ought to be done immediately.

18. And maybe she was a woman who did a mimic and impersonation act in a night club two years ago under the name of Maggie Moore!

19. You told me when you left the house that you were wearing that dress for the first time.

20. It's saying that when a woman gives the best part of her life to her job she's fairly apt to give the best part of her emotions to the man she works for whether she knows it or not.

21. I've been telling you ever since Martin beat me out in that election that I'd never be happy until I'd beaten him at something.

22. He called us all pirates and said that if we'd give up the treasure and set free the prisoners we could sail away wherever we wanted tonight.

23. If, in spite of the way I feel, you still want to go back to Chicago and spend the rest of your life paying off your debt of honor, that, of course, is up to you.

24. When one of his henchmen published an account of his adventures Morgan became incensed and sued for libel because he was accused of cruelty.

25. I'm sorry you can't agree with me, because whether you like it or not I don't see how I can afford not to accept the offer for your sake, darling, as much as for my own.

Reread the exercises of the first three chapters for groupings.

D. PERIOD FAULT

Punctuation, to repeat purposely for emphasis, is primarily for the eye. People engaged in conversation are never aware of the punctuation marks in their speeches. They talk in images and ideas, not in perfect, discernible sentences. For that matter, there is no rule anywhere—although seemingly one was once set up by teachers—that says a speaker must always come to a full stop at each and every period mark. Radio actors give themselves away as either neophytes or grammarians when they come to full stops at all periods. In the following examples notice how infrequently the period means a full stop.

1. JACKSON: You know darned well why she didn't want to tell him. She was afraid of what might happen. He might talk. He might cause trouble.

He might bring the police into the case. That's what's been worrying her.

2. JACOBY: I'm sure your daughter hasn't told you the truth.
   HELEN: That's a lie!
   JACOBY: I'm sorry, but the facts don't lie. You must look at the truth. You can't dodge it. Your daughter's in very grave danger.
   HELEN: I won't believe you. I can't. This is just a trap. You don't fool me!

3. MONTY: (IRRITABLY) Hello. Who is it?
   MAIZIE: (ON FILTER) Don't you know? Can't you guess? It's me. Maizie. What's wrong? Why're you so cranky?
   MONTY: I'm not feeling so good. I got a headache.
   MAIZIE: Why? What for? What caused it?
   MONTY: How should I know? Who knows what causes headaches? Look, I'm in a hurry. Call me tomorrow. Or I'll call you.
   MAIZIE: Why are you in such a hurry? I thought you wanted to talk to me. You told me to call you.
   MONTY: Look, I'm sick. I don't know what's the matter with me. I'm going to bed. I'm sorry.
   MAIZIE: Don't be sorry, Monty. Everything's all right. Tell you what — I'll come over.
   MONTY: No.
   MAIZIE: I'll grab a cab. It won't take me ten minutes. Then we can talk.
   MONTY: No, I told you! Look, Maizie, I have to hang up. I really do. Talk to you tomorrow.

4. ELIZABETH: After all the tension you've been under something had to happen. It always does. Nobody can go on at a high pitch forever. There's bound to be a let-down. Something snaps. That's what's happened to you.

5. MAX: You're not being fair, Ellen. And that isn't like you. This certainly isn't Annette's fault. I wish you could believe that.

ELLEN: Maybe you're right. I hope so. I hope so with all my heart. But I do know that before she came here all of us were very happy. We were having a grand time. You and the neighbors were getting on splendidly. We were all laughing. We'd never had such a good time. But the minute she came into this house everything changed. The trouble started.

6. FATHER: I'm telling you that boy has no sense of responsibility. He doesn't know what he's doing!

MURIEL: He does too know what he's doing! Arthur's the most responsible person I know. He's more responsible than either you or me. You're just making things up.

7. PETER: What's happened? What's wrong? We've never acted like this before now. We've never had fights. We've never shouted at each other like this.

AGNES: Let's not talk about it. We'll start in again.

PETER: Barbara was here today.

AGNES: I know. You told me. You told me three times. I was downstairs. I saw her come in. I was downstairs at the florist stand. I stayed down there. I waited for her to leave. I didn't want to see her. I think maybe I was afraid to see her.

8. RALPH: I hope we're dining in tonight. I don't feel like going out. And let's have dinner alone. No company. Just us two. I'm tired. I've had a tough day. I don't want to see anybody. I don't want to perform.

9. IRENE: I'm not young any more. I'm thirty. That's half a lifetime. And I'm not tied down. I have no children. No responsibilities. I can come and go as I please. Nobody can stop me. So what if I said to you: You made a gallant gesture. You married me. You bought me whatever money could buy. You tried to make me happy. But things just haven't worked out. They haven't worked out at all. Suppose we break it up? Suppose you go your way and I'll go mine?

10. HARRY: My father's pretty solid. Nothing ever shocks him. He goes along the same no matter what happens. I wish I were like him. I wish I could take things like this. But I can't. Everything's changed. I'm not the same guy I used to be. I'm different. I feel different. I think different. I'm a thousand years old. You don't understand that, do you? Nobody does.

E. GROUPING (speeches)

Notice how often in the following selections faulty grouping is the result of faulty breathing.

1. THE SECOND MRS. BURTON, #453*

MARION: Bill — Bill, it's me. Marion. (BEAT) You can't hear me, can you? Try, Bill. Try hard — because what I have to say to you is so important. I've been sick, Bill. Not you. I'm the sick one. I didn't know and nobody told me. Or if they did, I didn't know what they were talking about. I didn't feel sick — not like you — but way deep down inside of me I knew something was wrong. I knew that way down there some place I hurt. I hurt, and I cried, Bill. But I didn't know where or why — and I couldn't tell anyone because I didn't know where it was. And I still don't know. But I found out something last night. I found out what's been wrong. With us. With me. Oh, Bill, please try to hear me. Please try! It's so important, darling. If you try, and I try . . . Darling, listen. Listen. I love you, Bill. I love you. Do you hear that? I love you. I've never loved anything before in my life. But suddenly last night — this morning — I love you. No wonder we had such a hard time together, darling. We couldn't be right because I was so wrong. But we have a fair chance now, darling. Just like other people. Lillian and Jim. And Terry and Stan. There's some hope for us now. I can fix it so we'll be happy. (PAUSE) Oh, darling, you haven't heard a word, have you?

* By Martha Alexander. Reproduced through the courtesy of the author.

2. BEAUTIFUL SILENCE*

RANDY: From that moment I knew that the bomb had left its mark on me . . . that although there were no visible injuries . . . although my arms and legs and senses were as good as ever, something inside had changed. The sound of that ticking clock had brought it all back. The bomb was there again in all its ugliness . . . the odd-shaped nose, fused into the casing . . . the octagonal brass fitting at the tip. I could hear it again in the room with me — ticking . . . a sort of prelude to the sickening buzz that came just before the explosion . . . . I don't know how I ever got through that night. As I lay in bed it was all around me . . . never stopping, the rhythm of it jabbing into my mind like a needle . . . my heart picking up the tempo as it grew louder and louder, bouncing from wall to wall in the bedroom until I could almost feel the bed shake under me . . . . Twice I got out of bed, but there was no escaping it. The ticking followed me everywhere . . . in the kitchen, the library, the living-room. Louise was still asleep at six o'clock when I finally decided to see Dr. Lambert in London . . . .

3. TROILUS AND CRESSIDA†

CRESSIDA: Boldness comes to me now, and brings me heart: —
Prince Troilus, I have lov'd you night and day
For many weary months . . . . I was won, my lord,
With the first glance that ever — pardon me, —
If I confess much, you will play the tyrant.
I love you now; but not, till now, so much
But I might master it: in faith, I lie;
My thoughts were like unbridl'd children, grown
Too headstrong for their mother: See, we fools!
Why have I blabb'd? Who shall be true to us,
When we are so unsecret to ourselves? —
But, though I lov'd you well, I woo'd you not;
And yet, good faith, I wish'd myself a man,

* By M. H. Swanton. Reproduced through the courtesy of the author.
† From *Troilus and Cressida,* Act III, scene 2, by William Shakespeare.

Or that we women had men's privilege
Of speaking first. Sweet, bid me hold my tongue;
For, in this rapture, I shall surely speak
The thing I shall repent. See, see, your silence,
Cunning in dumbness, from my weakness draws
My very soul of conscience! Stop my mouth.

4. THE STORY OF GUS*

GUS: I'm a father, Theresa. If Maxie's your son, he's my son. I never thought a thing like this could happen to me, but all of a sudden I'm a father and everything I been doing don't seem right. I don't know, Maxie . . . I wish I could set an example for you. I — Excuse me. I want to go for a walk. I'll see you later. And enjoy yourself. Don't let me get you down. I just feel peculiar suddenly, being a father and all. I . . . I'll be right back.

5. WESTERN STAR†

NARRATOR: Americans are always moving on.
It's an old Spanish custom gone astray,
A sort of English fever, I believe,
Or just a mere desire to take French leave —
I couldn't say. I couldn't really say.
But, when the whistle blows, they go away.
Sometimes there never was a whistle blown,
But they don't care, for they can blow their own.
Whistles of willow-stick and rabbit-bone,
Quail-calling through the rain,
A dozen tunes but only one refrain:
"We don't know where we're going, but we're on our way!"

* By Arthur Miller. Reproduced through the courtesy of the author.
† By Stephen Vincent Benét. From *Western Star,* published by Rinehart & Company, Inc. Copyright, 1943, by Rosemary Carr Benét.

6. THE GHOST OF YANKEE DOODLE*

SARA: You get a walking stick. Not that you haven't fifty others already, but this one's rather special. Because it's descending from Paul's and my honeymoon in the Southwest, from the desert and sandstone and the wide, dry rivers Paul loved, from an Indian pueblo where the Chief was a friend of Paul's, and this was his wand of office from Abraham Lincoln. You can see the signature "A. Lincoln," engraved here on the top. And that's because, back in the Civil War — families were splitting on an issue then — the Confederates tried making Indian trouble for Lincoln. And Lincoln sent these walking sticks, one to each chief, like a feudal king swearing vassals to loyalty. And the tribes didn't make trouble and the chiefs still hand their staffs on to their successors . . . One day, long after Paul's death, this came through the mail. There weren't any more Indians left in that pueblo. I like to think that Lincoln would have given the Indians a more generous deal than the Senators of your generation gave them, dear Ned . . . . Now I'm started on this . . . . (SHE TURNS BACK TO THE CHRISTMAS TREE FOR TWO MORE PARCELS, ONE A BOOK, THE OTHER A FRAMED PICTURE.) John, my dear brother-in-law, and much better than any brother I've known about, will you accept this treasure I'd forgotten I owned? It's the very rare, very first edition of Huckleberry Finn, with the accidentally dirty picture in it that got it suppressed when it first came out, and that makes it what's called a collector's item, though I can't find any picture we'd call dirty now! Your father gave it to me my first Christmas here. To make up for the row he raised when Paul married an actress. I'd told him how Mark Twain wanted me to play Joan of Arc, and you know how your father worshipped Mark Twain. But I believe in passing the past along and making it somebody else's future! (THEN TO RUDI) I want you, Rudi, as the companion of my baser nature — don't misunderstand me, John, will you? — to have George Bellows' report on the immortal wallop Firpo handed Dempsey. I used to creep round with this print at night and hold it up to the walls and say to myself: "My God, what a sock that was!" But these walls never seemed to do Bellows justice! Here it is, Rudi dear, in memory of

* By Sidney Howard. Copyright, 1936, 1938, by Sidney Howard. Reprinted with the permission of Mrs. Sidney Howard.

the journey we made to see Schmeling knock out Joe Louis. (SHE IS SUDDENLY ANGRY) And how he knocked him out! And how he should have had his crack at Braddock! (THEN) Come in here, Joan, and get your Christmas present!

7. PSALM FOR A DARK YEAR*

OLD WOMAN: May I speak for a moment, having but a moment left to speak in? I too am listening for a horn to blow — one which will call me from this time and place to another time and place.

In this my ninety-second year, my eyes grown dim and my hearing poor, sleeping most of the time — the foothills of sleep before I reach the mountains — I am thankful for still clear memories both big and little, happy and sorrowful: of a dress that I wore once; of the night my mother passed away; of meeting Edward on a sleigh ride one December night when the moon was new and Mount Toby lay frozen under stars that seemed so low you could almost touch them — of the morning Ralph was born — of how little Edwina died of the diphtheria, delirious and crying for ice cream — of all the other memories, the many, many other things too full to hint at, too many to contain. I joke with my grandchildren when they come to see me now. I tell them I am like a minute-man — ready to go at a moment's notice.

God bless you every one.

8. THE STEEL WORKER†

GIORGIO: (VOICE DEAD . . . HOPELESSLY) And den for long time is no work. Layoff . . . no more smoke from mill chimney. No more song from furnace. Everytin', she's cold and quiet. No work, no work. I sit by home . . . I wait . . . I know de world need for de steel. Yah, de mill, she start again . . . She's got to! De peoples need good house, good tool, good everytin' de steel can make . . . Yah, so I wait . . . I wait . . . Some

* From *More by Corwin,* by Norman Corwin. Reproduced by permission of Henry Holt and Company, Inc. Copyright, 1944, by Norman Corwin.

† By Arch Oboler. Reprinted with the permission of the author.

day . . . (IN GROWING EXCITEMENT) And den one day de whistle blow! I run to door! My frien's call, "Giorgio, come on! De mill, she's open! De work, she start!" I grab my wife, my kids! I laugh! I jump! Right! I was right to wait! De time, she's come! De world wants steel again! Good steel! I run to de mill! "It's me!" I say. "I come for work! . . . Me, Giorgio Maslarovic!" Day say, "Sure, Giorgio! We got work for you . . . plenty of work." Ha ha . . . it's good . . . it's good! I run into de mill! I no can wait! My frien', da steel . . . I want to hear her! I <u>got</u> <u>to</u> <u>hear</u> <u>her!</u>

9. PORTIA FACES LIFE, #1698*

PORTIA: How can I say it so you'll — so you'll realize . . . (EARNESTLY) Dr. Cornwall, have you ever had to live on money that your wife earned? Have you ever wanted to give her all the nice things of life but couldn't because you believed you were a failure? That makes a man ashamed of being a man. I know because I've seen Walter go through it. I've seen him almost lose his pride, his self-respect. I've seen him to the point where he was almost convinced that trying was no use. And he's not weak, Doctor. He's more of a fighter than most men. But what I'm trying to tell you is this . . . it's not entirely behind him yet. He's not really established. His roots still aren't set in the ground . . . . He can't afford any more worries now. He's had enough! I'm not saying I won't tell him. I'm only saying that decision is mine, and I'll make it when I know more about the . . . about the situation. So please stop talking in circles, Doctor Cornwall, and tell me what's wrong?

10. THIS LAND IS MINE†

SORREL: I thought you were a confirmed bachelor like me. (AS ALBERT LOOKS UP AT HIM) Oh, like all young men I fell in love, but — she died — and I found a great comfort in my work. <u>Our</u> work. My family became this

* By Mona Kent. Reproduced through the courtesy of the author and General Foods Corporation.

† Taken from an RKO picture entitled *This Land Is Mine,* directed by Jean Renoir, screen play by Dudley Nichols, and reprinted by special permission of RKO Radio Pictures, Inc.

school — my books, my teachers — you, Miss Martin — my pupils — (SMILING) many of them grown up now. (VERY GRAVELY) You know it's a great thing to be a schoolmaster. It's a life-work. You sacrifice a lot of things, but you get a lot in return. And now I believe we're the most important people in our country. It's a time for sacrifice now, more than ever — and our real happiness lies in our doing our job well.

Our Mayor was in here this morning talking about duty — but I prefer to use the word job. Those books must be burned. Very well, we must burn them — We can't resist physically. But morally, within us, we can resist. We contain those books; we contain truth; and they can't destroy truth without destroying each and every one of us. We can keep truth alive if the children believe in us and follow our example. Children like to follow a leader — and they have two kinds of leaders today: We seem weak, we have no weapons, we don't march — except to air raid shelters — and our heroes are called criminals and shot against walls. The other leaders have guns, tanks, parades, uniforms; they teach violence, self-love, vanity, everything that appeals to the unformed minds of children — and their criminals are called heroes. That's a lot of competition for us. Love of liberty isn't glamorous to children. Respect for the human being isn't exciting. But there's one weapon they can't take away from us — and that's our own dignity. It's going to be a fight — it is a fight, but if the children admire us they will follow us. (WITH PROFOUND FAITH) We will win, Mr. Lory — (WHIMSICALLY) — or maybe we will get shot. But every one of us they execute wins a battle for our cause, because he dies a hero — (SMILING) — and heroism is glamorous for the children. (THEN HE CHUCKLES, SEEING ALBERT'S FACE ILLUMINATED BY HIS WORDS) I don't ask you to die, my friend. Not immediately. But if you think these things over I'm sure it will help you when we (HESITATING TO MENTION AIR RAIDS) — have trouble. (VERY MAN-TO-MAN) Do you think you can handle your class and be less nervous next time?

Chapter V. . MICROPHONE READING: MEANING (Continued)

1

In addition to grouping there are, in any arbitrary dissection of this matter of meaning, at least three other major factors pertinent to reading the dialogue of a radio play intelligently. If the units of thought are brought out by an awareness of the word groups, the subtleties of thought are brought out partly by changes in pitch, partly by emphasis and inflection, and partly by timing and pause. Yet all three of these factors are so inextricably combined in actual performance that it is difficult to separate definitely any one of them. Nobody has ever been able to put into recipe form the exact combination of the expressional elements involved.

To isolate the factors of changes in pitch, emphasis and inflection, timing and pause is also somewhat dangerous. The unwary student is all too likely, when moving from one topic to another, to mechanize his approach to reading. While concentrating on one factor at a time (it is necessary to do exactly that for practice) he is likely to forget that he is only "taking meaning apart," as one takes a watch apart, in order to see how it works. Rarely, when his attention is restricted to only one of the agents, is the actor communicating the whole meaning.

Nevertheless the factors of changes in pitch, emphasis and inflection, timing and pause must be separately examined, if but briefly. Only by improvement through practice in each of these factors can the radio actor demonstrate that he knows precisely what he is saying.

2

"Where there is subtlety of meaning, where there is delicacy of expression, and where there is refinement of sense and sensibility, there must be mastery of the change of pitch," in the opinion of Charles Woolbert. "Accuracy of meaning, fine distinctions of thought and feeling, charm, delicacy, and power—all rest heavily upon the ability of the interpreter to use the pitch changes of his voice with discrimination and sensitiveness."[1] The real meaning of words is in the intention of the speaker or writer, and the evidence of intention comes out largely in the pitch changes.

Most normal, everyday speech is characterized by variety in changes of pitch, and each change indicates the particular meaning the speaker attaches to his words. To the mind of the speaker many thoughts come crowding at almost one and the same time; the mind is always leaping from one idea to another, or from an idea to a qualification of it. All such new relationships and new directions in thinking are marked by appropriate vocal changes in the utterance. In reading dialogue, then, such meaningful vocal changes will occur only if the radio actor is aware of his *changes in thought,* only if he shifts his mind constantly from the old to the new. "Change, change, change" is the key to actual thinking and to valid microphone reading.

Change of pitch is defined as "the leap of the voice from one key to another during intervals of silence between words, phrases, and sentences."[2] These leaps occur often between phrases but most frequently between sentences. For example, notice the main changes of pitch required at the diagonal marks in the following speeches:

[1] Charles H. Woolbert and Severina Nelson, *The Art of Interpretative Speech* (New York: Appleton-Century-Crofts, Inc., 1927), p. 288.

[2] Bassett, *A Handbook,* p. 52; cf. Fairbanks, *Voice and Articulation Drillbook* (New York: Harper & Brothers), 1940, p. 179.

1. You're very observant —/ but then, of course you would be, being a writer./ I wonder what can be keeping Elaine? She said she'd be right down./ I think I'd better go up and see if she's all right.

2. Follow the road till you come to the mill./ I'll wait for you inside./ It's about a twenty-minute walk from your house./ Don't expect to see my car parked there. I'll leave it down the road somewhere.

3. We'll have to talk it over with Leslie./ It was she who insisted that clause be written in./ But Leslie Palmer's all right. I think she'll listen to reason./ Suppose you let me talk to her and see what I can do?

Find the changes in pitch in these selections:

1. Helen, look at our house. All the lights are on! I remember I turned them off when we left. Hey, there's a burglar in there! Come on. We'll go around back and sneak in the kitchen.

2. It's the best turkey ever — big and plump. And the best Christmas ever, too. It's pure heaven to be back here again. Peter, look. The snow's starting to fall again!

3. MRS. SMITH: (COMING ON) Is Harold out here in the kitchen?

   HELEN: No, he isn't, Mother. My goodness, what have you got there in that box?

   MRS. SMITH: Just some things that got out in the trash barrel. If he asks whether you know anything about who cleaned out his room, simply say you haven't been up there.

   HELEN: Is all that stuff from Harold's room?

   MRS. SMITH: Most of it. A little of it's from your father's. If those two were allowed to save everything they brought into this house, we wouldn't be able to move from one room to the other.

The importance of all such changes of pitch is quickly evident. Yet too many radio actors are limited to a bare minimum of pitch changes; they use many fewer in reading than in normal, everyday conversation. Too many radio actors are, unknowingly perhaps, addicted to the same few changes of pitch; they have a pitch or intonation pattern; they persist in making identical changes at more or less regular intervals. Furthermore, a considerable number of radio actors should guard against the almost imperceptible habit of taking the exact pitch of the preceding speaker.

For a wider and quicker vocal flexibility as the direct result of correct thinking, practice in concentrating on changes in pitch is essential.

3

"Stress," according to Grant Fairbanks' definition, "is used in a generic sense to refer to the relative prominence given to a sound, syllable or word by any vocal means and for any purpose whatsoever. *Emphasis* is logical stress for the purpose of expressing meaning and pertains primarily to words. *Accent* is syllable stress . . . ."[3] *Centering* is frequently stress applied to groups of words.

Emphasis, then, is "a matter of getting attention to the word or words which must stand out if the sentence is to have the right meaning." That is to say that in all speaking a word is to a phrase, to a clause, to a sentence, or even to an entire paragraph as a syllable to a word. Just as within a word certain syllables are stressed and others are unstressed, so within a phrase or larger group certain words are emphasized and others kept in the background. Definite, well-placed emphasis, therefore, is substantial evidence of a thorough understanding of what is being read. In fact, one test of an actor's mastery of a sentence or an entire speech is his use of emphasis. "Without proper emphasis there is no sure meaning that the listener must positively get."

The ways of emphasizing the new or key or idea-carrying words are several: (a) the prolongation of accented vowels, (b) force, (c) inflection, and (d) pause. In normal speech, however, all these forms of emphasis frequently combine in one word.

a) The use of prolonged vowels for emphasis is more often than not a mannerism. As a method of giving prominence to certain words it can be overdone. Notice how the voice is suspended, giving the effect of drawing out the tone, in the following examples:

> I'm *so* glad to see you.
> I'm so *glad* to see you.
> It's gonna be a g-r-e-a-t day!
> Is *ev*-erybody happy?
> She sat out there *all alone.*
> It was *mar*velous, simply *mar*velous!

b) Emphasis by vocal force, or pounding the principal word, is easy and elementary, but never the only way of emphasizing, and not always the best way. When radio actors utilize only force on the significant word—usually because it is underlined in the script—they frequently betray their own lack of conviction by straining to bring out a meaning externally. Emphasis by vocal force is correct if it is honest, but emphasis by inflection and pause are perhaps better methods, and add a necessary variety.

c) Inflection is defined as a vocal glide, "the rise or fall of the voice during the utterance of a word" without interruption of the phonation. Inflection of the stressed vowel discloses attitudes and relationships in the mind of the speaker. Jane Herendeen finds that

> . . . inflection therefore forms a running commentary upon the ideas expressed in conventional language; it is a discriminating critique upon thought; it is the intellectual life of speech . . . . The voice climbs high or it drops low in pitch; it twists and turns in the simple flow of everyday speech or in the heightened flow of emergency, but always it is properly involuntary. When one has assumed a definite mental attitude he need have no question about using the right inflection. He may as reasonably fear that his motor system will set him walking on his hands.[4]

In the following simple sentence note how many different meanings can be brought out by various inflections:

1. Yes, I voted for him.
   (Who says I didn't?)
2. Yes, I voted for him.
   (What of it?)
3. Yes, I voted for him.
   (Dubious; was I wrong?)

[3] Fairbanks, *op. cit.,* p. 218.

[4] Jane Herendeen, *Speech Quality and Interpretation* (New York: Harper & Brothers [1946]), pp. 92 and 91.

4. Yes, I voted for him.
   (I'll gain by it; thank Heaven!)

5. Yes, I voted for him.
   (But I'm sorry now I did.)

6. Yes, I voted for him.
   (He won; he's wonderful.)

7. Yes, I voted for him.
   (It's a secret.)

8. Yes, I voted for him.
   (I'm bitter about it.)

9. Yes, I voted for him.
   (What else could I do?)

10. Yes, I voted for him.
    (I was a fool.)

And so on and so on almost endlessly. Then, again, if the actor changes the word to be emphasized from "Yes" to "I," or to "voted" or to "him" he can by his inflections bring out additional important changes in the meaning of the sentence.

Only by study and a diligent search for the exact meaning intended by the character speaking (via the playwright) can the radio actor determine his emphasis.

The problem of correct emphasis is not, however, only a matter of giving the right kind of prominence to certain words—or even to certain phrases, clauses, or whole sentences. It is also a matter of keeping certain words of a sentence or of a speech subordinate. The elimination of overemphasis and overinflection is one of the most difficult tasks in all reading. Radio actors, especially when their lines are few, are inclined to make every word count, to make every word they speak important, with the result that little they say is shaped toward the expression of meaning. For genuine emphasis radio actors ought often to subordinate, and even to throw away, whole sentences, whole speeches, and whole scenes.

As Hiram Corson wrote in *The Aims of Literary Study:*

> Emphasis is regarded by many readers as the all important thing; but it is really the least important. Any untrained voice can emphasize. The difficult thing to do well is the opposite of emphasis—the slighting of certain subordinate parts of discourse. Whatever is sufficiently implied, or should be taken for granted, or has been anticipated, and, in short, all the outstanding relations of the main movement of thought and feeling, require to be slighted in expression, in order that they may not unduly reduce the prominence and distinction of the main movement. Only the well-trained voice can manage properly the background of what is presented; and if the background is properly managed, the foreground will generally have the requisite distinctness. When a reader endeavors to make everything tell, he makes nothing tell. Ambitious reading often defeats its own end.[5]

4

d) In reading for meaning, pause and timing are important enough to deserve special attention.

"Timing" is the esoteric word of all actors. "Ah, she has such beautiful timing." "Timing is something you are born with; you can't learn it." "Timing is—Oh, I don't know what it is exactly, but you can tell when someone has it." Apparently, as bandied about daily in the profession, the term "timing" is some magic word that describes the expertness by which certain radio actors bring out the meaning of what they say. Apparently it has something vaguely to do with pause. That is about all anybody knows about it—except that it is highly important in acting.

Timing, however, is not a mysterious something. As correctly defined by motion-picture director George Sidney, it is

> . . . simply making use of an understanding of the rhythmic processes of the human mind, as it anticipates, comprehends, enjoys or rejects, then rests before starting the rhythm again. The human body, with its pulsing heart, is a rhythmic mechanism. Time the elements of your appeal so they accord with these rhythms, and a response is inevitable.[6]

(Timing is, in addition, perhaps making use of an awareness of a listening audience.) The radio actor who has his mind on what he is saying, who has made the words on the mimeographed page his own thoughts and feelings, knows consequently when to start and

[5] Hiram Corson, *The Aims of Literary Study* (New York: The Macmillan Company, 1894), p. 123. Copyright, 1894, by The Macmillan Company. Used by permission of The Macmillan Company.

[6] George Sidney; quoted in New York *Herald Tribune,* September 26, 1943, p. V-3.

when to stop, when to accelerate and retard. He has a sense of timing. He knows, with Stark Young, that

> the distance at which our ear receives a word from one person that answers some word of another's a moment before is as much a part of the idea as the word itself . . . .
>
> The plain word *no* means simply negation or refusal, but by tempo and vocal tone other meanings are added. When a character asks, Are you certain of his guilt? and another answers *no,* he is speaking two languages, one the language of the word, which in this case remains the same; the other of music, by which the meaning can be changed at will. If he says *no* at once in a clear tone, *no* fifty seconds after the question and in a shrill tone, *no* one minute after the question in an angry tone, and so on, he is plainly saying different things, things of which the word is only a small part. The gradations and values of sound in the theatre are in their way as infinite and inexhaustible as music is.[7]

Pause, whether slight or dramatically long, exhibits the entire human mechanism actively at work, lets the audience share in that process, and, with all its varying degrees of suspense, drives home or reinforces the meaning. Pause, which can come either before or after a word or word group in order to set it off from others, is defined as "an element *in thinking* in which an impression is taken in or sustained and during which there is a cessation of speech."[8] Pause is never just a wait, a recess for the actor. "It is not a quiescent experience; it is a very active part of thought, a period of attention and impression. It brings a new impetus to speech and changes in tone and style in speaking."[9]

Perhaps the three most common causes of faulty timing, or bad pausing, are (i) wrong or haphazard breathing, (ii) nonthinking, and (iii) a lack of confidence in pure silence. If the radio actor will think out what he is saying, timing will in most instances take care of itself. If the actor knows that whenever a person has a new idea to express he always instinctively takes a breath and retains it in preparation for speech, and naturally replenishes it during pauses between his various ideas and shades of meaning, he will go far toward improving his sense of timing. Also, if he has something to put into the pause, some purpose, some point, some reaction, some impression, he will not be afraid to stop for whatever beat or length of time is necessary, and he will no longer be mechanized into measuring out the length of his pauses by counting.

Not only does the pause help to make sense; according to Woolbert,

> . . . it is also one of the best ways of showing feeling. The logic of your ideas confines you, most of the time, to pauses in certain places with no leeway for caprice or chance. But your feelings allow you wide latitude in stopping and breaking sentences and phrases apart. A speaker or interpreter *can* stop anywhere, and every stop gives a new and added meaning—whether it is intended or not: in any case, meaning.[10]

[7] Stark Young, *The Theatre* (New York: Doubleday & Company, Inc., 1927), pp. 32–33.

[8] Herendeen, *op. cit.,* p. 86.

[9] *Ibid.*

SELECTED READINGS

Barrows, Sarah T., and Anne E. Pierce, *The Voice: How To Use It, with Exercises for Tone and Articulation.* Magnolia, Mass.: Expression Co., 1933. Practice the exercises in Part IV, "Intonation," pp. 147–155, for developing attentiveness to pitch differences, for developing ability to vary pitch, for freeing the voice for pitch response, and for increasing inflection and range of voice.

Bassett, Lee Emerson, *A Handbook of Oral Reading.* New York: Houghton Mifflin Company, 1917. See Chap. III, "Pitch Variation," pp. 51–82, and Chap. IV, "Emphasis," pp. 83–101.

Coleman, H. O., "Intonation and Emphasis," *Miscellanea Phonetica* (Association Phonetique Internationale, London), I (1914), 6–26.

Cowan, Milton, "Pitch and Intensity Characteristics of Stage Speech," *Archives of Speech* (December, 1936), Supplement, pp. 1–9.

Dolman, Jr., John, *The Art of Acting.* New York: Harper & Brothers, 1949. Study Chap. X, "Reading the Lines," pp. 101–117.

Fairbanks, Grant, "Recent Experimental Investigations of Vocal Pitch in Speech," *Journal of the Acoustical Society in America,* XI (1940), 457–466.

Fairbanks, Grant, and W. Pronovost, "An Experimental Study of the Pitch Characteristics of the Voice during the Expression of Emotion," *Speech Monographs,* IV (1937), 87–104.

Gray, Giles W., and Ramona D. Tomlin, "The Improvement of Pitch Control in Speech," *Quarterly Journal of Speech,* XVII, No. 2 (April, 1931), 190–202.

Morris, A. R., "A Note on the Inflection of Julia Marlowe," *Quarterly Journal of Speech,* XX, No. 2 (April, 1934), 200–202.

[10] Woolbert and Nelson, *op. cit.,* p. 245.

Ortleb, R., "An Objective Study of Emphasis in Oral Reading of emotional and Unemotional Material," *Speech Monographs,* IV (1937), 56–68.

Root, Alfred R., "The Pitch Factor in Speech—a Survey," *Quarterly Journal of Speech,* XVI, No. 3 (June, 1930), 320–341.

Skeet, Edgar B., *The Melody of Speech; The Purpose and Effect of Inflection and Variation of Pitch in Speech.* London: Samuel French, 1927, 92 pp.

Smedley, Constance, *Greenleaf Theatre Elements II: Speech.* London: Gerald Duckworth & Company, n.d. Study the exercises in accent for *As You Like It* and Maeterlinck's *Aglavaine and Sélysette,* pp. 33–35, and for pitch in Shaw's *Arms and the Man,* pp. 43–44, and in Barrie's *Dear Brutus,* pp. 47–48.

Stanislavski, Constantin, *Building a Character.* New York: Theatre Arts Books: Robert M. MacGregor, 1949. Read, though the material is disappointing, Chap. VII, "Diction and Singing," pp. 78–103; Chap. VIII, "Intonations and Pauses," pp. 104–142; Chap. IX, "Accentuation: The Expressive Word," pp. 143–167; and Chap. XII, "Speech Tempo-Rhythm," pp. 217–237.

Tiffin, J., and M. D. Steer, "An Experimental Analysis of Emphasis," *Speech Monographs,* IV (1937), 69–74.

EXERCISES

In reading the following selections little or no concern should be given to either characterization or surrounding circumstances. The selections should be read only for logical meaning.

A. CHANGES, REVERSALS, TRANSITIONS

1. THE ALDRICH FAMILY, #405*

MR. ALDRICH: Well, Mrs. Johnson, that's your game — and rubber.

MRS. JOHNSON: Well, what do you know!

MR. JOHNSON: (COMING ON) Mrs. Aldrich, do you know a young fellow named Willie Marshall?

MRS. ALDRICH: Oh, yes!

MR. JOHNSON: Well, he's out in our front hall, and he says you want to see him.

MR. ALDRICH: What's that?

MRS. ALDRICH: Why, yes. I phoned him about ten minutes ago, Sam, when I was dummy, and asked him to come over. Will you excuse me a moment, please?

MR. ALDRICH: Alice, what do you want to see Willie Marshall for?

MRS. ALDRICH: (FADING) I'll be right back, Sam.

MRS. JOHNSON: Charles, didn't the phone ring while you were out in the hall?

MR. JOHNSON: Yes, and I'd like to know who's been handing out my private number. It was some young fool wanting to borrow a dollar.

MRS. JOHNSON: Really?

MR. JOHNSON: He said he couldn't wait until business hours.

MR. ALDRICH: Probably some prankster.

MR. JOHNSON: He didn't even know who I was. As soon as I told him my name he said he didn't really need the dollar — really — and hung up.

MRS. ALDRICH: (COMING ON) Well, are we going to start a new rubber?

MRS. JOHNSON: We might as well. It's your deal, Mrs. Aldrich.

MRS. ALDRICH: All right.

MR. ALDRICH: Alice, where's your bracelet?

MRS. ALDRICH: Why —

MR. ALDRICH: Weren't you wearing a bracelet a little while ago?

MRS. ALDRICH: Sam — I — (BRIGHTLY) How's the score, Mr. Johnson?

* By Patricia Joudry and Del Dinsdale, based on characters created by Clifford Goldsmith. Reproduced through the courtesy of the authors and Clifford Goldsmith.

MR. ALDRICH: Alice, didn't you hear me? Didn't you have a bracelet on just before you went out to the hall to speak to Willie Marshall?

MRS. ALDRICH: (SWEETLY) Sam, suppose we talk about it when we get home? We don't want to interrupt the game, do we?

2. APPOINTMENT*

MARK: Vincent!

VINCENT: Who — Mark! You startled me! What are you doing here?

MARK: More to the point — what are <u>you</u>? Let's pull into this doorway. How can you stand so conspicuously in such a public place? Why, the papers are full of your escape. Here, wear my hat to cover your eyes. Have you gone mad?

VINCENT: I'm here to kill a man. There's no time to explain. He'll come by any minute now.

MARK: To <u>kill</u> a man? Why, you'll be caught and shot in seconds.

VINCENT: I know that. I expect that. But if you're with me you'll be shot as well. Now there's the hour — he's already late. Listen, will you scram? I know what I'm doing.

3. TALES OF WILLIE PIPER, #5†

(RATTLING OF PANS)

WILLIE: (ANXIOUS TO PLEASE) Isn't there anything I can do to help you, Martha?

MARTHA: (NOT MAD, BUT DISTRAIT) Willie, I've told you I'll get this supper cooked much faster if you don't stand around the kitchen.

WILLIE: Oh. I thought maybe there was something I could do to help you.

MARTHA: I did want everything to be just right the first time I had Mr. Grindle to supper —

WILLIE: But it's going to be swell! Gee, look! You've got lots of food!

MARTHA: Yes, I know. After running all the way to the butcher shop to get there before he closed, and then all he had left was fillet of haddock.

* From *Thirteen by Corwin,* by Norman Corwin. Reproduced by permission of Henry Holt and Company, Inc. Copyright, 1942, by Norman Corwin.

† By Samuel Taylor. Reproduced through the courtesy of the author.

WILLIE: But you didn't have to go to all that trouble. Mr. Grindle doesn't care what he eats.

MARTHA: I'm not going to cry, I'm not going to cry, I'm not going to cry, I'm not going to cry.

WILLIE: What?

MARTHA: Nothing.

WILLIE: Besides, you fry fish better than anybody in the world! Don't you?

MARTHA: But I don't want to fry fish for Mr. Grindle!

WILLIE: (SUDDENLY REALIZING) Oh, you don't? Gee, I didn't realize — Have I done something wrong, Martha?

MARTHA: No, Willie, you haven't done anything wrong. It's just that I feel so . . . pushed; that's all.

WILLIE: Yeah . . . I ought to be shot.

MARTHA: Now, Willie, it isn't anything. We're going to have a nice supper. I've got an apple pie in the oven, and — and — It's going to be all right — really!

4. PORTIA FACES LIFE, #1820*

DAISY: She'll be havin' no trouble sleepin', will she, Walter?

WALTER: Good heavens, no. She'll drop off the second her head touches that pillow. But I don't like the way she looks, Miss Daisy. She's so white and thin.

DAISY: After what she's been through it's no wonder. A body can't be tearin' their life into bits and not show the strain of it for some time after. But don't you be worryin'. She's home now and we'll be takin' good care of her.

WALTER: We mustn't lose her again.

DAISY: Get along with you, Walter. In two weeks or so she'll be her old self again. Wait and see.

WALTER: She — she asked me if she'd walk again.

DAISY: It hurts, don't it, to see her like that . . . so slow and awkward. Her that used to walk so light and quick . . . like a queen.

* By Mona Kent. Reproduced through the courtesy of the author and General Foods Corporation.

WALTER: Yes. But instead of loving her any the less for it, I think I love her even more. I'd give anything, Miss Daisy, to help her walk again.

DAISY: And what one of us wouldn't? But faith, after the miracle we've seen today, Walter, why can't we believe that another one will happen?

WALTER: If it only would happen . . . for her sake. I'll call Dr. Cornwall and have him come in to see her this evening. Then we'll know just what her chances are. I'll call him right now.

5. SPELLBOUND*

J. B.: (IN A LOW VOICE) It's like looking into a picture book — an old one. And seeing the familiar pictures, one at a time. I went to Columbia Medical School. Had a girl with a giggle who, luckily, married my roommate, Ken. Oh, by the way, my name is John Ballyntine. Another thing — my army record is — all right. I was invalided out. I ran into Dr. Edwardes when I was in the Cumberland Mountains trying to recover from some kind of nerve shock I got from the plane crash. He was on vacation, but I asked him to help me and he invited me to go skiing with him. (AFTER A PAUSE) We went through New York and I vaguely remember going to lunch somewhere. I'm still a little vague about that lunch part. Then we arrived here and the accident happened at that spot . . . . I'm still a little foggy about it, but I do know that Edwardes was about fifty feet ahead of me when he went over — I saw him plunge.

6. SILVER THEATRE: *THE BOILING POINT*†

TREADWAY: I suppose, Miss Watson, it's the most sensational song ever written?

JEAN: No . . . I don't think so, Mr. Treadway.

TREADWAY: Well, that's refreshing.

JEAN: You see, whether you buy it or not isn't important. But I wish you'd at least see Richard — Mr. Dobbins . . . and . . . Well —

* From the screen play by Ben Hecht; suggested by Francis Beeding's novel, *The House of Dr. Edwardes.* Reproduced through the courtesy of Vanguard Films.

† By William Engvick. Reproduced through the courtesy of the author.

TREADWAY: And shut up and listen for a change?

JEAN: Yes, sort of.

TREADWAY: I'm disappointed, Miss Watson. I thought you were going to ask for my son's hand in marriage.

JEAN: But I don't love him, Mr. Treadway.

TREADWAY: You have my deep admiration. Very well, bring this songwriter around. I'll see him. After that it's up to him.

JEAN: Oh, no. He'll come by himself. I don't want him to know I've spoken to you, or even that I work here. You see, this is something he has to do on his own. I want him to learn to be confident and willing — to boil over.

TREADWAY: Whatever you say. I'll see him this afternoon. But I'll be sorry to lose you, Miss Treadway.

JEAN: Lose me?!

TREADWAY: When this Dobbins . . . boils over.

7. DAVID HARDING, COUNTER-SPY, #158*

ELRA: The top of the waves in the moonlight . . . like rows of silver . . .

(A WAVE POUNDING ON THE BEACH)

CARLTON: I've never seen you so happy, Elra.

ELRA: (LAUGHS) You flatter me. It is because your stomach is full. You feel good.

(ANOTHER WAVE)

CARLTON: It's more than that.

ELRA: And the sea — and the moon — and the water — and a woman — any woman.

CARLTON: That isn't so.

(A FAINT WAVE NOW)

ELRA: (BECOMING HARDER) I have seen you before, you know.

CARLTON: I've seen you, too — but I didn't dare speak until yesterday.

ELRA: I have seen you look at many women . . .

CARLTON: Eh —

ELRA: You have followed some —

* Excerpt from DAVID HARDING, COUNTER-SPY, written by Phillips H. Lord. Reproduced through the courtesy of Phillips H. Lord, Inc.

CARLTON: Oh, now, Elra, don't spoil all this.

ELRA: You are nice, but you are not very clever.

CARLTON: There's nothing to be clever about. Why should I — Oh. (PAUSE)

ELRA: (SNAP) What is the matter?

CARLTON: (VERY TENSE) That gun — where'd you get that?

ELRA: (HARD, FLAT) I have not asked you where you got the one that is in your pocket.

CARLTON: (SNAP) Put that away, Elra. What are you thinking of?

ELRA: (HARD, FIRM) You did not speak to me because you <u>liked</u> me. You wanted to know who I am.

CARLTON: Oh, so that's it?

ELRA: That is exactly it. You have been checking on many women in Tia Juana.

CARLTON: All right, I admit it. But I didn't speak to you for that reason. I liked you very much — too much.

ELRA: After I noticed you — I investigated, too.

CARLTON: (INTENSE, DAWNING) You — you aren't — !

ELRA: (GIVE IT ALL . . . BITTER, MAD) If you have been looking for Fraulein Gross — you have the honor to have met her.

CARLTON: (EXPLODING) You — you Fraulein Gross! What a fool I am!

ELRA: (HATRED) A bigger fool than you know!

(SHOT)

(NO GROAN: JUST EXHAUSTING OF BREATH)

8. ADVENTURES OF THE THIN MAN: *THE CASE OF THE BLEEDING LIPSTICK**

NICK: Gosh, Belinda, I haven't seen you for years.

BELINDA: Notice any improvements?

NICK: Yes, indeed. You've gotten so . . . so young.

BELINDA: Lovely lad! You've gotten younger, too, dear.

NICK: You think so, Belinda?

BELINDA: Especially around the forehead. Oh, flowers! How nice!

NICK: No, Belinda, darling. These are for my wife.

BELINDA: Oh, you've got one, too?

* By Milton Lewis, based on the characters originated by Dashiell Hammett. Reproduced through the courtesy of the authors.

NICK: Un-huh. Tonight's our anniversary. I'm meeting her at the Rhumba Blanca. Say, why'd you call me?

BELINDA: I need a divorce.

NICK: Why?

BELINDA: In alphabetical order Tony's a beast, a bum — cad, fool, goon, horror, an insect — old, poisonous, ratty, stupid, unspeakable, vulgar, wearisome, excruciating, yellow, and zo on.

NICK: You left out j and k.

BELINDA: So sorry. Jerk and krum.

NICK: He doesn't appeal to you, huh?

BELINDA: Nick, will you act as the other man in a divorce?

NICK: What!?

BELINDA: It shouldn't be hard, darling. As a detective you must have had so much experience at it.

NICK: Oh, no.

BELINDA: For old times' sake, Nick?

NICK: No. And putting your arms around me will get you nowhere.

BELINDA: Darling, when that gets me nowhere I'll blow my brains out!

NICK: Oh, nuts! You got lipstick on my shirt!

BELINDA: I love that shade on you. Looks grand, doesn't it?

NICK: Not to my wife on my anniversary. I'll be murdered! I can't get a new shirt at this hour . . . and I'll be late!

BELINDA: Here. These shirts just came for Tony. You can put one on.

NICK: Thanks. And listen to me, Belinda, this is out of my line. I only handle murders now.

BELINDA: Oh. Would you murder Tony for me, Nick?

NICK: Absolutely not!

BELINDA: But it'll save the lawyer's face. Know anyone who would?

NICK: Hey, what kind of a person are you, Belinda?

BELINDA: A woman — and very female, Nick.

B. EMPHASIS

Work in the following selections for variety in bringing out the main ideas via the key words.

1. MYSTERY THEATRE: *NOT QUITE PERFECT**

LARRY: It was perfect — a perfect crime. The police thought that in an exchange of shots I had killed the hold-up man and that he had killed my wife. But murder changes your life completely. Even though you commit a perfect crime as I did, there is no escaping the relentless, gnawing fear of being found out. (PAUSE) About a month later — while Esther and I were discussing our forthcoming marriage — the whole thing went to pieces.

2. THE ALDRICH FAMILY, #278†

MARY: Has Aunt Harriet gone?

MRS. ALDRICH: Yes, dear. She just left.

MARY: Mother, do you think <u>she</u> might have taken my box of chocolates?

MRS. ALDRICH: No, dear. Your Aunt Harriet is not in the habit of taking candy that doesn't belong to her.

MARY: Well, then I guess that leaves just three people that might have taken it.

MRS. ALDRICH: And who are they?

MARY: Either Henry or Homer or Charlie Clark. Or possibly all three.

MRS. ALDRICH: Now, Mary, that isn't exactly fair. You probably intended to put the box of candy in the sideboard and absent-mindedly put it some other place.

MR. ALDRICH: (COMING ON) Alice, why isn't there any soap upstairs?

MRS. ALDRICH: Any soap, Sam?

MR. ALDRICH: Yes, Alice. I'd like to wash my hands.

MARY: My goodness, Father, what is that you have all over your hands?

MR. ALDRICH: Why, nothing, Mary. It just seems to be — chocolate.

MARY: Chocolate?

MR. ALDRICH: I think it's chocolate.

MRS. ALDRICH: Sam, how did you get chocolate on you?

* By L. K. Hoffman. Reproduced through the courtesy of the author.
† By Clifford Goldsmith. Reproduced through the courtesy of the author.

MR. ALDRICH: I have no idea. I happened to look at my hand a little while ago and it was all chocolate. After all, is that important? Where will I find a piece of soap?

MRS. ALDRICH: (REALLY MAD) Dear, I don't think I've ever been so mad at you in my life!

MR. ALDRICH: Mad at me? What have I done?

MRS. ALDRICH: Sam, you know what you've done! You know very well what you've done!

MARY: Mother, do you think he did?

MR. ALDRICH: (FADING) Alice, all I want is a cake of soap.

(DOOR CLOSES OFF)

MARY: Mother, I can't believe it!

MRS. ALDRICH: I should have known, Mary, that your father couldn't be trusted with a box of candy in the house. He never could be. Let him have one piece and he loses all control and all character.

AUNT HARRIET: (OFF) Alice!

MRS. ALDRICH: (CALLING) Harriet, I thought you'd gone!

AUNT HARRIET: (COMING ON) Don't bother. I just slipped back into the hall closet and got my umbrella I left here last week.

MRS. ALDRICH: Oh, did you almost forget it again?

(DOOR OPENS ON)

AUNT HARRIET: Don't bother to come out on the porch with me.

MARY: Goodbye, Aunt Harriet.

AUNT HARRIET: I'm glad now I forgot my umbrella last week. It's just starting to rain.

MARY: Do you want me to hold your pocketbook while you put it up?

AUNT HARRIET: No, thank you. I can put it up.

(THE UMBRELLA OPENS AND THINGS DROP DOUBLY AND SINGLY TO THE FLOOR)

AUNT HARRIET: Alice, my goodness! What's falling on me?

MARY: Mother, look! Chocolates! Aunt Harriet, where did you get those?

AUNT HARRIET: Chocolates? Alice, is this my umbrella?

MRS. ALDRICH: Harriet, hold your head still!

AUNT HARRIET: Now what's happened?

MRS. ALDRICH: A couple of creams fell into your hat.

AUNT HARRIET: Well, my gracious, Alice! My gracious!

MRS. ALDRICH: What's the matter, Harriet? Stand still.

AUNT HARRIET: I can't. I can't! A chocolate went down inside my dress! Alice, where are they coming from?!

3. TO TIM AT TWENTY-ONE*

ELLEN: I beg your pardon, but I don't remember any gloves, sir.

MARSHALL: Well, I do. I distinctly remember taking them off and handing them to you.

ELLEN: I'm afraid you're mistaken.

MARSHALL: Now see here, young woman, I don't patronize this restaurant to be told I'm mistaken.

ELLEN: I don't expect you do. It happens you have no gloves.

MARSHALL: I don't relish being contradicted.

ELLEN: Neither do I. Sorry, but your gloves are not here. You'll probably find them in your coat.

MARSHALL: (RAISING HIS VOICE) Are you going to check carefully or do I have to call the manager?

ELLEN: You can call the manager if you like, but he's not a magician. He won't be able to produce gloves out of the air. Are you sure, sir, they're not in your coat?

MARSHALL: (SHOUTING) They are <u>not</u> in my coat — and besides, to whom do you think you're talking?

ELLEN: I haven't the faintest idea. My name's Tewksbury.

MARSHALL: What — Oh! Well, Miss Tewksbury, I've had just about enough! (SHOUTING) Manager! Manager! Come here at once! (DOWN) We'll see now whether it's possible to get a little cooperation or courtesy out of you.

ELLEN: Yes, sir, we'll see.

MANAGER: (HURRY ON) Oui, monsieur — ees it anything wrong, sir?

MARSHALL: (THE REASONABLE ACT: HE HAS BEEN OUTRAGED, BUT IS SHOWING FINE

* *From Thirteen by Corwin,* by Norman Corwin. Reproduced by permission of Henry Holt and Company, Inc. Copyright, 1942, by Norman Corwin.

CONTROL) My good man, I merely asked this girl to look for a pair of gloves which are somewhere in that check-room, since they are certainly not in this coat, and not only has she refused to oblige me, but she — (BREAKS OFF . . . PAUSE)

MANAGER: Yes, sir?

MARSHALL: (FLUSTERED) I — I beg your pardon. I'm so sorry. They're — they've been in my inside coat pocket all the time. (EMBARRASSED CHUCKLE) I — I'm sorry.

MANAGER: Ah, mais non, it ees all right, just so long you find your gloves. (FADING) Bonjour, monsieur, I am glad everything ees all right.

MARSHALL: (AFTER A PAUSE) Miss Tewksbury — my sincere — apologies.

ELLEN: Not at all, sir. We all make mistakes.

MARSHALL: Only some mistakes are more stupid than others.

ELLEN: (AMIABLY) Oh, it's all right —— forget it.

MARSHALL: Er — if you're still interested in knowing to whom you are talking — uh — the name is Marshall . . . Eric Marshall.

ELLEN: How do you do, Mr. Marshall?

MARSHALL: How do you do?

4. THERE SHALL BE NO NIGHT*

ERIK: Oh, Kaatri, don't let's sit here telling each other what our fathers say. We're old enough to make up our own minds, aren't we?

KAATRI: I don't know, Erik.

ERIK: You've made up your mind that we're going to be married, haven't you?

KAATRI: Yes. But — that's different.

ERIK: I'm glad it is different. The trouble with old people is — they remember too much — old wars, old hates. They can't get those things out of their minds. But we have no such memories. We're free of such ugly things. If there's going to be a better future, we're the ones who are going to make it. Kaatri ——

KAATRI: Yes, Erik?

* By Robert E. Sherwood. Reprinted with the permission of the author and the publisher, Charles Scribner's Sons.

ERIK: Next summer I'll stop being a student. I'll be a worker! And you and I will be married.

KAATRI: What will we live on, Erik?

ERIK: On what I make. It won't be much — but it will be enough. I'll be your man — and you'll be my woman.

KAATRI: We'll have a wonderful wedding, won't we, Erik?

ERIK: Yes, I suppose our families will insist on that.

KAATRI: It will be in the Agricola Church, and there'll be lots of flowers.

ERIK: Your father will be looking stern and magnificent in his colonel's uniform. And my father, in his black coat, looking bored. And Mother behaving like a grand duchess, and Uncle Kaldemar playing da-da-de-dum . . . . And then we'll escape from all of them, and go home, and have several children.

KAATRI: Erik!

ERIK: Oh, Kaatri! We'll be happy people, you and I. That's all that matters, isn't it, dearest?

KAATRI: Yes. No! It isn't all that matters!

ERIK: What else is there?

KAATRI: There's now . . . . There's this . . . . There may be war. Next summer may never come to us.

5. A WOMAN'S LIFE, #2082*

MADELINE: And do you think I came because I wanted to be amused or entertained? I came because I like you — like being with you, talking to you about . . . anything and everything.

SCOTT: And what did we talk about? Me! You haven't any idea of how much I'd been looking forward to tonight, Madeline. You can't have. Why did things have to turn out this way — involved and confused? Why couldn't everything have been the way it was the other night — out by the lake?

MADELINE: There are some things that you can't either force or recapture, Warren. Perhaps that's why . . . or perhaps we were trying too hard.

SCOTT: No, that's not it. I know what's wrong. I think I've known all evening. I haven't been able to break through — reach you, touch you — because I

* By Julian Funt. Reproduced through the courtesy of the author.

haven't once talked about the one thing that has any real meaning for me now . . . the thing that's been on my mind constantly for days now — you.

C. PRONOUN POUNDING

A common, unexplainable fault in emphasis, even among experienced radio actors, is the prominence constantly given the personal pronoun. The letter "I," perhaps because it is a capital letter, or perhaps for some egocentric reason, is too frequently stressed, with a consequent distortion of the meaning intended. The word "you" is also too often pounded by radio actors. The truth is that the pronouns are sometimes more important and sometimes less important than other words in a sentence, as the following exercises indicate.

1. ART: Mother, it's okay if I go out coasting with the guys for a while, isn't it?

GRACE: Well . . .

ART: It isn't very cold. I just looked at the thermometer.

GRACE: How cold is it?

ART: Twenty-eight. And it's getting warmer, I think.

GRACE: Then I don't see any reason why you can't, dear. Providing you dress warmly and don't stay out too long.

ART: I won't. I knew you'd let me go.

GRACE: You're quite a mind reader.

ART: Oh, I can figure out lots of things by myself.

GRACE: No doubt you can.

ART: Except — (HE STOPS)

GRACE: Except what, dear?

ART: I shouldn't say it, I guess.

GRACE: But what is it, darling?

ART: You won't get mad if I tell you?

GRACE: Why should I get mad?

ART: Maybe you won't like it.

GRACE: I can't tell until I hear what it is, Art.

ART: Well, I was just wondering. I mean — I can't figure out why that Mr. Capwell's been over here so much lately.

2. DICK: I'm very fond of you, Helen. I always have been.

HELEN: But, Dick, when one reaches our age —

DICK: I haven't changed.

HELEN: We all have, Dick.

DICK: I've never stopped loving you — caring — hoping. I can give you everything.

HELEN: But —

DICK: Even though I know you don't love me as I love you. I'm willing to take you this way.

3. HANK: Hey, Dan, how about a buffalo? I hear they're very chic.

CLERK: Buffalo! I've never heard of anyone wearing buffalo.

HANK: Oh, yeah. My Aunt Gussie used to wear one all the time.

DAN: Hank, the gentleman is not interested in your Aunt Gussie.

HANK: What you got against my Aunt Gussie, huh?

DAN: Wait a minute, Hank. Look, I don't think Sally would care for a disgusting animal like a buffalo.

HANK: But, Dan, buffaloes ain't disgusting. Are they, Mr. — uh —

CLERK: I'm sure I haven't the slightest idea. I've never known buffaloes intimately.

4. BOY: But you're tired, Betty. I can see that you're tired.

GIRL: All right, Harold. We'll sit down for a while.

BOY: Here. Here's a nice bench over here. We can look right over the lake.

GIRL: Yes . . .

BOY: Betty . . . do you want to go home?

GIRL: Go home? And have people say that you couldn't even — I certainly won't go home.

5. EDNA: What's the matter with you tonight?

FRANK: I'm sure I don't know, Edna.

EDNA: Well then . . .

FRANK: All I know is that this silly quarrel of yours is wrecking the whole family.

EDNA: Quarrel? What makes you so sure Nancy and I are quarreling?

6. MRS.: What do you want the book for?

MR.: I promised Archie he could have it, and I'm not going to give him the opportunity of saying I forget promises, too. Only I wish now I'd never made that promise.

7. TOM: Now that I think of it there's a good chance I might run into him. As a matter of fact, I'd better be running along now. Don't worry. I'll be home early. I promise you.

8. MAN: I can't believe it! I never thought she'd get mad at me just because I happened to forget her birthday. Why, I was only saying the other night how much I liked her. And why would I say a thing like that if I didn't mean it?

D. CONJUNCTION HITTING

Conjunction hitting is a second common, unexplainable emphasis fault. Nine of ten inexperienced microphone performers insist on hitting the frequent "and's" and "but's" in their speeches. Not that these two words are never important; often they are. Not that these two words are not constantly given a wrong importance in actual, everyday conversations; often they are. Conjunction hitting is a bad, because baseless, habit of speech. The following "and" and "but" selections should be read both the wrong and the right ways for a comparative examination of their respective values as evidence of correct thinking.

1. It seems to be my destiny to bring happiness to others when I myself have known nothing but unhappiness. And if it is my destiny — Well, there's no use trying to escape it.
2. Tell them it's all right to come in now, will you? And that Harry wants to see them.
3. I — I can't bear this place! And that dog! Such an ugly, beastly little creature!
4. This isn't what you wanted, I know. But you'll just have to make the best of it. I have.
5. I know for certain that he isn't going to do it. And what happened between you and her mother should have shown you the reason.
6. She's very fond of me. It's so obvious. And she's doing everything she can to make it pleasant for me.

7. On the surface that may seem like a little thing, but — Harold isn't a well man.

8. Oh, she's so — so aggressive — so unfeminine. But there's just a chance that the marriage will work out all right.

9. Always he fooled the people he was to conquer. He promised them he would never cross their borders. But — one by one, the lights went out in Europe.

10. I said to myself then, My husband is a soldier
And now I am a soldier, and I must win.
I thought of the world, of the earth and seas,
And those fighting with us on the earth and seas
And I wasn't afraid any more.

E. SUBORDINATIONS

Call these exercises in "the perspective of speech," since some phrases or clauses of a sentence—even entire sentences—are subordinate to other matter. Thinking implies the combination of principal things with subordinate things. Primer-style reading is the prime example of reading minus thinking.

1. NOTEBOOK*

WRITER: Many years ago I sat one day, in a sad mood . . . I went over the wishes that I wanted to realize in life. I found that the most important or the most delightful was the wish to attain a view of life (and — this was necessarily bound up with it — to convince others of it in writing) in which life, still retaining its natural full-bodied rise and fall, would simultaneously be recognized no less clearly as a nothing, a dream, a dim hovering.

2.

BILL: You've probably got more than you need already.

JEAN: A woman never has enough handbags, Bill. You should know that. There — your coat's all hung up now. Would you like to see our Christmas tree?

* By Franz Kafka.

3. CREDO*

NARRATOR: I believe that we are lost here in America, but I believe we shall be found. And this belief, which mounts now to the catharsis of knowledge and conviction, is for me — and I think for all of us — not only our own hope, but America's everlasting, living dream. I think the life which we have fashioned in America, and which has fashioned us — the forms we made, the cells that grew, the honeycomb that was created — was self-destructive in its nature, and must be destroyed. I think these forms are dying, and must die, just as I know that America and the people in it are deathless, undiscovered, and immortal, and must live.

4.

FATHER: It happened something like this. Or at least I think it did. A few years ago — maybe three, maybe four — things went from bad to worse for me. You all know what I mean. Well, one day I thought I'd go into town — talk it over with old Jimmy Welch. He was working in the bank then. You remember Jimmy Welch, don't you? The man who lived in the big house on the hill. Well, he was nice enough. He got me to make out a mortgage on our home.

5. SHERLOCK HOLMES: *THE MAN WITH THE TWISTED LIP*†

HOLMES: Then I shall reward you with a clear and concise statement of my problem. Mr. Neville St. Clair, age 37, the father of two children and an affectionate husband, is missing. He left his house — the Cedars, near Lee, our present destination — last Monday.

6.

MR. ANDERSON: Thank you, Albert, for a very colorful analysis of our teen-age problems. And if you ever happen to run across a solution for them, we'd be glad to hear it. Just a joke, Albert. You might well be proud of your son, Mr. and Mrs. Harris. And now for the second speaker on tonight's

* By Thomas Wolfe. Reprinted with the permission of Edward C. Aswell and Harper & Brothers.

† From the original story by Sir Arthur Conan Doyle, adapted for radio by Denis Green. Reproduced through the courtesy of Denis Green and the Executors of the late Sir Arthur Conan Doyle.

panel. That is, if he and the frog have parted company. I have the pleasure to present Buster Norton.

7. UNDER THE VOLCANO*

NARRATOR: Towards sunset on the Day of the Dead in November, 1939, two men in white flannels sat on the main terrace of the Casino drinking anis. They had been playing tennis, followed by billiards, and their racquets, rain-proofed, screwed in their presses — the doctor's triangular, the other's quadrangular — lay on the parapet before them.

8. A CHILD IS BORN†

INNKEEPER: And you keep singing songs!
Not ordinary songs — the kind of songs
That might bring in a litle bit of trade,
Songs with a kind of pleasant wink in them
That make men forget the price of the wine,
The kind of songs a handsome girl can sing
After their dinner to good customers
— And thanks to me, the inn still has a few! —
Oh, no! You have to sing rebellious songs!

F. THROW-AWAY LINES

Closely related to subordinations are throw-away lines, lines that merely fill in, that serve as the mortar between one important thought and another. Noel Coward, in his biography, *Present Indicative,* wrote that the one important thing he learned from American acting was the art of throwing away a line—saying a line so that the audience could hear it and yet know that it was an unimportant one. In the following examples the student should sense, even at a sight reading, which lines can be thrown away and which can not.

1. THE SECOND MRS. BURTON, #26‡

BILL: Greetings, Marion.

MARION: How are you, Bill?

* By Malcolm Lowry. Copyright, 1947, by Malcolm Lowry.

† By Stephen Vincent Benét. Copyright, 1942, by Stephen Vincent Benét. Published by the Walter H. Baker Company. All performance rights reserved.

‡ By John M. Young. Reproduced through the courtesy of the author.

BILL: Pretty good, thanks. Did you get my message? I spoke to Henrietta earlier.

MARION: She told me, Bill. I've been expecting you.

(DOOR OPENS ON)

And I'm highly flattered to think you'd come to see me today of all days.

BILL: Why so?

MARION: With all the work you must have in your new position at the store — to think you could even take a few minutes away from it. (PAUSE) Do let me take your coat, Bill.

BILL: I'll throw it on the chair, thanks.

MARION: If you like.

BILL: I can't quite get used to the idea of controlling the store, Marion. I still can't seem to believe it.

MARION: It's true though. It was in the paper this morning if you want confirmation.

BILL: I know. I saw it. Come sit here beside me.

MARION: Very well.

BILL: It's very strange — my feelings about having won.

MARION: I should think you'd be up in the clouds, Bill.

BILL: I thought I would be, too.

MARION: But aren't you?

BILL: No. That's what I want to talk to you about. That's why I came over.

2. DOUBLE INDEMNITY*

PHYLLIS: You handle just automobile insurance, or all kinds?

NEFF: All kinds. Fire, earthquake, theft, public liability, group insurance, industrial stuff, and so on right down the line.

PHYLLIS: Accident insurance?

NEFF: Accident insurance? Sure, Mrs. Dietrichson. I wish you'd tell me what's engraved on that anklet.

PHYLLIS: Just my name.

* By James M. Cain; screen play by Billy Wilder and Raymond Chandler. Special permission for use of this quoted material from *Double Indemnity* obtained from Paramount Pictures, Inc., producers of the motion picture *Double Indemnity*. Copyright, 1944, by Paramount Pictures, Inc. The play is based on the story *Double Indemnity* in the volume *Three of a Kind,* copyright, 1936, 1943, by James M. Cain, and reprinted with the permission of Alfred A. Knopf, Inc.

NEFF: As for instance?

PHYLLIS: Phyllis.

NEFF: Phyllis. I think I like that.

PHYLLIS: But you're not sure?

NEFF: I'd have to drive it around the block a couple of times.

PHYLLIS: Mr. Neff, why don't you drop by tomorrow evening about eight-thirty? He'll be in then.

NEFF: Who?

PHYLLIS: My husband. You were anxious to talk to him, weren't you?

NEFF: Sure, only I'm getting over it a little. If you know what I mean.

PHYLLIS: There's a speed limit in this state, Mr. Neff. Forty-five miles an hour.

NEFF: How fast was I going, Officer?

PHYLLIS: I'd say about ninety.

3. MYSTERY THEATRE: *THE THIRD WITNESS**

RUTH: Walking to the bus, Marian?

MARIAN: Un-huh. Let's go.

RUTH: Gee, gets dark early these days, huh, Marian?

MARIAN: I'll say.

RUTH: Kinda creepy in this neighborhood after office hours. No place for a girl to be walking alone.

MARIAN: Oh, I don't know. I don't mind.

RUTH: You're a strange one. Never could figure you out. (YAWNS) Dying to get home and curl up at the radio and hear what's going on in the world. Being cooped in an office all day sure cuts you off from — (PAUSE, SUDDEN SCARED UNDERTONE) Marian!

MARIAN: What?

RUTH: Don't look now, but — a man's following us. A masher, I think — in a car.

* By Joseph Ruscoll. Reproduced through the courtesy of the author.

4. WHEN A GIRL MARRIES, #1610*

MRS. BROWN: Mrs. Tibbs just drove me by. Now you know I'm a nuisance, but I just couldn't resist stoppin' in before I went home.

(DOOR CLOSES)

JOAN: We built a fire in the fireplace this afternoon. It was chilly indoors.

MRS. BROWN: My, but it looks nice!

JOAN: Sit down, won't you?

MRS. BROWN: I'm just about dead. If there's anything that tires me to the bone it's lookin' for dress material.

JOAN: Does Murray's have a nice selection?

MRS. BROWN: Well — he got some new cloth in, but I wouldn't say it was nice. I didn't find anything I wanted to buy and Mrs. Tibbs didn't either.

JOAN: What a shame to waste your afternoon that way . . .

MRS. BROWN: Mrs. Tibbs was just as tired as I was.

JOAN: Oh.

MRS. BROWN: So we stopped in at the Sweet Shop and had a cup of tea.

JOAN: I think it's so nice since they opened the back room.

MRS. BROWN: And it ain't expensive either.

JOAN: Mother Davis and I stopped by the other day.

MRS. BROWN: (PAUSE) Well, Mrs. Davis —

JOAN: Yes?

MRS. BROWN: You know how I hate to spread stories that might hurt anybody.

JOAN: I don't understand, Mrs. Brown?

MRS. BROWN: And you know I always call a spade a spade. Ain't nothin' like puttin' all your cards on the table, I always say. (PAUSE) Besides that, I think it's best to know a thing before it makes any headway.

JOAN: That's very true.

MRS. BROWN: So, bein' very frank, I'm goin' to speak my mind. And mark me, I'm only doin' it for your own good, dear.

JOAN: Let's get to the point, Mrs. Brown.

MRS. BROWN: That's just what I'm goin' to do, Mrs. Davis. Not more than half an hour ago I saw your husband in the Sweet Shop with one of the prettiest young women I ever laid eyes on. And let me tell you they was talkin' together as intimate as any two people could talk!

* By Elaine Carrington. Reproduced through the courtesy of the author.

5. ALL MY SONS*

FRANK: Hya.

KELLER: Hello, Frank. What's doin'?

FRANK: Nothin'. Walkin' off my breakfast. That beautiful? Not a cloud in the sky.

KELLER: Yeah, nice.

FRANK: Every Sunday ought to be like this.

KELLER: Want the paper?

FRANK: What's the difference? It's all bad news. What's today's calamity?

KELLER: I don't know. I don't read the news part any more. It's more interesting in the want-ads.

FRANK: Why — you tryin' to buy something?

KELLER: No, I'm just interested . . . to see what people want, y'know? For instance, here's a guy is looking for two Newfoundland dogs. Now what's he want with two Newfoundland dogs?

6. BRIGHT HORIZON†

CAROL: Life is very funny, Tillie.

TILLIE: It's all we have, though, isn't it?

CAROL: As Ethel Merman says, "La vie, la vie, la vie — we'd all be dead without it."

TILLIE: My idea is — if you really want to know what I think of this life . . . That's an awfully pretty bra you're wearing.

CAROL: I wonder they don't cut them all this way — on the bias. I've had this for years, but it was good to start with.

TILLIE: Give me that some day, and I'll take it to Madame Yolanda and see if she can't have some made for us.

CAROL: You were saying — about life?

TILLIE: Oh, yes. Well, it was nothing. Except that sometimes I think we're all fools.

CAROL: I know we are. My check dress would be all right for today, wouldn't it?

TILLIE: What are you doing?

* By Arthur Miller. Reproduced through the courtesy of the author.

† By Kathleen Norris. Reproduced with the permission of the author.

CAROL: Going with Larry to the country club to watch some tennis, and I suppose have lunch there.

TILLIE: Let's see what hat you're wearing.

CAROL: There on the dresser.

TILLIE: Yes, that's all right. The green checks go with the leaves on your hat, and the rose is good. Yes, we all seem to get our lives into tangles reaching for something, and when we get it . . . it isn't there. I'm going to clip this lock of hair off.

G. PAUSE

Various kinds of pauses are illustrated in the following selections.

1. PORTIA FACES LIFE, #1698*

CORNWALL: Mrs. Manning, sit down.

PORTIA: But —

CORNWALL: Sit down, please, and listen.

PORTIA: My appointment's at eleven and —

CORNWALL: Those headaches of yours are not a silly little thing . . . as you put it. You're very ill.

PORTIA: (PAUSE: THEN WOODENLY) Ill? I can't be.

CORNWALL: I don't like being brutally frank this way. I'm not usually, but your attitude, Mrs. Manning, makes it necessary.

PORTIA: (STUNNED) Ill!? But, Doctor —

CORNWALL: There's no need to be frightened. You have a chance . . . an even chance, I would say . . . providing we don't waste too much time. But I must see your husband ——

PORTIA: No.

(A PAUSE)

CORNWALL: What do you mean?

PORTIA: What's wrong with me?

CORNWALL: I'll go into it thoroughly —

PORTIA: You've got to tell me!

* By Mona Kent. Reproduced through the courtesy of the author and General Foods Corporation.

CORNWALL: As I explained before, Mrs. Manning, I shall furnish your husband with all the details.

PORTIA: No, Walter's not to be brought into this. So please stop talking in circles and tell me what's wrong — in plain layman's language.

CORNWALL: Very well — if that's how you want it. (PAUSE) Those headaches of yours . . . the lethargy that accompanies them . . . the feeling of numbness in the extremities . . . they're all . . . warning signals. If allowed to continue without treatment . . . the result will be . . . total paralysis.

PORTIA: Total —— Go on, Dr. Cornwall.

CORNWALL: It's enough for you to know that an operation — if successful — can prevent a paralytic condition. (PAUSE) There you have the situation briefly. I can explain it more fully in medical terms, if you wish.

PORTIA: No, I — I understand.

CORNWALL: If there's something you'd like to ask, I'll try to answer your questions as simply and truthfully as I can.

PORTIA: Yes, there is something.

CORNWALL: (WHEN SHE DOESN'T GO ON) What is it, Mrs. Manning?

PORTIA: Why did Dr. Watkins tell me there was nothing wrong?

CORNWALL: Well, he has his reasons — and from his way of looking at it . . . they were very good ones.

2. THE TRIDGET OF GREVA*

The three men are fishing.

LAFFLER: Well, boys, any luck?

BARHOOTER: By the way, what was <u>your</u> mother's name before she was married?

CORBY: I didn't know her then.

LAFFLER: Do they allow people to fish at the Aquarium?

BARHOOTER: You sure must know her first name.

CORBY: I don't. I always called her Mother.

BARHOOTER: But your father must have called her something.

CORBY: That's a hot one.

BARHOOTER: I wanted to ask you something about your sister, too.

CORBY: What about her?

BARHOOTER: Just anything. For instance, what's the matter with her?

CORBY: Who?

BARHOOTER: Your sister.

CORBY: I'm not married. (AFTER A PAUSE, BOTH LAUGH)

BARHOOTER: (TO LAFFLER) Do you know what we were laughing at?

LAFFLER: I have no idea.

BARHOOTER: I wish I knew who to ask.

LAFFLER: Mr Corby —

CORBY: Well?

LAFFLER: I often wonder how you spell your name?

CORBY: A great many people have asked me that. The answer is, I don't even try. I just let it go.

LAFFLER: I think that's kind of risky.

3. WHEN A GIRL MARRIES, #1606*

MRS. D.: If you had to pay for the coal you burn in that stove, it'd be a different story.

(PAUSE)

You've always been very free with other people's money, but when it comes to spending your own, that's another matter.

(PAUSE)

All right. Have you ever offered to pay me one cent since you've been living here?

(PAUSE)

You'd think once in a while you might bring me a box of candy — or a book

* By Elaine Carrington. Reproduced through the courtesy of the author.

to read. But do you ever think of me? No, you only think of your own selfish desires.

(PAUSE)

Well, why don't you say something?

4. ALTER EGO*

JOAN: (THIS IS SPOKEN IN A HOPELESS, WEARY TONE OF VOICE — THE DASHES BETWEEN PHRASES INDICATE WHERE PAUSES ARE MADE TO PERMIT THE BACKGROUND OF TRAIN MOVEMENT TO BE HEARD) Train after train — I would get off one train and on the other — I didn't care where I was going — I just wanted to get away, far away — train after train — until at last my money was almost gone (PAUSE) and I found myself in this city — (PAUSE FOR STREET SOUND EFFECT) Unknown — a thousand miles from home — but happy, because I thought I was free from her!

5. IN THE FOG†

ATTENDANT: (COMING ON) Good evening, sir. Fill 'er up?

DOCTOR: (IMPATIENTLY) No, please. Where's your telephone? I've just been held up!

ATTENDANT: No!

DOCTOR: Do you have a telephone?

ATTENDANT: Find one inside, pay station.

DOCTOR: Thank you!

ATTENDANT: (STOPPING HIM) Er . . .

DOCTOR: Well? You were going to say something?

ATTENDANT: Sort of looking fellers were they?

DOCTOR: Oh. Two big ruffians, with rifles. They won't be hard to identify. Bearded, both of them, faces and heads bandaged and covered with dirt and blood. Friend of theirs with a gaping chest wound. I'm a doctor, so they forced me to attend him.

ATTENDANT: Oh. (ODDLY KNOWING) Those fellers.

* By Arch Oboler. Reprinted with the permission of the author.

† By Milton Geiger. Reproduced through the courtesy of the author.

DOCTOR: Did you know about them?

ATTENDANT: Yeah, I guess so.

DOCTOR: They're desperate, I tell you, and they're armed!

ATTENDANT: That was about two miles back, would you say?

DOCTOR: Yes, just about that. Now if you'll show me where your phone is and tell me the name of that town I just went through (PAUSES ON QUESTIONING NOTE . . . NO ANSWER) I say . . . (ANNOYED) What town was that back there?

ATTENDANT: (ODDLY . . . QUIETLY) That was Gettysburg, mister . . .

DOCTOR: (STRUCK) Gettysburg!

ATTENDANT: (QUIET AND SOLEMN) Gettysburg, and Gettysburg battlefield. (PAUSE . . . FOR EFFECT) When it's light and the fog is gone, you can see the gravestones. Meade's men and Pickett's men and Robert E. Lee's.

DOCTOR: Then, those — those men —

ATTENDANT: On nights like this, well, you're not the first they've stopped in the fog, nor the last.

DOCTOR: (SOFTLY . . . DISTANTLY) Gettysburg, and the dead that never die!

ATTENDANT: That's right, I guess. (PAUSE . . . DEEP BREATH) Fill 'er up, mister?

DOCTOR: (DISTANTLY) Yes, fill 'er up . . . fill 'er up.

6. MIRACLE IN THE RAIN*

A soldier stands in a doorway alongside a girl he does not know. They both look at the rain. Finally, in a cheerful voice, not directed at her, he speaks.

SOLDIER: Look at her come down! Like a pack of horses coming down the home stretch! (A PAUSE) You know, a night like this makes this town look almost human. Listen to that rain — like firecrackers. There's nothing so good as a real rain — unless it's a blizzard. (PAUSE) I'd be out walking in it right now if I had any place to go. (HE LOOKS AT HER FOR THE FIRST TIME) Maybe that's the best time to walk in the rain, when you got no place to go.

* Television adaptation by Frederick Coe, of a story by Ben Hecht. Reprinted with the permission of the authors and The National Broadcasting System.

7. BABY SNOOKS SHOW*

SNOOKS: What are we doing down here, Daddy?

DADDY: Listen, we've got to get to the Mayor. They won't let us through the front entrance, but maybe we can find a way up through this basement. Here — what's this?

(DOOR OPENS ON)

DADDY: The dumbwaiter!

SNOOKS: (PAUSE — WORRIED) Daddy, why are you looking at me like that?

DADDY: (PAUSE — VERY SHMALTZY) Snooks, my little lamb chop . . . come a little closer. There's something I want to show you.

SNOOKS: Oh, no!

DADDY: Why not?

SNOOKS: 'Cause I ain't your little lamb chop unless there's a reason. And I think I know what the reason is!

DADDY: (REPROACHING) Snooks, you're not afraid to ride in that dumbwaiter, are you? (PAUSE) Well, are you?

SNOOKS: (PAUSE) Ain't I?

Reread the exercises in all the preceding chapters for additional practice in pitch changes, emphasis, and inflection.

* By Jesse Oppenheimer and Everett Freeman. Reproduced through the courtesy of the authors.

Chapter VI . . CHARACTERIZATION: ACTION

1

The problem of characterization must be considered next; it has been waiting out in the anteroom long enough. Thus far, in the discussions and the exercises, the radio actor has been learning about meaning—but he has been practicing only as himself. Perhaps as a result he has become better acquainted with himself, with the materials he must always use in acting. Now he is ready to start *acting*, to act *another person*, to characterize.

Unfortunately, the radio actor who rightly centers his efforts on characterization is immediately in a predicament; it takes time to work out a genuine characterization, and apparently there is no time for that in the broadcasting procedures. What can the actor do? Shall he, in his races against the clock, and following the practice of experienced radio performers, find effective substitutes for characterizations? Shall he, of necessity, hunt for short cuts? Turn on tricks? Shall he finally do what most radio actors are forced to do—cap this series of mistakes by foregoing any concern whatsoever with authentic characterizations?

The radio actor who is tempted thus to succumb to the prevailing custom of blithely forsaking characterizations can eventually argue that hardly any radio director knows enough about acting to be able to distinguish between effective personalities and technical skills, or between the "bag of tricks which every old hand carries and the stock of ideas and sense of character which distinguish the master-actor from the mere handy man."[1] He can always argue that radio actors "get by" with their pseudo characterizations because many directors, in the rush and pressure of production, are too fond of casting their plays largely by types: the low-voiced man as the menace, the motherly-sounding woman as the mother, the dignified old gentleman as the judge, senator, or doctor, and so on. Furthermore, he can quote directors like George Zachary, writing in *Variety*, to the effect that "radio has developed the most versatile group of actors known to the entertainment field" because you can give them a script and get a characterization the first time[!]. "Your capable radio actor can play an extraordinary number of characterizations at a moment's notice"[!]. He can continue quoting from Zachary and believe that

> . . . the radio actor lacks the opportunity for development of characterization he would have in the theatre. A radio performance is rehearsed briefly and then broadcast, and that's the end of it. The actor must therefore give a quick, vital impression of the part. I know of no radio actors whose performances improve perceptibly with rehearsal . . . . If an actor (and by this I mean a regular radio actor) doesn't get a characterization right with the first reading, there's no use trying to change him. [!] You can alter cues, bits of business, or the exteriors of the performance, but the characterization will remain the same.[2]

Nevertheless, the radio actor who succumbs to such tempting arguments and finally abandons his concentration on characterization will quickly become as vulnerable as the horde of his colleagues who have already succumbed: he can be eclipsed in a moment by any radio actor who can truly create a genuine character even under the stingiest of radio rehearsal periods.

Characterization has the same central importance in radio acting that it has in stage and screen acting. It cannot be brushed nonchalantly aside merely because people are in a hurry. The real attraction for listeners

[1] George Bernard Shaw, *Dramatic Opinions and Essays*, edited by James Huneker (New York: Brentano's, 1906), I, 135.

[2] George Zachary, *Variety*, January 22, 1941, p. 34.

at their radio sets, as for all theatre audiences, "is the exhibition of *character;* and the accurate presentation of character, with all of its contrasts, and mysterious tones, founded on study and observation, is what constitutes *acting.*"[3]

Whenever characterization in radio acting is minimized, for whatever cause, it is in grave danger of being eliminated.

2

Many actor candidates, when studying characterization, especially for the theatre, are assigned to observe for a time a small earthenware pitcher, and then to improvise an individual suggested by the qualities found in it. They are also asked to delineate a person who has the qualities found in a military march, in a carnation (white or red), or in a lemon drop. Perhaps such exercises are a helpful spur to the imagination, but as a practical approach to radio characterization, this "lemon drop" method seems a little pretentious, and roundabout, and foolish.

There is one basic truth, though, that the radio actor can learn from such esoteric exercises. This truth is that a characterization is properly born in the imagination and not in the ears. The exercises stress the fact that a radio characterization should emanate from the actor's mind and not merely from his mouth. This fact can stand considerable reiteration, because what Bernard Shaw wrote some time ago about stock actors applies today to more than a few radio performers.

> . . . it is . . . impossible for a human being to study and perform a new part of any magnitude every day . . . The stock actor solved the problem by adapting a "line": for example, if his "line" was old age, he acquired a trick of doddering and speaking in a cracked voice; if juvenility, he swaggered and effervesced. With these accomplishments, eked out by a few rules of thumb . . . he "swallowed" every part given him in a couple of hours, and regurgitated it in the evening . . . always in the same manner, however finely the dramatist might have individualized it . . . . His great contribution to dramatic art was the knack of earning a living for fifty years on the stage without ever really acting, or either knowing or caring for the difference between "Comedy of Errors" and "Box and Cox."[4]

[3] Percy Fitzgerald, *The Art of Acting* (London: The Macmillan Company, 1892), p. 69.

[4] Shaw, *op. cit.,* II, 393.

Nowadays too many radio actors translate themselves into other human beings by hurriedly applying vocal make-ups: they turn on certain speech tricks, and lo! with a twist of the tongue or the lips they create the dramatis personae. The actress learns "not how to interpret plays," but how to sound "sweet and gentle, or jealous and wicked, or funny, or matronly, or deaf and palsied . . . ." The actor learns how to sound "sprightly, or romantic, or murderous, or bucolic, or doddering . . . ."[5]

For instance, one radio actor, currently advertising his characterization wares via a printed circular, describes as follows the parts he is prepared to play:

OLD SOAK—Here's a jovial, hearty, W. C. Fieldsian character, designed for both adult and child audiences; can be played for comedy or pathos.

NERVOUS WRECK—A fluttery, harried neurotic; comic, or—for a twist—a villain; a touch of "swish" if desired.

BLUSTERING BULLY—A gruff, tough hombre, perfect as a loud-mouth villain; can also be played for broad comedy.

HIGH-PRESSURE SALESMAN—A fast-talking, energetic fellow who may easily be converted into a barker or pitchman.

MEEK MOUSE—A unique approach to the "Milquetoast" type gives this lovable, mild little man a piquant quality highly colorful for comedy—a sure-fire laugh-getter for audience shows.

AUTHORITATIVE STRAIGHT—Young, enthusiastic, strong properties give this "straight" an exciting freshness. Well adapted for documentary programs and high-lighted dramatic announcements.

OLD RURAL—Varying approaches to this character permit a wide interpretative range, from a straightforward country sheriff, through a New England philosopher, to a comic hillbilly.

SINISTER HEAVY—The soft, oily touch makes this scoundrel an ideal "con man," gambler, or politico.

MUDDLE-HEADED PROFESSOR—An excitable, absent-minded, scholarly type, his gnomelike voice quality creates an image perfect for programs of scientific fiction.

[5] George Bernard Shaw and Ellen Terry, *Ellen Terry and Bernard Shaw, A Correspondence,* edited by Christopher St. John (New York: G. P. Putnam's Sons, 1931), p. xvi.

AWKWARD YOUTH—An incredulous adolescent, scatterbrained if you like, with lots of vitality and a wide-eyed confusion at the simplest problems.

Any experience with radio actors will inevitably lead one to conclude that in nine of ten cases such characterizations are likely to be little more than cleverly external. They are applied only from the outside; they are the trite acting sounds that signify nothing; they are the ear and mouth diseases of radio.

Radio actors who take pride in the mere agility of their tongues and mouths, who can at the drop of a hat spew out all the cliché externals that are supposed to fit the individualized human beings a playwright has labored long to create for his particular play, only substitute a pseudo cleverness for perceptive creation. They should, for remedy, take a tip from the Japanese actor in the *Noh* plays who one day saw his adopted son and successor-to-be following an old woman down the street and copying her manner of speaking. When the actor asked the boy what he was doing, he replied that in this way he hoped some day to become a fine actor of woman's roles. Angry at this, the actor thundered: "In that way you will never play in the theatre! Forget the externals. Within your *mind* you must call up the conviction that you are old, and all the externals will follow."[6] He said what every radio actor ought to know: in the theatre you cannot achieve a characterization merely by changing your voice to guttural or by altering your speech to Kentuckian.

Working from without is no way for a radio actor to bring into being "that supreme sense of humanity which alone can raise the art work . . . into a convincing presentment of life."[7] He must create from *within*. As far back as 1892, Percy Fitzgerald wrote

Acting is popularly supposed by our journeymen to be a faithful . . . imitation of the figures before us in real life, with all their ways, tones, peculiarities of speech . . . and the rest . . . . But acting, in its true sense, is a very different thing. It is an intellectual process, and deals with what is within. It is the art . . . of exhibiting *character,* and all the phenomena of character. You cannot *copy* character, but you can reproduce it. Mere sevile copying of the outer crust is not acting . . . .[8]

The radio actor's job in characterizing is not to supply an idea with a peculiar sounding board but with a credible and natural and specifically *individualized* human being to utter it.[9] Actors who dodge that necessity by resorting to the cliché or the stencil commit the second current sin in radio acting. They turn to the generalized, to the familiar formula, to a tired old echo from some other play, until the air waves are dully crowded with recurring types, with the same old dummies mechanically resurrected.

Wise and rare indeed is the radio actor who is as positive as Shaw that

there is a definite conception of some particular sort of man at the back of all Shakespeare's characters. The quality of fun to be got out of Bottom and Autolycus, for instance, is about the same, but underneath the fun there are two widely different persons, of types still extant and familiar. Mr. L——— would be as funny in Autolycus as he is in Bottom, but he would be exactly the same in both parts.[10]

Some such definite conception of a *particular* person is also at the back of most playwrights' characters or can be added, must be added, by the actor.

Working in vague and wide generalities, then—in the cliché and the stencil—is "nothing but a new jug of hot water on very old tea leaves." Working thus, a radio actress ". . . . can play 'the heroine' under a hundred different names with entire success. But the individualized heroine is another matter."[11] Working for individuality, on the other hand, she can create "a distinct person about whose history the audience has learnt something,"[12] can leave it with some "sense of having made a new acquaintance."[13]

3

Moreover, what an audience is entitled to meet, via each actor, is not only a new person but *the* new person specified by the dramatist. Too many radio actors,

[6] Elsie Fogerty's introduction to her translation of Constant Coquelin, *The Art of the Actor* (London: George Allen & Unwin, Ltd., 1932), pp. 15–16.

[7] Shaw, *op. cit.,* II, 1–2.

[8] Fitzgerald, *op. cit.,* pp. 72–73.

[9] Shaw, *op. cit.,* II, 256.

[10] *Ibid.,* I, 173–174.

[11] *Ibid.,* pp. 109–110.

[12] *Ibid.,* II, 128.

[13] *Ibid.,* p. 357.

though, blandly overlook this premise of the art of acting and commit the third current sin in radio acting, that of always substituting themselves for the characters they are supposed to be acting. They present, ofttimes because they must work swiftly—purely egocentric characterizations. Celeste Barnett, a hypothetical radio actress, plays Mrs. Anderson on THE ALDRICH FAMILY, a stenographer on MR. DISTRICT ATTORNEY, a school teacher on WILLIE PIPER, and any number of other roles between the ages of thirty and forty-five; but always she is merely herself acting herself (even when she changes the level of her voice or varies her accent). Similarly, Howard Adam, a hypothetical radio actor, plays a business man on CRIME DOCTOR, a judge on MYSTERY THEATRE, or a janitor on A DATE WITH JUDY, and any number of externally similar roles; but always he is only himself playing himself (even when he drops his "g's" for one characterization and speeds up his pace of delivery or raises the volume for another).

This custom whereby the radio actor substitutes his own personal qualities for the role he is to enact is a more insidious evil, and a more predominant one, than either the "mouth" method or the cliché method of characterizing. The causes for such a plague of exhibitionism are two: first, it is always relatively easy for the radio actor to act himself, and he is often the only person he has time to act; second, it is always highly flattering for the actor to hope that the tuners-in are more interested in listening to him than to the unique individual created by the dramatist.

If the truth be known, the actor who is addicted to purveying only his own charms on the microphone is making a perilous presumption. That way lies failure as an artist. For example, the late Alexander Woollcott failed as an actor when he portrayed Sheridan Whiteside in *The Man Who Came to Dinner* mainly because he was content only to be himself, to exhibit his own personal characteristics. He failed, even though he was Woollcott himself acting the character of Woollcott, because he did not act Woollcott as George S. Kaufman and Moss Hart had drawn Woollcott. He did not characterize himself as he had been created through a temperament, from a point of view, and as a functioning part of a play. He did not act the playwrights' attitude toward Woollcott. He accepted himself, perhaps perforce, as a substitute for the character. In brief, Woollcott did not know how to characterize.

To take a second example, Stark Young has pointed out that

> in naturalistic roles an actor if he has the talent can go far on this basis of putting himself in the character's place and then expressing the emotion he feels in a given situation. Mr. David Warfield, for example, in *The Music Master* could by his imagination and dramatic sympathy put himself in the old man's place, could feel what he felt, and by his admirable craft could create all this for us. But when he tried Shylock that was another matter; his Shylock was a Ghetto father, with all the simplicity, intensity, fanaticism and pathos of his type. Mr. Warfield could give us what he felt in Shylock's place, and what he gave us was genuine and moving emotion. But the point is that he could not put himself in Shylock's place. He gave us what he felt as Shylock, but could not feel the Shylock of Shakespeare. He could not enter into this persecuted Jew in a seventeenth century fantasy, a character with his due ferocity and scars but seen, nevertheless, through the perspective of a Venetian comedy written by a Renaissance poet. The trouble, obviously, with this theory is its first term. Mere sincerity of intention does not necessarily put an actor into the character's place; nor does mere genuineness of emotion on the actor's part give us the right emotion for the character. After all, what we are interested in is the role, not the actor's feeling natural.[14]

Against this brainless but fashionable practice of the actor's substituting his own dulcet personality for whatever character the playwright carefully draws, Shaw, as usual, throws the last brickbat. In a letter to Ellen Terry he wrote, "Is it not curious that the only thing not forgivable in an actor is *being* the part instead of playing it?"[15] He went on elsewhere in his theatrical criticisms to observe that "Duse's private charm has not yet been given to the public. She gives you Cesarine's charm, Marguerite Gauthier's charm, the charm of La Locandiera, the charm, in short, belonging to the character she impersonates."[16]

For emphasis, then, it must be repeated that although the radio actor must remain himself in each and every role he creates, he must not remain himself *per se,* must not be *only* himself. He must use himself and his personal qualities of heart and mind only as a medium for the expression of his characterization. In other words,

[14] Stark Young, *The Theatre* (New York: Doubleday & Company, Inc., 1927), pp. 103–104.

[15] *Shaw-Terry, op. cit.,* p. 161.

[16] Shaw, *op. cit.,* I, 133–134.

the qualities of Miss Barnett and Mr. Adam, the hypothetical radio performers, should in acting be a means toward an end, and never the end itself. "An actor uses himself . . . his voice, and the elusive quality that goes with these, exactly as Titian uses paint or Haydn sound, to create a form for his idea."[17] He uses himself in order to create a purposive characterization in accordance with the new and unique recipe of the dramatist.

4

How then can the radio actor try to accomplish in a three- or four-hour rehearsal period what a stage actor rarely succeeds in accomplishing in a few weeks?

First of all, he must work swiftly, very swiftly. And he can hurry profitably as soon as he learns, and always remembers, that every radio play—despite its appearing to be only a pack of words, only long stretches of dialogue, only talk-talk-talk—is an organization of *actions,* a sequence of *actions.* That is to say, in all radio plays the characters are always doing things or attempting to do something, are overcoming conflicts in themselves, or going around external barriers, or adjusting what they are doing to certain obstacles, and so forth. People in plays are indisputably people *in action.* What a character does or tries to do in line with his objectives, or how he is set *in action* by the playwright, is his prescribed uniqueness, his individuality. Discover a character's actions and you disclose—or create—the character.

The plot of any play is a series of causes and effects; one person *does* something, and that action causes another person to *do* something. For example, at the moment the radio play opens, the villain slaps the hero. This is an effect, "the cause of which is unknown," according to Maren Elwood. "The slap remains an effect only as long as it bears no result. But the moment the hero does something about it, or responds, the slap becomes likewise a cause, the cause of our hero's response. *What the response will be depends entirely on the dominant character-traits of the hero.*"[18] In other words, what the hero *does* will reveal his character. "In turn, whatever our hero does is an effect that in time will become a cause, as soon as it brings about action on the part of the villain, that is, action that will characterize the villain."[19] Even in a less obvious, less melodramatic play, as Samuel Selden has observed, "At all times, even during the most intellectual, and therefore abstract, passages, there should be sensed vaguely, at least, the struggling of persons to search out other persons, to approach or to avoid things, to sink or to rise higher, and to extend or to curtail other people's action"[20]—to *do* something.

Yes, "plot is character in action," and revelations of character are deduced from action. As John Howard Lawson insists, "Not only is character, as Aristotle said, 'subsidiary to the actions,' but the *only* way in which we can understand character is *through the actions to which it is subsidiary.*"[21] He maintains further, "Characters can have neither depth nor progression except insofar as they make and carry out decisions."[22] No wonder Chekhov in one of his letters wrote this advice to a writer—advice that ought to be sent to every radio actor: "Avoid depicting the hero's state of mind; you ought to try to make it clear from the hero's action."

Therefore for a swift but genuine creation of the playwright's individualized person the radio actor must search out what his character does in response to the actions of others, how he reacts to different stimuli, how he pursues his objectives, and how he alters his actions in response to different people and various happenings. The job is that simple—and that difficult. As Ernest Hemingway wrote in *Death in the Afternoon,*

> . . . I found the greatest difficulty, aside from knowing truly what you really felt, rather than what you were supposed to feel, and had been taught to feel, was to put down what really happened in action; what the actual things were which produced the emotions you experienced.

Yet when Brunetière pronounced drama to be action, "the spectacle of a *will* striving toward a goal, and conscious of the means which it employs,"[23] he did not limit it to "bang-bang-bang, and another Indian bit the dust," nor to Eliza crossing the ice or ascending

[17] Young, *op. cit.,* p. 112.

[18] Elwood, *Characters Make Your Story,* p. 93.

[19] *Ibid.*

[20] Samuel Selden, "Surface and Under Imagery in Acting," *Theatre Annual* (1944), p. 34. Cf. the same author's *First Steps in Acting* (New York: Appleton-Century-Crofts, Inc., 1947), Ch. II, "Building the Stage Image."

[21] Lawson, *Theory and Technique of Playwriting,* p. 280.

[22] *Ibid.,* p. 287.

[23] Cf. Barrett H. Clark, *European Theories of the Drama* (Cincinnati: Stewart & Kidd Company, 1918), p. 407.

into heaven, nor to Mercutio and Tybalt dueling, nor to anything else merely physical. Action is internal as well as external. Stanislavski always said to his students, "You may sit without motion and at the same time be in full action."[24] The special truth for the radio actor is this, according to Maren Elwood: "The man who speaks even one truly *significant* word is as much in action as the man who throws the villain over the cliff from the thundering express train. Both are moving the story forward."[25] Dryden defined a character's action for all time when he concluded that "every alteration or crossing of a design, every new-sprung passion, and turn of it, is part of the action, and much the noblest, except we conceived nothing to be action till the players come to blows."[26] Action is not merely motion in the course of which man changes his position in space; action is also the consciousness of man when he changes his mental condition. Speech is action—is "something we *do* in a given situation."

5

Since, then, a human being in a radio play, as in life, is always in action, the radio actor can achieve a quick but worthy characterization when, so to speak, he hunts out his verbs. He ought to search out the verb for his every moment in the play, even for the moments when he is only listening. He ought to mark his script off into "French scenes"—a new scene starting at the arrival or departure of any character—and then find his verb for each of these scenes. Eventually he ought also to find the verb for his contribution to, and function in, the entire play. The more specific the verbs, the more definite will be the actions—and consequently the characterization.

For instance, you as a radio actor may be called on to give a long and academic dissertation on pragmatism. How you will deliver that speech *in character* will depend largely on what the character's *action* is at that time. The characterization will depend on the verb you use, a verb that the playwright invariably, if sometimes subtly, indicates if you will but search for it. Your verb for the speech on pragmatism can be "to instruct" your hearers, or to "show off" your own learning, or "to postpone" a crisis, "to bore" the assemblage purposely,

[24] Stanislavski, *An Actor Prepares,* p. 34.

[25] Elwood, *op. cit.,* p. 73.

[26] Clark, *op. cit.,* p. 187.

"to cover up" a personal grief, "to test" your own skill in instructing others, "to flirt" with a visiting lady, and so on. Each of these verbs will give you as the actor a different way of reading the speech. Each verb will give you your specific task, your action, and therefore your characterization. Change the verb, and you change the character. If you do not hunt for a verb, or even if you are not conscious of the exact verb while reading, you cannot know what your character is, because you cannot know what the character is *doing.* Your reading will be delivered only as something next on the page, something in a vacuum, by something that is not essentially human and not completely individualized. There will be no characterization.

Richard Boleslavsky as the teacher of acting for The Creature brings out this important point when he asks her at one of the lessons, "What scene in Ophelia do you feel least comfortable in?" When she replies, "The third act, the performance scene," he asks her what her action is. She replies, "To be insulted." He then tells her that she has selected the wrong *action,* that her action should be to preserve her dignity. "Ophelia is a courtier's daughter," he explains.

"The Prince of the reigning house is making unsuitable remarks to her publicly. He is master of her life, the more because she loves him. He can do whatever he pleases. But even if it pleases him to kill her, she will die with the dignity appropriate to her state. Your main action is not to break down, not to show weakness, or to *display publicly your intimate emotion.* Don't forget, the whole court watches Ophelia. Take all that now as your action."[27]

To sum up: you as a radio actor working out a characterization during the *tempus fugit* of rehearsals ought to write in the margins of your script the verb for perhaps every speech, or at least for each of the "French scenes" in which you take part. In addition, you ought to keep changing these verbs as you rehearse until you find, in each case, a better verb, a more accurate one. Then in front of the microphone you can play the "music of the action," but as Boleslavsky warns, "You would have to know the difference between 'I complained' and 'I scorned' and, although the two actions followed each other, you should be just as different in their delivery as the singer is when he takes 'C' or 'C flat.'"[28]

[27] Boleslavsky, *Acting,* p. 86.

[28] *Ibid.,* p. 61.

The important value in the use of these verbs to the radio actor is that "if you have your action confined within one single word, and you know exactly what that action is, you have it inside you on the call of a split second. How then can you be disturbed when the time comes for delivery?" How can you complain at the rude changes of time and scene in radio playwriting, or lose your character progression during the music bridge? "Your scene, or part, is a long string of beads—beads of action. You play with them as you play with a rosary. You can start anywhere, any time, and go as far as you wish, if you have a good solid hold on the beads themselves."[29] You will always have a good hold on the actions that alone make your characterization a new and individualized one.

It may be true, as Maren Elwood has observed, that characters tend to speak more or less alike—that is, without showing individualizing traits of behavior—when everything is going normally or smoothly. "But when characters are reacting emotionally to impacts or opposing forces, whether these stimuli rise from within themselves or from forces outside themselves, the actors will react characteristically, that is, *individually.*"[30]

SELECTED READINGS

Boleslavsky, Richard, *Acting; The First Six Lessons.* New York: Theatre Arts, Inc., 1933. See the Third Lesson, "Dramatic Action," pp. 49–64.

Elwood, Maren, *Characters Make Your Story.* Boston: Houghton Mifflin Company, 1942. Consult Chap. X, "Action and Reaction," pp. 92–100.

Firkins, O. W., "Action in Drama—What It Is and Is Not," *Theatre Arts Monthly,* XIV, No. 7 (July, 1930), 591–596.

Lawson, John Howard, *Theory and Technique of Playwriting.* New York: G. P. Putnam's Sons, 1936. There is much of value, though, from a writer's point of view, in Part III, Chap. I, "The Law of Conflict," pp. 163–168, and Chap. II, "Dramatic Action," pp. 168–173, as well as in Part IV, Chap. III, "Progression," pp. 244–262.

Rapoport, I., "The Work of the Actor," translated by Ben Blake and Lyuba Vendrovskaya, *Theatre Workshop,* I, No. 1 (October–December, 1936). Study especially pp. 21–38. The same material appears on pp. 49–66 in *Acting; A Handbook of the Stanislavski Method,* edited by Toby Cole (New York: Lear Publishers, Inc., 1947).

Stanislavski, Constantin, *An Actor Prepares,* translated by Elizabeth Reynolds Hapgood. New York: Theatre Arts, Inc., 1936. See Chap. III, "Action," pp. 31–50.

[29] *Ibid.*

[30] Elwood, *op. cit.,* pp. 75–76.

DISCUSSION

Discuss the following statements. First, working at the microphone, perhaps each student can attempt to read each statement as the utterance of a fresh and highly individualized human being. Secondly, each student can reread his selection in an attempt to achieve a characterization suggested by the class, but he should avoid the use of dialects or vocal tricks. Thirdly, each student can read his selection as himself.

1. ". . . . the most exasperating of all theatrical follies, the pet recourse of the spurious actor who goes to his make-up box for character and to some mimic's trick for his speech, [is] a stage foreign accent." (George Bernard Shaw)

2. "In the drama the actors act as substitute stimuli of flesh and blood. They are not substitutes for the persons whose names they carry . . . but substitutes for the teller's mental image of those persons." (Arthur Koestler)

3. "We sometimes see on the Academy walls the portrait of some successful trader, some local functionary, whose vacuous face, composed to a pompous dignity, and saucer-like eyes excite our mirth or ridicule; yet his friends recognize it as a perfect likeness, and the painter can truly say, 'I copied the man faithfully, exactly as I found him: there he is to the life.' Yet it is no likeness. Now suppose the sitter to have fallen into the hands of a real artist—a Sir Joshua Reynolds or a Sir Thomas Lawrence, or our own Frederick Leighton—the result would be very different. Such a painter would say to himself, 'This must be a successful man, for he has fought the battle of life well; he has encountered and triumphed over many difficulties; and must have shown sagacity, cleverness, shrewdness in his trade. When he composes himself to a formal attitude of dignity and strives to look "genteel," he will cease to be himself: his mind will be eclipsed, and his face assume a vacuity. But I will pierce to his real and better nature and show him with his faculties kindled and stimulated by his favorite calling.' And the portrait that is the result will be full of life, shrewdness, and intelligence. There is the difference between acting of character, and the exhibiting merely external accidents." (Percy Fitzgerald)

4. ". . . . play construction in drama of any intellectual quality has no other end than the effective presentment of character." (William Archer)

5. ". . . . of all the infuriating absurdities that human perversity has evolved, this painted-on 'character acting' is the only one that entirely justifies manslaughter." (George Bernard Shaw)

6. "The foundation of all emotional response . . . is characterization . . . it is characters that sell stories." (Maren Elwood)

7. The reason why *Eugen Onegin* "never quite came off, in spite of many touching passages, is that both authors were weak at the delineation of character . . . . The sustaining of dramatic interest without the aid of characterization, by feeling alone, no matter how varied this may be, has always seemed to me an undertaking to strain the expressive powers . . . ." (Virgil Thomson)

8. "Reduce any dramatic masterpiece to a simple statement of its plot and the story will seem so trite as hardly to be worth dramatization. For instance, a man of jealous nature, passionately in love with his young wife, is made by the lies and trickery of a friend to believe that his wife has been intriguing with another of his friends . . . . In a fury of jealousy the husband kills his wife and then himself . . . . It is, of course, the story of *Othello*—a masterpiece because Shakespeare knew Othello, Iago, Desdemona, and Cassio so intimately that by their interplay of character upon character they shape every scene perfectly . . . . All depends upon a careful study of the people involved. What must they do to give rise to such a situation—not each by himself, but when brought together under the conditions of the scene?" (From *Dramatic Technique,* by George Pierce Baker, published by Houghton Mifflin Company)

9. "Stendhal . . . locates or fixes his characters within the pattern of their mental habits . . . their habits of fearing or desiring, loving or fighting, their different ways of pursuing happiness." (Matthew Josephson)

10. ". . . . specific directions for character-drawing would be like rules for becoming six feet high. Either you have it in you, or you have it not." (William Archer)

EXERCISES

A. ORAL MAKE-UPS

In the following selections, discover whether or not the mere assumption of an oral disguise is enough for the adequate creation of a radio character. Is anything beyond a speech trick needed? If it is, indicate by your own approach to the reading, or from the suggestions of the class, what in addition can be done to attain a genuine characterization.

1. *Japanese:* A LESSON IN JAPANESE*

OFFICER: Naturally, we cannot be troubled to take you with us as prisoner, so — there can be but one answer . . . I must tell you my men wait for you on the other side of those trees — with bayonets . . . I give you — a gentleman's way out . . . Here is . . . a pistol. It contains — one bullet. You understand?

2. *British:* THE IMPORTANCE OF BEING EARNEST†

LADY BRACKNELL: Now to minor matters. Are your parents living?

JACK: I have lost both my parents.

LADY BRACKNELL: Both? . . . That seems like carelessness. Who was your father? He was evidently a man of some wealth. Was he born in what the Radical papers call the purple of commerce, or did he rise from the ranks of the aristocracy?

JACK: I am afraid I really don't know. The fact is, Lady Bracknell, I said I had lost my parents. It would be nearer the truth to say that my parents had lost me . . . I don't actually know who I am by birth. I was . . . Well, I was found.

LADY BRACKNELL: Found!

JACK: The late Mr. Thomas Cardew, an old gentleman of a very charitable and kindly disposition, found me, and gave me the name of Worthing, because he happened to have a first-class ticket for Worthing in his pocket at the time. Worthing is a place in Sussex. It is a seaside resort.

LADY BRACKNELL: Where did the charitable gentleman who had a first-class ticket for this seaside resort find you?

JACK: (GRAVELY) In a hand-bag.

* By Neal Hopkins.
† From the play by Oscar Wilde.

LADY BRACKNELL: A hand-bag?

JACK: (VERY SERIOUSLY) Yes, Lady Bracknell. I was in a hand-bag — a somewhat large, black leather hand-bag, with handles to it — an ordinary hand-bag in fact.

LADY BRACKNELL: In what locality did this Mr. James, or Thomas, Cardew come across this ordinary hand-bag?

JACK: In the cloak-room of Victoria Station. It was given to him in mistake for his own.

LADY BRACKNELL: The cloak-room at Victoria Station?

JACK: Yes. The Brighton line.

LADY BRACKNELL: The line is immaterial. Mr. Worthing, I confess I feel somewhat bewildered by what you have just told me. To be born, or at any rate bred, in a hand-bag, whether it had handles or not, seems to me to display a contempt for the ordinary decencies of family life that remind one of the worst excesses of the French Revolution. And I presume you know what that unfortunate movement led to?

3. *Ministerial:* RED ROSES FOR ME*

RECTOR: All things in life, the evil and the good, the orderly and disorderly, are mixed with the life of the Church Militant here on earth. We honour our brother, not for what may have been an error in him, but for the truth forever before his face. We dare not grudge him God's forgiveness and rest eternal because he held no banner above a man-made custom . . . Stand aside, and go your way of smoky ignorance, leaving me to welcome him whose turbulence has sunken into a deep sleep, and who cometh now as the water of Shiloah that goes softly, and sings sadly of peace.

4. *Southern:* 27 WAGONS FULL OF COTTON†

FLORA: I wouldn' dare to expose myself like that to the sun. I take a terrible burn. I'll never forget the burn I took one time. It was on Moon Lake

* From *Red Roses for Me,* by Sean O'Casey. Copyright, 1943, by Sean O'Casey. Used by permission of the Macmillan Company.

† From *27 Wagons Full of Cotton,* by Tennessee Williams. Copyright, 1945, by Tennessee Williams. Published by New Directions. Reprinted with the permission of the author's agent, Liebling-Wood.

one Sunday before I was married. I never did like t' go fishin' but this young fellow, one of the Peterson boys, insisted that we go fishin'. Well, he didn't catch nothin' but jus' kep' fishin' an' fishin' an' I set there in th' boat with all that hot sun on me. I said, stay under the willows. But he wouldn' lissen to me, an' sure enough I took such an awful burn I had t' sleep on m' stummick th' nex' three nights . . . I fell in the lake once, too. Also with one of the Peterson boys. On another fishing trip. That was a wild bunch of boys, those Peterson boys. I never went out with 'em but something happened which made me wish I hadn't. One time, sunburned. One time, nearly drowned. One time — poison ivy! Well, lookin' back on it now, we had a good deal of fun in spite of it, though.

5. *Jewish and German:* AWAKE AND SING*

BESSIE: (CALLING) Come in here, Schlosser. (SOTTO VOCE) Wait, I'll give him a piece of my mind . . . What's the matter the dumbwaiter's broken again?

SCHLOSSER: (SLIGHTLY OFF) Mr. Wimmer sends new ropes next week. I got a sore arm.

BESSIE: He should live so long, your Mr. Wimmer. For seven years already he's sending new ropes. No dumbwaiter, no hot water, no steam — In a respectable house they don't allow such conditions.

SCHLOSSER: (COMING ON) In a decent house dogs are not running to make dirty the hallway.

BESSIE: Tootsie's making dirty? Our Tootsie's making dirty in the hall?

SCHLOSSER: I tell you yesterday again. You must not leave her —

BESSIE: (INDIGNANTLY) Excuse me! Please don't yell on my ear! From now on we don't walk up the stairs no more. You keep it so clean we'll fly in the windows.

SCHLOSSER: I speak to Mr. Wimmer.

BESSIE: Speak! Speak! Tootsie walks behind me like a lady any time, any place. So goodbye . . . goodbye, Mr. Schlosser.

SCHLOSSER: (FADING) I tell you dot — I verk very hard here. My arms is . . .

BESSIE: Tootsie should lay all day in the kitchen maybe!

6. *Italian:* A BELL FOR ADANO*

BASILE: You have not seen my cart, have you, Mister Major? You would not forget it if you had seen it. It has four scenes painted on it — from the Holy Word, and they are all concerned with eating. There is the miracle of the loaves and fishes. There is the Last Supper. There is the widow's jar which never emptied no matter how much food she took out. There is the wedding at Cana where the water turned to wine. And all of the people in these pictures are fat people, because mine is the cart for food. I do not think it is sacrilegious that even Jesus himself is fat on my cart.

But now how can I put between the shafts my fat horse, whose name is General Eisenhower, in honor of our deliverer, and put my fat self on the seat and drive around with my pictures of fat and holy people — when the people of Adano are starving? This fills me with shame. (PAUSE) There is nothing in all the proclamations which says Americans came to Adano in order to make the people die of hunger — to die of thirst, is there? Thank you, Mister Major.

7. *French:* KING HENRY V†

KATHARINE: Your majesty shall mock at me; I cannot speak your England.

KING HENRY: O fair Katharine, if you will love me soundly with your French heart, I will be glad to hear you confess it brokenly with your English tongue. Do you like me, Kate?

KATHARINE: Pardonnez-moi, I cannot tell vat is 'like me.'

KING HENRY: An angel is like you, Kate, and you are like an angel.

KATHARINE: O bon Dieu! les langues des hommes sont pleines de tromperies.

KING HENRY: But, Kate, dost thou understand thus much English, — Can't thou love me?

* From the radio script by Paul Osborne, based on John Hersey's novel. Reprinted with the permission of Alfred A. Knopf, Inc.

† By William Shakespeare, V, 2.

KATHARINE: Is it possible dat I should love de enemy of France?

KING HENRY: No; it is not possible you should love the enemy of France, Kate; but in loving me you should love the friend of France; for I love France so well that I will not part with a village of it; I will have it all mine: and, Kate, when France is mine and I am yours, then yours is France and you are mine.

KATHARINE: I cannot tell vat is dat.

KING HENRY: No, Kate? I will tell thee in French; which I am sure will hang upon my tongue like a new-married wife about her husband's neck, hardly to be shook off. Quand j'ai la possession de France, et quand vous avez la possession de moi, — let me see, what then? Saint Denis be my speed! — donc votre est France et vous êtes mienne. It is as easy for me, Kate, to conquer the kingdom as to speak so much more French: I shall never move thee in French, unless it be to laugh at me.

KATHERINE: Sauf votre honneur, le Français que vous parlez, il est meilleur que l'Anglais lequel je parle.

KING HENRY: No, faith, is't not, Kate; but thy speaking of my tongue, and I thine, most truly falsely, must needs be granted to be much at one. Come, your answer in broken music, — for thy voice is music and thy English broken; therefore, queen of all, Katharine, break thy mind to me in broken English — wilt thou have me?

KATHARINE: Dat is as it sall please de roi mon père.

KING HENRY: May, it will please him well, Kate, — it shall please him well.

KATHARINE: Den it sall also content me.

KING HENRY: Upon that I kiss your hand, and I call you my queen.

8. *Irish:* OAK LEAVES AND LAVENDER*

MONICA: (SHUDDERING) I wish I could keep away from the thoughts of death: were you to go, I should be a desolate little ship lost on a lonely sea.

DRISHOGUE: It is inevitable we should think of what is everywhere around us.

MONICA: Oh, Drishogue, surely death cannot mean the loss of life!

DRISHOGUE: Perhaps not; I only know it means the loss of many lovely things:

* From *Oak Leaves and Lavender,* by Sean O'Casey. Copyright, 1947, by Sean O'Casey. Used by permission of The Macmillan Company.

the moving patterns of flying birds; the stroll through crowded streets, crudely strewn about, that the moon regenerates into silvered haunts of meditative men; the musical wile of waves rushing towards us, or slowly bidding us farewell; the wild flowers tossing themselves onto the field and into the hedgerow; the sober ecstasy, or jewelled laugh, of children playing; the river's rowdy rush or graceful gliding into sea or lake; the sun asthride the hills, or rainfall teeming down aslant behind them; a charming girl, shy, but ready with her finest favours — Oh, these are dear and lovely things to lose!

MONICA: They may be shadows of finer things to come.

DRISHOGUE: Give me but these, and God can keep whatever is behind them. But let us get away before the others come. We ought to go before the house awakens.

MONICA: (A LITTLE IMPATIENTLY) Oh, let them come! To be afraid of what we've done is to be like a young oak shivering in a summer breeze. Sometimes a quiet life becomes too precious to us all. Why should you fear the taunt in the rosy hours spent with the girl you like?

DRISHOGUE: And love, too, darling.

MONICA: For the time being, anyway.

DRISHOGUE: Till time has grown so old that things remembered lose their colour, and are growing grey.

MONICA: Dark woe to think how things have changed so sudden!

DRISHOGUE: And you must be as the Irish lass of twice a hundred years ago, who sold her rock and sold her reel and sold her spinning-wheel, to buy her love a sword of steel to fix him fitly in the fight for the rights of man.

MONICA: I'll have to do it soon enough; but first come, love, to my room again, to dream away from us a moment more of restless turnings to the sound of war; and give darkness another chance to hush a lover and his lass into the sweet secrecy of themselves.

DRISHOGUE: I ought to go before the house awakens. Look! The moon is pale and worn after dancing through the sky as the beauty of the night, and is bidding goodbye at the door of dawn.

MONICA: False dawn, with hate in all its lovely face!

9. *Characters from Dickens:* DICKENS QUIZ*

A. "What I want is facts. Teach these boys and girls nothing but facts. Facts alone are wanted in life. Plant nothing else, and root out everything else. Stick to facts, sir!" (Thomas Gradgrind)

B. "It is a far, far better thing that I do than I have ever done; it is a far, far better rest that I go to than I have ever known." (Sydney Carton)

C. "It was as true as turnips is. It was as true as taxes is. And nothin's truer than them." (Mr. Barkis)

D. "'Father' is rather vulgar, my dear. The word 'papa,' besides, gives a pretty form to the lips. Papa, potatoes, poultry, prunes, and prism are all very good words for the lips, especially prunes and prism." (Mrs. General)

E. "I am constantly being bailed out, like a boat. Somebody always does it for me. I can't do it, you know, for I never have any money; but somebody does it, God bless him!" (Harold Skimpole)

F. "Buy an annuity cheap, and make your life interesting to yourself and everyone else that watches the speculation." (Jonas Chuzzlewit)

G. "Whatever the world's opinions on the subject may be, Pip, your sister is a — fine — figure — of — a — woman!" (Joe Gargery)

H. "Don't ask me whether I won't take none, or whether I will, but leave the bottle on the chimley piece, and let me put my lips to it when I am so disposed." (Sairey Gamp)

I. "At present, and until something turns up (which I am, I may say, hourly expecting), I have nothing to bestow but advice." (Wilkins Micawber)

J. "I am a lone, lorn creetur, and everythink goes contrairy with me." (Mrs. Gummidge)

* From *Dickens Quiz,* by Howard Collins, *Saturday Review of Literature,* November 16, 1946.

Now, for the wide use of the imagination in characterization, here is a set of inhuman or fantastic roles for the radio actor to create.

B. FANTASTIC VOICES

1. MRS. MURGATROYD'S DIME*

A DIME: I'm nobody you'd remember. You've seen me and them like me all over the place, but never noticed us particularly, I bet. I'm a dime. But no ordinary dime — see? Most dimes don't rate much respect around. Good for a tip or a cup a' coffee and sinkers. Or a shoeshine. Or they're the thin dimes a lot of people ain't worth. Uh-uh. Not me. I'm kind of a special dime.

What's my name? Well, my official moniker is E. Pluribus Unum. But that's not what I call myself. I'm Mrs. Murgatroyd's dime. Who's Mrs. Murgatroyd? Say, don't rush me, don't rush me. I'll keep talking.

When I first get out of the Mint, I was just a kid. Y'know, shiny and new, ready for anything? I'm all excited the day I first enter civilian life — and so, bang! just like that I'm dropped in a kid's piggy bank. I stay there six months. Nearly went stir-crazy. Then one night the kid's old man breaks open the bank and goes on a spree. I bought a mug of beer on Third Avenue.

(CLINK ON BAR)

After that, everything gets a little hazy, I moved so fast. I was on a bus —

(BUS BELL)

Fifth Avenue. I bought a can of beans for a housewife —

(CASH REGISTER)

I took a fellow to an early-bird matinee. Yep, I even got religion. I was dropped into a collection basket — by a millionaire.

(SOUND OF DIME ON OTHER COINS)

Geez, I was glad he let go of me, too. He'd pinched me black and blue. Then I was all over the place. Bought a loaf of bread, got a girl a lipstick at the five-and-ten . . . You'd be surprised what a dime can do. The five-and-ten was nice. Saw a lot of the fellows there. We jawed about what was going on. One of the 1930 dimes kept complaining about the

* By John Latouche. Reprinted with the permission of the author.

country going to the dogs. Kept speechifyin' about disaster. He turned out to be a phony, anyway. Then they threw me out for change.

(CASH REGISTER . . . CLINK OF COIN ON COUNTER)

Gee, what a hot hand I landed in. The dame was in a hurry — she drops me in the street.

(SOUND OF DIME ON PAVEMENT AND ROLLING)

Didn't even look back. I lays there. Nobody cares. "E. Pluribus," I says to myself, "you've fallen low." And I had to fight to keep from bursting out crying like a common penny. But then — then it was Mrs. Murgatroyd clapped eyes on me.

2. BAMBI*

(The autumn wind is blowing through the bare branches of a large oak tree with a menacing hum. Near the tip of a high branch are the only two leaves left on the tree. The first leaf has the voice of a man, and the second leaf the voice of a woman.)

FIRST LEAF: Are you all right?

SECOND LEAF: Yes, I'm all right.

FIRST LEAF: But you're trembling.

SECOND LEAF: I'm not sure of my hold any more. It's so hard to hang on.

FIRST LEAF: You can rest awhile; the wind has stopped blowing.

SECOND LEAF: We seem to be the only two leaves left on our trees.

FIRST LEAF: Yes. But we can't complain. We've outlived many others.

SECOND LEAF: I wonder -- which of us will go first —

FIRST LEAF: Sh-h-h. Let's not think about such things. Let's remember how wonderful it all was.

SECOND LEAF: Yes, of course. Have I changed much?

FIRST LEAF: Not in the least. Here and there may be a little golden spot. But it's hardly noticeable . . . and it only makes you more lovely.

SECOND LEAF: Thank you. I don't believe you — not altogether. But I thank you because you're so kind. I'm just beginning to understand how kind you really are.

* From *The Art of Walt Disney,* by Robert D. Feild, published by The Macmillan Company.

(THE SOUND OF THE WIND INCREASES AGAIN)

FIRST LEAF: Listen — the wind has started again.

SECOND LEAF: Oh, I'm frightened. It blows so hard and I — I haven't the strength to fight against it. I'm so afraid.

FIRST LEAF: You mustn't be afraid.

SECOND LEAF: But why do we fall? What happens to us?

FIRST LEAF: I don't know. Some say one thing — some another. But nobody really knows.

SECOND LEAF: What is under us? Do we feel anything? Do we know about ourselves down there?

FIRST LEAF: I don't know. I'm only sure of one thing. We grew here for some reason. So there must be a reason — why we fall.

SECOND LEAF: Yes — there must be a reason. (A PAUSE) I think I'm going to fall now.

FIRST LEAF: Are you still afraid?

SECOND LEAF: No — no. I'm not afraid — any more.

3. BRETTON WOODS*

NARRATOR: This is once more an old-time story. First we'll show you how it was, then we'll show you how it can be. Once upon a time . . . there were three countries.

COUNTRY X: (A WOMAN) Country X . . .

COUNTRY Y: Country Y . . .

COUNTRY Z: And Country Z.

NARRATOR: Country X was a nice little country, but very little indeed. In order to get along at all, she had to trade with other countries. But she didn't have much to sell, and she couldn't get much for what she did sell. What she really needed was equipment for producing more. Could she borrow the money?

COUNTRY Y: (VILLAIN) Don't borrow the money, little Country X. Why borrow at all? Trade with me, dear little country. Trade with me and all will be well. What have you to sell to me?

* By Peter Lyon. Reprinted with the permission of the author.

COUNTRY X: I have raw materials, and that is all, alas, for I have no industry to manufacture goods of my own!

COUNTRY Y: (GLOATING) What could be better? You have the raw materials — I have the factories. I will pay you well. We will get along famously. Sign here, please.

COUNTRY Z: Just a moment! Be careful, little Country X! Do not deal with this villainous Country Y! All you will get will be tears and unhappiness! Deal with me, instead!

COUNTRY X: But I need equipment, machinery. Country Y will give me a good price for my raw materials, and then I can buy equipment and machinery from him. I think you are nothing but a rich fool, Country Z! Go away and peddle your papers.

COUNTRY Y: Well spoken, my dear. Sign here.

COUNTRY X: There! Now here are my raw materials. Pay me, please.

COUNTRY Y: Uh — pay you. Yes, yes, of course. Excuse me. I have an urgent call I must make.

COUNTRY X: Hey, pay me!

COUNTRY Y: Uh — yes. Just so. Pay you. I'll tell you what. I'll pay you in aspirin tablets and harmonicas. How's that? Fair exchange . . . no robbery . . .

COUNTRY X: I want machinery and equipment or cash on the barrel-head.

COUNTRY Y: (GETTING TOUGH) Machinery and equipment? I need that for plans of my own. I'll pay you in blocked marks.

COUNTRY X: Blocked marks? What are blocked marks?

COUNTRY Y: They're money, of course . . .

COUNTRY X: Good! What I wanted.

COUNTRY Y: . . . except, of course, that they must stay inside my borders. They'll be put to your credit, of course.

COUNTRY X: Credit! But I don't want credit! I want cash!

COUNTRY Y: You'll take what you get, and like it. Either aspirin tablets and harmonicas, or blocked marks. Remember, you signed the contract. Oh, yes, and by the way, I can't say I like your prime minister. Get rid of him. Kick the rest of the cabinet out, too, while you're at it. They've been doing entirely too much talking about non-aggression.

COUNTRY X: Now just a minute. I'll call my friend, Country Z.

COUNTRY Y: Country Z? Oh, yes. Now that I've got your raw materials, I was thinking about him. I think I'll just go and pick a fight with him.

4. ELSIE THE COW*

ELSIE: But anybody can give a party for a few pennies!

ELMER: I don't want to give any doggone party! I'm not spending my hard-earned cash to feed a bunch of broken-down relatives.

ELSIE: Now, dear, our party will be so good that even your relatives will say nice things!

ELMER: I don't want them saying nice things if it's going to cost me money.

ELSIE: But it won't, Elmer. You can entertain royally with a few glasses of those creamy, smooth-spreading Borden's Cocktail Spreads. Just serve them with a little imagination and —

ELMER: I don't like imagination with my cheese. I like bread.

ELSIE: But, angel, we can't use that much bread these days. And that's where the imagination comes in. We'll slice rosy-cheeked apples and crisp russet pears, and spread the slices with Borden's Cocktail Spreads. Vera-sharp is grand on apples, and Smokey is heavenly on pear slices.

ELMER: Apples! Pears! Why not potatoes?

ELSIE: A fine idea. We'll dress up potato chips with Blue Cheese Spread. And, for a special holiday touch, we'll sandwich a thick layer of creamy-rich Pimento Special between halves of walnuts. And fill crunchy celery with savory Olive Pimento Spread. There! Could you ask for anything more?

ELMER: Sure, I could! If I'm paying for this shindig, I want something sweet.

ELSIE: And you shall have it, darling. Nobody would think of giving a party without Borden's Ice Cream. It makes everybody feel so — so party-ish. It's such delightful refreshment and such grand food at the same time. Made with rich milk and cream —

ELMER: Look, Mrs. Lotsa-Talk! All I want to know is what flavor we're going to have?

* By Thelma Walker, from *Time* Magazine, November 11, 1946, p. 10. Reproduced through the courtesy of The Borden Company.

ELSIE: Since you're paying, you pick. All flavors of Borden's Ice Cream are delicious. For Borden's uses only the finest flavorings, the —

ELMER: Please, Elsie! Beulah and I have heard the Borden spiel a million times!

ELSIE: And you're likely to hear it a million more. For everybody everywhere is saying — if it's Borden's, it's GOT to be good!

5. FINIAN'S RAINBOW*

FINIAN: You're an imposter. You can't be a leprechaun. You're too tall.

OG: Yes, and I'm getting taller.

FINIAN: Naturally — gallivantin' about America. Everything gets bigger and better over here. What are ye after, anyhow?

OG: Alack, alack, alack — <u>and</u> willo-waly. I weep for Ireland.

FINIAN: You weep? Why, what's happened?

OG: No colleens smile and no children sing. A blight has fallen over Ireland.

FINIAN: The British are back!

OG: Never have I seen such a curse befall a folk, in all my round hundred and — (NUDGING HIS MEMORY) fifty-nine years. (WAILING) Alas, poor Ireland!

FINIAN: A fine lot of fairy folk you are, you and your associates, lettin' all this happen! Where's your magical power?

OG: We've lost it.

FINIAN: (OUTRAGED) You mean you've gone and lost the power to make wishes?

OG: (MISERABLY) Aye.

FINIAN: What has Ireland to live for now? Answer me that!

OG: Doom and gloom — (WAILING AGAIN) D-o-o-m and gl-o-o-m!

FINIAN: Who's the author of this foul outrage?

OG: A monster.

FINIAN: (HE WASN'T COUNTING ON THIS) A monster, eh? You mean the old flame-breathin' type, with the head of a dragon?

OG: Oh, no. This is a tiny wee monster, with the brain of a banker. (SLYLY) About your size.

* From *Finian's Rainbow*, by E. Y. Harburg and Fred Saidy. Reprinted with the permission of Alfred A. Knopf, Inc.

FINIAN: (HIS COURAGE UP AGAIN) Lead me to 'im! A tiny one, eh? Lead me to 'im! I'll sizzle his gizzard. (HE SIZZLES) I'll throttle his larynx. (HE THROTTLES) I'll rend him apart, vertebra by vertebra! (HE RENDS) Who is he? (A ROAR) Who is this monster?

OG: (COURTEOUSLY) Excuse me for pointing, Mr. McLonergan, but it's you.

FINIAN: Me!

OG: It's you who cast this curse on Ireland.

FINIAN: You're mad!

OG: You brought on the blight yourself when you stole our crock of gold — the little crock that gives us our power to wish.

FINIAN: Don't be superstitious, man; it's bad luck.

6. THE ODYSSEY OF RUNYON JONES*

VOICE: (BOOMING OUT ON P.A.) When you hear the time signal it will be exactly half past one-sixty-two on Uranus.

TIME: Fah! That was thirty-seven thousandths of a second late! Miss Chrono, make a note of that. We'll have to make it up in the year seven billion, three hundred two.

CHRONO: Yes, sir.

TIME: Now what was it you wanted, little man?

RUNYON: Well, sir, could you tell me how I could get to Curgatory, because my dog Pootzy —

TIME: Oh, yes. Was he a delinquent dog?

RUNYON: No, sir, a mongrel.

VOICE: (ON P.A.) When you hear the musical note it will be the hundred and seventy-second millionth anniversary of the birth of the first dinosaur.

(GREAT BOOMING OF THE CHINESE GONG)

TIME: Miss Chrono, remind me to send an anniversary message of felicitations to Mother Nature.

CHRONO: Yes, sir. Can I have time to go to lunch?

TIME: Later, later. (TO RUNYON) Where did you say the dog was?

* From *Thirteen by Corwin,* by Norman Corwin. Reproduced by permission of Henry Holt and Company, Inc. Copyright, 1942, by Norman Corwin.

RUNYON: In Curgatory. I just want to know how to get there.

(LOUD BUZZER ON . . . RECEIVER LIFTED)

TIME: Now what's that?

CHRONO: Main office. Chrono speaking.

TIME: My, my! Look at that green clock. It's getting toward morning on Neptune already.

CHRONO: . . . Yes, I'll tell him . . . Keep your shirt on. He's right here.

TIME: (TESTILY) Who's that? Who's on the phone?

CHRONO: Our agent on Alcyone. He says they need a shipment of sand very badly.

TIME: Why?

CHRONO: The sands of time are running low all through the Archipelago of the Pleiades.

TIME: Tell him we're digging some new pits on Mercury, and that he'll have his order in two shakes of a comet's tail.

CHRONO: (STILL OFF, RELAYS TIME'S MESSAGE, AND HANGS UP WHILE:)

TIME: Finest platinum sand in the system. Uh . . . (WITH SURPRISE) What are _you_ doing here?

RUNYON: Don't you remember, Father Time? I'm the one who is looking for my dog. I came —

TIME: Oh, yes, yes! Mr. Bones!

RUNYON: Jones.

TIME: You're from Earth, aren't you?

RUNYON: Yes, sir.

TIME: (SHARPLY) Well, then, I want you to know that I am heartily ashamed of the kind of time they have down there in Greenwich.

RUNYON: Yes, sir.

TIME: And I want you to understand why.

RUNYON: Yes, sir.

TIME: Because it's so _mean!_ It's _pretty mean time!_

Next the students should be trained to mark down in the margin of their books the verbs for their actions and reactions, and then to read their lines while concentrating on these verbs.

Then the same exercises should be read again with the students arbitrarily changing the verbs they use in order to see the change that is effected in the acting.

Then the same exercises should be read again with the class attempting to discover what verbs the actor had in mind while reading.

C. PREVIOUS EXERCISES

Turn back to the exercises for all the preceding chapters and read the selections at the microphone, giving full attention to the characterization problems. Mark down in the margins of the pages the verbs for your actions and reactions, and then read your lines while concentrating on these verbs.

Read the same selection a second and third time, arbitrarily *changing* your verbs to see what effect such changes have on the reading, on the characterization.

Read your selections a fourth time with still different main verbs and see if the class can discover what verbs you had in mind while reading.

D. IMPROVISATIONS

In the following experimental exercises for reactions to a stimulus—which are also exercises in actual listening—first read over and absorb completely the full situation. Then put into words at the microphone your response, your reaction—the thing that you do. Try to make your sentence-reaction say as much as possible.

Prepare this exercise first as yourself, in your own character. Find your personal verbs. Next assume another character and repeat your sentence-reaction with other verbs. Finally assume a third character in the same situation.

1. You hear your mother open the door to your boy friend and tell him that you are not at home.

2. You have been working on a physics experiment of great importance; it is now finished; you realize your success or failure. You telephone your superior, he answers. You speak. You repeat the situation, telephoning your wife or your husband, your closest friend.

3. You meet your brother for the last time in the death cell. You speak first as soon as the guard leaves. Next, repeat the exercise with yourself in prison as a reporter comes to get an interview.

4. A stage star has granted you an interview. You enter the dressing room and speak first.

5. You ask for a loan of ten dollars from (a) your father, (b) a good friend, (c) your worst enemy, (d) a stranger on the street, (e) the Chief Justice of the United States.

6. You are led up to the judges' stand and awarded an Oscar for your acting in motion pictures. After the applause, you address the gathering.

7. You are sitting in a restaurant booth viciously gossiping about a certain person. That person rises from the adjoining booth, comes over to your table. You speak first.

8. You have just finished painting a room in your friend's apartment. It is hot. You are dirty, exhausted, and irritated. Your friend suggests you come over tomorrow and paint the other room. You reply with one sentence.

9. A man rings your doorbell. You answer. After the greetings, he says that he is your father. But you are positive he is not; your father is dead.

10. You return to your apartment at night, after the theatre, unlock the door, and find the lights on and a stranger sitting in the chair by your fireplace.

11. You have just told your family about the prize scholarship you have won. The family insists that you cannot quit your job and leave home in order to study dramatics.

12. You have just heard the news that a good friend of yours has been killed in an accident. You leave your room, go down in the elevator, and meet him or her on the ground floor.

13. At the opera with your wife or husband you are bored; you want to go to a night club. You say you want to go. He or she refuses to go. You insist on leaving.

14. You have learned today that your mother is not truly yours. You return home and meet your foster mother. She asks you why you have come home so early.

15. You apply for a job. After a brief interview, the employer asks you to tell him why you consider yourself indispensable to his organization.

16. Make up at least three situations for the sentence-reaction: "What in the world — ! Harry, what are you doing here?"

17. You are writing a letter to your folks in which you say you are leaving home. You finish the letter, seal it, and are about to address it when your mother comes into the room and asks you what is in the letter. You answer.

18. You answer the telephone. You have been waiting for this promised call. You learn it is from the friend who had promised to phone you five hours before.

19. It is early morning. You have been down at campaign headquarters for the counting of the ballots. You have lost. You come home and meet your wife, and you know by the look on her face that she knows you have been beaten. You speak first.

20. You have been long in love with a man. One day he introduces you to his wife. You acknowledge the greeting, and then speak to him.

21. You speak a full sentence or two the moment after the door has been shut (1) on a person who has threatened to take away your job; (2) on an old society fool who has invited you to dinner.

22. You find the action for the sentence: "Shut off your radio, will you? What do you think this is? I'm trying to sleep."

23. You open your door, and a tottering old man, blood-covered, stumbles in, and falls to the floor at your feet.

24. After a long and tormented pause, the person with you says, "Say something." You do.

25. You wake up in a large gold room. You look around at all the elaborate furnishings. A symphony orchestra is playing near by. You see that your right arm is in a cast. A stranger comes up to your bedside. You speak.

Now turn the above improvisations into duets. Add a second actor to each of the situations. The first student will give the new, fresh, unprepared response to the given situation; the second student, as the other character in the scene, will respond to the first.

E. ACTION VERBS

In groups of two's and three's the students should prepare brief scenes for delivery in class at the microphone—scenes which they should repeat several times with changes in the verbs. Only by reading the same scenes with *different* verbs each time can they learn the decisive effect verbs have on characterization in acting.

Chapter VII . . MICROPHONE READING: ILLUSION OF THE FIRST TIME

1

Even when the radio actor completely understands the meaning (and perhaps the function) of his speeches, it is not easy for him to read them in performance and not sound patently as if he were reading them. Logical comprehension of content, though essential, is not sufficient to produce in acting the desired effect of people talking to people. Clarity in the communication of meanings will not in itself insure the necessary aliveness and immediacy of the conversational quality. Consequently, once the radio actor understands the meaning of his speeches, he must turn them into conversation, since a play, in one sense, is in its entirety a designed conversation.

In order not to sound as if he were merely reading, the actor at the microphone must do what he does in actual, everyday conversation, must have the same *mental activity* in the one as in the other. According to Wayland Parrish,

> As our minds create the thought we speak in conversing, so they must *re*create the thought we speak in reading. We must have a vivid, intense realization of the meaning of what we read *while we are reading it.* With all our mental force we must bear down on the thought at the moment of utterance. This is not merely to say that we should know the meaning of what we read. We may understand thoroughly the meaning of the Lord's Prayer, and yet recite it with our minds on the Sunday dinner waiting at home. If reading is to be real, the mind must be *present.* The chief cause of unreality is, in most cases, absent-mindedness."[1]

To do in reading what is done in conversing is not easy for the radio actor. He holds in his hands a mimeographed script that he has marked and become familiar with during the rehearsal period. His words are already set down for him, and he has practiced them again and again. Therefore at air time he is always fully aware of what he is to say and when he is to say it; and he is more or less certain of how he is going to say it. Yet the *character* the radio actor is representing does *not* know exactly when he is going to speak next, or for how long, or what he is going to say in the situation in response to others, or how he is going to say it. To the *character* various thoughts occur one by one, and, as the occasion arises or permits, he utters the thoughts he wishes to speak in whatever style he is able to command at the time.

Difficult though it may be, the constant and crucial task of the actor who knows exactly what he is going to say next is, as William Gillette insists, "to behave exactly as though he didn't; to let his thoughts (apparently) occur to him as he goes along, even though they are in his mind already; and (apparently) to search for and find the words by which to express those thoughts, even though these words are at his tongue's very end" or right there on the page in front of him. Living and breathing creatures have to find their words "with more or less rapidity according to their facility in that respect . . . . That is to say, the Whole must have that indescribable Life-Spirit of Effect which produces the Illusion of Happening for the First Time."[2]

Gillette's rule furnishes the foundation for the reality of *present-thinking* in all acting. Rarely has anyone said so much about acting in so little. In radio, which is a medium of intimacy, his conversational method is especially required. The radio actor must therefore base his reading, in style as well as in volume, on the conversational mode.

[1] Wayland Parrish, *Reading Aloud,* 2nd ed., rev. (New York: The Ronald Press Company, 1941), p. 40. Copyright, 1941, by The Ronald Press Company.

[2] William Gillette, *The Illusion of the First Time in Acting,* pp. 40 and 43.

2

The conversational method of acting, strangely enough, is relatively modern. Molière was an innovator in 1663, when he said in *L'Impromptu de Versailles,* "Here is this one speaking like a marquis! Didn't I tell you that your part was one in which you should talk naturally?" Even in 1765 John Rice had to combat Thomas Sheridan's lectures on mechanical elocution by asserting that the style of reading should be that of natural conversation; yet as late as 1775 Joshua Steele's "An Essay towards Establishing the Melody and Measure of Speech to be Expressed and Perpetuated by Certain Symbols," was extremely popular. Shortly before 1800 and thereafter, however, rhetoricians Hugh Blair, Whately, and others continued to insist that the best instruction was "to form the tones of public speaking upon the tones of sensible and animated conversation."[3] Charles Macklin also did much to reform acting by introducing natural speaking in the theatre; he would, for instance, "bid his pupil first speak the passage as he would in common life . . . and with nothing more than this attention to what was natural, he produced out of the most ignorant persons, players that surprised everybody."[4] Finally, during the later nineteenth century the growing predominance of the realistic style of play dialogue made conversational utterance in acting almost a requirement.

Although the history of the emergence of the conversational mode of acting, as prescribed by Gillette, is not too important, the reason for the development and acceptance of the mode is of immense significance to any twentieth-century actor.

[3] Cf. Hugh Blair's Lecture XXXIII (1783).

[4] Cf. [John Hill] *The Actor* (London: R. Griffiths, 1775), pp. 239–240.

Nowadays, theatre—including radio—audiences, possibly because of the advent of things psychological, have shifted their major interest from the ***results*** to the *processes* of stimulus and response as manifested in speech. They want to hear the thoughts and feelings of various characters in various situations *come into being.* To them speech must have in it a "livingness." To them the moments in a play are fundamentally magnetic only in so far as they are moments in which speech is being born and growing and changing—and revealing. To them truth is something they can hear happening now, not something that has previously happened and been warmed over and served again. To listeners nowadays the most exciting thing about the best acting is that in it the thoughts and feelings seem to come into existence right then and there. The audience can hear them a-borning.

This rare quality of human nature-in-the-process-of-becoming is the inimitable peculiarity—the fascination and glory—of all acting. Yet, since the radio actor has his speeches before him in the script instead of in his mind—since he has to read rather than to remember—it is much, much more difficult for him than for the stage or screen actor to capture and to communicate this livingness. To maintain the Illusion of the First Time is always his immense problem, his distinctive and emphatic problem.

What is there of value in the following typical speeches from such typical radio plays as WHEN A GIRL MARRIES* and THE ADVENTURES OF OZZIE AND HARRIET* except this livingness? What can the radio actor extract from them except the juices of genuine life?

* Reproduced through the courtesy of the authors.

1. IRMA: It's just a mother's worry — like an old hen clucking over her brood — with no more reason, I suppose.

2. THORNY: Hmm. (PAUSE) Oz, the measure of a man is to be able to admit he's wrong. After I left here today, I went home and thought the whole situation over carefully. Slowly I realized how cruel and selfish I'd been. I was man enough to change my mind and admit I was wrong.

3. PHIL: I told you, Mother, I don't want to talk about Kathy. I don't want any unpleasantness. And there's going to be some if we go into the matter any further.

4. WOMAN: Oh, yes, I've known Mr. Dunkel for a long time. When he comes in for an order, I always slip a fig into his bag. Is there anything you'd like?

5. JOAN: It's awfully hard for me to see someone else's point of view if it's built entirely for their own personal gain — Maybe I don't mean gain. Maybe I mean their own personal satisfaction. — But anyway, it upsets me completely when something like that happens in the lives of people who are close to me.

6. OZZIE: Come on, Nick, get off the couch. I want to lie down. You're not supposed to be up here anyway. Look at this couch. He's got it covered with hair. Thorny sat down on it last night with his blue serge suit and got up wearing a Harris tweed.

7. KATHY: Once love's happened, Phil, you can't just turn it off. You told me that once about Joan. You told me that even though you knew that Joan was happily married — even though you knew she never gave you a thought — you'd always love her.

8. MRS. D.: The whole thing's as plain as the nose on your face. Irma has ideas. Here's a good chance for her daughter to marry into a great deal

of money, and she's pressing it. Why, I wouldn't be a bit surprised if she put the whole idea into Kathy's head.

9. OZZIE: Harriet, look down the street. Mr. Dunkel homeward bound . . . hat straight on his head, starched collar . . . the creases in his blue serge cutting the wind. Wonder what he has in all those little packages he's carrying?

10. THORNY: But this isn't like you, Oz. You're the guy who always gives an opinion whether anybody wants it or — That is, I mean — You can't let your neighbors down this way.

So vibrant and persuasive is this quality of the livingness of speech as demonstrated by acting at its best that the writers of novels have recently been trying to capture it for their books. James Joyce and others have experimented with the well-known stream-of-consciousness technique. Gertrude Stein, going a step farther, has attempted to capture thoughts in the act of coming-into-being in passages like the following, from *Wars I Have Seen:*

> Medieval means, that life and place and the crops you plant and your wife and children, all are uncertain. They can be driven away, or taken away, or burned away, or left behind, that is what it is to be medieval. And being a pioneer has a little of the same not all the same but something of the same and when you are fifteen it is all very real, medieval and pioneer. And now and here in 1943, it is just like that, you take a train, you disappear, you move away your house is gone, your children too, your crops are taken away, there is nothing to say, you are on the road, and where are they, if you go there is nobody to say so, anything can come and anything can go and they can say yes and now, and they can say, go, they never do say come, but yes they do now, they say come now, and they have to come and they have to go, everything is all the same what can happen here can happen there, and what can happen there can happen anywhere and it does, beside it does.
>
> So at fifteen there comes to be a realisation of what living was in medieval times and as a pioneer. It is very near. And now in 1943 it is here.
>
> It is disconcerting to know and it gives you a funny feeling, that any time not only that you can be told to go and you go but also that you can be taken. Nevertheless you stay, and if you stay you do not go away. That was true in medieval times too.[5]

Literature, however, cannot yet do what all acting at perfection can do preeminently. Literature is still the *record* of a happening, the happening someone tells you about rather than the happening you yourself watch and hear. Literature is still the letter someone wrote to you four days ago, which you are now reading; it is not the letter writer actually talking to you over the long distance telephone with the thoughts and feelings coming into being right then and there.

Therefore this unique quality of acting, this livingness wooed by literature, must be cherished and perfected by the radio actor. This "becoming" cannot be taken for granted or forfeited. As the distinguishing feature of acting it must be centered and enlarged on by the radio actor. He must constantly strive for *present-thinking* via Gillette's rule for the Illusion of the First Time. He must see the actor's truth in Stendhal's statement: "I spoke much better as soon as I began each sentence without knowing how I should end it."[6]

3

The Illusion of the First Time does not, as is generally supposed, imply that the radio actor, in searching

[5] Gertrude Stein, *Wars I Have Seen* (New York: Random House, Inc., 1945), pp. 26–7. Copyright, 1945, by Random House, Inc.

[6] Stendhal (Marie Henri Beyle), *Armance;* quoted in Gide's *Journal,* translated by Justin O'Brien (New York: Alfred A. Knopf, Inc., 1948), II, 33.

for his thoughts and his words, ought to stumble, and halt, and repeat, and stutter, or otherwise fuzz up the author's lines with additional words. Allan Funt, originator of the CANDID MICROPHONE program, is exaggerating when he declares that dramatists have "never touched the true speech of real people," and that actors never "know how to speak it with all the *uhs* and *ahs* and embarrassments and variations of tone in everyday life."[7] If that is the way people actually converse, it is not the way they should converse in acting. Bernard Shaw always rightly criticized any actor who, in an attempt to give an air of naturalness and spontaneity to his dialogue, was too free in his use of repetitions and nervous stumblings.

Miss K.——— P.———, . . . was quite as natural; and yet she never wasted an instant, and was clear, crisp and punctual as clockwork without being in the least mechanical. I am on the side of smart execution: if there are two ways of being natural in speech on the stage, I suggest that Miss P———'s way is better than the fluffy way.[8]

The Illusion of the First Time implies (a) a hunting for thoughts and the words with which to express these thoughts. In the following examples only this search and discovery can impart livingness to the lines:

[7] Louise Levitas, "Little Mike Has Big Ears," *PM,* January 11, 1948, p. M–6.

[8] George Bernard Shaw, *Dramatic Opinions and Essays,* edited by James Huneker (New York: Brentano's, 1906), II, 272.

1. I know what you mean, I've spent more than one night in those — lower regions myself.

2. But you might have told me that — that you — (BEAT) I felt so alone, so completely, hopelessly alone last night. If I'd known that — you've been through something similar I might not have felt so — so utterly lost.

3. But I can't come over there now if she's there. Can't you — can't you send her on an errand or something for a while?

4. But you needn't worry about me. I can take care of myself today. I could do anything today. I feel so — I don't know . . . Mother earth.

The Illusion of the First Time implies (b) an awareness of the added thought, the additional something that was not in the speaker's mind when he started but *at the moment* pops into it and must be said, as in the following examples:

1. It <u>is</u> good coffee. I was making good coffee before you were born. And I'll tell you something — if you want to keep your Dan happy after you're married, you'd better have a good cup of coffee for him every morning.

2. It was awful while it was going on — real suffering — the worst kind of suffering. But it's wonderful now. Everything's different. Everything looks different. And I feel so different. So much — healthier.

3. Oh, my goodness! She must have slammed up the receiver on him. Not that I was listening to his private talk. And I hope you wouldn't ever be guilty of such a low trick either.

4. One more crack like that out of you and you can go antiquing by yourself. I don't like antiques anyway. And I don't like you very well today either.

The Illusion of the First Time implies (c) a sense of growth and progression, a building up, in many speeches. Thinking and utterance are often cumulative. One thing leads to another. Once the speaker is started, one thought quickly moves on to a new one. Often, spurred on by his own thinking, the speaker builds, without planning to do so, beyond his starting point or level to a fact or feeling that he did not intend to reach. Notice this "growth at the moment" in the following example:

I know Ted Miller — just the same. And I know who his mother is too. And I know where he lives. Or where he used to — before she threw him out. And besides that, I know who he calls. Terry Burton . . . Mrs. Stanley Burton . . . that owns the new Burton store. That's who he calls. And she's the reason his mother wouldn't let him live with her any more. I found out all about it last night.

The Illusion of the First Time implies (d) that a speaker in conversing often leaves one thought before it is completed because he wants to take up another thought or because he does not know exactly how to finish, as in the following examples.

1. I suppose you're right. I don't understand. But I wish —— Do you suppose a lot of people have been through — what I've been through last night, and I just haven't known it?

2. I never talked so that I could get you to understand what I wanted while I — while I — Maybe now . . . . There're a couple of things I ain't had enough of.

3. I don't blame her for getting back into the car. If I were in her — Well, will you take a look at that!

4. No, Hank, those bananas are for — Oh, well, what does it matter?

5. Jealous? I'm not — (BREAKS OFF) Well, maybe I am.

6. Mother, it looks like — Maybe she — I think we'd better call a doctor.

The Illusion of the First Times implies (e) a consciousness of the birth of new ideas. New ideas must come to the radio actor's *mind,* not merely next in the script. The new idea must come to the speaker an instant before he puts it into words and must not be anticipated. Notice the emergence of the new idea in the following examples:

1. Maybe by using her suspicions I could — Sure! Right then and there something clicked. I hit upon a plan.

2. But I've simply got to get that bracelet back. Look, I've got an idea. Why don't you and I pretend we're calling on her, see, and then —

3. HENRY: Every penny counts, Homer.
   HOMER: Look, why not borrow the money? From Mary, say?
   HENRY: Oh, no, Homer!
   HOMER: Why not, Hen? She's your sister, isn't she? That makes you practically flesh and blood.
   HENRY: But how could I cement relations with my mother on Mary's money? I know how I can raise the money! You see this box here?

4. MARK: Well, this free-lance business is all right in spots, John, but . . . we do all right.
   JOHN: I see. Mark, why don't you get a steady line in art? How about newspapers? Political cartoonists do well. Or say! Why don't you do a comic-strip? Good money in it if it catches on!

Several other matters that the Illusion of the First Time implies have already been examined, such as grouping and the period fault (in Chapter IV) and changes-reversals-transitions, emphasis, subordination, and pause (in Chapter V). They are all earmarks of thinking at the time of utterance (apparently) for the first time.

Four additional factors complete the final essentials for acting based on the conversational mode: the motivation for saying what is said, the attitude of the speaker toward what he is saying (both of which come more logically under the heading of Characterization), communion or contact with the person spoken to (which will be examined in Chapter VIII), and awareness of surrounding circumstances (the subject of Chapter X).

4

Finally, there is one point, so peculiarly radio's, that must be more than mentioned in connection with conversational reading. How much physical action should the radio actor indulge in while reading his lines at the microphone? The answer seems to be, once you have watched experienced radio actors perform, that physical action is virtually a necessity for full, vivid, conversational expression. Facial and bodily changes are, according to some theories, an inseparable part of the complete vocalization. Certainly they seem to add something essential in the way of livingness to the utterance. Certainly the radio actor can discover by practice that the simulated struggle adds something to the lines, that the merest indication of dance movements add something different, that hugging the body to keep warm adds something else, as does the limpness of sickness, the thrusting of the face forward into a strong wind, the stamping of the foot on certain words, the arching of the eyebrows before a certain sentence, and the narrowing of the eyes in anger, the distinct approximation of the rhythm of ice skating, the stance of an obdurate person, the pointing finger, the palsied shake of an old lady's head, and the "take" in the middle of a sentence. In short, the radio actor will discover that facial changes and bodily actions will help him to shape his speaking at the microphone toward livingness.

The conversational mode, with its *present-thinking* in the Illusion of the First Time, is probably the device Duse employed, the device, according to Stark Young,

> by which speeches in themselves overexplicit or pat or non-dramatic are made to fall apart, stricken or winged with pauses and sudden emphases, as if they were from the speaker's inmost impulse rather than from some still-born platitude or deliberate exegesis on the dramatist's part. In this way the actor may save the dramatist from himself as it were.[9]

SELECTED READINGS

Gillette, William, *The Illusion of the First Time in Acting, Papers on Acting I.* New York: Dramatic Museum of Columbia University, 1915, 58 pp.

Goodrich, Lawrence, "The Illusion of Real Talk," *Quarterly Journal of Speech,* XIX, No. 1 (February, 1933), 39–43.

Talley, C. Horton, "A Comparison of Conversational and Audience Speech," *Archives of Speech,* II (July, 1937), 28–40.

[9] Stark Young, *New Republic,* March 9, 1942, p. 332.

EXERCISES

Again, as in most of the previous exercises, no attempts should be made at characterization; the student should read as himself.

A. READING ARTICLES, LETTERS, AND THE LIKE

To start with what acting as conversation should *not* be, the following selections illustrate what the radio actor must do to make reading sound like *reading* instead of like conversation. In the following examples the actor is not uttering his own thoughts; he is reading what someone else has already thought out. Unfortunately, much radio acting, even in simulated conversations, sounds exactly like reading.

For practice in differentiating reading as reading from reading as conversation, perhaps an attempt can be made to turn each selection into present-thinking via the Illusion of the First Time.

1. THE WILD FLAG*

July 3, 1944.

We received a letter from the Writers' War Board the other day asking for a statement on "The Meaning of Democracy." It presumably is our duty to comply with such a request, and it is certainly our pleasure. Surely the Board knows what Democracy is. It is the line that forms on the right. It is the don't in Don't Shove. It is the hole in the stuffed shirt through which the sawdust slowly trickles; it is the dent in the high hat. Democracy is the recurrent suspicion that more than half of the people are right more than half of the time. It is the feeling of privacy in the voting booths, the feeling of communion in the libraries, the feeling of vitality everywhere. Democracy is the score at the beginning of the ninth. It is an idea which hasn't been disproved yet, a song the words of which have not gone bad. It's the mustard on the hot dog and the cream in the rationed coffee. Democracy is a request from a War Board, in the middle of a morning in the middle of a war, wanting to know what democracy is.

2. THE JOURNALS OF ANDRÉ GIDE†

January 3 (1892)

I am anxious to know what I shall be; I do not know even what I want to be, but I do know that I must choose. I should like to progress on safe and

* First published as an editorial in *The New Yorker,* copyright, 1944, by E. B. White, from *The Wild Flag* (Houghton Mifflin).

† Reprinted from *The Journals of André Gide,* Volume I: 1889–1913, translated by Justin O'Brien, by permission of Alfred A. Knopf, Inc. Copyright, 1947, by Alfred A. Knopf, Inc.

sure roads that lead only to the point where I have decided to go. But I don't know; I don't know what I ought to want. I am aware of a thousand possibilities in me, but I cannot resign myself to want to be only one of them. And every moment, at every word I write, at each gesture I make, I am terrified at the thought that this is one more eradicable feature of my physiognomy becoming fixed: a hesitant, impersonal physiognomy, an amorphous physiognomy, since I have not been capable of choosing and tracing its contours confidently.

O Lord, permit me to want only one thing and to want it constantly.

3. PORTIA FACES LIFE, #1774*

MRS. BLAKE: I can't wade through all this legal verbiage. All I'm interested in is what you've put down concerning — Oh, yes, this about Walter Manning . . . . (READING) "Five years ago his first wife, Arlene Harrison, sued for a divorce and obtained it on the grounds of non-support. At the time of the action Mr. Manning admitted for the record that the charges made by his wife were true. A month after the divorce was granted, he became engaged to Portia Blake, Richard Blake's mother and Walter Manning's second wife, now deceased. This engagement lasted for the term of some six months and was broken off suddenly when Mr. Manning accepted a position as war correspondent on the European front." That was a good point to make, Phillip. I'd forgotten all about that broken engagement.

4. DAVID HARDING, COUNTER-SPY, #160†

MR. B.: They're crazy! Crazy! It can't be!

MRS. B.: (TERRIFIED) What is it, James?

MR. B.: "Harry Winters to speak at Philadelphia auditorium tomorrow evening."

MRS. B.: (EXPLOSIVE) You must be reading wrong! It can't be that!

MR. B.: (READING EXCITEDLY) "Disappearance of Harry Winters — the murder of policeman — all a mistake. Harry Winters will lecture tomorrow night in the Central Auditorium of the atrocities he saw in German prison camps." (SLAMMING PAPER AROUND)

* By Mona Kent. Reproduced through the courtesy of the author and General Foods Corporation.
† By Phillips H. Lord. Reproduced through the courtesy of Phillips H. Lord, Inc.

(ALMOST A FIT) They're crazy! They can't do it! I never heard of such a thing!

MRS. B.: James — stop it. Stop! You've got to calm yourself.

MR. B.: How can Harry Winters speak? I'm Harry Winters. The fools — the dastardly fools!

MRS. B.: James, you mustn't! Please —

MR. B.: (GETTING CONTROL OF HIMSELF) I never heard of such a thing! What are they talking about?

MRS: B.: Read it — read it slowly . . .

MR. B.: (EASES UP AND CONCENTRATES) "The mystery — and the false arrest stories reported concerning Harry Winters' lecture on German atrocities have finally been solved. Police Officer Tufts — who was hit over the head at the time of Officer Connors' killing — has regained his memory and has told the United States Counter-Spies the correct version to the murder of his fellow officer."

MRS. B.: James — what does it all mean . . . ?

MR. B.: "Officer Tufts — while suffering from the blow on the head — became confused. He had recently attended one of the lectures given by Harry Winters — and was much affected by it, since he has a son of his own in a prison camp in Germany. Officers Tufts and Conners went out to investigate a suspect — and Conners was killed during the questioning — but that case and the case of Winters have no connection. Officer Tufts in his dazed condition — resulting from the blow — got confused between the two in first telling the story."

B. NARRATION

Most narration, while not conversation, should give The Illusion of the First Time, the effect of being thought out at the time of utterance. It must not sound as if it were being read from a manuscript page.

1. THE SECOND MRS. BURTON, #452*

ANNOUNCER: Mrs. Dugald's rooming house is well-known in Dickston. It stands big and rambling at the corner of Mulberry Street and Maple, six blocks away from Terry and Stan Burton's house — and a ten minute walk from

* By Martha Alexander. Reproduced through the courtesy of the author.

the middle of town where most of Mrs. Dugald's roomers work — in shoe stores and garages and drug stores and super-markets. Men, she likes to say, who first came to her door "like poor, penniless bairns, knockin' in the nicht." Men who were young — full of dreams and ambitions — and who, year after year, have stayed on and on in healthy, well-fed bachelor-contentment.

But this new lad — this Ted Miller he-called-himself — "wi' all his art traps and skittle" — he's a queer one for a young lad. Mrs. Dugald can't make him out. "He's no' been oot o' the house since the day he came."

But every afternoon, around three, Ted Miller leaves his hall bedroom and comes quietly down the long stairway to the nickel telephone in the downstairs hall. Mrs. Dugald's rooming house is quietest at that hour. The cleaning done, she's safely closeted in the kitchen preparing dinner, with the help of a high school girl he vaguely recognized when she was waiting on the table last night. But Ted hardly gives them a thought as he drops his nickel into the phone . . .

2. HOLLYWOOD DOCTOR*

ALICE: You know how it is when a bunch of us sit around the screen-writers' table in the studio commissary having lunch together. Sometimes we sit around, as Thurber says, not so much listening as waiting for an opening. But once in a while we hit on something really interesting.

This time, for instance, we were chewing the rag about familiar Hollywood characters, like Oscar, the bootblack, Joe, the literary head-waiter at Romanoff's, and Angelo, the friendly little dwarf who peddles papers on Hollywood Boulevard.

Somebody said, "Speaking of favorite newsboys, whatever became of Chester?"

Chester was a poor kid with a body gnarled and twisted like an old oak tree. You always used to see him standing outside the studio gates.

* From *Hollywood Doctor*, by Budd Schulberg, published by Harper & Brothers. Copyright, 1941, by Budd Schulberg.

We all used to like the way he held his papers firmly with his one good arm, the way he'd force his paralyzed face into a spunky grin.

"Boys," I said, "if I ever told you what happened to Chester, you'd all dash back to your offices and write it — it's that good."

"Go ahead," they all said. "Let's have it. We have plenty of time."

Well, there's nothing a screen-writer loves more than finding a good excuse for not going back to work, so I took a deep breath and I was off.

3. MYSTERY THEATRE: *THE GREAT GABBO**

FERRIS: So Gabbo got to be — good property, see? He goes swell on the circuit. We got so we're grossing half a grand a week, and we're getting set for movies and big houses when — this Rubina babe comes along. This happens about a year ago. We're playing Oswego. Rubina is with an acrobatic act. She just barely has enough brains to hold a hoop straight for the muscle boys to jump through. And her physical equipment doesn't give Miss America any worries either. But Gabbo? (PAUSE. FADING) Well, he buttonholes me one night after the act, see . . .

GABBO: (EXCITED) Mr. Ferris, I want an assistant for my act — a . . . woman assistant.

FERRIS: Gabbo, you're nuts! You're top billing now. A woman'll slow it up.

GABBO: (FIRM) But it's all settled, Mr. Ferris. I have already arranged it with Miss Rubina.

FERRIS: So Rubina joins the act. And from then on . . . it's a circus. The act slips like a mail-order face-lifting job. I'm worried, see? It's a good act, and it's dough out of my pocket to see the guy tossing more lines at the dame than at the dummy. The audience is giving with large doses of silence. Then one night I'm dodging the theatre manager in the wings when I hear Gabbo chinning with Rubina behind a prop. (FADING) I ain't proud. I listen.

* Reproduced through the courtesy of the authors, Frederic Methot and Ben Hecht.

4. BETWEEN THE SILENCE AND THE SURF*

NARRATOR: The American past, the past of all the American nations, contains more elements, and more characteristic elements, common to the continent as a whole, than any other continental past of which there is knowledge or record.

There is no other continent of the world, Europe or Africa or Asia, in which so great a number of living men share in the memory of a past common to all of them. There is no continental past from which such great and unforgettable events make up the common living memory of so many men.

Take, for one, the settlement of this continent. Men of undiluted Indian blood aside, there is no American of whatever race or tongue who does not share with every other American the memory of the experience, either in his own life or his father's life or his father's father's, of the settlement beyond the water — of the departure from a known world and the long crossing of the sea and the settlement in a world not known. It is not an experience which men forget even in centuries of time. And it was the same experience, or almost the same, on all the coasts of the American continent. In the first years, whether in Plymouth or in Brazil or in Virginia or Acadia, it was the experience of a world between the surf on one side, and the wilderness on the other — a world between two sounds — between the sound of the surf on the beaches where their boats had come aground ——

And the wind's sound in the grass or in the brush or in the forests where they still must go. The world of the first settlements was the narrow world between the silence and the surf, between the water and the wilderness — between the past cut off by water and the future closed by distance and by danger — but not closed.

* From *The American Story,* by Archibald MacLeish. Reprinted by permission of the publishers, Duell, Sloane, and Pearce, Inc. Copyright, 1944, by Archibald MacLeish.

5. SHERLOCK HOLMES: *THE MAN WITH THE TWISTED LIP**

WATSON: My story begins on a June night in 1889. My wife and I had spent a quiet evening at home, I remember, and it was just about the hour that a man gives his first yawn and glances at the clock when the tranquility of the scene was broken by the discordant jangling of our front door bell. It turned out to be a certain Mrs. Isa Whitney, an old friend of my wife's, who had come to us in trouble. Her husband, she told us, had been missing for forty-eight hours; and knowing him to be a victim of the shocking habit of taking opium, she was convinced that he was lying, drugged and stupefied, in some foul den amid the London waterfronts. She told me that her husband had mentioned frequently a place called the Bar of Gold in Upper Swandham Lane; so naturally that's where I began my search. I quickly located it and, after ordering my cab to wait, I entered the place. A strange sight met my eyes: Through the smoke-ridden gloom I could catch a glimpse of bodies lying in strange, fantastic poses as the men there smoked the pipes of death. Most of the unhappy creatures lay silent, but some muttered to themselves, and others talked together in strange low, monotonous voices . . .

C. ONE-SIDED CONVERSATIONS

1. MY FRIEND IRMA†

AL: Hello, Joe? Al . . . Got a problem. How do you keep a dame from running around with strange men? . . . Introduce them and then they won't be strange? No, no, Joe. Goes deeper than that. Want to get the lowdown on a guy named Robert Girard . . . Yeah, must have dough . . . Oh, you're looking him up in your little black book under P.S. — Potential Suckers? I'll wait . . . Un-huh, un-huh, un-huh . . . Ummmmmmmmmmmmm! Where does he live, Joe? . . . 2746 Park Avenue . . . No, Joe! Don't send Rub-Out Louie! Going to handle this personally. Goodbye.

* From the original story by Sir Arthur Conan Doyle, adapted for radio by Denis Green. Reproduced through the courtesy of Denis Green and the Executors of the late Sir Arthur Conan Doyle.

† By Cy Howard and Parke Levy. Reproduced through the courtesy of the authors.

2. SILVER THEATRE: *LEAVE IT TO ETHEL**

ETHEL: Penelope Garmud, please . . . Hello, Muddy? . . . Look, Muddy, can you take a letter . . . For Mr. Butler . . . I know he's dreamy, but I can't talk about him now . . . You can't . . . Okay, kid, some other time.

(JIGGLE-JIGGLE)

Give me Miss Murphy, please . . . Hello, Murph? . . . Busy? . . . Too bad. I wanted you to take a letter for Sally . . . Me take it? Shorthand and I have only a nodding acquaintance.

(JIGGLE-JIGGLE)

Try Miss Jelniph, please . . . Hi, Dimples. Can you take a letter for Sally Jones? . . . You can? Gee, that's great kid! . . . In an hour! But this has gotta be right now!

3. DUFFY'S TAVERN†

ARCHIE: (ON PHONE) Hello. Duffy's Tavern — where the elite meet to eat. Archie, the manager, speakin' . . . Duffy ain't here . . . Oh, hello, Duffy . . . Huh? You're goin' on your vacation? Where you goin'? . . . . Takin' Mrs. Duffy to Niagara Falls? . . . Duffy, you'll be the first man who ever went there an' brought his own barrel. I thought you was goin' to the beach on your vacation . . . You want to keep Mrs. Duffy away from the water? How come? . . . Last time she went swimmin' a tugboat tried to push her into the ferry slip . . . Well, look, Duffy, we're gettin' the place closed up for the summer . . . Yeah, we're packin' all the stuff away. Say, there's some free lunch left. What'll I do with it? . . . Give it away! Duffy, I been tryin' to do that all year. By the way, tell Mrs. Duffy we finely found her false teeth. Yeah, they was back of the radiator — clutchin' to a roast beef sandwich . . . Huh? . . . You're worried about burglars? Don't worry, Duffy. Before I leave I'm nailin' all the doors shut from the inside . . . How'm I gettin' out? Through the busted window, of course. Well, I gotta close up the joint, Duffy. I'll call you later. (RECEIVER DOWN)

* By Jerry Rice and William L. Stuart. Reproduced through the courtesy of the authors.

† Reproduced through the courtesy of Ed Gardner and his writing staff.

4. YEARS AGO*

MY FATHER: (GIVES A LITTLE START, STANDS RIGID AS A RAMROD, THEN BEGINS SPEAKING VERY CAREFULLY — THE FIRST TIME HE'S EVER USED A TELEPHONE) Hello? . . . Is that you, Dan? . . . Who? . . . Oh, is that you, Fan? . . . This is Jones . . . I'm telephonin' to you from Wollaston . . . From Wollaston . . . From Wollaston — where — I — live! . . . That's right. Clinton Jones . . . Can you hear me all right? . . . What's that? . . . What? . . . Oh, yes, I can hear you fine! . . . I'm telephonin', Fan, because I'd like to speak to your father, that is, if it's convenient . . . Oh . . . Well, what's a likely time for him to be back home again? . . . I don't want to put him to no trouble but it's somethin' a little urgent . . . All right, he can telephone to me late as he's a mind to. Our telephone number is — You got a pencil to write it down there? . . . All right, I'll go ahead. The number is six-five-seven . . . six, five, seven, party R . . . Quincy . . . That's right! All right now, Fan, if you're ready I'll hang up my end.

5. THE SECOND MRS. BURTON, #493†

MARION: Hello . . . Oh, Jim. Hello, dear . . . (DULLY) Oh, thank you. Happy Thanksgiving right back at you. Is Lillian there? . . . Oh, don't tell me she's cooking a turkey! Now I've heard everything . . . Oh, no. If she's all involved with a stove, don't call her. I don't have anything important to say . . . Yes — I'm very much alone today . . . No, he's having dinner at Stan's. I suppose Terry's doing a turkey with all the trimmings . . . Thank you, dear, but I'm afraid I have neither the spirit nor the appetite for a big Thanksgiving dinner . . . No, not particularly. I just wanted to talk . . . Well, if she wants to call me later, fine. I'll be here . . . Um-huh. Goodbye, Jim. Enjoy your turkey.

* By Ruth Gordon. Reprinted through the courtesy of Ruth Gordon and the publishers, Viking Press.
NOTE: This excerpt may be used only in the classroom and in no case on the radio or the stage, professionally or in any other way.

† By Martha Alexander. Reproduced through the courtesy of the author.

6. THE WELBURNS—CONFIDENTIAL REPORT*

JIM: (PLEASANTLY) Come in . . . Won't you sit down? May I ask you why you want to talk to me? . . . (BLANKLY) Wh-at? What did you say? A hero? I . . . You want to what? . . . Feature article — newspaper. Really, young man, I'm afraid they sent you to the wrong place. I — Yes, yes, my name's Jim Weldon, but I'm just a printer — really I'm not important at all, believe me! My wife will be home soon — she'll tell you — we're just plain ordinary small-town folks — anyone can tell you — the Welburns — we — (PAUSE, THEN SLOWLY) You really want to write about me? . . . People have told you what? . . . But that's not true — there's nothing to write about my life. It's been an ordinary life! Well, if you persist . . . I'll try to tell you . . . and when I'm through, I'm sure you'll understand there's nothing to write about because I'll prove it to you — how do the lawyers put it? — yes, with the evidence. The evidence of thirty years. For that was when we first came to this town (FADING) the town of thirty years ago . . .

D. HUNTING FOR THOUGHTS AND WORDS

Live conversation is never memorized: it forms itself as it goes along in accordance with active thinking. For an extempore quality both thoughts and words must be searched for, even though the search is a simulated one.

1. STUDENT: It's the one part I've wanted to play all my life. Don't you think I could do it, Miss Davidson?

   TEACHER: Well, I'm not so sure. I — I'm afraid your voice . . . wouldn't carry, Bill.

2. ANGELA: I can see by all the girls' pictures on your walls that you're really a ladies' man, aren't you?

   ROWAN: Oh, those. They don't mean a thing. I've always been looking for something . . . someone with class . . . like you.

   ANGELA: I can imagine.

   ROWAN: No, this is no gag. I mean it. Just by being here you make this room — Well, I don't know how to say it . . . something wonderful. You

* By Arch Oboler. Reprinted with the permission of the author.

give it a . . . kind of feeling. Like I — like I've arrived somewhere . . . somewhere I've always wanted to go.

3. DUNNIGAN'S DAUGHTER*

FERNE: The point is I feel I've failed with you. I feel all the time . . . I have to save myself with you. Sometimes — you're so —

CLAY: (A LITTLE SHARP, IMPATIENT) Well? What?

FERNE: Sometimes you're so warm and wonderful, it's like — it's like it was in the beginning. And then — a few minutes later — you're — remote . . . unreachable. I feel like a stranger. I feel I'm . . . intruding on you.

4. MYSTERY THEATRE: *TRIANGLE OF DEATH*†

CAROLE: Oh, Pete, I — I feel so good now. I don't know — I . . . Golly, the silly things that have been upsetting me today.

PETER: What things?

CAROLE: (EVASIVELY) Oh — little trifles — around the house . . . tradesmen and — you know.

PETER: (CONCERNED) Made you irritable?

CAROLE: That's it. But now my husband's come home, and — doctored it all away . . . and it's stopped pounding.

5. A WOMAN'S LIFE, #2084‡

BARBARA: No, I'm not tired, Tom. It's just that — Well, it surprised me a little, too — seemed as if you just got here.

TOM: And the funny part of it is that — Well, we haven't really been talking about anything either. Anything really important.

BARBARA: Perhaps that's why.

TOM: Keeping away from anything that makes for — Well, one of our blow-ups.

* By S. N. Behrman. Copyright, 1946, by S. N. Behrman.
† By Joseph Ruscoll. Reproduced through the courtesy of the author.
‡ By Julian Funt. Reproduced through the courtesy of the author.

E. ADDED THOUGHTS

People conversing do not recite set pieces. When they start to speak they rarely know how or where they will finish. Often a thought needs modifiers, expansions, additions. Most of the time speakers amend or augment what they have just said.

1. WESLEY: Air feels pretty good, doesn't it?

   HELEN: After that enormous dinner.

   WESLEY: That could have something to do with it. Probably has a lot to do with it. (PAUSE) It was a grand evening all right. Grand company. Grand talk. Quite a grand town you've got here.

2. ARTHUR: Dear, I'd like to get you a fur coat. I'd like to very much. But it's either a coat or having the front lawn re-seeded. And we agreed the lawn's in a lot worse shape than you are.

3. MARION: Now don't worry. And don't cry. There's nothing to be gained by that. The whole thing's very simple and understandable. The way your sister Ruth explains it, they're just taking inventory. You know, like a store that's changed hands — the new owner wants to know what his stock on hand is.

4. MOTHER: Why, that sounds lovely, dear. "An idle brain is the devil's workshop." Weren't you clever to think that up?

   DAUGHTER: Oh, I didn't think it up. It was Benjamin Franklin, or someone like that. But I don't think a Purdue man would know that, do you?

5. MAN 1: Where you goin', Joe?

   MAN 2: Goin' down to vote. Where do you suppose? And look, tell that gang of hoodlums down by the river not to hand me any marked ballots. I'm votin' my own way. See?

6. GERRY: He always looks kind of cross and serious, and he never has much to say. Not even "Boo." And every time I try to be polite and talk to him he just acts sort of bored, and I think he's a dope. Maybe he thinks I'm a dope, too.

7. CLERK: How about this lovely mouton?

MAN: Is that rabbit?

CLERK: Oh, no, lamb. And it's only seventy-five dollars. That's complete with the lady's initials embroidered on the lining.

8. MARTHA: I've never noticed anything particularly frightening about Jug. He's a nice dog.

WALTER: You're used to him. Elaine isn't. Dickie's got to teach that dog some manners. For that matter, it wouldn't hurt Dickie to learn a few himself. It wouldn't hurt any of us to learn a few manners.

9. GIRL: Well, I'll be darned if it isn't my old music teacher! Imagine meeting you in a place like this. And still looking as handsome as ever. A little more dignified perhaps, but as handsome as ever. And where did you get that gleam in your eye?

10. SANDY: Suppose some other girl came along in the meantime? What then?

SUE: Oh, I don't know. I'd just scratch her eyes out, I guess. That is, unless she was going to marry someone else the next day.

F. GROWTH OR PROGRESSION OF THOUGHT

1. THE ALDRICH FAMILY, #405*

MRS. ALDRICH: Sam, why — why don't we invite Miss Trevor up to dinner?

MR. ALDRICH: Now, Alice!

MRS. ALDRICH: Well, I think it would be a nice gesture. If she's a new teacher in town she probably doesn't know many people. And I'm sure she'd be glad to eat a home-cooked dinner.

MR. ALDRICH: But, dear — !

MRS. ALDRICH: Besides, she might take a personal interest in Henry.

MR. ALDRICH: But, Alice, I never know what to say to school teachers. Why not invite her over for tea some afternoon?

* By Patricia Joudry and Del Dinsdale, based on characters created by Clifford Goldsmith. Reproduced through the courtesy of the authors and Clifford Goldsmith.

MRS. ALDRICH: I wonder about tonight . . .

MR. ALDRICH: You mean this afternoon . . .

MRS. ALDRICH: No, dear, I mean tonight. As a matter of fact, I could probably call her at the school right now before classes begin.

2. THE THIRTEENTH FLOOR*

KITTY: The hall was empty. No one around! I started to run . . . down the narrow little corridor of the thirteenth floor. I pressed the elevator button, and waited. It seemed like hours instead of seconds. I wanted to go back down the hall and bang at doors . . . but I was afraid to take the chance.

(ELEVATOR HEARD)

Finally I heard the elevator. I felt as if I were standing on hot coals, and my insides wouldn't stay still! The hand of the clock above the elevator climbed slowly from 5 to 6 to 7. I was going crazy just standing there! From 7 to 8 to 9 to 10 . . . 11 to 12. Then my heart exploded. My legs were hardly able to hold my body up. The elevator had stopped at 12, and then it went on to — 14. Then I remembered that it wasn't going to stop. It couldn't stop at my floor . . . because . . . because in this building there wasn't any thirteenth floor!!

3. SILVER THEATRE: *CRYSTAL*†

VIRGINIA: You weren't working tonight . . . nor the other nights.

KEN: No . . . no, I wasn't.

VIRGINIA: That's your first lie, isn't it, Ken?

KEN: Do we have to call it that?

VIRGINIA: Yes. To someone else, perhaps, it's evasion . . . but for us it's a lie. The only thing that can destroy us and all our years together.

KEN: You're right. (PAUSE) Do you want to know about her?

VIRGINIA: I don't know. To know there is another woman is almost everything. Yes, tell me about her.

* By Winifred Wolfe. Reproduced through the courtesy of the author.

† By Robert Presnell, Jr. Reproduced through the courtesy of the author.

KEN: She's twenty . . . a piano student. Her name is Jeanie Tanaquille. She lives on Eighth Street . . .

VIRGINIA: Do you love her, Ken?

KEN: You don't know what a question that is. To say I love you implies I don't love Jeanie. To say I love Jeanie implies I don't love you. Neither is true. And . . . I really don't see how you can sit there so coolly and smile so brightly. I'd be breaking the furniture by now . . .

VIRGINIA: If you knew the carnage . . . the murderous devastation inside of me, you wouldn't invite it.

KEN: I'd understand it better.

VIRGINIA: It's easy to understand violence. Thinking is much harder. I — Ken, have you faced the fact that no matter how much thinking I do . . . I could never share you?

KEN: I haven't faced it because I'd never expect it.

VIRGINIA: Do you want your . . . freedom?

KEN: From you, Virginia? Can loss be freedom?

VIRGINIA: (UP A LITTLE) Please, Ken! No speeches. I know you're good with them.

KEN: (SOFTLY) No speeches, Virginia.

VIRGINIA: Why do you make me say it? Do you want a divorce?

KEN: No.

VIRGINIA: (BREAKING ONLY SLIGHTLY) Oh, Ken . . . Ken . . . I don't want to lose you. But how can I compete with youth? Ken . . . I'll wear red socks again, and dungarees . . . and . . . and take ferry rides, if that's what you'd like. But wearing a girdle too, Ken. Don't you understand? And wearing a mask!

4. ANN RUTLEDGE*

ANN: If it's what I imagine — then love's like the way the leaves stirred all last night — and the little sounds kept coming from far away. Or it's like how the hay smelled down at Tuttle's farm just after they finished mowing last week — or the way the sky looks on those clear, clear nights in

* From *Thirteen by Corwin,* by Norman Corwin. Reproduced by permission of Henry Holt and Company, Inc. Copyright, 1942, by Norman Corwin.

winter, all bright and glowing, and kind of pure — you know? Like warm blankets and soft pillows when you're all snug in bed and it's blowing a blizzard outside and there are icicles on the window. (A LITTLE LAUGH OF DELIGHT) Is it — is it anything like that, Mother?

5. DUNNIGAN'S DAUGHTER*

FERNE: He doesn't need you. He doesn't need me. He doesn't need anybody. And what if he does? Zelda, listen. For the first time in my life I feel I can choose. I can't tell you what a marvelous feeling it is. It's not Jim alone. I don't know about Jim yet. I'm not sure. What I am sure of is that I'm not going to be afraid any more. It's the difference between being alive and dead. Don't deny it to yourself, Zelda. Don't be afraid of being sorry afterwards. Don't be afraid of hurting even. Don't be afraid!

6. HAVING WONDERFUL TIME†

CHICK: Gee, I remember when I was a kid I had the world by the tail. I used to see rich men in their automobiles and I'd say to myself, "Don't worry, Chick. Some day you'll have a boat like that — only better. With your full name on the side, not just your initials." Or else I'd read about some famous man and I'd say, "O.K., O.K., Chick. There's no hurry. Ssh! Just take it easy, you'll get there and you'll even be famous." Funny, when you're a kid nothing seems impossible . . . Y'know, even after I was admitted to the bar I still thought I was a big-shot. I was a professional man, see? I had a sheepskin with my name on it in fancy letters — Charles Kessler, LL.B. The world was waiting for me! (SNORTS) Sure, it was! It was waiting — with a club in each hand . . . So now I have an education and a degree, and what good is it? I can't even get a job as relief investigator at twenty-five smackers a week. There're too many other lawyers ahead of me . . . It's all a lotta baloney. Study hard, they tell you. Get a lotta knowledge — knowledge is power. A lotta bunk I say!

* By S. N. Behrman. Copyright, 1946, by S. N. Behrman.
† By Arthur Kober. Reprinted by courtesy of Random House, Inc.

7. PORTIA FACES LIFE, #1784*

ALICE: I cleaned out Mrs. Clark's room the day after the undertakers took the body, and I found one of Janet's pearls under her mother's bed.

NILES: (LOW AND SHAKEN) Good Lord!

ALICE: I don't know whether she did it alone or if you came back and helped her. No matter how it happened I'm not blaming either of you. Old Mrs. Clark was a devil and she deserved being killed. The world's a lot better off without her.

NILES: (A LITTLE SICK) Alice, what you're saying is . . .

ALICE: Let me finish. That Miss Mitchell is as smart as a whip, and she's going to ask a lot of questions. But stall her off. Don't let her pin you down. And, please, Mr. Niles, please don't leave the house tonight without Miss Janet!!

8. MYSTERY THEATRE: *THE THIRD WITNESS*†

KOVACS: (SUDDENLY ALARMED) Chief, my gosh!

LIEUT.: What's the matter?

KOVACS: That cashier! The trail! Remember what Joe Larsen yelled out in the Courtroom?

LIEUT.: Huh?

KOVACS: What he'd do when he got out of stir?

LIEUT.: (ALSO ALARMED NOW) Good Lord, that's right!

KOVACS: Swore he'd come back and kill her, didn't he? For testifying against him!

LIEUT.: And those other witnesses, too! The doorman at the theatre and that old flower lady. They cooked his goose, too! The three of them! Kovacs, quick! Go find them! Bring them in at once! If Joe Larsen gets to them first, there'll be three very dead corpses!

* By Mona Kent. Reproduced through the courtesy of the author and General Foods Corporation.
† By Joseph Ruscoll. Reproduced through the courtesy of the author.

9. ROADSIDE*

HANNIE: When you first came along last night I kinda tuck to you . . . I thought you stepped right off a mountain some'eres. I thought you was full of shine like a scoured pot. I thought if you set, the sun ud set. Nen this mornin', when I heard you shootin' off yer head, I was mad as a settin' hen, fer about five minutes. 'N when I ast you jist now if you was blind's a bat, I mighta knowed the answer! Course you're blind as a bat — blind as forty-seven bats! If you wasn't you'd see I've hotfooted it clear here to Verdigree, waded th'ough weeds and bresh and got chiggers on me all the way from my feet to whur I set down! And whut fer? To try to get a fool of a man outa trouble that's had a landslide in his head and cain't even remember who he's supposed to be! Now, git outa my way!

10. THE ALDRICH FAMILY, #413†

MR. ALDRICH: Henry, let me explain one thing to you. You are to march right straight home, and go up to your room, and stay there — do you understand — until I tell you to come out!

HENRY: But, Father, the ten dollars!

MR. ALDRICH: And if I have to tell you once more to go home, just once more, you can forget about your allowance for the next six months!

HENRY: (FADING) Yes, Father. I'm going.

MR. ALDRICH: (CALLING) And the same applies if I catch you leaving your room. And don't stop to talk to anybody — and don't come back!

G. INCOMPLETE, BROKEN THOUGHTS

1. GEORGE: What I've done may be all wrong. I don't know. It may be that — All I know is that there may be some changes ahead for — for all of us. For you and Mother — especially for Bernice and me. (PAUSE) That is, if Bernice ever comes back to me. If she ever — Oh, what

* Copyright, 1930, by Lynn Riggs. All Rights Reserved. Reprinted by permission of the author and Samuel French.

† By Patricia Joudry and Del Dinsdale, based on characters created by Clifford Goldsmith. Reproduced through the courtesy of the authors and Clifford Goldsmith.

a mess I've made of everything! I guess I just — (HE STOPS SUDDENLY, UNABLE TO CONTINUE)

HELEN: George, you mustn't act like that. You haven't done anything wrong. Sit down. Please sit down.

GEORGE: I hated to tell you all this. I swore I never would. But the way you've taken it — Well, I just wish I had your courage — your ability to accept things that happen. I haven't. I — (PAUSE) I have to go now. Thanks a lot. I'll get in touch with you tomorrow.

2. CAPTAIN: Here, take my binoculars, boy. Take them and put them — Who's been in the cabin here?

MATE: No one that I know of, skipper. Not me.

CAPTAIN: Put the binoculars up there on the top shelf.

MATE: If I could take just a second of your time, Captain . . . I know where the treasure is.

CAPTAIN: The darned things aren't worth the — What did you say, Benson?

MATE: I said I know where the treasure is.

3. CLARIBEL: Mr. Smithers, what hotel are they going to stay at?

SMITHERS: Well, I tell you, Claribel . . . I did something a little extra-special for them. I got them a — Mind if I smoke?

CLARIBEL: No, sir.

SMITHERS: Thanks. I got them a room at the same hotel where the first Mrs. Smithers and I spent our honeymoon twenty-five years ago.

CLARIBEL: The very same one? Oh, Mr. Smithers, how wonderful! How really — Where is that?

SMITHERS: The Winona Hotel on Magnolia boulevard. A mighty fine hotel!

CLARIBEL: The Winona! But that hotel was torn down eight years ago!

SMITHERS: Yes, sir! I wrote them on Friday, and I said "You take care of — " Torn down! Claribel, did you say the Winona Hotel was torn down?

CLARIBEL: About five years ago.

SMITHERS: You're crazy! It can't be. You mean those two kids are — ! (YELLING) Claribel, we've got to rescue them!

4. MARION: Very well, if that's it. If you don't want me around —

TOM: Now, Marion! When did I say — It's just that I want to get away from — from people. And not be disturbed.

MARION: But if you hate crowds so much, why don't you take the car?

TOM: Because — Well, because crowded trains are fun when you go skiing. Everybody sings and — That is —

MARION: But didn't you say you wanted to get away from crowds?

TOM: I know what I said! I want to get away from certain crowds. I mean — but some crowds, well — You wouldn't understand.

5. WALTER: Say, listen, Arch, the reason I phoned — Well, a little bird told me you and Arthur were going away on a little fishing trip.

ARCH: Why — a — Why —

WALTER: And I've got George Marshall here with me, and — What's that, George? (PAUSE) Arch, George and I have been talking it over and —

ARCH: Listen, Walter —

WALTER: And I said to George, I said, why don't we phone Sam and Arthur and make this a foursome?

ARCH: Oh.

WALTER: Won't we have a great time?

ARCH: Why — a — Would you hold on for a minute, Walter? I just — I just noticed somebody in my office here.

6. HATTIE: Now stop worrying, Richard. You're worse than a — a — I don't know what. Oh, hello, Harry.

HARRY: You know, we ought to decide what time we're all going to get up in the morning. Then we can — we can — Frankly, I don't know what we can do next.

7. MRS. RAY: My husband asked me to ask you — How would you like to serve on the committee with him? That is, if you —

MR. HUNT: Mrs. Ray, I certainly appreciate that. I really do. But after all — Well, as a matter of fact I did have other plans. I — Don't look so disappointed.

MRS. RAY: I'm not disappointed, Mr. Hunt. I just — Well, I know he did look forward to — It's all right.

8. JEB: I want you to be — I want you to — I want — Oh, what's the use? The words just sort of stick in my throat.

BABS: I know what's wrong. You're just not romantic enough. You're not — Here, get down on one knee.

JEB: Like this?

BABS: Yeah. Now put your hand over your heart.

JEB: Like this?

BABS: Yeah. Now look me in my eyes and propose.

JEB: Very well. Babs, you're the most gorgeous woman I know. You're so pretty you — Well, you look like a picture. When I look at you I — I —

BABS: What's the matter?

JEB: Turn your face the other way, will you?

9. MRS. HAPGOOD: Oh, Bob, my little boy! My little boy!

MR. HAPGOOD: Bob, it sure is good — Wonder what all those soldiers in your squad'd say if they heard their Sergeant being called a little boy?

BOB: It's good to be back. It's — I can't tell you.

MR. HAPGOOD: Well, I guess — Well, it's — Give me your baggage checks, son. I'll go see about your trunk. You and your Mother maybe want to — I'll meet you both at the car.

BOB: Right, Dad.

MRS. HAPGOOD: Oh, Bob! Having you back is — ! Everything's going to be just the way it was before!

10. BETSY: I didn't think you'd be home. I thought maybe — I just had to phone you. And it isn't pleasant news. It's horrible! It's about — Ellen, do you remember that boy who used to bring around the sandwiches? The one who — The boy you said looked just like your brother? Well, he's — It's the most awful news!

H. NEW IDEAS

1. CONNIE: Well, you do live like a little mouse, don't you? Always staying home by the fire . . . never going out anywhere. And I never get to go out either. You've turned me into a little gray mouse too.

   HERBERT: Maybe you're right, Connie. In fact, I know you're right. You're absolutely right. What a way to live! What a way to make you live! Connie, you know what?

   CONNIE: What?

   HERBERT: If this were my vacation . . . I'd pick up right this minute, and we'd go off together to that little hunting cabin up in Vermont. (A SUDDEN THOUGHT STRIKES HIM) Say, why should my classes keep _you_ cooped up here? ("Huh?") Look, Connie, why don't _you_ go up to the cabin. Then I'll join you in four or five days. ("But — ") And, say, why shouldn't Jim go up with you and stay till I get there?

2. BRUCE: Well, gee whiz, why didn't my teacher tell me?

   MOTHER: I'm sure I don't know. Would you like some more milk?

   BRUCE: No, thanks. Mother, if I were to build a better mousetrap and could give you anything in the world you wanted, what would you want?

   MOTHER: Bruce, what's on your mind?

3. CHARLIE: You know, it makes me feel good inside just thinking about her. Especially about buying her a present.

   GEORGE: It does?

   CHARLIE: Sure. Especially one that's gonna cost four dollars.

   GEORGE: That's a lotta money.

   CHARLIE: Sure, it is. You know, they say a man's best friend is his dog. But, you know . . . I think it's really his mother.

4. MR. X. Thanks for warning me, Bill.

   MR. Y. Don't mention it. It was a pleasure. Say, how about my buying you lunch tomorrow?

   MR. X. Well, let's see . . . I think I'm free . . . Say, Joe, was my wife over at your house last night?

5. MR. DOW: There's the movie. Now where are we going to park?

ETHEL: There's a car coming out! No, it's just going in.

TOMMY: I'll tell you what, Mr. Dow. Why don't you and Ethel get out, and I'll park the car around the corner, and you two go in and save me a seat? Here's the money for the tickets. This time I'm paying.

6. MRS. HOTCHKISS: And, Max, with that chicken — You will be sure it's browned nicely, won't you? — With that chicken bring us a good white wine. And, Max, this is Mr. Altenhouse. Mr. Altenhouse is a banker. And a very close friend of mine of many years' standing. Mr. Altenhouse knows a good thing when he sees it. So I want you to see that he's served with the very best you have. And served promptly, Max. Mr. Altenhouse has been through some very harrowing experiences today. Mr. Altenhouse, if you're thinking of getting married, you must let me tell you all about women. Nobody knows a woman like another woman. So, Max, we want excellent service.

7. ROY: Are you falling for this guy?

BILLIE: I never thought of such a thing. Why do you ask?

ROY: Are you falling for anybody?

BILLIE: Mr. Austin never thinks of me except as someone who works for him. Mr. Austin is a gentleman. He considers me a friend.

ROY: I suppose he's going to adopt you?

BILLIE: I wish you wouldn't say things like that! I want you to consider me a friend, too.

ROY: You wait a couple of days, and I'll give you the low-down on Mr. Austin. You think he's a gentleman, do you? All right! Wait and see! I'm going to do a little detective work.

8. MR. WRIGHT: Here you are. My heaven's, that's the smallest I have. A ten dollar bill.

SALLY: You mean you can't give just sixty-seven cents? I haven't any change — at least not that much.

MR. WRIGHT: I'm sorry, young lady, but this is the smallest I have. Perhaps you'd better come back some other time?

SALLY: No —— no, I couldn't do that! Look, why don't I do this? Why don't I run down to a store and get your ten dollar bill changed?

9. EVA: Of course, Emily, you never did have any taste in things like that. Only a person with a very morbid mind could like grisly things. And now that that's settled, let's talk about something —

EMILY: Yes, Alice? What is it?

ALICE: (SLIGHTLY OFF) Mrs. Peters says to tell you dinner will be ready in about twenty minutes, ma'am.

EMILY: Thanks, Alice.

EVA: That song you were working on, Emily — you remember? The one you told me about. Have you finished it?

10. BOY: You mean you're not mad at me any more?

GIRL: You can put it like that, if you wish.

BOY: That's swell! That's the way things ought to be. How'd you like to go to the movies tonight?

GIRL: That'd be wonderful!

BOY: Look, we could go to the movies, and then maybe go dancing afterwards!

I. CONVERSATIONAL SELECTION

THE SECOND MRS. BURTON, #470*

(MUSIC: LEAD IN)

(DOOR OPENS; SLIGHT PAUSE; CLOSES)

STAN: (DEEP SIGH) Wheeeew — this has been some day.

TERRY: And dinner time and nothing in the house to eat.

STAN: (WEARILY) I don't care, Terry. I'm so glad to get home. I'd settle for a fried egg sandwich and not say a word. (FLOPS DOWN ON COUCH WITH A SIGH)

TERRY: (MOVING AROUND) That's probably just about all you'll get. Stan — Darling, if you're going to lie there on the couch, take your shoes off, won't you?

STAN: (MUTTER) They're not touching anything.

* By Martha Alexander. Reproduced through the courtesy of the author.

TERRY: (THROW AWAY) That's what you always say. But I'm forever finding heel prints on the slipcovers just the same.

STAN: (MUTTERED TEASE) Um, all right. Nag-nag-nag.

TERRY: Would you like to have a fire in the fireplace and eat in here?

STAN: Um-huh. Might be sorta nice.

TERRY: Then you'll have to bring in some wood. There's only one log here.

STAN: Changed my mind. Just's soon eat in the kitchen. (BEAT: SOFTLY) Come here.

TERRY: I have to find us something to eat, darling.

STAN: Come here first.

TERRY: There isn't time, Stan. It's after six —

STAN: Who's in a hurry? Brad isn't here. There's just you and me. What difference does it make if we don't eat till midnight?

TERRY: It doesn't make <u>any</u> difference to <u>me</u>. You're the one who's always fussing about wanting dinner <u>exactly</u> at six-thirty.

STAN: (THROW AWAY) Well — my personality's changing. Come here. Sit down.

TERRY: (SMILE) Are you starting a new seven year cycle?

STAN: Um-huh. It's gonna change my luck, too. I'll be a rich man in seven years. (ADDING) Maybe. (BEAT) Maybe not, too.

TERRY: (MUMBLE) Aw — oo — oh!

STAN: What's the matter?

TERRY: Earrings. The spring's too tight.

STAN: Then why do you wear 'em? Gimme. I'll fix it.

TERRY: They never hurt till I take them off. Can you fix 'em?

STAN: I can <u>try</u>. Both of them too tight?

TERRY: Um-huh. Don't break them.

STAN: That isn't my goal, dear. You haven't as much faith in my fix-it talent as Brad used to have when he was little. He spent the first five years of his life bringing me things to fix.

(NOTE: TERRY'S IN A QUIETLY UNHAPPY-WITHOUT-APPARENT-REASON MOOD — ALMOST NOSTALGIC IN QUALITY)

TERRY: (SLIGHT PAUSE) I wish <u>I'd</u> known Brad when he was little.

STAN: He was a cute kid. There. Try that one. (BEAT) Any better?

TERRY: Um-huh. I think so. Thank you, darling. (BEAT) What else did Brad do when he was little?

STAN: Huh? Oh, I don't know. What do you want to know?

TERRY: Anything. Everything. Did he turn a dish of mashed potatoes and gravy over on top of his head? Most children do at least once.

STAN: Um-huh. He did. And had a lovely time patting it smooth after the dish fell off. And he stuck his finger in an open floor plug once — just to see what would happen. He found out. There. Try that one.

TERRY: (BEAT) It feels wonderful, darling. Thank you very much. (BEAT) Tell me some more.

STAN: About Brad? Well, let me see. He had an imaginary dog for a while once. But it finally ran away, I think. Its name was Spot — and it had to be imaginary because he wanted to take it to bed with him, and Marion wouldn't let him take a real dog. (THOUGHTFULLY) I'm not sure what Spot's eventual fate was. Maybe he just vanished.

TERRY: (BEAT) What else?

STAN: Well — I pulled all his baby teeth for him. That was always quite an occasion. We used the string and door knob method. (CORRECTION) String-doorknob and <u>nickel</u> method. I got pretty good at it by the time we got to his molars.

TERRY: (SLIGHT PAUSE) What else?

STAN: Why — I don't know, honey. I guess he was pretty much like most kids. Maybe a little more spoiled than most. I don't know. Why? Why all this sudden interest in Brad's early childhood?

TERRY: I don't know. I just wish — (BREAKS OFF) Darling — I love Brad. I feel — very close to him — closer sometimes than others. I don't feel at all like a "step-mother."

STAN: Well, I'm glad you don't, honey. I think — I think you mean a lot more to Brad than just a "step-mother" in that tone of voice.

TERRY: Do you? Do you really, Stan?

STAN: Why — Terry, what <u>is</u> this? What's it all about? What's on your mind? What's happened?

TERRY: Nothing. Nothing's happened. Only — when I see Brad with Marion — it's — it's so <u>different</u> from the way he is here. It's almost as if he's two different people. He so <u>obviously</u> adores Marion. I couldn't help noticing them this afternoon. When she cried, he cried. When she looked tense, he looked tense. When she smiled, he smiled. And I kept wondering — is that good? — or is that bad?

STAN: And what conclusion did you reach?

TERRY: I don't know. I'm still wondering. What do you think, darling?

STAN: (BEAT) Well — Marion's apt to have a pretty strong emotional effect on most anybody.

TERRY: (SLIGHT PAUSE, CAREFULLY) How did you feel about our leaving Brad with her this afternoon?

STAN: All right. I thought it was pretty obvious that he wanted to stay. And — she said she wanted him to. So as far as I was concerned that settled it. She hasn't paid much attention to the poor kid all summer. I thought she — Well, now that Bill's dead, she might start making it up to him. (BEAT, FROWNING) Why, Terry? How did you feel about it?

TERRY: I — (CONFESSION) I thought it was a mistake.

STAN: Why? After all, she is his mother.

TERRY: I know, I know. And I haven't any good, concrete reason for feeling that way. But I did — and you asked me and I told you. (DEEP SIGH) Are you about ready for a fried egg sandwich?

STAN: (BEAT) No. I want to know what's going on in your head?

TERRY: I just told you, darling, as much as I know. There isn't anything else.

STAN: (BEAT) I think there is. What is it, Terry? You're not — jealous of Marion — and the way Brad feels about her, are you?

TERRY: Jealous? (BEAT) Well, I don't know. Maybe I am. Would it be "jealousy" if I felt that —

STAN: (FINISHING FOR HER) That you'd make a better mother for Brad than she does?

TERRY: That — being less erratic — less emotional — calmer — I might — (BREAKS OFF) Oh, I don't know, Stan. Maybe I'm just plain jealous. I admit — it — hurt me a little bit to see the way Brad is willing practically to kneel down and worship Marion in return for one kind word from her. It hurts me — not because I want him kneeling and worshiping me. I don't! I wouldn't let him. Not for a single minute. But I — I can't help wondering why he doesn't show any of that tendency with us. Is he unhappy — living with us, Stan? Does he — simply tolerate us?

STAN: You know that isn't true, Terry. Brad said he wanted to live with us. He preferred living with us.

TERRY: (CORRECTING) He preferred us to Bill Sullivan. Not to Marion.

STAN: Well, that's natural. After all, honey, Marion is his mother, and nothing'll ever change that.

TERRY: But — the way she — she feeds herself on his emotions. It isn't good, Stan. I know it isn't.

STAN: (A LITTLE DEFENSIVELY) Nevertheless, she's his mother and she has a right to —

TERRY: (STRONG, CUTTING IN) She doesn't have a right to ruin —

STAN: (CUTTING IN, SHARPLY) She has a right to treat him any way she wants to, Terry, and you can't interfere.

TERRY: (SLIGHT PAUSE, DOWN) No, I can't interfere. I have no right — to say anything.

STAN: (SLIGHT PAUSE, TRYING TO SMOOTH OVER HIS PREVIOUS SHARPNESS) What you say may be absolutely true. I don't say that Marion's the "ideal" mother. Not by a long shot. However — I do believe that Brad needs her — in a way that he could never need you, Terry, no matter how much he learned to love you. You simply can't get away from the fact that —

TERRY: (FINISHING FOR HIM) — After all, she is his mother. I know, dear — very well. Just the same I'd like to tell her a few things on the proper —

STAN: (CUTTING IN) Well, you can't.

TERRY: (BEAT) Yes — I know that, too. I have no "right" to say a word.

STAN: (SLIGHT PAUSE) Is that what's bothering you, Terry? The fact that you love Brad as if you were his mother — and yet have no right to say anything?

TERRY: (BEAT) Yes. Yes, it does bother me. (SHAKING) I can't help it, Stan. It — it — I feel — cheated. It isn't fair.

STAN: What isn't fair?

TERRY: (SLIGHT PAUSE, CONTROLLED) Oh, nothing. I — I'm just — (BEAT . . . DEEP SIGH, DULLY) Shall we eat?

STAN: Not till we've gotten this thing straightened out. Just what is it that you think isn't fair?

TERRY: I don't know, dear. I honestly don't know. But that's the way I feel.

I can look at the facts and tell myself in a clear, firm voice the very same things you've been saying to me. And I know they're true. I haven't the right to say a word about Brad. "After all, he's not my child." But that doesn't help, darling. It doesn't even touch the way I feel.

STAN: (SLIGHT PAUSE) Well — uh — what do you think would?

TERRY: I don't know. Maybe nothing would. Maybe it's a feeling that I just "have to get over." I guess I — I forgot that Brad had just been borrowed from Marion for a while. I guess it's time I reminded myself. Because it seemed pretty obvious to me this afternoon that she wants him to live with her again now that Bill's gone. Didn't it to you?

STAN: Yes — it did. And I think she's perfectly justified in wanting him back now. After all, Bill Sullivan was the only reason she let us have Brad in the first place.

TERRY: (IMPATIENTLY) "After all, after all — " That's what I must keep saying to myself. (BEAT) All right. I'll say it to myself all the time I'm frying our eggs. "After all" everything is just the way it should be. But I wonder if I'll ever make myself believe it?

STAN: I can't see that it's so difficult to understand or believe.

TERRY: (CHOKING) But Brad is your son. You have a child. (BREAKING) I don't.

STAN: Terry! (BEAT) Is that what's wrong?

TERRY: (THROUGH TEARS, PARTLY SELF-DISGUST) Oh, I don't know. This whole day has been — (DOESN'T FINISH, CRIES SOFTLY UNDER)

STAN: (GENTLY) It hasn't been a very easy day, I admit. I can't see that memorial services are much different from regular funerals when it comes to wear and tear on the nerves. (BEAT) Don't cry, honey. Or maybe I should say, "Sure, go on and cry. Get it out of your system." You'll feel much better afterwards.

TERRY: (THROUGH TEARS) No, I won't. Oh, Stan — I want a child. Oh — desperately I want one! Our child. That's all that's wrong with me. Yes, I — I am jealous of Marion — and of every other woman who's —

STAN: (CUTTING IN) Terry. (BEAT, FIRMLY) Now we've been all through this before. There's no point in going into it again. I've told you how I feel — and I haven't changed. I won't change. I feel very strongly about it, Terry.

TERRY: And I feel strongly about it, too, Stan!

STAN: But I'm considering a great deal more than my own personal wishes. Brad's had just about all the tough breaks a kid can stand. But that's one he won't have to stand. Now — dry your eyes and — let's go see what we can do about those fried egg sandwiches.

TERRY: (SLIGHT PAUSE, DOWN) I'll fix them. You stay here and rest.

STAN: But I'd rather help you.

TERRY: (FIGHTING A FRESH OUTBURST OF TEARS) But I don't want you to help me! That doesn't solve a thing!

STAN: (BEAT, TOUCHY) Okay. If that's the way you feel about it. I have no objections to — taking it easy.

(MUSIC: IN)

Chapter VIII . . MICROPHONE READING: CONTACT

1

When, in *An Actor Prepares,* Director Tortsov asks, "Have you never put out your emotional antennae to feel out the soul of another person?"[1] he emphasizes an element of acting that is peculiarly the concern of the radio actor. On stage or before the cameras actors can, with practice and concentration, more or less easily communicate with one another during a scene: they can "size up one another"; they can contact one another eye to eye; they can watch the facial expressions and gestures and movements of their partners; they can see the other character in his make-up and costume; they can move away or toward him; and so on. Such intercommunication of the dramatis personae is impossible in radio. Often two actors performing a scene are stationed at different microphones; often, though speaking directly to each other at the same microphone, an eye-to-eye contact is denied them since their eyes are rather constantly glued to the mimeographed script page.

In spite of these seemingly unsurmountable obstacles, the radio actor must communicate with, must contact, the person to whom he is speaking when he reads his sentences. The conversational mode of acting demands, in addition to (1) a "full realization of the content of your words as you utter them," and (2) an illusion of happening for the first time, (3) "a lively sense of communication." When this third element is lacking, according to James A. Winans, "we may describe the delivery as *soliloquizing,* not *communicative,* or *indirect.*"[2]

In life conversation is the means of communication among people. At the microphone the playwright's dialogue should be transformed into that same sort of communication. Conversation is the *exchange,* with or without interruption, of thoughts and feelings; words are not uttered in a vacuum, in isolation. Conversation is give-and-take, is at least a duet instead of a solo, is an unbroken flow. In conversation you give to another person and get back from that person a something as concrete as a pencil that you may give him and that he may take, examine, and then return to you. Conversation is communion with another, is *contact* with another. A commonplace in everyday life, it must be striven for constantly with the actor's every resource at the microphone.

This contact with another person can be achieved in radio only by the most intensely concentrated use of the imagination. In order to establish contact with his partner the radio actor must therefore do two things: (a) he must imaginatively adapt himself differently to the different people he addresses, must concentrate on what Mrs. Pat Campbell called "that most difficult of technical difficulties, the subtle tones, tempo and manner, which indicate the difference of feeling towards each character in the play"; and (b) he must listen (apparently for the first time) to what is being said in the scene, must discover the truth in the old saying that "you can learn to act by learning to listen to what is being said to you."

2

Adapting oneself to the different people addressed is a fundamental of all acting and offers no distinctive difficulties for the radio actor. Certainly he knows that his different attitudes toward different people variously shape the way he reads his lines. Certainly in his performances he illustrates the truth that a sentence or speech is read in different ways depending on whether he is talking to a loved one, a stranger, a bill collector, an employer, an avowed enemy, the President of the United States, or someone else. As Stanislavski advises,

[1] Stanislavski, *An Actor Prepares,* p. 188.

[2] James A. Winans, *Public Speaking,* rev. ed. (New York: Appleton-Century-Crofts, Inc., 1926), pp. 31 and 32.

"If you are called upon to deal with a stupid person you must adjust yourself to his mentality, and find the simplest means with which to reach his mind and consciousness. But if your man is shrewd, you should proceed more cautiously and use subtler means so that he won't see through your wiles."[3]

This adaptation to the person addressed can be quickly illustrated by the following examples. The first is from Episode #120 of Agnes Ridgeway's THOSE WE LOVE:*

[3] Stanislavski, *op. cit.*, p. 215.

* Reproduced through the courtesy of the author.

KATHY: Les says you want me to match some yarn.

EMILY: Will you have time, dear?

KATHY: Yes, sure! Les has an operation up at Springdale at two-thirty, so I'm thumbing a ride.

EMILY: When does Frank get back?

KATHY: He thought tonight. He's got a meeting of his deacons tomorrow.

EMILY: Oh. (TO THE BABY) Yes, dear, Auntie sees the rattle. Come and see Auntie, Tom? (LAUGHING SOFTLY) That's a darling!

KATHY: It's funny, isn't it? . . . You never had a child of your own . . . and yet he seems to fit right into you. All babies do . . .

EMILY: (SMILING) Well, perhaps you and Kit conditioned me rather early in my life. Besides, babies know who loves them, don't they, Tom . . . (LAUGHING) Yes, that's my nose! Noses are funny-looking things, aren't they?

In Episode #465 of Martha Alexander's THE SECOND MRS. BURTON the whole color of the nurse's line, "Maybe you'd rather wait for your mother in the lounge. It's right here at the end of the hall," depends on her attitude toward the young boy, Bradley. Similarly, Bradley's speeches to the nurse, to his mother, and to his stepmother are given their shape and their quality in accordance with his different attitudes toward these three people.

A change of attitude peculiar to radio—the leap from a scene to narration—is illustrated in the following example from Joseph Ruscoll's *Primer for Murder,** which appeared on MYSTERY THEATRE.

* Reproduced through the courtesy of the author.

DONNIE: (GAILY) Oh, Herbert, you're an angel! I've misjudged you so! When do we start packing?

HERBERT: Right now is as good a time as any. (HE LAUGHS TOO) Come on — come on, you two! Get started. The trunks — get your trunks packed!

(MUSIC: STING)

HERBERT: Yes, they got out their trunks all right. (SIGHS) And that's when it happened. They went away all right — but out of this world. Trunk murders, remember? Two bodies were found!

Such obvious attitudes toward the person addressed are clear enough to the radio actor; he can't miss them. Nevertheless, he is likely to go wrong by forgetting that all attitudes toward other characters are not that obvious, by forgetting that attitudes toward other characters, however subtle, *always* exist. In other words, Emily in the first illustration is likely to show her attitude toward the baby, but she is all too likely to forget her attitude toward Kathy. Emily has an attitude toward Kathy, and Kathy has an attitude toward Emily. The best acting will bring out those attitudes.

Once the radio actor has found his attitude toward the character he is addressing he can correctly contact him. These contacts, or confrontations, are the tension of drama. Contact is established if, according to Stanislavski, while speaking to the person who is playing opposite you, "you learn to follow through until you are certain your thoughts have penetrated his consciousness. Only after you are convinced of this . . . should you continue to say the rest of your lines."[4] The radio actor, unable to add with his eyes what cannot be put into words, naturally has an extremely difficult job in making such contacts and penetrations. He can accomplish them only by using his imagination.

3

All actors must learn to listen. This rule is an old one and a simple one. It is so simple that most actors take it for granted, say "Yes, yes, I know I should listen," and then go on acting under the misapprehension that they are listening when, if the results are examined, they have never truly listened all the time they have been performing.

To listen in acting means to listen as in daily conversation. To listen in acting means not only to listen to others when you are not actively in the conversation but to listen to others precisely because you are participating in the conversation. To listen in acting means to *take in, each time afresh,* the words and thoughts and feelings and attitudes and motivations and objectives of your partner. To listen in acting means that you must be *newly* aware of the lines said to you even though you have heard them repeatedly during rehearsal.

Such listening at the microphone is essential if the flow of communion between people is to be maintained. Many actors, though, establish contact with their partners only when they are reading their own lines. "But let the other actor begin to say his," observes Stanislavski, "and the first one neither listens nor makes an attempt to absorb what the second is saying. He ceases to act until he hears his next cue. That habit breaks up constant exchange because that is dependent on the give and take of feelings both during the speaking of lines, and also during the reply to those already spoken, and even during silences."[5]

Listening in radio, however, differs vastly from listening on stage or on the movie set. Of course, the radio actor actually listens, in so far as he can, to what is being said in the scene—and most especially to what is being said directly to him. Yet he can and must listen in another way. Since he has his partner's speeches before him on the script page, he listens by following the lines as they are being read to him. *He listens by reading.* The skilful radio actor does not commit the common fault of jumping over all speeches on the page except his own; he does not, as soon as he finishes his own lines, immediately skip to the cue for his next speech, and then wait and listen only for that cue. He listens by following all the words. He therefore speaks when he does in reply to what has been said, to what he has heard, to what he has read. He does not speak merely because his lines come next on the page.

A final point for the radio actor to remember is that the audience cannot see him listening. Denied this advantage of the stage and screen actor, the radio performer can prove that he has been listening only by the way in which he reads his responses to other lines. The difference between lines that are born of listening and lines that only "come next in the script" is prodigious.

SELECTED READINGS

Read in *An Actor Prepares,* by Constantin Stanislavski, translated by Elizabeth Reynolds Hapgood. (New York: Theatre Arts, Inc., 1936), Chap. X, "Communion," pp. 182–209, and Chap. XI, "Adaptation," pp. 210–228.

[4] *Ibid.,* p. 190.

[5] *Ibid.*

EXERCISES

A. SOLILOQUIES

In order to experience and to know thoroughly the values of contacting another person for the full conversational shaping of his utterance, the radio actor might well begin with some readings in which communication with another actor is absent. Perhaps he can in this way discover the differences between communion and noncommunion.

1. THE SECOND MRS. BURTON, #485*

TERRY: (SOTTO) A simple matter of choice. You take or you give. You love or you're loved. Simple. Nothing to it. Man's greatest gift. Choice. "Which hand do you take?" They start us early — making choices. Teaching us how it's done. You can't have both. That's your trouble, Terry, old girl. You want both. That isn't the way the game's played. You know that. But nobody ever explained to you why the rules <u>had</u> to be the way they are. That's the trouble. You want what's in both hands. And why not? That's what they forget to tell you. It's the same way with that "You can't have your cake and eat it, too" business. All right — you can't have <u>all</u> your cake at a special given moment if you've just eaten <u>all</u> your cake. But why can't you have a slice now and then and save some — and when your supply begins to get low — take another one? That's what nobody ever bothered to explain. Why can't you — "take" sometimes — and "give" sometimes? Why do you have to stay on one side or the other? Why can't you — love and be loved? Isn't life big enough — and strong enough — to hold that much love all at once? Sure, it is. It's happened. What about — Abelard and Heloise? Well — <u>they</u> didn't turn out so well. But — what about Elizabeth Barrett and Robert Browning? <u>They</u> turned out all right. They <u>thrived.</u> So that proves it. It <u>can</u> happen. (BEAT) But — I guess it takes a special breed of people. Poets, maybe. Maybe it can only happen to poets — who don't care about — money and — the old Burton Store — and things like that. Maybe — I should have married a poet. Because — I don't think there's much chance that Stan and I — will ever go down as one of the great romances of history. If heaven's our destination — we'll have to slip through another entrance. (BITTERLY) And it'll probably say "Burton Store" over the door. (SLIGHT PAUSE)

* By Martha Alexander. Reproduced through the courtesy of the author.

Elizabeth Miller's right. Stan doesn't need me. I knew she was right when she said it — but I couldn't tell her so. Why couldn't I? Why did I resent it — when I already knew it was the truth? Why didn't I come right out and say, "Yes, I know. I've thought about it myself?" I don't suppose it's "my secret." Probably everybody in Dickston has thought about it — one time or another. I don't feel guilty about it. I'm sorry. I wish he did. But I can't help it if he doesn't. I just haven't got the things he needs. I'm not even good luck for him. He was better off in every way before he knew me. I guess I'm actually — "bad luck" for him. Everything he values — he had more of before he knew me. Hmf! A fine help-mate I turned out to be. (BEAT) What did I do wrong? Where'd I go off? I wanted so much to — to be good for him. (DEEP BREATH) But nothing's been the way I thought it would be. I guess — maybe — nothing ever is. You can't have your cake and eat it, too. Maybe you — can't have your dream and live it too.

2. HENRY IV, PART I*

PRINCE HENRY: I know you all, and will awhile uphold
The unyok'd humour of your idleness:
Yet herein will I imitate the sun,
Who doth permit the base contagious clouds
To smother up his beauty from the world,
That, when he please again to be himself,
Being wanted, he may be more wonder'd at,
By breaking through the foul and ugly mists
Of vapours that did seem to strangle him.
If all the year were playing holidays,
To sport would be as tedious as to work;
But when they seldom come, they wish'd-for come,
And nothing pleaseth but rare accidents.
So, when this loose behavior I throw off,
And pay the debt I never promised,

* From Shakespeare's play.

By how much better than my word I am,
By so much shall I falsify men's hopes;
And, like bright metal on a sullen ground,
My reformation, glittering o'er my fault,
Shall show more goodly and attract more eyes
Than that which hath no foil to set it off.
I'll so offend, to make offence a skill;
Redeeming time when men think least I will.

3. THE SECOND MRS. BURTON, #513*

MARION: (SOTTO: WRITING A LETTER) "Dear Lillian. I can assure you that if I had anything better to do this bright sunshiny Christmas morning, I wouldn't be writing you, dear. You should see the miserable, prosperous-looking derelicts — of which I am one — who wander up and down the aisles, smiling feebly at anyone who will smile back and exchange an equally feeble 'Merry Christmas' with them. It's sad, Lillian — and I've never felt more sorry for myself than I do at this minute. Incidentally, thanks very much for the atomizer. So far it hasn't spilled a drop in my purse — and I investigate it every hour or so, having nothing else to do. I suspect that all of us in this car are snobs — afraid of being snobs if we dare indicate that we'd like to start a conversation. I'm sure this attitude doesn't exist in the day coaches — because every time the doors open between the cars I can hear singing — laughter. Not good, but lively, at least. For a few minutes, a while ago, I vaguely entertained the idea of going into the coaches just to see what it was like in there. But then I noticed the man sitting caty-corner across the aisle from me . . . "

4. THE SECOND MRS. BURTON, #506†

STANLEY: (HALF-ASLEEP IN BED, SOTTO ON FILTER) Is this feeling — this — this sense of comfort and well-being that I always have with Terry — the thing that Marion calls "selfish"? Or is it this feeling that Marion's looking

* By Martha Alexander. Reproduced through the courtesy of the author.
† By Martha Alexander. Reproduced through the courtesy of the author.

for — and thinks we could find together — if we had another chance? Did I ever feel it with her? I can't remember. I must have — at first. But I don't remember it. (BEAT) She wants a decision tomorrow. Tomorrow . . . . Gee, Brad seemed happy tonight. He's a good kid — and we've given him a pretty rough time. I guess we haven't — taken our "duty to society" very seriously so far. I guess we have been — pretty doggoned selfish.

5. THE ORACLE OF PHILADELPHI*

ANN RUTLEDGE: Not long before Abe and I were to be married, I fell sick and died of the fever, and they put me in a lonely grave in the burying ground seven miles away, and on a black night of wind and rain he came to me and threw himself on the ground and beat his fists and cried my name. And I tried to say to him to be brave and go on without me and to believe in himself because one day he would be great with the greatness of America. And I didn't think he could hear me because there was dust in my throat, and outside the wind was tumbling. But he heard me.

6. OVERTONES†

Harriet is a cultured woman; Hetty is her primitive self. Both characters can be portrayed by one actress. Margaret is a cultured woman; Maggie is her primitive self. Both characters can be played by the same actress. According to the author, "The voices of the cultured women are affected and lingering, the voices of the primitive impulsive and more or less staccato."

HARRIET: How well you are looking, Margaret.

HETTY: Yes, you are not! There are circles under your eyes.

MARGARET: How well you are looking, too.

MAGGIE: You have hard lines about your lips. Are you happy?

HETTY: Don't let her know that I'm unhappy.

* From *Thirteen by Corwin,* by Norman Corwin. Reproduced by permission of Henry Holt and Company, Inc. Copyright, 1942, by Norman Corwin.

† From *Overtones,* by Alice Gerstenberg. Copyright, 1913, by Alice Gerstenberg and renewed in 1941. This selection is intended solely for study purposes and it may not be produced in any manner without the written permission of, and payment of royalty to, the author's agents, Longmans, Green and Company, 55 Fifth Avenue, New York 3, N. Y. Reproduced by permission.

HARRIET: Why shouldn't I look well? My life is full, happy, complete —

MAGGIE: I wonder.

HETTY: Tell her we have an automobile.

MARGARET: My life is complete, too.

MAGGIE: My heart is torn with sorrow. My husband cannot make a living. He will kill himself if he does not get an order for a painting.

MARGARET: You must come and see us in our studio. John has been doing some excellent portraits. He cannot begin to fill his orders.

HETTY: Tell her we have an automobile!

HARRIET: Do you take lemon in your tea?

MAGGIE: Take cream. It's more filling.

MARGARET: No, cream, if you please. How cozy!

MAGGIE: Only cakes! I could eat them all!!

HARRIET: How many lumps?

MAGGIE: Sugar is nourishing.

MARGARET: Three, please. I used to drink a very sweet coffee in Turkey and ever since I've —

HETTY: I don't believe you were ever in Turkey.

MAGGIE: I wasn't, but it's none of your business.

HARRIET: Have you been in Turkey? Do tell me about it.

MAGGIE: Change the subject.

MARGARET: You must go there. You have so much taste in dress you'd enjoy seeing their costumes.

MAGGIE: Isn't she going to pass the cake?

MARGARET: John painted several portraits there.

HETTY: Why don't you stop her bragging and tell her we have an automobile?

HARRIET: Cake?

MAGGIE: At last!

MARGARET: Thank you.

HETTY: Automobile!

MAGGIE: Follow up the costumes with the suggestion that she would make a good model for John. It isn't too early to begin getting what you came for.

MARGARET: What delicious cake!

HETTY: There's your chance for the auto.

HARRIET: Yes, it is good cake, isn't it? There are always a great many people buying at Harper's. I sat in my automobile fifteen minutes this morning waiting for my chauffeur to get it.

MAGGIE: Make her order a portrait.

MARGARET: If you stopped at Harper's you must have noticed the new gowns at Henderson's. Aren't the shop windows alluring these days?

HARRIET: Even my chauffeur notices them.

MAGGIE: I know you have an automobile. I heard you the first time.

B. LEAPS FROM NARRATION TO CONVERSATION

An attitude toward, and a contact with, a partner is highly important and readily discernible in the kind of acting, peculiar to radio, in which the speaker moves from narration to scene dialogue.

1. MY FRIEND IRMA*

JANE: The last time I filled out an application blank . . . next to Name — I put Jane Stacy. Next to Occupation — stenographer. Education -- grade school, high school, and college. I have a roommate. Name — Irma Peterson. Occupation — stenographer. Education — grade school, high school, and back to grade school. Now don't misunderstand me. Irma is a wonderful girl, and I love her. But there are times . . . Well, for instance, the other day I said: "Irma, I see where they've abolished poultryless Thursday." And Irma said:

IRMA: Yes. Now Al can call me "Chicken" again.

JANE: See what I mean? Right now we're both in our apartment. I'm just relaxing, and Irma . . . Well, Irma's thinking. I can always tell when Irma is thinking. "Irma, honey, what are you thinking about?"

IRMA: About my Christmas shopping.

JANE: Christmas shopping!? Aren't you a little premature? Thanksgiving isn't even here yet.

IRMA: That's just it. I don't like to run around right after I eat.

JANE: I'm sorry I asked.

* By Cy Howard and Parke Levy. Reproduced through the courtesy of the authors.

2. SILVER THEATRE: *CRYSTAL**

KENNETH: I wanted to tell her at once that I already knew her . . . already loved her. But all I said was, "Sorry . . . I didn't know anyone was in here."

JEANIE: It's all right.

KENNETH: I'm going to Washington Square . . . the Mews. Are you going that far?

JEANIE: Yes, almost.

KENNETH: Would you let me ride with you? It's . . . so hard to find a cab.

JEANIE: Yes . . . it is. Of course you may ride with me.

KENNETH: (LOW) Her voice was soft and a little husky . . . like a whisper trying to steal out between her words. I couldn't stop looking at her. I couldn't accept the familiarity of her face and the fact that we were strangers. And I couldn't bear to sit there in silence. Inanities pour from a man who is controlling himself in obedience to conventions, and I became a fountain of them. (UP) This is quite a rain, isn't it?

JEANIE: Yes.

KENNETH: I don't believe I've seen a rain like this all year.

JEANIE: Oh?

KENNETH: When it rains this hard, you might as well not struggle. Just take it . . . and change clothes when you get home.

3. WHEN A GIRL MARRIES, #1606†

ANN: (TO MOTHER AND JOAN) I felt so much better when I left here. I thought — I could face anything. I took a lot of time driving home. I almost — felt like I used to, like I did when Pete was alive. And then it happened. I no sooner got in the house when she started to nag me. I knew what would happen if I didn't get up to my room. (FADING) So I went upstairs and closed the door. But she followed me . . .

(LOUD KNOCK ON DOOR)

MRS. DUNN: Open the door!

ANN: I told you, Mrs. Dunn, I'm unpacking.

MRS. DUNN: That makes no difference. I want to talk to you, and I'm going to!

* By Elaine Carrington. Reproduced through the courtesy of the author.

† By Robert Presnell, Jr. Reproduced through the courtesy of the author.

(GROWING HYSTERICAL) I won't be treated this way by anyone! This is my home, and I demand some respect if — if you want to continue to live in —

(DOOR OPENS SUDDENLY)

ANN: What do you mean by that?

MRS. DUNN: I mean exactly what I say.

ANN: I think — we'd better have a long talk. Now wait a minute, Mrs. Dunn!

MRS. DUNN: No, I won't. I've been afraid to open my mouth in my own home — afraid to say what's what when I'm paying the bills. But now I'm going to change.

ANN: (LAUGHING) Afraid! That's ridiculous.

MRS. DUNN: No, it isn't. There's a look that comes in your eyes that frightens me. If you're going to continue to stay here, you're going to change. You're going to change completely, understand?

ANN: (BACK, HYSTERICAL AGAIN) And then — and then — oh, dear God! (SHE SOBS)

JOAN: There-there, dear.

ANN: I couldn't help it.

MOTHER: We'd better take her upstairs.

ANN: Please let me stay here tonight. Please do. Please let me stay here!

JOAN: Of course you'll stay here tonight.

ANN: I can't talk any more now. (SOBBING) I can't!

4. THE BIG STORY: *MURDER ON SEVENTY-SEVEN**

GRAHAM: (ALMOST HYSTERICALLY) He killed my wife, do you understand! Shot her down in cold blood right before my eyes! Left her bleeding to death in the highway . . . !

FRANK: (SHARPLY) Mr. Graham!

GRAHAM: (AFTER A PAUSE, QUIETLY) I'm sorry.

FRANK: Sure, I don't blame you for feeling that way. But how did it all happen? What were you doing on Route Seventy-Seven?

GRAHAM: (DULLY) Yesterday was a special kind of day, Mr. Winge. You see . . . it was my wife's fortieth birthday. And about six o'clock I came home from the office . . .

(DOOR CLOSES ON)

* By Max Ehrlich. Reproduced through the courtesy of the author and the producer of BIG STORY.

GRAHAM: (CALLING) Ellen! Oh, Ellen!

ELLEN: (OFF) Yes, dear. I'm coming. (COMING ON) Just setting the table for — Why, Albert! Roses! You brought me roses!

GRAHAM: Happy birthday, Ellen.

ELLEN: A dozen American beauties! Oh, Albert, what a wonderful surprise!

GRAHAM: (CHUCKLING) Think so, Ellen? Wait'll you hear what else I got for your birthday.

ELLEN: Albert, you darling! What?

GRAHAM: You remember that farm down near Oregon you've wanted for years? Well, I just bought it for you as a birthday gift.

C. INTERRUPTIONS

Most conversations are interrupted constantly with one speaker breaking in on another. Conversations are rarely a series of perfect completions. The secret of effective interruption is attentive listening. As a listener the actor must distinguish between the cue that brings on his response and the cue for starting to speak; they are not always identical.

Much dialogue in a play should have in it a sense of interruption, each actor speaking up more or less unexpectedly. This sense of interruption, this flow of give-and-take, can be simulated by the radio actor if he smartly picks up his cues, if he will say what he has to say before another person has a chance to speak up or to continue.

Radio actors need extensive practice in scenes like the following, from Mona Kent's PORTIA FACES LIFE* and Martha Alexander's THE SECOND MRS. BURTON.†

1. WALTER: I . . . I just don't want you asking any favors of John Breen, that's all.

   PORTIA: I don't understand. He's a very good friend of mine, and —

   WALTER: (INTERRUPTING) And he was also your law partner.

   PORTIA: Yes, but —

   WALTER: (INTERRUPTING) I don't want you feeling that you owe him anything.

   PORTIA: Oh, Walter, really that's —

   WALTER: (INTERRUPTING) No, Portia, I mean it. You gave me your word you were through being a lawyer. And you're not going back on it.

2. WALTER: Since you feel, obviously, that I haven't the right to criticize Dickie, why —

* Reproduced through the courtesy of the author and General Foods Corporation.

† Reproduced through the courtesy of the author.

PORTIA: (INTERRUPTING) But you do have the right, Walter. And I'm not taking any attitude about anything. I'm only trying to be fair about —

WALTER: (INTERRUPTING) Fair? If you think that putting all the blame on Miss Arden for what happened is being fair, what on earth's happened to your sense of values? It's entirely —

PORTIA: (INTERRUPTING) She shouldn't have screamed as she did! And she had no right to say the things —

WALTER: (INTERRUPTING) And I say Dickie has no business letting that dog of his jump all over —

PORTIA: (INTERRUPTING) When she called him a beastly little creature that was —

WALTER: (INTERRUPTING) I don't care if it was Elaine Arden, or —

PORTIA: (INTERRUPTING) For heaven's sake, Walter, at least let me finish what I'm trying to say instead of interrupting me every time I open my mouth.

WALTER: What's the point of talking about it at all? Dickie's your son. He can't possibly do any wrong! All right, Portia, from now on his discipline is strictly in your hands. I won't have any part of it!

(A DEAD PAUSE)

PORTIA: I wonder what's taking Byron and Kathie so long. That fainting spell of Elaine's can't have lasted all this time.

(PAUSE)

WALTER: (TURNING OFF) I think I'll go in and —

PORTIA: (INTERRUPTING) Walter.

(PAUSE)

WALTER: Well . . . What is it?

PORTIA: Walter, darling, we're quarrelling. And what about? Why?

3. STAN: The last time we talked about him you thought he was the greatest news analyst in America, the most brilliant commentator on the air, the most —

TERRY: As a commentator I still think he's fine. But that doesn't make him a wonderful <u>man</u>.

STAN: What did he do that made you change your mind?

4. BILL: Aw, you make me sick — the whole worthless bunch of you. You don't know what it means to —

LILLIAN: (CUTTING IN) I'm afraid you'll have to excuse me, Bill. It's later than I thought. I have an appointment.

BILL: Don't worry. I'm not staying. I've got better things to —

LILLIAN: Bill, who was it that told you I have Marion's rings?

5. TERRY: Yes, I know they've gone to look for berries, but do you know where?

MRS. MILLER: Well, when Ted was a little boy he used to go out on the old mill road. That's out by —

TERRY: Yes. I know where it is. Do you think they might have gone there today?

6. MYSTERY THEATRE: *DIG YOUR OWN GRAVE**

HANNAH: It's that young Betty Heath! ("Betty — ?!") That little actress across the street! ("Now listen — ") Don't lie! I saw it with my own eyes, didn't I?

ERIC: You mean about the —

HANNAH: Yes, about the dog just now!

ERIC: But I can explain that. ("Not to me, you can't.") Hannah, for heaven's sake, where are you going?

HANNAH: Across the street. ("No!") To scratch her eyes out!

ERIC: (CALLING) Hannah, you'll disgrace us before the neighbors! ("Disgrace!") I swear I don't even know the lady!

D. TOPPING AND UNDERPLAYING

Topping is the technical term for what happens in actual conversation when one speaker retaliates with more force, insistence, volume, or presence than does his partner. Topping means raising the level of speech. It is the reverse of "coming in under," or lowering the level of speech.

Both these changes of volume in utterance are ingredients of natural conversation; they are also technical devices for the structure of a scene.

Most radio actors need considerable practice in avoiding the bad habit of taking their tone of voice from that of the preceding speaker. This habit is often unconsciously formed

* By Joseph Ruscoll. Reproduced through the courtesy of the author.

when they merely half listen to the volume and tone used by their partners. Only by listening with special care and concentrating their efforts on using a different tone can they avoid copying.

1. BABY SNOOKS*

DADDY: Hmmmmmmmm. Well, Congress has finally settled down to some good hard work. Wonder how this Republican Congress will do? What do you think, Vera?

MUMMY: May I have the society page, dear?

DADDY: Well, that's a normal answer for you. I make a pertinent observation on the events of the day, and you're not even listening to my question.

MUMMY: Apparently you didn't listen to mine either. I said — may I have the society page?

DADDY: You may not.

MUMMY: What!

DADDY: Vera, why can't I come home once and sit down with a complete paper without everybody grabbing pieces of it?

MUMMY: Because there's only one paper and more than one person who wants to read. If you want to be so selfish —

DADDY: Ohh, here. I'll tear it off for you.

2. THEATRE GUILD ON THE AIR: *I REMEMBER MAMA*†

KATRIN: Mama . . . Papa . . . Nels! I've sold a story!

MAMA: A story?

NELS: What?

PAPA: No!

KATRIN: I've got a letter from the agent, with a check for — (GASPING) Five hundred dollars!

NELS: Five hundred dollars!

PAPA: My!

* By Jesse Oppenheimer and Everett Freeman. Reproduced through the courtesy of the authors.

† From *I Remember Mama,* by John van Druten. Copyright, 1944, 1945, by John van Druten. Adapted from Kathryn Forbes's *Mama's Bank Account.* Both published by Harcourt, Brace and Company, Inc. Radio adaptation by Erik Barnouw, in H. William Fitelson (ed.), *Theatre Guild on the Air,* published by Rinehart & Company, Inc.

MAMA: Katrin . . . is true?

KATRIN: Here's the letter.

NELS: What will you do with five hundred dollars?

KATRIN: I'll buy Mama her warm coat, I know that. And we'll put the rest in the Bank.

NELS: (KIDDING) Quick. Before they change their mind and stop the check. (ALL LAUGH)

KATRIN: Will you, Mama? Will you take it to the Bank downtown tomorrow? — What's the matter?

MAMA: I do not know how.

NELS: Just give it to the man and tell him to put it in your account, like you always do.

MAMA: Sure . . . sure . . . but —

PAPA: You tell them . . . now, Marta.

KATRIN: Tell us what?

MAMA: (DESPERATELY) Is no Bank Account! Never in my life have I been inside a bank!

NELS: What!

KATRIN: Mama, you always told us . . .

MAMA: I know. But was not true. I tell a lie.

NELS: But why, Mama?

MAMA: Is not good for little ones to be afraid . . . not to feel secure . . . But now . . . with five hundred dollar . . . I think I can tell.

KATRIN: Mama!

MAMA: You read us the story. You have it here?

3. IT HAPPENED ONE NIGHT*

ELLIE: It's the first time I've ridden "piggy-back" in years.

PETER: This isn't "piggy-back."

ELLIE: Of course it is.

PETER: You're crazy.

* From the screen play by Robert Riskin, based on a novelette by Samuel Hopkins Adams. *It Happened One Night* was produced by Columbia Pictures Corporation. Used with permission.

ELLIE: (AFTER A SILENCE) I remember distinctly Father taking me for a "piggy-back" ride —

PETER: And he carried you like this, I suppose?

ELLIE: Yes.

PETER: (WITH FINALITY) Your father didn't know beans about "piggy-back" riding.

ELLIE: (AFTER ANOTHER SILENCE) My uncle — Mother's brother — had four children . . . and I've seen <u>them</u> ride "piggy-back."

PETER: I don't think there's a "piggy-back" rider in your whole family. I never knew a rich man yet who was a good "piggy-back" rider.

ELLIE: That's silly.

PETER: To be a "piggy-backer" it takes complete relaxation — a warm heart — and a loving nature.

ELLIE: And rich people have none of those qualifications, I suppose?

PETER: Not a one.

ELLIE: You're prejudiced.

PETER: Show me a good "piggy-back" rider and I'll show you somebody that's human. Take Abraham Lincoln, for instance. A natural "piggy-backer." (CONTEMPTUOUSLY) Where do you get off with your stuffed-shirt family? Why, your father knew so much about "piggy-back" riding that he —

ELLIE: (PERSISTENTLY) My father was a <u>great</u> "piggy-backer."

PETER: Hold this suitcase a minute.

(HE DELIVERS A RESOUNDING SMACK ON HER BACKSIDE, SO THAT ELLIE LETS OUT A YELP)

PETER: Thank you.

4. THE ADVENTURES OF THE THIN MAN: *THE CASE OF THE CHILLING CHEWING GUM**

COOKIE: (SINGING)

(DOOR KNOCK OFF)

COOKIE: (CALLING) Who is it?

EB: (OFF) This is Sheriff Ebeneezer Williams.

COOKIE: The Sheriff! (CALLING) Is my singing that lousy?

EB: (OFF) 'Tain't so bad. You just made one mistake.

COOKIE: What's that?

* By Milton Lewis, based on the characters originated by Dashiell Hammett.

EB: You're singing in the wrong bathtub.

(DOOR OPENS ON)

COOKIE: Who says so?

EB: (ON) Oh. Glad to see you're wearing a bathrobe.

COOKIE: I'm queer like that. I always wear a bathrobe when I take a bath.

EB: What's your name?

COOKIE: Cookie . . . on account of I'm just a mouthful.

EB: Well, look, Cookie, I don't like to turn you out wearing only a bathrobe.

COOKIE: Why not? I look good in a bathrobe.

EB: This is my room. You'll have to leave.

COOKIE: I won't do it.

EB: But, Cookie — !

COOKIE: You know what you are? You're an old wolf!

EB: You reckon so?

COOKIE: A man of your years and dignity! You know what I'm going to do?

EB: What?

COOKIE: What any girl does when she don't know what to do! Scream! (SCREAM) Help!

5. CANDLE IN THE WIND*

CISSIE: Mademoiselle, is it true you can buy fruit and cheese and butter on the streets in New York? All you want?

MAISIE: Yes.

CISSIE: From open wagons on the streets?

MAISIE: Yes.

CISSIE: Could one person buy all that was on the wagon?

MAISIE: If he wanted to.

CISSIE: Have you seen this yourself?

MAISIE: Oh, yes.

CISSIE: Have you ever bought all that was on a wagon?

MAISIE: Well, in my time I've made a terrible consumption of butterfats and cheese, but never by the wagon-load.

* By Maxwell Anderson. Copyright, 1941, by Maxwell Anderson. Reprinted with the permission of Anderson House.

CISSIE: I think if I ever saw it I'd buy a whole wagon-load, and take it home. I shall never stop being hungry.

MAISIE: You'll find that you can't eat much at a time. Woman wants but little food and drink, but she just wants that little fairly regular.

CISSIE: Of course, for me America is only a dream.

MAISIE: I used to walk around on it, so it must be solid.

CISSIE: It may be that you walked in a dream. I myself have walked there in a dream. They say when you dream in English, then you are no longer German. Then you can be an American.

MAISIE: There may be something in that.

CISSIE: I dreamed once that I walked among the food wagons, and spoke English — spoke it clearly — and asked for ice cream. And the man filled a great vase with ice cream, and it piled up and up and up — like a white cloud, and when I reached for it, it blew away. I woke up, and now I'm always hungry, and I cannot dream in English again.

6. THE THIRTEENTH FLOOR*

KITTY: Let go of my arm. You're digging your nails in it.

NICKIE: Sorry, Baby. Maybe I don't know my own strength.

KITTY: (SCARED) What do you want? How did you get here?

NICKIE: (FADING) One thing at a time. Don't rush me.

(KEY IN LOCK)

NICKIE: (OFF) There.

KITTY: What'd you lock the door for?

NICKIE: (COMING ON) I don't like interruptions. You never used to either, when you were alone with me . . . Remember, Kitty?

KITTY: I don't remember nothin'!

NICKIE: Yeah, I know. You got a memory like a faucet. You turn it off and on . . . off and on . . . Wonderful! Take me, for instance. I got the kind of memory you can't turn off. It keeps running all the time . . . And the longer it runs the hotter it gets. It's so hot now, Kitty, it'll scald you.

KITTY: Look, Nickie —

* By Winifred Wolfe. Reproduced through the courtesy of the author.

DUERR, EDWIN

RADIO AND TELEVISION ACTING
CRIT, THEORY & PRACTICE

RINEHART — N.Y. — (1950)

NICKIE: I am looking. You're still a nice looking number. I always did like the way your waist curves in the middle, and how white your neck is . . .

KITTY: You didn't come here to tell me —

NICKIE: And the way you toss your hair over your shoulder like it gets in your way. Go ahead, Kitty. Toss your hair back for Nickie.

KITTY: What are you trying to do? Dangle me on a string —

NICKIE: Yeah, still a good looking number. I don't look so hot, do I? Think maybe I lost a little weight?

KITTY: Let me tell you — — (PLEADING)

NICKIE: And my face is kind of pasty looking? That's because you don't get much chance for fresh air . . . sweating what's left of time away in a death cell.

KITTY: If I scream the police will come and get you. If you come near me, I'll scream!

NICKIE: You won't scream.

KITTY: No? Come one step closer and I'll show you!

NICKIE: You won't scream because there's not that much sound left in you. It's all frozen and sticking in your throat like an ice cube — because you're afraid . . . afraid of me. Try screaming, Kitty!

KITTY: I — — I — —

NICKIE: See. What did I tell you?

KITTY: Nickie, I can help you. I can hide you here so they won't find you. Then I can help you get away, Nickie. Anywhere you want. I promise, Nickie. Don't come near me. Please!

E. ATTITUDES, COMMUNION, CONTACT

In the following two excerpts notice Marion's different attitudes toward, first, a friend, and then, second, her former husband when telling them the same information and making the identical request. This difference is expressed not only in her words but in her attitude toward each of the men. Such attitudes are present, though not so clearly, in all scenes of a play.

1. THE SECOND MRS. BURTON, #393*

GREG: Don't mention it. Can you share your rock with me?

MARION: Sit down.

* By Martha Alexander. Reproduced through the courtesy of the author.

GREG: This is a nice spot. Wonderful waterfall. Good to know about. Do many people come out here?

MARION: Not during the day. At night I understand it's fairly popular with the high school crowd.

GREG: Nothing is ever quite so deserted as a deserted mill. I wonder why?

MARION: I haven't much time, Greg. I have to be back in town for lunch.

GREG: Very well. Deserted mills postponed. What's on the morning's agendum? I hope you notice the care with which I handle Latin.

MARION: (BEAT) Bill's threatened to kill me.

GREG: What? (LAUGHING) Oh, no! Not really?

MARION: What's funny about that?

GREG: (STILL LAUGHING) Doesn't it amuse you?

MARION: It certainly does <u>not</u>. And I don't think it would amuse you either, Greg, if you could have heard him and seen — as I did — that he meant it.

GREG: (DISMISSING IT) Awh — Bill won't kill you, Marion. Forget it. Every man threatens to kill his wife once in a while.

MARION: (SLOWLY) And every once in a while — a man <u>does</u> kill his wife.

GREG: (BEAT, MORE SOBERLY) Granted.

MARION: I have no desire to be included in that group —

GREG: I can see your point. (BEAT) But I think you're wrong about Bill. He's not the type.

MARION: He's the most frightening man I've ever known in my life.

GREG: Frightening, yes. But that doesn't make him a murderer.

MARION: It hasn't — <u>yet</u>.

GREG: (BEAT) What brought on this particular threat?

MARION: (SLIGHT PAUSE) I was — planning to go to New York for a week — to look for a job. I made the mistake of telling him so.

GREG: Is that all?

MARION: He saw it as the final step — in our separation.

GREG: Oh. He won't let you go, huh?

MARION: He can't keep me. He can't keep me if I — if I can borrow some money somewhere. He can't watch me every second, can he? He has to look after the store. If I can — borrow some money, I'll — simply go along for a while — pretending that I've — reconsidered. And — as soon as he's convinced that I'm not still planning to leave — I'll — disappear.

GREG: Then what?

MARION: I'm — not absolutely certain yet. I'll probably — go somewhere where he'd never think of looking for me — establish my residence — and apply for a divorce. I could — work it out some way, I think, so that he wouldn't be notified until it was too late. But that would take money — and he's already stopped my checking account.

GREG: I don't understand why any man wants to keep a wife who doesn't want to stay with him. Maybe I should forget about the Balkans this summer and write a book in praise of bachelorhood?

MARION: Peculiarly enough — Bill loves me. And men are notoriously bad losers at love.

GREG: We'll put that statement up here in the same pigeon hole with deserted mills — to be discussed later. We are not in agreement, my sweet.

MARION: (BEAT) Can you help me, Greg?

GREG: Help you what?

MARION: Can you let me have a thousand dollars?

GREG: A thousand dollars? Marion, you flatter me. I would gladly give you a thousand dollars — if I had it. But I don't. I'm in debt up to my eye-brows. You know that. I always am. One of the reasons I came to Dickston for the summer was to save money. That is — to save my bills from getting any higher.

MARION: Haven't you saved <u>anything</u>? With your income —

GREG: Darling, how can I afford to save anything when I haven't yet learned how to afford to pay my bills?

MARION: I told you a long time ago you should live on a budget.

GREG: I do. But I habitually underestimate "incidentals." You have no idea how expensive my incidentals can be.

MARION: (BEAT) Are you telling me the truth? You haven't got a thousand dollars?

GREG: Cross my heart. I'm sorry, Marion. I wouldn't even know where to get it for you. Unless I were to hit Bill for it. But I doubt if he'd let me have it, don't you?

2. THE SECOND MRS. BURTON, #395*

STAN: You aren't planning to make a habit of dropping in here at the store unexpectedly, are you?

MARION: It seems to be the only way I can ever see you alone any more.

STAN: Why should we see each other alone, Marion? Our only point of contact now is — Brad. And I thought we had reached at least a temporary solu —

MARION: (CUTTING IN) I didn't come to talk about Brad today.

STAN: (BEAT) Oh?

MARION: (SLIGHT PAUSE, THIS IS TOUGH GOING) I'm in trouble, Stanley — serious trouble.

STAN: With Bill?

MARION: Yes.

STAN: I'm not surprised.

MARION: He's — threatened to kill me — before he'll let me leave him.

STAN: (SLIGHT PAUSE) He'd never do it. He's too big a coward.

MARION: Bill's not a coward, Stanley, and you know it.

(DISTANT RUMBLE OF THUNDER UNDER)

STAN: So — you're not leaving him after all. Is that it?

MARION: Of course I'm leaving him. I'm more determined than ever. But — I'll have to have help.

STAN: (GUARDEDLY) What kind of help?

MARION: Money.

STAN: That's why you've come to me? (BOWING) Thanks.

MARION: Is there anyone else I could go to?

STAN: It seems to me almost any of your friends have a healthier bank account than mine.

MARION: Can you name one that would lend me a penny without bragging about it all over town? Bill mustn't know about this, Stan. He mustn't find out that his threats haven't stopped me.

STAN: (SLIGHT PAUSE) What are your plans? (ADDING) Or don't you want to trust me with them?

MARION: Can I trust you, Stanley?

* By Martha Alexander. Reproduced through the courtesy of the author.

STAN: That's for you to decide.

(SOUND: THUNDER IN CLOSER.)

STAN: Oh-oh! It's getting close. I'd better put that window down.

MARION: (QUICKLY) No, don't.

STAN: Why not? (BEAT: TOLERANTLY) Oh, yes. I remember now. You and summer storms. All right. The windows stay open but if the floor gets soaked, you'll have to stay and mop it up.

MARION: Do you hate me, Stanley?

STAN: At the moment or — generally speaking?

MARION: Just answer my question.

STAN: Well — I have moments —

MARION: Of what?

STAN: Hating you.

(SOUND: BRING IN RAIN UNDER)

MARION: And in the other moments?

STAN: (BEAT) I guess I don't think about you at all.

MARION: (BEAT) I don't believe you.

STAN: (SHRUG) That's too bad. A smarter woman would.

MARION: (DEFENSIVELY) I don't think I've ever been considered stupid.

STAN: I didn't say you were stupid. I simply meant to imply that you're smart about all the wrong things.

MARION: (BEAT, MOVING AROUND) I don't know what that means — and I don't think I want to. (ABRUPTLY, EARNESTLY DEMANDING) What's the matter with me, Stan? Why don't I have any friends real enough to count on when I need help? Why do men — either love me — or hate me?

STAN: Why ask me, Marion? My judgment of you has been outstandingly inaccurate for years. (THROW AWAY) You'd better come away from that window. You'll get wet.

MARION: I don't care. I love it. (BEAT) It would be tempting — if this window were only high enough to guarantee instant death for anyone who jumped out of it. (ABRUPTLY) Stan, will you lend me a thousand dollars?

STAN: A thousand dollars?? Me?!

MARION: Well, don't look as if I've just asked for your head on a silver platter. A thousand dollars isn't much money.

The attitudes of the main characters toward one another, and toward common problems, make up one of the main reasons for the popularity of the following program and the excellence of the acting.

3. MY FRIEND IRMA*

AL: Why waste time dealing with the hired help? Go to the top — that's my policy. Go to the top. Do you think Pike's Peak would ever have been discovered by a deep sea diver?

IRMA: But, Al, what do you mean — go to the top?

AL: Go to the owner.

IRMA: Then we can't go to the top. We have to go to the bottom. The owner's been dead for fifteen years.

JANE: Irma, he means go to the bank, the people who control the property.

IRMA: But if we do that, Jane, Mrs. O'Reilly will be fired.

JANE: Look, honey, I know what you're thinking. We all like Mrs. O'Reilly, but evidently the feeling isn't mutual.

AL: Jane's right. You can't be sentimental about these things, Irma. You're paying rent. You should get your money's worth. She's got no right treating you like this. You're not veterans.

JANE: Well, there's only one answer. It's survival of the fittest. If we expect to live through the winter, we simply must take action.

AL: Tell you what to do, kids. Draw up a petition and take it to the bank.

IRMA: I don't think that'll do any good.

JANE: Why not?

IRMA: Mrs. O'Reilly will never sign it.

JANE: Irma, only the tenants have to sign it, and if we get the Martins upstairs it'll be unanimous.

AL: Good. You and Irma go upstairs and talk to them while the Professor and I draw up the petition.

JANE: Al, for once you're talking sense. Come on, Irma.

IRMA: All right, Jane. What shall I wear?

JANE: What will you wear? Irma, we're only going upstairs.

IRMA: I know, Jane, but it's freezing down here, and they say the higher up you go the colder it gets.

JANE: Don't worry, honey. If things get rugged just yell "Mush!" Come on.

* By Cy Howard and Parke Levy. Reproduced through the courtesy of the authors.

In the following two selections notice the different attitudes one person has toward different people.

4. DAVID HARDING, COUNTER-SPY, #164*

DAD: (FILTER) Hello . . .

LAURA: Oh, hello, Daddy.

DAD: (AMAZED) Laura?

LAURA: Daddy, how much longer are you going to be in Boston?

DAD: (STILL AMAZED) Why — a couple of days . . .

LAURA: Then I can't wait. I've got to tell you. Guess, guess!

DAD: (DUMBFOUNDED) What are you talking about?

LAURA: (SLIGHT PAUSE — THEN THE TERRIFIC NEWS) Charlie Bendix has asked me to marry him!

DAD: (PAUSE — AMAZEMENT) What?

LAURA: He asked me this afternoon. I've only known him six weeks, but, Dad, he's the most wonderful person!

DAD: (VERY SERIOUS) Now, Laura — I'll want to talk to you.

LAURA: And he's not in love with me because of your money either, Dad. He's the handsomest man I ever saw — and he's more fun to be with! Every woman looks at him when he passes . . . There's nobody like him. (GETTING COLDER AND COLDER . . . EACH WORD SLOWER UNTIL LIKE ICE) And I'm sure everything will be all right. I — I know it will be. And — a — (PAUSE)

DAD: (PAUSE — THEN SPOKEN AS IF SOMETHING TERRIBLE HAD HAPPENED) Laura!!

LAURA: (BITES EVERY WORD . . . GREAT ANGER HELD IN . . . LIKE STEEL) I can't tell you now. I'll tell you when I see you. Goodbye.

(RECEIVER DOWN)

CHARLIE: (SUBDUED CHUCKLE)

LAURA: (REALLY MAD) Charlie Bendix! I'm mad at you! I didn't hear you come in.

CHARLIE: (CUTE — TEASING) I didn't intend you should.

LAURA: But — ?

CHARLIE: I thought I'd surprise you . . . and steal a little kiss. (PLAY IT . . . REALLY MOCKING) I didn't know I was going to hear my bride-to-be (TEASING) so beautifully describing me!

LAURA: (EVIDENTLY VERY EMBARRASSED . . . STUNNED . . . STILL MAD, BUT EXCUSING HERSELF) Well — I just had to say it. I had to sell Dad.

* Written by Phillips H. Lord.

CHARLIE: (PLAYFULLY SMILING) Am I good looking?

LAURA: (POSITIVE) No.

CHARLIE: Oh, yes, I am. Don't all the women look at me when I go by?

LAURA: They certainly do not!

CHARLIE: (CHUCKLES . . . VERY MOCKING) There were a lot more nice things you could have told your Dad about me, you know.

LAURA: (VERY SERIOUS . . . COMPLETE SUDDEN CHANGE . . . PAUSE) Charles . . .

CHARLIE: (TEASING ABOUT HER SERIOUSNESS) Um . . . I get the tone.

LAURA: Don't. I'm very serious. (VERY TENSE AND FLAT) There's something I've got to talk to you about.

CHARLIE: (TRYING TO PASS IT OFF JOVIALLY) Oh, now, it can't be that serious.

LAURA: But it is. It's terribly serious. I — I don't know what it means.

*** ***

(DOOR OPENS ON)

LAURA: Yes?

HARDING: Are you Miss Laura Deke?

LAURA: Yes. Who are you?

HARDING: A friend of Charlie Bendix.

LAURA: (PAUSE — BREATHLESS) Charlie — Bendix?

HARDING: Yes. I want to talk to you about him.

LAURA: (PAUSE — THEN FIRM BUT DIGNIFIED) You go back and tell Charles I don't ever want to see him — or talk to him again. Or any of his friends. And that ends it.

HARDING: Just a minute, Miss Deke. (SIMPLY AND EARNESTLY) I know something about Charlie going away (SLIGHT PAUSE) I think you ought to know.

LAURA: (PAUSE — HEAVY BREATH — MAD) He could have written . . .

HARDING: There's something very important, Miss Deke, that you don't know. (PAUSE) May I come in?

LAURA: (AFTER A LONG PAUSE) All right.

(DOOR CLOSES)

LAURA: Who are you?

HARDING: David Harding — of the United States Counter-Spies.

LAURA: (AMAZED) What!?

HARDING: Yes, and I want to ask you a few questions about Charlie.

LAURA: (VERY FEARFUL) I — I — — Well . . . (SUDDENLY SUSPECTING CHARLIE A SPY) What's the matter?

HARDING: (PAUSE) You were in love with Charles Bendix, weren't you?

LAURA: I — I don't know.

HARDING: The truth.

LAURA: (SWALLOWS — LOW) Yes.

HARDING: But there was something about Charles that worried you, wasn't there? (PAUSE) Wasn't there?

LAURA: (SUPPOSEDLY WANTING TO DEFEND HIM) Well . . .

HARDING: (KINDLY) What was it?

LAURA: (LETTING OUT A LITTLE PENT-UP EMOTION AND HURT) I — I couldn't understand certain telephone calls he used to get . . . and he . . . he'd have to leave, and he wouldn't tell me why . . .

HARDING: Did you suspect him of anything?

LAURA: Oh, no, no! (PUZZLED) But I couldn't understand it.

HARDING: (POINT . . . PAUSE) But you really did love him?

LAURA: (PAUSE — REAL TENDER FINALITY) Yes — very, very much.

HARDING: Well, Miss Deke — I feel I must tell you — Charles Bendix was one of my best agents.

LAURA: (PAUSE) A — what?

HARDING: Charles was one of my agents — a Counter-Spy.

LAURA: (GREAT SHOCK . . . REALIZING SHE DOUBTED HIM) No — no . . .

HARDING: He was under orders not to talk.

LAURA: (STILL DAWNING) I — I — don't under . . . Charles was a government agent?

*** ***

DAD: (ON FILTER — COMPLETELY BROKEN) No, no! I didn't do it. I didn't kill Charlie Bendix! I'll talk. I'll turn government witness. I'll tell you who the big boss is!

PETERS: (ON FILTER) It isn't a man. It's a woman.

DAD: Yes, it's a woman. It's —

PETERS: Fraulein Harriet Grocket — one of the cleverest woman spies of them all — who has been posing as your daughter!

LAURA: (OVERHEARING THIS — A GASP)

DAD: Yes, yes! I admit it.

LAURA: I'll kill him! I'll kill him — !

HARDING: (PANTING) I'll take that gun! That's why you wanted me to drive you back to the apartment so you could kill him before he talked.

LAURA: You tricked me, you, you — !

HARDING: (RATHER FAST, MAD BUT CLEAR) You little fiend! You discovered Charlie Bendix was a Counter-Spy and pretended to fall in love with him so you could check on him. We hoped you'd go into action and we could get you. Instead — you had him killed first.

LAURA: I just wish it had been you! If it had been you, I'd have done it myself!

5. MYSTERY THEATRE: *THE MAN WHO MURDERED IN PUBLIC**

(PAPERS BEING RIFFED)

MARTLEPLUG: (OVER SOUND OF PAPER AND UNDER BREATH — TO HIMSELF) First, the town of Ilfracombe, then Bognor, now it's Paignton. And all the same way — and the same man!

VOICE: (COMING ON) Well, Inspector Martleplug. Still studying those stuffy accident files. Whatever do you see in them?

MARTLEPLUG: Murder!

VOICE: Oh, I say now!

MARTLEPLUG: Doubt it? Look! Those three reports. Identical. Three women, all servant girls, drowned. All with a man named Macartney.

VOICE: So? There are hundreds of identical accidents every summer.

MARTLEPLUG: Two of the women insured . . . .

VOICE: Husbands insure their wives as a matter of course.

MARTLEPLUG: Perhaps, but I think this Macartney bears talking to.

(MUSIC: BRIDGE)

(KNOCK ON DOOR . . . PAUSE AND REPEAT . . . THEN OPEN DOOR ON)

GEORGE: Yes?

MARTLEPLUG: Mr. Macartney?

GEORGE: I'm George Macartney.

MARTLEPLUG: (PLEASANT) Mr. Macartney, I'm Inspector Martleplug of Scotland Yard. May I come in?

* By Roy Vickers, adapted by Frederic A. Methot. Reproduced through the courtesy of the authors and the publishers of *Ellery Queen's Mystery Magazine*.

GEORGE: (PLEASANT) I was just about to leave. However, Scotland Yard comes first, I'm sure. (CLOSE DOOR ON)

MARTLEPLUG: I'll come straight to the point, Mr. Macartney. Our records reveal that you have . . . uh . . . had the singular misfortune of being the . . . er . . . sole survivor in three drowning incidents.

GEORGE: Oh, dear! I had rather hoped to forget about them.

MARTLEPLUG: I shouldn't wonder. Can you shed any light on the . . . er . . . coincidences?

GEORGE: It fairly beats me, Mr. Martleplug, and that's a fact. You'd think that after a thing like that happened once, it couldn't possibly happen again.

MARTLEPLUG: True.

GEORGE: It used to haunt me. That's why poor Madge persuaded me to go out again . . . to overcome my horror of water. But why talk about it?

MARTLEPLUG: That's why I've come . . . to talk about it, Mr. Macartney.

GEORGE: (TONE BECOMES NORMAL, KEEN, BUSINESSLIKE) I see! But I don't care to talk about it, Inspector. It's too painful.

MARTLEPLUG: Not nearly so painful as a rope.

GEORGE: I tell you I won't discuss it, Inspector. If you don't like that, why don't you arrest me for murder? (PAUSE) I'll tell you why you don't. Because . . . you have no evidence. (LAUGHS) You'll never hang me, Martleplug, because you haven't any evidence and you can't get it! (LAUGHS)

Each of the next two selections should be read by the students perhaps three or four times—with a definite change in attitudes on the part of the characters toward each other for every reading. Only by practicing such exercises—in which the attitude "regulator" is changed while the speeches and everything else remain constant—can the student discover the tremendous effect communion has on utterance.

The two selections are only samples of the kind of dialogue that the students should be assigned to bring to class—excerpts from plays in which the attitudes of two characters toward each other can be variously changed—to help them understand the variety of effects that can be achieved in conversational reading.

6. MIRAGE*

CARL: We'll get off on safe subjects — the sea, the weather, the moon, June, the number of days to Christmas!

* By Arch Oboler. Reprinted with the permission of the author.

LINDA: Exactly!

(SOUND OF WALKING ON THE SAND)

CARL: We'll start with the sea. Calm, isn't it?

LINDA: Don't walk so fast, Carl, please.

CARL: Oh, oh, I forgot! Sand must be ruining your slippers!

LINDA: No, the beach is packed so hard — I'm quite all right. Just don't walk so fast!

CARL: Right! Fine place the Hunters have here!

LINDA: They do have successful parties.

CARL: Hunter bought this place right before '29. Tried to unload it all through the depression — couldn't get even enough to cover the land value.

LINDA: Did you hear about Ivy's debut? Margaret naturally wanted to have it at the Claremont, but Tom insisted on their country place!

CARL: Poor Tom! Dropped plenty in that Amalgamated merger! Amazing — man of his experience not knowing that you can't disturb the capital investment of an organization . . .

LINDA: (INTERRUPTING) Now just a minute, Mr. Laughlin! If you're thinking of starting on capital investments again, I'd better remind you that this conversation is limited — to — remember — June — moon . . .

7. COLUMBIA WORKSHOP: *A DRINK OF WATER**

MAN: (COMING ON) How do, young lady. Very pleasant, isn't it?

CLARE: What? Oh! Yes, yes. You aren't the one who — No, of course not . . . Uh . . . where did you come from?

MAN: Oh, just strolling. It's my holiday. Enjoying the beauties of nature . . . very much indeed. Miss . . . er . . . my name is Pope. Who are you looking around for?

CLARE: No one. But there was a young man I thought might . . .

MAN: Young! I hope you don't take me for an old man. Not exactly a chicken maybe, but . . . Don't get up. Please.

* From *A Drink of Water,* dramatic version copyright, 1939, by Max Wylie; original story by Wilbur Daniel Steele, *A Drink of Water* first appeared in *Harper's Magazine* and in the collection of Wilbur Daniel Steele stories, *The Man Who Saw through Heaven,* copyright, 1919, 1924, 1925, 1926, and 1927, by Wilbur Daniel Steele. In *Columbia Workshop Plays,* edited by William Coulter; copyright, 1939, by Columbia Broadcasting Company, Inc.

NOTE: Permission to reprint must be obtained from Columbia Broadcasting System, Inc., and Harold Matson.

CLARE: No, it was a young man . . . He pulled me out . . . He scared me . . . I just wanted . . . Well, I wanted to say "thank you."

MAN: Young man. Pulled you out, did he? Too bad. Too bad. He's gone on down the beach, I guess.

CLARE: Oh, well, it doesn't matter. I was just about to go into the cottage.

MAN: Oh. Don't let me drive you away.

CLARE: (FADING) No, no. It's quite all right . . . I was just going anyway.

F. CONFRONTATIONS

Intensive contact of one actor with another is illustrated in the next excerpt. Such confrontations, even when lesser in degree, should be sought out by the actor in the scenes that he must play.

1. LADIES IN RETIREMENT*

ELLEN: Albert, I've got something to say to you.

ALBERT: Are you going to take down my breeches and give me a dozen?

ELLEN: Don't you wish you could pay for your misdeeds that way?

ALBERT: You take me too seriously, you know. Half the time I'm only fooling.

ELLEN: One has to take a thief seriously.

ALBERT: Oh, come, Auntie! We don't want to go all over that again, do we? I'm not proud of myself. We're all miserable sinners, aren't we? You used to tell me that often enough when I was a little boy. I'm not going about in sack-cloth and ashes for the rest of my life!

ELLEN: I've been to London today.

ALBERT: (WITH INTEREST) Have you? Why didn't you tell us? You are a dark horse. Have you been on a spree?

ELLEN: No. I've been on your account. I've been to a shipping company.

ALBERT: (WIDE-EYED) A shipping company — on my account?

ELLEN: Yes. I've bought your passage to Canada.

ALBERT: (UP IN ARMS) But I don't want to go to Canada!

ELLEN: (COLDLY) I don't think you've very much choice, have you?

* By Reginald Denham and Edward Percy. Copyright, 1940, by Edward Percy (pseudonym for Edward Percy Smith) and Reginald Denham. Copyright, 1940, by Random House, Inc. Copyright, 1941, revised, by Edward Percy (pseudonym for Edward Percy Smith) and Reginald Denham.

NOTE: Reprinted by permission of the authors and of Dramatists Play Service, Inc. The amateur acting rights of *Ladies in Retirement* for the United States and its Territories and Possessions and the Dominion of Canada are controlled exclusively by the Dramatists Play Service, Inc., 6 East 39th Street, New York 16, N. Y., without whose permission in writing no performance of it may be made.

ALBERT: (HALF JAUNTILY THIS TIME) I'm quite happy here for the time being.

ELLEN: (VERY DIRECTLY) I'm not quite happy having you here.

ALBERT: But I thought we'd agreed. I was to lie low till the Gravesend business blew over. Time enough for a passage abroad in a month or so.

ELLEN: I've changed my mind.

ALBERT: Well, I think you might have discussed it with me first.

ELLEN: I didn't see any need. I'm paying the piper.

ALBERT: But what's made you change your mind?

ELLEN: Well, in the first place, you play the fool so much with Louisa and Emily that you'll have them chattering about your being here. And you know what that'll mean. The wrong sort of word to the tradesman or the nuns and we shall have the police down on us. And I can't do with any scandal here.

ALBERT: (PROTESTINGLY) Oh, but isn't that a bit thin? They're not very difficult to keep an eye on.

ELLEN: You forget Emily goes for long walks. You don't know who she talks to.

ALBERT: But surely there's more to it than that, Auntie? There must be!

ELLEN: Yes. There's Lucy. She's even more dangerous than your aunts.

ALBERT: Oh, Lucy won't give me away.

ELLEN: Are you in a position to be sure?

ALBERT: (VERY SURPRISED) What do you mean?

ELLEN: You know well enough what I mean. You wouldn't mind adding Lucy to your conquests, would you?

ALBERT: (WITH EXAGGERATED INNOCENCE) It never so much as occurred to me. I've hardly noticed the girl.

ELLEN: Don't lie, Albert. I've watched you whispering together. I saw the way you eyed her the first evening you came. I've seen her setting her cap at you ever since. I'm not going to have that sort of thing going on under my roof!

ALBERT: Well, all I can say, Auntie, is — it must be your mind. We're as innocent as the driven snow . . .

ELLEN: (WITH SUPPRESSED RAGE) You hateful little hypocrite!

ALBERT: Can't one have a joke and a bit of a lark with a girl without being accused of ruining her?

ELLEN: (SHARPLY) I never said you'd ruined her. Have you? Am I a little behindhand in sending you away?

ALBERT: (PROTESTING ONCE MORE) Now, look here. If you go on talking to me like this, I shall get quite cross. I'm doing my best to keep my temper as it is.

ELLEN: (CONTEMPTUOUS) Your temper! You can't pull wool over my eyes, Albert! Now, listen. You'll start tomorrow. I'm coming with you. Bates will be here directly after breakfast.

ALBERT: (NOW THOROUGHLY ALARMED) But I daren't go up to London! I might be recognized.

ELLEN: You're not going to London. Bates will drive us to Maidstone. Then we'll make our way across country by coach to Southampton. There's a boat leaving for Quebec on Friday. I've got your ticket. I've got everything.

ALBERT: (GRUMBLINGLY) By Jove, you are a hard woman, Auntie.

ELLEN: Perhaps I am. Perhaps circumstances have made me so. And you haven't helped to make me any softer.

ALBERT: I don't know why you're suddenly so down on me.

ELLEN: (QUIETLY, BUT WITH GREAT BITTERNESS) I've got to know you better. I've watched you very carefully the last few days. You're not a bit sorry for what you've done. You haven't shown a spark of gratitude to me. You're thoroughly callous. You've demoralized your aunts. Goodness knows what harm you've done that young girl. You've nosed about the house and spied on everybody. If I hadn't put my cash box in a very secure place I'm quite sure your light fingers would have found a way to it. And I'm saying this to my sister's son!

ALBERT: (HALF WHIMPERING) You are full of the milk of human kindness, aren't you? I suppose you realize I've never had a chance — brought up as I was. It's not my fault if I'm ambitious.

ELLEN: (SCORNFULLY) Ambitious!

ALBERT: Yes. Ambitious. I don't want to be downed all my life — with other people's footmarks all over me. I want to be on top. And I'm going to be!

ELLEN: Well, you're not going to climb there on my shoulders! I've made up my mind, and it's no use arguing with me. You're going out of this house before you're a day older.

ALBERT: (PLUCKING UP HIS COURAGE) I see. That's what you think. Does it occur to you that I may not go?

ELLEN: Well, I can't throw you out physically, but I can always send for the police.

ALBERT: Somehow I'd got the impression you didn't want the police here.

ELLEN: Does that mean you refuse to go?

ALBERT: Well, I certainly shan't go tomorrow morning.

ELLEN: I'm afraid you'll have to.

ALBERT: No. On second thought I'm quite content to stay for the time being. I'm getting fond of the place. The air suits me. You can't bluff me, you know.

ELLEN: (ANGRILY) I'm not bluffing you, Albert. I'm ordering you to go.

ALBERT: Order — my foot! I'll tell you what I think of your reasons for wanting me out of the house. Bunkum!

ELLEN: What do you mean?

ALBERT: There's another you haven't mentioned, isn't there? A sounder one.

ELLEN: (FACING UP TO THE ISSUE) Yes. There is.

ALBERT: Ah, now we're getting down to brass tacks! It's about Miss Fiske, isn't it?

ELLEN: Yes, it is. (QUITE NATURALLY) I met her in town today. She's comin back.

ALBERT: (ABSOLUTELY STAGGERED) You met her in town, you say?

ELLEN: Yes. Why shouldn't I?

ALBERT: (NONPLUSSED) No reason.

ELLEN: I had to take her some money that came for her.

ALBERT: I'd got it into my head that she'd gone for good.

ELLEN: Who gave you that idea? It's her house. There's never been any question of her not coming back.

ALBERT: Well, in that case, why spend the last half hour abusing me? Why not tell me straight away I'd got to go because she was coming back?

ELLEN: I didn't want you to know anything about it.

ALBERT: Why not?

ELLEN: You're such a chatterbox. You'd go blurting it out to your aunts. And it would be fatal if they got to know about it now. Because — don't you see? — it means that they've got to go too. They'll be dreadfully upset about it. You know what they are. And I shall have to break it to them very gently.

ALBERT: (ALMOST CONVINCED) Oh, well, there's nothing for it, then. My little country holiday has obviously come to an end. I'll have to thank you for your loving care, Auntie, and kiss you goodbye. I don't know what the blazes I'll do in Canada. But I suppose one can starve there as well as anywhere else.

ELLEN: I shall give you something to start on. I can't do less — for Rose's sake. I've no doubt you'll pick up a living somehow. There's a bit of the Greek in you, Albert. He thrives where the Jew starves, you know.

ALBERT: I'll do my best to deserve your good opinion, Auntie. And I suppose I ought to be grateful.

ELLEN: I'm not asking for that.

ALBERT: Well, I'd better get some sleep, hadn't I? I'm going to have a tiring day tomorrow. Do we kiss good night?

ELLEN: No.

ALBERT: I say! You're looking rather played out. Hadn't you better toddle off, too?

ELLEN: (WITH AN EFFORT) I'm just coming. I've got to lock up.

ALBERT: (FADING) Oh, I forgot to tell you. I had a funny dream last night, Auntie.

ELLEN: What was that?

ALBERT: (OFF) I dreamt Miss Fiske was dead.

ELLEN: (FACING HIM COOLLY) Oh?

Chapter IX . . CHARACTERIZATION: MOTIVATION

1

Discovering the right actions is only a part of the approach to characterization. The best radio performer (or best stage or screen actor) concentrates on more than what his character is doing at the major moments of the play. He has to know to some extent *why* his character is doing exactly what he does. He therefore focuses his attention concurrently on motives.

Human motivation, however, is a complex matter. Is motive the action itself? Or does motive stimulate and evoke behavior? Or does motive include both the stimulus and the reaction? These are labyrinthine questions the answers to which can be left to such specialists in motivation as Burke, Dewey, James, Lewin, McDougall, Woodworth, and others. It is sufficient for the radio actor to realize that behind his character's every action, or accompanying it, is a reason, a cause, a purpose. In character portrayal, therefore, the actor "must not only carry out the action and deliver the words of his part . . . he must compel himself *to have the same objectives as the character he is playing*."[1]

The actor who merely does what the script parentheses or directors instruct him to do, who merely acts out "in general" the verbs he has found for himself—who merely suffers for the sake of suffering, or merely boasts, or taunts, or flatters, or insinuates, or pokes fun, or chastizes, or informs—is only abortively creating a character. He is carrying out an action, yes; he is, for instance, running—but he is not yet certain whether he is running from a bear, or for a bus, or in a track meet. To ignore or to take for granted a character's objectives, as given in the context of the play, is to disregard his secret, and significant, aspects. Only by searching out the underlying motivations, only by understanding *why* his character suffers, boasts, taunts, flatters, insinuates, pokes fun, chastizes, informs, or runs can the actor completely capture the person he has been assigned to create. An actor does what he does in a play in accordance with the *aims* of the character he is interpreting.

"Motive to a character is what gasoline is to a car—it gives the character vitality and the ability to go places under his own power,"[2] writes Maren Elwood; and a character will come to life only when he moves under his own power. "Without strong motives to impel your characters to act as they do, you cannot build suspense, drama, emotion, climax."

Speech is something we *do* with a motivation in a given situation. According to Malinowski,

> Language is a social activity. A statement spoken in real life is never detached from the situation in which it has been uttered. For each verbal statement or feeling is actual *at that moment and in that situation,* and necessary for some reason or other to be made known to another person or persons—in order, either to serve purposes of common action, or to establish ties of purely social communion, or else to deliver the speaker of violent feelings or passions. Without some imperative stimulus of the moment there can be no spoken statement. In each case, therefore, *utterance and situation* are bound up inextricably with each other and the context of the situation is indispensable for the understanding of the words.[3]

In working out his characterization, then, the radio actor, like all actors, is forced to go beyond the discovery of the right verbs for his actions to the uncov-

[1] I. Rapoport, "The Work of the Actor," translated by Ben Blake and Lyuba Vendrovskaya, *Theatre Workshop,* I, No. 1 (October-December, 1936), p. 22.

[2] Elwood, *Characters Make Your Story,* p. 119.

[3] Bronislaw Malinowski, "The Problem of Meaning in Primitive Languages," in C. K. Ogden and I. A. Richards, *The Meaning of Meaning,* rev. ed. (New York: Harcourt, Brace and Company, 1947), Supplement, p. 307.

ering of the motivations for them. Not until he digs his character's *aims* out of the text can he hope to create a convincing characterization.

2

When the actor has searched out his character's objectives—when he has discovered what his character is doing, *and why*—he will as a result almost automatically discover the right way of performing the action, or saying the lines, and thus reveal the author's character to others. In the generally accepted opinion of I. Rapoport the elements of the actor's characterization job are three: "(1) Action—What I am doing. (2) Volition—Why I am doing it. (3) Adjustment—How I am doing it (form, character of action)."[4] The first two elements, action and motivation, are always consciously determined by the actor from the script; once he knows them, the third element, the adjustment or the how, arises voluntarily.

For example, (1) you bang your fist on the table (2) in order to quiet the meeting; (3) the corresponding adjustment arises (the form, the character of the blow, the way in which you strike the table). Now let the action, the verb, remain the same, but change the motivation. (1) Again you bang the table, but this time (2) in order to test its firmness, to appraise it; (3) a new adjustment follows—the new bang on the table will be unlike the first. Again keep the same action but change the motivation. (1) Bang your fist on the table (2) in order to play a joke on a friend who is dozing there, or in order to swat a fly there; (3) a new adjustment, a new way of banging the table, will automatically follow in each instance, and these last two bangs on the table will differ greatly from each other. In short, when the motivation changes, the form or quality of the same basic action changes; the motivation shapes or regulates the action, differentiates it from somewhat similar actions.

(One important point to note, however, in the aforementioned example, is that you as the actor must never anticipate *how* you will do what you are called on to do . . . or *how* you will say your next speech in the script. In hunting for the adjustment between what you are doing and why you are doing it you must never plan it beforehand. Instead, you must concentrate only on the *why* of what you are doing or saying. Then in most cases the proper adjustment, the revealing action, will arise quite independently.)

Take another example of motivation shaping the quality or form of the action—this time an auditory rather than a visual one. Suppose that in your radio script you are called on to say *in character* the sentence: "Go out into the yard and see." You have already discovered from the play's context that your verb, your action, is (1) "to beg" your partner to go out into the yard. You also know the difference between "to beg" and "to invite," between "to beg" and "to tease," and so on. But as yet you will not be able to put your action correctly into words, to speak the sentence in character; you can only "beg" in general. However, once you discover that your purpose in begging is (2) an urgent desire to be left alone to brood, (3) the corresponding adjustment, the how-to-read the sentence in character, follows. Again, if (1) you beg your partner to go (2) because you must make a secret telephone call, (3) a different way of reading the line will follow; or, if (1) you beg him to leave (2) so that you can enjoy the surprise you have prepared for him out in the yard, (3) another way of saying the line will follow.

Now suppose you discover that your action verb for the same sentence is not "to beg" but (1) "to order" your partner to leave? You as the actor can, of course, order him to leave in general, can order for the sake of ordering, can order because the script directions tell you to do so, but until you know why you order your partner out you cannot say the line convincingly in character. Nowhere is there any such action as ordering someone out in general, or without motivation. Therefore you must find the purpose behind your action, the motivation behind the line. If (1) you order your partner to go into the yard (2) because you are positive that that is the only way of convincing him of a truth by something he will find there, then (3) a right way of saying the line will appear. Similarly, if (1) you order him out (2) because you are ill and don't want to answer any more of his nagging questions, (3) a new adjustment and a new way of saying the sentence in character will come into being.

In short, the right motivation will in large measure always correctly shape the character's action, will furnish the "how" for what he does. In radio these cor-

[4] Rapoport, *op. cit.*, p. 23.

rectly performed actions via utterance reveal the character.

3

Two supplementary reasons compel the actor to focus his attention on the discovery and delineation of his character's motives. The first is that since people want desperately to understand one another, the perennial purpose, and appeal, of all fiction is the disclosure of human motives. Critic J. Donald Adams is sure that "most of us are endlessly interested in the motives which prompt people to act as they do; we want to know what makes the wheels go round. Sometimes we can make a pretty shrewd guess, but just as frequently we are baffled."[5] Worthy radio characterization should therefore give an audience the opportunity of seeing what they have so many times expressed the desire to see when they have said, "How I'd like to know what is going on in his mind." In this *motive* behind the chance word or the sigh or the speech is all the evidence we can often be afforded of that secret life which every person lives—and in which his happiness and misery reside.

The second is that the actor is obliged to divulge the motivations for his character's physical or mental action in order best to make an audience feel strongly toward the character. An audience will have sympathy for, or have no interest whatsoever in, or will hate, a character only in so far as it can follow his reasons for doing what he does. In every play, according to John Howard Lawson, the emotional participation of the audience is a kind of identification, a "living in the character," but neither the dramatist nor the actor can

> . . . induce this experience by an appeal to the sentiments and prejudices of the audience. Identification not only means "more than sympathy," but something which is essentially *different* from sympathy. To show us a distorted view of a character, to convince us that he is kind to his mother and gives candy to little children, does not cause us to live *in* the character. Identification means sharing the character's *purpose,* not his virtues.[6]

Although by now most radio actors have been bludgeoned into acknowledging the fact that motivation is indispensable to building a true characterization, there always will be some actors who will balk at all "this motivation stuff." They will argue, "In life people often act unconsciously, unaware of the causes that determine their behavior. So why shouldn't people in a play act in the same way?" Such objectors are lamely assuming that because people in life rarely know their own motivations or only dimly apprehend or understand them, they act without motivations. The truth is that even when a person in life is unaware of his motives they are always present as the strongest regulator of the form and quality of his actions, and thus always expressive of his uniqueness. If the actor carries out his character's actions unaware of the causes, that is, suffers for the sake of suffering, or begs or orders merely in general and without purpose, he cannot uniquely shape the actions that, when totaled, will reveal the character. Therefore what is often unknown to the *character,* though always present and regulatory, must be known to the *actor.*

What is more, the motives behind and shaping a character's individualized actions must be taken *from the playwright.* For instance, in life Julius Caesar may actually never have fathomed the motivations for what he did, and never have been required to fathom them; but specific motivations, or regulators, for his conduct were not consequently absent; Caesar was Caesar, and mostly remembered for what he characteristically did. In art, however, in a play by Shaw, where the character called Caesar may rarely, if ever, apprehend the scheme or the progression of his own motivations, the actor who is creating Caesar must search out, first and last, *the motives assigned to the character by Shaw* (and not by Shakespeare, nor by Freud, nor by the psychologists, nor by Caesar's actual heredity or environment, nor by the purely personal experience of actor George Spelvin). If he does not do this he cannot bring the character into unique and functional and convincing existence. For the actor there is no other way of discovering the differentiating shape for the actions of Shaw's Caesar, for regulating the "how" of his behavior in the play. In order to create a character the actor has to know the character; to know the character he must know the character's motivations, and to know the character's motivations he must go primarily to the playwright.

Thus the objectors to "all this motivation stuff" are bumptious; they have yet to learn that the actor's professional motivation, his purpose in playing, is to win

[5] J. Donald Adams, New York *Times,* January 10, 1946.

[6] John Howard Lawson, *Theory and Technique of Playwriting,* (New York: G. P. Putnam's Sons, 1936), p. 285.

audience approval for his skill *in disclosing the motivations of his character* as functional to the playwright's design, to the communication of his temperament, his attitude toward experience. An actor who does less—who acts "unconsciously," who speaks into the microphone without prescribed and precise motivations—is guilty of what Henry James called "the platitude of mere statement."

4

To be sure, the motives of even the simplest men are too complex and too multiple ever to be presented in their entirety in a brief radio play. Consequently for each of his characters the playwright usually selects only one or two dominant aims as necessary to the expression of his over-all attitude or idea. He places his emphasis only on what is essential for his purpose in writing the play; other attributes of his characters he often subordinates or omits. As a result the radio actor has to search out—and has time to search out—only one or two dominant aims, urges, or needs, together with perhaps some of their mutations and accompaniments.

In their scientific approach to this subject psychologists have concluded that for each person there is usually a single compelling urge that determines his line of action and is responsible for all the changes in his life. Wendell White, for instance, in his *Psychology in Living,* has made up one of many such lists of man's basic needs:

a) A sense of personal worth—the desire for recognition or applause from our fellows
b) An interesting life—the desire for varied experiences
c) Love—the desire for affection and comradeship
d) Activity—the desire for sensory and motor experiences, or the pursuit of something worthwhile
e) Physical well-being
f) A livelihood
g) Security[7]

In other words, some men have a fundamental need for affection, some for power, some for wealth, some for fame, some for joy, and so on. One or more of these general objectives, or life-drives, are usually behind the smaller, concrete, daily objectives; always they color and shape them. Because they are present—a dominant objective or two for each person—they can and must be discovered by the actor. "Whatever way you tabulate these urges, they are the roots of all activity. Sometimes we have simple reasons for our actions and sometimes very complex ones, but in all cases, whether evident or not, there is an instinctive urge that is a relentless driving force. Because it is usually guided by emotion rather than the cold logic of the mind, it is all powerful and often ruthless in its methods."[8]

This superobjective, this dominant motive or character trait behind all the little, ever-changing, span-of-the-play motives for action, is what the actor creating a character must dig out, even in the brief time allotted for the rehearsal of a radio play. He can usually find this objective, often only implied, by adding up, so to speak, the motivations for all the action verbs. All the minor motivations will disclose the major one.

This search for the dominant objective or character trait was carried on relentlessly by Nazimova whenever she studied a new role. She explained that "at first I am nothing. I have to reconstruct my whole self into this woman I am to portray—speak with her voice, laugh with her laughter . . . ." She maintained that an actor must know everything there is to know about a character's thoughts. She traced the *origin* of each line, each word, each thought; she analyzed the minutest *cause* behind the emotion. Nazimova sought to determine first about a character: "What is she thinking, what her inner response is, her feeling, when some other character is holding the stage. Once you know what she *is,* what she *does* becomes easy to interpret . . . . You see that she . . . must . . . speak with a certain inflection."[9] What Nazimova did for a stage characterization the radio actor must do for a microphone characterization—only more swiftly. What is true for one medium is true for the other.

Once the actor has found the dominant motive or character trait, he begins, as Coquelin says, to make up his personage.

> He borrows from his author, he borrows from stage tradition, he borrows from nature, he draws on his own stock of knowledge of men and things, on his own experience and imagination; in short, he sets himself a task. His task once set, he has his part; he sees it, grasps it.

[7] Wendell White, *Psychology in Living* (New York: The Macmillan Company, 1947).

[8] Elwood, *op. cit.,* p. 117.

[9] Eustis, *Players at Work,* pp. 52–53.

Moreover, what is of paramount importance in radio, with its brief scenes and great time lapses and quick transitions after musical bridges, once he has absorbed the dominant character trait, the actor is always ready to perform.

He can take up his part, no matter when, and instantly excite the desired effect.[10]

5

In the last analysis, though, the actor, having found the one or more dominant character traits for the character he is to portray, must always come back to himself. His final problem in characterization is the relating of the character traits he has assembled from the text to his own qualities as a person, though this does not mean substituting his own qualities for the qualities of the character. Knowing thoroughly the person he is to create is perhaps half of the job of characterization; knowing himself and how to relate his own qualities to those of the character is the other half.

When Helen Hayes, according to Morton Eustis, feels that she knows the person she is to portray as well as she knows herself, "and preferably better; when, in her mind's eye, she can see the character as clearly as if she held a photograph of the woman before her eyes" [or in radio: when, in her mind's ear, she can hear the character as clearly as if she were eavesdropping on her, not in life, but in the various situations of the play], "then she starts to consider the problem of relating Helen Hayes, the woman and actress, to the conception she has formed."[11] Alfred Lunt created the character of Harry Van in *Idiot's Delight* by piecing him together —accent and personality—"from three people I used to know in vaudeville. I took something from each one of them and added a general impression *based on my own experience*."[12] When Burgess Meredith is given a part to characterize,

. . . his immediate reaction is in the first person singular: "How am I going to deliver this line?" And most important of all, *"What am I?"* He first obtains certain instinctive reactions about the character and the playing. His next move is to determine "What characteristics of this person do I know from my own feelings?" No part was ever written, he believes, which does not have in its main conception some relationship to the actor's own personality. The character may be weak, strong, arrogant, supercilious, snobbish, headstrong. The actor himself may not be any one of these things in whole, or even in part. But, certainly, he will have had moments in his life when he experienced the emotions those qualities produce.[13]

The actor, then, must finally discover "wherein the person he is attempting to bring to life is similar to himself and others, and wherein different from himself and others."

6

What a radio actor specifically does in achieving a characterization, and does in only a few hours, cannot be set down here in a specific step-by-step recipe. There is no definite order, or foolproof check list, of perceiving and understanding and assimilating. Many things are discovered at one and the same time; many last things come first, and many first things last. With the experienced radio actor the entire process of discovering the ingredients for a valid characterization is probably somewhat instinctive. The primerlike 1-2-3's of a rigid method have become blurred into an intuitive approach to the problem. This is all to the good.

The relatively inexperienced or imperfect radio actor, however, will certainly find it advisable to follow, for some length of time, an arbitrary check list of things to do in order to characterize truly. Later—but never in too short a time—the actor seeking perfection may find that practice will eventually transform the drudgery of a somewhat dull process into something more and more instinctive, into something intuitively reliable and luminous.

The check list for effecting a convincing characterization in radio differs importantly from the same process in the legitimate theatre. In the theatre the actor usually, or ideally, starts his investigation of the character he is to portray by doing five things:

1) First he reads the play carefully as the story of the actions, conflicts, and progressions of certain human beings. He centers his attention, not on his own character, but on the entire play.
2) Next he finds the point, or the idea (not the moral!), of the play—the attitude toward experience on the part of the playwright.

[10] Constant Coquelin, *Art and the Actor* (1880), translated by Abby Langdon Alger, *Papers on Acting II* (New York: Dramatic Museum of Columbia University, 1915), p. 57.

[11] Eustis, *op. cit.,* p. 16.

[12] *Ibid.,* p. 42.

[13] *Ibid.,* pp. 95–96.

3) Then he studies the design of the play, its structure, the relationship between the various parts, and the function of his role in the whole design.
4) Then he ascertains the kind of play it is—for example, comedy, melodrama, fantasy, farce, tragedy. He decides the play's dependence on distortion or style or sense of period. He measures the play's closeness to the realistic method.
5) Finally he centers his attention on his own role, on the actions and motivations, the surrounding circumstances, and so forth.

Unfortunately, all these procedures, with the possible exception of the fifth, are denied the radio actor in the preparation of his role. There simply is no time for them. Since the radio actor does not receive his script before the first cast reading, he cannot study it; he cannot keep thinking about his characterization, now from this angle, now from that, for a long period of time, and in the lonely places. He cannot become acquainted with his character as Lynn Fontanne does:

> Suddenly . . . walking in the park or motoring to the theatre, you discover something about the character you never knew even existed. In a flash, you derive a new slant on an action, a motive. Bit by bit you sink deeper into the person. You see that you are wrong in one scene; the woman could never use that tone of voice.[14]

This lack of a gestation period for the creating of a character is the radio actor's ominous and irreparable handicap. Given only a few crowded hours for rehearsal, and denied the time in which to engage in the fivefold investigation of the legitimate actor, the radio performer still must set up his own swift process for effectively working out a fresh and individualized and authentic characterization. Starting with the sight reading at the first cast rehearsal of the script, he can do, in one way or another, the following things:

1) First, the actor can mark off his script into units, into its component parts, by dividing it into "French scenes"—a new scene for the arrival and departure of any character. For each new "scene" he can draw a horizontal line across the script page.
2) Then as he first reads—and *never* in character the first time—he can learn from the text such items as his character's age and health and occupation, his chief pleasures, peculiar habits, complexes, problems, education, fears, home life, race and religion, political or social opinions, and philosophy of life.
3) Next he can discover for each "scene" he is in his emotional relations toward all the other characters in the scene, and how responsive his character is to other people, whether he is an extrovert or introvert, pessimistic or optimistic, intellectual or emotional, how changeable, and so forth.
4) As soon as possible he can find the precise verb for his character's main action in each "scene," together with the motive behind it. These actions and motivations he can jot down in the script margins.
5) Then, adding up his findings: (a) what is said or implied about the character in the script, (b) the character's attitudes toward, and responses to, other characters, and (c) the major actions and their motivations—he can in most instances dig out his character's dominant objective.
6) Next, he can work *backward* from this dominant character trait and see all the actions and relationships in a new but prescribed light.
7) Then he can decide wherein the character to be portrayed is similar to himself and others and wherein he differs—and build accordingly.
8) Finally he can determine his character's function in the play as expressive of the playwright's attitude or idea. Sometimes, too, he can find his own comment to add thereto.

Coquelin, in summing up this process of characterization for the stage, sums it up also for radio acting:

> When the actor has a portrait to paint, a part to study—he must first, by a careful and repeated reading of the whole play, steep himself in the intentions of the author, disentangle the importance and the reality of the character, realize his plane of action in the plot, see him, in a word, as he *must* be; then he has obtained his model. Now, like the painter, he realizes the likeness not on canvas, but on himself . . . . He has got to make Tartuffe speak as he hears him speak, and in order to think out the action of the part he must make himself . . . listen, think—from the very soul of Tartuffe.[15]

7

Two warnings, however, must be given the over-anxious and ambitious radio actor. The first, all the characteristics of a person are rarely evident and frozen at the start of a play—to remain so throughout. Almost

[14] *Ibid.*, p. 36.

[15] Coquelin, *op. cit.*, p. 33.

always the various character traits are *gradually* revealed. The actor therefore must give his attention to the *continuing* development of his character. As William Archer has pointed out, the development of character means

> . . . not change, but rather unveiling, disclosure . . . a dramatic crisis ought to disclose latent qualities in the persons chiefly concerned in it, and involve, not, indeed, a change, but, as it were an exhaustive manifestation of character . . . A drama ought to bring out character as the photographer's chemicals "bring out" the forms latent in the negative.[16]

The second, no actor in a radio play—or in any other kind of play for that matter—can put in *everything* about a character. Since no playwright ever puts in everything but selects only what is useful to his purpose, no actor should try to include everything he can imagine about the character. Sometimes, yes, a leading character demands extensive delineation; sometimes he is complex in that he has two or more dominant and conflicting traits. As a rule, though, a radio character is fairly simple, exhibiting only meagerly a single dominant trait. For a background or flat character sometimes there is no dominant trait at all. The secret is to include in the characterization only as much motivation as is needed for the purposes of the play.

SELECTED READINGS

Richard Boleslavsky has some valuable advice in "The Fourth Lesson: Characterization," in his *Acting; The First Six Lessons* (New York: Theatre Arts, Inc., 1933), pp. 65–88.

Lajos Egri's *The Art of Dramatic Writing; Its Basis in the Creative Interpretation of Human Motives* (New York: Simon & Schuster, Inc., 1946) emphasizes characterization in Chap. I, "Premise," and Chap. II, "Character," pp. 1–120.

Maren Elwood discusses characterization from the writer's point of view in *Characters Make Your Story* (Boston: Houghton Mifflin Company, 1942). Consult Chap. I, "The Importance of Characterization," pp. 1–9; Chap. II, "The Creative Process of Characterization," pp. 9–18; Chap. III, "First Steps in Characterization," pp. 19–28; Chap. VII, "Listen to Him Speak," pp. 65–72; Chap. VIII, "When Characters Meet," pp. 73–81; Chap. IX, "Thoughts Are Things," pp. 82–91; Chap. XII, "Motives Make the Man Go," pp. 115–128; Chap. XVII, "Emotion and Characterization," pp. 171–183.

Morton Eustis offers some engaging reading in *Players at Work; Acting According to the Actors* (New York: Theatre Arts, Inc., 1937). There are chapters on the stage work of Helen Hayes, Alfred Lunt and Lynn Fontanne, Nazimova, Katherine Cornell, Ina Claire, and Burgess Meredith.

Sophie Rosenstein, Larrae A. Haydon, and Wilbur Sparrow include, in *Modern Acting: A Manual* (New York: Samuel French, Inc., 1936), two worthwhile chapters: VI, "Characterization," pp. 65–80, and X, "Problems in Characterization," pp. 105–113, including exercises.

Constantin Stanislavski, in *An Actor Prepares,* translated by Elizabeth Reynolds Hapgood (New York: Theatre Arts, Inc., 1936), is sometimes helpful in Chap. VII, "Units and Objectives," pp. 105–119; Chap. XII, "Inner Motive Forces," pp. 229–236; Chap. XIII, "The Unbroken Line," pp. 237–245; and Chap. XV, "The Super-Objective," pp. 256–265. His second book, *Building a Character,* translated by Elizabeth Reynolds Hapgood (New York: Theatre Arts Books: Robert M. MacGregor, 1949) is disappointing; but examine Chap. I, "Toward a Physical Characterization," pp. 3–8; Chap. II, "Dressing a Character," pp. 9–19; Chap. III, "Characters and Types," pp. 20–33; and Chap. X, "Perspective in Character Building," pp. 167–176.

Stark Young has some stimulating reading in his chapter, "Character Acting," in his *Theatre Practice* (New York: Charles Scribner's Sons, 1926), pp. 73–94.

[16] William Archer, *Play-Making* (Boston: Small, Maynard and Company, 1912), p. 373.

EXERCISES

A. STATEMENTS

In the following exercises give a full characterization, in so far as it is imaginatively possible, to the utterance. Center your full attention on the motivation of the action. In your readings change in as many ways as possible the volition—the why I am doing it—of each action to see what adjustment follows. Then change the action itself.

1. When a true genius appears in the world, you may know him by this sign — that the dunces are all in confederacy against him. (Jonathan Swift)

2. A man doesn't learn to understand anything unless he loves it. (Goethe)

3. The reward of the general is not a bigger tent, but command. (O. W. Holmes, Jr.)

4. Of all manifestations of power, restraint impresses men most. (Thucydides)

5. If we begin with certainties, we shall end in doubts; but if we begin with doubts, and are patient in them, we shall end in certainties. (Bacon)

6. The artist, like the God of the creation, remains within or behind or beyond or above his handiwork, invisible, refined out of existence, indifferent, paring his fingernails. (James Joyce)

7. I sometimes think that the most plaintive ditty has brought a fuller joy and of longer duration to its composer than the conquest of Persia to the Macedonian. (Walter Savage Landor)

8. Helen, when she looked in the mirror and saw the withered wrinkles which old age had made in her face, wept, and wondered to herself why ever she had been twice carried away. (Leonardo da Vinci)

9. It requires a very unusual mind to undertake the analysis of the obvious. (A. N. Whitehead)

10. The world is neither wise nor just, but it makes up for its folly and injustice by being damnably sentimental. (T. H. Huxley).

11. Pursue, keep up with, circle round and round your life, as a dog does his master's chaise. Do what you love. Know your own bone; gnaw at it, bury it, unearth it, and gnaw still. (Thoreau)

12. The superior man understands what is right; the inferior man understands what will sell. (Confucius)

13. When you swear, swear seriously and solemnly, but at the same time with a smile, for a smile is the twin sister of seriousness. (Plato)

14. Anybody can make history; only a great man can write it. (Oscar Wilde)

15. . . . . if a sparrow come before my window, I take part in its existence and pick about the gravel. (Keats)

16. As a cousin of mine once said about money, money is always there but the pockets change; it is not in the same pockets after a change, and that is all there is to say about money. (Gertrude Stein)

17. There are two kinds of taste, the taste for emotions of surprise and the taste for emotions of recognition. (Henry James)

18. Be entirely tolerant or not at all; follow the good path or the evil one. To stand at the crossroads requires more strength than you possess. (Heine)

19. A man can be given only what he can use; and he can use only that for which he has sacrificed something. This is the law of human nature. So if a man wants to get help to acquire important knowledge or new powers, he must sacrifice other things important to him at the moment. (Ouspensky)

20. The Don Juans eternally seeking some new object of passion, the men and women desperately trying to lose themselves in drink, promiscuity, sensuality — in all of the excess of flesh and power — are, more often than we suspect, lonely children lost and naked in a world that has never

woven a garment of love for them and that has relentlessly driven them down the empty corridors of the years, desolate and alone. Penetrate behind the mask of men of ruthlessness and of power, who seem to move from conquest to conquest, and it will often be seen that their soul is really an army in retreat, fleeing from loneliness to loneliness. (From Peace of Mind, by Joshua Liebman. Published by Simon and Schuster, Inc. Reprinted with permission.)

B. MOTIVATIONS

In the following exercises, in order to create the characterization, the students should read from the motivations behind the actions. In order to show potency of motivation they should read each scene at the microphone at least three times with a *different* motivation for the action or actions each time.

1. THE DEATH OF AUNT AGGIE*

Two sailors are on shore leave down at Joe's place in Honolulu.

BIG BRAIN: Hey, Harry. Lookit!

HARRY: What's with you, Big Brain?

BIG BRAIN: Pipe the dames. Looka the grass skirts. Brooklyn was never like this.

HARRY: Yeah.

BIG BRAIN: Just like in the movies. I never would have believed it. But ain't they liable to catch cold, just wearing that shredded wheat?

HARRY: Don't kid yourself, Big Brain. When those wahines start shaking that stuff it gets warmer than a sixteen-inch gun turret after a full salvo.

BIG BRAIN: Yeah? What was that word you called them — Mahoneys?

HARRY: No! No! Wahines. Means girls in Hawaiian.

BIG BRAIN: Yeah?

HARRY: Yeah. You see —

MABEL: (OFF) Harry! Hello, Harry.

HARRY: Mabel!

BIG BRAIN: But, Harry, I don't see —

HARRY: Look, Big Brain, here's a quarter. Go drown yourself in a bucket of suds.

BIG BRAIN: Okay. I don't need a brick wall to fall on me. (FADING) If you want me I'll be over talking to one of the Mahoney girls.

* Original radio script by Ranald MacDougall. Copyright, 1949, by Columbia Broadcasting System, Inc.

HARRY: I don't want you. (A PAUSE) Gee, it's nice to see you again, Mabel.

MABEL: (COMING ON) It's nice to see you, Harry. How've you been?

HARRY: Ah, what's the use of complaining, I always say. How are things with you, Mabel?

MABEL: I can't kick. (A PAUSE) Long time no see, Harry.

HARRY: Yeah. Two years at least.

MABEL: Two years and five months. I kept track.

(MUSIC: STARTS)

HARRY: Wanna struggle this one with me, Babe?

MABEL: (LAUGHING) Same old Harry. You know I don't like you to call me that.

HARRY: I forgot. How's this — may I have the pleasure of this dance, Sugar?

MABEL: That's better.

HARRY: Gee, it's nice to see you again, Mabel.

(MUSIC: SWELLS UP; VIOLINS SWEEP IN AND OVER, MAKING IT A TENDER AND LYRIC THEME)

2. THE BATTLE OF THE WARSAW GHETTO*

NARRATOR: (SIMPLY) My name is Isaac Davidson and I lived in the Polish city of Lublin with my wife Dvora, and Samuel, our son. When Poland fell they herded us into a cattle car and transported us to the Ghetto of Warsaw . . . We went to the tenement in the Twelfth District . . . to the place we were going to live. We went up the stairs of the tenement, and Samuel and I waited in the hall, while Dvora spoke to the woman who lived there.

DVORA: They said you would know where we are supposed to stay.

WOMAN: Come in. This is where you stay — in this room.

DVORA: But you live here.

WOMAN: In this corner. The other corner is yours.

DVORA: But I thought . . .

WOMAN: You don't know how lucky you are. This room has a window.

DVORA: Perhaps we shouldn't trouble you. Maybe . . . some other place.

WOMAN: (LAUGHING BITTERLY) You'll find out. Before they walled the Ghetto, fifty thousand people lived in these slums.

* By Morton Wishengrad. Reprinted through the courtesy of the author.

DVORA: Yes, but —

WOMAN: Do you know how many are here now? Five hundred thousand! A half million! I know a man who sleeps in a vault in the cemetery. Don't be a fool. Come in. It's still better than the cemetery.

3. INSIDE A KID'S HEAD*

RITCHIE: (AGED TEN, COMING ON) Now look here, King John! You've been actin' awful bossy lately! An' we barons are gettin' pretty sick of it!

KING JOHN: (FIRMLY) What does thou propose, Sir Ritchie? Thou hast no right to challenge the King of England!

RITCHIE: Well now, your Majesty, we barons have been talkin' this over, jes' between ourselves. An' we come to the conclusion the people oughta have somethin' to say about what's goin' on.

MARY JANE: (AGED TEN) Please, Father! Why don't you do as Sir Ritchie asks? He's so handsome!

KING JOHN: This is none of thy concern, Princess Mary Jane! My liegemen, this is treason!

RITCHIE: Jes' get down off your high horse, King John! All we're askin' yuh to do is put your name on this hunk of paper, so's folks don't have to worry about you not treatin' 'em right. Now, I happen to have a fountain pen right here in my suit of armor. If you'll jes' sign on the dotted line . . .

KING JOHN: I refuse! Thou art traitors! All of you!

RITCHIE: (VERY MATTER-OF-FACT) We mean business, King John! You better sign, or we'll have to get tough!

KING JOHN: Does no man remain loyal to his King?

RITCHIE: We're loyal, King John. But we jes' don't like the idea of you havin' your own way all the time. We want some say-so, too! That's only fair!

MARY JANE: Sir Ritchie is right! Sign, Father!

KING JOHN: Very well, Sir Ritchie. Give me the pen.

(SCRATCH OF PEN)

KING JOHN: (POUTING LIKE AN ADOLESCENT) There! Take your old paper!

* By Jerome Lawrence and Robert E. Lee. Reprinted with the permission of the authors.

MARY JANE: Sir Ritchie — you're so wonderful!

RITCHIE: (TOSSING IT OFF) Oh, it was nothin'. Gentlemen! (AS IF SPRINGING A DRAMATIC PIECE OF INFORMATION) Gentlemen! We shall call this — the Magna Carta!

4. GRANDPA AND THE STATUE*

SHEEAN: (SLIGHT BROGUE, OFF) A good afternoon to you, Monaghan.

MONAGHAN: How're you, Sheean, how're ya?

SHEEAN: (COMING ON) Fair, fair. And how's Mrs. Monaghan these days?

MONAGHAN: Warm. Same as everybody else in summer.

SHEEAN: I've come to talk to you about the fund, Monaghan.

MONAGHAN: What fund is that?

SHEEAN: The Statue of Liberty fund.

MONAGHAN: Oh, that.

SHEEAN: It's time we come to grips with the subject, Monaghan.

MONAGHAN: I'm not interested, Sheean.

SHEEAN: Now hold up on that a minute. Let me tell you the facts. This here Frenchman has gone and built a fine statue of Liberty. It cost the Lord knows how many millions to build. All they're askin' us to do is contribute enough to put up a base for the statue to stand on.

MONAGHAN: I'm not throwin' me good money away for somethin' I don't even know exists.

SHEEAN: Now what do you mean by that?

MONAGHAN: Have you seen this statue?

SHEEAN: No, but it's in a warehouse.

MONAGHAN: And how do I know it's in this here warehouse at all?

SHEEAN: You read your paper, don't you? It's been in all the papers for the past year.

MONAGHAN: Ha, the papers! Last year I read in the paper that they were about to pave Butler Street and take out all the holes. Turn around and look at Butler Street, Mr. Sheean.

* Taken from *Grandpa and the Statue*, an original radio play, written by Arthur Miller for Du Pont's CAVALCADE OF AMERICA.

SHEEAN: All right. I'll do this. I'll take you to the warehouse and show you the statue. Will you give me a dime then?

MONAGHAN: Well . . . I'm not sayin' I would, and I'm not sayin' I wouldn't. But I'd be more likely if I saw the thing large as life, I would.

SHEEAN: (PEEVED) All right, then. Come along.

(MUSIC: UP AND DOWN AND OUT)

5. MR. LEDFORD AND THE TVA*

LEDFORD: How you gettin' along, Uncle Joe, now?

KIRBY: (A DEEP, OLD VOICE: IT RUMBLES AND RATTLES WITH AGE AND POWER AND CONVICTION; EACH WORD IS WEIGHTED AND CONSIDERED) Oh, purty well. I'm gettin' kinda come down to the feeble days though; but I'm still purty healthy and hearty.

LEDFORD: Still able to work some?

KIRBY: Yes . . . Made a purty good little crop this yur. Of course, y'know, I'm jest a boy yit, jist goin' on eighty-one years old.

LEDFORD: Jest a boy yet!

KIRBY: Yes. (HE GRINS)

LEDFORD: Well, that's fine! What do you think about the old days and the modern days of today? Which do you like the best?

KIRBY: (AFTER A PAUSE AND THINKING IT OVER) Well, that's sort of a hard question with me. I don't know whether I can correctly answer it or not. Now, some of the old times, I like 'em pow'ful well, but some of 'em — I like modern times mighty well, much better. (HE HAS HIS TEETH INTO HIS IDEA NOW AND HE RUNS ALONG SWIFTLY) I can't see how I could live if my wife had to go back an' make clothing an' make everything with her fingers like my mother did — just couldn't do it — never could have done it . . .

LEDFORD: (THROWING IT IN) I guess not.

KIRBY: It don't look to me like — we raised a good crowd of children an' she jest had her hands full an' she had a good cook stove or a range. When me an' my wife was married — I had bought this land before we's married, but that's been back about fifty-three or fo' years ago — 'Course

* By Alan Lomax. Reprinted with the permission of the author.

money was pretty hard an' debts was hard to pay. An' me an' my wife, nary one, had no house stuff scarcely, just enough to sort of do with. An' I had corn — I didn't have no wheat. The year before we was married, I didn't make much. I kinda baffled about — an' I had enough on hand to pay for the land all except seventy-five dollars, but seventy-five dollars were hard to git.

LEDFORD: Uh-huh.

KIRBY: . . . an' we lived hard an' paid for our little home an' got to whur we could buy furniture an' most anything, an' we've had a very plenty ever since — (RISING FEELINGS) But we jest starved there an' now for some — the government er somebody to come along an' say. "You must jest get out of here an' give us possession." It sounds unjust to me!

LEDFORD: (AFTER A PAUSE) B'lieve in bein' free!

KIRBY: Yes, I do. An' I b'lieve in givin' 'em a chance to worship God accordin' to the dictates of his own heart, jest as our old Con-sti-tu-tion say.

LEDFORD: Yeah.

KIRBY: That's what I b'lieve in.

LEDFORD: (AFTER A PAUSE) Well, I b'lieve it's gettin' late, Uncle Joe, and I'm going to have to go on home now.

KIRBY: (CHANGING HIS TONE AND SWINGING INTO THE MOUNTAIN HOSPITALITY FORMULA) Why not stay all night with me? It's been s'long since you bin to see me an' we're old friends an' —

LEDFORD: I certainly would enjoy stayin' all night with yuh, but I can't stay tonight. I'll come back, though, sometime, and I will stay all night and we'll talk more.

KIRBY: All right — I can jest — if I can't fill you on meat and bread, I sho can on hot air!

LEDFORD: (CHUCKLING) All right, that'll be fine.

6. PARIS INCIDENT*

VOICE 1: (HUSHED) Tomorrow night will be the time. The dynamite will be ready.

* By Norman Rosten, from *The Treasury Star Parade,* edited by William A. Bacher, published by Rinehart & Company, 1942. Reproduced with the permission of the author and The Treasury Department.

VOICE 2: How many guards?

VOICE 1: Two or three. It will be dangerous.

VOICES: "I will go." — "No — I!" — "Let me go!"

JOAN: No, I will do it.

VOICE 1: This is a man's job.

JOAN: It may be easier for a woman. They will suspect a woman less.

VOICE 1: It is too dangerous.

JOAN: Are we to be afraid of that word? Let the man or woman speak who has not seen the face of danger, or heard its voice, or slept upon its bed. Let me go. Some of you have children. Remain with them a while longer. Let me go first.

(MUSIC: BACK TO NARRATIVE MOOD)

JOAN: (ON CUE) It was easy to decide, Pierre. You didn't speak a word — at first. How were you to say no? Each of us knew the meaning of our lives, and the value of them — each of us understood. That last evening, Pierre . . .

(MUSIC: SOFTLY FADE OUT)

JOAN: Neither of us slept . . .

PIERRE: Do you remember, darling, our first summer, near the sea? How we lay awake, listening to the waves, and the gulls weeping over the water . . .

(MUSIC: IN SOFTLY . . . DEBUSSY)

JOAN: Our first vacation . . .

PIERRE: . . . Our first picnic . . .

JOAN: We had such a wonderful day!

PIERRE: The people . . .

JOAN: . . . the children.

PIERRE: The roller coaster and the carousel . . .

JOAN: And the hawkers!

PIERRE: . . . the eating and drinking . . .

JOAN: . . . and the wonderful tiredness. Then back to our house.

(MUSIC: SOFTLY OUT)

PIERRE: The warm still nights . . .

JOAN: All the world seemed asleep.

PIERRE: And now, no one sleeps. (BURSTS OUT) I can't lose you now!

JOAN: No —

PIERRE: I never wanted anything else in life — to be near you forever . . .

JOAN: Pierre, darling — ! (SHE TRIES TO STOP HIM)

PIERRE: I won't let you go! I'm not a coward, but there's so little we have left —

JOAN: (TEARFULLY) And yet we must give that little . . . all of us.

PIERRE: Joan — you will come back to me . . . You will do it and come back!

JOAN: I shall try. I shall pray to come back . . .

(MUSIC: SOFTLY BACK TO NARRATIVE THEME)

JOAN: You left early for work. I felt your kiss upon my cheek, Pierre, and I heard you whisper something. I wish I could remember what it was now. There is so little time for remembrance . . . Do not be angry that I left before you returned.

(MUSIC: MOOD CHANGES)

7. BULLDOG DRUMMOND*

DRUMMOND: I stand here in the quiet of early evening, looking at the Andrews' house for the last time. Tomorrow its unhappy history comes to an end at the hands of a wrecking crew. And with its dark walls will go the last trace of the burning hatred that dwelt within them — a hatred which reached its climax in a story I have called — "Last Will and Testament."

(MUSIC: BUILDS TO A STAB AND OUT)

ANDREWS: "I, Mark Andrews, being of sound and disposing mind, do hereby make my last will and testament. Item One: My entire property — "

ELLEN: (PROTESTING) Uncle Mark, please!

ANDREWS: (ARCHLY) What's the matter, Ellen? Does this reading of my will offend your sensibilities?

ELLEN: I — I — Well, it's just that —

JOHN: What Ellen wants to say, Uncle Mark, is that here you are reading your own will and you're still —

ANDREWS: Alive? Is that what you wanted to say, John?

JOHN: Yes.

ANDREWS: (COLD) Very touching! As if you really cared — any of you.

* Original story by Milton Lewis. Reproduced through the courtesy of the author. The character of Bulldog Drummond is the property of the Sapper Estate and is used here with special permission.

EVERETT: (CALM) It's unusual, Uncle Mark, to say the least.

ANDREWS: But it doesn't offend you, does it, Everett?

EVERETT: Not at all.

ANDREWS: Nothing ever did offend you, Everett. Yes, as I recall, even as a child you —

EVERETT: (BORED) Really, must we go through that again? Please continue. I'm sure Ellen and John are equally anxious to hear how they came out in the disposition of your wealth.

ELLEN: (OUTRAGED) Everett!

JOHN: Now just a minute. Uncle Mark, you mustn't pay any attention to him.

ANDREWS: You needn't put on the outraged act, either of you. I've called you here this evening because I thought I'd enjoy the pleasure that few men have reserved for themselves — the pleasure of seeing the manner in which my own living heirs receive the conditions of my will.

EVERETT: My time's limited. Shall we get on with it?

ANDREWS: Very well. (READING) "I, Mark Andrews, being of sound and disposing mind, do hereby make my last will and testament. Item One: My entire property, both real and otherwise, I bequeath to my oldest living heir, Everett Andrews."

JOHN: (SHOCKED) Everett? Your entire estate? But, Uncle Mark — !

EVERETT: But what, John?

JOHN: At least I thought that Ellen and I deserve some consideration.

ANDREWS: I've considered you, John — both you and Ellen. (READING) "Item Two: In the event of the death of the oldest living heir, the above mentioned legacy shall be transmitted to the next eldest, John Andrews."

JOHN: (SARCASTIC) You're too kind.

ANDREWS: There's more. (READING) "Item Three: In the event of the demise of the second eldest the legacy shall be bequeathed to the youngest of my heirs, Ellen Andrews."

EVERETT: Well, now that that's settled, I'll be on my way. (COOL) Uncle Mark, my deepest gratitude.

ANDREWS: Just a minute, Everett. I'm not through.

EVERETT: Huh?

ANDREWS: There's one more provision. (READING) "Item Four: In the event that

I, Mark Andrews, survive my sixty-fifth birthday, the above mentioned items shall be without force and effect, and my entire estate I bequeath to the Willard Community Foundation."

JOHN: (BIG) Well, that is interesting, eh, Everett?

(PAUSE)

ANDREWS: No remarks, Everett?

EVERETT: Should I act surprised? I knew you'd put a joker in it somewhere.

JOHN: (IRONIC LAUGHTER) My deepest sympathy, Everett.

ELLEN: John, please! Must there always be this hatefulness among us?

JOHN: But, Ellen, now I'm really beginning to enjoy this little session. If I remember correctly, Uncle Mark, your sixty-fifth birthday is on the twenty-second of this month.

ANDREWS: Precisely — a week from today. And it might please you all to know that my doctor reports that I'm in splendid health.

EVERETT: There was an item in this morning's paper. A man keeled over in the street . . . and was dead . . . (SNAPS HIS FINGER) just like that.

ANDREWS: But, Everett, remember my doctor's report.

EVERETT: The newspaper item said the man had been in apparent good health. The cause of death was unknown. (SLOW) So you see, my dear uncle . . .

ANDREWS: Yes . . . ?

EVERETT: Perhaps by your sixty-fifth birthday next week there may yet be reasons for condolences instead of greetings.

(MUSIC: SWEEPS IN QUICKLY)

8. TOMMY RIGGS AND BETTY LOU*

BETTY: There's nothing to worry about, Uncle Tommy. Don't act so nervous.

TOM: What makes you think I'm nervous? I always bite my nails.

BETTY: But you don't always bite mine.

MAN: (COMING ON) How do you do, folks. I understand you need a lawyer? I'm Crampton Pumperdink of Pumperdink, Pumperdink, Pumperdink and Dink.

BETTY: Who's Dink?

MAN: He's only a half brother.

TOM: Thanks, Mister, but we've got a lawyer.

* By Bill Danch. Reproduced through the courtesy of the author.

BETTY: And besides, Uncle Tommy didn't steal that spade. It belongs to him.

MAN: That makes no difference. When you get up in front of that judge he's going to say to you, "Thirty dollars or thirty days."

BETTY: We'll take the money!

MAN: If you want my legal opinion of your legal chances —

TOM: Please, Mister, go away.

MAN: Okay, but you're missing your big chance. Don't you want to take advantage of a great mind? I've just written a new law book.

TOM: A new law book?

MAN: Yes. I call it "Loopholes of 1946."

TOM: Look, Mister, we're not interested.

MAN: Okay, but if you change your mind, you'll find me across the hall in the jail.

BETTY: What are you doing in jail?

MAN: Thirty days. (FADING) Well, good luck.

BETTY: Don't worry, Uncle Tommy. I got my boy friend Wilbur to be a character witness for you!

TOM: Wilbur? Betty Lou, whose side are you on? Mrs. MacIntyre, where's our lawyer — Ambulance O'Shea?

MAC: Oh, I got rid of him. He's no good. Two of his clients were hanged last week.

BETTY: Gee! They hung two men?

MAC: Sure. His slogan is "Swing and Sway with Ambulance O'Shea!" Oh, oh, careful! Here comes Mrs. Wingate, the old crab.

WIN: (COMING ON HAUGHTY) So! There you are! You thief in cheap clothing!

BETTY: Don't you talk about my Uncle Tommy like that!

WIN: You just wait until I get up to testify!

MAC: You better tell the truth!

WIN: I'll do more than that! When I get up on that witness chair and cross my legs, you know what the judge will think, don't you?

MAC: Yeah. He'll think the witness chair has six legs.

WIN: And as for you, Mister Riggs (FADING) Just you wait!

BETTY: Gee, we're really in trouble now. I wish Wilbur would get here with that speech he's rehearsing.

(GAVEL)

MAN: Here ye, hear ye, hear ye! Magistrate's Court, fourth district, is now in session, Judge Wilson presiding. Next case: Mrs. Wingate vs. Tommy Riggs. Court calls Mrs. Wingate.

WIN: Here I am. Go ahead, Your Honor. Ask me anything.

JUDGE: First chair I ever saw with six legs. Mrs. Wingate, where do you live?

WIN: 202 Maple Drive, Your Honor.

JUDGE: 202 Maple Drive. And now comes a very important question.

WIN: Yes?

JUDGE: Any vacancies?

WIN: No.

JUDGE: Next witness, please!

BETTY: Oh, gee, it's Wilbur! My very special boy friend!

WILBUR: Hello. (SNIFFS)

(GAVEL NOISE)

JUDGE: Order in the court! Order in the court!

BETTY: Your Honor, can I speak to Wilbur first?

JUDGE: This request is highly irrelevant, immaterial, impertinent — and —

BETTY: I knew you'd let me, Your Honor! Look, Wilbur, have you memorized your speech?

WILBUR: Uh-huh!

BETTY: What's the first thing you're going to do when you get on the stand?

WILBUR: I'm gonna cross my legs . . . like this.

BETTY: Wilbur! You're using adhesive tape to hold up your socks!

WILBUR: Uh-huh.

BETTY: Well, why do you use adhesive tape?

WILBUR: Thumb tacks hurt!

BETTY: But, Wilbur, why have you got your handkerchief hanging out of your sleeve?

WILBUR: Because.

BETTY: Why don't you keep your handkerchief in your back pocket?

WILBUR: What! And squash my pet poodle?

BETTY: Well, anyway, you look good for the trial. How did you get so nice and clean?

WILBUR: I was diggin' clams.

BETTY: But how would digging clams get you clean?

WILBUR: The tide came in!

BETTY: Wilbur, how can you be so stupid?

WILBUR: It ain't easy!

(GAVEL POUNDS)

TOM: Come on, Betty Lou. It's time for Wilbur to take the stand.

BETTY: Now, remember, Wilbur, don't forget your speech.

WILBUR: I won't.

TOM: (SOTTO) Yes, Wilbur, get me out of this!

JUDGE: All right, young man, take the stand. Now, your name?

WILBUR: Wilbur.

JUDGE: And you were born — ?

WILBUR: Uh-huh!

JUDGE: What does your father do?

WILBUR: Nothing.

JUDGE: What does your mother do?

WILBUR: Yells at him!

JUDGE: Never mind that. Tell the Court in your own words what you think of Tommy Riggs.

WILBUR: Your honor, COMMA, I have known Tommy Riggs for years, COMMA, and he has always been fair and honest.

JUDGE: Are you sure this testimony hasn't been rehearsed?

WILBUR: Oh, no, Your Honor. PAUSE AND TURN FULLY AROUND AND LOOK JUDGE RIGHT IN THE EYE. Tommy Riggs is too nice a man to be guilty of such a crime . . . BRUSH AWAY A TEAR WITH YOUR RIGHT HAND.

JUDGE: Mr. Riggs, I've heard your character witness, and I'm not impressed. I think this witness has been corrupted.

WILBUR: Oh, no, Judge, it's just the hair tonic I'm wearing.

JUDGE: Leave the stand!

9. PEPPER YOUNG'S FAMILY, #2379*

GIRL: Mr. Trent . . . There's a lady to see you. She's in the reception room.

CARTER: A lady? Who?

* By Elaine Carrington. Reproduced through the courtesy of the author.

GIRL: (SILENTLY OFF) Mrs. Baker.

CARTER: Here? At this time of the morning?

GIRL: Yes, sir.

CARTER: Will you bring her here to my office?

GIRL: Yes, sir.

CARTER: (FADING) Thank you very much.

(FOOTSTEPS ON CORRIDOR — ON . . . HOLD — THEN)

GIRL: (TO MERRY) Mrs. Baker, Mr. Trent will see you. Will you come this way?

MERRY: Oh . . . yes.

(FOOTSTEPS ALONG CORRIDOR)

GIRL: His office is right down here.

MERRY: Thank you.

(FOOTSTEPS STOP)

GIRL: Here — here we are. You go right in, Mrs. Baker.

MERRY: Thank you, very much.

GIRL: (FADING) You're very welcome.

(DOOR OPENS ON)

MERRY: Hello, Carter.

CARTER: (OFF) Hello, Merry.

MERRY: I suppose you think it's awfully early for me to drop in on you.

CARTER: (OFF) Well, I just got here myself. Come in. Sit down.

MERRY: Thank you.

(DOOR CLOSES ON)

CARTER: (OFF) Here. Sit right here.

MERRY: Yes. Oh, Carter, don't look at me. I look a sight. But honestly, Carter, I haven't been able to sleep nights. I've been in such a state.

CARTER: I'm sorry to hear that. (COMING ON)

MERRY: No, you're not. You're annoyed at me for coming here to your office. I can tell.

CARTER: Well, I didn't expect you, that's all. But if there's something I can do for you —

MERRY: Oh, Carter, there's so much you can do for me. Somebody's got to help me. I'm so completely alone with the children. I don't know what to do or which way to turn.

CARTER: What do you mean?

MERRY: Well, I haven't heard a word from Steve — not a word. I don't know what to do.

CARTER: Well, you can't be worried about money. I thought you said he'd deposited some money for you and that you didn't have to worry about that?

MERRY: Oh, I supposed he had — but where does that leave me as far as he and I are concerned? Why can't he meet me and talk things out? Why can't we discuss what both of us want to do?

CARTER: I think it's pretty evident what Steve wants to do. He wants to quit.

MERRY: But walking out on me like that! It's so humiliating to have your husband just walk out. I never thought anyone would walk out on me. If there was any walking out to be done, I wanted to be the one to do it.

CARTER: Well, you can't change what's happened. You can only go on from there.

MERRY: Go on to what? What have I got to go on to? Carter, you don't know how desperately lonely I am — how desperately worried. I feel as if — as if I'd lost all power to attract anyone — as if I were — finished — as if I were through.

CARTER: You know better than that, Merry. You're young and darned attractive.

MERRY: Oh, do you really think so?

CARTER: Of course, I think so. You'll find another guy.

MERRY: I don't want another guy. I can't think of anything worse than getting involved emotionally with a man again. It would just mean that I'd get hurt in the end. All I want is to have you help me over this period! Carter — stand by until Steve and I arrange our affairs. Because I may as well have a divorce as go on this way.

CARTER: I'm sure your lawyer can advise you about that better than I can.

MERRY: I'm not asking for your advice, Carter. I really came down this morning to ask for your friendship.

CARTER: Merry, you know perfectly well that Peggy and I will always be your friends as long as you live.

MERRY: _Peggy_ and you?

CARTER: That's right.

MERRY: What's the matter with you, Carter, that you have to hide behind your wife?

CARTER: I don't understand.

MERRY: Why should you bring Peggy into this? You know that she hates me.

CARTER: You're wrong about that, Merry. She's the one who suggested that I call you up and see you whenever I can. She hasn't raised a single objection to our friendship — not one.

MERRY: She hasn't?

CARTER: No.

MERRY: Well, she's far cleverer than I thought.

CARTER: What's that?

MERRY: Nothing.

CARTER: Look, Merry, why don't you come and have dinner with us tonight instead of staying alone up there in that big house?

MERRY: No, thank you. I'm afraid I wouldn't feel as free to talk in front of Peggy. I'm afraid a family party isn't what I need at the moment.

CARTER: Well, would you like to go out to lunch sometime?

MERRY: Carter, don't you understand? I'd like you to spend a little time with me. Just let me talk out my heart — say what's in my mind to somebody — try to figure out what I'm going to do for the rest of my life.

CARTER: Merry, you know as well as I do that that's something you'll have to work out for yourself. Nobody can do that for you. For you especially, I mean. You're a gal who's going to do exactly as she sees fit for the rest of her life and you're not going to take any advice from a bozo like me, or anyone else.

MERRY: In other words, you've promised Peggy not to see much of me alone — is that it?

CARTER: You're crazy if that's what you think, Merry. I just got through telling you that Peggy was the one who suggested I see you alone as often as I like.

MERRY: And that scared you, didn't it?

CARTER: Well, it surprised me, I'm free to admit.

MERRY: And you never thought that Peggy was doing it on purpose to —

CARTER: To what?

MERRY: To make you react this way — to make you unwilling to see me alone.

CARTER: Merry, I think I've been unwilling to see you alone ever since Steve left.

MERRY: Why is that?

CARTER: For many reasons, but I think one reason is because Steve came to see Peggy.

MERRY: Oh, that.

CARTER: Yes. I know he wouldn't have come to see her unless he were deeply interested in her.

MERRY: (LAUGHING) Imagine your being jealous of Peggy! If it's Steve you're worrying about, you needn't. He's far away. He won't be coming to see Peggy again.

CARTER: I hope not.

MERRY: So you think you'd better stay at home to make sure?

CARTER: We aren't getting anywhere, Merry, talking this way. I trust Peggy, and she trusts me. I don't have to stay at home to keep watch on her. But I do know she might misunderstand a deep friendship between you and me at this time when your husband is no longer around.

MERRY: I see, Carter. So you're giving me the brushoff, too.

CARTER: Well, I certainly wouldn't put it that way.

MERRY: Why not? Facts are facts, aren't they? You've got to face them. And for some reason you're afraid of me.

CARTER: Very much afraid, Merry. But more than anything else, I'm afraid of Peggy — afraid of doing anything that will throw her for a loss — that would hurt her. Y'see, I love my wife.

MERRY: I see. Well, thanks, Carter. You needn't go on. (LAUGHS) Thanks for the memory . . .

10. MARY AND THE FAIRY*

(This is the story of Mary Pooter, a good girl who worked at the perfume counter in a five-and-ten-cent store and took to heart everything she read and everything she saw and everything she heard. Consequently she was worried about what four out of every five have, and coffee nerves, and pink toothbrush, and dry skin, and telltale signs, and she was afraid of offending, and of what might happen if she didn't insist on the name . . .

One day she sent in twenty-five wrappers of Crinkly-Crunkly's delicious wholesome Scotch-bran bread with a letter of exactly twenty-five words, explaining why she liked it. Later she learned that her letter had won the contest that week, and that the Crinkly-Crunkly Good Fairy would call on her on Wednesday evening at 8 o'clock ready and eager to grant her Five Wishes absolutely free of charge.—N.C.)

* From *More by Corwin,* by Norman Corwin. Reproduced by permission of Henry Holt and Company, Inc. Copyright, 1944, by Norman Corwin.

MARY: (EXCITEDLY) Oh, dear! Now what? I've gone and won the Good Fairy contest! The Good Fairy is going to visit me!

(EIGHT BELLS; THEN DOORBELL)

MARY: (DITHEREDLY) Why, that must be the Good Fairy now! And very punctual.

(STEPS TO DOOR; DOOR OPENS ON)

FAIRY: Does Mary Pooter live here?

MARY: Yes, I'm Mary Pooter.

FAIRY: I'm the Good Fairy from the Crinkly-Crunkly Bread Company.

MARY: I was expecting you. (A NERVOUS TITTER) Won't you come right in?

FAIRY: Thank you.

(DOOR CLOSES ON; THEY WALK — ONLY ONE PAIR OF FOOTSTEPS, SINCE FAIRIES DO NOT LEAVE FOOTPRINTS)

MARY: (APOLOGETICALLY, AS THEY WALK) This place isn't very attractive, I know, but I'm getting a new slipcover for the sofa next week. Uh — won't you sit down?

FAIRY: Thank you. (LIKE AN INSURANCE SALESMAN CLOSING A DEAL) Now, Miss Pooter, if you will sign these papers we can get started immediately on your wishes.

(RUSTLE OF PAPERS)

FAIRY: I have to be out of here by nine, because I have three more calls to make in this district tonight.

MARY: Oh. Where do I sign them?

FAIRY: Right on the bottom where it says X . . . Now this one is a company quit-claim in case by any chance you should wish to get into some kind of accident. So's the company will not be held responsible.

MARY: I see.

FAIRY: And this one is a report I have to turn in to the head of my department to show I was here.

MARY: Oh, yes.

FAIRY: And this last one — giving us the right to use your name among the indorsers of C.C.R.B.

MARY: C.C.R.B.?

FAIRY: Crinkly-Crunkly Raisin Bread, a new product to be added to the line effective September fifteenth.

MARY: Oh, yes, I see . . . Heaven's sakes, I feel so important, signing all these papers.

FAIRY: Thank you very much. Now, Miss Pooter, will you kindly state your wish?

MARY: (SLIGHTLY EMBARRASSED) Well, I — I don't exactly know how to say it, but I — Well . . . .

FAIRY: Are you embarrassed about something?

MARY: Yes, ma'am.

FAIRY: But why should you be embarrassed?

MARY: Because — Well — you see, you don't look much like a real fairy to me.

FAIRY: What did you expect I'd look like?

MARY: Well, I thought you'd at least have wings — kind of shiny-like? — and you'd be dressed all in white, and have a magic wand or something.

FAIRY: But I do have wings and a wand.

MARY: You do?

FAIRY: Here, let me take off my wrap. I always fold my wings back under my wrap, or I'd be too conspicuous. There . . . see?

MARY: Oh, how nice! They're very pretty. Like dragonfly wings. May I touch one, please?

FAIRY: Well . . . yes, but don't stroke it against the grain.

MARY: Oh, my, it's beautiful. They're shorter than I would have thought.

FAIRY: That's because I'm an amphibian fairy. I don't fly much.

MARY: Amphibian?

FAIRY: Yes; and here's my magic wand. I have to keep it in a case with a zipper . . .

(SOUND OF ZIPPER)

FAIRY: . . . because it gets dusty and loses its ultra-shortwave powers. When you make a wish I tap you with it on the forehead.

MARY: (ADMIRINGLY) It's like a baton, isn't it?

FAIRY: Yes. And now I'm afraid we'd better get on with your wishes, because my time is short. What's your first wish?

MARY: Well, you see — I — er — Well, ma'am, I come from a poor family and we —

FAIRY: Sorry, but in money matters we have a maximum fortune agreement with the Federal government by which we don't grant wishes for fortunes in excess of twenty-five dollars, because of the obvious inflationary results if we permitted every contest winner to become a millionaire.

MARY: Well, that's all right — I was just going to wish for some of the things I had to miss because I had to quit high school in the second year to work in an office.

FAIRY: You mean you want a high school diploma?

MARY: No — I'd like to sound more educated, that's all. You know — to be able to talk about plays and books and culture and all things like that, and not be a — Well, a wallflower, and the kind of a girl that men — that men forget.

FAIRY: I see. Well, I'm very sorry but we can't grant any complex wishes. Only one thing at a time.

(May Heaven protect this play . . . from a Mary who sounds like a radio ingenue. I can think of nothing drearier than the sweet young Claudias of the air who are endlessly emoting, endlessly in trouble, endlessly irradiating B_1 and light wherever they go.

Mary . . . is a plain girl who has had to sweat for $14.85 a week ever since she was fifteen years old. She is not pretty, bright, aggressive, and she knows it.

Mary is lonely. She has dreamed of romance and glamour, hugged a pillow in bed, looked with envy and self-pity upon happy couples in the park . . . Mary lives in a prefabricated house of dreams. She is encouraged by full-page assurances that a *vita nuova* will open up for her the minute she smells nice.

Mary should be in her thirties, warm, hopeful, querulous, gullible, transparent. She is not a dope, not a silly child. Your listener must feel sorry for Mary, never impatient with her or contemptuous. It is important that Mary should never sound dyspeptic or metallic or unpleasant. She is not sexy, yet not sexless . . . She must be actress enough to accommodate anxiety, twittering excitement, disappointment, self-reproach.

The Fairy has a hard lot. Her voice quality—half fatigue, half ennui—can immediately convey everything there is to know about life in the Crinkly-Crunkly Exploitation Department. At first the Fairy is completely perfunctory toward the girl.—N.C.)

Chapter X . . MICROPHONE READING: CIRCUMSTANCES

1

Once the radio actor is in character he will vary the reading of his lines in accordance with the conditions under which he speaks. He must, as the phrase goes, be aware of the imaginary circumstances that precede and surround his utterance. These circumstances function importantly in further shaping the how of what he says. For example, the actor may understand thoroughly his action and the motivation for it, may know the precise meaning of his lines, may speak them conversationally with an Illusion of the First Time, and may fully contact his distinctly individualized partner; yet he will say his lines one way if he is suffering from a splitting headache and another way if he has just finished eating a huge Thanksgiving dinner; he will say them one way if he has very recently been thwarted in his love life and another way if just yesterday he was elected United States Senator; he will converse one way if he is lying in bed half awake and another way if he is riding on a merry-go-round; he will speak one way if he is standing for the first time on the rim of the Grand Canyon and another way if he is sitting in a funeral parlor.

This point is so elementary that many radio actors apparently can't be bothered awarding much attention to it. "Circumstances?" they ask. "Sure—so what? Shall I read the lines faster or slower? Loudly or softly?" Nevertheless, in radio acting the circumstances that surround the speeches—precisely because they are unseen—merit more than a quick brush-off. Furthermore, the prevailing circumstances of a scene are not brought out merely by changes in tempo or volume. They come into the lines, and shape them, only as the result of a compulsory and concentrated use of the imagination.

This depiction of the conditions under which the lines are spoken is the unique problem of the radio actor. His colleagues on stage and on the screen do not, to the same degree, have to put all of a certain mood or physical state of the character into the words; they are assisted greatly by the mere fact of being seen; they can always rely on help that is visible. For mood and inner states they have recourse to such things as the beam on the face, the slump of the body, the spring and bounce of the walk, the glaze of the eyes, the nervous fluttering of the hands. For all gestures, or movements, or changes of position they need only, for instance, to run, or to lie on a sofa, or to hammer a nail, or to fox trot around the room, or, truly, to carry out any called-for action, and the audience can watch, and can add what it sees to what it hears. For the scene in which they are performing, and the atmosphere that it induces, the stage and screen actors can place their faith in the actual locale or the scene painter's design—and the property man's gadgets. The radio actor, on the other hand, has to put his somewhat visible moods and all his various "business," and the scene or locale into the lines he speaks. If they are not in his words they are nowhere; if they are not in his voice they do not exist. This denoting via speech of all his moods, his gestures and movements and changes of position, and his locales is the new and distinctive necessity that differentiates the radio performer's kind of acting from all other kinds.

2

The disclosure of inner states, of current moods, is perhaps a part of the entire field of characterization (as discussed in Chapters VI and IX). It is sufficient to remind the actor that the father who comes on the microphone to join his family at the breakfast table with a "Good morning, everybody. What's new today?"

will read the two sentences in different ways depending on different preceding or surrounding circumstances. If he has cut himself while shaving he will be in one mood; if earlier he has had a bitter tiff with his wife he will be in another mood; if he has already glanced at the stock market reports to find that he has made $6,000 he will be in still another mood; if he is wearing a new Easter outfit he will be in a different mood; if he wishes to impress his daughter's girl-friend guest he will be in another mood, and so on. The proper reading of the two sentences comes, of course, from the right action and the right motivation.

3

The depiction of physical action is, however, a problem peculiar to the radio actor. Standing in front of a microphone with the script in his hand, he has to simulate hoeing weeds in a garden, climbing up a ladder, peeling potatoes, racing downhill on a bobsled, wrestling, dropping heavily into a chair, and innumerable other activities. Only when the actor vividly uses his imagination, plus as much physical action as is necessary or possible, can he properly read the following apparently simple speech from THE ADVENTURES OF OZZIE AND HARRIET:

OZZIE: (IN A BUS, CALLING) Rogers Road! Let me out, please. Eh — pardon me. Getting out! Oaf! Pardon me. Thank you. Out, please!!

or this scene from THE ADVENTURES OF THE THIN MAN: *The Case of the Flying Baby,** by Milton Lewis,

* Reproduced through the courtesy of the author.

DIANA: You must be out of your mind to leave a child alone like that!

(CRACK)

Ow! (STRUGGLING) Let go of me!

NORA: (STRUGGLING) Now — maybe you'll —

DIANA: Let go of my hand! Don't bite. Ow!!

NORA: (BREAKING AWAY) There! I've got your gun.

DIANA: Ow, my hand!

*** ***

and the following one from *Now You See Her,** by Paul Monash (on MYSTERY THEATRE):

* Reproduced through the courtesy of the author.

(CLATTER OF GLASS FALLING)

ELAINE: The juice . . . There's something — it's been drugged! I — (CHOKING) I'm growing dizzy . . . I — I — can't breathe . . . (BIG SIGH) Can't move . . . !

KING: Elaine . . . Elaine! (TRIES TO STAND) My legs . . . Can't — can't stand! Must get . . . to phone . . . Can't . . . can't . . . (GROANS)

(BODY FALL)

Surely the imagination is as susceptible of improvement by practice as our judgment or our memory. Only by rightly and fully imagining can the radio actor depict via his voice his unseen actions. Only thus, and in his small way, can he approach the sensitivity and the penetration of a Virginia Woolf who could imagine, in her short story, called "The Mark on the Wall," how it feels to be a tree:

I like to think of the tree itself; first of the close dry sensation of being wood; then the grinding of the storm; then the slow, delicious ooze of sap; I like to think of it, too, on winter's nights standing in the empty field with all leaves close-furled, nothing tender exposed to the iron bullets of the moon, a naked mast upon an earth that goes tumbling, tumbling, all night long. The song of birds must sound very loud and strange in June; and how cold the feel of insects must feel upon it, as they make their laborious progresses up the creases of the bark, or sun themselves upon the thin green awning of the leaves . . . .[1]

4

Painting the scene of the action via his voice is the most difficult chore the radio actor must perform at the microphone. So difficult is it, in fact, that most radio actors forego it, although in so doing they forego some of the essential subtleties of their craft.

Only by using the imagination can the actors properly set the scene for the following excerpt from THE ADVENTURES OF THE THIN MAN: *The Case of the Sinister Perfume,** by Milton Lewis:

[1] Virginia Woolf, in *A Haunted House* (New York: Harcourt, Brace and Company, Inc., 1944), p. 45.

* Reproduced through the courtesy of the author.

(SMALL EXPLOSION OFF)

NORA: What's that?

NICK: It sounded like an explosion. Do you smell smoke?

NORA: (SMELLING) Yes! Nick, look up there!

NICK: I should have realized this is their only way out. They've set the place on fire! Come on! We've got to get out of here!

NORA: We can't go back the way we came! The stairs are full of smoke!

(EXPLOSION . . . FIRE)

NICK: (COUGHING) Come back here! There may be another way out.

NORA: All right. (COUGHING) But we'd better find it soon! You can hardly breathe in here.

NICK: Wait a second. There's a window up there. (COUGHING) Here . . . If you climb up on this packing case you can reach it.

NORA: (CLIMBING UP) All right. Give me a boost.

NICK: (HELPING HER) There! Now kick through the window.

(GLASS BREAK ON)

NORA: (COUGHING) It leads to a sort of backyard.

NICK: Go through and wait for me. I'm right behind you.

NORA: (OFF) All right. Come on, Nick. It's safe.

NICK: (EFFORT) Here I am. (DEEP BREATHS) Whew! It feels good to breathe fresh air again. (BOTH OF THEM BREATHE DEEPLY) Come on, Baby. All we have to do is get over that fence and onto the street.

(FIRE SIRENS COME ON)

NORA: Look at the building we just left. You can see the flames now all right.

NICK: Yes. And someone must have turned in an alarm. (RUNNING) Come on back to the apartment, Nora. We've got a date with a murderer!

Only imaginatively can radio actors set definitely in the listener's eye the scene and positions for the actors in the following sketch from THE SECOND MRS. BURTON, #392,* by Martha Alexander:

* Reproduced through the courtesy of the author.

TERRY: I can tell you right now — there's little chance the painting will look like _you_.

TED: Try it anyway. Pick your pose. How do you want me?

TERRY: (LIGHTLY) Well — if I must study you, I'd rather have you looking at me with a smile in your eyes.

TED: Okay. (SOFTLY) Like this?

TERRY: (SUDDENLY THROWN) No. No, that isn't so good. Maybe — maybe it would be better — if you look — (ANY PLACE BUT AT HER) — toward your house —

TED: Anything you say.

TERRY: (STILL TENSE) Yes — that's better. Lift your chin a little. There. That's fine. Now — _think_ about something. Anything.

TED: (QUIETLY) I am. I've been thinking about it for days. (BEAT) Thank you, Terry — for letting me know I _can_ still fall in love. I'd begun to doubt it. But now — I don't have to worry about it any more. Thanks. (BEAT) Sure is a beautiful day, isn't it?

Depending on the actors' imagination, the following scene from A WOMAN'S LIFE, #2086,* by Julian Funt, can be located in front of a living room fireplace, in a crowded restaurant, in a cemetery at midnight, on a beach in the blistering sun, hanging onto straps in a noisy streetcar, or in a number of other places.

* Reproduced through the courtesy of the author.

CAROL: (SMILING) Well, how are you today?

SCOTT: To tell you the truth I don't really know. Still a little dazed . . . or in a mild state of shock. That's . . . Well, one of the things I want to talk to you about — find out whether I made any sense last night. I remember meeting you and Michael . . .

CAROL: You were wonderful, Warren. Really. Just bubbling over with it — as excited as sixteen years old.

SCOTT: Hmmm. Not very becoming to a man of my years.

CAROL: What years?

SCOTT: Mine. I didn't really stand on my hands or walk along the top of a picket fence, did I?

CAROL: Of course not.

SCOTT: That's good. Because there were times when I wanted to. (SIGH) Thank heaven I don't have any pressing work to get out! I imagine it'll be several days before I really start functioning again.

CAROL: I think it's just marvellous — for both of you.

SCOTT: Do you really, Carol? Honestly?

CAROL: I certainly do. Michael and I stayed up till all hours talking about it. You need someone, Warren . . . have for some time now. Someone who will give you all the love and understanding and encouragement that you've been starved for. Someone like Madeline.

SCOTT: Yes, that's certainly true. I just never thought I'd ever find anyone that — But what about her? Is it fair to her?

CAROL: Fair? Don't you think she needs someone too? She's a very warm person, Warren . . . and she's been very lonely. I think, without even knowing it, that she's been looking for someone too. Someone like you — someone who needs her and whom she can love and cherish and respect.

SCOTT: Thanks, Carol, for saying that.

By imaginative practice, then—for there is no other extant advice for the portraying of mood, physical action, or scene—the radio actor must learn not to skip but to search out all the *necessary* attendant circumstances. Of course he must know when overelaboration of detail is beside the main point. It is both pointless and relatively impossible for the actor to build up a plain "Yes, sir" so that it delineates a character who was vaccinated yesterday in the city clinic by a red-nosed doctor whose mother was an angry Armenian.

EXERCISES

A. CIRCUMSTANCES

1. WHEN A GIRL MARRIES, #1335*

IRMA: Doctor, I have to get up. I'm all right.

DOCTOR: Suppose you tell me what's worrying you first? There's something on your mind, Mrs. Cameron — something that's got you down this way.

IRMA: Steve —

DOCTOR: Steve's in California, Mrs. Cameron. You remember that.

IRMA: (FAINTLY) Yes, California . . .

DOCTOR: Now if you'll just put out this arm — that's right. We'll see what your blood pressure's doing.

IRMA: No — I'm all right! I want to get up.

DOCTOR: Suppose you let me take your blood pressure first.

IRMA: I can't, Dr. Frank. I'm fine now.

DOCTOR: It'll only take a minute.

IRMA: Steve — Steve — !

DOCTOR: I'm afraid Steve isn't around, Mrs. Cameron. Now let's see what the reading is . . . (PAUSE) Umph . . . Um.

IRMA: I have to get up! I have to!

DOCTOR: Mrs. Cameron, you're going to have to stay <u>very</u> quiet for the time being.

IRMA: No — I — I can't! There are things I have to do.

DOCTOR: Right now the only thing you're going to do is rest.

IRMA: Dr. Frank, I can't — !

DOCTOR: That is if you want to get back on your feet in a couple of days.

IRMA: I have to be all right! I have to be well!

DOCTOR: Then I want you to listen to me. I'm going to give you a hypodermic, Mrs. Cameron. Then after you've <u>rested</u> <u>all</u> <u>night</u> I'm coming back and see how you are in the morning.

IRMA: Don't, please — !

DOCTOR: It isn't going to hurt at all.

IRMA: I'll be all right without it.

DOCTOR: I'm afraid you won't. Besides, this is going to do you a lot of good.

* By Elaine Carrington. Reproduced through the courtesy of the author.

IRMA: I can't stay in bed — !

DOCTOR: (FIXING HYPO) Mrs. Cameron, this is an order. I don't want to alarm you, but there's something at the moment that isn't working right. And unless you want to be in bed for quite a spell, I want you to do exactly what I tell you.

IRMA: I can't, Doctor! I have to get up!

DOCTOR: Now this won't hurt, Mrs. Cameron. It'll just make you relax.

IRMA: No — !

DOCTOR: Hold your arm still. (PAUSE) Now that wasn't very bad, was it?

IRMA: Dr. Frank — ?

DOCTOR: Yes, Mrs. Cameron? . . . You don't want to tell me what's worrying you, do you?

IRMA: Nothing. (VOICE FADING) I'm just so terribly — terribly tired . . .

DOCTOR: You'll be better once you rest.

IRMA: Tired . . .

DOCTOR: Of course you are.

IRMA: (DROPPING OFF) Very tired . . .

DOCTOR: Well, I'll stop in and see you again first thing in the morning.

2. THE SECOND MRS. BURTON, #272*

Read this scene under many different circumstances; for instance, (a) with Terry and Stan walking down a street, her arm locked through his, during a light, flaky snowfall; (b) during a freezing blizzard or rainstorm; (c) with the two people seated in front of a cozy fireplace; (d) riding in a rattling subway; (e) whispering at a concert.

TERRY: I'm glad you liked the Warrens, Stan. They're wonderful people. We all went to school together.

STAN: I never would have guessed it.

TERRY: Now, Mr. Burton — !

STAN: All the stories you reminisced about — your good old childhood days together — sliding down trees and down hills in the winter — and how you helped each other with your homework, and how you and Elise Warren were cheerleaders . . .

TERRY: Was it really so bad?

* By John M. Young. Reproduced through the courtesy of the author.

STAN: Bad?

TERRY: Did we bore you positively to distraction?

STAN: Not at all. I enjoyed every minute of it.

TERRY: Poor boy! We didn't give you much of a chance, did we?

STAN: I don't mind. It's not too bad, having the shoe on the other foot for a change.

TERRY: Explain that statement.

STAN: I mean — all this past year in Dickston you've been listening to tales of my school days. Isn't it only right and just that I should hear of your mysterious past from some actual eye-witnesses, too?

TERRY: There's nothing mysterious about my past. Or should I pretend there is?

STAN: Just be yourself, my pet. That's a hundred percent all right with your husband.

3. MYSTERY THEATRE: *THE CREEPER**

In addition to reading this scene under various circumstances, such as Mrs. S and Georgia speeding down a street in an automobile, sitting across the table from each other, talking across an alleyway, in a movie theatre, or on the telephone, add such antecedent circumstances as that the two of them mistrust each other, one is suspicious of the other, one is in low spirits, and they have just met for the first time.

MRS. S: Yes, isn't it terrible! I'm simply frightened to death myself.

GEORGIA: At least if I had a double lock — but the night one doesn't work.

MRS. S: Oh, really? I have a chain lock besides. And still I —

GEORGIA: The way it is I sit and shiver when there's a sound at the door. I can't get a locksmith. They're all so busy. Mr. Frank on the corner promised to, but didn't know when. Why are they all so busy?

MRS. S: Well, my dear, because every woman in the neighborhood's changing theirs too. It's simply a nightmare. But don't you worry. We'll stay together this afternoon till our husbands come home. Think of it — we've never visited though we live right across the hall from each other. Isn't that like a big city, for heaven's sake? Or would you rather I dropped in on you?

GEORGIA: Well, I don't —

MRS. S: Make it yours then. Isn't it horrible? The ghastly things they're saying — the theories? One doesn't know what to think next. You believe the latest?

GEORGIA: The latest?

MRS. S: That maybe it's a woman — the Creeper.

GEORGIA: A woman!?

MRS. S: Can you beat it? I can't imagine how in the world the police figure that, for heaven's sake, can you?

4. JOYCE JORDAN, #345*

Read the following selection in accordance with as many different antecedent and surrounding circumstances as possible.

MRS. RILEY: Like an angel she looks, Mrs. Maggs.

MRS. MAGGS: Ain't it so, Mrs. Riley? Such a lovely white dress she has on.

MRS. RILEY: It's the one she was to wear in the piano recital. Mrs. Cleary made it over from an old one of Lola's, and it looks as good as new, I'm thinking.

MRS. MAGGS: Mrs. Cleary always was one to do miracles with a needle. And it's a blessing she could, poor thing, with such a family to keep going.

MRS. RILEY: What I've always said exactly. She was telling me about the dress not three days ago. She got the ribbon new at a sale at Grimes' store. And how proud she was at the way the dress turned out! Little did she think what it would be used for.

MRS. MAGGS: Don't I know? What a shock it was to hear. Joe was working with Mr. Cleary when he got the news. And when he told me I just had to sit down I was that dumbfounded. "No," I said. "No, Joe, it can't be!"

MRS. RILEY: The very same with me. Of course, she's always been what you might say a frail sort of child. But never did I think she'd go like this.

MRS. MAGGS: That pneumonia is a terrible thing. Quick as lightning.

MRS. RILEY: So it is. But have you heard, Mrs. Maggs, that the sickness may not have been so bad as people think?

* By Agnes Eckhardt. Reproduced through the courtesy of the author, and the producer, Himan Brown.

MRS. MAGGS: What do you mean by that, Mrs. Riley?

MRS. RILEY: You haven't heard?

MRS. MAGGS: Heard what?

MRS. RILEY: Well, you know that Dr. Milldermaul has always taken care of Sharon when she's been sick?

MRS. MAGGS: Yes . . .

MRS. RILEY: But this time, when that cold she had got so much worse, Dr. Milldermaul was out of town.

MRS. MAGGS: Oh? Then she didn't have a doctor?

MRS. RILEY: Oh, they got one. But the point is — how good was she?

MRS. MAGGS: She?

MRS. RILEY: Uh-hmm. It so happens that when Mrs. Cleary went to the Tunka house to use the phone, them not having any, Dr. Joyce Jordan was visiting there. And when Mrs. Cleary couldn't get Dr. Milldermaul, Dr. Jordan came instead.

MRS. MAGGS: Dr. Jordan?! Why, isn't she the one folks say — ?

MRS. RILEY: Paralyzed Jim Bradley's arm deliberately? That she is!

MRS. MAGGS: Oh, I'd never want her to take care of a child of mine. Or anybody I held dear to me, for that matter.

MRS. RILEY: Nor would anybody. But when you're beside yourself with worry as Mrs. Cleary was, you'll take most anybody.

MRS. MAGGS: So she came and the child died.

MRS. RILEY: Uh-hmm! It just don't ring right to me.

MRS. MAGGS: To me either. Seeing the child was all right the day before, seems like a good doctor could have pulled her through.

MRS. RILEY: My feelings to a "t", Mrs. Maggs.

MRS. MAGGS: What a terrible tragedy, Mrs. Riley! The Clearys'll never get over her death.

MRS. RILEY: Never.

MRS. MAGGS: Look at that poor woman now.

MRS. RILEY: Well, at least, she's been able to let go of herself and have a good cry. It's Lola Cleary I'm worried about. See her sitting over there in the corner by herself? She hasn't moved all evening. And not a tear out of her this whole time.

MRS. MAGGS: Why do you suppose she's taking it so quiet?

MRS. RILEY: Still waters runs deep, Mrs. Maggs. That's the kind it goes worse with. Her hurt's so far down inside she can't bring it to the surface. She fairly worshipped her little sister. If only she could have a good cry, how much better she'd feel!

MRS. MAGGS: I guess you're right, only — Mrs. Riley, who's that woman just come in the door? See her? She's walking up to the casket.

MRS. RILEY: That I do. And the fine lady is none other than Dr. Joyce Jordan!

MRS. MAGGS: No!?

MRS. RILEY: I never forget a face. How do you suppose she'd have the nerve to come here?

5. THE ALDRICH FAMILY, #425*

It is mid-morning on a hot day. The scene opens under an oak tree on the Aldrich front lawn . . . .

HENRY: (LAZILY) Homer . . .

HOMER: Yeah?

HENRY: Look.

HOMER: Where?

HENRY: Up.

HOMER: Do I have to move?

HENRY: No, you can stay right there on your back and look straight up. See that leaf that's floating down?

HOMER: Oh, yeah.

HENRY: It's going to land right on your face.

HOMER: Yeah . . .

HENRY: Aren't you going to move?

HOMER: I don't know. What's an oak leaf more or less?

HENRY: Here it comes. It's going to land on me. No, it's going to land on you. (PAUSE) Homer.

HOMER: Yeah?

* By Patricia Joudry and Del Dinsdale, based on characters created by Clifford Goldsmith. Reproduced through the courtesy of the authors and Clifford Goldsmith.

HENRY: It's on your eye.

HOMER: I know. It feels nice and cool.

HENRY: It does?

HOMER: I wish one would fall on my other eye.

HENRY: Gee, look at these ants.

HOMER: Where?

HENRY: In this ant hill. Lean over me and you can see them.

HOMER: Never mind. I believe you.

HENRY: Boy, is it hot!

HOMER: I'll say!

6. THE SECOND MRS. BURTON, #394*

STAN: (SOFTLY) Good night, Terry — darling.

TERRY: Good night — Stan.

STAN: (DEEP, SLEEPY BREATH) Umm — Did you set the alarm?

TERRY: Um-huh.

STAN: Seven?

TERRY: Um-huh.

STAN: (HALF ASLEEP) Good. I was late this morning.

TERRY: (SLIGHT PAUSE) Doesn't Jane Winters open the store all right if you're late?

STAN: Um-huh. But I'd rather be there.

TERRY: (BEAT) Why?

STAN: (NOT CARING) I don't know. Pride of ownership, maybe.

TERRY: You depend on Jane for other things.

STAN: Um-huh.

TERRY: Why not let her open the store every morning? Why not let that be a regular part of her job?

STAN: In time — maybe. Not tomorrow.

TERRY: (BEAT) Stan —

STAN: Hum?

TERRY: Why hasn't Jane ever married?

* By Martha Alexander. Reproduced through the courtesy of the author.

STAN: Good heavens, I don't know. I never asked her.

TERRY: She's a nice looking girl. Hasn't anyone ever been interested in her?

STAN: I don't remember. (BEAT) Why?

TERRY: I was just — wondering.

STAN: Well, what do you say we wonder about Jane's love life tomorrow. I'm going to sleep. Good night.

(SOUND: BRIEF KISS)

TERRY: Good night. (SLIGHT PAUSE) Stan —

STAN: (JUST A GRUNT) Um?

TERRY: People are talking about you and Jane.

STAN: (MUMBLE) What are they saying?

TERRY: That she's — in love with you.

STAN: (SNORT) Humf.

TERRY: That she — has been for years.

STAN: Humf.

TERRY: That — <u>that's</u> the reason she left Bill Sullivan and came to work for you — for nothing.

STAN: I'm paying her now.

TERRY: But — she was <u>willing</u> to work for nothing. That's the important thing.

STAN: (BEAT) People always talk.

TERRY: But — it <u>was</u> an <u>overly</u> — generous move on her part. Don't you think?

STAN: No, I think it's exactly the sort of thing Jane <u>would</u> do.

TERRY: For <u>you</u>.

STAN: She's loyal to me — that's all. Good night, honey.

7. TALES OF WILLIE PIPER*

(<u>MUSIC</u>: <u>THE DAY DREAM BEGINS</u>)

WILLIE: (WORRIED) What am I going to do? I can't even think any more. I'd fight for her, but I can't even get a chance to fight. And here we are on Boston Common . . . Bunker Hill must be up that way . . . and somewhere over there Paul Revere stood with his horse, waiting to ride to Lexington and spread the alarm. I guess it'd be different if Martha and I were living then . . .

(<u>MUSIC</u>: <u>CARRIES THROUGH FOR A MOMENT AS HE PAUSES, THEN</u>)

* By Samuel Taylor. Reproduced through the courtesy of the author.

WILLIE: . . . . the eighteenth of April, seventeen seventy-five . . . and Martha and I would be living in a little house in Lexington.

(MUSIC: FADES OUT)

WILLIE: And then late at night . . . one o'clock in the morning . . .

(HORSE'S HOOVES FAINTLY)

. . . we hear a horse coming down the country road, and someone pounds on our door . . .

(POUNDING ON DOOR OFF)

PAUL REVERE: (STYLIZED) Awake! Awake! The British are coming!

WILLIE: And Martha'd be scared, and she'd say . . .

MARTHA: (STYLIZED) William! What's that noise? What's the matter?

WILLIE: (STYLIZED) It's someone at the front door, Martha.

(POUNDING ON THE DOOR OFF)

PAUL REVERE: To arms! To arms! The British are coming!

WILLIE: It sounds like Paul Revere. Martha, hand me my musket.

(HORSE'S HOOVES FADE OUT)

MARTHA: William! You're not going out there and fight?

WILLIE: And I'd say to her . . . Martha, I've got to. It's freedom we're fighting for. The right for every American to come and go as he pleases.

(MUSIC: FAINTLY, FIFE AND DRUM IN "SPIRIT OF '76")

MARTHA: But, William — !

WILLIE: Won't you see what I mean, Martha? I've got to fight. So that if you and I ever want to go down to Boston and stop at a tavern for the night, no one can keep us from having a room.

WILLIE: And then I'd take my musket and go, and she'd stand in the door looking after me.

MARTHA: (FADING) William, please be careful.

WILLIE: And I'd gather on the green with all my minute men . . . and they'd be nervous, but I'd keep them calm. And then the British would come marching up the road . . . .

(MUSIC: CHANGE TO STEADY BEAT OF DRUMS)

WILLIE: And they'd stop and look at us, and the leader of the British'd yell . . .

GENERAL: (QUITE ENGLISH) I say there! Lay down your arms! Disperse, you rebels!

WILLIE: And I'd say to my men . . . stand your ground. Don't fire unless fired upon.

MARTHA: (A LOUD SNEEZE) Ka-choo!

WILLIE: But if they mean to have a war —

MARTHA: Ka-choo! (SORRY FOR HERSELF) Willie . . .

WILLIE: (STARTLED) Huh?

MARTHA: You might at least say "Gesundheit!"

WILLIE: Oh, I'm sorry, Martha. I was thinking. Are you catching cold?

MARTHA: I don't know.

WILLIE: Here, let me put my arm around you.

MARTHA: All right. Ka-choo!

WILLIE: (TENDERLY) Gesundheit, darling.

MARTHA: (SNIFFLING) Thank you, Willie.

8. MYSTERY THEATRE: *THE BRIDE WORE BLACK**

BLISS: Come on. Why don't we go out on the terrace? Corey's got a wonderful terrace. Don't know how he makes the dough to afford it.

COREY: I don't play the stock market.

BLISS: Well, that's one way. Come on, Nora. Show you the lights of the big city from the terrace.

NORA: All right. I like to look at lights.

BLISS: That's the girl.

COREY: I'll come along, too.

BLISS: Three's company. No, I mean's a crowd.

COREY: Yes, but it's my terrace.

(TERRACE DOOR OPENED ON . . . FOOTSTEPS . . . FAINT WIND EFFECT . . . DOOR CLOSED)

NORA: It's wonderful out here! But I'm a little chilly. Would one of you please bring my wrap?

BLISS: Corey's the host.

NORA: Would you?

COREY: Well . . .

* Adapted by Paul Monash from a story by Cornell Woolrich. Reproduced through the courtesy of the authors.

NORA: Please.

COREY: Yes, of course. Which one is it?

NORA: It's a blonde mink . . . initials N.R.

COREY: (FADING) Okay. I'll be back.

(DOOR OPENED OFF . . . CLOSED . . . WIND SUSTAINED)

BLISS: Doesn't seem so chilly out here to me.

NORA: It really isn't. It's just that I wanted to talk to you . . . alone.

BLISS: Oh.

NORA: About something important . . . very important.

BLISS: Important? What's important?

NORA: You. Some things about you. About you and a murder.

BLISS: A murder! Me and a murder?! What are you talking about?

B. PHYSICAL ACTION

1. INNER SANCTUM: *BURY ME NOT**

JANE: Let go of my arm!

ED: Don't be a fool. It's too dangerous to let you go. You might stab me in the back.

JANE: What?!

ED: The way you did Ritchey and Miss Gavin.

JANE: What are you talking about?

ED: You, dear. You called Dunphy just now so you could put the blame on me.

JANE: No!

ED: Don't lie to me! I suspected you of killing Ritchey all the time. That's why I brought you here. I thought Miss Gavin might get you to talk.

JANE: Let me go!

ED: Not until you tell me why you killed her. Why did you do it, Jane? I know you hated Ritchey. But what did you have against Miss Gavin?

JANE: Nothing!

ED: Was she the woman Ritchey fell in love with? Tell me! Was she the one who took Ritchey away from your sister and broke up their marriage?

JANE: Please, Ed — let me go! I'll tell you everything if you let me go!

* By Robert Sloane. A radio presentation, not an adaptation of an Inner Sanctum Mystery novel. Reproduced through the courtesy of the author and Simon and Schuster, Inc., Publishers.

ED: All right, Jane. I'll let you go. (THEN SHARPLY) But first you're going to drop that gun! (EFFORT)

JANE: No! You can't make me!

ED: Drop it, I said!

JANE: Ed, stop! Stop twisting my wrist, or I —

(GUN SHOT)

JANE: (IN PAIN) Ohhhh! Oh, Ed . . .

ED: Jane! Jane, darling!

JANE: (EFFORT) It's all right, dear . . . I know it was . . . an accident . . . and yet . . . it had to be this way . . .

ED: Jane . . .

JANE: No, no . . . listen. Ritchey and Gavin were in love — shamelessly. That's why I killed them. Their love took away my sister's life . . . and I took theirs . . .

ED: You poor kid!

JANE: I don't care . . . it doesn't matter any more. At first I tried to make it look as if my sister's body had come back from the grave . . . but they found out too soon. Even the diary wasn't any use after that . . .

ED: You wrote in that diary?

JANE: Yes . . . I wrote it, Ed . . . to make me look innocent. But you see . . . the diary told the truth. I am going to die . . . tonight.

(BODY FALLS)

2. FIGHTING SENATOR*

(CAR DOOR SLAMS . . . CAR DRIVES OFF . . . FOOTSTEPS ON GRAVEL . . . OTHER STEPS APPROACH, THEN STOP)

SAM: Where you going, Senator?

JEFF: To a — What do you men want?

SAM: Nothing, Senator. Just —

JEFF: No, you don't!

SAM: That's what you think!

* By Arnold Perl. Reproduced with the permission of the author and Louis G. Cowan, Inc.

(A SOCK . . . JEFF HITS BACK)

CROWD: AD LIBS.

JEFF: You men think you can —

SAM: Quick, Chuck, quick! He —

(JEFF SOCKS HIM . . . FOOTSTEPS RUNNING ON)

CHUCK: Get him from the back, you dope! Okay, wiseguy!

(MORE STRUGGLE, SOCKS)

JEFF: (EXERTION)

CHUCK: Sap him, you dope, sap him!

(A VICIOUS CLOCK ON THE HEAD)

JEFF: (GOES DOWN GROANING)

SAM: (A BEAT) You wanna finish him off?

CHUCK: We can't. Somebody might of seen us.

SAM: Well, we can't —

CHUCK: Okay, so we can't. Don't stand there. Kick him, you dope. Kick him where it'll do the most good.

SAM: (SAVAGELY) Okay, Chuck. I was only asking.

(A VICIOUS KICK)

JEFF: (A GROAN OR TWO)

3. THE ADVENTURES OF OZZIE AND HARRIET*

OZZIE: What's that wonderful smell?

EMMY: Those are some cookies my mother asked me to bring to the Thornberrys'.

OZZIE: Cookies?

(PAPER BAG SOUND)

OZZIE: Yes, they are cookies.

EMMY: Care to try one, Mr. Nelson?

OZZIE: Thank you. (EATING) You see, just what I was talking about. Things like this are too rich for you. Chocolate is one of the richest foods . . . very bad.

EMMY: Some of them are vanilla.

* By Ozzie Nelson and Staff. Reproduced through the courtesy of Ozzie Nelson.

OZZIE: Huh? (EATING) Oh, you're right. Well, even vanilla is too rich. In fact, I'd say that the vanilla is just as sweet as the — Let's see. (CHEWS . . . COUGHS) No, the chocolate is richer. Very bad for you. I'd better eat another vanilla to sort of neutralize it. (EATING) No wonder people get sick so easily.

EMMY: How long is Mr. Dunkel going to stay, Mr. Nelson?

OZZIE: Oh, until his wife gets back. Here's a broken one. (CHEWING) No use throwing it away. Or unless Mr. Dunkel suddenly decides to —

EMMY: That one's chocolate.

OZZIE: (MOUTHFUL) Emmy Lou, don't you think a man should spend Thanksgiving with his family if possible?

EMMY: Oh, of course.

OZZIE: I'll see you later.

EMMY: Where are you going?

OZZIE: Oh, I don't want to keep you, Emmy Lou. You've got an errand.

EMMY: Not any more. Mind if I throw this empty bag into your garbage can?

OZZIE: Not at all. And don't forget what I told you about rich foods. Goodbye.

EMMY: Just a minute, Mr. Nelson. You've got crumbs on your coat. I'll brush them off.

OZZIE: Don't you touch me! I'll find them!

4. MY FRIEND IRMA*

AL: (CRYING) Professor! Stop crying.

KROPOTKIN: (CRYING) Who's crying? I've got an allergy. Anything that makes me sad makes me cry. (STILL CRYING) Janie, how could you think of doing such a horrible thing to such a wonderful woman?

JANE: (CRYING) Me? Why, it was all Irma's fault. She's always saying she's cold.

IRMA: (SOBS) Jane, do you think I'd do that to my own mother?

JANE: Oh, what's the difference? (SNIFFING) There's no point in our standing around crying like a bunch of fools. She was fired because she wanted to help us. Every time I think of what we were on the verge of doing, I almost hate myself.

* By Cy Howard and Parke Levy. Reproduced through the courtesy of the authors.

5. MYSTERY THEATRE: *THE FOUR FATAL JUGGLERS**

GORDON: (YAWNING: TO HIMSELF) Five o'clock. Oh, Lord! (YAWNS AGAIN) Say, you guys . . . wake up. Come on . . . Come on . . . get up. (SOME SLEEPY STIRRING) It's five o'clock. Come on, Dave.

DAVE: (SOUNDING GROGGY) Aw, let me sleep. Too cold . . . sleepy . . .

GORDON: You'll feel better in a few minutes. You want to bag a few ducks, don't you?

DAVE: Oh . . . (BIG YAWN) . . . Oh, okay.

GORDON: Come on, Bob, off and on them.

BOB: (YAWNING) I'm stiff as a board.

GORDON: We've got a fine, exciting day ahead of us. You don't want to miss any of it.

BOB: That's right . . . I don't. What time is it?

GORDON: Five o'clock.

BOB: Oh, no!

6. MYSTERY THEATRE: *THE BRIDE WORE BLACK*†

MITCHELL: There . . . that's the kind of music I like. Now for a drink and —

JULIE: Here's yours. (GIVES IT TO HIM) How about a toast?

MITCHELL: Okay. Here's to a long life . . . and a merry one.

JULIE: (IRONICALLY) Yes . . . a long life. (MITCHELL DRINKS)

MITCHELL: Aren't you having any? What's the matter? It's not bad stuff.

JULIE: I . . . I was just thinking . . .

MITCHELL: Thinking? About what?

JULIE: About our first meeting.

MITCHELL: Yeah, I've been wondering about that too. Where did I ever see you before?

JULIE: On the steps of a church.

MITCHELL: Ugh! My stomach — !

JULIE: What's wrong?

MITCHELL: Nothing, nothing. Just a pain in my stomach. It'll go away. What did you say about a church?

* By Paul Monash. Reproduced through the courtesy of the author.

† Adapted by Paul Monash from a story by Cornell Woolrich. Reproduced through the courtesy of the authors.

JULIE: I said . . . you saw me on the steps.

MITCHELL: (PAIN REACTION) Don't mind me. It's just a cramp. Never get them but — (CONTROL) What were you doing . . . at the church, I mean?

JULIE: Getting married. Do you remember?

MITCHELL: Married? No, I — (PAIN AGAIN) This is the funniest thing! All of a sudden, too. It's burning!

JULIE: Do you remember . . . the church . . . the wedding . . . and then right after?

MITCHELL: (IN PAIN) Look . . . something's wrong! My whole stomach — it's on fire! Gotta call a doctor. Can't understand this . . . Gotta call a doctor!

JULIE: No, you're not going to call a doctor.

MITCHELL: Get out of my way! (EFFORT) Look out!

JULIE: You're too late for a doctor.

MITCHELL: Too late? What'd you do? (FEAR AND PAIN MIXED) What'd you do to me? What for? I don't even know you . . . I don't . . . I don't . . . ! (BODY FALLS)

JULIE: Yes, you do know me. I'm Mrs. Nick Killeen.

MITCHELL: (SOMEWHAT OFF . . . VERY WEAK) Nick Killeen . . . Nick — . . . Don't understand.

JULIE: Don't you . . . ? You don't remember Nick Killeen? And the girl on the steps . . . in her wedding dress?

MITCHELL: (GETTING DISTANT) You've got me . . . mixed up . . . mixed up . . . (DEEP BREATH . . . SHARP PAIN REACTION . . . AND SILENCE)

7. DAYBREAK*

SURGEON: All right . . . start the transfusion and give him a hypo of adrenalin. (PAUSE) Get the large kidney clamps and the heavy ligature ready. (PAUSE) Suction.

(SOUND OF SUCTION IN . . . THIS IS A STEADY HISS OF AIR WITH FAIRLY STEADY GURGLE OF LIQUID BEING SUCKED UP A TUBE . . . PAUSE . . . SOUND OF CLAMP BEING APPLIED . . . CLAMP HAS RATCHET — CATCHES LIKE A HANDCUFF BUT MAKES A SMALLER, CLEANER SOUND)

* From *Thirteen by Corwin,* by Norman Corwin. Reproduced by permission of Henry Holt and Company, Inc. Copyright, 1942, by Norman Corwin.

SURGEON: Sponge. (PAUSE)

JONES: The pulse is becoming imperceptible . . . heart sounds very feeble.

SURGEON: Inject some coramin into the veins.

JONES: Yes, sir. (PAUSE) Doctor, the heart sounds are not audible.

SURGEON: Massage his heart. (PAUSE) Sponge.

ANESTHETIST: Pupils are widely dilated, Doctor.

JONES: There's no response from the heart at all.

ANESTHETIST: Doctor, the patient has ceased breathing.

SURGEON: Well, we did all we could.

8. THE ALDRICH FAMILY, #396*

(A BICYCLE BELL)

MR. ALDRICH: Come on, Will. Put on a little speed, and we can coast all the way down this hill!

MR. BROWN: (SLIGHTLY OFF) I'm right behind you, Sam.

MR. ALDRICH: (PUFFING) What's the matter? Can't you go any faster?

MR. BROWN: (PUFFING) The trouble is — this bike of Homer's is just held together by pieces of string.

MR. ALDRICH: Yes?

MR. BROWN: He can never be bothered lifting it down off the veranda. He just rides it down the steps.

MR. ALDRICH: Is that right? He'll break his neck one of these days.

MR. BROWN: (COMING ON) Yeah, maybe he will.

MR. ALDRICH: Now — from here on we can coast.

MR. BROWN: What a relief!

MR. ALDRICH: Isn't this a grand day though, Will? You'd think it was the middle of July.

MR. BROWN: Sam, look!

MR. ALDRICH: What?

MR. BROWN: That big pile of leaves at the side of the road. Let's ride our bikes through it.

MR. ALDRICH: Sure thing, Will. That's a good idea.

* By Patricia Joudry and Del Dinsdale, based on characters created by Clifford Goldsmith. Reproduced through the courtesy of the authors and Clifford Goldsmith.

MR. BROWN: Here I go!

(BIKES GO THROUGH LEAVES)

MR. ALDRICH: Hah! Just listen to that! Look, Will, no hands.

MR. BROWN: Boy, there's nothing like playing hookey from work on a morning like this.

MR. ALDRICH: I just hope Henry and Homer weren't planning to use their bicycles this morning.

MR. BROWN: They won't use them. They never use them any more.

MR. ALDRICH: By the way, did you instruct your secretary, Will?

MR. BROWN: Yes, I told her to tell everybody I was in conference. She thought I was crazy.

MR. ALDRICH: So did mine. (THEY BOTH LAUGH) Will, stop your bike a second. Take a look over there.

MR. BROWN: An apple orchard!

(THE BIKES STOP)

MR. ALDRICH: Isn't it a beauty? The last apples of the season.

MR. BROWN: Remember when we were boys, Sam?

MR. ALDRICH: I know exactly what you're going to say. There was no thrill in the world like helping yourself to a few apples.

MR. BROWN: Yes, sir, I've spent the happiest hours of my life up in an apple tree.

9. THOSE WE LOVE, #120*

EMMETT: (LAUGHING AS SHE BEGINS AGAIN, SINGING AT TOM) "There were four-and-twenty sailors, a-shipping on the deck,
And they were white and pretty nice, wi' rings about the neck;
And the captain was a duck, wi' a jacket on his back!
When the ship began to move, cried the Captain, "Quack! Quack! Quack!"

(SHE LAUGHS, WITH TOM CROWING HAPPILY)

LESLIE: (OFF FROM DOORWAY, APPLAUDING AND LAUGHING) Bravo, Mrs. Emmett!

EMMETT: (TURNING TO LAUGH) Och, I didna hear you come up, Doctor! That was a request number. (LAUGHS)

* By Agnes Ridgeway. Reproduced through the courtesy of the author.

LESLIE: (COMING ON) I remember it. You sang it to my daughter . . .

EMMETT: (LAUGHING) Aye. Miss Kathy thought of it just now.

KATHY: Are you going now, Leslie?

LESLIE: In a few minutes, darling. I've just time to say hello to my son.

KATHY: Nice . . .

LESLIE: (SMILING) Having yourself a time, Thomas? Mmm? (LAUGHS)

KATHY: Daddy, Tom?

TOM: (TALKS TO LESLIE)

LESLIE: Where's Daddy's big boy, hm? (THEY LAUGH A LITTLE) Yes, water's wet, isn't it! (SMALL LAUGH)

EMMETT: (FADE) I'll go down now, Miss Kathy. I want to make some soup for Amy's lunch.

KATHY: (SMILING UP AT HER) Okay, Mrs. Emmett.

EMMETT: (FROM DOORWAY) Guid-bye, Tom.

KATHY: Here, shake bye-bye. Bye-bye, Mrs. Emmett . . . .

TOM: (TALKS TO HER)

EMMETT: (LAUGHING) Aye, it's a big wee mannie! Bye-bye, dear . . . (SLIGHT PAUSE)

KATHY: All right, Tom, I guess you're clean . . .

LESLIE: Hold his towel, and I'll fish him out. Come on, Tom, aaall-y up! (LAUGHING) That's my baby! Your mommy has a nice, warm towel waiting.

KATHY: This part he isn't so crazy about . . . (AS TOM PROTESTS) Hey, none of that! (SINGING HEAVILY IN IMITATION OF MRS. EMMETT) Ohhh, the Captain was a duck, with a jacket on his back! (LESLIE LAUGHING) And when the ship da-da-daah, daaaah, the Captain said QUACK-quack-quack-quack-quack-quack . . . (SHE DOES IT FAST, DONALD DUCK STYLE — IT ENDS IN A KISS ON TOM'S NECK. KATHY AND LESLIE LAUGH) Ooooooh, I could eat you! I guess the nursery's warm enough for him . . . .

LESLIE: Yes, the house is warm all over today.

(SOUND: THEIR FOOTSTEPS JUST BARELY SUGGESTED)

LESLIE: Your Aunt Emily called up a few minutes ago — just before my patient came.

KATHY: Oh, I thought it was somebody for you.

LESLIE: She wants you to match some yarn or something up in Springdale.

KATHY: Oh, sure . . .

(SOUND: FOOTSTEPS OUT)

LESLIE: She's bringing it over. I offered to pick it up, but she's going over to Landises' anyway.

KATHY: Oh, yes, they're planning for the church fair! Auntie and Mrs. Landis have the needlework table.

LESLIE: Oh . . .

KATHY: A little talcum powder, Tom?

TOM: (PROTESTS SQUIRMING)

KATHY: Ah, gwan, you do, too, like it!

LESLIE: Here, son, here's your rattle . . .

(SOUND: SMALL SOUND OF RATTLE)

10. MYSTERY THEATRE: *THE MAN WHO MURDERED IN PUBLIC**

(CLANK OF OARLOCKS, GASP, AND A FEW SPLASHES)

GEORGE: (SHARPLY) Have a care, Elsie. You'll —

ELSIE: (SQUEALS) The oar! George, the oar! It's overboard! Catch it!

GEORGE: (SLIGHTLY OFF) I . . . can't . . . reach . . . (SHARPLY) Don't lean on this side! You'll —

ELSIE: (SCREAMS)

(SPLASH . . . MUFFLED CRIES)

GEORGE: (OFF AND COMING ON, SPLUTTERING) Elsie! Elsie, are you all right? I'm coming. Don't struggle!

(SWIMMING SOUNDS)

ELSIE: (ON SPLUTTERING) Don't! Stay away from me!

GEORGE: (ON) Here. Turn about . . . on your back.

ELSIE: (SCREAMS IN PANIC) Stay off! Let go of me, you ugly little brute! I'll —

(GRUNT FROM ELSIE AND THUD OF FLESH INDICATES BLOW TO GEORGE'S FACE . . . CONTINUOUS SWIMMING SOUNDS)

GEORGE: (UNBELIEVING) Ugly little brute! (SINISTER) You called me that five years ago. And you struck me! Brute, am I?

(BETWEEN CLENCHED TEETH)

* By Roy Vickers, adapted by Frederic A. Methot. Reproduced through the courtesy of the authors and the publishers of *Ellery Queen's Mystery Magazine.*

Brute? You shouldn't have said that, my girl! (WITH PHYSICAL STRUGGLE IN VOICE) I'll brute you, you soft, white mealy little fool! You she-devil! (LAUGHS HYSTERICALLY) Brute, eh! (LAUGHS)

ELSIE: You're drowning me! Let go! (SCREAMS, SPLUTTERS, SPLASHES) Help! Help! (CUT OFF SHARP) Hel -- ! (INCREASED THRASHING) Don't! Dear Heaven, don't! (LONG GURGLING INTAKE OF BREATH)

11. HOP HARRIGAN, #881*

(FADE IN STEADY DRONE OF PLANE AND HOLD)

JAMESON: (COMING ON) Are we anywhere near the canyon, Hop?

HOP: Should be just about over it, Colonel Jameson. Stand by with a flare, Tank.

TANK: Right.

HOP: Open the side window and let her go when I give the word.

TANK: Check.

(WINDOW SLIDES OPEN — HIGH WHINE OF WIND)

TANK: Window's open.

HOP: Okey, let it go!

(HISS OF FLARE)

TANK: She's away!

HOP: Look sharp now.

TANK: There it is, Hop! To the left!

JAMESON: Is that the canyon?

HOP: Yes, sir. The transport crashed at the bottom of it.

JAMESON: And you expect to run the paraplane through that canyon?

HOP: It can be done, sir. There's enough wing clearance. Hang on now. We're going through.

(PLANE DRONE UP IN DIVE)

TANK: Want me to close the window, Hop?

HOP: No. Stand by with another flare.

TANK: Okey.

HOP: (PAUSE) Hang on. I'm banking in!

(CHANGE LEVEL OF PLANE — ECHO THROUGH CANYON)

* By Albert Aley. Reproduced through the courtesy of the author and the producer, Robert Maxwell Associates.

TANK: We're in!

HOP: Drop the flare!

(HISS OF FLARE)

TANK: She's away!

JAMESON: Where's the wreckage you saw, Hop?

HOP: I didn't see the whole wreck — only the plane wing.

TANK: Should be right under us.

JAMESON: I don't see anything but snow.

TANK: Me neither.

HOP: Let another flare go, Tank.

TANK: Check.

(HISS OF FLARE)

TANK: It's over.

HOP: Well?

TANK: Nothing yet.

HOP: That's funny.

TANK: Are you sure you got the right canyon?

HOP: Positive.

JAMESON: There's nothing down there now, Hop.

TANK: Hey, wait! Jumping Jennies!!

HOP: What is it, Tank?

TANK: (ALMOST A PRAYER) Oh, no! Oh, no, it can't be! It can't be!

(PLANE DRONE UP AND FADE)

12. THE SECOND MRS. BURTON, #194*

(HORSES TROTTING)

BRADLEY: Boy, what a day! What a day!

TERRY: (SLIGHTLY OFF) It's super, isn't it?

BRADLEY: I'll say!

TERRY: (COMING ON) Shall we walk them a while now, Brad?

BRADLEY: Well . . .

* By John M. Young. Reproduced through the courtesy of the author.

TERRY: Let's walk them to the bend. Then we can canter right up to the Falls.

BRADLEY: Okay. Easy, Duchess. Easy, old girl!

(BLITZ IS UNHAPPY . . . HE ACTS UP, SNORTS)

BRADLEY: Gee, that Blitz still doesn't act so good, does he?

TERRY: Easy, Blitz. Whoa, boy! Whoa, boy!

(THE HORSE SLOWS DOWN)

TERRY: Oh, he's all right, Brad. Just a little stubborn; that's all.

BRADLEY: Yeah.

(THE HORSES ARE WALKING NOW)

BRADLEY: He sure has got the fire in his eye. Much better than this Duchess . . . She acts like she was asleep on her feet.

TERRY: Let's not go over that again, Brad. She's a fine little horse.

BRADLEY: How's about letting me ride Blitz from here to the Falls?

TERRY: Not a chance.

BRADLEY: How's about letting me ride him part way home after supper?

TERRY: Not on your tintype!

BRADLEY: (SMILING) I bet you I could.

TERRY: That's something you'll never know . . . a bet we'll never make.

BRADLEY: Want to dare me to try it, Aunt Terry?

TERRY: No, siree. (CHUCKLING) Are you always as stubborn as this, Brad?

BRADLEY: Am I stubborn?

TERRY: I don't know where you get it.

BRADLEY: From Dad maybe. He's stubborn, too, sometimes.

TERRY: We settled the question of your riding Blitz about four times to my knowledge, yet still it comes up.

BRADLEY: I just think I'm getting pretty good; that's all.

TERRY: Well, you have improved.

BRADLEY: That's because you're a good teacher.

(BLITZ SNORTS AND SKITTERS)

TERRY: Whoa, Blitz. Easy there! What's the matter with you? Cut that out.

BRADLEY: Boy — !

TERRY: Steady, boy. Steady there! That's the good horse.

BRADLEY: Boy, he likes to cut up all right.

(BLITZ IS ALL RIGHT NOW)

TERRY: And that's precisely why, Mr. Bradley Burton, I'm not going to allow you to ride him. Those jodhpurs must have given you too much confidence.

BRADLEY: Yeah, I guess they have. Gee, they're neat, Aunt Terry! You were swell to give them to me. You've been swell about everything.

(A PAUSE)

TERRY: That's — that's the nicest thing you could possibly say, Brad. (PAUSE) I think you're pretty swell too. (PAUSE) Oh, look. There's the Falls just up ahead. Let's break into that canter now, shall we?

(THEY CLUCK THE HORSES . . . SNORTS . . . THEN A CANTER)

BRADLEY: Yipppppeeee! We're off!

(THE HOOFBEATS COME UP LOUD)

Bring to class additional scenes with difficult circumstances or physical actions in them.

C. CROWDS

FIGHTING SENATOR*

MIKE: (A GIRL) (FURIOUS) I thought so. Am I a sucker? Walked out, that's what he did. Just plain walked out on it! Now I've seen everything.

EVANS: You don't mean that!

MIKE: Don't you see it? Rouse the town, get a meeting to fight this thing, and then walk out on it. Could there be a better way to ruin a reform movement? Could Big John Munster have picked a slicker man for the job?

CROWD: "WHERE'S JEFF TYLER?" "LET'S GO HOME."

EVANS: What are we going to do?

MIKE: I said I'd speak and I'll speak. The first thing I'm going to do is expose our friend, Jeff Tyler, for the coward he is.

EVANS: Miss Logan, let me speak first. The crowd is unruly. I mean they know me.

MIKE: All right — if you want to — all right.

CROWD: (MORE AD LIB PROTESTS: "LET'S GO HOME." "IS TYLER YELLOW?")

MIKE: (ON P.A. AS SHE SPEAKS, CROWD QUIETS DOWN) Attention please. This meeting was called by Senator Jeff Tyler —

CROWD: (LOUD BOO'S)

* By Arnold Perl. Reproduced with the permission of the author and Louis G. Cowan, Inc.

MIKE: — and it's still possible he may get here. Right now I'd like to introduce Mr. George Evans, a man you all know and respect. Mr. Evans.

CROWD: "AH, GO HOME, EVANS."

EVANS: (ON P.A.) Friends: this is an unhappy event for me as well as for you. The necessity to call a meeting to protest the action of people of this town is a great shock to me.

CROWD: (CATCALLS: "CAN'T HE TALK?" "WHERE'S TYLER?" "IS HE YELLOW?")

VOICE: (FROM THE CROWD) Where's your yellow-livered Senator? He started all this. Where is he?

EVANS: Please, please!

VOICE: Where's your outside agitator? Where's your "Fighting" Senator?

VOICE: What's he doing — starting something so he'll get elected Governor?

CROWD: "YEAH," "WHERE IS HE?" — (THE CROWD GETS OUT OF HAND)

MIKE: We'd better call it off, Mr. Evans.

EVANS: But we can't. This is — (LOUD) Please, please! May I have your attention —

VOICE: (WOMAN, SHRILL) It's Senator Tyler — look at him!

CROWD: (AD LIB AMAZEMENT: "WHAT HAPPENED TO HIM?" "LOOK AT HIM.")

MIKE: Jeff!

EVANS: He's bleeding, he's —

MIKE: (IN A RUSH, CALLING) Jeff, what happened? What did they do? Who did it? Jeff!

EVANS: He'd better get to a hospital —

JEFF: (OFF) No!

MIKE: Jeff, you can't —

JEFF: (COMING ON) Yes, I can. They left me in the alley there — and — two GI's there — this sergeant and —

MIKE: Don't try to talk. You the one?

SERGEANT: Yes, ma'am. Willie and me found him there. They must of — I don't know — kicked him in the head, Miss. We wanted to get to a hospital, but he said get him here — so we —

MIKE: Well, he's got to — Jeff, you can't just stand here and —

JEFF: I've got to talk to the crowd, Mike.

MIKE: No.

CROWD: "GO ON, GET HIM OUT OF HERE . . . . " "WE DON'T WANT HIS KIND HERE." "NOBODY WANTS TO HEAR WHAT YOU GOT TO SAY, TYLER."

JEFF: I've got to speak, Mike.

MIKE: But, Jeff, you can't —

JEFF: I'll be okay.

MIKE: One of you men help him. (INDICATING) Sergeant —

SERGEANT: Sure, Miss. Easy, Senator.

JEFF: I'm okay.

EVANS: Look out. That man's throwing a stone — look out!

(SOUND: A STONE THROWN. MISSES JEFF. CRASHES ELSEWHERE.)

VOICE: Get off that platform!

SERGEANT: I'll get that guy, Senator. You go ahead and speak. Stop that man. (OFF) Okay, Senator, go ahead. We'll take care of this guy.

Chapter XI . . EMOTIONAL AND COMEDY ACTING

1

Emotional acting (the extreme of straight or serious acting) differs in important essentials from comedy acting. A radio actor's approach to reading a role in a straight, serious, or tragic play is not the same as his approach to playing a part in a comedy or in a farce. Although many actors somehow fail to note or to adjust to this basic dissimilarity between the two kinds of acting, it is more or less admitted everywhere.

An awareness of the difference lies behind Athene Seyler's questions to Stephen Haggard: "Have you noticed that young people usually find comedy more difficult than serious parts? . . . . Now why should inexperienced young people find it easier to lose themselves in the portrayal of a serious character than in a comic one?"[1] The awareness has always been evident in the old truth that every clown longs to "do something different" and act in tragedy; it is evident today in the desire of most radio actors who perform regularly in daytime serials such as WHEN A GIRL MARRIES or in evening dramatic programs such as GANGBUSTERS to act in comedy half-hours like MY FRIEND IRMA. A yearning for a "different" kind of acting explains also why most of the funny people in, for instance, THE LIFE OF RILEY, hope some day to be cast for a serious part in a show like SUSPENSE. The difference between the two ways of performing is constantly implied by a comment like this, from the director to his THE ALDRICH FAMILY cast: "You're all performing that scene as if it were a soap opera or a scene from a straight play! Remember—you're acting in a comedy."

That emotional acting differs from comedy acting is, however, not all the actor must know. He must understand wherein the two kinds of acting differ, so that he can change, for example, from soap opera or straight playing to comedy playing. He must be sure, in one way or another—by instinct, or from experience, or from theory—what these fundamental differences are. Perhaps only a few great actors have excelled equally in playing dramatic and comedy roles, but every performer ought to learn how to attack the two kinds of acting. The differences between them, fundamental to all playing, therefore need to be more than casually examined. Moreover, an acquaintance with these differences can illuminate the whole art of acting.

Any examination, however, of emotional acting or of comedy acting is a perilous pursuit. All that one can hope to do is to venture out into the depths of psychological and philosophical theory and, taking care not to become engulfed, return in quick time with a few tidbits that may prove helpful.

2

If, as E. F. Carritt says, "The subject of art is emotion and emotion is its effect,"[2] Bernard Shaw is correct in declaring that the circulation of feeling is more important to the actor than the circulation of blood.[3] As he wrote to Ellen Terry,

> . . . the greater the actress the greater is her power of seizing on every emotional impulse and . . . amplifying it as a microphone . . . amplifies sound . . . . The story of Mrs. Siddons terrifying the shop assistant by the intensity with which she asked, "Will it wash?" is quite probable.[4]

[1] Seyler and Haggard, *The Craft of Comedy,* p. 18

[2] E. F. Carritt, *The Theory of Beauty* (London: Methuen & Company, Ltd., 1914), p. 287.

[3] George Bernard Shaw, *Dramatic Opinions and Essays,* edited by James Huneker (New York: Brentano's, 1906), I, 69.

[4] George Bernard Shaw and Ellen Terry, *Ellen Terry and Bernard Shaw; A Correspondence,* edited by Christopher St. John (New York: G. P. Putnam's Sons, 1931), p. x.

Elsewhere he went on to point out:

It takes years of practice to develop this power of emotional expression; for most educated women have been trained to fight against emotional self-expression because it is a mode of self-betrayal. Now self-betrayal, magnified to suit the optics of the theatre, is the whole art of acting.[5]

In order, then, to portray the necessary feelings and emotions called for by the script, an actor ought to know, if only in general, that the three major aspects of the affective life are (1) attitudes, (2) feelings, and (3) emotions, which can be briefly described as follows:

1) An attitude, always present in what an actor says, has been defined by Daniel A. Prescott as

. . . a mental and neural state of readiness, organized through experience, exerting a directive or dynamic influence upon the individual's response to all objects and situations with which it is related.

The attitude is incipient and preparatory, rather than overt and consummatory. It is not behavior but the precondition of behavior. It may exist in all degrees of readiness from the most latent, dormant traces of forgotten habits to the tension or emotion which is actively determining a course of conduct that is under way.

Without guiding attitudes, the individual is confused and baffled. Some kind of preparation is essential before he can make a satisfactory observation, pass suitable judgment, or make any but the most primitive reflex type of response. Attitudes determine for each individual what he will see and hear, what he will think and what he will do.[6]

2) Feelings, which come and go, rise and fall, in each character during the action of a play, are vaguely perceived sensations of pleasantness and unpleasantness that are less violent than emotions.

Feelings may be taken to be indicators of how well the basic equilibria are being maintained . . . of whether or not conditions are optimum for the maintenance of those dynamic physiological processes that are characteristic of the organism . . . . Feelings range from unpleasant to pleasant as behavior is blocked or facilitated; they vary with the quality and intensity of sensory stimulation; they grow out of organic conditions in the viscera and are changed as these conditions are modified through autonomic stimulation.[7]

3) Emotions—of which perhaps rage, fear, and love are the major—are "adjustive reactions of the body attempting to adopt the body economy as a whole to the demands of the situation."[8] They involve intensive visceral behavior or marked bodily changes of "feeling," "choc," or "upset." "Choc" is the name for "Poorly coordinated responses elicited by stimuli not reacted to by the organism in its immediate past, such as 'shock' or 'start.'" "Upset" is "the condition of an organism brought about by a series of stimuli which cannot be reacted to adequately, with consequent disassociation of . . . usually integrated behavior patterns."[9]

The first important fact that the actor can learn from these statements has been expressed elsewhere in the James-Lange theory, that "*bodily changes follow directly the perception of the exciting fact, and that our feelings of the same changes IS the emotion*"; or, as William James "in this crude way" phrased it, ". . . we feel sorry because we cry, angry because we strike, afraid because we tremble . . . ."[10] Perhaps the theory is not quite so simple, and not entirely tenable, but it is sufficiently sound to teach the actor a basic law of his profession: in order to portray an emotion *he must apparently undergo bodily changes.*

The second important fact is that, as Carney Landis points out, "no pattern of expression . . . may be said to characterize any situation or emotion of any one individual or group of individuals." The actor can conclude from it that he cannot successfully act out an emotion "in general" but *must imaginatively and in character perceive the stimulus or the exciting fact that evokes the emotion.* As I. Rapoport insists, for instance, fear is an emotion "which arises in a person as a result of some external phenomena threatening danger," or from the inexplicable. But there are as many varieties of fear as there are people and causes. It is one thing to be frightened by a frog . . . and quite another thing to be frightened by an explosion. A young girl's fright differs from that of a healthy lad. Every person has his own individual expression of this or that feeling under any given set of circumstances.[11] The radio actor should therefore "never seek to be jealous, or to make love, or

[5] Shaw, *op. cit.*, I, 409.

[6] Prescott, *Emotions and the Educative Process*, pp. 805–806.

[7] *Ibid.*, p. 13.

[8] *Ibid.*, p. 18.

[9] See Landis, *The Expression of Emotion*, pp. 312–351.

[10] William James, *Principles of Psychology* (New York: Henry Holt & Company, Inc., 1890), II, see 447–454.

[11] I. Rapoport, "The Work of the Actor," *Theatre Workshop I*, No. 1 (October–December, 1936), p. 26.

to suffer, for its own sake"; he should never charge "himself with feelings without any reference to his lines."[12] All strong feelings or emotions result from something that has gone before; they result from the way in which action is either blocked or facilitated. On the stimulus, the exciting fact, the actor must concentrate all his attention and imagination. Then and then only can he work up and portray the true emotion.

3

Today much is made of the actor's use of his "emotion memory." For many actors it seems to be the precious secret for successfully portraying any emotion called for by a script. Unfortunately, the theory of the "emotion memory" can be as harmful to the actor as it is helpful. Often he does not realize that the term is merely a synonym for "imagination"; he takes it to mean something else; he somewhat constantly defines it as only "memory." Memory and imagination, needless to say, are not interchangeable words. In accepting the truth that "feelings drawn from our actual experience and transferred to a part are what give life to the play,"[13] the actor who is an addict to the "emotion memory" theory is all too likely to center his entire attention on remembering his own emotions and transferring them to the part instead of concentrating upon transmuting them for the part. This difference between transferring and transmuting the remembered personal emotions is crucial. In so far as the "emotion memory" theory emphasizes the imaginative transmutation of remembered emotions it can be extremely helpful to some actors. When the theory emphasizes and limits itself to merely a vivid power of recall it is egotistic, puerile, and uncreative.

According to the theory, probably first pronounced by the French psychologist Thèodule Ribot near the start of the century, and made much of by Stanislavski and his followers,

Just as your visual memory can reconstruct an inner image of some forgotten thing, place, or person, your emotion memory can bring back feelings you have already experienced. They may seem to be beyond recall, when suddenly a suggestion, a thought, a familiar object will bring them back in full force.

Since you are still capable of blushing or growing pale at the recollection of an experience, since you still fear to recall a certain tragic happening, we can conclude that you possess an emotion memory.[14]

Boleslavsky illustrates this point with his story of a certain couple who had been married when they were very young:

He had proposed to her one fine summer evening when they were walking in a cucumber patch. Being nervous, as nice young people are apt to be under the circumstances, they would stop occasionally, pick a cucumber and eat it, enjoying very much its aroma, taste and the freshness and richness of the sun's warmth upon it. They made the happiest decision of their lives between two mouthfuls of cucumbers, so to speak . . . .

Long years of life and struggle came; children and, naturally, difficulties. Sometimes they quarrelled, and were angry. Sometimes they did not even speak to each other. But their youngest daughter observed that the surest way to make peace between them was to put a dish of cucumbers on the table. Like magic they would forget their quarrels, and would become tender and understanding.[15]

Since, according to the theory, all people have "emotion memories," the actor is often wrongly led to the conclusion that all he has to do in order to portray truthfully a certain emotion is to remember out of his past the strongest emotion nearest to it in quality. If, for example, he has to portray the fear of a man awaiting execution in a dungeon, it suffices for him to remember the most outstanding instance of impending terror that he can recall from his own experience, such as his waiting as a child for a dreaded whipping from his father. The fear of the paternal punishment will then be wrongly substituted for the character's fear of execution.

What the actor should do, according to *Modern Acting; A Manual,* is to recall such details as

a) hearing his father making preparations in the next room,

b) dryness in his mouth, and

c) seeing the door through which his father will come.

From these he is able to recreate the emotion of fear. Next,

[12] Shaw, *op. cit.,* I, 167.

[13] Stanislavski, *An Actor Prepares* (New York: Theatre Arts, Inc., 1936), p. 155.

[14] *Ibid.,* pp. 158–159.

[15] Boleslavsky, *Acting,* p. 37.

He must center his attention on the general feeling of fear and its manifestations to such an extent that that emotion dominates him. The details which helped him recall it are forgotten for the moment in the intensity of the new stress.

Now with that feeling still strong within him the student goes on with the action in the dungeon. The important thing is to continue the new action at the moment when he experiences fear rather than at the moment when he is involved in the mechanics of recreating fear.[16]

What the actor so often actually does, however, in trying to follow through with the "emotion memory" theory, is to forget the final step, is to neglect the *new action,* is to substitute fear of a whipping for fear of death in the electric chair, is to overlook the truth that his kind of fear may not be the same as his character's. He makes the mistake of omitting the specific stimulus for his character's fear, one of the regulators of its quality.

In other words, it may be true, as Boleslavsky insists, that a sensitive artist, in order to arouse himself to the right emotional state in which to act Othello killing Desdemona, need only be able to remember how he was driven to kill an annoying mosquito once at an outdoor picnic. Nevertheless, the secret of Boleslavsky's advice, often overlooked or misunderstood, comes in his last sentence: "The rest is the work of magnification, imagination, and belief."[17] In other words, the remembrance of an earlier emotion is nothing more than a springboard for the creation of the emotion called for by the script. What the actor does with the emotion *after* he has recalled it is the important thing. If he remembers but cannot also imagine he is creatively crippled. In short, and to repeat for emphasis, memory and imagination are not synonyms. Their meanings are as distinctly different in acting as they are, for instance, in literature where memory is what the writer of an autobiography largely uses; imagination is what the novelist relies on.

The authors of *Modern Acting; A Manual* stress the actor's dependence on this point. As an illustration of how imagination should be joined to memory in the portrayal of an emotion they use an actress who has been assigned the role of Ase in Ibsen's *Peer Gynt;* the scene is that in which Ase dies.

The particular circumstances are: Ase is old, worried for Peer's safety, happy to have him with her, in pain, uncomfortable in the cramping quarters of the small bed which belonged to Peer as a child. At moments she is transported into the dream world that Peer creates for her as he weaves the story of the ride to St. Peter. Her attention is broken, however, now by pain, now by fright at approaching death. In the final moments she is weakened by the emotional strain; she falls back limply against the bed and says to Peer, "I'll lie back then and trust me to you, my boy." Let us take the problems of interpretation in this scene.

From her *memory* she draws this: 1. The actress recalls her severest illness and her weakest moments. 2. . . . the relief of relying on the nurse present. 3. . . . the satisfaction of having her mother present. 4. . . . another time when she sat in a crowded automobile for hours at a time. 5. She remembers the pain of a burn received from hot sealing wax. 6. She recalls the fear of endangering her mother's health through her own illness. 7. . . . her childish absorption in fairy tales.

From her *observation* she draws the following: 1. The picture of old age. 2. Norwegian characteristics. 3. The furnishings of the room.

It will take her *imagination,* however, to: 1. Intensify the feelings accompanying illness, weakness, and pain that she is actually able to recall. 2. To visualize the person, the feelings and the circumstances as one. 3. To transfer all the experiences to the character. 4. To believe in the result as truth.[18]

4

The old debate on whether the actor should truly feel the emotion he is portraying goes futilely on and on. Many actors, especially the young, who have the notion that "they must feel the thing they are trying to do, and then act it according to their feelings," who "dislike to think that the mind arranges and designs the final expression of the moment of acting," are, like the character in Somerset Maugham's *Theatre,* always a little shocked to learn that some performers do not actually feel the emotions they are acting.

When I was just a kid, I was fourteen, I was standing one night in the wings watching you act. It must have been

[16] Rosenstein, Haydon, and Sparrow, *Modern Acting,* p. 30. Copyright, 1936, by Samuel French. All rights reserved. Reprinted by permission of the authors and Samuel French.

[17] Boleslavsky, *op. cit.,* p. 44.

[18] Rosenstein, Haydon, and Sparrow, *op. cit.,* pp. 27–28. Copyright, 1936, by Samuel French. All rights reserved. Reprinted by permission of the authors and Samuel French.

a pretty good scene, you said the things you had to say so sincerely, and what you were saying was so moving, I couldn't help crying. I was all worked up. I don't know how to say it quite, I was uplifted; I felt terribly sorry for you, I felt a bloody little hero; I felt I'd never do anything again that was beastly or underhand. And then you had to come to the back of the stage, near where I was standing, and tears were streaming down your face; you stood with your back to the audience and in your ordinary voice you said to the stage manager: What the bloody hell is that electrician doing with the lights? I told him to leave out the blue. And then in the same breath you turned round and faced the audience with a great cry of anguish and went on with the scene.[19]

And today's horde of Stanislavski disciples simply does not know what to make of the methods of a great actor like Edmund Kean, of whom critic Lewes wrote:

People generally spoke of him as a type of the "impulsive actor." But if by this they meant one who abandoned himself to the impulse of the moment without forethought or prearranged effect, nothing could be wider of the mark. He was an artist, and in Art all effects are regulated. The original suggestion may be, and generally is, sudden and unprepared—"inspired" as we say; but the alert intellect recognises its truth, seizes on it, regulates it . . . . Kean vigilantly and patiently rehearsed every detail, trying the tones until his ear was satisfied . . . and having once regulated these he never changed them. The consequence was that, when he was sufficiently sober to stand and speak, he could act his part with the precision of a singer who has thoroughly learned his air.[20]

Quintilian started this "to feel or not to feel" argument in the first century when he declared that the actor moves others only by first being moved himself. Then Diderot and Coquelin defended the paradox that you can be a great actor only on the condition that you have complete self-mastery and the ability to express feelings that you do not feel—perhaps feelings that you cannot feel—"by which last is meant that the actor can by synthesis build up an image of emotions that are beyond human perfection." Finally, in the twentieth century, Stanislavski, pushed along by psychology, returned to Quintilian's point of view. There is no way of definitely settling the controversy. The only practical conclusion is Stark Young's:

One man can experience an emotion repeatedly with more readiness than another; one has less need than another to feel the emotion at the moment in order to act it . . . .[21]

But feeling the scene is something that no actor can forever depend on . . . . And even if he could be sure of the right excitement within himself, he must remember that the art of acting does not consist only of what is felt—much of it lies in the external means by which feeling is conveyed.[22]

All that we can ask of the actor is that he should discover what the emotion is and possess the means of conveying it to us.[23]

In order to convey an emotion to an audience the actor must give the *effect* of feeling it. How he achieves that effect is his own business. As Salvini explained when he said that he recited the monologue before the murder of Desdemona without any emotions whatsoever,

It is only that I know how to say it so as to make others believe in my sincere emotion. And once I did feel it, too . . . when I studied the role! Then I felt it completely, even to the point of physical pain. But after I have mastered it, I no longer worry about anything. I have it at my fingers' ends. I play the emotion the way the pianist plays the piano, without looking at it.[24]

5

Perhaps the essential difference between emotional and comedy acting is this: in the former the prime requisites are sensibility, imagination, and a belief in the truth of the action; in the latter the prime requisites are sensibility, imagination, high spirits, and a belief in the lack of proportion or in the distortion of the action. In other words, when Harold Lloyd said once, on being asked what he did to make people laugh,

[19] Somerset Maugham, *Theatre* (New York: Doubleday & Company, Inc., 1937), p. 259. From *Theatre*, by S. Somerset Maugham. Copyright, 1937, by W. Somerset Maugham. Reprinted by permission of Doubleday & Company, Inc.

[20] George Henry Lewes, *On Actors and the Art of Acting* (London: Smith, Elder & Company, 1875), pp. 6–7.

[21] Stark Young, *Theatre* (New York: Doubleday & Company, Inc., 1927), pp. 113–114.

[22] Stark Young, "Minor Exhibitionists," in *Glamour* (New York: Charles Scribner's Sons, 1925), p. 99.

[23] *Ibid.*

[24] Max Martersteig, *Der Schauspieler* (1900), pp. 68 ff.; as quoted in Lorenz Kjerbühl-Petersen, *The Psychology of Acting*, translated by Sarah T. Barrows (Magnolia, Mass.: The Expression Company, 1935), p. 200.

"Act natural in an unnatural situation," he assuredly meant that the actor should pretend that the action is natural *all the time he is sure that it is not natural.* For example, the actor sitting in a room and pretending that a man is behind the door intent on murdering him can play the scene straight, or seriously, from a belief in truth that is in balance, or he can play it for comedy from a belief in truth that is obviously out of balance. As Athene Seyler wrote to Stephen Haggard, "If the actor is really frightened the audience will be frightened too; but if he knows subconsciously that his fear is out of proportion to the danger the audience will enjoy it."[25] The straight or serious actor gets inside a part; the comedy actor stands both inside and outside a part.

This is not to say that the actor of comedy must try primarily to be amusing. John Hill's 1755 rule is as applicable now as it was then: "To succeed perfectly, the player must disguise to his audience, in a proper degree, his intent of raising a laugh, and his expectation of doing it."[26] He must believe in his action and the situation; he must, as Shaw advises, play his comic part "like a true actor: by the simple but very unusual method of playing it from its own point of view." The accomplished comic actor

. . . plays Osric from Osric's own point of view, which is that Osric is a gallant and distinguished courtier, and not, as usual, from Hamlet's, which is that Osric is a "waterfly."[27]

Surely it is clear, if anything histrionic is clear, that Dogberry's first qualification must be a complete unconsciousness of himself as he appeals to others.[28]

To say that a comic character needs complete reality in the playing is to state "the fundamental law of all acting, comic or serious." "Surely all artistic creation must be founded on truth; but one can regard truth from different angles." Seyler and Haggard point out, nevertheless, that the roots of all comedy are lack of balance, distortion, overemphasis or underemphasis, and surprise.

Now, all these things are only relative to something else: the truth. So that you must first see the truth of a character before you can upset its balance. But you must *believe* in the distorted view of the truth that you have discovered.[29]

. . . . take your Victorian lady as truth, and ask her to turn from you and pick up a pin from the floor, so that all you see of her is her bustle! Here is emphasis on one aspect of her without altering her measurements, which is the essence of comedy.[30]

Having drawn the character a little out of proportion you must passionately believe in that measurement as the correct one. I think that your true comedian does both these things at once; that is to say, he is aware instinctively that the emphasis he is laying on one side of his portrait distorts it, and yet he offers it as a true likeness. The "standing outside"—the approach to the character—is the first process. The second process is concerned with presenting this view, and depends on what we call technique. It is the craft of appearing to believe in the balance of a thing that one knows is out of balance.[31]

If you stand outside Epidohov in Chekhov's *The Cherry Orchard,* for example,

. . . his fears are ridiculous; you know that a spider can easily be brushed away, and that Epidohov will never use his revolver. But he himself magnifies a spider into a real menace and believes that he might one day kill himself. If you play the part from the inside (as he sees life and himself) it may well be a tragic performance of a man bordering on insanity. But if you are aware of him from outside as a foolish, impotent, harmless fellow all the comedy will be apparent.[32]

All such advice about comedy acting is perhaps best summed up in Milton Berle's rule, "You can't build comedy on comedy—that's basic," and Charlie Chaplin's admonition, "If what you're doing is funny, don't be funny doing it."

Of course, comedy playing is so much a matter of technique, or practical execution, that it is almost useless to theorize about it. Comedy acting demands the high spirits of pace in the playing and of topping one another's tones. It needs the right rhythm for the retort. It depends heavily on give-and-take among two or more players and nearly always comes out right as "the effect of a line spoken by one and the reactions of the others." Seyler and Haggard give an example of

[25] Seyler and Haggard, *op. cit.,* p. 16.
[26] [John Hill] *The Actor* (London: John Griffiths, 1755), p. 181.
[27] Shaw, *op. cit.,* II, 323.
[28] *Ibid.,* p. 428.
[29] Seyler and Haggard, *op. cit.,* p. 14.
[30] *Ibid.,* p. 25.
[31] *Ibid.,* p. 15.
[32] *Ibid.,* p. 16.

how a lack of this comic technique ruined a potentially bright and merry scene:

> The old father and the young cub of a son were having an argument with the daughter about her boy friend. It was three minutes of what one might call quick-fire repartee and ought to have gotten a laugh every few lines. But it didn't come off because the girl who was playing the daughter, instead of taking the broad tone of the other two, elected to play the part with complete sincerity, and the hesitations, the little movements, the low voice which she used (which would have been charming in a straight scene) simply let the ball drop instead of returning it good and hard to her colleagues.[33]

Yet whatever the values of technique in comedy acting, and they are many, "if your understanding of the humour of a character is lacking, . . . no technical accomplishment will enable you to present it faithfully."[34] Therefore the actor trying comedy should,

> . . . firstly, have a firm trust in the comedic quality of his part, and secondly, assured expectation that the audience will respond. These will make him able to impart his private opinion (*i.e.* delight in) his interpretation.[35]

6

The gnawing questions that this discussion of emotional and comedy acting raises are these: Why cannot the straight or serious actor also "stand outside" his part while playing it and believing in it? How else can he play from an idea, or add his comment thereto? On the brink of answering them one must stop. They are questions the answers to which are endless and esoteric—questions that can provoke thought if not produce a dogmatic solution.

SELECTED READINGS

Emotions:

Allport, G. W., "Attitudes," in Carl Murchison (ed.), *Handbook of Social Psychology.* Worcester, Mass.: Clark University Press, 1935, pp. 798–844.

Archer, William, *Masks or Faces? A Study in The Psychology of Acting.* London: Longmans, Green and Company, 1888, 232 pp. An investigation of "emotionalist" and "antiemotionalist" acting.

Bard, Philip, "The Neuro-humoral Basis of Emotional Reactions," in Carl Murchison (ed.), *Handbook of General Experimental Psychology.* Worcester, Mass.: Clark University Press, 1934, pp. 264–311.

Blanton, Smiley, "The Voice and the Emotions," *Quarterly Journal of Speech,* I, No. 2 (July, 1915), 154–172.

Boleslavsky, Richard, "The Second Lesson: Memory of Emotion," in his *Acting; The First Six Lessons.* New York: Theatre Arts, Inc., 1933, pp. 29–48.

Cannon, W. B., *Bodily Changes in Pain, Hunger, Fear, and Rage* (2nd ed.). New York: Appleton-Century-Crofts, Inc., 1929, 311 pp.

Claparede, E., "Feelings and Emotions," in *Feelings and Emotions; The Wittenberg Symposium.* Worcester, Mass.: Clark University Press, 1928, pp. 124–139.

Darwin, Charles, *The Expression of the Emotions in Man and Animals* (1872). New York: Appleton-Century-Crofts, Inc., 1899, 372 pp.

Dunbar, H. F., *Emotion and Bodily Changes.* New York: Columbia University Press, 1935, 595 pp.

Kjerbühl-Petersen, Lorenz, Chap. X, "The Problem of Emotion and the Attempts to Solve It," and Chap. XI, "Significance of the Illusion of the Act in the Several Creative Phases of His Work," in *Psychology of Acting; A Consideration of Its Principles as an Art,* translated by Sarah T. Barrows. Magnolia, Mass.: Expression Co., 1935, pp. 157–201, 202–238.

Landis, Carney, "The Expression of Emotion," in Carl Murchison (ed.), *Handbook of General Experimental Psychology.* Worcester, Mass.: Clark University Press, 1934, pp. 312–351.

Langfeld, H. S., "The Role of Feelings and Emotions in Aesthetics," in *Feelings and Emotions; The Wittenberg Symposium.* Worcester, Mass.: Clark University Press, 1928, pp. 346–352.

Luria, A., *The Nature of Human Conflicts.* New York: Liveright Publishing Company, 1932, 431 pp.

Lund, F. H., *The Emotions of Men.* New York: McGraw-Hill Book Company, 1930, 348 pp.

MacDougall, William, *Energies of Man.* New York: Charles Scribner's Sons, 1932, 305 pp.

Meier, N. C., *Studies in the Psychology of Art.* University of Iowa Studies in Psychology No. 17, *Psychological Monographs,* XLV, No. 1, 1933.

Paulhan, F., *The Laws of Feeling* (1887). New York: Harcourt, Brace & Company, Inc., 1930, 213 pp.

Prescott, Daniel A., *Emotion and the Educative Process.* Washington, D.C.: American Council on Education, 1938, 323 pp.

Reymert, M. L. (ed.), *Feelings and Emotions; The Wittenberg Symposium.* Worcester, Mass.: Clark University Press, 1928, 446 pp.

[33] *Ibid.,* p. 45.
[34] *Ibid.,* p. 18.
[35] *Ibid.,* p. 36.

Ribot, T. A., *The Psychology of the Emotions.* London: Walter Scott, Ltd., 1897, 455 pp.

Rosenstein, Sophie; Larrae A. Haydon; and Wilbur Sparrow, Chap. IV, "Imagination" (Emotion Memory), in *Modern Acting; A Manual.* New York: Samuel French, Inc., 1936, pp. 26–47.

Ruckmick, C. A., *Psychology of Feelings and Emotions.* New York: McGraw-Hill Book Company, Inc., 1936, 529 pp.

Watson, J. B., *Psychology from the Standpoint of a Behaviorist.* Philadelphia: J. B. Lippincott Company, 1919, 429 pp.

Woolbert, Charles H., "A Behavioristic Account of Intellect and Emotion," *Psychological Review,* XXXI (July, 1924), 265–272.

Young, Stark, "Minor Exhibitionists," in his *Theatre Practice.* New York: Charles Scribner's Sons, 1926, pp. 62–68.

Comedy:

Bergson, Henri, *Laughter; An Essay on the Meaning of the Comic* (1900), translated by Cloudesley Brereton and Fred Rothwell. New York: The Macmillan Company, 1914, 200 pp.

Cooper, Lane, *An Aristotelian Theory of Comedy* . . . . New York: Harcourt, Brace & Company, Inc., 1922, 323 pp.

Dolman, John, Jr., "A Laugh Analysis of 'The School for Scandal,'" *Quarterly Journal of Speech,* XVI, No. 4 (November, 1930), 432–445.

Feibleman, James, *In Praise of Comedy; A Study of Its Theory and Practice.* New York: The Macmillan Company, 1939, 284 pp. A highly useful book.

Freud, Sigmund, *Wit and Its Relation to the Unconscious* (1905), translated by A. A. Brill. New York: Dodd, Mead & Company, Inc., 1916, 388 pp.

Gaver, Jack, and Dave Stanley, *There's Laughter in the Air! Radio's Top Comedians and Their Best Shows.* New York: Greenberg, Publisher, 1945, 291 pp. Scripts, mostly in condensed form, for twenty-one comedy programs from Fred Allen to Ed Wynn.

Gregory, J. C., *The Nature of Laughter.* London: Kegan Paul, 1924, 241 pp.

Grieg, J. Y. T., *The Psychology of Laughter and Comedy.* London: G. Allen & Unwin, 1923, 304 pp.

Lamb, Charles, "On the Artificial Comedy of the Last Century" (1823), in *Essays of Elia.*

Meredith, George, *Essay on Comedy and the Uses of the Comic Spirit* (1877). New York: Charles Scribner's Sons, 1918, 326 pp.

Seyler, Athene, and Stephen Haggard, *The Craft of Comedy.* London: Frederick Muller, Ltd., 1943, 86 pp. Required reading for actors.

Smith, Willard, *The Nature of Comedy.* Boston: Chapman & Grimes, 1930, 191 pp. A helpful survey of theories.

Sully, James, *An Essay on Laughter.* London: Longmans, Green & Company, 1902, 441 pp.

EXERCISES

A. TYPICAL EMOTIONAL SCENES

1. MYSTERY THEATRE: *CORPUS DELICTI**

(FOOTSTEPS PROCEEDING DOWN LONG ECHOING CORRIDOR . . . THEN . . . KEY IS INSERTED IN LOCK AND TURNED . . . JAIL DOOR IS SWUNG OPEN)

GUARD: You can go in now. You can have half an hour.

MIKE: A half hour? But —

GUARD: Sorry. The Warden says that's the best he can do. Even for you, Lt. Connors.

MIKE: All right.

(DOOR CLANGS SHUT . . . KEY IS TURNED IN LOCK)

GUARD: (FADING) I'll be back. You can call if you want to leave before then.

MIKE: (AFTER A MOMENT, PLEADING ALMOST TENDERLY) Jim . . . . (HE WAITS, THEN WITH MORE URGENCY) Jim . . . (HE WAITS AGAIN, THEN ALMOST DESPERATELY) Jim, for the love of God . . . !

JIM: (HIS VOICE TIGHT WITH EMOTION) Mike, I — (THE WORDS WON'T COME. THEN, FEELING HIS BROTHER'S ARM TIGHT AROUND HIM, HE BREAKS)

MIKE: (ALL COMPASSION) Jim! Jim boy, you've got to tell me. You can tell me.

JIM: (TIGHT) There's nothing to tell.

MIKE: (PLEADING) You can tell your own brother. Don't you see — this is my business, Jim. I'm not a police detective for nothing. I could help.

JIM: It's too late, Mike. (STRANGELY CALM NOW) In two days it'll be all over. They say they give you a shot of something before they take you to the chair. They say you hardly even know what's going on.

MIKE: (RAGING) But you didn't do it. I know you didn't. You're taking the rap for that cheap lying dirty little —

JIM: (SHARPLY) Mike!

MIKE: (GRUDGINGLY) Oh, all right. Sorry!

JIM: Don't talk about her like that, Mike. If you knew how sweet she is, you'd —

MIKE: Jim, I know you didn't kill her husband. I don't know what happened, but I know you didn't do it. Why won't you tell me? Jim, what can I say to Mother? I've got to tell her something. She's waiting at home now.

* By Don Agger. Reproduced through the courtesy of the author.

JIM: All right. If I tell you, will you promise me something?

MIKE: Anything.

JIM: Promise me you'll tell no one but Mother, and not even her until I'm . . . until after . . . (HE SWALLOWS HARD) the day after tomorrow.

MIKE: I promise. (EAGERLY) Jim, what happened that night?

JIM: Well, as you probably know, I met Mary about six months ago. (LOW, STEADY) I love Mary more than anything in the world. And she loves me.

MIKE: (INDIGNANT) She loves you enough to let you take the rap for her!

JIM: Please, Mike!

MIKE: All right. Go on.

JIM: She told me she'd asked her husband for a divorce, but he wouldn't give

(MUSIC: SNEAK)

it to her. She was terribly unhappy. Then this night she called, and . . . Well, I'd never heard her sound that way before.

(MUSIC: STING AND CONTINUED B.G.)

MARY: (FILTER) Jim, Jim, come to me. Quickly, darling! I need you.

JIM: Mary, what's the matter!

MARY: (FILTER) I can't tell you — over the phone. Just come, please!

JIM: I'll be right over.

(MUSIC: STING AND UNDER)

I rushed out and grabbed a cab. I couldn't imagine what had happened. When I got there, Mary met me at the door. She was trembling. She led me to the living-room.

(MUSIC: STING AND HOLD)

MARY: Jim! It's Martin. He's . . . he's . . . Oh, Jim, look!

JIM: Martin, her husband, was lying on the floor, his head all bloody. There was a heavy candelabra nearby with blood on it. He was dead!

(MUSIC: UP IN CLIMAX AND OUT)

MARY: I didn't mean to kill him! We'd quarreled again. And he said such terrible things, about you . . . and me. He kept screaming names at me. Then he started to beat me, and —

JIM: Mary! Oh, you poor darling. Your face . . . it's all bruised.

MARY: He kept hitting me. I grabbed the candelabra and told him to stay away. But he kept coming toward me. I didn't want to do it. (SHE WEEPS HYSTERICALLY)

JIM: Mary, you've only done what everyone has a right to do. It was self-defense. We'll call the police!

MARY: (IN HYSTERICAL FEAR) No!

JIM: But, Mary —

MARY: No, not the police! (A LITTLE MORE CALMLY) They'd never believe me. They'd say I did it — because of us. (FLARES UP AGAIN) They'd put me in prison! They'd — ! Don't let them do it!

JIM: (REASONABLY) Now look, Mary, try to be reasonable. We've got to call the police. There's no other alternative.

MARY: Very well then. But you'd better go now, and leave me to face it alone. Your being here'll only make it worse.

JIM: (PROTESTING) But, Mary —

MARY: I used to believe you, Jim, when you said you loved me . . .

JIM: I'll do anything. You know I will. I love you so terribly. I'll do anything!

MARY: Do you mean that?

JIM: Yes, I do.

MARY: All right. (SLOWLY) Jim — Jim, what if there weren't any body . . . ?

JIM: What do you mean?

MARY: If there's no corpus delicti, they can't find anybody guilty. They won't even be sure there's <u>been</u> a murder. (PAUSE) I'm not asking you to do anything. You're quite free to leave this house — this minute. (WITH CONTEMPT) I'll be careful not to involve you. I'll manage by myself — somehow.

JIM: Don't say things like that. I'll do anything. You know I'll do anything! (HELPLESSLY) Only . . . what can we do?

2. CANDLE IN THE WIND*

MADELINE: Yes, Madeline — you must learn to live without Raoul. If there's to be no Raoul, you must learn to live without him. He would forgive your gray hairs, for his own is graying now. He would forgive those crow-tracks around your eyes, for the crows have torn at him too. But nobody

* By Maxwell Anderson. Copyright, 1941, by Maxwell Anderson. Reprinted with the permission of Anderson House.

else would forgive you, Madeline. The crowds won't forgive. They will say that you are old. Raoul would forgive you, Madeline, but there is no Raoul. Wipe out those lines, and weep less in these sleepless nights, for you must go forward without him. That is your lesson, Madeline. Learn it by heart, and never forget. I can't, I can't — I can't! (SHE BREAKS DOWN AND CRIES)

3. THE SEARCHING WIND*

SAM: (WITH GREAT PASSION) I love this place. And I don't want any more fancy fooling around with it. I don't want any more of Father's mistakes, for any reason, good or bad, or yours, Mother, because I think they do it harm. I was ashamed of that clipping. But I really didn't know why. I found out tonight. I am ashamed of both of you, and that's the truth. I don't want to be ashamed that way again. I don't like losing my leg, I don't like losing it at all, I'm scared — but everybody's welcome to it as long as it means a little something and helps to bring us out some place. All right. I've said enough. I love you both. Let's have a drink.

4. MIRACLE IN THE RAIN†

ART: Ruth! I'm glad you could come. Do you mind just standing here? I've only got about ten minutes.

RUTH: Ten minutes . . . ?

ART: I'm leaving. They just told me half an hour ago, and I'm supposed to be on my way to the boat now. I can say I got lost for a few minutes.

RUTH: You're leaving? For where?

ART: Overseas. I've only got time to say goodbye. Listen — write me, will you?

RUTH: Yes . . .

ART: Send your letters to this address. (HE HANDS HER A SLIP OF PAPER) They'll

* By Lillian Hellman. Reprinted with the permission of the author and the publishers, The Viking Press, Inc.

NOTE: This excerpt may be used only in the classroom and in no case on the radio or on the stage, professionally or in any other way.

† Television adaptation by Frederick Coe of a story by Ben Hecht. Reproduced with the permission of the authors and the National Broadcasting Company.

be forwarded. And don't worry if you don't hear from me for some time. I'll be off the mailman's route for quite a while.

RUTH: Oh, Art . . . !

ART: I'm wearing the lucky piece you gave me — the genuine Roman coin. So you don't have to worry about anything, and I don't, either, darling. Write me . . . please. I'll think of you every moment.

RUTH: Yes . . .

ART: I love you, Ruth. You don't know how wonderful you are. Nobody does. Only me.

(THEY EMBRACE . . . HE LEAVES . . . HER EYES FOLLOW HIM)

RUTH: Art . . . goodbye . . .

5. MYSTERY THEATRE: *LUCKY GUY**

BARTENDER: (COMING ON) Sorry, bud . . closing up for the night. We've . . (DOES TAKE) Uh . . . it's you.

CRANE: Yeah, it's me. We're going to have a talk. Sit down there. (MUMBLED PROTEST) Sit down there . . at that table.

BAR: (LITTLE FRIGHTENED) Look, what's eating you? What's with that gun?

CRANE: We're going to play a little game — you and I. (SHARP) Sit down! (BARTENDER SCRAMBLES INTO CHAIR) Did you ever hear of Russian Roulette?

BAR: No. Are you crazy? You off your nut?

CRANE: Maybe I'd better explain the game to you. First, I break open this gun. See?

(BREAKS OPEN GUN . . TAKES OUT CARTRIDGES)

CRANE: Then I take out five cartridges. Five. Count them. Then I spin the cylinder, and I close the gun. Now, how good are you at arithmetic? ("Arithmetic?") Yeah, how many bullets do I have left in the gun?

BAR: Okay, you got one left. What about it?

CRANE: I'm going to ask you some questions. Whenever I know you're lying to me, I'm going to put the gun to your head and pull the trigger. The first time I pull it the chances are one out of six you get killed. The second time they're one out of five if you don't get it the first time.

* By Paul Monash. Reproduced through the courtesy of the author.

BAR: I ain't got nothing to tell you! You're just blowing your top.

CRANE: Start talking! That night I was in here — the girl steered me here . . and there was someone waiting . . maybe in one of the other booths. Who was it?

BAR: There wasn't no one. Listen, I'd tell you —

(CLICK OF GUN HAMMER)

CRANE: That's the first lie. Now you've got a one out of five chance of getting killed.

BAR: I'd tell you, wouldn't I? What are you going to do . . kill an innocent guy?

CRANE: Okay, I'll try again. Whoever it was probably followed me and the girl out of the bar. Who was it? (COUPLE OF BEATS) Come on . . who was it?

BAR: No one. I swear . . no one . .

(CLICK OF GUN HAMMER)

CRANE: It's one out of four now. The odds are getting shorter. Another chance. How much did you get paid to forget? (BEAT) How much? (BEAT) Okay!

BAR: Wait! Three . . three hundred bucks. ("That's better!") Listen, Crane, if they'd —

CRANE: (CUTTING IN WITH SATISFACTION) Never mind that. Now just spill it. Who was here? Who was here the night that girl got killed? Who followed me out to the street? Who was it? My wife?

BAR: No, it wasn't your wife.

CRANE: Then who was it?

BAR: It was her brother . . Ed Eastman. Now for the love of heaven, will you put that gun away?

(MUSIC: BRIDGE . . AND BEHIND)

6. ROCKET TO THE MOON*

STARK: Poppa's coming over. He wants to see me.

BELLE: What about?

STARK: He didn't say.

BELLE: You might have told him we're going home.

STARK: I'll call him back and tell him.

BELLE: But you don't want to go home.

* By Clifford Odets. Copyright, 1939, by Clifford Odets. Reprinted by permission of Random House, Inc.

STARK: (OVER-PATIENT) I'll call him back and tell him.

BELLE: (INSISTENTLY) Do you . . . ?

STARK: (FINALLY, IN A TWISTED VOICE) No, Belle, I don't. That's a shack on the beach, and this is a shack. Don't be angry. It won't do us no good to quarrel again. I know you're my wife, but it's like we're enemies. We're like two exposed nerves!

BELLE: (BITTERLY) It's my fault!

STARK: (QUIETLY) Much more mine. I don't know what happened. I thought about these things a lot these past few months. You expect many things from marriage, but I can't give them. I feel a moral obligation but I don't know what to do. These scenes go on. We're always worried. We're two machines counting up the petty cash. Something about me cheats you. I'm not the man to help you be the best woman it's in you to be. So your attitude's justified. I know I owe you a lot, Belle —

BELLE: (BITTERLY) Hallelujah!

STARK: (ANGER MOUNTING DESPITE HIMSELF) Now I realize I've had a guilty feeling for years. "Marriage is the only adventure open to the coward," a certain man says. He made a mistake. You have to be a hero to face the pains and disappointments. (AS SHE TRIES TO SPEAK) No, let me finish. Because now I'm really guilty . . . I mean with this girl —

BELLE: (QUICKLY) That's enough!

STARK: I can't lie any more.

BELLE: That's enough! Do you hear me? Enough!

STARK: (INSISTENTLY) I have to tell you —

BELLE: But you don't love her! (PAUSE — THEN SHE CONTINUES IN FEARFUL AGITATION) You don't love her! The girl was here all day. You were close together and you fell into that thing. I can forget it; I can forget it, Ben. I'm your wife. It doesn't involve our whole relationship. We can have many happy years together. I'll do anything you want. We're young — we have our life together in common, our ten years. We can talk it out — we're civilized beings. I'll never mention it. We'll both forget it. We need each other, Ben. We . . . (WAVERING, SHE IS A SPOUT OF WATER)

STARK: (EMBRACING HER) Belle, dear, dear, dear, dear . . .

BELLE: (STARING AT HIM) It was only a thing of the moment, wasn't it? Wasn't it? Do you hear me — wasn't it?

STARK: (ANYTHING TO BLOT OUT THE PALE GHOST BEFORE HIM) Yes, yes!

BELLE: (AFTER A PAUSE, WILDLY) I'll wait for her. When is she coming back?

STARK: (FRIGHTENED) I'll take you home, Belle. We'll go home.

BELLE: When is she coming back?

STARK: I don't know.

BELLE: (WILDLY) You don't know? Did you tell me you don't know? I'll sit and wait for her.

STARK: (AFTER A PAUSE) Belle, you can't do that. We'll talk about it tomorrow. We'll be more sensible —

BELLE: Do you love her?

STARK: (TWISTING) . . . It can't be settled in a minute, Belle.

BELLE: (WHITE TO THE LIPS) What can't be settled?

STARK: I don't know what. I have a responsibility . . .

BELLE: Your first responsibility's to me! You hear that?

STARK: I have to know what to do, Belle, and —

BELLE: To do? You don't know what to do? You're in doubts? You have the slightest doubt?

STARK: (WRITHING) I don't know what —

BELLE: (INSISTENTLY) Give me the key to the car!

STARK: I'll go down with you.

BELLE: Give me the key!

STARK: The car's across the street. I'll take you down . . .

BELLE: Stay here.

STARK: Downstairs to the car.

(SHE SLAPS HIM STRONGLY AGAINST THE FACE . . . HE IS SILENT)

BELLE: When you know what to do . . . I'll be at Milly Heitner's apartment.

(DOOR SLAMS OFF)

7. THE SECOND MRS. BURTON, #463*

MARION: I've been saying for a long time — that I <u>hate</u> Bill. But that isn't true, Lillian. I <u>don't</u> hate Bill. I don't hate anyone in the world — but <u>myself.</u> <u>I'm</u> what I hate. I <u>detest</u> myself. That's what I found out last night. I hate myself <u>so</u> <u>much</u> — that I haven't anything left over to love

* By Martha Alexander. Reproduced through the courtesy of the author.

with. But I didn't know that. I thought it was just the other way — until last night. I thought — (BREAKS OFF: COMPLETELY DEJECTED) Oh, I thought a lot of things. After you went to sleep. For hours and hours after you went to sleep. (BEAT) And the worst of it is — (CHOKES UP) now that I know the truth — I don't know what to do about it. When I — when I used to think it was Stan — that was simple. I divorced him. And then — thinking it was Bill — I could plan to leave him. But now — knowing that's not true, knowing it wasn't Stan or Bill — but myself I hate — what can I do about it? I can't divorce myself. I can't — (BREAKS. CRIES. THEN REGAINS PARTIAL CONTROL) The only thing I can do is — tell Bill I know. I want to tell him. I want to tell him that — it wasn't his fault. I only wanted to believe it was. I had to believe it was. I didn't have anything else to believe. Now I — I want to tell him that — if I could have loved anyone, I would have loved him. (BEAT) I want to tell him that, Lillian, before I go home. Whether he hears me or not — I want to tell him that. (BEAT) You needn't wait if you don't want to. It may take some time — a long time — to say all the things I want to say —

(NOTE: GIVE THE EFFECT OF A FADE HERE, NOT BY AN ACTUAL FADE, BUT BY A KIND OF RUNNING OUT OF ENERGY AND BREATH: SPENT)

B. COMEDY LINES

1. THE MERCHANT OF YONKERS*

Students often need to practice the brightness and buoyancy, the timing and the click, necessary to the delivery of comedy lines.

1. Mr. Vandergelder, will you please sit still one minute. If I kill you it'll be practically unintentional.

2. Pardon my expression: money's like manure, which isn't worth anything until it's spread about encouraging young things to grow. Do you see what I mean?

3. Show me your hand. Lord in Heaven! What a life-line! Just look at it. From here to here. It runs right off your hand. I don't know where it goes. Ha-ha-ha! They'll have to hit you on the head with a mallet. Ha-ha-ha!

* From *The Merchant of Yonkers*, by Thornton Wilder, published by Harper & Brothers. Copyright, 1935, by Thornton Wilder.

4. Dolly, one of those Ermengardes wasn't a dear little girl at all. She was a boy. Well, that's what life is: disappointment, illusion.

5. There's a woman over there, Mr. Vandergelder — civilization hasn't touched her.

6. Yes, being employed is like being loved. You know someone is thinking about you the whole time.

7. I had an employer once. He watched me from eight in the morning until six at night — just sat and watched me. Even my mother didn't think I was as interesting as that.

8. Barnaby, you might as well know right now that everybody except us goes through life kissing right and left all the time.

9. I tell you, Minnie, it's a terrible thing to be suspected of being a wicked woman for fifteen years. It puts ideas in your head.

10. Oh, I don't want to take a bath. I always catch cold. Ambrose, remember the other time?

11. Everybody's asking me if my name's Miss Van Huysen. I think that's a matter I can decide for myself.

12. What can I do? I'm at a new hotel where they don't know me; and I've never been here before. Stop eating that chicken! I can't pay for it!

13. I sometimes ask myself seriously if there's any faith in womankind at all. I've a good mind to go around dressed in men's clothes so as to escape attention.

14. Oh, I'm as disappointed as you are. I — can't — eat — a — thing! What -- have — you — ordered?

15. Yes, you can put your arm around my waist for a minute, just to show that it can be done in a gentlemanly way. But I might as well warn you: a corset's a corset.

16. Rudolph, write this down: Neapolitan ice-cream, hothouse peaches, champagne, and a German band. Have you another German band?

17. I shan't trouble you again, Mrs. Malloy, and vice versa.

18. He has only one fault, as far as I know. He's hard as nails. But apart from that, as you say, a beautiful nature, ma'm.

19. Peter Malloy — God rest him! — was a fine arguing man. I pity the woman whose husband slams the door and leaves the house at the beginning of an argument. Peter Malloy would stand up and fight for hours at a time. I'll say that for him. He'd even throw things, Minnie — and there's no pleasure equal to that. Yes, yes — when I felt tired I'd start a good bloodwarming fight, and it'd take ten years off my age . . .

20. Take a last look at your girlhood home, dear. I remember when I left my home. I gave a whinny like a young colt and off I went.

21. Oh, Mr. Vandergelder, I can't wait for you to lay eyes on her. A treasure. A dove. And what a foot! Smaller than mine, if I do say it. Never wears a dress lower than this — (STRIKES HER CHIN) No one has ever seen more of her than that. Her own mother hasn't.

22. Her father — God be good to him — was the best undertaker in Brooklyn. Respected, esteemed. He knew all the best people — knew them well, even before they died.

23. Did you ever watch an ant carrying a burden twice its size? What excitement eh! What patience! What will! Well, that's what I think of when I see a woman running a house. What giant passions in those little bodies — what quarrels with the butcher for the best cuts -- what fury at discovering a moth in a cupboard! Oh, oh, believe me! If women could harness their natures to something bigger than a house and a go-cart, — heck! — they'd change the world.

C. TYPICAL COMEDY SCENES

1. THE ADVENTURES OF OZZIE AND HARRIET*

OZZIE: Gimme three more balls.

BROWN: Listen, mister, you been here two hours already. I promised my wife I'd be home for dinner an hour ago. Give up, will you? I'm hungry.

HARRIET: Well, there must be something wrong. This astrology book says today is Ozzie's lucky day. You sure those bottles aren't glued down or something?

* By Ozzie Nelson and staff. Reproduced through the courtesy of Ozzie Nelson.

BROWN: Glued down! Listen, lady, I've got them teetering so close to the edge that if he comes within five feet of them the breeze'll knock 'em down.

OZZIE: I'm gonna win one of those kewpie dolls if it takes me a week!

BROWN: Here I'll give you a kewpie doll free, a gift, no charge. Take it. Just let me go home and eat dinner.

OZZIE: I don't want it free.

BROWN: (GROANS)

OZZIE: It's the principle of the thing. I want to win it fair and square.

BROWN: I'll tell you what I'll do. I'll give you a free throw on the house. Here's a free ball.

OZZIE: A free ball! That's what's wrong — these baseballs. They're irregular! That's why I can't get accuracy!

(CONTINUES — AD LIBBING)

BROWN: Pick any ball you like. Throw a basketball! Throw the counter! Only throw something and lemme go home, will you?

HARRIET: Go ahead, dear. Maybe one more will be lucky. After all, this astrology book says . . .

OZZIE: That book again! That's what I wanna throw — that book. Give me that astrology book!

HARRIET: Ozzie!

OZZIE: (GRUNTS)

(SOUND OF THE BOOK HITTING METAL)

OZZIE: That's what I think of that book and —

(SOUND OF GONG, BELLS, SIREN, ETC.)

(MUSIC: FANFARE)

HARRIET: Ozzie, what's that? Look, skyrockets!

OZZIE: A picture of General MacArthur!

MAN: (OFF, THROUGH LOUDSPEAKER) Will the party who made that last throw please step forward to the main platform? He has won the grand prize.

OZZIE: I knew I could do it! I was figuring the wind velocity all wrong. And I got the curve just right, and —

MAN: (COMING ON) Are you the gentleman who made that last throw?

HARRIET: Yes, that's him, that's him!

MAN: Well, sir, here are your prizes . . . This huge basket of assorted canned goods, a twenty-five dollar War Bond, a bowling ball donated by Kelsey's Bowling Palace, and a season's pass to Happyland Amusement Park.

OZZIE: All that? What did I hit?

MAN: You didn't hit anything. You just made the millionth throw in the Park. Now if you'll just stand over here so we can take a picture for publicity . . .

2. TOMMY RIGGS AND BETTY LOU*

BETTY: Gosh, Uncle Tommy, I'm sorry I made Mrs. Wingate mad.

TOMMY: That's all right, Betty Lou. I understand. But in spite of Mrs. Wingate I've got to get into that club.

CECIL: (OFF) Greetings and salutations, neighbors!

TOMMY: Oh, why can't we ever lose that pesky neighbor of ours?

BETTY: (CALLING) Hello, Mr. Simpson. How did you ever get away from your wife today?

CECIL: (COMING ON) How did I ever get away from my wife? Don't be silly! I come and go as I please. She doesn't wear the pants in our family! I'm the man around the place! She can't keep me in the house! I do exactly as I please! (GIGGLE) I filed my handcuffs off.

BETTY: Mr. Simpson, Uncle Tommy's having trouble getting into the Newport Beach Club.

CECIL: Yes, I know what he's up against. I once tried to get into a very exclusive hunting club. Why, just to be a junior member you had to shoot five lions.

BETTY: How could you become a senior member?

CECIL: You had to shoot five junior members.

TOMMY: Mr. Simpson, could you help me —

CECIL: No, I'm afraid I couldn't help you today, Mr. Riggs. I'm tired out . . . I'm exhausted.

TOMMY: Did you ever try taking vitamin pills for energy?

CECIL: Yes, I did, but they never work.

BETTY: Gee, they don't?

* By Bill Danch. Reproduced through the courtesy of the author.

CECIL: No, my body gets all pepped up and raring to go, but my mind just lays there and says, "Sit down, and stop making a sap of yourself."

BETTY: Well, gee, how do you ever get anything done around the house, Mr. Simpson?

CECIL: Oh, that's easy. Just this morning I fixed the refrigerator.

TOMMY: What was wrong with it?

CECIL: It was eating the tomatoes.

BETTY: Did you get it fixed?

CECIL: Sure. Now it doesn't eat tomatoes any more. It eats bananas.

BETTY: Gee whiz!

CECIL: But I can fix that. I'm going to get myself a new refrigerator. Keep up with the times — that's my motto. This is a fast moving world. Here it is 1942 already.

BETTY: But, Mr. Simpson, this is 1946.

CECIL: Say, it's moving faster than I thought! Goodbye, Mr. Riggs. Goodbye, Betty Lou.

(MUSIC: BRIDGE)

TOMMY: Look, Betty Lou. Who's that climbing out of that swimming pool?

BETTY: It's Wilbur! My very favorite boy friend!

TOMMY: Oh, no!

BETTY: (CALLING) Wilbur! Hello, Wilbur!!

WILBUR: (COMING ON) Hello. (SNIFFS, LAUGHS)

BETTY: Gee, Wilbur, you're always sniffling. Haven't you got a handkerchief?

WILBUR: Un-huh. But it's in my back pocket.

BETTY: Well, why don't you use it?

WILBUR: My nose won't reach that far.

TOMMY: And, Wilbur, look at your eyes. They're all red.

WILBUR: I know. I couldn't sleep a wink last night.

BETTY: Why couldn't you, Wilbur?

WILBUR: Brrr! Those cold feet on my back!

BETTY: But don't you sleep alone, Wilbur?

WILBUR: Un-huh.

TOMMY: Well, then, how could you have cold feet on your back?

WILBUR: I'm double-jointed.

TOMMY: Now look, Wilbur, I'm very anxious to get into this beach club. I want you to be very careful what sort of impression you make. Do you understand?

WILBUR: Uh-huh.

BETTY: Gee, Wilbur, I wish you'd worn another bathing suit!

WILBUR: What's wrong with this one? Look at all the pockets it's got.

TOMMY: Yes, but what's that big bulge in your left pocket?

WILBUR: A milk bottle.

BETTY: And what's that bulge in the other pocket?

WILBUR: The milk.

BETTY: Wilbur, how can you be so stupid?

WILBUR: It ain't easy.

3. mr. ace and JANE*

JANE: Well, Sally, something's gotta happen pretty soon. After all, a girl's only young once in a while, you know.

SALLY: But, Jane, these fellows you have me meet never come out with anything I can put on my finger.

JANE: Well, we'll try Eddie. Here's the elevator now. Look young.

SALLY: Okay, Jane.

(ELEVATOR DOOR OPENS ON)

EDDIE: Going down.

JANE: Hello, Eddie.

EDDIE: Oh, hello, Mrs. Ace.

JANE: This is my cousin, Sally Anderson. This is Eddie Benson.

EDDIE: Pleased to meet you.

SALLY: Haha. How do you do.

JANE: Well, Eddie, aren't you gonna invite us in?

EDDIE: Uh — sure — if you're going down.

JANE: Well — we don't know if we will or not. We just don't pick up rides with anybody that comes along.

EDDIE: Didn't you ring for the elevator?

JANE: Haha. Fresh. Isn't he, Sally?

* From Chapter 33 of "mr. ace and JANE" by Goodman Ace. Reproduced through the courtesy of the author and Columbia Broadcasting System.

SALLY: Haha fresh.

(BUZZER RINGS)

EDDIE: Somebody's buzzing for the elevator on the fourth floor. I'll have to take it down.

JANE: My, the elevator business is rushing, isn't it, Eddie?

EDDIE: They really have me working for my thirty-seven-fifty a week.

JANE: Is that all you make? How can you get married on that?

EDDIE: Who's getting married?

SALLY: Haha fresh!

JANE: Have you ever thought of going into business for yourself — like buying your own elevator?

EDDIE: I'm not interested in running an elevator. I'm studying law. That's where I expect to make my money.

(BUZZER RINGS)

I have to go now. Are you riding down?

SALLY: Yes, we were just gonna —

JANE: No, Sally! Goodbye, Eddie. Oh, what a wolf you are!

(ELEVATOR DOOR CLOSES)

SALLY: Jane, what did you do?

JANE: Sally, I told you — you gotta play hard to take. Come on, let's go back in the apartment and we'll figure out what to do next. He's a nice, quiet, respectable fellow, isn't he?

SALLY: On thirty-seven-fifty a week what else can he be?

JANE: But that's only until he becomes a lawyer. If he gets a case he'll make a lot of money, and that's where you come in, Sally.

(DOOR OPENS)

Come in, Sally.

4. THE JOHNNY MORGAN SHOW*

(SOUND OF RUNNING FOOTSTEPS)

MORGAN: Gloria, Gloria!

(POUNDING ON DOOR)

* By Louis Melzer, Benny Ryan, and Johnny Morgan. Reproduced through the courtesy of Johnny Morgan.

MORGAN: Gloria, where are you? Open the door. Something's happened!

(DOOR OPENS ON)

GLORIA: Why, Johnny, what's all the excitement?

MORGAN: Look what I found . . . a wallet!

GLORIA: Oh, how wonderful! Where did you find it?

MORGAN: (QUICKLY AND HYSTERICALLY) I was walking along Tenth Avenue at eleven o'clock . . . or Eleventh Avenue at ten o'clock . . . or maybe it was Eighth Avenue at seven o'clock. It was awful dark, and I looked down and I saw a wallet. It was laying right there . . . in the gutter. I saw it, the wallet. I saw it with my own eyes!

GLORIA: Johnny, wait a minute! Take it easy. Now speak slowly and calmly . . . and tell me . . . exactly . . . what happened.

MORGAN: (VERY SLOWLY) Well . . . I was walking along the sidewalk minding my own business when I looked down and what do you think? (SUDDEN EXCITEMENT) I saw this wallet. It was laying there in the gutter . . . right there in front of me. I saw it! There it was. It was on Eighth Avenue at nine o'clock or Ninth Avenue at ten o'clock.

GLORIA: Johnny, Johnny, wait a minute! Now this is what happened. You found a wallet.

MORGAN: Who told you?

GLORIA: You did.

MORGAN: That's right. I knew I told somebody. See, it's a real expensive wallet!

GLORIA: Is the owner's name on it?

MORGAN: Let's see. Yeah. It belongs to a fellow named Al . . . . Al Iggatore.

GLORIA: Johnny, that says, "Alligator." It's alligator skin. Is there any money in it?

MORGAN: Certainly! It must have a lot of money in it. Feel how fat it is. Why, there must be a hundred thousand dollars in it . . . Maybe two hundred thousand!

GLORIA: Oh, now you can buy me an engagement ring.

MORGAN: Why, I'll buy you one for each finger.

GLORIA: And will you buy me a silver fox too?

MORGAN: Silver fox! I'll buy you a solid gold one! We'll have the best of everything. This winter I'll be wearing mink underwear with the fuzzy side in.

GLORIA: (COYLY) Johhny, then we can get married . . . and have three children.

MORGAN: We'll have five children.

GLORIA: Three children.

MORGAN: Five.

GLORIA: Three!

MORGAN: Say, whose wallet is this anyway?

GLORIA: Johnny, why don't you take a look and see how much is in it?

MORGAN: Oh, no, Gloria. I couldn't look in the wallet.

GLORIA: Why not?

MORGAN: For two reasons. First, I'm too honest.

GLORIA: And what's the second?

MORGAN: If I open it up and it's empty, I'll drop dead!

5. THE ALAN YOUNG SHOW, #19*

(TYPEWRITERS: NEWSPAPER OFFICE BABBLE)

ALAN: Gee, what a busy newspaper office. Let's see now who should I — Oh, there's the girl that helped me last time. Pardon me, Miss, I wonder if you can help me?

GIRL: He wonders if I can help him, he wonders.

ALAN: Look, Miss — By the way, what's your name?

GIRL: My name is Narcissus Vanderpyle, my name.

ALAN: I see. Well, Narcissus, I have a wonderful story for your paper. It's about an adventure I had as a boy.

GIRL: Gee, it sounds fascinating, gee it —

ALAN: No, you don't understand, Narcissus. This was an adventure. One day I came face to face with a wild animal. I could feel his breath on my neck.

GIRL: I been in parked cars, too, I been. Of course they never take me out again of course. I never had a steady boyfriend, I never. Something about me seems to keep them away, something about . . . .

ALAN: Hey, was your mother frightened by a repeater pencil?

* By Al and Sherwood Schwartz. Reproduced through the courtesy of the authors.

GIRL: If you're asking me for a date the answer is yes.

ALAN: Look, Narcissus, you've got it all wrong.

GIRL: That's why no man ever asks me for a date. That's why.

ALAN: What do you mean?

GIRL: I got it all wrong, I got.

ALAN: Please . . . . just tell me where I can find the editor?

GIRL: The editor is a very busy man, the editor. But just go right through that door over there. Sometimes it sticks in this weather, it sticks — so pull hard. You jerk the door open, you jerk.

ALAN: Thanks, Narcissus. I'll find the place, I'll find.

(FOOTSTEPS ON)

ALAN: Oh, here's his office. "Van Nuys Gazette. Editor-in-Chief. B. B. Busby."

(KNOCK ON DOOR)

MAN: (OFF) Come in . . . . come in . . . . come in.

(DOOR OPENS ON)

ALAN: Pardon me . . . . Mr. Busby.

MAN: (COMING ON) Speak up, young man. I haven't got all day. I'm a busy man. Always on the go, always on the go. Busy Busby they call me. Gotta run this place all by myself — nobody's competent, nobody's competent. When I'm not down at the Police Station chasing ambulances, I'm flying off to Washington to interview Congress. I'm Busy Busby that's me. Well, what do you want?

ALAN: Well, Mr. Busby, I have a story —

MAN: Just a minute. Gotta use the phone. (RECEIVER LIFTED) Hello, copy desk. (BEAT) Wipe out the lead story on page one. Get in touch with rewrite. Hold up the magazine section. And send up Mr. Thompson. I want Thompson up here right away.

(RECEIVER DOWN)

ALAN: Well, Mr. Busby, I —

MAN: Sit down, Thompson. You must be tired.

ALAN: Mr. Busby, I'm Alan Young.

MAN: Oh, I beg your pardon. What did I come here to see you about?

ALAN: You didn't come to see me. I came here to see you.

MAN: Oh. Cigar?

ALAN: I don't smoke.

MAN: Cigarette?

ALAN: I don't drink either. I mean, Mr. Busby, I've got a story that —

MAN: Just a minute, young man. (RECEIVER LIFTED) Hello, comic section? How many times have I told you about the paper shortage? You've got to condense the comics. You heard me. Condense. Condense. I don't care if Little Orphan Annie has to sleep on the same brick with Vitamin Flintheart. Goodbye.

(RECEIVER DOWN)

ALAN: Mr. Busby . . .

MAN: Oh, you still here, Thompson?

ALAN: My name is Alan Young. I killed a bear when I was six years old.

MAN: Where's Thompson? I told them to send Thompson up here.

ALAN: I guess you didn't hear me, Mr. Busby. I shot the bear with a bow and arrow. And not many bears are killed by archery.

MAN: Oh, yes, archery, archery. Listen to him all the time on Duffery's Tavern.

ALAN: Mr. Busby, I thought that would make a great story.

MAN: Story? What story? Always interested in a story.

ALAN: I killed a bow and arrow named Thompson with a six-year-old bear — No, I mean I killed a bear at the age of six.

MAN: Sit down, Thompson. You must be tired.

ALAN: I know this sounds astonishing, but I can give proof of the whole incident.

MAN: Amazing story, amazing. Have you got a picture?

ALAN: No, but I know where I can get one, Mr. Thompson . . . . I mean Busby.

MAN: Wonderful . . . . wonderful! Came exactly at the right moment. The Adventurer's Club is holding a convention right here in town.

ALAN: I know — and Hubert's the President.

MAN: Anybody who killed a bear at the age of six belongs in the Adventurer's Club. The Van Nuys Gazette will be proud to sponsor your admittance.

ALAN: Gee, me a member of the Adventurer's Club! I'll be as good as Hubert Updike.

MAN: Get hold of that picture at once. I want to print it in the Van Nuys Gazette.

ALAN: Sure — it'll be in the next mail.

MAN: Remember you'll be upholding the honor of Van Nuys in the Adventurer's Club. I've got work to do now. Nice to have met you, Mr. Uh . . . Mr. Uh.

ALAN: Busby.

MAN: Oh yes, Mr. Busby. Goodbye.

ALAN: Goodbye.

6. THE MAN WITH A PLATFORM*

MAN: I propose a model school for junior executives to be known as the Professional School of Rugged Individualism and Fox and Hounds Academy. Take 'em young, say at nine or ten, and drill it into 'em. When a lad matriculates at P.S.R.I.F.H.A., he is in for a dynamic career. No time wasted on non-essentials. The little stinker can't help growing up to be an industrial magnate or a district attorney or a sponsor of a serial program . . . For example, the arithmetic class would get away to a flying start, like this —

MATH PROF: All right, guys! Now there's a science called arithmetic, which includes adding and subtracting and all things like that. Ordinarily we'd teach this to you, but for some years now there have been machines on the market which can add faster than any six math professors put together. So what's the point of learning how to add? Class dismissed.

MAN: And then there's the advanced writing class. We would hire an expert for this course, whose opening lecture would be —

HUTCHINS: Gentlemen, writing is tough. As you get along in life and rise to positions of affluence, you'll have more and more important things to say and will need more and more help in saying them. Therefore you will hire ghost writers. And since you'll eventually have statements and articles written for you, you might as well start in having them written for you now. Directly following cocktails, you will be introduced to the ghost writers assigned to you for this term. Your ghost writers' homework for tonight will be to prepare a thousand-word theme on the subject, "Playing the Game Clean."

* From *More by Corwin*, by Norman Corwin. Reproduced by permission of Henry Holt and Company, Inc. Copyright, 1942, by Norman Corwin.

MAN: Nothing would be too good for the boys at Fox and Hounds, so we'd also have a class in reading . . . listed in the catalogue as English 41. This would be under the tutelage of Miss Fragrance Depew, whose semester would begin in the following manner —

DEPEW: (SEXY DAME) Boys . . . every generation in the history of civilization has contributed writing of some kind or other to what is loosely known as culture. Culture — get it? This means the world is practically filthy with all kinds of literature. There's too much to read. Therefore, in order to find time to play the horses, as you will learn to do in Throgg's course, Pari-mutuel 67, we will have to condense our studies. You will read short synopses of Shakespeare's plays and one-line descriptions of great poems. You will also get complete digests of novels and a box-score and break-down of the world's best essays. These will come in handy little folders which may be carried conveniently inside your racing forms. That is all (SIGNIFICANTLY) for now.

MAN: The geography course would be another innovation. Professor Carrington Timkins, who's been around, would start things rolling with a keynote lecture —

TIMKINS: Buddies, geography is okay for them as likes it. It is studied on maps a good deal of the time, and if things was even-steven I'd have some maps here this morning so's we could begin studyin' it. But maps is bein' changed so fast there's no point in goin' out on a limb and studyin' it, now is there, fellers? Class is dismissed until further notice.

MAN: Our music class would be up-to-date, naturally, and abreast of the times. Miss Marylou Susabelle Betty-mae Brown would teach those junior executives a thing or two —

MARYLOU: Yayus. Now, Beethoven's Sixth Symphony, as y'all knows, comes from Disney's "Fantasia." Also Tchaikovsky's Andante Cantabile comes from "Moonlove." Stephen Foster was played by Don Ameche, and Gilbert and Sullivan comes from the "Hot Mikado." Now for our next study of classical composition, the entire class should cover the new Warner Brothers release at the Bijour Theatre, "The Life of Chopin," starring Don Ameche.

Chapter XII . . MOTION

1

The well-trained radio actor should encounter no great difficulty in learning to perform for the television cameras, or, what will be more likely, in shuttling back and forth between the two kinds of acting. He may at first, of course, especially if he is without extensive film or stage experience, be a little frightened by the demands of this newer medium, by the fact that in television he has to forego "slow speech," as Conrad calls it in *Lord Jim,* for "the instantaneous effect of visual impression." The demands, however, are not so formidable as they are sometimes made to seem, nor so esoteric. For instance, because the radio cast of THE GOLDBERGS always played as if the stories were being lived—tinkling their cups and saucers and spoons, opening and closing doors, giving a shampoo, and so forth—the change-over to television, according to Gertrude Berg (Molly), "called for no important change . . . in acting technique from the radio version."[1]

The first truth, then, and a reassuring one, that the radio actor in television will discover is that everything he has so far studied about reading—the material of most of the previous chapters—is absolutely indispensable to, and the foundation for, his video work.

The second and new truth he will discover is that, to some extent at least, "the playwright's art lies not so much in supplying the actor with lines to be spoken as in supplying him with situations he can express without speech," that "the words are the supplement of motion," merely explaining it and giving it character and color, that the actor must open up his speeches *to let the play in.* He will become acquainted with the values of movement, gesture, and facial expression. He will therefore have to tackle the new problem of being seen while he is speaking his memorized lines.

Give an actor who performs for the eye as well as for the ear a speech such as "My dear Mrs. Smith, I am so pleased to see you again. I trust you are well. And your mother? She is well?" and he will see it, as the stage actor does, as "an open framework for motion, of which the words are plot necessities and amplification." He will consequently memorize his part somewhat as follows:

> My hat is in the curve of my left arm. The wrist of my right glove is turned down and the fingers are loosened. I part the door curtains with my right hand. I enter. I pause. I glance around the room. I see Mrs. Smith. I bow. I say, "My dear Mrs. Smith." I draw off my right glove. I walk forward to meet her. I take her hand. I say, "I am so pleased to see you again." She goes to her chair. I walk to the table. I put down my hat. She sits. I say, "I trust you are well." I remove my left glove and lay both on the table. I say, "And your mother?" I come round the end of the table to my chair. I sit. I say, "She is well?"
>
> And he will do it with . . . speed and fluency . . . and still seem leisurely and careless about it all.[2]

Memorization, however, is not the main problem here. Memorization should pose no problem at all for the actor. Yet there are in every cast those ever-recurring persons with a boogie-boo about learning their "sides" (largely because they do not listen to what is said to them), who take them home and burn the midnight oil conning single sentences and single speeches over and over until they achieve, in the end, with sweat and tears, merely a predictable artificiality. The only quick and happy and correct way to get "up" in a role is to memorize the words and the motions *simultaneously* and *in context* (which means in constant relation to surrounding circumstances, characterization, motivation, and line of action). This can best be done at the regular daily rehearsals, which for the average half-hour television play add up to four hours a day for five

[1] Gertrude Berg, "TV and Molly," *Variety,* July 27, 1949, p. 46.

[2] Mitchell, *Creative Theatre,* pp. 160–161.

days a week "dry" or off camera, plus approximately six hours on performance day before the cameras. That is sufficient time to memorize most parts in most plays.

The main and new problem for the radio actor in television is motion. Although it is true that the video director, primarily interested as he must be in pictures for the cameras, sets most of the motion—telling the actors where and when and how to cross and stand and sit, which direction to face, and how to group themselves—there is still much that the actor himself has to know about the subject. There is a skill that must be acquired. "To walk in a certain manner, to fix a certain expression or a certain gesture, requires the nice coordination of scores of muscles; and muscles, to respond accurately to command, must be trained." It is not the director, but Duse herself, who can draw from a critic the comment that she

> . . . produces the illusion of being infinite in variety of beautiful pose and motion. Every idea, every shade of thought and mood, expresses itself delicately but vividly to the eye; and yet, in an apparent million of changes and inflections, it is impossible to catch any line of an awkward angle, or any strain interfering with the perfect abandonment of all the limbs to what appears to be their natural gravitation toward the finest grace. She is ambidextrous and supple, like a gymnast—a panther; only the multitude of ideas which finds expression in her movements marks off humanity from the animals, and, I fear I must add, from a good many gymnasts.[3]

2

Some thinkers about the theatre take the extreme view that "pantomime, in the larger sense of action based on emotional thought, is . . . the reason for the theatre's existence."[4] Roy Mitchell, for one, firmly contends that "the theatre's essential art is motion." "Motion itself," he writes, "is the peculiar and exclusive property of the theatre which can by the use of the human body, the most plastic and expressive of forms, embody its miracle in actual motion." "Deny motion and you have no theatre at all."[5] And scene designer Robert Edmond Jones, in his stimulating *The Dramatic Imagination,* pointedly makes up a story about the leaders of a Stone Age tribe who have just killed a lion:

> The lion's skin lies close by, near the fire. Suddenly the leader jumps to his feet. "I killed the lion! I did it! I followed him! He sprang at me! I struck him down with my spear! He fell down! He lay still!"
>
> He is telling us. We listen. But all at once an idea comes to his dim brain. "I know a better way to tell you. See! It was like this! *Let me show you!"*
>
> In that instant drama is born.[6]

Yet no one needs attempt to decide emptily which is more important to the theatre—and especially to television—the voice or the body, the sound or the motion. All that is important to you, the radio actor who prepares for the video cameras, is that you must concentrate for a while on the potentialities of pantomime. You can best do this by skipping with a sigh of relief the detailed theories of François Delsarte, Emile Jaques-Dalcroze, and Vsevelod Meierhold and by simply outlining for yourself, perhaps with some amazement, the five kinds of motion essential to all video acting. They can be listed as follows:[7]

I. Motion within the actor—swirl, the *"goingness* of a vital current" inside him; not just personality, not just the body's emotional vibrations as it reacts to external or internal stimuli, but the power by which an actor draws or relinquishes the spectator's interest.
II. Axial motion in the actor—posture, starting and stopping, sitting, rising, degrees of relaxation and tension—to which must be added all "stage business" such as sewing, lighting a cigarette, fixing a broken chair, and so forth
   A. As prescribed by the playwright
   B. As added by the actor (or the director)
      1. For characterization, state of mind
      2. For meaning
         a. Emphasis (or subordination)
         b. Changes in thought or relationships
         c. Suspense or anticipation
         d. Contrast, etc.
      3. For comedy
      4. For style

[3] George Bernard Shaw, *Dramatic Opinions and Essays,* edited by James Huneker (New York: Brentano's, 1906), 1, 138.

[4] Alberti, *A Handbook of Acting,* pp. 32–33.

[5] Mitchell, *op. cit.,* pp. 156–157, 164.

[6] Robert Edmond Jones, *The Dramatic Imagination* (New York: Duell, Sloan & Pearce, Inc., 1941), p. 46.

[7] See Mitchell, *op. cit.,* pp. 186–190.

III. Gesture—including facial expression
  A. As prescribed by the playwright
  B. As added by the actor (or the director)
    1. For characterization
    2. For meaning
    3. For comedy
    4. For style
IV. Movement from one place to another
  A. As prescribed by the playwright
  B. As added by the actor (or the director)
    1. For characterization
    2. For meaning
    3. For comedy
    4. For style
    5. For composition (principally by the director)
      a. Control of attention
      b. Emphasis (or subordination)
      c. Function in the design
      d. Rhythm
      e. Tempo
      f. Pictorial effect (or "stage" conventions)
      g. Camera shots
V. Motion by the cameras (only by the director)
  A. Close-ups, medium shots, long shots, panning, dollying
  B. Switches from one camera to another

About two of these types of motion essential to television the actor can do little or nothing. "Swirl" he either has or has not; and the placement and movement of the various cameras are not his immediate concern. All the other motions, however, are either designated by the script or the director, or invented by the actor. The actor, therefore, has to be capable of (1) inventing physical actions suitable to his function in the play and of (2) motivating his prescribed and invented actions in relation to his characterization, surrounding circumstances, line of action, medium, sense of truth, and sense of grace.

In television acting, obviously, the body must cooperate with the mind. It must be capable of expressing all sorts of nuances of meaning in support of the words. Yet "too often, through a lack of training in pantomimic expression, the attitude of the body will express one thought and emotion, the movement another. . . . This makes a hodge-podge of both character and emotional values. The problem is to have the whole body express one emotional idea at a time."[8] The point is that in television the bodily movements, the gestures, and the facial expressions can speak to an audience as effectively as, and sometimes more effectively than, the words.

In short, then, television acting demands that the actor should be a person with a flexible, sensitive and powerful body, a person who knows instinctively what a tense and what a relaxed gesture is. He must be able to follow any intricate movement of the arms and upper part of the body, and at the same time be able to run, stand, jump, kneel and fall down swiftly and easily. He should have sensitive, expressive hands and fingers, complete control of the facial muscles, and know a great deal about folk dancing. Finally he should be able to *improvise* interestingly and variedly but always "justifying" his gestures, relating them to some meaning.[9]

No wonder Maria Ouspenskaya is reported to have done acrobatics an entire winter in order to visualize the governess in Chekhov's *The Cherry Orchard.* No wonder Shaw could go into raptures over a performer's rare physical talent or physical command. After watching Mrs. Patrick Campbell act one of her roles he was convinced that she

> . . . could thread a needle with her toes at the first attempt as rapidly, as smoothly, as prettily, and with as much attention to spare for doing anything else at the same time as she can play an arpeggio.[10]

3

Most of the books on pantomime that systematically list and diagram the various expressive positions of the body, head, feet, and hands are not much more helpful to the student who wants to learn how to move and gesture than Gilbert Austin's outdated *Chironomia, or A Treatise on Gesture,* published in 1806. Poppycock such as the "right foot (advanced before the left foot about the breadth of the narrowest part of the foot) forms with the left an angle of about 75 degrees," though well-meant, is external, artificial, and eminently foolish. Instead of trying to find the "set" positions for each emotion or thought, the wise actor will engage in life study. He will make a practice of constantly and carefully observing the expressive movements of people around him in everyday circumstances.

8 Alberti, *op. cit.,* pp. 33–34.

9 Galpern, "Body Training for Actors," p. 47.

10 Shaw, *op. cit.,* I, 192.

> Life study as related to acting means observing and recording mentally and physically the reactions and characteristics of all classes of human beings. The eyes and ears are the agents through which the observations are made and the body is the instrument for recording the studies observed.[11]

However, when as a television actor you engage in the long habit of keenly observing and honestly reproducing the postures, movements, gestures, and facial expressions of various people in all sorts of circumstances, you must do so with two warnings indelibly in mind. The first is that you must not make the common mistake of inferring

> . . . that everyone in anger (for instance) does exactly the same thing; for obviously no two persons in anger are identical in the complex of feelings, but that certain "constants" and those being the major elements or expression, appear in all anger states. . . . If this were not so, we could never tell the state of another person or know the effect of our words or actions upon others.[12]

Nor could we ever correctly communicate to others, either intentionally or unintentionally, our responses to surrounding and internal stimuli. In watching people, then, you must always be searching for a "theme with a variation," for a motion—a walk, a gesture, a facial expression—that is both fresh and revealing.

The second warning is that in observing your models you must not make the other common mistake of copying bodily actions only *per se*. If you are ever to use effectively on camera what you find, you must penetrate to the cause or the motivation behind the posture, the movement, the gesture, the facial expression.

> The study of life must be through observation of the objective to the subjective of the one studied; or from the study of movement and voice of an individual to the character, thought, and feeling which prompts voice and action; but when an actor portrays the life study he should be able to reveal the subjective personality through the objective action.[13]

In other words, the actor should guard against using a gesture merely because he has seen someone else use it; he should use it only when he can motivate it and thereby reveal the character. Bodily action without justification may well be clever and interesting mimicry, but it is always beside the main point.

In practicing your life studies you must know something else: you must be aware of the difference between motion as raw material and motion as translated into theatre terms, or into camera terms. For instance, the perfect copying, even with added motivations, of a girl impatiently waiting for a friend on a busy street corner is only the raw material for the enactment of the same situation before the television cameras. In movement, as in speech, complete and authentic copying is not acting. The mysterious and ineffable and creative "X" must be added in order to translate the one into the other.

The most expert life studies brought to class, and applauded and "ohed and ahed" over, are—make no mistake about it—never acting. Such studies, such exercises, such copying, are only the preparation for acting. Take another instance: you may say of a classmate that he has honestly recorded and imaginatively motivated his life study of a man getting on a bus, finding his purse, paying his fare, and going to his seat. You may conclude that you know the kind of man he is portraying from the pantomime you have just watched. The real test of your fellow class member as an actor, though, will come when you say to him, "Now translate that life study into acting before the cameras." Every expert in observing, copying, and successfully communicating to others the essence of a real-life person must finally be asked, "What changes in your life study would you make if you had to *act* that man in that situation?"

The recurring point, as discussed in Chapter I, is that there is a crucial difference between life and art. When you engage in life studies, when you observe and record the movements of people around you, you must proceed from motivated copying to something else, or as an actor you will give undue prominence to minor details, that is, you will bring into bold relief much that should be subjected. What that "something else" is can be somewhat easily defined as follows: when you are asked to turn your life study into acting you will attempt to move and gesture in terms of your medium and in terms of your functional part in the expression of a playwright's idea. That is to say, before he can *act*, and not just reproduce, the situation of the man getting on the bus your fellow class member would have to be

[11] Alberti, *op. cit.*, pp. 100–101.
[12] Bridge, *Actor in the Making*, pp. 15–16.
[13] Alberti, *op. cit.*, p. 101.

given, or to work out by himself, the playwright's *point* in the scene. In order to translate his life study into acting, the student would by elimination, addition, combination (all in accordance with the character's function), "and a sense of stage-values added to his creative imagination, transform these so-called natural movements into artistic stage pantomime."[14]

It is most important always to remember that acting is a form not only of expression, but of communication. Hence the inadequacy of the advice to act naturally. The natural action of the woman discovering the pearls she had stolen were only paste would perhaps communicate nothing to an audience. Half the significant things we do . . . are not expressed in such a way as to communicate to others what they really mean . . . all great acting is illumination of character, not merely imitation of obvious forms of behavior. . . . This condition demands of the actor certain adjustments which do not trouble the man in the street. There must be exaggeration, elimination of factors not directly relevant to the design and the playing up of actions, sound, colors, beyond their intrinsic naturalness.[15]

The difference between the man in the street or in the bus is, as Bernard Shaw insists, an important one:

When the layman walks, his only object is to get to Charing Cross; when he makes a gesture, it is to attract the attention of a cab driver or a bus-conductor; when he speaks it is to convey or demand information, to tell a lie, or otherwise further his prosaic ends; when he moves his hands it is to put up his umbrella or take out his handkerchief. On the stage [or before the cameras] these merely utilitarian purposes are only simulated: the real purpose is to produce an effect on the sense and imagination of the spectator.[16]

What the actor on camera adds to or subtracts from his life study, his remembered observation, for the purpose of theatrical communication *of the point he is making* is the yardstick not only of his understanding but of his creativity. It is the one and only valid test of his imaginative powers; and memory has never yet been a synonym for imagination.

In fact, movement in front of the camera is at times so unlike natural movement that the television actor may often have to go so far as to forsake honesty for falseness. Cameras, as Hume Cronyn discovered, lie; and the television actor must often be prepared to aid in this deception. As Cronyn explains,

A move which would be utterly false on stage, which goes directly against every reasonable impulse, may be camera-wise effective and necessary. In *Shadow of a Doubt* I had a scene in which I sat down to gossip to a neighbor while he and his family had dinner. During the meal, I said something upsetting to the character played by Teresa Wright. She turned to me with unexpected violence. I stood up in embarrassment and surprise and automatically took a step backward. However, at the point of the rise, the camera moved in to hold us in a close two-shot, and to accommodate it—that is, to stay in the frame—it became necessary for me to change that instinctive movement so that when I got up from the chair, *I took a step toward the person from whom I was retreating.* Because of my inexperience and the falseness of the move, this made a hazard for me in the middle of an otherwise simple scene. I was convinced that the action would look idiotic on the screen, but I was wrong. When I saw the rushes, I had to admit that the occasion passed almost unnoticed even by me.[17]

The faculty, or power, of turning carefully observed and recorded life studies into acting by complying with certain inescapable technical and *artistic conditions*

. . . without being so preoccupied with them as to be incapable of anything else is hard to acquire, and can be perfected only by long practice. . . . The habit can never become as instinctive as keeping one's balance, for instance, because failure in that for even an instant means a fall, so that the practice of it is lifelong and constant: whereas the artistic habit lapses more or less in the absence of an audience, and . . . can be forgotten for long periods without any worse consequences than a loss of charm which nothing may bring to the actor's attention. The real safeguard against such lapses is a sense of beauty—the artistic sense—cultivated to such a degree of sensitiveness that a coarse or prosaic tone, or an awkward gesture, jars instantly on the artist as a note out of tune jars on the musician. The defect of the old-fashioned systems of training for the stage was that they attempted to prescribe the conclusions of this constantly evolving artistic sense instead of cultivating it and leaving the artist to its guidance. Thus they taught you an old-fashioned stage walk, an old-fashioned stage way of kneeling, of sitting down, of shaking hands, of picking up a handkerchief, and so on, each of them supposed to be the final and perfect way of doing it.

[14] *Ibid.*, p. 34.
[15] Bridge, *op. cit.*, pp. 9–10.
[16] Shaw, *op. cit.*, I, 206.
[17] Cronyn, "Notes on Film Acting," p. 46.

The end of all that was, of course, to discredit training altogether. But the neglect of training very quickly discredits itself; and it will now perhaps be admitted that the awakening and culture of the artistic conscience is a real service which a teacher can render to an actor. When that conscience is thoroughly awakened and cultivated, when a person can maintain vigilant artistic sensitiveness throughout a performance whilst making all the movements required by the action of the drama, and speaking all its dialogue graphically without preoccupation or embarrassment, then that person is a technically competent artistic actor, able to play a part of which he hardly comprehends one line, in a play of which he knows nothing except his own words and speeches and cues thereto, much more intelligently and effectively, as well as agreeably, than a statesman with ten times his general ability could. He can only be beaten, in fact, by the professional rival who has equal skill in execution, but has more numerous and valuable ideas to execute.[18]

4

Most television performers can improve their powers of physical expression for the cameras immeasurably if for a while they will give some specific attention to practicing facial expressions, gestures, and walks.

Since television, largely because of the small frames of the home receiving sets, is compelled to use more close-ups than are ordinarily used on the motion-picture screen, the video actor needs, perhaps most of all, an expressive face. To some extent that can be acquired. Daily practice in varied expressions can correct the appalingly common "dead-pan," the face with the lazy muscles, the face that seldom changes, that rarely reflects varying thoughts and moods. Most faces, it is true, can register the more obvious emotions, such as anger, horror, great joy, pain, and the like; but for television they must be trained to show all the more subtle shades of meaning and feeling. The actor's face must be so sensitive, expressive, and mobile that it can reflect a character's every thought and emotion until the viewers can literally *see* the personality. Only constant practice can loosen the blank face until "it won't be long before it will reflect your thoughts without being reminded."

Only daily practice before a mirror can lead you to discover and to correct any bad facial habits, such as biting the lips, frowning, screwing up one side of the mouth, twitchings, drooping eyelids, and the like.

[18] Shaw, *op. cit.*, I, 205–207.

All television actors could improve their camera effectiveness if they would practice regularly in registering on their faces those constantly recurring surprises that are the most frequent and fundamental reactions asked of a character in any video script.

Surprise is unexpected and instantaneous: it is the shortest in duration, because it quickly passes into something else. Surprise checks one emotional vibration and allows the inception of another. Surprise is the initial emotion occurring with every new idea. . . . Surprise occurs even when one is thinking, as when new ideas enter the mind.[19]

Surprise is the *visual* Illusion of the First Time. Surprise, like the multitude of other transitions from one thought to another, from one emotion to another, from one circumstance to another, from contacting one person or another, and so on, can best be registered by the face—and must be registered there effectively and constantly. So crowded with transitions is any portrayal of a character in a play, because a play is necessarily much more compressed than life, that you may almost define your camera characterization as a series of transitions expressed by the face. Transitions in front of the camera, moreover, must be more definite and clearly marked than they are in life, lest the audience not catch them or not quite understand them.

In your practicing, however, in loosening up your facial muscles, you must be warned, not at first, but in time, not to overdo. The danger of "mugging" is ever present. It is necessary, therefore, to know that

In "closeup" very little becomes very much; a whole new range of expression is opened up to the actor. He can register with . . . a glance, a contraction of a muscle, in a manner that would be lost on the stage. The camera will often reflect what a man thinks, without the degree of demonstration required in the theatre.[20]

As for gestures, most actors new to television are likely at first either to gesture too much—to fidget, to twiddle, to overelaborate—or to be "sticks," with their hands, wrists, and arms completely frozen. Rarely is there a happy medium between the two. In time and with practice most actors can be taught to use their hands freely and expressively. A longer time, though, is usually required to learn not to gesture too much—to

[19] Alberti, *op. cit.*, pp. 42–43.

[20] Cronyn, *op. cit.*, p. 46.

learn what Maugham's Ashenden knew: in the theatre it is useless to make a gesture that has no ulterior meaning. Most of all, television actors have to guard against making pointless or unrestrained gestures, since, "natural though they may be to the actor himself," they "only blur the design of his part, make his performance unclear, monotonous and uncontrolled."[21]

For rightness in gesture perhaps the student, in going about his life studies, might to some extent follow dancer Nijinsky's advice and "watch children if one wishes to learn the proper way of using the hands beautifully, because children are always unself-conscious." Perhaps then in performance before the cameras television actors would gesture with effectiveness, authority, and grace—without constant recourse to individual mannerisms or clichés.

Expressive hands can be marvelously adroit actors. When the late Osgood Perkins played Sganarelle in *The School for Husbands* he spread his hands, palms up, in amused contempt for the simple-mindedness of Ariste; he warned Valere off with an index finger like a dagger; he kept Isabelle "where she ought to be" with a downward drive of a thumb. His hands grew "too old, too old" in the ballet; he clenched his fist, and then opened it in a two-fingered leer; he threw back his wrists and minced his fingers absurdly; he curved his hands tenderly as he assured Isabelle he would marry her tomorrow morning.

As for walking, the television actor need only know that the way he walks should exhibit his character. Yet not enough attention is customarily given to walkings. Actors are, for the most part, content to use their own walks, for better or for worse. They forget to create, when the occasion permits, a highly individual walk for the character they are playing. One has only to recall the brilliant footwork of Charles Laughton in *Henry VIII* to discover what a potent adjunct to characterization a walk can be, how quickly and frankly it can express the inner man. A way of walking can say things words cannot say. In Sherwood's *Reunion in Vienna,* for instance, it was Alfred Lunt's walk at his final exit, without words and without gestures, that said all that was necessary. As he strode regally through the doorway, he was the restored Hapsburg, the triumphant lover. Similarly, when Lynn Fontanne, standing there a moment trying to decide whether or not to follow her lover, took two steps she told by the way she walked all that was in her mind and heart.

The television actor should also learn how to stand still in front of the cameras. Fidgeting with the feet, shifting the weight from one foot to another, tapping the toes, and so on, are not only distractions but evidence of a first-rate amateur.

In rehearsing for a television play the actor should repeatedly "walk through" his part. In memorizing his meanings he cannot neglect his pantomime. Even before actual rehearsals begin he should, whenever possible, visualize his part by "walking through" it.

Hume Cronyn, for instance, has reported:

> There are some scenes which an actor cannot study or conceive of playing without considering the character's movement in detail, so intermeshed are words and activity. What can you do when the director is not available for discussion of such a scene beforehand, when it's not even possible to familiarize yourself with the set because it won't be up, let alone dressed, until the day it's to be used? . . . I find it best to plan your own set at home, indicate the furniture, plan your own simulated props, imagine your fellow actors and *rehearse.* Walk through whatever pattern of activity seems logical to you, explore the possibilities, decide on a course, and turn up for work with an idea. It may have to be changed . . . but the chances are that much of your work you have done will . . . achieve a more successful result than if you offer [the director] nothing other than memorized lines and sublime negativity in regard to the scene's execution.[22]

5

For efficient conducting of rehearsals there is a common language for stage movement that the television actor must learn. This terminology, taken over from the legitimate theatre, allows the actor to coordinate himself with the other members of the cast and to follow quickly and definitely the instructions of the director. Fortunately, this combination list of rules or conventions is not a long one. The main points to be remembered are:

Unless specifically instructed to do so, the actor must never look directly into the camera lens.

To move "down" is to move toward the camera; to move "up" is to move away from the camera.

[21] Stanislavski, *Building a Character,* p. 69.

[22] Cronyn, *op. cit.,* p. 47.

To move "forward" or "backward" is to move in the direction you are, or are not, facing.

To move "left" or "right" is always to move to the actor's left or right.

To cross "above" or "below" is to cross behind or in front of another actor, property, or piece of furniture.

To "steal" is to get into a desired position in such an inconspicuous manner as not to attract attention to the move. (Or it may mean speaking with the face turned a bit more toward the camera than it would be naturally.)

To "open-up" is to swing more of the body or face around to the camera, presenting more front.

To "turn in" is to turn away from the camera, presenting more profile or back.

To make "a quarter-turn" is to turn from full face on camera halfway to profile.

To make a "half-turn" is to turn from full face on camera to profile.

To make a "three-quarter turn" is to turn from full face on camera to a point halfway from profile to full back.

To "share a scene" with another actor is to present one half or three fourths of the face or body, like the partner, to the camera.

To "give a scene" to another actor is to be down from the latter and turned three-fourths away from the camera.

To "cover" is to get in front of an actor, property, or piece of furniture. (It is usually bad to cover another actor; but the responsibility for such a bad position is largely the upstage actor's since he can see whether or not someone is between his face and the camera lens.)

To "step out" or to gesture correctly is usually to do so with the upstage foot or hand.

6

Finally, in all his pantomime the television actor must learn to relax. Ease in execution is the signature of the genuine artist. Yet every actor has to battle, again and again in all the movements of his performances, the old ogre of tension. Especially in television with its many pressures and confusions—the clock relentlessly ticking away, the cameras rolling here and there, booms reaching out and dropping down, instructions constantly being signaled, actors and numerous crewmen scurrying hither and yon—a first and only performance and no more chances to rectify errors—will the actor find that to relax is practically impossible. Eventually, though, he must learn to relax if his physical and vocal expressive powers are to function unimpaired.

The television actor need not worry too much about stage fright. Everyone has stage fright.

> The effect on an ordinary man of making him suddenly conscious of the artistic aspect of his movements and speech is to plunge him into a condition of terror and bewilderment in which he forgets how to do anything. It gives him stage fright, in short. Take a humble tradesman who has demolished his boiled mutton and turnips for half a century without misgivings. Invite him to meet a peer or two at dinner in Grosvenor Square, and he will refuse dish after dish because he no longer feels sure of how he ought to eat it.[23]

Stage fright is only the sensitive recognition of responsibility in the middle of strange surroundings; as such it is good; as such it will quickly pass once the performer concentrates on his job at hand.

The tension that the actor must fight is the tension that occurs when the actor "attempts to solve his task without understanding it." Tension is born again and again during a performance whenever the actor, coming on an important passage or scene, feels that it contains much, that something extra must be expressed. Just exactly what is to be *done* in the passage or the scene he does not know. Consequently he begins to strain; he puts all his muscles to work; therefore tension sets in and either inhibits or displaces the right expression of the required emotion.

Only two methods have so far been found helpful in overcoming this tension. The first: the actor must practice exercises in control and relaxation of his muscles. He must observe himself in action and systematically remove all unnecessary muscular tension. The second: for his tension passages or scenes the actor must simplify what he is attempting to do until he can verbalize it as a well-understood *physical* task that he can execute by simple actions. Once the actor understands what he is truly supposed to *do* in a specific passage or scene, and can concentrate on doing it with economy and grace, he will be well on the way to achieving relaxation.

[23] Shaw, *op. cit.*, I, 208.

Yet the pursuit of relaxation in acting is a never-ending one.

A few happy beings are born with it, but the majority of beginners and young players have to battle tenseness every inch of the way for years. Beginning with a general tenseness from top to toe you work until it is eliminated in everything but your hands; you succeed in chasing it out of them, and find it turns up in your toes! If you banish it from your throat it will lodge in your solar-plexus, effectively killing all true flow of emotion! Stanislavski fought for twenty years for the relaxation which he at last so perfectly achieved.[24]

SELECTED READINGS

General:

Alberti, Madame Ewa, *A Handbook of Acting; Based on the New Pantomime.* New York: Samuel French, 1932, 205 pp. This *Handbook* is perhaps dated, but there are some valuable suggestions in Chap. IV, "Emotional Vibrations," pp. 52–61; Chap. VI, "Transitions or the Change in Thoughts and Emotions," pp. 78–96; and Chap. VIII, "Re-Creations from Life . . . ," pp. 97–120.

Aubert, Charles, *The Art of Pantomime,* translated by Edith Sears. New York: Henry Holt & Company, Inc., 1927, 210 pp.

Boleslavsky, Richard, *Acting; The First Six Lessons.* Theatre Arts Books, 1933. Read "The Fifth Lesson—Observation," pp. 89–102.

Bridge, William H., *Actor in the Making.* Magnolia, Mass.: The Expression Company, 1936, 115 pp. A handbook on improvization with reading and drills in bodily expression, life study, and improvization.

Broadbent, R. J., *A History of Pantomime.* London: Simpkin, Marshall, Ltd., 1901, 226 pp.

Cannon, Walter B., *Bodily Changes in Pain, Hunger, Fear and Rage* (2nd ed.). New York: Appleton-Century-Crofts, Inc., 1929, 311 pp.

Chisman, Isabel, and Hester E. Raven-Hart, *Manners and Movements in Costume Plays.* London: H. F. W. Deane & Sons, The Yearbook Press, Ltd., 1934, 122 pp.

Craig, Gordon, *On the Art of the Theatre.* Boston: Small, Maynard & Co., 1911. Read "The First Dialogue" (1905), pp. 137–181.

Cronyn, Hume, "Notes on Film Acting," *Theatre Arts Monthly,* XXXIII, No. 5 (June, 1949), 45–48.

Dolman, John, Jr., *The Art of Play Production* (rev. ed.). New York: Harper & Brothers, 1946. Examine Chap. VI, "Planning the Action," pp. 96–109; Chap. VII, "Stage Movement," pp. 110–125; and Chap. VIII, "Stage Business," pp. 126–135.

Dunbar, Helen Flanders, *Emotions and Bodily Changes* (3rd ed.). New York: Columbia University Press, 1946, 595 pp.

Findley, Elsa, "Rhythmic Practice," *Theatre Arts Monthly,* XI, No. 9 (September, 1927), 710–714.

Galpern, Lasar, "Body Training for Actors," *Theatre Workshop,* I, No. 2 (January–March, 1937), 43–54.

Mitchell, Lee, "Some Principles of Stage Fencing," *Quarterly Journal of Speech,* XXVIII, 4 (December, 1942), 437–441.

Mitchell, Roy, *Creative Theatre.* New York: The John Day Co., Inc., 1929. Read Chap. X, "The Art of Motion," pp. 155–69, and Chap. XII, "Motion Germinal," pp. 185–194.

Pardoe, T. Earl, *Pantomimes for Stage and Study.* New York: Appleton-Century-Crofts, Inc., 1931, 395 pp.

Pudovkin, V. I., *Film Acting,* translated by Ivor Montagu. London: George Newnes, Ltd., 1935, 153 pp.

Selden, Samuel, *A Player's Handbook.* New York: Appleton-Century-Crofts, Inc., 1934. Study Chap. III, "Training for Expressiveness—The Body," pp. 137–158, and "Exercises: Part II—Pantomimes for the Expressive Body," pp. 159–180.

The Stage in Action. New York: Appleton-Century-Crofts, Inc., 1941. See "The Player Dancing," pp. 41–98.

Stanislavski, Constantin, *Building a Character,* translated by Elizabeth Reynolds Hapgood. New York: Theatre Arts Books, 1949. Consult Chap. IV, "Making the Body Expressive," pp. 34–44; Chap. V, "Plasticity of Motion," pp. 45–67; Chap. VI, "Restraint and Control," pp. 68–77; Chap. XI, "Tempo-Rhythm in Movement," pp. 177–216; and Chap. XIII, "Stage Charm," pp. 238–241.

Young, Stark, *Glamour.* New York: Charles Scribner's Sons, 1925. Study "Movement in Acting," pp. 65–68. The same article also appears in his *Theatre Practice* (New York: Charles Scribner's Sons, 1926), pp. 39–42. Also read "Wearing Costumes," pp. 95–106 in the latter book.

Television:

Allan, Douglas, *How to Write for Television.* New York: E. P. Dutton & Co., Inc., 1946, 244 pp.

Bettinger, Hoyland, *Television Techniques.* New York: Harper & Brothers, 1947. Suggested reading for Chap II, "The Medium," pp. 11–17; Chap. III, "Pictorial Composition and Continuity," pp. 18–45; Chap. IV, "Video Techniques," pp. 46–71; and Chapter VIII, "Producing the Play," pp. 153–179.

Dupuy, Judy, *Television Show Business.* Schenectady, N. Y.: General Electric Company, 1945, 246 pp. A

[24] Eva Le Gallienne, *At 33* (New York: Longmans, Green & Company, Inc., 1934), p. 110.

handbook of programming and production based on five years' experience at station WRGB, the General Electric station.

Eddy, William C., *Television; The Eyes of Tomorrow.* New York: Prentice-Hall, Inc., 1945, 330 pp. Discussion of the history and development of television, engineering, staging, and the like, with a glossary of terms.

Hubbell, Richard W., *Television Programming and Production.* New York: Rinehart & Company, Inc., Murray Hill Books, 1945, 207 pp. Includes an examination of television in relation to the theatre, motion pictures, and radio, as well as some helpful material on the problems of the television camera.

Madden, Cecil, "Television; Problems and Possibilities," The *B. B. C. Quarterly* 2 (January, 1948), 225–228.

Maugham, W. Somerset, *Quartet.* Screen plays by R. C. Sherriff. New York: Doubleday & Company, 1949. The four short stories and their film treatments are valuable reading for an acquaintance with camera techniques.

Smith, Bernard B., "Television: There Ought to Be a Law," *Harper's Magazine,* 197 (September, 1948), 34–42. A prediction of the immense effect television may have on the habits of the American people and on the entertainment and communications industries.

EXERCISES

A. FACIAL EXPRESSIONS

1. In front of a mirror practice saying, with varying shades of intensity, and under different circumstances and to different people, such sentences as "I hate you!" "You cheat!" "I absolutely refuse to go," "I don't believe you," "Why do you say that?" and so forth.

   Try saying, in similar fashion, such sentences as "I'm so glad," "We had a wonderful time," "It's really a spring day," "Congratulations," "You mean I won?" and so forth.

   Try saying these and similar sentences in your mirror—but this time contradict the words with your facial expression.

   Say in front of the mirror, "Really," and by your facial expression make it mean a dozen different things.

   Finally merely *think* all the preceding and similar sentences, and try to communicate your meaning.

2. Tie a scarf over your face like a Turkish woman's veil, and see in the mirror what your eyes and forehead can do to register such reactions as struggle (mental or physical), surprise, anger, fear, questioning, pain, unhappiness, confusion, doubt, and so on. Try to register your moods with the *minimum* of expression.

3. Imagine you hear and react facially to

   a. A mouse gnawing on wood.
   b. A clap of thunder.
   c. A friend unexpectedly calling on you.
   d. The loud screech of automobile brakes.
   e. Someone tiptoeing up behind you.
   f. A cry from the baby's bedroom.
   g. An angry crowd outside.
   h. A steady drip of water overhead.
   i. Static on your radio.
   j. A soprano hitting "high C."

4. Imagine you see and react facially to

   a. A plane falling.
   b. A startling newspaper headline.
   c. A dog coming toward you.
   d. A prize gladiola.
   e. Blood from a cut on your arm.
   f. A birthday present you unwrap.
   g. A moth hole in your coat.
   h. A photograph of a friend's child.
   i. Flames next door.
   j. Robin Hood in person.

5. Imagine you smell and react facially to

   a. A bakery.
   b. Gasoline.
   c. Banana oil.

d. A skunk.
e. Fresh rain.
f. A favorite cheese.
g. Smoke from burning cloth.
h. Strong perfume.
i. Dinner cooking, perhaps cabbage or cauliflower.
j. A chest lined with cedar.

6. Imagine you taste and react facially to

a. Bitter medicine.
b. Cold soup.
c. Lemon.
d. Scalding hot coffee.
e. Slightly burned string beans.

7. Imagine you touch and react facially to

a. A snake.
b. Velvet.
c. A hot pan handle.
d. Someone's pulse.
e. Ice.

8. Repeat each of the preceding reactions (a) with three widely different characterizations and then (b) with each of the characters in at least two different sets of surrounding circumstances.

9. Repeat each of the preceding facial reactions, first, for a close-up, and then for a medium or long shot.

10. Bring to class five additional examples of facial reactions "3," "4," and "5" for the members of the class to watch and identify.

11. Practice indicating by facial expression, without lip movements, such simple sentences as

a. I'm afraid to go in there.
b. I'm hungry.
c. Where'd he say he was going?
d. Isn't he the cutest dog!
e. I lost the tickets.
f. You win; I give up.
g. Ouch! That hurts!
h. What are you doing here?
i. Whew! I'm hot!
j. You mean I don't have to stay?
k. How could you ever think that about me?
l. You're not telling the truth.
m. Please let go of me.
n. You mean . . . she's dead?
o. Hurry up! We're late.

12. Repeat each of the preceding and similar sentences (a) with three widely different characterizations and then (b) with each of the characters in at least two different sets of surrounding circumstances.

13. Repeat each of these facial expressions, first, for a close-up, and then for a medium or long shot.

14. Bring to class at least five additional expression sentences, as in "11," for the class to identify.

15. Respond facially to such sentences as

    a. You stole my purse.
    b. Get out of this room and stay out.
    c. You've been elected editor.
    d. I don't believe a word you're saying.
    e. I'm glad to say your friend will recover.
    f. Hands up!
    g. I apologize; you were right.
    h. Why don't you say something?
    i. You were there all the time?!
    j. I've got measles.

16. Improvise ten such startling, or ordinary, sentences for your partner and watch his facial reactions.

17. Repeat "15" and "16" (a) with three widely different characterizations and then (b) with each of the characters in at least two different sets of surrounding circumstances.

18. Repeat all these facial reactions, first, for a close-up, and then for a medium or long shot.

19. Watch a slowly opening door through which enters

    a. A king in royal regalia.
    b. An escaping convict.
    c. Your best friend you thought was in Europe.
    d. A bill collector.
    e. A strange, six-year-old child.
    f. The President of the United States.
    g. A most attractive boy (or girl).
    h. A circus clown.
    i. Dr. Fu Manchu.
    j. Your child with a broken arm.

20. Enter and react facially to

    a. A cathedral.
    b. A new summer cottage you've rented.
    c. A beautiful, cool forest.
    d. A haunted house by night.
    e. A stadium from the top row.
    f. A doctor's office.
    g. A picture gallery.
    h. Your dining room.
    i. A cave.
    j. Heaven.

21. Repeat "19" and "20" (a) with three widely different characterizations and then (b) with each of the characters in at least two different sets of surrounding circumstances.

22. Repeat all these facial reactions, first, for a close-up, and then for a medium or a long shot.

23. With a partner enact, for facial expressions only:

    a. A wife annoyed at her husband's boredom at a symphony concert.
    b. A messenger boy watching a young lady open and read the contents of a telegram.
    c. A fond parent watching his child, seated on the auditorium platform, being praised by the school principal.
    d. The young Queen Victoria when, for the first time, she watches Albert shave.
    e. A friend who comes to see you in the hospital and finds you horribly disfigured.
    f. A student watching a band conductor demonstrate how to hold a baton.
    g. A girl watching a friend show her a dress she could possibly wear to a party.
    h. Yourself, watching a critic who disapprovingly examines your painting.
    i. Yourself, staring at a person opposite you on a street corner who is staring at you.
    j. Yourself, watching your friend watch a ball game.

24. Justify—find a motivation for—five facial expressions that the class gives you.

25. Read any of the solo speeches of the previous chapters and watch, or let the class watch, what happens to your face.

B. GESTURES

1. Imagine a six-foot figure "8" placed horizontally, and then vertically, before you—then overhead, or at your side. In each instance follow the lines of these "8's" with one or both arms in all possible directions. Practice this exercise frequently for a feeling of freedom and relaxation.

2. Practice gesturing like a child, a teen-age youngster, a young person, a middle-aged person, an elderly person, an effete person, an excited person, a thoughtful person, a conceited person, a regal person, a sick person, a person in pain, and so forth.

3. Repeat all these gestures (a) with three widely different characterizations and then (b) with each of the characters in at least two different sets of surrounding circumstances.

4. Repeat the gestures, first, for a close-up, and then for a medium or long shot.

5. Bring to class examples of unusual gestures you have observed; then justify each of them.

6. Next translate each real-life gesture into a camera gesture for a specific purpose in a characterization you are creating.

7. Practice the many functions of the hands, such as to define, to indicate, to mold, to detect, to hold, to caress, to affirm or assert, to deny, to conceal, to reveal, to reject, to support, to protect, and so on.

8. Discover the relaxed positions your hands take when you are seated.

9. Carry out such manual activities as

   a. Knocking on a door.
   b. Eating an ice-cream cone.
   c. Searching through a drawer for lost papers.
   d. Picking up a bird's nest.
   e. Ironing a shirt.
   f. Eating spaghetti like an Italian.
   g. Sewing on a button.
   h. Holding a baby.
   i. Pointing.
   j. Arranging flowers in a vase.
   k. Shelling peas.
   l. Reading Braille.
   m. Drinking a cocktail.
   n. Lighting a cigarette in the wind.
   o. Pouring tea.

10. Bring to class five different gestures that are shaped by the costumes you imagine you are wearing.

11. Repeat all these manual activities (a) with three widely different characterizations and then (b) with each of the characters with at least two different surrounding circumstances.

12. Deliver any of the solo or long speeches from the previous chapter exercises (a) with no gestures, (b) with your own gestures, and (c), finally, with characterization gestures.

C. SITTING

1. Practice sitting well back in your chair, so that your weight is on the bottom of your thighs and not on the back of your spine.

   (A girl should usually sit with one foot extended slightly in front of the other. A man should usually sit with both feet planted on the floor in the same plane.

   A girl should not, unless in character, cross her knees in sitting.)

2. Practice trying to sit down, not with your feet together, but by standing with one foot slightly forward. Rise slightly on your toes, bend your knees slowly, and tilt your trunk forward as your leg muscles lower your body onto the chair.

3. Practice sitting without looking into your chair just before you sit (and thus breaking the audience's attention). Reach your chair, usually, before you are to sit; then when you sit, lightly touch the chair with the back of your leg, and sit without looking down.

   (Men should not pull up their trousers when they are sitting down unless it is definitely in character.)

4. Practice getting up from a chair by first placing one foot in front of the other; then lean forward, putting the weight on your front foot; then push up with your rear foot and lift yourself up, putting forward your rear foot for the first step.

5. Practice sitting like a child, a teen-age youngster, a young person, a middle-aged person, an elderly person, a conceited person, an athletic person, a thoughtful person, a crude person, a tense person, a regal person, a sick person, and so forth.

6. Next translate these real-life sittings into camera sittings.

   (Know that it is easiest to fall out of character in your risings and sittings.)

7. Bring to class examples of sittings you have observed; first justify each of them, and then turn each one into acting.

8. In sitting, are there any distinctive attitudes for an army officer, a Hindu, an old maid, a bank clerk, a ballet dancer, a judge, a jockey, a European peasant, a dock worker, an athletic girl, a model, a mortician, a club woman, a burlesque comic, and so forth?

D. POSTURE

Practice throwing back your shoulders by rotating the palms of your hands outward as they hang at your side. Now inhale, inflating your lungs, expanding your chest. Hold in the muscles of your paunch. Then plant your feet parallel to each other and distribute the weight on the balls of your feet. Vary the position by putting one foot slightly forward.

E. WALKS

1. Practice the two methods of walking:
   a. In the first kind of walk, after your foot is placed, pointing straight ahead, in the forward position without weight, you can, by raising the heel of your back supporting leg, shove or propel your trunk weight onto the forward leg. This raising of the heel of the back leg to propel the weight of the trunk forward into space, until it rests over the advanced foot, is known as the propulsive step.
   b. In the second kind of walk, which starts from the same foot-forward position, you plant the fore part or ball of your foot on the floor, gripping it so firmly that your forward leg is able, by means of the grip, to draw your trunk forward by gradual pulls exerted successively by the muscles of your lower leg and thigh. This "pawing" method of pulling the weight of the trunk forward is known as the suction step.

2. Discuss Nijinsky's statement that "women have the tendency to put the tip of the toe to the ground first, to give the impression of grace and lightness, instead of first putting the heel down, which gives firmness and natural rhythm to the body. This is the way one should walk. . . ."

3. Practice walking like a child, a teen-age youngster, a young person, a middle-aged person, an elderly person, an effete person, a crude person, a lazy person, a tense person, a regal person, a sick person, a person in pain, and so forth.

4. Repeat these walks (a) with three widely different characterizations and then (b) with each of the characters in at least two different sets of surrounding circumstances.

5. Are there any walks identified with any professions or classes of society?

6. Bring to class three examples of walks you have observed and justify each one; then translate them into acting.

7. Demonstrate three walks and let the class decide your different moods.

8. Bring to class the walks of a person
   a. Scurrying in the rain.
   b. Strolling in the park.
   c. Tiptoeing down a hall.
   d. Walking "on eggshells."
   e. Ploughing through mud.
   f. Hiking in deep sand.
   g. Waiting to meet someone.
   h. Hiking the last long mile.
   i. Carrying a book on top of his head.
   j. Treading on slippery ice.

9. Practice making all varieties of entrances and exits.

10. Practice walking, without words, through a number of the short scenes of the previous chapters.

F. TRANSITIONS

1. Start to leave your house, but discover that it is freezing cold outside. Go to the closet, find and put on your overcoat; discover it isn't yours. Take it off, find yours, put it on; find a note in one of the pockets, read it.

2. See someone opposite you on the streetcar, stare at him a few seconds thinking he looks like someone you know. When he turns to you, smile at him; when he stares back at you, realize he is not the person you thought he was. Then decide you do know him, that you met him somewhere recently. Try to remember his name or where you saw him. Smile at him again, with no response but a glare. Decide you don't know him. Look around to see if anyone has been watching you.

3. In a hospital read an adventure of Peter Rabbit aloud to a sick young friend; show your scorn for such juvenile doings together with your genuine and undisguised interest in finding how the story will turn out.

4. Turn on your radio for your favorite program, listen to the conclusion of the preceding one, the "station break," and then get ready for the start of your own favorite show. Another program comes on. Dial several other stations without finding your program. Pick up your newspaper, read the radio log, and learn that your program is not listed for tonight. Then, noticing the date on the paper, realize this is the wrong night.

5. Sit looking at your watch, knowing that an execution is taking place in exactly one minute. Look up at the lights to see if they will dim. On the dot hear a scream. Then realize it was just a neighbor calling someone. Next hear a different scream, from another direction. Realize you're jumpy.

6. Riding in an automobile, watch first the scenery; then see a rare license plate on the car ahead, a charming house on the left, something strange at the roadside ahead that turns out to be a dead rabbit; then read the oncoming road sign; discover you are on the wrong road.

7. At your desk start to write out a check. First be pleased at your large bank balance as shown on your check stub; then be unsure as to exactly how to make out the check;

find the bill, examine it, be amazed at the strange spelling of the company name. Start to write, but discover that your pen is a leaky one. Get another pen but discover that the point is bad. Start writing with a third one, but stop as if you heard someone call you. It is no one. Start to write again. Spell the name wrong.

8. Go to your refrigerator for an evening snack only to discover nothing at all in it except one solitary bottle of milk. Wonder what happened to all the provisions that ought to be there. Pour yourself a glass of milk, drink it, and discover it is buttermilk, which you dislike. Wonder again what happened to all the provisions. Then remember.

9. Read a popular novel; turn a page and read a few sentences until you find it doesn't make sense. Try to find out why not; reread the passage several times until you discover that a page is missing. Find the missing pages wrongly inserted further along in the book. Start to read again. The phone call you've been waiting for rings. Answer. The voice is a complete surprise to you.

10. Listen to your lawyer tell you, in imagination, that you look fine, and so forth. After this introduction he says that he has something important to tell you, something shocking. He finally tells you that your mother isn't really your mother, that she adopted you. He explains that your real mother is very rich and now wants to claim you, but your foster mother refuses to give you up. Then the door opens and a strange woman comes in. You think it is your real mother. The lawyer introduces his secretary.

11. Bring to class two original pantomimes that are rich in surprises and transitions.

12. Read again some of the exercises from the preceding chapters and notice how much you can accomplish by the addition of pantomime.

G. VIBRATIONS

Without moving one muscle

1. Listen to several different kinds of phone calls, such as
   a. Two old ladies gossiping.
   b. A plot to take your life.
   c. Your best friend praising you to someone.
   d. A police call.
   e. A bore who just won't stop talking.

2. Decide to commit suicide.

3. Watch someone you absolutely detest play the piano.

4. Sit with your lover at the edge of a lake at night.

5. Listen to someone berate you furiously; you know that he is right.

H. RELAXATION

1. Notice how much muscular energy it takes to move a chair from place to place in your room, and then how much surplus energy you expend on the same operation when you are watched by others.

2. Observe the different amounts of muscular energy expended in carrying out certain activities in private and then in public, such as

   a. Putting on your coat.
   b. Opening and closing a door.
   c. Lighting a cigarette.
   d. Drinking a cocktail.
   e. Raising a window shade.

3. Sit on a chair with your muscles perfectly relaxed, making only the effort to sit upright. See for yourself (and let the class see) whether your arms, neck, shoulders, face, and leg muscles are relaxed.

   Now, letting every muscle remain as it was, tighten the muscles of one hand, then the muscles of your feet, your shoulders, and so on. Continue this until your entire body is tense.

   Then reverse the process until again the entire body is relaxed.

4. Take a variety of positions or poses, standing, sitting up straight, squatting, kneeling, creeping along (in groups and with and without props) and notice and name the tense muscles in each position.

5. At a given signal, perhaps a hand clap, strike some pose, spontaneously, unexpectedly, and even foolishly. Then observe yourself, and relax your muscles, exerting only the minimum effort required to maintain the pose.

   Next, repeat the same pose, but this time find a motivation for it. See whether or not the added motivation does not tend to lessen the tension.

Chapter XIII . . MICROPHONE READING: STRUCTURE (DIRECTING)

1

Many radio and television actors are so concerned with exhibiting themselves that they seldom bother with the structure of a play. Worse than that, they will rarely let anyone help them preserve by their performances the true nature of the play in which they are appearing. Let someone try to explain to them their character's function in the playwright's *design,* and immediately they turn either pugnacious or blank. Let a director advise them about such structural matters as change of beat, contrast, pace, picking up cues, pointing a line, reversals, rhythm, subordination, style, or pictorial composition, and at once they answer with an air of superiority, "We're not interested in doing all those artificial things. We want to be natural."

Such indignant and trite retorts usually come from immature actors, are the impotent though well-intentioned peeps of the young who have newly fallen in love with an abstraction called "Truth" but have not yet discovered that in art Truth has form. Such innocent arguments ignore the fundamental fact that all actors must "play the playwright," must offer adventitious assistance not only to what he says, but also to *how* he says it, to *how he has organized his saying of it.* According to Theodore Komisarjevsky's reasoning, the advocate of only honesty, sincerity, or naturalness in playing—usually the pupil of Stanislavski—"neglects the form and rhythm of the play and substitutes his own remembered, intellectual states in place of those of the author."[1]

Two examples taken from the criticisms of Stark Young serve to indicate why the actor must often forsake a sole allegiance to "feeling natural" and give some attention to the form or structure of the play. First, in those scenes of Shaw's *Back to Methuselah*

> . . . where the Brothers Barnabas explain their doctrine, much would be gained if the actors sat still, took each other's speech up immediately, with distinct and precise enunciation, and heightened the speed at which the lines are given. This would be artificial, yes, but that has no point, for the scenes in themselves are patently dialogue statements of ideas . . . trying to make these scenes seem real can accomplish only a childish rubbish of illusion.[2]

Second, in the New York production of Pirandello's *Henry IV,*

> . . . the expository scene spoken by the four pages failed of its dramatic function because of the actors' individualizing their speeches, making, or trying to make, them proceed from themselves. By this they lost the speed and continuity right for the scene; what we got was four people more or less expressing themselves on a point, where we should have gotten the effect of a point streaming through a brain, with the various arguments clashing and running against each other.[3]

In other words, an actor must know that a play has both form and content, that it is what it is because of how it says what it says. Consequently in his feeling and his speaking each character in a play must not only be true to nature; he must also be true to the formal relationships of the play's structure. As H. Granville-Barker has observed, a play always has two aspects:

> . . . its aspect in action—this being how it is primarily and normally presented to us—and in the perspective of our recollection of it. While we are watching it, and yielding to the spell of its illusion, our appreciation of the characters will be dominantly emotional. In recollection . . . emotion yields to judgment; for then we see them rounded and complete, and in a settled relation to the whole scheme of the play. The actor must also acquire this double view

[1] *Encyclopaedia Britannica* (1944), I, 139.

[2] Young, *Theatre Practice,* p. 43.

[3] Young, *The Theatre,* p. 131.

of a character; though he must consider it in its second aspect first, if he is, as he acts it, to develop it consistently, to relate its various phases one to another.[4]

Some point there is, then, in advising all actors to pay more than a little attention to the architecture of the play in which they are performing. A knowledge of the design or form of the play can help in correctly shaping the reading of the lines—can change the reading perhaps only a mite, but change it nonetheless. A mite added to acting is like a mite added to the length of a nose.

The radio or television actor gets this sense of the play's structure from his director. One of the main reasons for the director's being at the conference table or in the control booth is to bring out the organization of the play for the authentic and complete communication of the playwright's individual idea. What the busy actor has no time to do for himself the director must somehow do for him. Moreover, the director is often the only one who can, in a measure, acquaint him with all the formal factors necessary to his playing, because he usually has the advantage of having studied the script thoroughly (everyone hopes!) the night before the rehearsal. He has more hours than the actors in which to discover what is in the script, what came out of the writer's mind and heart, and how it has all been carefully designed. He can lie on his stomach in front of the script for hours and hours of coffee and concentration, and examine and re-examine it until finally he is an authority on it. Therefore at rehearsals he has the right to insist, not only on truthful readings, but on right relationships, changes of beats, climaxes, contrasts, rhythms, toppings, and so on.

In brief, since radio and especially television actors must lean so heavily on the director, they ought to know what, at best, he is trying to accomplish.

2

Toward directing, most actors usually take one of two attitudes. Either they agree with George S. Kaufman that "the whole business of direction is overrated . . . a play is supposed to simulate life, and the best direction is that which is so effortless and natural that it simply isn't noticed at all. Once it begins to call attention to itself, something is wrong."[5] Or they agree with Stark Young that "when a play emerges from the hands of a director it has undergone a restatement of itself, a translation into the terms of the theatre, and the importance of the thing added will measure the importance of the director . . . . Directing is an art or it is nothing."[6] To some actors a director is merely the kind, remembering individual who has cast them in the roles they are scheduled to play; to others "radio is essentially a director's, not an actor's, medium"; and television is entirely a director's medium.

Whatever the attitude of the performers, the fact is that ever since the beginning the director has been the one man who takes the script from the mimeographer's and, in varying degrees, tells the actors what to do so that he can recreate the play in his own technical terms. Since "there is no such thing as a play directed exactly as it is written any more than there is a landscape painted as it really is" or a symphony conducted exactly as it has been set down by the composer, the director is the chief person responsible for joining his imagination to that of the author's and finding one way of bringing the play to an audience "its parts justly related and its idea expressed." No two people can ever successfully lead a script to the microphone or cameras; nor can any cast of eight variously take it there any more than eight people can jump onto one horse and simultaneously ride it off in eight different directions.

A director unifies the many contributions and relationships of a group engaged in bringing a playwright's script into theatrical being. His job is (1) as coach, to get the best interpretative reading out of his individual actors—the unique sound and skill of each of them. This he does by patient explanation and sympathetic encouragement, by coaxing some with a box of chocolates, by threatening others with a hefty baseball bat, or by using any other egocentric or self-humbling device that works in the brief time allotted him. His job, beyond coaching, is (2) to get out of the script via the actors *as a team* the values his thoughtful scrutiny and emotional explorations have found to be contained therein. This he does by discovering the playwright's

[4] H. Granville-Barker, *Prefaces to Shakespeare, Third Series: Hamlet* (London: Sidgwick & Jackson, Ltd., 1936), pp. vi-vii.

[5] George S. Kaufman, "What Is Direction, Anyhow?" in *Producing the Play*, edited by John Gassner (New York: The Dryden Press, Inc., 1941), pp. 70–71.

[6] Young, *Theatre Practice*, p. 128.

idea, and the design of its expression, and then by guiding all the readings and, in television, all the motions, accordingly.

In television this responsibility of the director's is at least only partly appreciated by actors. They will quickly admit that he must work out the visual composition of the play, but they will just as quickly balk at letting him work out its oral composition. In this attitude they join most radio actors in ignoring the director's responsibility for guiding the right reading, for adhering to the right *formal* expression of the play. This distrust by actors of the director's sense of oral structure is often the fault of the directors themselves. Many a radio director skips any acquaintanceship with form. Often he does no more toward achieving a right reading of a script than cast it and, then, stop watch in hand, cut it down to time size. Obviously this is not the sort of directing that can honestly command respect. It is a purely mechanical task, a chore for a small boy. At other times the director does little more than sit before the talk-back in his glass-enclosed control booth, booming to his cast, "Faster there" and "Louder, please"; or, "The correct pronunciation is 'dju-ty' "; or "Your script says 'Laughing' there"; or "Too close to the mike"; or "Let's change 'and' to 'but' "; or "Darling, you were wonderful!" Too frequently for comfort this sort of directing, centered on assorted trivialities, ignores the kind of play at hand, its characterizations, its texture and structure. It skims the surface. It completely misses the point. It overlooks the unifying of the play around the theatrical expression of an idea.

A director who is not the commander of the sounds as well as the motions of all the characters in his play is nothing.

3

Television actors need not bother too much about how and why a director arranges his camera pictures; they need only motivate what they are given to do as part of the composition. But, like all radio actors, they must be somewhat acquainted with the various ways in which directors go about shaping the *reading* of the play. They can perhaps best do this by discovering how radio directors perform this oral task. What is true of them is similarly true of television directors. The first type of director is born of the fact that today's theatre is predominantly, if not entirely, realistic. A theatre based on resemblance and reproduction, it thrives on the duplication of the kind of speaking we have all at one time or another heard as the only method whereby the playwright and the actor can express what they wish to express. Of course, selectivity, rearrangement, and perhaps some heightening are included in the realistic method, but fidelity to the actual sounds of life is the only basis on which it functions. Truth to life in the way things are said is all that matters.

According to this theory, any man who knows what the speech of actual people is like can, alas, with common sense and a little patience, usually become a radio director. All he needs to do is listen, and then say to the actor that this sentence or that speech was not natural, was not sincere, was not honestly thought out and felt and said in accordance with the character's true-to-life objective and circumstances. Thus, and thus only, he directs; and finally, when the entire cast as an ensemble has approximated verisimilitude—when each actor thinks of what he is saying while he is saying it, and listens to the other actors and responds; when the tempos and the tones, the changes of beat and the pauses, are lifelike; when hesitancies and slips are present as they are in everyday utterance; and when speeches and cues purposely overlap as a positive replica of the authentic—finally, when what is actually audible in life has been phonographed, the actors have been perfectly directed!

This know-what-people-sound-like-in-real-life kind of directing is discouragingly popular with most actors today. The four reasons for this popularity are easy to uncover. The first is that the actual talk of human beings is tangible; its reproduction is something definite, something concrete, for the actor to aim at. Any goal less substantial can be too esoteric and too difficult to achieve. Not that the reproduction of truthful speech is easy. Mimicry involves great skill; it demands constant and careful practice. And once expertness is acquired, it is easily recognized and evaluated, inasmuch as the director, or any listener, can judge for himself when the actor has reproduced with honesty the speech of real people.

The second reason is that most directors leave to their own devices those actors who are experienced and sufficiently proficient in giving out over the air all the nuances of actual speech. Once the actors know their business of imitating the tones and timing and inflections of real people, most directors are content; and any directing that lets the actors alone is humanly certain to be attractive for a while, but only so long as the actors themselves remain short-sighted.

The third reason is that this know-what-people-sound-like-in-real-life kind of directing is, in a way, both important and necessary, although not the final perfection of directing. It is the rich *preliminary* to all interpretation. You as a performer need to work from a knowledge of truth to nature. Always you need to be reminded how to relive sharply, fully, and with belief the truth of the experience you are enacting. Always you need to know what the actual is before you can transform it into something else, something new, something theatrical. To put this another way, two tensions are continually pulling every actor in opposite directions: you must be true to nature, and you must be true to art. You can err by being pulled too far in either direction, and perhaps the more grievous error is to depart too far from nature. Therefore, you need to retain for your own purposes your contacts with reality; you need to be reminded by a director of the necessity of keeping these contacts fresh, and genuine, and original. In so far as this kind of directing accomplishes such a purpose it is worth while.

The fourth reason is that the know-what-people-sound-like kind of directing has about it an odd prestige derived from the popularity of the Stanislavski system of acting. Stanislavski taught in the legitimate theatre; yet some of his principles, under cover of darkness, have crept into radio and video. For a moment, then, the basic point in his theory must be examined because of its dominant influence on today's acting.

In *An Actor Prepares* Stanislavski teaches his students to "avoid falseness . . . avoid everything that runs counter to nature, logic, and common sense!"[7] For instance, he advises his students in one of the exercises that "if every little auxiliary is executed truthfully, then the whole action will unfold rightfully."[8] He tells them he does not believe the exercise in which one of the students counts some imaginary bank notes; and then he proceeds to deepen that student's "physical actions, movement by movement, second by second, until coherent sequence" is achieved and the class can see "to what an extent of realistic detail you must go in order to convince our physical natures of the truth of what you are doing . . . ." However, the student's truthful physical actions—finding the end of the string, and not too suddenly; rolling it up carefully and laying it beside the pile of notes; tapping the money for some time on the table in order to make neat piles; counting the hundreds first since there are usually ten to a packet; and counting no more quickly than the most expert cashier could have counted the crumpled, dirty old bank notes—may lead him—probably do lead him—to experience the validity of the playwright's source of material. Whether this is all there is to *acting* is the forgotten question. Yet it is the only important question.

To be blunt about it, this truthful playing by the accurate execution of every little auxiliary is not the end-all of acting on the stage or in front of the microphone. It is only the *material* that the actor uses for his creative endeavors. By no means is it the final measuring stick of the truth or success of a physical action on stage, or on camera, or of a sentence or speech read on microphone.

The know-what-people-sound-like-in-real-life radio directors, adhering to Stanislavski's "Faith and a Sense of Truth" admonition, are always totally unaware that the bank notes would be counted—and that any speech would be read—one way in a scene from a Norman Corwin farce and another way in a Corwin high comedy; and in still another way in a play by Arch Oboler; the bank notes would be counted one way—and any speech would be read one way—in a Bernard Shaw play written when he was thirty years old, and another way in a play written when he was sixty; and one way in a Millard Lampell play as directed by Mr. X, and another way in the same play as directed by Mr. Y; and yet differently if the scene containing the notes—or the speech—came near the beginning of the play and not near the end; and again differently if the scene is to be emphasized and not subordinated. The variations are endless.

What the Stanislavski director always forgets is that while an audience may acknowledge a hundred and one lifelike accuracies in the cast's reading of a script, it will, in the long run, wish for something in the acting that engages the mind more fully.

Today's realistic director, then, can demand of you

[7] Stanislavski, *An Actor Prepares* (New York: Theatre Arts, Inc., 1936), p. 152.

[8] *Ibid.*, pp. 126 ff.

as an actor faith and a sense of truth, a belief in your motivations and emotions and way of speaking, a sincere inner feeling; in brief, he can ask you to be true to nature without once helping you serve the designed idea of the play, without once guiding you to express it, except perhaps accidentally. The realistic director coaches his actors to be true to nature, but he is never sure that they will be true to nature that has already been interpreted in a distinctive way and in a particular medium.

Take a simple example. The following few speeches are from a scene in THE ALDRICH FAMILY,* by Clifford Goldsmith:

* Reproduced through the courtesy of the author.

OPERATOR: (ON FILTER) Number, please?

HENRY: Well, look, may I ask who this is?

OPERATOR: This is the Operator. What number do you want?

HENRY: Well, could you do me a favor? Could you transfer any calls that may come for me at the Aldriches over to Homer Brown's house?

OPERATOR: I'm sorry, but we can't possibly do that.

HENRY: Well, do you happen to know Charlie Clarke?

OPERATOR: Yes.

HENRY: Well, he's a friend of mine, see, and his sister works there at the phone company. So does that make any difference?

OPERATOR: I'm Charlie Clarke's sister.

HENRY: Oh, you are? You are! Well, I'm Henry, see? And I've got an unusual case here. My father's driven me out, see. He's driven me out — and somebody very important is trying to get me.

OPERATOR: Is it an emergency call you're expecting?

HENRY: Boy, I'll say it is!

OPERATOR: I'll take it up with the Supervisor, and explain the circumstances.

HENRY: Gee, thank you very much. Goodbye.

OPERATOR: Goodbye.

Two actors reading this brief scene can discover any number of true-to-life characterizations for the two people involved; they can invent a limitless number of honest circumstances to guide the scene in its playing; they can set up whatever sincere over-all objectives they wish. For instance, if you were the woman in the cast, you could, as an exercise:

1) Model the Operator on a real operator; on your own comic conception of an operator; on ten widely different women you know; be yourself as Operator.

2) Read the Operator as if she were at the last ten minutes of her shift; as if she had just fought with her Supervisor; as if she knew Henry; as if she had a toothache; as if it were very sultry at the exchange; as if she were instructing, by her example, a new Operator.

If you were the boy in the cast you could:

1) Variously change the characterization and circumstances of Henry in a similar fashion.

2) Locate Henry at various phones; place Homer near by, listening, or a strange woman there waiting to

talk next on the telephone; let Henry know he is not liked at all by Charlie Clarke's sister; make this the third time Henry has called this very same Operator.

3) Change the objective Henry has in mind in as many ways as possible, making urgent or otherwise the necessity for his getting the call.

As an actor you could attempt all these things until you found the truth in the scene, until finally you were reading sincerely and with belief in all the objective circumstances the playwright has included in the script. And your director would probably be delighted because his two actors sounded like two real people talking to each other.

Finding the truth in the scene will, however, never be enough. It will serve perhaps—it will "get by," but it will not be the best kind of acting. The true director cannot stop there. He has to say to his two actors something like, "Now that we have the feel of the scene, the truth of the experience and the characters, let's turn it all into *acting*. Let's make it Clifford Goldsmith. Let's make it farce comedy. Let's turn it into theatre. Let's find the design. Let's act from the recipe of (a) reality, (b) interpreted, and (c) expressed in a distinctive way. Let's make it approach art." The director must know—and the actors must know—that the capture of the right structural qualities in this ALDRICH FAMILY scene—the atmosphere, the theatricality, the comic click and pace, the texture of the playwright's attitude toward adolescence, the buoyant brightness, and the warm and inventive heightening—is essential. All these additional qualities go beyond mere fidelity to actual life. They proceed toward formal unification around the play's central and individual idea. The achieving of such unification is every top director's job, the one thing his actors should expect of him.

The same point in acting and directing can be made in the preparation of the following two scenes. The first is from *The Boiling Point,** by William C. Engvick, as produced on SILVER THEATRE:

* Reproduced through the courtesy of the author.

JEAN: Oh, dear! Excuse me! I didn't dream you were right behind me. Sorry I bumped into you.

RICHARD: I enjoyed it.

JEAN: I got off on the wrong floor. This is the seventeenth.

RICHARD: Gee, I'm on the wrong floor, too.

JEAN: That's what I thought. I wanted to see if you were following me . . . and you are.

RICHARD: You make a great leader.

JEAN: I'm sorry, but you're wasting your time . . . I think.

RICHARD: Shall I ring for the elevator?

JEAN: Oh, no, I'll do it. I can't accept favors from strange young men.

RICHARD: I'm not strange — really. I've watched you in the elevator lots of times.

JEAN: Yes, I know. I've watched you watch me.

RICHARD: You have? That's wonderful!

JEAN: But it's got to stop. I'm late for work, and I'm not interested. (INTERESTED) Who are you, anyway?

RICHARD: Well, I'm from Utica . . .

JEAN: Yes, I know . . . .

RICHARD: I'm a song-writer . . . .

JEAN: A song-writer!

RICHARD: And all this week I've been trying to get up nerve to . . . .
What do you do?

JEAN: I'm a secretary.

RICHARD: Yeah? What office?

JEAN: A song publisher's.

This scene can be prepared and perfected in any number of true-to-life ways. It must be remembered, though, that when you and the others in the cast have discovered, after an hour of various readings, that there is never one way—surely not only the first glib way—of reading a scene; when all of you can read the scene honestly, or naturally, or sincerely, there will still be more to do with the acting of it. For the purposes of an exercise, and to emphasize his point broadly, the director might next give you an idea or design that he sees in the scene and that must be accented. He might ask that the scene be tossed off, be thrown away, as a very subordinate part of the whole design. He might ask for anything that would make the scene interesting theatrically instead of being just natural.

The next scene is taken from Roy Vickers' story, *The Man Who Murdered in Public,** as adapted for radio by Frederic Methot:

* Reproduced through the courtesy of the author and the publishers of *Ellery Queen's Mystery Magazine.*

GEORGE: May, why not chuck it all and marry me?

MAY: I — I'm not sure, George, that I should leave my parents and chuck my job. You tell me you have no money, but —

GEORGE: But I've no employment? What matter? I have enough to care for you, May . . . and your parents. And I have a surprise for you tonight!

MAY: A surprise, George?

GEORGE: Yes. Something I've kept all these years . . . for just such a girl as you, May. Here. It belonged to my mother.

MAY: Glory, what a beauty! I've always adored bracelets. Oh, George, it's rubies!!

There ought, of course, to be some differences in the reading of the scene if it takes place on the street instead of in front of a fireplace, at a public lecture instead of on a hillside, in a rowboat instead of in the cold wind beside an icy lake, and so on. There ought, furthermore, to be something in the reading to indicate the attitudes of the two people toward each other—are they in love, is he trying to impress her, is she a spy trying to learn about him, does he want to know if she recognizes the rubies, does she know he stole them from her? The possibilities of motivation are legion. Yet whatever the truths of the scene, whatever the correspondences to reality, the director will again have to tell his performers to play the scene as farce, as comedy, as melodrama, as documentary, or whatever else it may be in the theatre.

Directing that is content only with talk-as-it-sounds-in-real-life, eminently important as this consideration is, has not effected the change in acting, however subtle it may be, that transforms nature into art.

4

Some such transformation of nature into art is effected by the second type of oral director, who places his ear right smack in the middle of his audience. This director joins Mother knitting in her rocking chair beside the fireplace, or Mabel and Joe in their automobile, or the ranger lonely at night in Yellowstone, or an invalid in bed, or the various fans who follow the show regularly. He is interested primarily in producing an effect on Thackeray's "great baby, the public." Perhaps he centers his efforts on addressing millions of listeners, all the while remembering critic A. B. Walkley's notation to the effect that the crowd "has a mind and character of its own which differ from the mind and character of its individual members."[9] Perhaps he centers his attention on only one individual, on the ideal audience that Molière is supposed to have found in his cook, Bernard Shaw in his chambermaid, William Gillette in the man in the street, and Tolstoy in the *moujik*—"a respected, wise, and educated country laborer." Whatever his center of attention, his main purpose is always to provoke from his hearers a sustained attention and immediate appreciation. Wringing from the play all the structural excitement he possibly can, he aims to "put it over."

Virgil Thomson, the composer and critic, has perfectly identified this kind of director in his analysis of Toscanini's conducting.

> It opens few vistas to the understanding of men and epochs; it produces a temporary, but intense, condition of pure auditory excitement. The Maestro . . . reads all music in terms of its possible audience effect. The absence of poetical allusions and of historical references in his interpretations is significant, I think, of a certain disdain for the general culture of his individual listeners. [Toscanini emphasizes] . . . those musical aspects that have a direct effect on everybody . . . . Like Mendelssohn, he quite shamelessly whips up the tempo and sacrifices clarity and ignores a basic rhythm, just making the music, like his baton, go round and round, if he finds the audience's attention tending to waver. No piece has to mean anything specific; every piece has to provoke from its hearers a spontaneous vote of acceptance. This is what I call the "wow" technique.[10]

[9] A. B. Walkley's *Dramatic Criticism* (London: John Murray, 1903), p. 21.

[10] Virgil Thomson, "The Toscanini Case," in his *The Musical Scene* (New York: Alfred A. Knopf, Inc., 1945), pp. 57–61; see also the same article, New York *Herald Tribune*, May 17, 1942, p. IV–4.

Knowing his elementary psychology of attracting and holding the attention of others, this "wow" type of director centers all his skill on sudden contrasts in timing and volume of utterance wherever the listener's attention might flag. His devices are unexpected retardations and quickenings, obvious juxtapositions, definite pianissimos and fortissimos, suspenseful pauses, a pace and a dynamic that cannot be ignored. He emphasizes design. In demanding of you, his actors, your full technical resources, this director is at the opposite pole from the one who asks only for truth to nature.

This type of director is very conscious of the play's form; he knows its structure, its shape. He senses that in every script—beneath the plot, the scenes, and the situations—there is an abstract pattern. He studies "the layout of a play as if it were a musical composition." Just as Toscanini abstracts the essential outline of a score, this director abstracts the essential outline of a script. The whole accent is on structure. Unity, coherence, and emphasis are the qualities that must be brought out. Attention is only infrequently given to ornamentation, to the details contributory to the expression of an idea, to texture. The play must be delivered to its audience only in broadly effective strokes. Sometimes it does not seem to matter what the audience centers its attention on so long as it is attentive. The play must get across, it must arrive. All this brings back the old story of delivering eggs across the street. You can carry them there in a basket, or you can shoot them there from a cannon. By either method the eggs will arrive at their destination. A neglected point, however, is the condition of the eggs at the time of their arrival.

"This extraction of a play's formal essence," this "playing a piece for shape . . . gives (if the piece has any shape at all) the most exciting effect that can be produced. It is the same procedure as that of directing a melodrama on the stage, character and dialogue being kept at all times subsidiary to the effects of pure theatre, to the building up in the audience of a state of intense anxiety that is relieved only at the end of the last act." It is a method of directing that is frankly theatrical. This is its only virtue. However, any kind of oral directing that sacrifices content for an emphasis on form cannot be the highest type of directing, because it frequently sacrifices the *quality* of the thing the playwright is trying to say.

The trouble with this "wow" kind of directing is that it has standardized a basic technique that

. . . is applicable to any piece in the world, whether one understands its spirit or not . . . the radical simplification of interpretative problems that all this entails has changed orchestra conducting from a matter of culture and of its personal projection into something more like engineering. Young conductors don't bother much any more to feel music or to make their musicians feel it. They analyze it, concentrate in rehearsal on the essentials of its rhetoric and let the expressive details fall where they may, counting on each man's skill and everybody's instinctive musicianship to take care of these eventually. Poetry and nobility of expression are left for the last, to be put on as with an eye-dropper or laid on like icing, if there is time. All this is good, because it makes music less esoteric. It is crude because it makes understanding an incidental matter; but it is a useful procedure and one wholly characteristic of our land and century.[11]

This "wow" directing can be displaced only by directing that recognizes structure, not as something that can merely grasp and hold the attention of an audience, but as something that can hold the attention to what the playwright is saying.

5

The third and very rare kind of directing tries to discover and restate in theatre terms a "play's essential character and the style that expresses this character; to every element in the play the director means to give its special quality and intention."[12] More than aiming merely to be faithful to nature, or merely to hold and excite an audience, the third type of director seeks to interpret the play. He aims to get over to an audience the unity of the playwright's form and content.

Interpretation has been aptly called the reconstruction of the playwright's vision. The director as interpreter knows that in a script he must recognize not only the facts but the quality of the original experience. He knows that the playwright's responses to the truth of nature have been individualized, personalized. His premise is that "strictly literal reproduction is impossible, since the very process of translation into a medium . . . necessitates some modification, and since, moreover, some selection of subject-matter, angle of vision, and the like is unavoidable."[13] He is aware that different authors, using the same source material, using the same facts of experience, will always say a different thing or say the same thing differently because their attitudes toward the identical experiences will be different. This unique attitude toward experience on the part of each playwright is what the interpretative type of director tries to discover.

The search is not an easy one. No final script, as written, can give complete information to the interpreter. Certain intangibles cannot fully be expressed in words. The radio director has to analyze his script carefully, in all its component parts, retracing in so far as it is possible to do so the steps taken by the playwright in designing the script. On every page—in each scene, and situation, and character, and speech—he asks why the author did thus and so, or why he did it this way instead of another way. In so doing he can come close, in a slowly accumulating way, to finding the quality of the playwright's mind.

How does the better director go about interpreting a script? First, as G. Wilson Knight has found in studying Shakespeare's plays, "It is natural in analysis to pursue the steps of the tale in sequence, noticing the logic that connects them, regarding those essentials that Aristotle noted: the beginning, middle and end." This analysis is, of course, necessary, but every play script has something else to be studied, "a set of correspondences which relate to each other independently of the time-sequence" or story. "This I have called the play's 'atmosphere.'"[14] These correspondences have to do with the organization of the original experience into a medium, into something said in the form of a play. They have to do with the peculiar way in which the writer has put together his material in order best to convey to others his own personal attitude. They have to do with the form of the play that is always inextricably bound up with the quality of the content of the play.

An attitude toward experience, an idea, cannot be communicated without first being cast into an intelligible form. Form makes for clarity of expression via the medium. Form "is a question of harmony mostly,

[11] *Ibid.*

[12] Young, *Theatre Practice,* p. 129.

[13] Theodore Meyer Greene, *The Arts and the Art of Criticism* (Princeton: Princeton University Press, 1940), p. 418.

[14] Knight, *The Wheel of Fire,* p. 3.

of just proportions, significant emphasis, congruities and arresting contrasts."[15]

According to John Dewey, form can be defined as

> . . . the operation of forces that carry the experience of an event, object, scene, and situation to its own integral fulfillment . . . . The problems of discovering the nature of form is thus identical with that of discovering the means by which are effected the carrying forward of an experience to fulfillment. When we know these means, we know what form is.[16]

This most important prerequisite of the interpreter has been called "form-mindedness." Only the director who knows the structure or form of a play knows how to say to an audience the precise thing that he wants to say to them; he senses that the form in which a thing is said is part of its meaning.

The interpretative director must, therefore, see the story with its contrasts, reversals, confrontations, discoveries, expositions, subordinations, transitions, themes and variations, and the like as part of a *design*. He must find the pattern below the level of plot and character, the pattern that brings the idea into communicable meaning and existence. He must find how the separate elements are held together in such a way that a unified experience, a total meaning, will result. The interpretative director knows that the best playwright aims

> . . . at an organization of parts, however numerous and diverse or few or homogeneous, such that every part stands in evident relation to the whole and clearly contributes to the total effect. What we admire in the masters is their ability to create works in which so many artistic units and relations are fused into so organic an artistic whole, in which so many variations are introduced not for their own sake but as contributory factors to the final unity of the artistic effect.[17]

He knows that

> minor artists and imitators, apart from the significance of such ideas as they possess, are what they are because they are able to put the essential characteristic not through all the parts of a work, but only in this part or that.[18]

In other words, the interpretative director searches out each of the playwright's artistic motivations. He asks a "Why?" of the entire formal organization. Once he finds in the complex organization of a writer's script the contribution of each part or unit and its relationship to other parts, once he understands wherein it is impossible either to take away or to add anything without injury, he is on the right track toward knowing and feeling the quality of the unifying idea.

This director senses that the final value of the play as a whole

> . . . depends upon the reciprocal relations of its elements: each needs, responds to, demands every other element . . . . In short, the meaning of the whole is not something additional to the elements of the work of art, but their co-operative deed.[19]

He knows that

> . . . mutual adaptation of parts to one another in constituting a whole is the relation which, formally speaking, characterizes a work of art.[20]

He agrees with Dewey that

> . . . relation . . . fixes attention upon the way things bear upon one another, their clashes and unitings, the way they fulfill and frustrate, promote and retard, excite and inhibit one another. In art, as in nature and in life, relations are modes of interaction. They are pushes and pulls, they are contractions and expansions; they determine lightness and weight, rising and falling, harmony and discord.[21]

For the interpretative director relation is an affair of influence and mutual modification.

> Hence the relations which unite the ideas and elements to one another are artistically as important as are the units themselves.[22]

To come at this fundamental point in interpretative directing in another way: each and every different moment in a play can be true to nature and also attention-catching. Moment by moment each speech may be digested and justified. The intentions that move the various actors may be clear and honest, the transitions they effect may be convincing, and the situations may

[15] H. Granville-Barker, *On Dramatic Method* (London: Sidgwick & Jackson, Ltd., 1931), p. 158.

[16] Dewey, *Art as Experience*, p. 137.

[17] Greene, *op. cit.*, pp. 403–404.

[18] Young, *Glamour*, p. 78.

[19] DeWitt Parker, *The Analysis of Art* (New Haven: Yale University Press, 1926), pp. 34–35.

[20] Dewey, *op. cit.*, pp. 134–135.

[21] *Ibid.*, p. 134.

[22] Greene, *op. cit.*, p. 140.

be meaningful and exciting. Each moment may well make a theatrical statement. Yet no statement in a play is ever singular and lonely. Each statement is related in some way to all other statements. Each statement in one way or another contributes to the others, is a functional part of a design so carefully organized that it can thereby convey to others an attitude, an idea, an essence, a characteristic. What is more, this design is used deliberately or intuitively by the playwright as essential to the expression of what he has to reveal. This unifying attitude or idea connects all the parts; it connects all the moments each to each in serial progression. It is the theme, or unifying drive, or line of action that the better director must sense in order properly to interpret the script. Only when it is found can the author's *dramaturgy* reveal itself.

Dance critic John Martin is correct in saying,

> The essential basis of dramatic form is reducible to the following simple formula: the presentation of a leading theme, the introduction of a counter theme in direct opposition to it, a clash between the two, and the emergence of one of them as victor.[23]

In other words, every play as form is a movement toward something. The "movement toward something" is what the interpretative director always attempts to discover and to bring out in the wee bit of time at his disposal. When, in his directing, he centers his attention and efforts on "the movement toward," he works with the constantly progressive *changes in relationships.* When he centers his attention and efforts on the "something," he is properly concerned with *climax.* In every worth-while play everything moves toward the climax, which is "the concrete realization of the theme in terms of an event," according to John Howard Lawson.

> In practical playwriting this means that the climax is the point of reference by which the validity of every element of the structure can be determined. Every event, every element of the action, reacts upon, remolds, and revitalizes the climax itself.[24]

The interpretative director therefore constantly searches for the sometimes almost intangible *relationships* in the formal organization of a story that unify it into the expression of an individual attitude toward experience. He tries to make each part of the play basically true to nature, and each part attractive and communicable to an audience, but most important of all, he attempts to make each part contribute toward a total designed interpretation of reality.

[23] John Martin, *Introduction to the Dance* (New York: W. W. Norton & Company, Inc., 1939), pp. 24–25.

[24] John Howard Lawson, *Theory and Technique of Playwriting* (New York: G. P. Putnam's Sons, 1936), pp. 183–184.

6

One final and important point needs to be made about the close relationship between the director and the actor: the first must not make the second into a puppet. The wise director will always know "that the more he can use in his scheme of the play the actor's own stuff, the better." He will always want more of each individual actor's own quality and unique kind of creation in so far as these are compatible with the over-all expression of the idea in the play.

Perhaps it is more to the point to declare that no actor should ever lazily permit himself to be a mechanical robot in serving the director. Whatever the actor must try to achieve for the director in bringing the play into designed existence, he must do with understanding, and not with blind obedience. The actor always has the priceless responsibility of being himself in performance, and he must not forfeit that responsibility. He has the right to know what he is attempting to do, and why. He has the right also to do it in his own fresh and individual way.

Thus it may be said that the formal unification of the interpretation of a play, of an attitude toward experience, is the principal goal in directing. The best directing, however, is that which "brings the actor's own truth to the creation of the larger truth" of a designed idea.

SELECTED READINGS

Waldo Abbot's standard textbook, *Handbook of Broadcasting,* 2nd ed. (New York: McGraw-Hill Book Company, Inc., 1941) has a general chapter on "Directing the Radio Play," pp. 145–159.

Hoyland Bellinger examines television procedure in *Television Techniques* (New York: Harper & Brothers, 1947). Study especially Chap. II, "The Medium," pp. 11–17; Chap. IV, "Video Techniques," pp. 46–71; Chap. VII, "Directing and Producing," pp. 120–152; and Chap. VIII, "Producing the Play," pp. 153–179.

John S. Carlile has written a textbook, *Production and Direction of Radio Programs* (New York: Prentice-Hall, Inc., 1940), 397 pp.

Norman Corwin has some excellent practical production notes at the end of each of his plays in the three volumes.

Albert Crews' textbook, *Radio Production Directing* (New York: Houghton Mifflin Company, 1944), 550 pp., contains material on basic equipment, sound effects, and general production procedures as applied to radio talks, musical programs, news and special event programs, dramatic and variety programs, and the like. Read "Directing the Dramatic Program," pp. 187–209.

John Dewey's *Art as Experience* (New York: Minton Balch & Co., 1934) is worth reading for a point of view on form. See Chap. VI, "Substance and Form," pp. 106–133, Chap. VII, "The Natural History of Form," pp. 134–161.

Bonamy Dobree examines speech rhythms, mostly blank verse, in *Histriophone; A Dialogue on Dramatic Diction* (London: Leonard and Virginia Woolf, Hogarth Press, Ltd., 1925), 40 pp.

Edwin Duerr discusses "Stanislavski and the Idea," in *Studies in Speech and Drama in Honor of Alexander M. Drummond* (Ithaca: Cornell University Press, 1944), pp. 31–53.

Elsie Fogerty writes on *Rhythm* (London: Allen & Unwin, 1937), 245 pp.

Rosamond Gilder discusses "Style in Acting," *Theatre Arts Monthly,* XXI, No. 9 (September, 1937), 722–728.

Richard Hubbell, in *Television; Programming & Production* (New York: Murray Hill Books, Inc., 1945), discusses "The Nature of Television," pp. 11–53; "The Camera," pp. 57–82; and "Video Technique and Theory," pp. 85–146.

G. Wilson Knight is informative in his *The Wheel of Fire; Essays in Interpretation of Shakespeare's Sombre Tragedies* (London: Oxford University Press, 1930). See Chap. I, "On the Principles of Shakespeare Interpretation," pp. 1–18. In his *The Imperial Theme; Further Interpretations of Shakespeare's Tragedies Including the Roman Plays* (London: Oxford Press, 1931), read Chap. I, "On Imaginative Interpretation," pp. 1–31.

Arch Oboler includes some pointed "Notes on Acting and Production," in *This Freedom; Thirteen New Radio Plays* (New York: Random House, Inc., 1942), pp. xiii–xxv.

Constance Welch explains "Some Experimental Work in Speech Rhythm." *Quarterly Journal of Speech,* XI, No. 2 (June, 1925), 247–252.

Stark Young has written two important articles: Chap. X, "The Director," in his *The Theatre* (New York: Doubleday & Company, Inc., 1927), pp. 121–138; and Chap. VII, "The Art of Directing," in his *Theatre Practice* (New York: Charles Scribner's Sons, 1926), pp. 127–155). The same article is included, in his *Glamour; Essays in the Art of the Theatre* (New York: Charles Scribner's Sons, 1925), pp. 155–182.

But more important, for an understanding of ideas in art, is his essay, "Seeing the Point," in the latter volume, pp. 69–87.

B. E. Zakhava discusses some first-rate "Principles of Direction," as translated by Rose Siegel, in *Theatre Workshop* I, No. 3 (April–July, 1937), 43–56; and in I, No. 4 (September–October, 1937), 14–33. Both articles are included in *Acting; A Handbook of the Stanislavski Method,* edited by Toby Cole (New York: Lear Publishers, Inc., 1947), pp. 182–217.

EXERCISES

A. STRUCTURE OF SPEECHES

A student actor can begin to sense the structure of a play by examining the arrangement of his speeches. For a beginning he might note that, because of the highly condensed nature of every play, a large proportion of the speeches "look two ways." In other words, the first part is usually a response to the partner's thought; the remainder of the speech often takes up a new thought and thus quickly moves the dialogue and the play forward. Especially in sight reading should the young actor be constantly on the lookout for this type of change in thought. Find the forward movement in the following selections.

1.

ELAINE: I understand so well what he's going through. Life has treated me wretchedly, too. And tied to that woman! She goes out of her way to make Walter feel small and ashamed.

DONALD: He wouldn't have to feel that way if you were here, Elaine. And it's only for such a few days. Surely, for his sake you can put up with it for that long.

2.

SECRETARY: Yes, there were several calls on the Towne case. And your wife and Johnny also called.

BOSS: Yes? What did my wife want?

SECRETARY: She wanted you to stop at the butcher's.

BOSS: What for?

SECRETARY: Wouldn't it be meat, Mr. Chapel? I couldn't quite understand Johnny's call though. I got the impression he wanted to know what muskrats like.

3.

SALLY: You're going to San Francisco? When did you decide?

RAY: It was decided for me. Mr. Murchins said so. You didn't really think I'd go without saying goodbye, did you?

4.

SOLDIER: You have harmed only the body of my country. Her spirit still rises above the ruins of her cities. She does not know defeat — but you will know defeat!

GENERAL: You ghosts cannot frighten me! Why do you return to earth this way? On another peace mission?

5.

GIRL 1: He doesn't care for me one little bit.

GIRL 2: Oh, yes, he does. I'm sure he does.

GIRL 1: No, he doesn't. I can tell. And what did the paper mean this morning by saying he's going to leave town?

6.

HE: Was that all you wanted to know?

SHE: Yes, dear, that's all. Now run along and get your things on. I'll see who's at the door.

7.

DRISCOLL: Words are harmless things, Miss Parks.

PARKS: But it isn't the words, Captain Driscoll. It's the intentions behind them. I need your help desperately!

8. THE PHILADELPHIA STORY*

GEORGE: I suppose I ought to object to this twosome?

DEXTER: That would be most objectionable. Well, any time either of you wants more advice, you'll find I have a most understanding ear. Goodbye.

9. ALL MY SONS†

ANN: Then what's wrong? You've got to tell me . . . Even in your letters there was something ashamed.

CHRIS: Yes, I guess I've been ashamed. I — I don't know how to start to tell you. It's mixed up with so many other things. It goes so far back.

10. THE PIRATE‡

SERAFIN: I cannot believe destiny would be so perverse — to give me the vision and then to snatch it away.

MANUELA: Destiny is often perverse. It is even malicious. You live by your wits. I am a housewife. I love routine. I couldn't possibly live as you do.

SERAFIN: Can it be, Manuela, that you want to settle down? Very well.

MANUELA: I can't imagine you settled down. Keep to the life you really love. We're not for each other.

* From *The Philadelphia Story*, by Philip Barry. Copyright, 1939, 1940, by Philip Barry and Ellen S. Barry; by permission of Coward-McCann, Inc.

† By Arthur Miller.

‡ From *The Pirate*, by S. N. Behrman, by courtesy of Random House, Inc.

B. SCENE OR PLAY STRUCTURE

Find and bring to class scenes that depend to some extent for their theatrical effectiveness on such technical matters as change of beat, climax, contrast, exposition, pace, picking up cues, pointing a line, reversals, rhythm, subordination, style, and topping.

C. DIRECTION

What usually happens when the actor, having had his script only for an hour, reads his scene one way when the director, having carefully studied the entire script for many more hours, attempts to get the actor to play the scene in another way? A battle of egos—stalemate—tension.

Almost always the cause of such ever-recurring flare-ups is the fact that the actor has his eyes on only his own role, while the director has his ears on that particular character's—or that scene's—function in the over-all design of the play. The actor and the director are often looking at the same thing from different points of view.

In all such situations the actor should promptly try to understand what the director wants done with the scene, or the reading, and then try to do it to the best of his ability (*not* as some actors are inclined to do—in the worst way possible in order to prove the director wrong!).

If, finally, the actor cannot effectively do what is asked of him—but *not* merely because he does not feel natural doing it—an adjustment will have to be effected.

In radio and television time is always short; moreover, if the actor believes "the play's the thing," he will know that the director's requests are more important than any one actor's "feeling natural." He must realize that the director should know the play, should know what he wants.

In short, young actors need to learn how to play any character and any scene in many different ways, in accordance with various over-all designs, in ways removed from their customary way of playing "naturally," in ways that they have perhaps never even dimly realized the role or the scene could be played. They must be endlessly and imaginatively flexible. No actor can come up with the one right way, the one only way, of reading a speech or a scene.

For each of the following exercises—plus many of the other exercise scenes in this book—the instructor should assign a cast and at least one additional director, perhaps two.

The directors should be assigned several days in advance of the practice rehearsal so that they will have an opportunity to study the script for all the values contained in it. The cast, however, should not be assigned until just before the scene is to be read.

On the day the scene is to be directed, the instructor should let the cast first read the exercise with a minimum of comment from the director. After this first reading he should let the director give the instructions. Then the cast will read again, perhaps at the microphone, and attempt to carry out the director's ideas.

Next the second director should direct the same scene with the same cast.

Then the third director, or someone in the class with a different idea of how the scene should be played, should take over.

The cast should always try to deliver what each of these directors wants, discussing with him only the points that they honestly believe are completely in the wrong.

Some time limit should be set for the completion of each of these rehearsals in order constantly to impress on the student that nowadays both the cast and the director are, unfortunately, always working against the clock.

1. A WOMAN'S LIFE, #2085*

CAROL: (OFF) Warren! Oh, Warren!

SCOTT: (TURNING) Yes? Oh, Carol. Hello . . . or rather hello again.

MICHAEL: (COMING ON) Where have you been? I thought you were going right home.

SCOTT: I was. I did. And I am. How about coming in with me?

CAROL: Not now, Warren. It's too late. What do you mean?

SCOTT: Nothing except that . . . Well, things happened. They do, you know — wonderful, wonderful things — when we least expect them. And . . . Can't you come in — for just a few minutes? There's something I want to tell you.

MICHAEL: It really is too late, Warren. We stayed on at Gus's, talking, after you left and . . . Can't you tell us here?

SCOTT: Yes, I could. And, in a way, it's fitting. It's something I want the whole world to know. The thing is . . . Well, now I do have something to celebrate — something much more important than the contract for the hospital at Stockton.

CAROL: Don't keep us in suspense, Warren. Tell us.

SCOTT: Perhaps it won't surprise you . . . though I still can't believe it myself. And I can't possibly expect you to get as excited about it as I am . . . but . . . Well, Madeline and I are going to get married.

MICHAEL: (INCREDULOUS) What?

CAROL: Warren!

SCOTT: I told you I didn't believe it myself . . . but, unless I'm sleepwalking this very minute, it's true.

MICHAEL: But . . . but how did it happen? When?

SCOTT: Just a few minutes ago. I don't know whether you knew — even suspected — but I've been in love with her for some time now. Probably from the first day I met her. I asked her to marry me early this evening. She wouldn't — couldn't — give me an answer. Then, after I left you, she phoned me and . . . Well, she finally said yes.

* By Julian Funt. Reproduced through the courtesy of the author.

CAROL: Warren, that's the most exciting, most wonderful . . . It's the bride who's supposed to be kissed, but —

(SHE KISSES HIM)

SCOTT: (MOVED) Carol . . .

MICHAEL: Put it there, Warren. I won't wish you all the luck in the world. It seems to me you've got it already. But I can congratulate you.

SCOTT: Thank you, Michael. Thank you both. I . . . I'm getting all choked up again . . . the way I did with . . . Would it embarrass you to see me weep?

CAROL: No, Warren.

SCOTT: I'm not going to — really. It's just that . . . Well, it's all so wonderful that it frightens me a little. First the contract. Then Madeline. And now meeting you — the two people I wanted to tell more than anyone in the world.

CAROL: Things do change, Warren. And always for the better. Have you set a date yet?

SCOTT: No. Nothing. We just know that it's going to be — that it's got to be!

2. A STUDY IN BITTERNESS*

(MUSIC: SOFT AND GENTLE. LET IT FLOW FOR A FEW BARS, THEN UNDER)

MA: (QUIETLY) Hello, Joey.

JOE: Hello, Ma.

MA: (BREAKING A LITTLE) Joey, darling . . . Joe . . .

JOE: Okay, Ma . . . I'm okay. Come on, lift your face up. Let me look at you. You got skinny, Ma. You look like a chorus girl.

MA: You all right, Joey? You feel all right? You look tired.

JOE: What are you talking about? I've just been touring the continent. I'm just back from a vacation in sunny Italy, the healthiest climate in the world. It says so in the guide books.

MA: Joey . . .

JOE: Come on, sweetheart, let's go home.

(MUSIC: UP TO TIE-OFF THE SCENE, AND OUT)

JOE: (SATISFIED GRUNT) Ah, that corn bread! Terrific! Once O'Keefe got some

* By Millard Lampell. Reprinted with the permission of the publishers, Julian Messner, Inc.

meal from an Italian farmer, and I tried to make some of this stuff. It was terrible.

MA: Is that the boy you wrote about?

JOE: Yeah, Jocko. He got knocked off his last mission. He always did have lousy timing. (PAUSE) What's the matter?

MA: He's dead. How can you talk that way about somebody who's dead?

JOE: (LITTLE LAUGH) I don't know. You just . . . Look, Ma, forget it. Pass the corn bread.

(MUSIC: A CHORD, AND TREMOLO SUSPENDED UNDER)

JOE: Oh, this bed, this wonderful bed! Back in Italy one time I laid down for a snooze under a parked half-track, and along comes one of those stinking 88's . . .

MA: Not now, Joey. Tomorrow's Sunday. I won't even go to church. I'll just stay home and we can talk all day.

JOE: Okay. Yeah, sure. Tomorrow.

(MUSIC: FINAL CHORD, DIMINISHING SLOWLY AND OUT)

JOE: Morning, Ma.

MA: Did you sleep all right, Joey?

JOE: Not so good. Takes a little time to get used to a bed again. Looks like rain, huh? Good day to just loaf around.

MA: Joey, I completely forgot. This afternoon I have to go out.

JOE: Why? What's the matter?

MA: I just completely forgot. It's my turn to take a cake to the boys.

JOE: To do what?

MA: Some of the women in the neighborhood . . . we've been taking turns baking cakes for the boys out at the camp, the German prisoners of war. They seem so lonely out there.

JOE: (TIGHT) You . . . bake cakes for them . . . ?

MA: I kept thinking how it would be if you were in a prison camp.

JOE: (SLOWLY) Me and them, huh?

MA: It only takes a couple of hours. I'll drive out and come right back.

JOE: Yeah.

MA: You can walk around and take a look at the neighborhood again.

JOE: (HARD) Yeah, sure.

MA: Is anything wrong, Joey?

JOE: No, nothing's wrong. You better go.

("In the part of Joe . . . it is important to give the character a maturity and dignity. He isn't wistful and he isn't naïve. And the bitterness is no quick, casual thing . . . . The bitterness grows in spite of Joe, and he knows it and worries about it."

"Joe's mother isn't a stereotype. She's warm and sincere toward her son. She just doesn't know anything about the war, that's all. Believe me, there are thousands like her."—M.L.)

3. MY FRIEND IRMA*

AL: Hiya, Richard.

RICHARD: (COMING ON) Hello. I hope this is important, Al. You took me away from a very big conference. What is it?

AL: It's important enough, Richard. Sit down. I want to talk to you like a father.

IRMA: Oh, Al, we're not even married yet!

RICHARD: (EXCITED) What's all this about?

AL: Now don't get excited, Richard. How old are you?

RICHARD: What difference does it make?

AL: It's very important.

RICHARD: All right — I'm thirty-two.

AL: When were you thirty-two?

RICHARD: October.

IRMA: October? Al was thirty-two in April. So he was around longer than you.

RICHARD: So what?

AL: Richard, let me put it to you this way. All through the ages man has never been able to figure out woman. Man, as you know, has always been honest, trustworthy, and clear-headed. That's why woman is known as the opposite sex.

IRMA: Do you happen to know where Jane is at this very moment?

RICHARD: Sure. She's out with Mr. Robert Girard, a big prospective client of mine, and I'm meeting them later at El Morocco.

IRMA: You mean you know about it?

* By Cy Howard and Parke Levy. Reproduced through the courtesy of the authors.

RICHARD: Know about it? I arranged the whole thing. This is one of the most important deals of my whole career. Say, you two haven't been up to anything, have you? (PAUSE) Why are you breathing so heavily?

AL: Adenoids.

RICHARD: Adenoids!?

AL: Yes. Had 'em taken out when I was a kid and I miss 'em.

RICHARD: I've got a feeling something's wrong. Irma, you're staring at me as if you're out of your mind.

IRMA: Yes, I had it taken out when I was a kid and I miss it.

RICHARD: Well, from the looks of the two of you I know something's wrong. And I'm going to find out what it is!

4. DAVID HARDING, COUNTER-SPY, #160*

(EVERY WORD OF MR. AND MRS. BROWN MUST BE VERY DISTINCT . . . BUT THEY MUST GIVE US A FLAVOR OF SITTING IN A CROWD AND WATCHING THINGS HAPPENING)

(GENERAL HUBBUB OF GREAT CROWD)

MR. B: I hear this man Winters is quite a lecturer, Mona.

MRS. B: Yes, James. He's late in beginning.

MR. B: Look — that isn't —

MRS. B: Why, that must be him coming out on the stage.

(CROWD QUIETS DURING NEXT TWO LINES)

MR. B: Um . . . I wonder what's going on, Mona?

MRS. B: Shush. He's going to speak.

HARDING: (NOTE — ALL OF HARDING'S LINE OFF — GREAT PROJECTION AND ECHO) All doors to this auditorium are now to be closed . . . and to be guarded by United States government men. These are government orders.

(MURMUR IN CROWD . . . LOW BUT GREAT IN SIZE)

MRS. B: Why, James . . . !

MR. B: I can't understand it, Mona.

MRS. B: I thought Harry Winters was going to lecture?

MR. B: Ssh! The man's going to speak again.

(CROWD MURMUR QUIETS)

* Written by Phillips H. Lord.

HARDING: I would like to introduce myself — David Harding, Chief of the United States Counter-Spies.

(GREAT APPLAUSE)

This is a most unusual situation . . . and I'll have to ask you all to co-operate. If any disobey orders, it will be necessary to use force.

(REACTION)

HARDING: This lecture as announced tonight — was a false announcement . . . made in the interest of national security. We have reason to believe that Harry Winters — who is really an enemy agent and murderer — did not dare leave Philadelphia after the murder day before yesterday. This announcement of a lecture tonight was to trap him . . . for we felt quite positive that Winters, being in Philadelphia, would attend. We sincerely hope he is here in the hall tonight.

(OUTBURST OF EMOTION WITH MUCH APPLAUSE — TRICKLING OFF)

MRS. B: (EXCITED) James . . . did you ever hear of such a thing!

MR. B: (SARCASTIC) It's exciting, isn't it, Mona? To think that man Winters might be in this hall.

MRS. B: Do you suppose he'll shoot?

MR. B: I guess everyone's just as excited as we are.

5. PORTIA FACES LIFE, #1508*

KATHIE: (SOFTLY, WITH A HINT OF WISTFULNESS) She's very pretty.

DR. BYRON: (HE WASN'T LISTENING) What did you say, Kathie?

KATHIE: How is her pulse now?

DR. BYRON: It's getting stronger. She should regain consciousness in a very few minutes. But what did you say to me a second ago?

KATHIE: Just that . . . Miss Arden . . . She's lovely.

BYRON: Oh, yes . . . yes . . . very.

KATHIE: Don't you think so?

BYRON: Hmmm . . . as a type, yes. But I personally don't care for types. To me a woman must be individual to be beautiful.

KATHIE: But I thought — (SHE STOPS EMBARRASSED A LITTLE) What I mean is . . . She said you were such old, dear friends . . .

* By Mona Kent. Reproduced through the courtesy of the author and General Foods Corporation.

BYRON: (HE CHUCKLES) We are, but just friends. That's how it's always been.

KATHIE: Oh. Well, after all . . . it's really none of my business, Norman.

BYRON: Why isn't it?

KATHIE: What you've done with your life in the past — what right have I to ask questions about it?

BYRON: What I do with my life in the future is much more important . . . to both of us, Kathie.

(PAUSE)

KATHIE: What do you think, Norman? Is she regaining consciousness?

BYRON: Her breathing's getting deeper, and her color's much better.

KATHIE: What's the matter with her?

BYRON: The matter?

KATHIE: I mean . . . what's wrong? What causes these fainting spells?

BYRON: Shock more than anything.

KATHIE: Shock, Norman?

BYRON: She's a very shy, extremely sensitive person, and I don't think she ever completely got over the shock of Peter Townsend's suicide.

KATHIE: Was she in love with him?

BYRON: I don't think there'll ever be anyone for Elaine but Peter Townsend.

6. THE ALDRICH FAMILY, #405*

(DOORBELL RINGS OFF)

MRS. ALDRICH: Oh, my goodness! There's Miss Trevor. Sam, you'll have to answer it.

MR. ALDRICH: I? But, Alice, what will I say to her?

MRS. ALDRICH: (FADING) Say anything, Sam, but answer the door!

MR. ALDRICH: (CALLING) What's her name again?

MRS. ALDRICH: (OFF) Miss Trevor!

(DOORBELL COMES ON . . . DOOR OPENS ON)

MR. ALDRICH: Oh! (POLITELY) Yes?

MISS TREVOR: How do you do.

MR. ALDRICH: How do you do.

* By Patricia Joudry and Del Dinsdale, based on characters created by Clifford Goldsmith. Reproduced through the courtesy of the authors and Clifford Goldsmith.

MISS TREVOR: I've been invited for dinner. I'm Ruth Trevor.

MR. ALDRICH: You're Miss Trevor? Why, you don't look like a — I mean — Come in! Come in, Miss Trevor!

MISS TREVOR: Thank you.

(DOOR CLOSES ON)

MR. ALDRICH: (BEAMING) Well! Well, well! Here — let me take your coat, Miss Trevor!

MISS TREVOR: Certainly. Are you Mr. Aldrich?

MR. ALDRICH: Yes.

MISS TREVOR: You don't look old enough to have a son Henry's age.

MR. ALDRICH: Well, that's very — That's — No? — Did I tell you how glad we are you could come, Miss Trevor?

MRS. ALDRICH: (COMING ON) Miss Trevor, how do you do. I'm Mrs. Aldrich.

MISS TREVOR: How do you do, Mrs. Aldrich. It was so nice of you to invite me.

MR. ALDRICH: Not at all! When Henry told us about you, I said to Mrs. Aldrich, "We must invite Miss Trevor up to dinner!"

MRS. ALDRICH: What?

MR. ALDRICH: I said, "Why not tonight! Let's give Miss Trevor a real welcome to Centerville!"

MRS. ALDRICH: Why, Sam!

MR. ALDRICH: Let's all go in the living-room and sit down, Miss Trevor, ("Thank you") and you can tell us all about yourself. I understand you teach History, don't you? ("Why, yes . . .") Ah, History! When I was in Princeton — not that I was an honor student mind you, but —

7. MYSTERY THEATRE: *CHECK NUMBER B 131**

(CAR DOOR OPENS AND SLAMS SHUT: CAR STARTS)

DAN: Thanks. Thanks a lot for the lift.

ALICE: Going far?

DAN: To New York. You going that far?

ALICE: No, I'm not. Sorry. But I can take you twenty miles on your way.

DAN: Every little bit helps.

* By George and Gertrude Fass. Reproduced through the courtesy of the authors.

ALICE: Yes, I guess it does.

DAN: You're not scared? Picking up a guy like me? I'm not dressed so well.

ALICE: Should I be scared?

DAN: Oh, no.

ALICE: Well, I'm not. As a matter of fact, I didn't look at your clothes when I stopped for you. I looked at your face.

DAN: Looked honest, huh?

ALICE: Not only that . . .

DAN: (UNDERSTANDING) Oh. Say, I sure wish you were going to New York. We could have a great time there.

ALICE: Could we?

DAN: You may think because I'm dressed like a tramp I am a tramp. Broke. But that's where you're wrong. I've got lots of money waiting for me. I'll have it just as soon as I get to the city. Yep, I've got a stake there waiting for me . . . a big stake.

ALICE: That's nice. Someone die and leave you a fortune?

DAN: You might say that. Oh, you might say that. (LAUGHS)

ALICE: Then, I'm sorry I'm not going to New York. I'm on my way to my country place. I've got a little summer house near Gloucester.

DAN: Oh. You . . . staying there . . . all alone?

ALICE: Most of the time.

DAN: Isn't it . . . lonely?

ALICE: Yes, it might be . . . a bit lonely.

DAN: Well, look — I don't have to get to New York today. I could get in tomorrow . . . or the day after.

ALICE: Are you angling for an invitation?

DAN: I just thought . . . That is, if you wanted company . . . .

ALICE: I don't know. I guess you could come to lunch . . . and stay for a swim maybe.

DAN: I could? Say, that's swell!

8. MYSTERY THEATRE: *THE BETRAYER**

ALICE: (TALKING INCESSANTLY) Albert, I think our rooms are <u>lovely!</u> And this dear old place, Chinn House — why, it's absolutely charming! Don't you think so, Albert? And I'm so glad that long trip is over with. I hate long auto tri ——

WINSTON: (INTERRUPTING) Alice, please!

ALICE: Oh, my poor dear, I'm sorry! Your nerves must be on edge. I think it was that long drive . . . A long drive can do that, you —

WINSTON: (INTERRUPTING) Alice, in Heaven's name, stop that prattle!

ALICE: Albert!

WINSTON: I'm sorry. I'm just tired . . . and this rotten weather doesn't help any. Why don't we go downstairs for a drink?

ALICE: Oh, that's a splendid idea! A night like this calls for something warm inside. (FADING) Perhaps a hot rum toddy might do the trick. Or, on the other hand, if you don't like toddies . . .

(<u>MUSIC:</u> <u>IN</u> <u>TO</u> <u>WASH</u> <u>OUT</u> <u>ALICE</u> <u>. . . .</u> <u>TIME</u> <u>PASSAGE</u>)

ALICE: (COMING ON) And, of course, as I've always told father, there's nothing like a week in the country. Fresh air is so good for your health. Don't you think so, Albert? Exhilarates you, I mean. And then, of course —

WINSTON: (INTERRUPTING) Alice, what do you say we leave tonight and go back to London?

ALICE: But, Albert, we've only been here three days!

WINSTON: Oh? Somehow I got the idea it had been much longer than that.

ALICE: Really? Did you now, Albert? Now isn't that strange! Because, after all, we came on a Tuesday and this is Thursday; so Tuesday, Wednesday, and Thursday are three days, aren't they, Albert? And furthermore —

WINSTON: (ALMOST SHOUTING) Alice, please!

(<u>MUSIC</u>: <u>UP</u> <u>AND</u> <u>DOWN</u> <u>AND</u> <u>INTO</u>)

(CAR MOTOR ROARS . . . CARRY IN BG)

ALICE: This is such a beastly night for driving. All this rain! I think we'd have been better off to have stayed at Chinn House until morning. Don't you think so, Albert? (FADING) Don't you think it would have been better if we had stayed at Chinn . . .

* By Robert J. Mitchell and Gene Levitt. Reproduced through the courtesy of the authors.

(CAR MOTOR RISES OMINOUSLY TO DROWN OUT ALICE)

(MUSIC: UP WITH CAR MOTOR . . . THEN CROSSFADE WITH)

(CAR MOTOR IN AT HIGHER SPEED NOW . . . CARRY IN BG)

ALICE: I really don't think you should drive so fast, do you, Albert? I mean you're an excellent driver and all that, but don't you think it's dangerous, Albert? (FADING) I mean with the rain and the fog the road is so slippery that . . .

(MOTOR ROARS STILL HIGHER)

(MUSIC: UP MORE . . . CARRY IN BG AND BUILD UNDER FOLLOWING)

ALICE: Albert, please . . . don't drive so fast . . . Please . . . !

(TIRES SCREECH INTO SKID)

ALICE: Albert! Look out . . . the bridge! (TERROR) Albert! Look out!! (SCREAM)

(GREAT RIPPING CRASH)

(MUSIC: SMASH . . . DOWN TO SOMBER BRIDGE)

Because of the accident Alice Winston becomes another person, a Mrs. Joan Scott. Apparently she has forgotten everything about her past. She is no longer a young chatterbox, but a mature, rather dignified lady. But Winston has criminal reasons for pretending to everyone that his wife was truly killed and that Alice is not Alice but Mrs. Scott. He cannot let the truth come out.

The following scene takes place several months later in New York City.

(CAR MOTOR RUNNING STEADILY . . . HOLD IN BG . . . RAIN)

WINSTON: Well, Mrs. Scott, did you enjoy the performance?

ALICE: Yes, it was very good. Did you like it?

WINSTON: I thought it splendid. Of course, I can't go along with Carter's rabid praise. As a matter of fact, I find him something of a bore. That's why I preferred not joining them afterwards. I hope you didn't mind?

ALICE: No, not at all. What with this rain and the excitement of the evening I'd just as soon be driving home.

WINSTON: The rain? Does it bother you, Mrs. Scott? I mean is there anything in particular about it that you find annoying?

ALICE: (VAGUELY) I don't know . . . It's strange . . . hard to explain . . .

WINSTON: (STERNLY) Why is it strange, Mrs. Scott?

(CAR MOTOR UP FASTER . . . CONTINUE TO RISE IN BG)

ALICE: I can't say.

WINSTON: You mean you won't!

ALICE: Please, Mr. Winston, watch the road.

WINSTON: Never mind my driving, Mrs. Scott! Think about my question! Think, Mrs. Scott! Think about —

(MOTOR UP MORE . . . TIRES SCREECH IN SHORT SKID)

ALICE: Albert! Look out! The bridge! (SCREAM) Albert!!!

(CAR BRAKES TO STOP SHARPLY)

WINSTON: (PAUSE . . . DELIBERATE) What are you talking about, Mrs. Scott? (BEAT) There is no bridge!

(MUSIC: SMASH AND UP TO OMINOUS BRIDGE)

(KNOCK ON DOOR SLIGHTLY OFF)

ALICE: (CALLING) Come in.

(DOOR OPENS SLIGHTLY OFF)

WINSTON: (SLIGHTLY OFF) How do you feel this morning, Mrs. Scott?

(DOOR CLOSES)

ALICE: I don't know. I'm very uneasy — troubled.

WINSTON: (COMING ON) I'm worried about you too. Last night in the car you seemed to have had an hallucination. You were so terrified . . . spoke of a bridge . . .

ALICE: I know. I realize now it was something I dimly remember from my past.

WINSTON: Oh? (PAUSE) What's that in your hand, Mrs. Scott?

ALICE: This scratch pad?

WINSTON: Let me see it. It's covered with scribbling.

ALICE: I've been so nervous this morning. I guess I did it unconsciously.

WINSTON: Yes, I guess we all — (HE STOPS WITH A SHARP INTAKE OF BREATH)

ALICE: What is it?

WINSTON: These two words! Why did you write them down? Chinn House.

ALICE: I don't quite know. They have to do with the bridge and my past. It all seems to come to me, then escape me again. I know if I just concentrate I'll remember.

WINSTON: (HEAVILY) Yes, I guess you will remember. (DECISIVELY) Mrs. Scott, I'm going to help you. Sit down here.

(CHAIR SCRAPE)

Now close your eyes and concentrate.

ALICE: All right.

WINSTON: Keep your eyes closed. I've something here in my desk I want to show you. (FADING) It might help you. Keep your eyes closed. Keep concentrating . . .

(HE HAS GONE OFF, OPENING DESK DRAWER)

ALICE: (ON) Mr. Winston . . . Chinn House . . . it's coming back to me, I think. I was there . . . with a man . . . a honeymoon . . . Yes . . . !

WINSTON: (COMING ON) Don't open your eyes, Mrs. Scott. Go on. Keep talking.

ALICE: Yes, a honeymoon! Why, I do remember. I do! (THEN ECSTATICALLY AS THE CHATTER-BOX YOUNG CHARACTER) Oh, Albert! I remember! The wedding! Wasn't it a lovely ceremony! Just you and Bishop Randall and our very good friends. That's the way a marriage should be. Don't you think so, Albert?

(TREMENDOUS ROARING ECHO OF GUN GOING OFF)

ALICE: (GROANS . . . DYING) Albert . . .

(BODY FALLS)

9. THE SECOND MRS. BURTON, #443*

ANNOUNCER: Bill Sullivan is still confined to his bed, following a heart attack of several days ago. A small table has been pulled up to the side of his bed — and on the table a checker game is in slow progress. At Marion Sullivan's request Elizabeth Miller is "sitting" with him this afternoon — but try as she will she finds "entertaining" him too big a job for her.

ELIZABETH: It's your move again, Bill.

BILL: Um. Sorry. What time is it now? Five yet?

ELIZABETH: Five after. I just took one of your kings.

BILL: Um. So you did.

ELIZABETH: Are you tired, Bill? Do you want to stop playing?

BILL: Would you mind, Liz? You don't have to entertain me, you know. Wonder what's keeping Marion? I thought she'd be home by now.

ELIZABETH: I guess she'll be here pretty soon.

BILL: You don't have to wait, Liz. I'll be all right — if you want to go.

ELIZABETH: I don't want to go, Bill. I want to stay as long as you want me to.

* By Martha Alexander. Reproduced through the courtesy of the author.

BILL: You're a nice girl. You know something, Liz — death is about the most impersonal thing there is. You know that?

ELIZABETH: I haven't thought about it much — yet, Bill.

BILL: Well, I have. And I can tell you something else, too. I'm a failure, Liz. I've got money — a little "class" — I've got a lot of power in this town — but I'm a failure. You know why? Because nothing in this world matters but human relationships. That's all. Just human relationships. Nothing else is worth that. (SNAP FINGERS) And I haven't got a human relationship that's worth that either. If this ticker of mine had gone dead on me the other night — you want to know something? There wouldn't a been a single tear shed in this whole town.

ELIZABETH: (LOW) I would have cried, Bill.

BILL: Would you? Yeah — I believe you would have. That's good to know. You're a nice girl, Liz. I've always said that. You're a nice girl.

10. A CHILD IS BORN*

INNKEEPER: I do not understand it. They are gone.
They did not even look at me or pause
Though there's no other inn.
They follow the poor shepherds to the stable.

WIFE: They would not tarry with us — no, not one.

INNKEEPER: And yet —

WIFE: Peace, husband. You know well enough
Why none would tarry with us.
And so do I. I lay awhile in sleep
And a voice said to me, "Gloria, gloria,
Gloria in excelsis Deo.
The child is born, the child, the child is born!"
And yet I did not rise and go to him,
Though I had waited and expected long,
For I was jealous that my child should die
And her child live.
And so — I have my judgment. And it is just.

INNKEEPER: Dreams.

WIFE: Were they dreams, the shepherds and the kings?
Is it a dream, this glory that we feel
Streaming upon us — and yet not for us.

LEAH: Now, mistress, mistress, 'tis my fault not yours.
You told me to seek the strangers in the stable
And see they had all care but I — forgot.

SARAH: Kissing your soldier!

LEAH: Sarah!

SARAH: I am sorry, Leah.
My tongue's too sharp. Mistress, the fault was mine.
You told me also and I well remembered,
Yet did not go.

WIFE: Sarah.

SARAH: I did not go.
Brooding on mine own wrongs, I did not go.
It was my fault.

INNKEEPER: If there was any fault, wife, it was mine.
I did not wish to turn them from my door
And yet — I know I love the clink of money,
Love it too well, the good, sound, thumping coin,
Love it — oh, God, since I am speaking truth,
Better than wife or fire or chick or child,
Better than country, better than good fame,
Would sell my people for it in the street,
Oh, for a price — but sell them.
And there are many like me. And God pity us.

WIFE: God pity us indeed, for we are human,
And do not always see
The vision when it comes, the shining change,
Or, if we see it, do not follow it,
Because it is too hard, too strange, too new.
Too unbelievable, too difficult,
Warring too much with common, easy ways,

And now I know this, standing in this light,
Who have been half alive these many years,
Brooding on my own sorrow, my own pain,
Saying, "I am a barren bough. Expect
Nor fruit nor blossom from a barren bough."
Life is not lost by dying! Life is lost
Minute by minute, day by dragging day,
In all the thousand, small, uncaring ways,
The smooth appeasing compromises of time,
Which are King Herod and King Herod's men,
Always and always. Life can be
Lost without vision but not lost by death,
Lost by not caring, willing, going on
Beyond the ragged edge of fortitude
To something more — something no man has seen.
You who love money, you who love yourself,
You who love bitterness, and I, who loved
And lost and thought I could not love again,
And all the people of this little town,
Rise up! The loves we had were not enough.
Something is loosed to change the shaken world,
And with it we must change.

(THE VOICE OF DISMAS, THE THIEF, BREAKING IN . . . A RATHER QUIZZICAL, INDEPENDENT VOICE)

DISMAS: Now that's well said!

INNKEEPER: Who speaks there? Who are you?

DISMAS: Who? Oh, my name is Dismas. I'm a thief.
You know — the starved, flea-bitten sort of boy
Who haunts dark alleyways in any town,
Sleeps on a fruit sack, runs from the police,
Begs what he can and — borrows what he must.
That's me!

INNKEEPER: How did you get here?

DISMAS: By the door, innkeeper,

The cellar door. The lock upon it's old.
I could pick locks like that when I was five.

INNKEEPER: What have you taken?

DISMAS: Nothing.
I tried the stable first — and then your cellar,
Slipped in, crept up, rolled underneath a bench,
While all your honest backs were turned — and then —

WIFE: And then?

DISMAS: Well — something happened. I don't know what.
I didn't see your shepherds or your kings,
But, in the stable, I did see the child,
Just through a crack in the boards — one moment's space.
That's all I can tell you.
(PASSIONATELY) Is he for me as well? Is he for me?

WIFE: For you as well.

DISMAS: Is he for all of us?
There are so many of us, worthy mistress,
Beggars who show their sores and ask for alms,
Women who cough out their lungs in the cold,
Slaves — oh, I've been one! — thieves and runagates
Who knife each other for a bite of bread,
Having no other way to get the bread,
— The vast sea of the wretched and the poor,
Whose murmur comes so faintly to your ears
In this fine country.
Has he come to all of us
Or just to you?

WIFE: To every man alive.

DISMAS: I wish I could believe.

SARAH: (SCORNFULLY) And, if you did,
No doubt you'd give up thieving!

DISMAS: Gently, lady, gently.
Thieving's my trade — the only trade I know.
But if it were true,

If he had really come to all of us —
I say, to all of us —
Then, honest man or thief,
I'd hang upon a cross for him!
(A SHOCKED PAUSE. THE OTHERS MUTTER)
Would _you_?
(ANOTHER PAUSE)
I see that I've said something you don't like,
Something uncouth and bold and terrifying,
And yet, I'll tell you this:
It won't be till each one of us is willing,
Not you, not me, but every one of us,
To hang upon a cross for every man
Who suffers, starves and dies,
Fight his sore battles as they were our own,
And help him from the darkness and the mire,
That there will be no crosses and no tyrants,
No Herods and no slaves.
(ANOTHER PAUSE)
Well, it was pleasant, thinking things might be so.
And so I'll say farewell. I've taken nothing.
And he was a fair child to look on.

WIFE: Wait!

DISMAS: Why? What is it you see there by the window?

WIFE: The dawn, the common day.
The shepherds and the kings have gone away.
The great angelic visitors are gone.
He is alone. He must not be alone.

INNKEEPER: I do not understand you, wife.

DISMAS: Nor I.

WIFE: Do you not see, because I see at last?
Dismas, the thief, is right.
He comes to all of us or comes to none.
Not to my heart in joyous recompense

For what I've lost — not to your heart or yours,
But to the ignorant heart of all the world,
So slow to alter, so confused with pain.
Do you not see he must not be alone?

INNKEEPER: I think that I begin to see. And yet —

WIFE: We are the earth his word must sow like wheat
And, if it finds no earth, it cannot grow.
We are his earth, the mortal and the dying,
Led by no star — the sullen and the slut,
The thief, the selfish man, the barren woman,
Who have betrayed him once and will betray him,
Forget his words, be great a moment's space
Under the strokes of chance,
And then sink back into our small affairs.
And yet, unless _we_ go, his message fails.

LEAH: Will he bring peace, will he bring brotherhood?

WIFE: He would bring peace, he would bring brotherhood
And yet he will be mocked in the street.

SARAH: Will he slay King Herod
And rule us all?

WIFE: He will not slay King Herod. He will die.
There will be other Herods, other tyrants,
Great wars and ceaseless struggles to be free,
Not always won.

INNKEEPER: These are sad tidings of him.

WIFE: No, no — they are glad tidings of great joy,
Because he brings man's freedom in his hands,
Not as a coin that may be spent or lost
But as a living fire within the heart,
Never quite quenched — because he brings to all,
The thought, the wish, the dream of brotherhood,
Never and never to be wholly lost,
The water and the bread of the oppressed,
The stay and succor of the resolute,

The harness of the valiant and the brave,
The new word that has changed the shaken world.
And, though he die, his word will grow like wheat
And every time a child is born,
In pain and love and freedom hardly won,
Born and gone forth to help and aid mankind,
There will be women with a right to say
"Gloria, gloria in excelsis Deo!
A child is born!"
Come, let us go. What can we bring him?
What mortal gifts?

LEAH: (SHYLY) I have a ribbon. It's my prettiest.
It is not much, but — he might play with it.

SARAH: I have a little bell my father gave me.
It used to make me merry. I have kept it.
I — He may have it.

DISMAS: My pocket's empty and my rags are bare.
But I can sing to him. That's what I'll do
And — if he needs a thief to die for him —

INNKEEPER: I would give all my gold.
I will give my heart.

WIFE: And I my faith through all the years and years,
Though I forget, though I am led astray,
Though after this I never see his face,
I will give all my faith.
Come, let us go,
We, the poor earth, but we, the faithful, earth,
Not yet the joyful, not yet the triumphant,
But faithful, faithful, through the mortal years!
Come!

PLAYS AND RECORDINGS

PLAYS

The following list of easily available published radio plays is recommended for classroom productions.

A. SOLO MAN

1. *The Steel Worker,* by Arch Oboler, in Max Wylie (ed.), *Best Broadcasts of 1938–39.* New York: Whittlesey House, 1939, pp. 388–390.
2. *Man with a Gun,* by Charles Vanda and Russ Johnson, in Douglas Coulter (ed.), *Columbia Workshop Plays.* New York: Whittlesey House, 1939, pp. 245–247.

B. SOLO WOMAN

1. *The Dark Valley,* by W. H. Auden, in Max Wylie (ed.), *Best Broadcasts of 1939–40.* New York: Whittlesey House, 1940, pp. 33–43.
2. *Anatomy of Sound,* by Norman Corwin, in *More by Corwin.* New York: Henry Holt & Company, Inc., 1944, pp. 223–248.
3. *Mrs. Murgatroyd's Dime,* by John Latouche, 1 m or 1 w, in William A. Bacher (ed.), *The Treasury Star Parade.* New York: Rinehart & Company, Inc., 1942, pp. 35–37.

C. MEN

1. *Nine Prisoners,* by William March, adapted by Brian J. Byrne, 11 m, in Coulter, *Columbia Workshop Plays,* pp. 271–297.
2. *In the Fog,* by Milton Geiger, 4 m, in Wylie, *Best Broadcasts of 1939–40,* pp. 24–29.
3. *The Eddie Doll Case,* by Phillips H. Lord, 10 to 12 m, plus bit doubles, in Wylie, *Best Broadcasts of 1938–39,* pp. 369–385.
4. *Grandpa and the Statue,* by Arthur Miller, 5 m, 5 boys, in Erik Barnouw (ed.), *Radio Drama in Action.* New York: Rinehart & Company, Inc., 1945, pp. 267–281.
5. *Mr. Ginsberg,* by Arch Oboler, 5 m, voices, in Oboler's *Fourteen Radio Plays.* New York: Random House, Inc., 1940, pp. 193–213.

D. LARGE GROUPS

1. *The Face of America,* by Thomas Wolfe, adapted by William A. Bacher and Malcolm Meacham, 2 m, 1 w, and chorus, in Bacher, *The Treasury Star Parade,* pp. 143–150.
2. *Radio Primer,* by Norman Corwin, many voices, in *Thirteen by Corwin.* New York: Henry Holt & Company, Inc., 1942, pp. 27–50.
3. *Typhus,* by Bernard Victor Dryer, 15 m, 2 w, and many voices, in Barnouw, *Radio Drama in Action,* pp. 317–333.
4. *Cartwheel,* by Vic Knight, 34 roles, in Coulter, *Columbia Workshop Plays,* pp. 245–259.
5. *The Lonesome Train,* by Millard Lampell, narrator, singer, 1 m, chorus, and voices, in Barnouw, *Radio Drama in Action,* pp. 239–250. Also in Millard Lampell, *The Long Way Home* (New York: Julian Messner, Inc., Publisher, 1946), pp. 151–163.
6. *The Fall of the City,* by Archibald MacLeish, 5 m, and many additional voices, in Coulter, *Columbia Workshop Plays,* pp. 349–378. Also in Joseph Liss (ed.), *Radio's Best Plays* (New York: Greenberg, Publisher, 1947), pp. 3–31; and published separately (New York: Rinehart & Company, Inc., 1937).
7. *Meridian 7–1212,* by Irving Reis, 12 m, 8 w, and additional voices, in Coulter, *Columbia Workshop Plays,* pp. 31–62.
8. *Open Letter on Race Hatred,* by William N. Robson, 11 m, 4 w, bit parts, in Barnouw, *Radio Drama in Action,* pp. 59–77.
9. *Columbus Day,* by Orson Welles, in collaboration with Robert Meltzer and Norris Houghton, 3 m, 1 w, and many voices, in Barnouw, *Radio Drama in Action,* pp. 1–15.
10. *The March of Time,* many voices, in Wylie, *Best Broadcasts of 1938–39,* pp. 137–154.

E. SHORT PLAYS

1. *Pepper Young's Family,* by Elaine Carrington, 4 m, 4 w, in Wylie, *Best Broadcasts of 1939–40,* pp. 303–310.
2. *To Tim at Twenty,* by Norman Corwin, 3 m, 1 w, in *Thirteen by Corwin,* pp. 249–257.
3. *The Return of Danny O'Brien,* by Millard Lampell, 2 m, 1 w, in his *The Long Way Home,* pp. 45–55.
4. *Against the Storm,* by Sandra Michael, 2 m, 1 w, in Barnouw, *Radio Drama in Action,* pp. 348–351.
5. *The Twilight Shore,* by Milton Geiger, 1 m, 2 w, in Wylie, *Best Broadcasts of 1938–39,* pp. 342–349.

F. HALF-HOUR PLAYS

1. *Above Suspicion,* by Sherwood Anderson, 5 m, 3 w, in Ernest Boyd (ed.), *The Free Company Presents.* New York: Dodd, Mead & Company, Inc., 1941, pp. 269–301.
2. *The Snow Goose,* by Paul Gallico, adapted by William A. Bacher and Malcolm Meacham, woman narrator, 5 m, 1 w, in Bacher, *The Treasury Star Parade,* pp. 197–207.
3. *Ann Rutledge,* by Norman Corwin, 7 m, 2 w, and voices, in *Thirteen by Corwin,* pp. 191–207.
4. *Daybreak,* by Norman Corwin, 8 to 10 m, 3 w, extras, in *Thirteen by Corwin,* pp. 134–355. Also in Liss, *Radio's Best Plays,* pp. 157–171.
5. *Mary and the Fairy,* by Norman Corwin, 3 m, 2 w, in *More by Corwin,* pp. 3–20.
6. *El Capitan and the Corporal,* by Norman Corwin, 3 m, 2 w, and extras, in his *Untitled and Other Radio Dramas.* New York: Henry Holt & Company, Inc., 1947, pp. 79–102.
7. *Murder in Studio One,* by Norman Corwin, 8 m, 3 w, in *More by Corwin,* pp. 305–326.
8. *My Client Curley,* by Norman Corwin, adapted from a story by Lucille F. Herman, 7 to 10 m, 3 w, and voices, in *Thirteen by Corwin,* pp. 265–287. Also in Wylie, *Best Broadcasts of 1939–40,* pp. 3–22.
9. *Untitled,* by Norman Corwin, 8 m, 4 w, in *Untitled and Other Radio Dramas,* pp. 47–63.
10. *You Can Dream Inc.,* by Norman Corwin, 7 m, 3 w, in *Untitled and Other Radio Dramas,* pp. 253–268.
11. *Helen Keller,* by Ethel Deckleman, 2 m, 7 w, in Liss, *Radio's Best Plays,* pp. 273–286.
12. *The Hitch Hiker,* by Lucille Fletcher, 3 m, 5 w, and voices, in Liss, *Radio's Best Plays,* pp. 325–335.
13. *The Ghost of Benjamin Sweet,* by Pauline Gibson and Frederick Gilsdorff, 6 m, 3 w, in Coulter, *Columbia Workshop Plays,* pp. 149–179.
14. *A Trip to Czardis,* by Edwin Granberry, adapted by James and Elizabeth Hart, 4 m, 2 boys, 1 w, in Coulter, *Columbia Workshop Plays,* pp. 3–30. Also in Wylie, *Best Broadcasts of 1938–39,* pp. 24–42.
15. *The Clinic,* by Ted Key, 6 m, 4 w, extras, in Wylie, *Best Broadcasts of 1939–40,* pp. 87–107.
16. *The Last Day of the War,* by Arthur Laurents, 6 m, 2 w, in Barnouw, *Radio Drama in Action,* pp. 91–110.
17. *Inside a Kid's Head,* by Jerome Lawrence and Robert E. Lee, 8 m, 2 boys, 4 w, and voices, in Barnouw, *Radio Drama in Action,* pp. 181–201.
18. *Farewell to Altamont,* by Elizabeth Lomax, 6 m, 3 w, in Liss, *Radio's Best Plays,* pp. 255–267.
19. *The Trojan Women,* by Euripides, as translated by Edith Hamilton and adapted by Harry MacFayden, 2 m, 12 w, in Wylie, *Best Broadcasts of 1938–39,* pp. 549–576.
20. *Sometime Every Summertime,* by Fletcher Markle, 5 m, 3 w, in Liss, *Radio's Best Plays,* pp. 351–365.
21. *And Adam Begot,* by Arch Oboler, 2 m, 1 w, in his *This Freedom.* New York: Random House, 1942, pp. 49–68.
22. *Baby,* by Arch Oboler, 5 m, 4 w, many voices, in his *Fourteen Radio Plays,* pp. 163–185.
23. *Catwife,* by Arch Oboler, 6 m, 2 w, in *Fourteen Radio Plays,* pp. 87–109.
24. *Mirage,* by Arch Oboler, 1 m, 1 w, in *Fourteen Radio Plays,* pp. 237–256.
25. *Mr. Whiskers,* by Arch Oboler, 5 m, 4 w, in *Fourteen Radio Plays,* pp. 119–144.
26. *This Precious Freedom,* by Arch Oboler, 3 m, 2 w, and voices, in *Fourteen Radio Plays,* pp. 145–162.
27. *The Negro Domestic,* by Roi Ottley, 5 m, 1 boy, 3 w, in Barnouw, *Radio Drama in Action,* pp. 353–368.
28. *The People with Light Coming Out of Them,* by William Saroyan, 10 m, 3 w, in Boyd, *The Free Company Presents,* pp. 1–23.
29. *His Honor the Mayor,* by Orson Wells, 9 m, 3 w, and voices, in Boyd, *The Free Company Presents,* pp. 143–175.
30. *A Drink of Water,* by Wilbur Daniel Steele, adapted by Max Wylie, 7 m, 4 w, in Coulter, *Columbia Workshop Plays,* pp. 181–213.

G. FULL-HOUR PLAYS

1. *Ah, Wilderness,* by Eugene O'Neill, adapted by Arthur Arent, 9 m, 5 w, in H. William Fitelson (ed.), *Theatre Guild on the Air.* New York: Rinehart & Company, Inc., 1948, pp. 173–201.
2. *I Remember Mama,* by John Van Druten, based on *Mama's Bank Account,* by Kathryn Forbes and adapted by Erik Barnouw, 6 m, 6 w, in Fitelson, *Theatre Guild on the Air,* pp. 359–394.
3. *The Guardsman,* by Ferenc Molnar, translated by Grace L. Colbron and Hans Bartsch, and adapted by Arthur Miller, 3 m, 3 w, in Fitelson, *Theatre Guild on the Air,* pp. 67–97.
4. *This Lonely Heart,* by Arch Oboler 4 m, 2 w, and additional voices, in *Fourteen Radio Plays,* pp. 7–46. Also in Wylie, *Best Broadcasts of 1939–40,* pp. 69–85.
5. *On Borrowed Time,* by Paul Osborn, based on the novel by Lawrence Edward Watkin and adapted by Paul Peters, in Fitelson, *Theatre Guild on the Air,* pp. 137–169.

RECORDINGS

A. PLAYS

1. *On a Note of Triumph,* by Norman Corwin. Martin Gabel, narrator; large cast, Columbia M–575.
2. *Ethan Frome,* by Owen Davis (Edith Wharton). Scenes. Raymond Massey and Ruth Gordon, Decca DU–730.
3. *Sorry, Wrong Number,* by Lucille Fletcher. Agnes Moorhead, Decca DAU–2.
4. *Victoria Regina,* by Lawrence Housman. Scenes. Helen Hayes and cast, Decca DU–730.
5. *Medea,* by Robinson Jeffers. Judith Anderson and cast, Decca DAU–12; LP 9000.
6. *America Was Promises,* by Archibald MacLeish. MacLeish, Linguaphone L–14.
7. *You Are There* (*The Signing of Magna Carta* and *The Battle of Gettysburg*), by Robert Lewis Shayon. John Daly, Ken Roberts, Don Hollenbeck, Quincy Howe, Ned Calmer, and others, Columbia MM–822, 823.
8. *The Rivals,* by R. B. Sheridan. Scene. Walter Hampden and Bobby Clark, Harvard Vocarium.
9. *Abe Lincoln in Illinois,* by Robert E. Sherwood. Raymond Massey and cast, Victor M–591.
10. *The Importance of Being Earnest* and *Lady Windemere's Fan,* by Oscar Wilde. Scenes. John Gielgud and Edith Evans, Decca DV–8.
11. *The Skin of Our Teeth,* by Thornton Wilder. Scenes. Florence Eldredge and Frederic March, Decca DU–730.

B. GENERAL

1. *Tales from the Old Country,* by Sholem Aleichem. Howard Da Silva, Decca DU–5.
2. *The Pied Piper of Hamelin,* by Robert Browning. Ingrid Bergman, Decca DA–450.
3. *Gettysburg Address,* by Abraham Lincoln. Melvyn Douglas, Victor DM–1088; Charles Laughton, Columbia S–271M; Raymond Massey, Linguaphone L–26; Orson Welles, Decca A–439.
4. *Second Inaugural Address,* by Abraham Lincoln. Raymond Massey, Linguaphone L–26.
5. *The Crisis,* by Thomas Paine. Paul Muni, Victor 10–1005.
6. *Poems and Prose,* by Dorothy Parker. Ilka Chase, Victor Mo–971.
7. *The People, Yes,* by Carl Sandburg. Sandburg, Decca DA–273.
8. *Leaves of Grass,* by Walt Whitman. Selections. Ralph Bellamy, Victor M–955.
9. *The Song of Songs.* (Bible). Orson Welles, Decca DU–10.
10. *The Voice of Poetry,* Selections. Edith Evans, Columbia M–375.
11. *Dramatic Sketches* (Lincoln's Letter to Mrs. Bixby, The Sermon on the Mount, Latouche's *The Statue of Liberty* and *The Fog*). Judith Anderson, Victor 10–1005.

C. SHAKESPEARE

1. *Hamlet.* Selections. John Barrymore, Victor 6837; Maurice Evans, Columbia M–340; J. R. Firth, Linguaphone RER–24; John Gielgud, Decca DAU–7; Laurence Olivier, Victor DM–1273.
2. *Henry V.* Laurence Olivier, Victor DM–1128.
3. *Julius Caesar.* Orson Welles and the Mercury Theatre cast, Columbia C–10.
4. *King Lear.* Selection. John Barrymore, Victor 6837.
5. *Macbeth.* Maurice Evans and Judith Anderson, Victor M–878; Orson Welles and Mercury Theatre cast, Columbia C–33; Flora Robson (selection), Harvard Vocarium.
6. *Merchant of Venice.* Orson Welles and the Mercury Theatre cast, Columbia C–66; Portia's speech on mercy, I. C. Ward, Linguaphone RER–24.

7. *Merry Wives of Windsor.* Stratford-on-Avon Festival Company, Britam BA–1.
8. *Othello.* Paul Robeson, Jose Ferrer, and Uta Hagen, Columbia MM–554.
9. *Richard II.* Maurice Evans and cast, Columbia MM–303; Startford-on-Avon Festival Company, Britam BA–3.
10. *Romeo and Juliet.* Selections. John Gielgud, Decca LP 9001.
11. *The Tempest.* Stratford-on-Avon Festival Company, Britam BA–2.
12. Various Scenes. (*As You Like It, Julius Caesar, Macbeth, Merchant of Venice, Romeo and Juliet,* and *Taming of the Shrew*). Otis Skinner and Cornelia Otis Skinner, Victor M–753.
13. Various Scenes. John Gielgud.

    As You Like It, II, 7, "A fool, a fool . . . " and Jacques' speech.

    Hamlet, II, 2, Hamlet's speech. (Also on Decca DAU–90025.)

    ———, IV, 4, Hamlet's speech. (Also on Decca DAU–90024.)

    Henry IV, I, 3, Hotspur's speech.

    Henry V, III, 1, King Henry's speech.

    ———, IV, 3, King Henry's speech.

    Merchant of Venice, I, 1. Gratiano's speech.

    Midsummer Night's Dream, II, 1, Oberon's speech.

    Othello, I, 3, Othello's speech.

    Richard II, II, 1, John of Gaunt's speech. (Also on Decca DU–730.)

    ———, III, 3, King Richard's speech.

    The Tempest, IV, 1, Prospero's speech.

    Linguaphone L–12

INDEXES

INDEX TO EXERCISES

Acting or nonacting, 10–30
Action, 161 ff.
Added thoughts, 187–188, 202–203
Attitudes, communion, contact, 222, 241–253

Breathing, 36–37, 39–43

Changes, reversals, transitions, 127–133
Characterization, 161 ff., 267 ff.
Circumstances, 290–305
Comedy lines, 337–339
Comedy scenes, 339–350
"Coming on," 71–73
Communion, 222, 241–253
Confrontations, 253–257
Conjunction hitting, 141–142
Contact, 222, 241–253
Conversational selection, 214–220
Crowds, 318–320

Direction, 375–377, 386–405

Emotional scenes, 329–337
Emphasis, 134–139
Eye or ear material, 10–30

Facial expressions, 361–364
"Fading," 73–77
Fantastic voices, 170–177
Foreign accents, etc., 163–170

Gestures, 364–365
Grouping (sentences), 110–111
Grouping (speeches), 114–120
Growth or progression in thought, 203–208

"Hisses," 43–44
Hunting thoughts and words, 187, 200–201

Illusion of the First Time, 193 ff.
Improvisations, 178–180
Incomplete thoughts, 189, 208–212
Interruptions, 232–235

Kisses, 94–95

Leaps from narration, 230–233
Letters, 191–193
Listening, 178–180
"Livingness" of speech, 185–189

Meaning (sentences), 109, 127 ff.
Mispronounced words, 50–52
Motion, 361–369
Motivations, 267–288

Narration, 193–197, 230–233
New ideas, 212–214

"Off" microphone, 77–82
One-sided conversations, 197–200
Oral make-ups, 163–169

Pantomime, 361–369
Pause, 149–154
Period fault, 111–114
Physical action, 305–318
Pitch changes, 38
Posture, 366
Pronoun pounding, 139–141
Pronunciation, 50–52
Pronunciation, Characteristic, 52

Rate of speaking, 52–58
Reactions, 178–180
Reading articles, letters, etc., 191–193
Reading faults, 103–109
Relaxation, 368–369
"Relaxed throat," 37–38
Reversals, 127–133

Shouts, screams, loudness, 90–94
Sibilants, 43–44
Sight reading, 10–30
Sitting, 365–366
Soliloquies, 225–230
Statements, 267–269
Structure, of scenes and plays, 385
of speeches, 383–384
Subordinations, 142–144

Telephone calls, 197–199
Through doors, 82–86
Throw-away lines, 144–149
Tone, 37
Topping, 235–241
Transitions, 127–133, 367–368
Typical radio material, 10–20

Underplaying, 235–241

Verbs, 161 ff.
Vibrations, 368
Voice qualities, 43–49

Walks, 366–367
Whispers, 86–90

INDEX TO SELECTIONS AND AUTHORS

Ace, Goodman, 343–344
Adams, Samuel Hopkins, 237
Adventures of Ozzie and Harriet, The, 40–41, 185–186, 290, 307–308, 339–341
Adventures of the Thin Man, The, 86–88, 94, 132–133, 238–239, 290, 291–292
Agger, Don, 329–331
Alan Young Show, The, 346–349
Aldrich Family, The, 24–25, 56–58, 65, 74, 78–80, 85, 127–128, 134–136, 203–204, 208, 300–301, 311–312, 375, 392–393
Alexander, Martha, 45–46, 47, 52–53, 106–107, 114, 193–194, 199, 214–220, 225–226, 227–228, 233–235, 240–245, 292, 301–302, 336–337, 398–399
Aley, Albert, 315–316
All My Sons, 148, 384, 398–399
Alter Ego (in *Ivory Tower and Other Radio Plays*), 152
American Story, The, 196
American Vaudeville, 13
Anatomy of Sound, The, 22–23
Anderson, Maxwell, 239–240, 331–332
Ann Rutledge, 205–206
Appointment, 128
Arent, Arthur, 64
Arrow Shirts, 18–19
Art of Murder, The, 23–24
Art of Walt Disney, The, 171
Arthur Godfrey's Talent Scouts, 28–29
Awake and Sing, 165–166

Baby Snooks Show, The, 86, 154, 236
Bambi, 171–172
Barnouw, Erik, 236–237
Barry, Philip, 384

Bartsch, Hans, 63–64
Battle of the Warsaw Ghetto, The (in *Radio Drama in Action*), 270–271
Beautiful Silence, 76–77, 115
Beeding, Francis, 130
Behrman, S. N., 201, 206, 384
Bell for Adano, A, 166
Benét, Stephen Vincent, 48–49, 116, 144, 399–405
Benoff, Mac, 86
Betrayer, The, 395–398
Between the Silence and the Surf (in *The American Story*), 196
Big Story, The, 90–91, 232–233
Boiling Point, The, 130–131, 376–377
Borden Company, The, 174
Boswell, James, 20–21
Bretton Woods (in *Radio Drama in Action*), 172–174
Bride Wore Black, The, 304–305, 309–310
Bright Horizon, 148–149
Brown, John Mason, 101
Browning, Robert, 25–26
Bulldog Drummond, 276–278
Burke, Thomas, 108
Bury Me Not, 18, 305–306
Byrne, Brian, 42–43

Cain, James M., 145
Candid Microphone, 26–27
Candle in the Wind, 239–240, 331–332
Cantor Show, The Eddie, 12–13
Carrington, Elaine, 89–90, 147, 151–152, 185–186, 231–232, 281–285, 295–296
Case of the Bleeding Lipstick, The, 94, 132–133
Case of the Chilling Chewing Gum, The, 238–239
Case of the Crowded Coffin, The, 86–88
Case of the Flying Baby, The, 290
Case of the Sinister Perfume, The, 291–292
Cavalcade of America, 272
Chandler, Raymond, 145–146
Check Number B131, 393–394
Chekhov, Anton, 104
Child Is Born, A (in *Radio Drama in Action*), 144, 399–405
Clinic, The (in *Best Broadcasts of 1939–40*), 80
Clisbee, Florence, 24–25
Cluett, Peabody & Company, 18
Coe, Frederick, 153, 332–333
Colbron, Grace I., 63–64
Collins, Howard, 169
Columbia Workshop, 42–43, 48–49, 62, 75–76, 252–253
Comic Strip Murder, The, 93–94
Cook, Joe, 13–14
Corwin, Norman, 22–23, 29–30, 40, 118, 128, 136–137, 176–177, 205–206, 228, 284–288, 310–311, 349–350
Covan, Jenny, 104
Credo, 143
Creeper, The, 82–83, 297–298
Crystal, 105–106, 204–205, 231

Danch, Bill, 278–281, 341–343
Daniel Webster and the Sea Serpent (in *Columbia Workshop Plays*), 48–49
David Harding—Counterspy, 71, 131–132, 192–193, 247–250, 390–391
Daybreak, 310–311
Death of Aunt Aggie, The (in *The Best One-Act Plays of 1943*), 73–74, 269–270
Deckleman, Ethel, 72
Dell, Jeffrey, 64
Denham, Reginald, 253–257
Descent of the Gods, 29–30, 40
Dickens, Charles, 169
Dig Your Own Grave, 235
Dinsdale, Del, 56–58, 65, 74, 85, 127–128, 203–204, 208, 300–301, 311–312, 392–393
Disney, Walt, 171
Double Disaster Clause, 73, 92–93
Double Indemnity (in *Best Film Plays—1945*), 145–146
Doyle, Sir Arthur Conan, 143, 197
Drink of Water, A (in *Columbia Workshop Plays*), 252–253
Duffy's Tavern, 198
du Maurier, Daphne, 14
Dunnigan's Daughter, 201, 206

Eckhardt, Agnes, 298–300
Eddie Cantor Show, The, 12–13
Ehrlich, Max, 90–91, 232–233
Elinson, Izzy, 12–13
Elsie the Cow, 174–175
Empty Noose, The (in *Radio's Best Plays*), 43
Engvick, William, 130–131, 376–377

Face, The (in *Radio's Best Plays*), 101
Fall of the City, The, 21–22, 88–89, 103–104
Fass, George, and Gertrude Fass, 393–394
Feild, Robert D., 171
Fighting Senator, 306–307, 318–320
Finian's Rainbow, 175–176
Forbes, Kathryn, 236
Forester, C. S., 64
Four Fatal Jugglers, The, 309
Freeman, Everett, 154, 236
Funt, Allan A., 26–27
Funt, Julian, 71–72, 94, 138–139, 201, 292–293, 386–387

Gardner, Ed, 198
Geer, William D., 19
Geiger, Milton, 73, 92–93, 152–153
General Foods Corporation, 24, 55, 119, 129, 149, 192, 207, 233, 391
Gerstenberg, Alice, 228–230
Ghost of Yankee Doodle, The, 117–118
Gide, André, 191
Gilbert, Douglas, 13
Godfrey, Arthur, 28–29
Goldsmith, Clifford, 56, 65, 74, 78–80, 85, 127, 134–136, 203, 208, 300–301, 311–312, 375, 392
Goldsmith, Oliver, 52
Gordon, Ruth, 199
Gordon MacRae Show, The, 16–17
Granberry, Edwin, 62
Grandpa and the Statue (in *Radio Drama in Action*), 272–273
Great Gabbo, The, 195
Great Mellagio, The, 67
Green, Denis, 143, 197
Greenleaf Theatre Elements II, Speech, 52
Gregory, Ethel Harris, 67
Guardsman, The, 63–64

Hammett, Dashiel, 86, 94, 132, 238
Hands of Mr. Ottermole, The, 108
Harburg, E. Y., 175–176
Harrison, Joan, 14–15
Hart, James, and Elizabeth Hart, 62
Haunted House, A, 291
Having Wonderful Time, 206
Hecht, Ben, 130, 153, 195, 332–333
Helen Keller, 72
Hellman, Lillian, 332
Henry IV, Part 1, 101, 226–227
Henry V, 166–167
Hershey, John, 166
Hoffman, L. K., 108, 134
Holland, Gerald, 64–65
Hollywood, Doctor (in *The Writer's Radio Theatre, 1941*), 194–195
Hop Harrigan, 315–316
Hopkins, Neal, 163
Horla, The (in *The Writer's Radio Theatre, 1941*), 46–47
Howard, Cy, 95, 197, 230, 246, 308, 389–390
Howard, Sidney, 117–118

I Remember Mama, 236–237
Importance of Being Earnest, The, 163–164
In the Fog, 152–153
Inner Sanctum Mystery Radio Show, The, 18, 46–47, 305–306
Inside a Kid's Head, 271–272
Intermission Talk: Philharmonic Society (in *Best Broadcasts of 1938–39*), 27–28
International Silver, 11–12
Interview in *PM*, 17–18
It Happened One Night (in *Twenty Best Film Plays*), 237–238
Ivory Tower (in *Ivory Tower*), 48

Joe Cook's Baseball Yarn, 13–14
Johnny Morgan Show, The, 344–346
Joudry, Patricia, 56–58, 65, 74, 85, 127–128, 203–204, 208, 300–301, 311–312, 392–393
Journals of André Gide, The, 191–192
Joyce Jordan, 298–300
Jurist, Ed, 78–80

Kafka, Franz, 142
Kelly, George, 64
Kent, Mona, 55–56, 119, 129–130, 149–150, 192, 207, 233–235, 391–392
Key, Ted, 80
Kober, Arthur, 206

Ladies in Retirement, 253–257
Lampell, Millard, 104–105, 387–389

Lardner, Ring, 150–151
Last Inca, The (in *Radio's Best Plays*), 101
La Touche, John, 170–171
Laurents, Arthur, 101
Lawrence, Jerome, 271–272
Leave It to Ethel, 67–68, 198
Lee, Robert E., 271–272
Lesson in Japanese, A (in *The Treasury Star Parade*), 163
Levitt, Gene, 395–398
Levy, Parke, 95, 197, 230, 246, 308, 389–390
Lewis, Milton, 46–47, 86–88, 94, 132–133, 238–239, 276–278, 290, 291–292
Liebman, Joshua, 268
Life of Samuel Johnson, The, 20–21
Little One, The (in *Radio's Best Plays*), 81–82
Lomax, Alan, 273–274
Lord, Phillips H., 71, 131–132, 192–193, 247–250, 290–291
Lost Shoe, The, 26–27
Lowry, Malcolm, 144
Luck of Adelaide Bartlett, The, 23–24
Lucky Guy, 333–334
Lyon, Peter, 172–174
Lyons, Kenny, 28–29

MacDougall, Ranald, 73–74, 269–270
MacLeish, Archibald, 21–22, 74–75, 88–89, 103–104, 196
Mama's Bank Account, 236
Man behind the Gun, The, 73–74
Man with a Platform, The, 349–350
Man with the Twisted Lip, The, 143, 197
Man Who Murdered in Public, The, 250–251, 314–315, 377
Man Who Saw through Heaven, The, 252
Many a Watchful Night (in *Radio's Best Plays*), 101
March, William, 42
March of Time, The, 19–20
Markle, Fletcher, 61, 106
Mary and the Fairy, 284–288
Melzer, Louis, 344–346
Merchant of Yonkers, The, 337–339
Meridian 7-1212, 75–76
Methot, Frederic A., 93–94, 195, 250–251, 314–315, 377
Michaela, 41–42
Miller, Arthur, 63–64, 72–73, 116, 148, 272–273, 384
Miracle in the Rain, 153, 332–333
Mirage, 251–252
Mitchell, Robert J., 395–398
Molnar, Ferenc, 63–64
Monash, Paul, 53–54, 84–85, 290, 304–305, 309, 309–310, 333–334
Morgan, Al, 81–82
Morgan, Johnny, 344–346
Mouse That Played the Minuet, The, 16–17
mr ace and JANE, 343–344
Mr. Ledford and the TVA (in *Radio Drama in Action*), 273–274
Mrs. Murgatroyd's Dime, 170–171
Murder on Seventy-seven, 90–91, 232–233
My Friend Irma, 95, 197, 230, 246, 308, 389–390
My Last Duchess, 25–26
Mystery Theatre, 53–54, 67, 73, 82–83, 84–85, 92–93, 93–94, 108, 134, 146, 195, 201, 207, 222, 235, 250–251, 290, 297–298, 304–305, 309, 309–310, 314–315, 329–331, 333–334, 393–394, 395–398

Nelson, Ozzie, 40–41, 185–186, 290, 307–308, 339–341
Nemesis, 53–54
New York *Star*, 17–18
Nichols, Dudley, 119–120
Nine Prisoners, 42–43
Norris, Kathleen, 148–149
Not Quite Perfect, 134
Notebook, 142
Now You See Her, 84–85, 290

Oak Leaves and Lavender, 167–168
Oboler, Arch, 48, 61–62, 91–92, 118–119, 152, 200, 251–252
O'Brien, Justin, 191
O'Casey, Sean, 164, 167–168
October Morning (in *Radio's Best Plays*), 104–105
Odets, Clifford, 165–166, 334–336
Odyssey of Runyon Jones, The, 176–177
On Borrowed Time, 80–81
O'Neill, James, 15–16
Oppenheimer, Jesse, 86, 154, 236
Oracle of Philadelphia, The, 228
Osborne, Paul, 80, 166
Overtones, 228–230

Paris Incident (in *The Treasury Star Parade*), 274–276
Parker, Dorothy, 105
Payment Deferred, 64–65
Peace of Mind, 268
Peck, Ira, 17–18
People with Light Coming Out of Them, The (in *The Free Company Presents*), 39
Pepper Young's Family, 281–285
Percy, Edward, 253–257
Perl, Arnold, 43, 306–307, 318–320
Peters, Paul, 80–81
Peterson, Paul, 16–17
Philadelphia Story, The, 384
Pirate, The, 384
PM, 17–18
Portia Faces Life, 55–56, 119, 129–130, 149–150, 192, 207, 233–235, 391–392
Presnell, Robert, Jr., 41–42, 105–106, 204–205, 231
Primer for Murder, 222
Psalm for a Dark Year, 118

Quillan, Joe, 12–13
Quillan, Johnny, 12–13

Rapp, Johnny, 12–13
Rebecca (in *Twenty Best Film Plays*), 14–15
Red Roses for Me, 164
Reis, Irving, 75–76
Renoir, Jean, 119
Rice, Jerry, 67–68, 198
Riders to the Sea, 108–109
Ridgeway, Agnes, 222, 312–314
Riggs, Lynn, 208
Riskin, Robert, 237–238
Roadside, 208
Roberts, Kay, 11–12
Rocket to the Moon, 334–336
Rosten, Norman, 274–276
Roughhead, William, 23–24
Ruscoll, Joseph, 82–83, 146, 201, 207, 222, 235, 297–298
Ryan, Benny, 344–346

Saidy, Fred, 175–176
Saroyan, William, 39
Saturday Review of Literature, The, 169
Schulberg, Budd, 194–195
Schwartz, Al, and Sherwood Schwartz, 346–349
Searching Wind, The, 332
Second Mrs. Burton, The, 45–46, 47, 52–53, 106–107, 114, 144–145, 193–194, 199, 214–220, 225–226, 227–228, 233–235, 240–245, 292, 296–297, 301–302, 316–318, 336–337, 398–399
Shakespeare, 101, 115–116, 166–167, 226–227
She Stoops to Conquer, 52
Sherlock Holmes, 143, 197
Sherwood, Robert E., 14–15, 137–138
Show-Off, The, 64
Silver Theatre, 18, 105–106, 130–131, 198, 204–205, 231, 376–377
Sloane, Robert, 18, 305–306
Smedley, Constance, 52
Sometime Every Summertime, 61, 106
Special to Hollywood (in *This Freedom*), 61–62
Spellbound (in *Best Film Plays—1945*), 130
Stark, Sheldon, 48–49
States Talking, The (in *The Free Company Presents*), 74–75
Steel Worker, The (in *Best Broadcasts of 1938–39*), 118–119
Steele, Wilbur Daniel, 252
Story of Gus, The (in *Radio's Best Plays*), 72–73, 116
Stuart, William L. (Bill), 67–68, 198
Study in Bitterness, A (in *The Long Way Home*), 387–389
Swanton, M. H., 76–77, 115
Synge, John M., 108–109

Tales of Willie Piper, 77–78, 83–84, 128–129, 302–303
Taylor, Deems, 27–28
Taylor, Samuel, 77–78, 83–84, 128–129, 302–303
Teichman, Howard M., 101
Theatre Guild on the Air, The, 63, 80, 236
There Shall Be No Night, 137–138
Third Witness, The, 146, 207
Thirteenth Floor, The, 204, 240–241
This Land Is Mine (in *Twenty Best Film Plays*), 119–120
Those We Love, 222, 312–314
Three Sisters, The, 104

Time Magazine, 174
To Tim at Twenty-One, 136–137
Tokar, Norman, 78–80
Tommy Riggs and Betty Lou, 278–281, 341–343
Triangle of Death, 201
Tridget of Greva, The, 150–151
Trip to Czardis, A, 62
Troilus and Cressida, 115–116
27 Wagons Full of Cotton, 164–165
Two on a Clue, 107

Under the Volcano, 144

van Druten, John, 236–237
Vickers, Roy, 250, 314, 377
Vites, Louis, 107

Walker, Sam, 18–19
Walker, Thelma, 174–175
Waltz, The, 105
Watkin, Lawrence Edward, 80
We the People, 15–16
Welburns—Confidential Report, The (in *The Writer's Radio Theatre, 1941*), 200
Western Star (in *Radio's Best Plays*), 116
When a Girl Marries, 88–89, 147, 151–152, 185–186, 231–232, 295–296
White, E. B., 191
Wild Flag, The, 191
Wilde, Oscar, 163–164
Wilder, Billy, 145–146
Wilder, Thorton, 337–339
Williams, Tennessee, 164–165
Wishengrad, Morton, 101, 270–271
Wolfe, Thomas, 143
Wolfe, Winifred, 204, 240–241
Woman's Life, A, 71–72, 94, 138–139, 201, 292–293, 386–387
Women Stayed at Home, The (in *This Freedom*), 91–92
Woolf, Virginia, 291
Woolrich, Cornell, 304, 309
Wylie, Max, 252–253

Years Ago, 199
Young, John M., 144, 296–297, 316–318
Young Show, The Alan, 346–349

INDEX TO SUBJECT MATTER

"Accent" defined, 123
Acting (Boleslavsky), 7, 160, 323, 324
Acting defined, 5
Acting naturally, 1 ff., 351, 355, 373 ff.
Action, 155 ff.
Actor, The (Hill), 97, 184, 326
Actor and director, 381
Actor in the Making, 354
Actor is himself, 158–159
Actor Prepares, An, 1, 160, 221, 323, 374
"Actor's Creative Work, The," 31
Actor's salaries, 6
Actual speech, 373 ff.
Adams, J. Donald, 261
Added thoughts, 187–188
Aeschylus, 4
Aims of Literary Study, The, 124
Alberti, Madame Eve, 352 ff.
Aldrich Family, The, 60, 69–70, 158, 321, 375–376
Alexander, Martha, 25, 222
Alger, Abby Langdon, 262
Alving, Mrs., 3
American College Dictionary, 100
American Federation of Radio Actors, 6
Amphitryon, 4
Analysis of Art, 380
Archer, William, 162, 264
Ariste, 357
Aristotle, 6, 8, 159, 379
Aristotle on the Art of Poetry, 6
Armance, 186
Art, 2 ff., 325
  defined, 2–3, 7–8
  vs. nature, 2, 5 ff., 354 ff.
Art of Acting, The (Fitzgerald), 99, 156
Art of Acting, The (Irving), 98
Art and the Actor, 263
Art of the Actor, 157
Art as Experience, 380
"Art of Fiction, The," 7
Art of Interpretative Speech, The, 121
Arts and the Arts of Criticism, The, 3, 379
Articulation, 33–34
Artificial reading, 98
Artistic sense, 355
Artist's attitude, 2 ff.
Ase, 324
At 33, 359
Atmosphere, 379
Attitude defined, 322
Attitudes, 221 ff.
Audience, 6, 378
Austin, Gilbert, 353

Back to Methuselah, 371
Bacon, Francis, 7, 267
Baker, George Pierce, 162
Barrault, Jean-Louis, 2
Barrows, Sarah T., 34, 325
Basic needs, 262
Bassett, Lee Emerson, 97, 98, 100, 101, 121
Bear, Johnny, 1
Beethoven, 3
Behrman, S. N., 4
Being the part, 158
Bell, Clive, 8
Bentley, Eric, 97
Berg, Gertrude, 351
Berle, Milton, 326
Beyle, Marie Henri, 186
Black Lamb and Grey Falcon, 8
Blair, Hugh, 184
Blake, Ben, 259
Bodily changes, 322
"Body Training for Actors," 353
Boleslavsky, Richard, 7, 160, 323, 324
Box and Cox, 156
Breathing, 125 ff.
Bridge, William H., 354, 355
Brunetière, Vincent, 159
Building a Character, 355
Burke, Kenneth, 259

Campbell, Mrs. Pat, 221, 353
Candid Microphone, 187
Careless reading, 100
Carrington, Elaine, 35
Carritt, E. F., 321
Casarine, 158
Cassio, 162
Cassou, 4
"Centering" defined, 123
Chaplin, Charles, 326
Characters Make Your Story, 159, 259
Characterization, cliché and stencil, 157
  from the dramatist, 157 ff.
  external, 156–157, 161
  illumination, 355
  verbs, 160–161, 177–178, 181, 259 ff.
  from within, 157
Charm, 158
Chekhov, Anton, 35, 159, 326, 353
Cherry Orchard, The, 326, 353
Chironomia, 353
"Choc," 322
Christ of the Andes, 70
Clark, Barrett H., 159, 160
Climax defined, 381
"Closeup," 356
Cohn, Janet, vii
Coleridge, S. T., 8
Collingwood, R. G., 7
Comedy of Errors, A, 156
Communication, 2, 100, 355, 379
Composition, oral, 373 ff.
Confucius, 268
Conrad, Joseph, 351
Contact, 6, 221 ff.
Conversational method, 183 ff., 221 ff.
Cooper, Lane, 6
Coquelin, Constant, 157, 262–263, 264, 325
Corot, Jean, 2
Corson, Hiram, 124
Corwin, Norman, 3, 35, 66, 374
Cott, Ted, 60
Coulter, William, 62
Coward, Noel, 4, 144
Craft of Comedy, The, 321 ff.
Craven, Thomas, 4, 8
Creative Theatre, 351
Crime Doctor, 158
Cronyn, Hume, 355, 356, 357
Cues, radio, 66

D'Annunzio, Gabriele, 35
Date with Judy, A, 158
da Vinci, Leonardo, 267

Death in the Afternoon, 159
Delsarte, François, 352
Democracy and Education, 99
Desdemona, 162, 324, 325
Design, 2, 371 ff.
Dewey, John, 8, 99, 259, 380
Dialogue, 97 ff., 121 ff.
Dickens, Charles, 2
Diderot, Denis, 160
Directing, interpretative, 379–381
realistic, 373–377
"wow," 378–379
Director, 352–353
and actor, 381
Director's job, 372–373
Distances from microphone, 60–61
Dogberry, 326
Dominant aim, 262 ff.
Dramatic Criticism, 378
Dramatic form, 381
Dramatic Imagination, The, 352
Dramatic Opinions and Essays, 33, 155, 187, 352
Drinkwater, John, 4
Dryden, John, 160
Duse, Eleanora, 158, 190, 352

Ear, appeal to, 6
Edman, Irwin, 7
Electra, 4
Elements of Rhetoric, 98
Eliot, George, 2
Ellen Terry and Bernard Shaw, 34, 156, 321
Elocution, 98
Elwood, Maren, 159 ff., 259, 262
Emotion, 3, 158, 161, 263, 321 ff., 359
vs. anti-emotion, 324–325
defined, 322
Emotion memory, 322
Emotions and the Educative Process, 322
Emphasis, 121 ff.
Encyclopaedia Britannica, 371
Epidohov, 326
Ervine, St. John, 4
"Essay towards Establishing the Melody and Meaning of Speech," 184
Eugen Onegin, 162
Euripides, 4
European Painting and Sculpture, 4
European Theories of the Drama, 159
Eustis, Morton, 262 ff.
Exhibitionism, 158
Expression of Emotion, The, 322

Facial expression, 351 ff.
Fairbanks, Grant, 32, 33, 121, 123
Feeling the emotions, 324 ff.
Feeling natural, 371–372, 386
Feelings, 3, 125, 158, 162, 259, 322, 354
Fielding, Henry, 1
Fields, W. C., 156
"Film Acting, Notes on," 355
First Steps in Acting, 159
Firth, J. R., 100
Fitelson, H. William, 64
Fitzgerald, Percy, 99, 156, 157, 161
Fogerty, Elsie, 157
Fontanne, Lynn, 264, 357
Form and content, 371 ff.
Forster, E. M., 7
Forum Magazine, 62
"French scenes," 160, 264
Freud, Sigmund, 261
Fry, Roger, 8
Funt, Allan, 187

Galpern, Lasar, 353
Gangbusters, 321
Garrick, David, 1
Gassner, John, 372
Gauthier, Marguerite, 158
Gesture, 351 ff.
Gide, André, 2, 186
Gillette, William, 183, 184, 186, 378
Glamour, 325, 380
Goethe, Johann, 97, 267
Goldbergs, The, 351
Goldsmith, Clifford, 35, 376
Granville-Barker, H., 371–372, 388
Greene, Theodore M., 3–4, 379, 380
Grouping, 100 ff.
Growth and progression, 188–189

Haggard, Stephen, 321, 326 ff.
Hamlet, 1, 160, 326, 372
Handbook of Acting, A, 352
Handbook of Oral Reading, A, 97, 121
Hands, 356–357
Hardwicke, Sir Cedric, 5
Harpagon, 2
Harrison, Jane, 7
Haydon, Larrae, 323–324
Hayes, Helen, 263
Heine, Heinrich, 268
Hemingway, Ernest, 159
Henry IV (Pirandello), 371
Henry VIII (Laughton), 357
Herendeen, Jane, 123, 125
Hill, John, 97, 184, 326
History of Tom Jones, The, 1
Hofmannsthal, Hugo von, 4
Holmes, Oliver Wendell, 100, 267
Homer, Winslow, 2
How to Audition for Radio, 60
Huneker, James, 33, 155, 187, 321, 352
Hunting for words, 187
Huxley, T. H., 267
Hyman, Stanley Edgar, 7

Iago, 3, 162
Ibn-Zahav, Ari, 4
Ibsen, Henrik, 3, 324
Idea, 4, 5, 159, 262, 263, 264, 252, 254 ff., 327, 372, 373, 379, 382
Identification, 261
Idiot's Delight, 263
Illusion of the First Time in Acting, The, 183
Imagination, 7, 9, 156, 221, 223, 262, 289, 323, 324, 355
Imitation, 31–32
Improvise, 353
Inaccurate reading, 100
Incomplete thoughts, 188–189
Inflection, 121 ff., 123
Institutio Oratoria, 97
Interpretation, 3 ff., 379 ff.
Introduction to the Dance, 381
Introduction to the Phonetics of American English, An, 34
Irving, Henry, 98, 99
Isabelle, 357
It Seems Radio Is Here to Stay, 66

James, Henry, 7, 262, 268
James, William, 259, 322
James Family, The, 7
James Joyce, 2
James-Lange theory, 322
Jameson, House, vii
Jaques-Dalcroze, 352
Jeffers, Robinson, 4
Jewell, Edward Alden, 8
Johnson, Nunnally, 13
Jones, Robert Edmond, 352
Josephson, Matthew, 162
Journals of André Gide, The, 186
Joyce, James, 186, 267
Julius Caesar, 261
Justification, 260 ff., 353 ff.

Kaufman, George S., 372
Kean, Edmund, 325
Keats, John, 268
Kemble, Fanny, 5
Kenyon, Samuel, 34
Kjerbühl-Peterson, Lorenz, 325
Klein, Luce, and Arthur, Klein, 2
Knight, G. Wilson, 379
Knott, Thomas Albert, 34
Kober, Arthur, 1
Koestler, Arthur, 161
Komizarjevsky, Theodore, 371

Lady of Belmont, The, 4
Lampell, Millard, 374
Landis, Carney, 322
Landor, Walter Savage, 267
Landry, Robert J., 6
Laughton, Charles, 357
Lawrence, Thomas, Sr., 161
Lawson, John Howard, 159, 261, 381
Le Gallienne, Eva, 359
Leighton, Frederick, 161
Le Juene, C. A., 7
Levin, Harry, 2
Levitas, Louise, 187
Lewes, George Henry, 325
Lewin, Thomas, 259
Liebman, Joshua, 268–269
Life of Riley, The, 321
Life study, 353 ff.
L'Impromptu de Versailles, 184
Lincoln, Abraham, 4
Listening, 221, 223, 233
Literature, 186
"Little Mike Has Big Ears," 187
Living Voice, The, 98
"Livingness" of speech, 184 ff.
Lloyd, Harold, 325–326
Locandiera, La, 158
Lord Jim, 351

Lowell, Amy, 8
Lunt, Alfred, 263, 357

McDougall, William, 259
McGill, Earle, 59
Mackenzie, H. F., 4
Macklin, Charles, 184
Malinowski, Bronislaw, 259
Man Who Came to Dinner, The, 158
"Mark on the Wall, The," 291
Marking radio scripts, 66–68, 98–99
Marner, Silas, 2
Martensteig, Max, 325
Martin, John, 381
Masefield, John, 98
"Master Key to Understanding, The," 33
Matthiessen, F. O., 7
Maude, Aylmer, 3
Maugham, Somerset, 4, 8, 324–325, 357
Meaning, 97 ff.
Meaning of Meaning, The, 259
Mechanical reading, 98–99
Medium, importance of, 4, 354–355
Meierhold, V., 352
Memorization, 6, 351, 357
Memory, 324
Mendelssohn, Felix, 378
Mental activity, 183 ff.
Mercutio, 160
Meredith, Burgess, 262
Microphone positions, 59 ff.
Microphones, 59–60
Milton, John, 6
Mimicry, 1, 3, 7, 157, 354, 373
"Minor Exhibitionists," 325
Mitchell, Roy, 351, 352
Modern Acting, 323–324
Molière (John Batiste Poquelin), 2, 4, 184, 378
Monotonous reading, 98
Moreau, Gustave, 8
Morrow, Marjorie, 6
Moses, Montrose J., 5
Motion, kinds of, 352–353
Motivation, 354
Movement, 351 ff.
Movement terminology, 357–358
Mr. District Attorney, 158
Muckey, Floyd S., 32
Music Master, The, 158
Musical Scene, The, 378–379
My Friend Irma, 321
Mystery Theatre, 60, 69, 70, 158

Nathan, George Jean, 2
Natural Method of Voice Production, The, 32
Naturalistic roles, 158
Nature into art, 1 ff., 377 ff.
Nazimova, Olga, 262
Nelson, Severina, 121, 125
New ideas, 189
New Republic, The, 190
New York *Herald Tribune,* 4, 378
New York *Times,* 6, 124, 261
New Yorker, The, 1
Newton, Eric, 4, 7
Nijinsky, 357, 366
Noh plays, 157
"Notes on Acting and Production," 59, 99
"Notes on Film Acting," 355

Objectives, 259 ff.
Oboler, Arch, 59–60, 99, 374
O'Brien, Justin, 186
Observation, 324, 354 ff.
Odyssey of Runyon Jones, The, 66
Ogden, C. K., 259
On Actors and the Art of Acting, 325
On Dramatic Method, 380
O'Neill, Eugene, 3, 4
Ophelia, 160
Oral composition, 373 ff.
Osric, 326
Othello, 4, 102, 162, 324, 325
Ouspenskaya, Maria, 353
Ouspensky, 268

Pantomime, 352 ff.
Parker, De Witt, 380
Parrish, Wayland Maxfield, vii, 32, 33, 98, 100, 101, 102, 183
Partial Portraits, 7
Partridge, Mr., 1
Pause, 121 ff., 190
Peace of Mind, 268–269
Peer Gynt, 324
Perkins, Osgood, 357
Perl, Arnold, 35
Personality, 7, 158, 352
Photogenic face, 7
Physical action, 190, 290–291, 352, 374
Picasso, Pablo, 7
Picasso, 3
Pirandello, L., 371
Pitch changes, 121 ff.
Pitch levels, 33
Plato, 268
Plautus, 4
Play architecture, 371 ff.
Players at Work, 262
Play-making, 265
Playwright, 3–4, 31, 157–158, 160, 261–262, 264, 352–353, 371 ff.
Playwright as Thinker, The, 97
Plot, 159
PM, 187
Point, 355
Portia Faces Life, 60
Prefaces to Shakespeare, 371–372
Prentiss, Henrietta, 33
Prescott, Daniel A., 322
Present Indicative, 144
Primer of Phonetics, 101
Principles of Psychology, 322
"Problem of Meaning in Primitive Languages," 259
Producing the Play, 372
Projection, 6, 59–60
Pronouncing Dictionary of American English, 34
Proportion, 326
Psychology of Acting, The, 325
Public Speaking, 221
Punctuation, 101

Quinn, Don, 35
Quintilian, 97, 100, 325

Radio acting defined, 5–6
Radio directing, 371 ff.
Radio Directing, 59
Radio readings, 10
Rank, Otto, 8
Rapoport, I., 259, 260, 322
Rate of speaking, 34–35
Reactions, 159
Reading Aloud, 32, 183
Reading faults, 97–100
Realistic director, 373–377
Realistic theatre, 373 ff.
Reality, 3, 4, 373 ff.
Reed Club, John, 8
Reflections on the Actor's Art, 1
Rehearsal schedules, 67–70
Relationships, 379–381
Relaxation, 358–359
"Relaxed throat," 32
Reunion in Vienna, 357
Reynolds, Sir Joshua, 161
Rhythm defined, 7
Ribot, Théodule, 323
Rice, John, 184
Richards, I. A., 259
Riders to the Sea, 2
Robinson-Duff, Frances, 32
Roosevelt, Franklin D., 35
Rosenstein, Sophie, 323–324
Rousseau, J. J., 2
"Royal Roads to Acting," 5

St. Augustine, 2
St. John, Christopher, 34, 156, 321
Salvini, Tommaso, 31, 325
Schauspieler, Der, 325
Schoenfeld, Bernard C., 70
School for Husbands, The, 357
School for Scandal, The, 35
Scrooge, 2
Sea of Cortez, 1
Second Mrs. Burton, The, 60, 69, 222
Selden, Samuel, 159
Sensibility, 2, 7, 9
Seyler, Athene, 321, 326 ff.
Sganarelle, 357
Shadow of a Doubt, 355
Shakespeare, William, 3, 4, 6, 35, 101, 158, 162, 261, 326, 372, 379, 409–410
Shaw, George Bernard, vii, 8, 33, 34, 155, 156, 157, 158, 161, 162, 187, 261, 321, 322, 323, 326, 352, 353, 355–356, 358, 371, 374, 378
Sheridan, Thomas, 184
Sherwood, Robert E., 4, 357
Shylock, 4, 158
Shylock and His Daughter, 4
Siddons, Mrs., 321
Sincerity, 158, 371, 373
Sophocles, 4

Sparrow, Wilbur, 323–324
Speech, as literature, 186
"livingness" of, 184–186
Speech Quality and Interpretation, 123
Stanislavski (K. S. Alekseev), 1, 160, 221, 222, 223, 323, 325, 357, 371, 374
Steele, Joshua, 184
Stein, Gertrude, 186, 268
Steinbeck-Ricketts, 1
Stendhal (Marie Henri Beyle), 162, 186
Stimulus, 321–322, 324, 354
Stravinsky, Igor, 8
Streetcar Named Desire, A, 31
"Stress" defined, 123
Style in voice, 35
Sudakov, I., 31
Sullivan, J. W. N., 3
Superficial reading, 99
"Surface and Under Imagery in Acting," 159
Surprise, 356
Suspense, 321
Sweet, Henry, 101
Swift, Jonathan, 267
Sydney, George, 124

Talent, 6–7
Talma, François, 1
Tartuffe, 264
Technique, 5, 59 ff., 221
Television acting, 6, 351 ff.
Television directing, 371 ff.
Tempo, 35, 125
Terry, Ellen, 34, 156, 158, 321
Thackeray, W. M., 378
Theatre (Maugham), 324–325
Theatre, The (Young), 5, 31, 125, 158, 371
Theatre Annual, 159
Theatre Arts Monthly, 2, 5
Theatre Guild on the Air, 64
Theatre Practice, 1–2, 31, 35, 371, 372, 379
Theatre Workshop, 259, 322
Theory of Beauty, The, 321
Theory and Technique of Playwriting, 159, 261, 381
Thinking, 98, 121 ff.
This Fascinating Radio Business, 6
This Freedom, 59
Thomas, Charles K., 34
Thomson, Virgil, 162, 378–379
Thoreau, Henry David, 268
Thucydides, 267
Timing, 7, 121 ff., 124
Titian, 159
Tolstoy, Leo, 3, 378
Tone, vocal, 31, 32–33, 125
Tortsov, 221
Toscanini, Arturo, 378–379
"Toscanini Case, The," 378
Transitions, 6, 356
Truth to nature, 374
Turney, Robert, 4
"TV and Molly," 351
Two Views of Education, 6
Tybalt, 160

Understanding Picasso, 4
U.S. Department of Labor, 6
"Upset," 322

Valere, 357
Van, Harry, 263
Variety, 155, 351
Vendrovskaya, Lyuba, 259
Verisimilitude, 373
Voice, 7, 31 ff., 98
Voice and Articulation Handbook, 32 ff., 179
Voice balance, 60
Voice: How to Use It, The, 34

Walkley, A. B., 378
Walks, 357
Warfield, David, 158
Wars I Have Seen, 186
Waves, The, 99
West, Rebecca, 8
What Is Art . . . , 3
Whateley, Richard, 98–99
Wheel of Fire, The, 379
When a Girl Marries, 321
White, Wendell, 262
Whitehead, A. N., 267
Whiteside, Sheridan, 158
Wilde, Oscar, 268
Wilhelm Meister, 97
Williams, Tennessee, 31
Winans, James A., 221
Woodworth, Robert S., 259
Woolbert, Charles, 121, 125
Woolf, Virginia, 99, 291
Woollcott, Alexander, 158
"Work of the Actor, The," 259, 322
"Wow" directing, 378–379
Wright, Teresa, 355

Young, Stark, vii, 1–2, 5, 8, 31, 35, 125, 158, 159, 190, 325, 371, 372, 379, 380

Zachery, George, 155
Zola, Emile, 2